The Book of
Chagford

A TOWN APART

Iain Rice

HALSGROVE

First published in Great Britain in 2002

DEDICATION

To the memory of my late father, Alex P. Rice,
now at peace in Chagford churchyard.

British Library Cataloguing-in-Publication Data
A CIP record for this title is available from the British Library

ISBN 1 84114 193 3

HALSGROVE

Halsgrove House
Lower Moor Way
Tiverton, Devon EX16 6SS
Tel: 01884 243242
Fax: 01884 243325
email: sales@halsgrove.com
website: http://www.halsgrove.com

Old Walls, Chagford, c.1930.
(Thorn Collection)

Printed and bound in Great Britain by Bookcraft Ltd, Midsomer Norton.

CONTENTS

Chagford High Street in the early years of the twentieth century, with the cut-down stumps of the pinnacles still in place on the church tower. The archway in the churchyard wall at the left originally formed part of the access to the 'flushing tank' for the town water-supply leat which ran along the wall – originally an open channel, but culverted beneath the pavement by this time. [Thorn Collection]

The Strand – the upper part of Chagford Square linking the High Street and Mill Street – in about 1920, with the cars of the first motor tourists mingling with traditional horse-drawn traffic. The larger emporium at the left is Webbers, founded in 1891, with Bowdens beyond at the top of Mill Street. [Frith Collection]

ACKNOWLEDGEMENTS

The author would like to thank the following for valued assistance freely given:

Revd P.L. Baycock, latterly Rector of Chagford.
Leonard Brommell, Esq., Great Tree Farm, Chagford.
Dick Collins, Esq., Acre, Chagford.
Brian and Judith Cosford, Chagford.
Julia Endacott, Churchwarden and Captain of the Tower, St Michael's Church.
Tim Garrett, Esq., Rendells, Chagford.
Mrs Liz Haws, Chagford.
Jane Hayter-Hames, Rushford Barton, Chagford.
Maurice Hill, Esq., East Coombe Farm, Chagford.
Anthony Lloyd Hill, Esq., Morchard Bishop.
Peter Hill, Chagford Parish Council.

Peter Kay, Teignmouth.
A & L Martin, butchers, Chagford.
David Meldrum, Whiddons, Chagford.
Ivan and Mary Mortimore, Higher Shapley Farm, Chagford.
Gordon and Jackie Mortimore, Higher Shapley Farm, Chagford.
Judy Pool, Ring o'Bells Inn, Chagford.
Graham Reynolds, Chagford Primary School.
Laurette Rice, Gardeners, Chagford.
Pauline Spear, Moorlands, Chagford.
Anne Thorn, Chagford Postmistress.
Douglas Thorn, former Chagford Postmaster.
Chris Webber, Webbers, Chagford.
Van der Steen Hall, Architects, Chagford.
The Staff at the West Country Studies Library and Devon Record Office, Exeter.

The famous cromlech at Spinster's Rock, Shilstone. This is the burial chamber of a Neolithic tomb, but is here seen in its Victorian 'restored' form. The roof of Shilstone Barton can be seen in the background. (Thorn Collection)

Chagford from Rushford on a tranquil summer's day before the swimming pool was built. Rushford Mill just appears on the far right, the end wall shored up with timber props. The house on the left is Mr Reed's 'Teign View', while the town proper extends no lower than Monte Rosa – the secondary school and, later, Lamb Park, were built on the fields in the centre of this picture. This is a Chapman postcard, c.1925. (Thorn Collection)

Mill Street, Chagford, looking downhill towards the Moorlands Hotel and Rose Cottage from outside the Methodist Chapel, whose noticeboard is just visible in the right foreground. The shop seen here is Lewis' Dairy, one of two in the town at this time. (Thorn Collection)

AUTHOR'S NOTE

Spelling has, historically, been nothing like so consistent as it is in modern English usage. In the various sources consulted while compiling this book, many variations in the spelling of Chagford family and place names were encountered; hence, it is difficult to decide on a 'correct' spelling. Generally, I have used the common modern spellings except where quoting directly from a source or when a specific spelling is used in a particular context, as in titles such as Endacott House or the Endacott Charity – other references being to 'Endecott' and even 'Endicott'. 'Whyddon' and 'Whiddon' are likewise interchangeable, as are 'Perret' and 'Perrot'.

Many place names reflect a gradual corruption of an original. Chagford itself was 'Kagefort' to the Saxons, and Chaggesford in medieval times. 'Shapley' started out as the Latin 'Escalpulae' (meaning on the escarpment or shoulder of the hill) which, by the time of the Domesday survey was 'Escapaleia'. It later became Scapelie and then Shapleigh in medieval times and had apparently arrived at Shapley by the end of the seventeenth century. Modern Withecombe has been rendered, at various times, Withycombe, Widdycoombe or Widecombe, while Rushford started as Risford or Rishford. The River Teign was, in earlier times, the Tain, and there are many other similar examples. Many Chagford place names also gain and loose a terminal 'e' here and there on a seemingly casual basis, as at Waye, Weeke or Thorne.

In the early-nineteenth century, several Chagford street names were also changed or misquoted for a period: thus Lower Street became known as Post-Office Street while, at the same time, Southcombe Street was referred to as Sidcombe Street. The side of the Square furthest from the church is sometimes known as North Street, while the section of roadway across the top of the Square linking the High Street and Mill Street was styled for a while as the Strand. Pit or Pitt Street was the section of Mill Street in the deep cutting or pit, while what is now Nattadon Road is also known as Dennis Park. Perhaps the oddest thing about Chagford street names is the lack of a 'Fore Street', an almost-universal name for the main way into a Devon township.

Chagford Post Office – but not in Post-Office Street. This name was used for a while to describe Lower Street, when the office was, briefly, situated in Eliza Pratt's shop. It soon moved to the High Street and then, finally, to the Square. (Thorn Collection)

An all-but-deserted Chagford High Street on a beautiful summer's day in the early 1950s, with the Three Crowns displaying AA and RAC hotel signs as well as the 'name lantern' over the door. Beyond the hotel is St Katherine's Hall – at this time still in use as the Infant School – and the old Post Office and saddlery shop. The Mill Street branch of the town leat originally followed the churchyard wall on the left. (Thorn Collection)

'A truly rural place'. In spite of the sophistication of some of its buildings and the unusually cosmopolitan nature of its population, the true essence of Chagford is still that of a small country market town nestled into the landscape – a facet of the place readily apparent in this summer view, also dating from the 1950s and taken from the lower slopes of Meldon Hill. (Thorn Collection)

INTRODUCTION

I came to live in Chagford, fresh from college, in 1971, and the ensuing three decades have done nothing other than increase my fascination for the place. Every farm, every track, every mysterious hump or hollow in the ground and almost every stone of the town has, it seems, a story to tell.

This book is not an attempt at a definitive history of Chagford; far from it, for there is so much to explore, research and write about that the biggest problem has lain in deciding not so much what to include as what to leave out. Rather, the aim has been to produce a historical sketch of Chagford, biased toward the last 150 years and largely based on the rich collection of photographic material that is only now coming together into a cohesive archive. The result, inevitably, reflects my own particular interests, connections and fields of research.

The most recent attempt to encapsulate Chagford's long history, entitled *A History of Chagford*, was written in 1981 by Jane Hayter-Hames. This gives a detailed and scholarly – but highly readable – account of the town's origins and development and deals far more fully with the medieval period. It is expected that this excellent work will soon be back in print, and it is likewise hoped that this volume will be perceived as complementary to it.

Iain Rice, Carpenter's Cottage
New Street, Chagford.
May 2002

Building the rick at Higher Shapley Farm, August 1946.
(Courtesy of Mortimore family)

Prehistoric Chagford. Fernworthy Stone Circle probably dates from the period of the Beaker people, about 2000BC. It is thus of an age comparable to Stonehenge. When this picture was taken, c.1895, the circle was on open moorland, but now it lies in a clearing within Fernworthy Forest. (Meldrum Collection)

'Scorhill Sacred Circle' at Teignever is one of the best-known antiquities in the Chagford district – although it is actually situated in Gidleigh Parish. (Thorn Collection)

ONE

❧

AN HISTORICAL INTRODUCTION

Chagford has long been a place known above its station. For a small moorland market town with well under 2,000 inhabitants (a population which the Council for the Protection of Rural England would classify as a 'Small Village'), it has a fame far beyond its size or status. The reasons for this are numerous but all derive from a unique and chequered history, to which this book can be no more than a brief introduction.

Chagford's is a long story, although not as long as some places in Devon. Stone-Age man left few traces on Dartmoor, but there are the remains of several settlements within the Chagford parish boundary that date back to as long ago as 3000BC. These Neolithic people were the first true settlers of the area, as they practiced a very basic form of agriculture and thus created permanent homesteads. They used flint tools and pottery, and the presence of flint (not found naturally in the Dartmoor area) indicates not only that they travelled widely but also that they traded with other groups. There is much similarity between the artefacts found in this area and those found in parts of Dorset, South Wales and the Cotswolds, so this period probably marked the beginnings of trade and saw the first use of the ancient north-south trackway on the route of which Chagford lies.

The Neolithic settlers were the first to leave monuments, normally associated with burial rituals; the famous cromlech at Spinster's Rock, Shilstone, dates from this period. It may originally have formed a chamber within a barrow or earth mound, and contained burial artefacts. When it was first recorded, the cromlech was surrounded by small stone rows, although these may have been a later

A Dartmoor single-slab granite clapper bridge of archaic pattern. This example spans the Wallabrook (Welshman's Brook) next to a ford on the borders of Chagford and Gidleigh parishes at Teignever.

addition. They were unfortunately displaced, probably by farm improvements in the nineteenth century.

THE BRONZE AGE

The Neolithic people were followed, in around 2000BC, by a further and more sophisticated wave of settlers who possessed all of the Neolithic skills but with an important addition. These were the Beaker people, classified thus on the characteristic shape of their pottery. However, their real significance comes from their ability as monument builders and as the progenitors of the first culture to use metal artefacts – that of the Bronze Age. It is these settlers who are credited with the erection of the most characteristic and enduring of Dartmoor landmarks; the stone rows and circles for which the moor as a whole, and Chagford in particular, later became famous among antiquarians.

These monuments display evidence of considerable sophistication not just in their execution but also in their planning and alignment, which shows a developed mathematical skill and the use of a predictive calendar. There are many periodic astrological alignments that accord with the orientation of these enigmatic stones, and it is suggested that only peoples with a developed system of agriculture would be thus preoccupied with the seasonal cycles and their measurement and prediction. Other monuments dating from this era include cairns – piles of stone erected on prominent points, almost certainly for navigational purposes on the open moor – and kistvaens, small stone chambers. These have been associated with burial

The ancient ford on the Upper Teign at Teignhead. The bridge, although of the archaic granite-slab 'clapper' construction, dates only from 1808, but this crossing lies on the line of a track onto the High Moor in use since prehistoric times. In this postcard view dating from c.1900, the exposed farmstead of Teignhead is visible on the hillside – one of the remotest setttlements on the moor. (Meldrum Collection)

A popular early-twentieth-century postcard of Rushford, showing the 'steps', an ancient river crossing on an existing prehistoric trackway that passed close to the site of the town and led, eventually, to North Bovey. (Meldrum Collection)

sites and the use of cremation urns – again, a sophisticated practice for an ancient people.

The Beaker people developed their skills and mixed with further arrivals from Europe to become the true Bronze Age people, which is in all probability when the mineralogical importance of Dartmoor first emerged. Bronze is an alloy of copper and tin, both found in readily accessible forms in the surface outcroppings of the moor, and this almost certainly contributed to the relatively extensive settlement of the upland areas throughout this period. The trading links brought about by the presence of what were then immensely valuable raw materials were extensive, reaching as far as the Mediterranean areas of southern Europe; artefacts of Mediterranean origin have been uncovered on Dartmoor, while the trading links between the neighbouring Cornish tinners and the Phoenicians are well-established.

It is also from this time that we identify the first characteristic type of Dartmoor settlement: the circular stone huts found singly or in tight-knit groups that made up the early enclosed villages. The remains of these hut circles and enclosures are widespread throughout the Chagford district, with particularly prominent examples at Kestor and Fernworthy. Other evidence left by these peoples includes cultivation terraces, or lynchets, and larger, roughly-walled enclosures that also bear the marks of agricultural activity. Over the ensuing century, further peoples arrived in the Dartmoor area from mainland Europe. Each wave brought with them new skills and knowledge, and the age of bronze gave way to that of iron around 400BC. These new arrivals spoke a Celtic language, and were the first of what were to become the last and most dominant settlers of the Chagford area in prehistoric times, the Celts.

CELTIC CHAGFORD
– THE IRON AGE –

The particular characteristics of the Celtic peoples lay both in their practical skills as metalworkers and farmers and in their developed language and social system. Their society was organised in discreet groups under chieftans, a primitive progenitor of the feudal system that persisted in England throughout the Saxon and medieval period. The Celts were also a warlike people with a distinct warrior class; they built settlements that were strategically sited and defensible, as at the twin Iron-Age fortified villages of Cranbrook and Prestonbury. Later known as 'castles', these two sites dominated the heights either side of the Teign Gorge, a main access route onto the moor. As with their Bronze-Age forebears, the Celts found many of the resources they needed on

the moor, including iron ore, which occurred particularly along the north-eastern boundary of the granite.

These Iron-Age Celts gradually gained dominance over the Bronze Age peoples without, apparently, either displacing them or subjugating them; rather, they appear to have been assimilated into the new culture and to have contributed to its evolution. Thus, the history of the Chagford region from the arrival of the Beaker peoples until the start of the Roman invasion in 55–54BC seems to have been one of steady development of a relatively stable society and culture resting on the twin foundations of metal-working and agriculture, underpinned by a strong social and military order. Metal implements allowed more intensive agriculture to develop, and the characteristic field pattern of small, roughly square enclosures that evolved around the moor edge is accepted as being of Bronze Age and Celtic origin. These early reclamations from the moorland formed the basis of many later Saxon or Norman farms; such ancient steadings are usually distinguished by a place name ending in 'worthy', a Saxon name given to an enclosed place.

The original religion of the Celts was in the pagan tradition now generally referred to as 'Druidic'. This tradition has long been associated with many of the types of monument found on and around Dartmoor. The presence of Druids is also commemorated in a number of local place names such as Druids Well at Middlecott, which may indicate that Celtic settlement had penetrated the lower-lying forest areas from the more open Dartmoor heights. Middlecott is one of the oldest settlements in Chagford, well established before the time of Domesday. It is interesting that the inn at Drewsteignton latterly known as the Drewe Arms was, until the arrival of the wealthy Julius Drewe in the early years of the twentieth century, called the 'Druid's Arms', and the whole Drewsteignton area has strong Druidic associations.

THE ROMANS AND THE
DARK AGES

The Celts, however warlike, were no match for the discipline, tactics and equipment of the Roman legions. When the later Roman expeditions of 48–47BC set out to subdue the inhabitants of south-west England, the pragmatic Celts soon settled for a nominal subservience to Rome as preferable to persecution and extinction. Besides, the Romans did not seem greatly interested in the Celtic settlements on Dartmoor, an area which they seem to have regarded as too inhospitable to merit any but the most cursory attention. So the existing Celtic population, now officially the Roman tribe of the

Dumnonii, were able to carry on much as before under their new masters. The main Roman settlement and military base in Devon was at Isca Dumnoniorum – Exeter – and then pushing on further west they went well to the north of Dartmoor, where Nemetostatio, an outpost on the site of North Tawton, became the centre of the Roman taxation district to which Chagford belonged. However, given the scattered and primitive nature of the Dartmoor settlements and the insignificance of their small-scale scratchings at the surface of the moor's mineral wealth, it seems unlikely that Chagford or its hinterland contributed much to the Imperial Roman exchequer.

After half a millennium of relative stability under Roman rule – a period which left virtually no discernable mark on Celtic Chagford above a handful of coins – the occupation of Britain ended with the fall of Gaul around AD500 and the consequent isolation of the Roman garrisons and civilian population in England. The Romans swiftly withdrew, leaving behind them a rich infrastructure but a political and cultural vacuum, which resulted in the chaotic period known generally as the Dark Ages. This was an epoch throughout which there was no centralised order of society in England, but rather a fragmented, often-warring collection of distinct and different peoples organised on tribal lines or in small kingdoms.

In the South West, where the impact of the Romans had been relatively limited, there was greater continuity and order than was the case elsewhere. This is an epoch which has left virtually no written records, few monuments or artefacts and an intriguing jumble of legends, among them the most enduring of all – that of King Arthur and the Round Table. There are many versions of this legend and sites associated with the fabled Arthurian court include Glastonbury and Tintagel. Glastonbury's unique location, as a lone hill in the centre of a great and fertile plain, gave it a religious and cultural significance extending well back into prehistory, so most modern scholars are inclined to give it Arthurian precedence. However, some have suggested that Arthur may well have been a Celtic-derived king of Dumnonia with his seat on Dartmoor, and given the comparative wealth and stability of the area this supposition may hold a grain of fact.

This was also a time during which the Dartmoor area's chief links were with other established Celtic settlements, notably Wales, Cornwall and Brittany. For a period, the far south-west was effectively Welsh and was even known briefly as West Wales (Gorllewin yr Cymru). The not-infrequent Dartmoor and Cornish place name constituent of walla or wallas reflects this link, being a description of someone or something belonging to the Welsh. There are further links in the place names, with such obvious correlations as the Devon coombe, fold and pool with the Welsh cwym, ffald and pwll. The Christian faith had also begun to take hold of the whole Celtic world,

This view of Chagford from the stumpy stone tower – a 'folly' – on the crest of Rushford Hill has appeared on countless postcards. It clearly shows the situation of the town, set some way above the river bank on the lower slopes of Meldon and Nattadon Hills. This situation has its orgins in the Saxon manorial settlement of Kagefort, which probably dated from around the middle of the eighth century. Chagford House can be seen amid its woods to the left of the church, and Meldon Hall stands stark on the hillside above the town. (Thorn Collection)

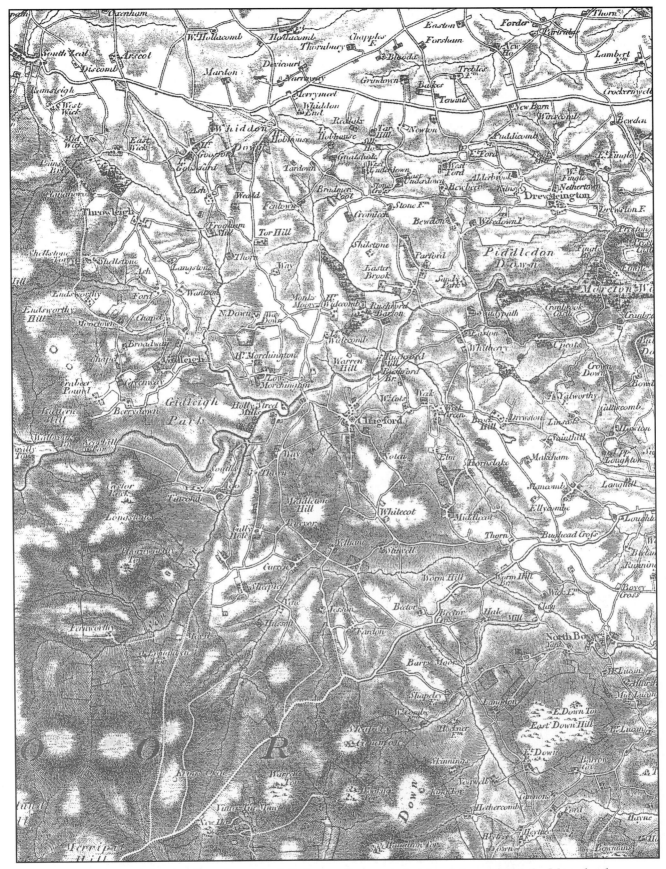

The Chagford district, from the original Ordnance Survey undertaken between 1805–9. Many local place names altered at this time due, it is said, to the difficulties experienced by the OS surveyors in comprehending the local dialect. They recorded what they thought they had heard!

initially during the Roman occupation, and flourishing further during the course of the 200-year interregnum of the Dark Ages. Christianity seems to have quite rapidly displaced the old Druidic culture, spread effectively by the evangelising of a new race of travelling Celtic scholars and pilgrims arriving from Ireland and France.

SAXON CHAGFORD

With the arrival of the first small groups of Saxons from the east around AD600 we enter the period of Chagford's recorded history. As was the case when the Celts arrived, this seems not to have been an invasion in the accepted sense of the word, but rather a gradual infiltration and absorption of one culture by another. Certainly there were skirmishes, but there was no sustained military overthrow of one people by an invading army. Saxon Devon was largely built on Celtic or Roman foundations, and on the fringes of Dartmoor the two cultures seem to have complemented each other rather than to have been in direct competition. The Saxons, with their roots in the great forests of Northern Europe, were predominantly a woodland people; practised in the arts of forest clearance and settlement. They cultivated irregular-shaped clearings in the forest and built using wood rather than stone. They kept cattle and oxen in small enclosures and developed a form of subsistence agriculture that was simply not possible on the upland areas held by the Celts.

The Saxons settled the area far more widely than any previous people and soon introduced the first recognisable system of local and regional government seen since the departure of the Romans. This was based on the manorial system of 'hundreds', which defined and recorded the different areas of land in a series of charters, by which means the landholdings were allotted to a new elite class of lords of the manor. The charters define the holdings in the form of a written description of the boundary using existing landmarks, and thus form the earliest surviving records of landholdings. They show that some of the new Saxon feudal lords held or acquired several manors and held sway over a subservient workforce of several hundred people. In the face of this organised hierarchical system, the old Celtic tribal network soon declined and crumbled, and by AD800 Saxon dominance over the area was virtually complete. Certainly, in all the earliest records – including the Domesday Book – the names of the landowners are without exception Saxon in origin, and most of the ancient Celtic place names have been usurped or modified by Saxon successors.

The town from Waye Barton, looking towards the range of non-granitic hills separating the upper and lower Teign valleys, terrain which the river penetrates by the Teign Gorge. The picture shows development on Manor Road at the start of the twentieth century – the bulk of the large Victorian Italianate villa 'Ferndale' is prominent with, behind it, Edwardian 'Beverley'. To the right, built on from the end of New Street, Meldon Road has extended as far as the large Edwardian block including 'Ingledene' and 'Fernleigh'. (Courtesy Pauline Spear)

This view of the Upper Square and the old 'Shambles' dates from 1860, and is one of the earliest known photographs of Chagford. The thatched shambles in the centre of the Square incorporated the market office and public slaughterhouse and, like many of the structures infilling the Square, was by this time somewhat dilapidated. The Mill Street branch of the town leat is also prominent in the foreground; this was paved over as a culvert (later made into a piped main) during the reconstruction of the Upper Square and Market House in 1861–2. At the left rear, behind the shambles, the trees in the churchyard are clearly visible through what should have been the roofs of a further row of cottages, destroyed by fire in early 1860s; the site is now occupied by the modern Post Office. The burned-out shell of the cottages can just be made out. This picture was taken at the height of the depression affecting the woollen trade and agriculture in the mid-Victorian period, reflected in the shabby state of the cottages and the Royal Oak Inn along the south-eastern side of the Square. (Thorn Collection)

THE FOUNDATION OF CHAGFORD

The genesis of the modern town cannot with any certainty be placed much earlier than around the middle of the eighth century. The name Chagge-Ford (Kage-fort) is Saxon in origin – meaning, literally, furzy or thorny ford. So the town probably started out in the middle of the Saxon period as nothing more than a convenient crossing point on the River Teign, where one of the ancient trackways linking more important centres forded the river.

In the Saxon and Norman periods, important centres almost always had religious foundations, with Glastonbury towering over all in the West Country. At that period all roads reputedly led to Glastonbury, which exerted a profound influence over a surprisingly wide area when it is remembered that the only means of transport were by foot or on

horseback. Other religious centres were springing up all over the west at this time, with monasteries being founded at Buckfast in the eleventh century, Torre in the twelfth and Buckland in the thirteenth. Crediton was already an important religious centre and had a monastery by the eighth century, and Exeter was likewise important in monastic terms from a very early period.

There is little recorded of early Chagford until the Domesday Survey in 1086. The only previous mention is its allocation to the hundred of Wonford in the ninth century. The Domesday Book lists five Saxon settlements in the area of which only one, Chagesford (Kagefort) was close to the original river crossing – recorded as already being bridged during this period – and hence formed the probable site of any settlement that might at that stage have developed. The Saxon manor, with its wooden buildings, has left no discernible trace apart from

Left: One of the best-known and most characteristic of Chagford postcard views is this portrait of the Market House dating from around 1890. The large block on the corner of North Street, that later housed Rowe's bakery and tearoom, has not yet been built. The leat has been piped, but the street lighting (installed after 1893) has yet to appear. (Meldrum Collection)

Right: The 1862 Market House, built at the instigation of George Hayter-Hames. This part of the structure, now the public conveniences, was then the business premises of Mr Middleweek the antique dealer. The rear of an artillery-wheeled touring car of early 1920s vintage can be seen on the right, intriguingly displaying a prominent 'GB' plate – a very rare fitment at this date, when few cars ventured abroad. (Thorn Collection)

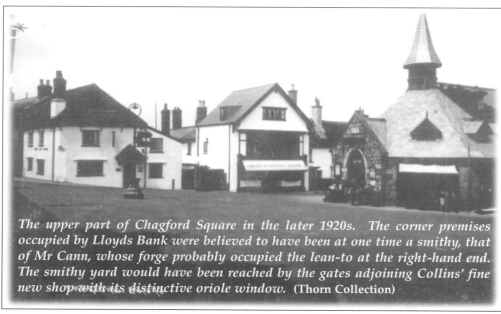

The upper part of Chagford Square in the later 1920s. The corner premises occupied by Lloyds Bank were believed to have been at one time a smithy, that of Mr Cann, whose forge probably occupied the lean-to at the right-hand end. The smithy yard would have been reached by the gates adjoining Collins' fine new shop with its distinctive oriole window. (Thorn Collection)

Above: *Chagford Square and Market House around 1952, showing the simpler replacement bay window of Collins' grocery stores. The chalkboard by the entrance to the Market House gents advertises a coach trip by 'Moorland Heather', Chagford's own tour operator. The view also has some very interesting motor traffic. Parked in the Square are an early Series I Land Rover, a 1949 MG TC and a very rare Ford Prefect shooting brake with a 'woody' body; all these vehicles have since become highly sought-after collectors' pieces, while the registration number alone of the Land Rover would today fetch thousands of pounds!* (Thorn Collection)

Below: *Another well-known Chagford postcard, of slightly later date than the previous view – the electric street lighting is now in place, while the Royal Oak has ceased to be an inn. The Ring O' Bells is also not functioning as a public house at this time – it is being used as Collins' butcher's shop. Animals were killed in the yard behind the inn. Next to Collins' are the premises of James Perrot, fishing-tackle maker and Dartmoor guide.* (Meldrum Collection)

Right: *Chagford Market House and the Square in the 'big snow' of 1963, when the town was completely cut off for several days. This was a not-uncommon occurence in earlier times – there are several instances recorded in the school logs – but the last time snow isolated Chagford was in 1984; the recent climatic trend to milder winters makes substantial or protracted snowfall on Dartmoor very rare.* (Thorn Collection)

Above Right: *Chagford High Street in the grip of the 1963 snows; quite impassable.*

the characteristic regular field pattern associated with Saxon cultivation.

Christianity had by now virtually eclipsed all other religions and held sway over both the remaining Celtic peoples and the newly-arrived Saxons. The two cultures blended over the period AD700 to around AD1000, with both the Germanic Saxon language and the Celtic tongue being absorbed as elements of early English. Scholars, churchmen and persons of rank still used Latin, and virtually all written records, books or documents are in this language.

Given the importance and strength of the Christian faith in this part of Devon – Chagford is, after all, only 12 miles from Crediton, then a dominant Christian centre – it seems more than likely that there was a church of some sort extant at Chagford before the foundation of St Michael's in 1261. On the evidence of the few surviving Saxon churches (most notably Greenstead-Juxta-Ongar in Essex) it is probable that this was a simple and rugged timber building constructed from whole tree-boles set vertically, with a thatched roof. With the construction of the first stone church on the same site in the thirteenth century, all traces of any such ancient building would have been hidden.

CHAGFORD – THE TOWN

The oldest buildings extant in the modern town of Chagford date back no further than the mid-fifteenth century. It is likely that the structures these succeeded were of a less-than-permanent nature – either wooden structures of limited life or small and primitive stone buildings that had outlived their purposes. However, the town plan, with the triangular market-place beside the church with a pattern of radiating streets, is highly characteristic of an early-medieval settlement. If there had been a castle or fortified manor house at the foot of Nattadon Hill, it would be pretty much a textbook example!

This suggests that the real growth period of Chagford was centred on the thirteenth and fourteenth centuries, with the town reaching maturity in the fifteenth. This accords not only with the fabric and layout that now exists, but also with the period of comparative wealth and stability arising from the working of the stannary and the emergence of the woollen industry.

The likely extent of the town at this period is open to speculation, but it is probable that it did not extend far beyond the nucleus of the Square. Bishop's House, the oldest parts of which Pevsner describes as 'late-medieval', was probably on the edge of the built area until the seventeenth- and eighteenth-century expansion of Chagford that created New Street and Lower Street. Much of what we see today dates from the seventeenth to the nineteenth centuries, with the age of the buildings on New and Lower Streets generally decreasing as they get further from the Square. This new construction did absorb some older buildings, including a medieval inn in New Street and an ancient farmyard in Lower Street. Dating the ordinary terraced cottages of the town can be difficult, as the traditional plan and construction of these remained static over a long period, with buildings constructed as late as 1850 being all-but-identical to those erected 200 years earlier.

The town has evolved continuously since the medieval period, although modern planning controls have now placed a limit on further expansion. The nineteenth and twentieth centuries saw a number of older buildings rebuilt, modernised or replaced, while part of the market-place was also built up. Early photographs of the Square show a lot more thatch and traditional frontages than can be seen at the beginning of the twenty-first century – these features were lost through the construction of relatively modern buildings such as the 1930s block on the south-east corner of the Square, the Victorian structure in pale-cream Marland brick next to the Three Crowns (reputedly on the site of the old Stannary Courthouse) and the current 'mock Tudor' frontage to Bowden's shop, which hides a variety of much older buildings behind.

This is generally true of parts of the Square, Mill Street, and even Lower Street and New Street, where ancient structures lie behind the modern frontages or are absorbed within them. There are a number of 'drangs' – narrow alleys barely a yard wide – with cottages or outbuildings on both sides, while in Gregory's Court – approached through a nineteenth-century archway off Mill Street – there is a miniature square with further ranges of older buildings to the rear. The jumbled roof lines and fascinating accretion of structures lying behind the more recent façades are a fascinating study; a good example is the contrast between the façades of the buildings fronting the south-eastern side of the Square, and the same group as viewed from the churchyard.

Although Chagford suffered several serious fires in the seventeenth and eighteenth centuries which damaged or destroyed a number of buildings in Lower Street, Southcombe Street and New Street, the town escaped the widespread conflagrations that afflicted many Devon towns such as North Tawton and Moretonhampstead. The widespread use of thatch for roofing always posed a severe fire risk, but Chagford's granite structures were not as prone to total destruction as the cob buildings common in the surrounding districts; they could often quite simply be restored or rebuilt after fires, which is why Chagford does not exhibit many of the obvious signs of past conflagrations seen in many other places.

MODERN CHAGFORD

An outline history of the main aspects of Chagford's farming, trade, industry and institutions is given in the ensuing chapters, which will hopefully go some way towards explaining the evolution from medieval stannary to modern touristic and cultural centre. There is no doubt that the tremendous improvements in Chagford's transport links, especially by road, in the last 30 years of the last century has probably had a greater impact on the town than any development occurring in the previous millennium. Far from being remote and relatively inaccessible, modern Chagford is little more than a three-hour journey from London, and is within easy and rapid reach of many parts of the British Isles.

This has underpinned and strengthened Chagford's role, first assumed in the nineteenth century, as a particularly desirable place to visit or take up residence. Under the protection of National Park status, Dartmoor has retained much of its romantic grandeur, although the advent of mass tourism and the accompanying swamping by motor traffic has inevitably had an adverse impact on both the moor and the town. Your author has, for the past decade, been attempting to obtain a photograph of the frontage of the Ebeneezer Hall in Southcombe Street unencumbered by parked cars – so far without success!

The proliferation of notices, codes, limits and worthy exhortations (Take Moor Care!) that seem an inseparable part of modern life have also somewhat sullied the rugged and primitive aspects of the moorland environment. Furthermore, what Pevsner – who wrote of Chagford in 1952 that its centre was 'pleasantly unspoilt by through traffic or undesirable development' – would have had to say of the chaotic parking, the unhappy imposition of corporate logos and colour schemes and the depredations of the plastic-window salesmen, is probably best left as speculation!

Nevertheless, in spite of it all, Chagford has continued to display that unique streak of against-the-grain independence and spirit that have long characterised this oddly charismatic little town, resisting the imposition of unwelcome change, promoting a lively cultural and economic life, and happily continuing, at least on the sporting field, the age-old rivalry with its neighbour Moreton-hampstead. Long may it continue.

An aerial view of Chagford taken in the 1930s, clearly showing the 'triangular tee' plan of High Street/Mill Street, the Square, and Southcombe and Lower Streets. In the Square, the Market House and attendant trees stand out, with what looks like the GWR bus from Moretonhampstead waiting outside – the only vehicle in the Square. Collins' grocery emporium is prominent to the left, with the dark thatch of 'Lydstone' – formerly the King's Arms Inn – behind. The block of buildings at the extreme right lower corner is the Globe Hotel with the Buffalo's hall and cottages at the rear of the courtyard. The line of Orchard Farmhouse and Orchard Terrace is clear, with the farm buildings of Orchard Farm to the rear of the terrace and Orchard Meadow – the site of post-war council-housing – to the right. At the upper left of the picture, the big shed behind Rock House built to house the GWR buses, shows up clearly, fronted by the allotments of Cranley Gardens. The big house at the extreme top of the picture by the avenue of trees is Monte Rosa, with the Moor Park Hotel opposite. (Thorn Collection)

Above and below: *Two views of the High Street and the Three Crowns Hotel from a similar view-point but separated by 40 years. In the upper view, dating from about 1885, the open channel of the town leat is just discernible in the shadows at the foot of the churchyard wall; the slab bridge over this giving access to the south-west gate of the churchyard can also be made out. At this date the channel down Mill Street was also still open, while the leat flowed beneath the Upper Square in a simple granite-slab culvert. (Thorn Collection) The lower view dates from the later 1930s, before the wartime scrap drive claimed the iron railings from outside the Three Crowns. The leat has long been piped and paved over, and the old Royal Oak has been replaced by the block of shops which was built in about 1935. (Meldrum Collection)*

Above: *The porch of the Three Crowns is probably Chagford's second most-recognisable structure after the Market House. What later became a forecourt is here still a garden, although the heavy growth of creeper that once covered the porch is missing. The inn was originally the town house of the Whyddon family and dates from the sixteenth century.* (Meldrum Collection)

Right: *The old butcher's shop outside the Three Crowns, built on the forecourt of the inn. This structure was removed in the early 1950s, having served for a time as Splatt's Dairy.* (Thorn Collection)

The Strand, Chagford, around 1900. The name Strand was used for the upper part of the Square in Chagford's 'spa' days. At the left is the old Royal Oak, which had ceased to be an inn at the end of the nineteenth century. Note the lack of a footway on the churchyard side of the High Street, where the old leat channel has not long been replaced by a water main. The village constable — complete with uniform cape — is in conversation with a baker's roundsman. The butcher's shop stands in front of the Three Crowns Hotel; it later became a dairy. Cattle were both milked and slaughtered in the inn yard at this time. Gale's shop (in the centre behind the horseman) published the postcard from which this view is taken. Interestingly, the original card bears the legend 'printed abroad' — quite uncommon at this date. (Thorn Collection)

Chagford High Street looking towards the Square with the old Post Office (Robert Thorn's saddlery and harness shop) in the centre. The porch in the foreground is that of the old Church House, now Church Stile Cottage; there was once a stile in the churchyard wall, adjacent to the south-west gate opposite the Three Crowns. (Meldrum Collection)

73129. CHAGFORD, HIGH STREET.

Chagford High Street around 1922, with a solitary car drawn up outside the Globe Hotel. The Three Crowns sold City Ales (prominently!) and the church tower now has simple battlemented corners; the rotten pinnacles were finally done away with in the 1914 reworking of the whole tower that saw a new concrete roof cast in place, and the bells re-cast and re-hung in a new cage. (Meldrum Collection)

Left: *The Lower Square, taken from the archway of Dartmoor Lodge in the 1920s, showing the group of buildings that replaced the fire-damaged cottages after 1861. The earlier of these is the Post Office (not built as such; it became so in 1892), while the three-storey 'villa' with vague Italianate overtones later provided 'superior apartments', bed & breakfast and a restaurant and shop on the ground floor. The Post Office houses the public telephone and telegraph office, and has acquired a splendid stamp machine – but has yet to be graced with the telephone box that now stands in the angle between the office and the restaurant.* (Thorn Collection)

Right: *Cannon House – at one time the Three Cannons pub – and the Lower Square, taken from an upstairs window of the Post Office. This block of Victorian buildings replaced a series of somewhat ramshackle cottages and outbuildings that had gradually infilled the triangular lower part of the Square during the seventeenth and eighteenth centuries. A few of these older buildings survive on North Street and in the apex of the triangle.*
(Thorn Collection)

Left: *The lower part of Chagford Square in the mid 1920s, with Mr Densham's house, Dartmoor Lodge, directly ahead, the Post Office to the right and Mr Gray's shop on the left, selling jewellery, watches and clocks, ironmongery and Shell motor spirit, among other things!*
(Thorn Collection)

Below: *A Frith postcard view of Chagford Lower Square and Post Office dating from c.1958, although the card was not posted until 1971. The Morris Minor post van is one of the unique GPO versions, specially built with an opening windscreen – 'to aid visibility in falling snow!'*
(Thorn Collection)

Above: *The Lower Square and Post Office before the First World War, with the pavement surfaced in sea cobbles – very durable but not very comfortable to walk on. The frontage of Dartmoor Lodge is heavily overgrown with clematis on trellising at this date, and also has a small front garden area with paling fence, now taken into the pavement area. Note the original electric street-light fitting bracketed off the corner of Mr Gray's shop.* (Thorn Collection)

Below: *The Market House and Lower Square in the severe snows of March 1947.* (Thorn Collection)

Above: *Chagford Lower Square in the mid 1930s. The telephone box adjacent to the Post Office has yet to be installed (the public telephone was then in the old Telegraph Room at the rear of the Post Office). The splendid car on the right is a 14hp Vauxhall of about 1932 vintage, and in the background can be seen a Devon General bus waiting to depart, probably to Exeter.* (Thorn Collection)

Left: *The 1960 winter, with the telephone box that replaced the internal phone in the Post Office now in place. This is Mr Tyke, the County Council's road lengthman, who had an unenviable job in these conditions.* (Thorn Collection)

Right: *North Street is the short length of roadway running out of the main Square on the western side, again seen in the severe winter of 1963. Collins' grocery store is on the left and Rowe's (later Miller's) bakery straight ahead.* (Thorn Collection)

Left: *North Street in about 1980. The lower two buildings seen in the row on the left were for several years the premises of F.G. Pearse, Motor Engineer; the wide alcove that now forms the shop doorways used to house a set of kerbside petrol pumps. The garage itself was behind, with access by a narrow alleyway, and utilised a range of older buildings that had formerly housed several of Chagford's traditional craftsmen, including the workshop of John Callard, 'Ironmonger, Brazier and Tinsmith'.* (Thorn Collection)

Left: *Mill Street c.1890. 'Mr Berry's House', later part of the Moorlands Hotel, has some of its windows blanked out, probably to avoid tax. The thatched building at the junction of Mill Street and Manor Road, Rose Cottage, was a popular subject for postcards due to its picturesque nature, evident in this view. The road ahead lead to Gidleigh via Pit Street and Chagford Bridge.* (Thorn Collection)

Right: *Rose Cottage and the road junction c.1910. The late-Victorian block of three-storey houses including 'Tregare' is now in being on Mill Street.* (Meldrum Collection)

Chagford, A well known Cottage.

Above: *Mill Street around 1960, looking down the hill towards Rose Cottage. 'Mr Berry's House', with its windows reinstated, is now the Moorlands Hotel, latterly a residential home.* (Meldrum Collection)

Above: *The upper part of Mill Street, in a view taken from outside the Buller's Arms. The pillars and railings on the right are in front of the Methodist Chapel, while the archway beyond the shop frontage leads on to Gregory's Court and forge. The Buller's Arms was formerly the Baker's Arms, being re-named to honour Sir Redvers Buller's part in the Boer War; the adjoining house was re-named 'Ladysmith' at the same time. Rose Cottage has lost its thatch for slates.* (Meldrum Collection)

Left: *Mill Street, c.1950. 'Claremont', the house seen here on the right was built in 1831 and was home to the Chagford medical practice for over 130 years.* (Thorn Collection)

Right: *New Street not long after the turn of the twentieth century, with Acre to the right. A number of cottages seen as thatched in this view now have slate roofs. The second cottage on the left with a porch was the Police House. Stone's 'factory' lay behind this cottage and those adjoining.* (Meldrum Collection)

Left: *Southcombe Street 'en fete' for the Coronation in 1952. Hill's bakery is directly facing the camera, with Southcombe House at the left and the front garden of Rock House to the fore.* (Thorn Collection)

Right: *New Street, Chagford, c.1950. The Turnlake is just out of view on the left and allotments still occupy Acre – the site was developed in 1979–80. The 1860 school was opposite the first cottage on the right-hand side of the road. The 1936 Ward Lock 'Red Guide' described New Street as 'a poor, mean and run-down quarter of the town'.* (Thorn Collection)

Left: *Lower Street, Chagford, with the Bishop's House prominent on the right, so called as it was used as the lodging for the Bishop of Crediton when he visited the parish. It is a fine medieval longhouse with seventeenth-century additions.* (Meldrum Collection)

Below: *Meldon Road and Dennis Park from Buda Farm, with the ridge of hills behind Moretonhampstead in the background.*
(Thorn Collection)

Above: *This view of Chagford was taken from just below Meldon Hill House, c.1928; the road in the foreground is the lane up Meldon at Knowles' Corner – it looks very different today as there are now sizeable trees on both sides of the road here. The newly-built houses of Dennis Park (now Nattadon Road) are prominent on the lower slopes of Nattadon Hill to the right.*
(Thorn Collection)

Dennis Park in the snows of 1947, with Nattadon rising steeply behind and Padley (Meldon) Common in the foreground. (Thorn Collection)

Orchard Meadow, Chagford, built in 1951–4 by the Okehampton Rural District Council on the home field of Orchard Farm; the house and yard of the farm lie behind the row of houses at the rear of this view.
(Thorn Collection)

Orchard Meadow again with the unique 'Octagon' houses on the right. This block of single-storey homes was built on the side of the hill and had garages beneath the lower side – an unheard-of provision for council-houses in 1954! The group of Chagford ladies shown here includes Avril Meredith and Hetty Rice, but the occasion is not recorded. (Thorn Collection)

The highest bridge over the Teign is at Teignhead Farm, a traditional Dartmoor clapper dating from 1808, adjacent to a ford on the downstream side. Manga Hill is on the left in this view, with the slopes of Kennon Hill straight ahead. (Meldrum Collection)

Right: *Leigh Bridge, over the mouth of the South Teign River at its confluence with the North Teign. This view looks downstream on the South Teign, which is very rocky and rapid just here.* (Meldrum Collection)

Left: *The old timber bridge at Holy Street that gave access to Holy Street Mill – a structure suited only to pedestrians and lightly-laden pack ponies. Access to the mill for wheeled vehicles was always by means of a track along the bank of the river.* (Meldrum Collection)

Two

Rivers, Bridges & Mills

The Teign – in the upper valley of which Chagford lies – is a classic upland river rising high on Dartmoor. There are two branches of the river, both dropping steeply off the moor to their confluence at Leigh, just west of Chagford. The South Teign has two tributaries rising at Sittaford and above Hurston, which combine at Fernworthy. The stream comes off the edge of the moor below Thornworthy and runs between Yardworthy and Teignworthy, dropping down past Yeo Farm and thence through the woods between Coombe and Northill to Leigh. The North Teign rises much further out on the moor in the great basin below Cut Hill that also spawns the Dart and the Tavy, coming down from the high moor at Teignhead, where the remote farmstead was abandoned during the Second World War. The river runs into Gidleigh Parish as it leaves the Chagford Newtake, and forms the parish boundary for much of the stretch between Batworthy and Leigh Bridge. The holed Tolmen Stone and twin clapper bridges at Teignever, and the nearby stone circle at Scorhill (all actually in Gidleigh) were famous landmarks that drew the romantically inclined to Chagford in the nineteenth century.

The River Bovey also flows through Chagford Parish, although at a much higher level than the Teign as its source is close to the edge of the moor in the south-east corner of the parish. The Bovey rises in a bowl of moorland between Lakeland and Fernworthy, on Chagford Commons. As was frequent practice, this river also forms a boundary, between the parishes of Chagford and North Bovey, and it soon leaves Chagford Parish to run down through North Bovey and Manaton.

Chagford town lies around 100 feet above the Teign, climbing the south side of the valley towards the twin hills of Meldon and Nattadon. The town's Saxon name is, of course, derived from its origins as a place where the river was traversed. In fact, there are a number of fording-places over the river in the vicinity of the town, of which the easiest is at Rushford, where the river is in a placid reach and spreads wide and shallow. The stepping-stones here are a well-known landmark and form a link in an ancient trackway that comes down from the heights of Withecombe and heads towards North Bovey.

FERNWORTHY RESERVOIR & FOREST

Water extraction from Dartmoor really started in a major way at the end of the nineteenth century with the construction of the great dam and its 117-acre lake at Burrator on the southern moor, completed in 1898. Other schemes followed, but it was not until 1927 that Chagford was affected, when Torquay Corporation built an intake works on the South Teign River just below Fernworthy Farm, which had already been abandoned to forestry by that date. This was connected by a pipeline to the lowest of the Trenchford Reservoirs, further down the Teign Valley between Hennock and Trusham.

In 1934, after this initial supply had proved inadequate, the Corporation returned the South Teign and Fernworthy with a proposal to dam the valley below the farm, thus creating a 76-acre lake capable of maintaining a supply of two and a half million gallons per day. Parliamentary powers for this undertaking were obtained in the same year, and construction work finally commenced in 1936. The scheme involved the flooding of most of the remaining land of Fernworthy Farm, and the buildings were

The original Fernworthy bridge (Thorn Collection)

33

demolished. It was necessary to build a new road to Teignhead Moorgate, as at that time Teignhead was still being farmed, while the newly-established forestry plantations in the area also needed access. Fernworthy Reservoir was established in order to maintain river flows at suitable levels to allow extraction further downstream at the waterworks complex at Trenchford throughout the year, especially in the summer when peak demand from the many holiday-makers in Torquay often coincided with low river flows.

Construction of the dam was beset with difficulties. The original intention was to build an all-masonry structure using stone quarried on site. A deep pit was opened up on the lands of Metherall Farm, with an aerial ropeway system to take the stone to the dam site. However, the Metherall granite proved too porous for dam-building, so the final structure was actually constructed in concrete and faced with granite. It is 65 feet high, of 'stepped' construction, and incorporates a small turbine for power generation. It was the last granite-faced dam built on Dartmoor.

As well as the problems with the Metherall granite, the works also suffered a catastrophic inundation of water and silt following a tremendous thunderstorm on 4 August 1938. This precipitated over three inches of rain over the area in eight hours; on some parts of the moor, the rainfall was said to have been nearer six inches. Before work could resume, two million gallons of water and 13,500 cubic feet of silt had to be cleared. The dam was finally finished in 1942 after the war had caused further delay – many site workers were called up and transport restrictions hampered work. It cost £246,000, some £66,000 over budget.

Fernworthy Reservoir lies at the heart of one of the largest and oldest plantations on Dartmoor. After the First World War, the Forestry Commission had been set up to ensure that Britain would not in future be dependent on imported timber supplies. The new Commission began to advise and negotiate

The Tolmen Stone at Teignever near Chagford. A tolmen is a stone with a hole through it, in this case worn by the grinding action of smaller stones moved by the rushing water. (Meldrum Collection)

with major landowners, which, on Dartmoor, meant the Duke of Cornwall. In 1919, the Duke agreed to plant over 5,000 acres of the moor with conifers. Fernworthy Forest, together with smaller plantations at Frenchbeer, was created by the Duchy in 1919–20 using Sitka Spruce and Douglas Fir, and by 1930 Fernworthy itself had extended to more than 800 acres. Further planting at the higher levels (above 1500 feet) extended Fernworthy by another 100 acres or so just after the Second World War, bringing the trees almost to the summit of Sittaford Tor. It was only the conferring of National Park status on Dartmoor in 1951 that saw further afforestation halted.

Fernworthy Reservoir today is an important trout fishery and a centre for bird-watching and conservation as well as being popular with visitors. The ancient Fernworthy stone rows, stone circle and the primitive hut circles of Fernworthy Iron-Age village were famous in the nineteenth century, when Dartmoor became the focus for antiquarians. Some of these ancient ruins have disappeared in the forest, but the stone rows and the circle at Fernworthy Down have survived in a clearing.

Left: A view of Fernworthy dam when almost new, taken from the slopes of Metherall Down. The sides of the valley in front of the dam were landscaped by Torbay Corporation and are now heavily grown with burberis and rhododendrons. (Courtesy of the Northway Family, Middlecott)

Looking along the top of Ferworthy dam towards Thornworthy Tor. The intake system seen here projecting on the inner face of the dam has now been removed, as today the reservoir is purely used to maintain river flows. (Thorn Collection)

Here is the later Fernworthy bridge on the occasion of one of its periodic appearances from beneath the waters of the lake – this was in the summer of 1989. (Courtesy of the Mortimore family, Shapley)

Left: *The waters of Fernworthy lake looking towards the dam. The picture was taken during a beating of the parish bounds; this part of the exercise necessitating the use of a boat. (Thorn Collection)*

Right: *A closer view of the dam showing the massive stepped construction and the broad spillway. Despite appearances, this is a mass-concrete structure and is only faced with local granite, which proved too porous for dam-building. (Courtesy of the Mortimore family, Shapley)*

CHAGFORD BRIDGES

Both branches of the Teign and the River Bovey are bridged at several points in Chagford Parish, some of these crossing points being of extremely ancient origin. The highest bridge upstream is Teignhead Clapper on the North Teign, built in 1808 out on the open moor when Teignhead Newtake was enclosed and the farm – one of the most remote on Dartmoor – was established. This packhorse and foot bridge crosses the North Teign where the trackway to the farm drops down from the Fernworthy moorgate to cross the river before climbing back up to the farmstead on the western side. Teignhead bridge was never replaced by a structure capable of taking wheeled traffic; the farm did not prosper and there is a rough ford adjacent to the bridge that probably sufficed for those few vehicles that attempted the trip.

Further back along this same trackway was a single-arch stone bridge over the South Teign leading to Fernworthy Farm, a structure which was rebuilt in the late-nineteenth century to take carts. It was subsequently submerged in the upper reaches of the new reservoir, but at times of drought the drowned bridge re-emerges from the waters; in the exceptionally dry summer of 1976, it was possible to walk over it dry-shod. Today, the furthest upstream bridge on the South Teign is a twentieth-century steel-and-concrete structure immediately below the Fernworthy dam, erected as part of the dam access works. About a mile below this is a modern footpath bridge. Then comes the bridge at Yeo Farm, a single arch which was rebuilt and widened in about 1829. A further mile downstream is Leigh Bridge, rebuilt as a relatively substantial single stone arch after floods damaged the original two-arch structure in the mid 1860s. Apart from the Teignhead clapper and the single-slab bridge at Teignever, the North Teign is crossed only by a modern footbridge on the Mariner's Way footpath in Gidleigh Woods, and by stepping-stones at Gidleigh Steps below Murchington before reaching Leigh.

The first bridge over the combined South and North Teign Rivers was at Holy Street, a simple wooden affair on stone piers suited only to pedestrians and light pack animals. This bridge fell into neglect and disappeared between the wars after the closure of Holy Street Mill, to which it gave access. The first of the surviving ancient bridges is Chagford Bridge, on a site recorded as having been bridged as early as

the eleventh century. This is where the main trackway from Chagford to the north and north-west crosses the Teign Valley, which at this point is steep-sided and narrow, making it a difficult fording-place. The present granite structure dates from about 1600 and has three arches, with piers either side of the main stream. On the Chagford side it is approached by a slightly elevated causeway, and this roadway is rarely known to flood. Chagford Bridge is just over 7.5 feet wide between the parapets, which incorporate v-shaped refuges on each pier. This width is common to many old Dartmoor bridges (North Bovey bridge is exactly the same) and is a dimension probably derived from the width of a laden packhorse when carrying hay, furze or faggots on a back-frame or 'crook'. This bridge has been known somewhat prosaically in more recent times as 'Factory Bridge', due to its proximity to the large woollen mill – the factory – built between 1800 and 1820.

The single-slab granite clapper bridge over the North Teign river at Teignever, looking downstream towards Chagford.
(Thorn Collection)

The other ancient granite bridge leading out of Chagford is at Rushford, a little way above the ford where the river is narrower. This is a twin-arched structure with a substantial central pier of cutwater design, and was originally known as 'Narrow bridge' – which may indicate that it had an original roadway width of 7 feet or less. This bridge was modified and widened during road improvements in 1836–40. Supplementary arches were added outside the main structure to take new parapet walls, increasing the roadway width to around 9 feet. The original structure exists within these supplementary arches and parapets and still supports the load. Although the approach is embanked on the town side, once over the bridge the road drops to the level of the riverside meadows. This stretch of road is prone to flooding from the elevated mill leat to Rushford Mill and is frequently impassable between Rushford bridge and the mill.

The most substantial bridge over the Teign is at Doggamarsh or Dogmarsh and dates from 1809 – a little before the construction of the Whiddon Down to Moretonhampstead turnpike. This bridge – which replaces an older one probably constructed in the early-seventeenth century – is a substantial affair, a broad stone arch sweeping over the river in a single span of some 40 feet. As with many eighteenth- and nineteenth-century structures, it today carries loads undreamed of by its constructors, while with a car-riageway of some 18 feet it is wide enough for most modern traffic to pass. Again, the road approaches

The sixteenth-century Chagford Bridge, in a view dating from the early-twentieth century. Nowadays the trees do not crowd so close around the bridge abutment and the ivy has been cleared. This is recorded as a bridging site as early as the eleventh century, so the present structure is not the original. It is also likely that this is close to the original crossing point of the Teign at 'Chagge-Ford', although it is difficult to decide exactly where this might have been; the river flow on this reach has been drastically altered by the weirs built at Holy Street and above Rushford. (Meldrum Collection)

Left and Below: *Rushford or Narrowbridge, as altered during the improvements to the road from Sandy Park to Chagford around 1840. The additional shallow-crowned masonry arches added either side of the original structure to allow the parapets to be rebuilt on a wider spacing are clearly visible, as are the substantial cutwaters added to the central pier. (Meldrum Collection)*

are built up slightly above the level of the surrounding meadows, which keeps the turnpike clear of floodwater.

The River Bovey is, in its Chagford stages, a mere infant of a river compared to the Teign. It is bridged twice within the parish, the highest crossing point being the ford at Lettaford on the old trackway from Moorgate to Shapley – part of the Mariner's Way. The first bridge is at the foot of Stiniel Down. This is a single-arched nineteenth-century stone bridge that almost certainly replaces a clapper bridge on an ancient crossing-site; a broad, shallow ford is adjacent, and the approach from the Stiniel side is on a relatively substantial causeway. Stiniel Bridge enjoys a picturesque situation and has been a popular spot for picnics for at least the last 150 years.

A little further downstream is Beetor Bridge, another nineteenth-century replacement of an older bridge, although its alignment to the road is somewhat awkward – a feature shared with Yeo Bridge in Chagford and several other similar structures elsewhere in the area. They were probably built thus to keep them reasonably square to the river banks, avoiding the complication of having to construct an arch on a violently-skewed angle, which is a difficult undertaking. The resulting 'kink' in the roadway did not cause a problem for horse-drawn vehicles, but has caught out more than one tripper's coach in recent times!

CHAGFORD CORN-MILLS

Not surprisingly for a parish blessed with a number of swift-flowing streams, Chagford at one time or another has had several water-powered corn-mills, most of which are still extant and, indeed, at least two – at Yeo and Holy Street – have water-wheels that remain in workable order. Throughout most of its recorded history Chagford is listed as having four corn-mills within the parish boundary, but it is likely that these were not always the same four. Water-powered mills are adaptable, and the power generated can be used for a wide variety of purposes, either simultaneously or in succession, as at Yeo. Mills were also prone to damage or destruction – fire and flood being the usual causes.

As with all technology, water-mills underwent considerable development, especially in the nineteenth century when the science of hydraulics emerged and more efficient designs of water-wheel became available. These new wheels, often iron-framed and much broader than the old all-wooden wheels, were developed alongside better bearings and iron rather than wooden gearing. Such developments reduced friction and increased the capacity of the machinery to transmit high power. Some mills were rebuilt and modernised to take advantage of these developments, as at Rushford where earlier mill machinery was replaced and a wide undershot wheel installed

Above: *The highest mill on the Teign is Yeo Mill, on the South Teign River. This is an early mill site but the existing structure dates from the early nineteenth century and remains substantially intact. The present wheel is a 15-foot overshot type installed in 1877.* (Rice Collection)

Above: *Rushford Mill, c.1906. This Valentine's postcard view was one of a selection published in book form by Robert Hole Thorn, the Chagford Postmaster. The wheel here was undershot, of quite a wide breast. The mill proper was relatively small and the machinery was later adapted for other uses including sawmilling.* (Thorn Collection)

Holy Street was the best-known and most photographed (and painted) of Chagford's water-mills – not on account of technical interest or efficiency, but rather because of its picturesque situation and rustic charm. These two postcards date from around 1890–1900 and show the primitive nature of the installation, with the overshot wheel of around 15 feet in diameter fed by a wooden launder. (Above left: Rice Collection. Above right: Meldrum Collection)

to take advantage of the large leat and plentiful water supply. Other mills that were unsuited to modernisation – such as Holy Street – became uneconomic and unable to compete in the face of the new 'super mills', which could grind corn more quickly and in far greater volume.

Chagford's oldest mill sites were probably at what is now Rack Park on the Teign and at Holy Street, where power probably originally came from a steeply-falling tributary stream of the Teign. Batworthy, where machinery is still extant, also seems likely to be of ancient origin as it occupies a situation typical of early mills, on a stretch of water with a relatively steep fall. This made it possible to use a simple undershot wheel working directly in the stream, thus avoiding the need for extensive impounding works and the construction of leats or launders. The existing installation at Batworthy is relatively modern, although remains of older machinery exist. It is driven by a still-flowing leat from the Bovey, and a modern wheel has been installed for power generation purposes.

Early stream-mills were somewhat limited in that the power produced was directly proportional to the rate of flow of the waterway – a factor which was largely out of the control of the miller. Later mills relied on a pound, usually a section of the river whose level was artificially raised by a weir, but otherwise supplied by creating a reservoir above the desired working level and fed by one or more sources. Pound-mills were assured of a more consistent water supply, and the mill could work at or near its full capacity whatever the river flows; only a prolonged drought – where the overall flow was so reduced as to be less than the extraction rate needed to drive the wheel for a reasonable period each day – would affect the working.

Yeo Mill was the highest upriver and most distant of Chagford's mills, situated on the South Teign not far below the point where it left the open moor. The site was a mill from about the mid-sixteenth century (c.1545), although the extant structure probably dates back to around the late-seventeenth century and has been, successively, a corn-mill, a sawmill and – in a very small way – a power station. It is still workable, both to generate modest amounts of electric current and to saw logs. The current wheel is a composite wood-and-iron overshot wheel of 13 feet diameter by 40 inches breast dating from 1877, when it replaced an older wooden wheel. Yeo is basically a stream-mill, although it is fed by a widened leat above the road level which would have formed a small pound – enough to keep a reasonably consistent supply at times of low flow.

Batworthy Mill on the Bovey was also somewhat remotely situated, which suggests early origins. Later mills were generally erected at locations where they were easily accessible by road. Early mills, however, relied on the packhorse to deliver the raw grist and to remove the finished product, and thus tended to be built close to or even as part of the farms they served. It may well be that Batworthy is a very ancient mill site indeed, as it lies adjacent to some of the earliest areas of settlement on the edge of the moor in both Chagford and North Bovey Parishes. Records of water-driven corn-mills extend back into prehistory, and there could quite possibly have been a crude corn-mill here as early as the pre-Saxon period following the Roman departure. We know that the Celtic farmers of this period were raising crops of rye and, later, oats. There are records of a not-dissimilar upland corn-mill operating at Babeny, near Poundsgate, before 1303.

A mill site is recorded at Holy Street as long ago as the eleventh century. The surviving structure is not that ancient, but it is certainly an early mill, with a narrow overshot wheel typical of those dating from the sixteenth century. For power, it relied on a small and quite lengthy leat cut from the river near Gidleigh Park. The water-wheel at Holy Street is about 15 feet in diameter by 2 feet breast, situated on the end wall of the main mill building and fed by a wooden launder. The building itself was constructed in part in stone with an upper storey of weatherboarding under a thatched roof. It probably possessed only one set of stones, and had difficult access either over the somewhat insubstantial bridge at Holy Street or along a track from the north end of Chagford Bridge. It was, however, picturesque in the extreme, and became a popular subject for postcards like the one reproduced here. The mill fell into disuse in the early years of the twentieth century (believed to have closed in 1906) and became ruinous. In recent times it has been restored and the wheel is used to generate power.

RIVER WEIRS & MILL POUNDS

River weirs to create pounds were built at three points on the Teign: Holy Street – to supply the succession of mills on the south bank of the river at what is now called Factory; about half a mile above Rushford, to supply Rushford Mill; and at Doggamarsh, for the large corn-mill later erected there. These mills all used undershot wheels, where the water was fed in below the level of the shaft. As such, they did not require a great fall of water. Such wheels date from the time when it was realised that the wheel only developed real power over half its effective diameter, and that a wide but smaller-diameter wheel working breast or undershot from a plentiful water supply could be made more efficient than a tall, narrow wheel fed from above, or 'overshot'.

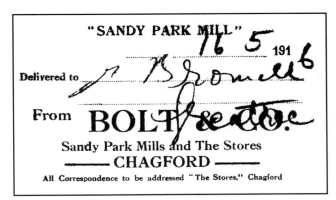

Sandy Park Mills was the trading name of the large mid-nineteenth-century corn-mill at Dogmarsh (Doggamarsh). Bolts were the millers; they also ran the 'Stores' in Chagford, selling foodstuffs, farm necessities, ironmongery, lamp oils and other sundries. (Courtesy of Leonard Brommell, Great Tree)

Rushford Mill is a typical small eighteenth-century corn-mill. The building is intact and has been structurally restored, now forming part of the complex of modern agricultural buildings at the hamlet of Rushford. It is probable that the existing mill arrangements date from the mid- to late-nineteenth century; the broad undershot wheel is now missing, although the leat still flows. With a large river pound giving a good water supply, this was probably the best-sited of all Chagford's older mills – convenient for the town and easily accessible from the main arable farms in the parish. It ceased grinding in the early years of the twentieth century, being latterly worked only for immediate farm use. Rushford is currently the site of Chagford's open-air swimming pool, built in 1934 and fed with water by the old mill leat.

The largest corn-mill to work in Chagford was the relatively modern structure erected at Doggamarsh, Sandy Park, in the nineteenth century, quite possibly following the opening of the adjacent turnpike and the new river bridge; the older bridging site was a little further upstream. This is, in all probability, an older mill site, and the big new corn-mill would have superseded a smaller farm mill. This was known as Sandy Park Mill, although that name might also be associated with the still-extant mill at Furlong – now a house – which, along with the whole hamlet of Sandy Park, is technically in Drewsteignton Parish.

The new mill at Doggamarsh certainly traded as Sandy Park Mill, at least for a period, and with good road links soon came to serve a wide area. It has a substantial breastshot water-wheel, fed by a large leat and launder from a pound on the river about a quarter of a mile upstream. The wheel worked an extensive set of gearing driving several sets of stones (not all simultaneously – large modern mills of this type usually possessed different sets of

stones for different types of feedstock or grist) as well as sack hoists, riddlers and possibly other machines such as chaff-cutters for producing animal feeds. This mill operated into the twentieth century, finally ceasing work in 1917. It was subsequently converted into an hotel. The leat, launders, wheel and weir are all extant, and were used for power generation in the 1930s.

THE WOOLLEN MILLS

The earliest recorded mill in Chagford was a fourteenth-century tucking-mill on the river bank just below Chagford Bridge. It is probable that this was a stream-mill relying directly on river flow which, in the period before the impounding of this length of the river to form the reservoir for Rushford Mill, would have been swift-flowing. There is also a possibility that another early tucking-mill existed on the Padley Brook on the higher side of the road from the town down to Chagford Bridge – known as Mill Street – on the site of what is now Millpond. The name of the street itself suggests that these are old mill sites predating the existing structures. Some records suggest these were originally corn-mills, but it may be that the exact classification of the mills was unclear or, in fact, they were changed from one use to another.

Both these early sites came to be part of the main complex of the Chagford woollen mills established by Mr Berry in the opening years of the nineteenth century. These included a mill actually in the town, beside the junctions of Mill Street and Manor Road. From the descriptions of the works established here, this mill was driven by a leat later integrated into the town water supply system, which suggests a modest wheel of low power, as none of the streams feeding this network have a high enough flow to work any but a small water-wheel. It seems probable that this was simply a small combing-mill, a process not requiring great power. The next lower site at Millpond became the original fulling-mill of the Berry complex and, as the modern name suggests, possesses a substantial pound. This water was undoubtedly used for cloth-finishing purposes, but there may also have been a fulling frame here driven by a further small wheel. Fulling was the process of finishing and bulking-up the fabric by abrasion, and involved the washing, bleaching or dyeing of finished cloth.

The heart of the Berry Mill complex was the 'Factory' at Factory Cross, a substantial woollen mill built in the early years of the nineteenth century over a broad leat taken off the river at Holy Street; this may have superseded an earlier, smaller leat as the weir at Holy Street shows signs of pre-dating the existing leat. The 'Factory' was powered by a large undershot wheel of 14 by 14 feet which, taken with the capacity of the leat and the healthy river flow, would have made for a very powerful installation. This mill, opened not long after Mr Berry set up business in 1800, operated regularly until 1848 and then spasmodically until about 1880. The wheel was finally converted for electricity generation in 1891. The buildings here have since been largely demolished, although parts of the complex survive in the hunt kennels that now occupy the site. For electricity generating purposes, the converted mill-wheel was later replaced by a small turbine fed by the mill leat, which is still extant.

Largest of the extant mill buildings in Chagford is the substantial 'Blanket Factory' at the foot of Rack Park, on the site of the earlier corn and/or woollen mill. This was the last of Mr Berry's mills, opened about 1820 and fed by the same leat from the river at Holy Street. Again, this used an undershot wheel, probably of similar size to that at the Factory Cross mill, given that it used the same water supply. The wheel powered a range of machinery including fulling and carding machines and the looms and presses for the production of woollen cloth, blankets, serges and felts. This mill finally ceased work around 1880 and has since been largely converted into housing.

Above: *The outfall of the tail race at Factory, on the mill leat which fed both this woollen mill and the later Lower Factory. It also provided the power for Chagford's miniscule hydro-electic station, the turbine and generator being housed in the small concrete structure in the background.* (Rice Collection)
(Document Courtesy of Leonard Brommell Esq., Great Tree)

HYDRO-ELECTRICITY IN CHAGFORD

The first electrical installation in the Chagford district was set up by Mr G.H. Reed, who had arrived in the area in 1890. Mr Reed described himself on his letterhead as – among many other things – an electrical engineer, and in 1891 he justified this description by installing a generating plant at Factory, driven by the old 14 x 14 foot undershot wheel of Mr Berry's mill. There are conflicting accounts of the technical details of this plant, which attracted widespread attention at the time. One description had the system working at '2,000 volts DC' – a frightening thought. It was certainly a DC plant, the design of alternators for AC current generation being at that time in its infancy, but the operating voltage was probably somewhere around 100 volts. The power was taken into the town on overhead lines and used to provide limited street lighting as well as power to individual buildings. These included Cranley House (built in 1862), where the remains of the original wiring from the DC installation were discovered by the owner in 1984.

Chagford was widely claimed to be the 'first town west of London to have its streets lit by electricity', which may well be so. However, it was not the first large-scale installation in the district; that honour goes to the 110V DC plant installed in Okehampton by Mr Geen some time before 1888. This substantial hydro-electric plant was driven by the East Okement River and provided power not only to Mr Geen's sawmill – the original purpose of the installation – but also to neighbouring houses and businesses. Both these pioneering installations became part of the West Devon Electricity Supply Company in 1930, and were eventually absorbed into the South-Western Electricity Board. The Chagford site was modernised by the installation of a turbine and conversion to AC generation in 1914. It was rebuilt again after the West Devon company took over in 1930, the turbine and generator being relocated to the existing small building to allow the mill site to be cleared. Eventually, the tiny Chagford hydro-electric station came to be the smallest generating unit feeding power into the national grid – all 33KW of it! It is still intact, although no longer in active use.

Not long after Mr Reed's electricity plant at Factory was established, a pioneering private installation was undertaken by Mr Wallace Perryman at Yeo Mill. In 1893 he installed a simple DC dynamo, arranged to be driven from the old overshot water-wheel, providing power to light the house and farm. This plant originally worked at 100 volts DC, a common value for early installations; it was later upgraded to 110V, and is still in workable order at the time of writing.

These small-scale hydro-electric enterprises pale into insignificance against the proposals of the Dartmoor and District Hydro-Electric Supply Company. If this scheme – proposed by Dr John Archibald Purves in 1919 – had come to fruition, hydro-electric generation in the area might have become more significant. However, the proposal, which called for eight reservoirs at various points on the moor and several power stations, including one at Leigh Bridge, would have destroyed many of the beauties of the area. The scheme rumbled on for nearly 20 years, being finally rejected by the House of Lords in 1937.

THE RIVER FISHERY

The creation of weirs to feed the various mills to some extent 'tamed' the river in the vicinity of Chagford, giving broader, slow-flowing reaches that have proved to be a huge asset to anglers. The Teign is a salmon river, and an important trout fishery with good stocks of native brown trout and, in season, sea trout as well as coarse fish. The banks are largely managed by the Upper Teign Fishing Association, and rod licences can still be obtained at Bowden's shop in the town, as has been the case for very many years.

Both coarse and flyfishing, on a wide variety of waters, has long been one of the traditional attractions of the Chagford district to visitors of a sporting bent, and several of the local hotels are well-known in angling circles. James Perrot, the famous Dartmoor guide of the late-nineteenth century, was also a well-known maker of fishing tackle, sold from his premises in Chagford Square. Chagford waters were then famous for the quantity, size and tenacity of their fish. Surely a fitting end to this quick dip into their clear, cool depths is by emulating Jane Hayter-Hames in her 1981 *History of Chagford* and quoting from the delightful letter written by an enthusiastic angler in 1910 to Revd Hayter-Hames, then riparian owner at Rushford:

Druid Arms,
Drewsteignton,
Devon

18 June 1910

Dear Sir,

Thank you not only for the permit, but for the cordiality accompanying it.

I was out yesterday and was very surprised. I am not a specialised 'carpist' but this should be the carp angler's paradise. The pool swarmed with them and I'm sure there must be monsters there. Something, which I tried hard to catch a glimpse of for a long time, broke me badly, and I was using salmon wire. There are no sea-serpents there, I suppose!...

A typical stretch of fishing water in the Chagford district, from an old postcard entitled 'Mountain Stream near Chagford' – probably the lower reaches of Blackaton Brook.
(Meldrum Collection)

Chagford farmland viewed from Rushford. Arable land and meadows on the lower slopes of the river valley, give way to rough common grazing land at higher altitudes. The changeover from arable and pasture to hill land generally occurs at 6–700 feet above sea level, although modern farming practices have produced improved pasturage and some arable land on the higher ground. (Meldrum Collection)

Chagford farmland from Nattadon, showing the broad tract of good arable land lying north and east of the town. Land seen here is from Rushford, Withecombe, Greatastones, Weeke and Whiteabury farms in the Chagford Parish, the more distant land lying in Moretonhampstead or Drewsteignton. Most of the long narrow fields running down from Meldon Road towards Padley Common are 'open fields' and hence form part of the common grazing between August and November. (Thorn Collection)

THREE

FARMS & AGRICULTURE

The *White's Directory of Devon* for 1850 describes Chagford's agriculture thus:

The parish comprises 7,492 acres, of which 5,732 acres are old enclosures and well cultivated; 1,271 acres are in pasturage and tillage on Dartmoor; 359 acres are waste, and 129 acres are in roads & co'

Presumably the buildings of the town constitute the '& co'. This might suggest a basically arable agriculture, but of course the summary fails to mention the common grazings and extensive sheepwalks on Dartmoor, on which much of Chagford's economy has always depended. In fact, the farm economy of the area has long been split between the mixed holdings on the low ground and the hill farms on the moor edge, a distinction which still holds today.

EARLY FARMING

Dartmoor was first exploited for agriculture and husbandry in the Neolithic period, in around 3000BC. The people in this era practiced a primitive form of cultivation to produce very limited crops, mostly coarse rye, on small areas of cleared ground associated with settlements on the fringes of the high moor. The first organised development of agriculture dates from the Bronze Age, when the high moorland was far more populous than the surrounding heavily-wooded low ground. The moor is littered with relics of this period of settlement – monuments, burial sites, hut circles, pounds, reaves (bank and ditch boundaries), enclosures and the distinctive stigmata of terraced cultivation. It was not until the Celtic period of the later Bronze Age and the Iron Age that what we recognise as the 'modern historic' settlement and clearance pattern began to emerge, creating the underlying elements of the distinctive moorland-fringe landscape commonly referred to as 'in-country'.

Early agriculture on Dartmoor came in two basic forms: herding of livestock for meat, wool and hides; and the small-scale cultivation of subsistence crops,

particularly rye and oats, on areas of cleared ground. This marginal arable land was either won from open moorland or the surrounding areas of scrub woodland. Such early-Celtic farmland is characterised by small, squarish fields bounded by stone-faced hedgebanks – a pattern still clearly discernible at many places in Chagford Parish. The banks are built from freestone, individual pieces of weathered granite found lying haphazardly over the surface of the moor or among the roots of trees. For purposes of cultivation, these boulders have to be removed, which is a laborious process that has been going on almost continuously for the last 2,000 years. The ancient and characteristic Dartmoor hedgebank was as much a convenient way of disposing of the piles of unwanted stone as it was a means of enclosure.

In the vicinity of Chagford, this pattern of agricultural settlement seems to have started on the more sheltered areas of the moorland in the middle Bronze Age, around 3000BC, and continued under Celtic influence throughout the Roman period.

Sheep have always been a staple of Chagford's economy and local breeders have, over the years, refined their flocks to produce animals of exceptional quality and hardiness. This is Maurice Hill of East Coombe with prize ewes on land at Withecombe, with Meldon Hill and Chagford in the background. (Courtesy of Maurice Hill Esq., East Coombe)

These early moorland enclosures were augmented by the Saxon woodland clearances of the seventh and eighth centuries, characterised by larger but less regular fields on the lower ground. Such clearance was obviously a slow process, as at the time of the Domesday survey in 1086 there were only five farm settlements listed in what became Chagford Parish: Chagford, Rushford, Middlecott, Shapley and Teigncombe. It is interesting that two of these farms – Shapley and Teigncombe – are situated relatively high up on the shoulder of the moor and probably grew from Bronze Age or Celtic clearances, while Chagford, Middlecott and Rushford are on the easier land of the valley bottom and thus are probably Saxon in origin. This would suggest that even at this early date, the split nature that has always characterised Chagford farming was evident, with the pure hill farms concentrating on stock rearing for trade, while, at the lower levels, a more mixed pattern of subsistence agriculture was established.

There is relatively little high-grade arable land in Chagford Parish, even today after more than a millennium of steady improvement. Most of the cultivation is concentrated on banks of the Teign and its immediate tributaries towards the valley bottom, and on the easily-graded land rising towards Whiddon Down: Leigh, Holy Street, the Withecombes, Rushford, Great Tree, Doggamarsh, Whiteabury, Greatastones, Adley, Weeke, Yellam, Horselake, Middlecott and Westcott became the main arable holdings. Away from the main watercourses the land rises steeply, with a further series of farms straddling the divide between the easier ground of the valley and the hill land proper: Nattadon, Down Park, Higher Middlecott, Batworthy, Uppacott, Weddicott, Yellands, Downes, Broadhalls, Stiniel, Tunnaford, Waye Barton, Buda, Beechlands, Thorn, Hole, Collihole, Outer Down, East and West Combe, Yeo, Northill and Southill and the Murchington farms all fall into this category. These farms were mixed, running stock on the higher grazing and on small commons like Weeke, Stiniel or Waye downs or on the open moor, while at the same time working the lower ground for cereal and root crops, meadow hay, orchards, fatstock raising and dairying.

Higher still, on the southern shoulder of the valley where it rises to the moorland edge, come the true hill farms. Many of them are at or above the 1,000-foot contour and have little or even no arable land. Such farms include Corndon, Beetor, Jurston, Lingcombe, Hurston, Shapley, Metherall, Fernworthy, Teignhead, Thornworthy, Teignworthy, Frenchbeer, Yelfords, Teigncombe, Brimstone Down and Batworthy-in-the-Moor. The main business of these farms was the running of sheep on the open moorland of the Dartmoor Commons, to produce what became an increasingly valuable commodity – wool.

This marked a fundamental characteristic of Chagford hill-husbandry even from the earliest

An ancient enclosure bank on Northill Farm, Chagford, built with stone cleared from the land. This is the characteristic form of Dartmoor bank that goes back to Celtic times – the large boulders (grounders) topped with smaller stones to level up the bank-top, crowned with a hedge of thorn or beech. (Rice Collection)

times: that of specialism, of producing what in the modern vernacular would be described as a 'cash crop', as opposed to the pure subsistence farming practiced elsewhere. The success of Chagford's agriculture thus greatly depended upon the success of the town as a centre of trade and, later, manufacture. There is no doubt that the granting of the Stannary Charter in 1305 was a major impetus to Chagford's agricultural development, as it made the town a de facto trading centre and hence a natural site both for a market and as a centre for the emerging trade in woollen cloth. An early example of 'added value' in farming is that much of the yarn was spun and the cloth woven on the farms themselves.

MEDIEVAL FARMING IN CHAGFORD

So the real growth in farming in the Chagford district came with the development of the woollen industry from the thirteenth through to the seventeenth century. The growth occurred not only in the hill farms producing wool, but in the mixed farms that produced food – such staples as flour, meat and dairy products. Many of the farm settlements date from this period, and a number of important buildings – such as Bishop's House in Lower Street, the Whiddon House (now Three Crowns) and, of course, St Michael's Church – remain as testimonials to this period of growth and prosperity. In the sixteenth century Chagford had a large number of farmsteads of one sort or another, some of which were right in the heart of the town. A number of ancient farmhouses can be seen among the more prosaic town buildings, including Bellacouch, Bishop's House and Orchard. During this period, the range of crops grown was extended to include barley and, later, wheat.

Most of the farms in and around Chagford were small affairs, some of the hill holdings consisting of little more than a farmstead and half a dozen small fields, probably totalling no more than 20 or 30 acres. Their main reliance was on the common grazing of the moor. Even the valley farms were generally of modest size, although historically farming everywhere worked on a far more restricted scale than is the modern norm. It was a very labour-intensive business, and the possibilities for expansion were limited by the available horse- and man-power, as well as the relatively poor nature of much of the ground and the difficulties of access. Dartmoor's climate has never made for the easiest of farming – an apocryphal local description being 'six months' winter followed by six months' bad weather.'

The soils of the Chagford area (loam over granite, according to Charles Vancouver) are predominantly acidic in nature, which has always limited arable production. From the medieval period, a number of 'manures' were spread to dress the land in an attempt to improve the soil balance. As well as straightforward farmyard manures, wood ash was widely used. Indeed, many farms had an ash house in which the residue from domestic fires was stored for this purpose. Characteristically, these are small round 'beehive' structures, as at Nattadon Farm. However, some farms had larger, rectangular or square buildings with a pitched roof, an example of which survives at Frenchbeer. Unlike more favoured areas, the poor transport links of medieval

Chagford did not permit the importation of alien manures such as lime, marl or sea sand, widely used elsewhere in Devon.

Dartmoor Farmsteads

The ancient Dartmoor farms were compact and self-contained. They were centred around the highly characteristic 'longhouse' that is found at the heart of virtually all old Devon steadings. The longhouse originally combined the farmer's living quarters, a shippon and a fodder store or 'tallet' in one long, low building. It was usually built diagonally across the slope, with its back against a sheltering hillside. The accommodation was arranged down the slope, divided into two parts by a cross-passage: animals one side, people the other. Normally, the habitable part of the house was uphill from the shippon, ensuring that manure and other undesirables drained away from the living quarters.

In their earliest form many longhouses did not possess a chimney and a Saxon roof hole was relied upon to allow the smoke from cooking fires to escape. Over the centuries the buildings became far more sophisticated and were usually rebuilt and extended. Alternatively, the original longhouse was abandoned or used simply as a barn or shippon, being replaced by a newer building nearby. On some farms, such as Yeo, several distinct dwellings can be traced. By the seventeenth century most longhouses had a substantial fireplace and chimney added to the living space. Subsequently, a new larger shippon

The epitome of a traditional Dartmoor farm: Nattadon, Chagford, in an absolutely stunning Chapman postcard dating from about 1920, with the buildings in immaculate order. Note the conical thatched ash house at left, a fine example of this traditional Dartmoor feature that is happily still extant (see also The Book of Lustleigh*). The thatched hipped-roof barn has been lost, however, and the scene today unfortunately lacks much of the charm so evident in this picture.* (Thorn Collection)

Right: *One of the best-known of Chagford's ancient longhouses – Stiniel, showing the use of the slope to position the living quarters of the farmer (the far end) above those occupied by his stock. Note the truly massive granite block incorporated in the front wall of the building adjacent to the door – a sign of antiquity but also an enigma; how was a piece of granite this large quarried and raised on site?* (Rice Collection)

Left: *East Coombe farmhouse, Chagford, set tight against the slope of Waye Hill where it drops down to the South Teign Valley. This is a typical siting for a Dartmoor farmhouse – set at a slight diagonal on the slope to give both shelter and a slight fall over the length of the building. In earlier times, this helped drainage of that part of the building housing the animals.* (Courtesy of Maurice Hill Esq.)

Above: *There are three farmsteads in close proximity at Middlecott, one of the original Saxon manors (Mitel-cote) mentioned in the Domesday Book. This is the farmhouse at Higher Middlecott – a farm held for generations by the Northway family. This view from about 1920 is taken from the farm's highly-productive vegetable garden.* (Courtesy of the Northway Family, Middlecott)

was often built at the downhill end, at right-angles to the existing building. The original shippon was then taken into the house to extend the living area, resulting in the classic layout of a cross-passage with rooms either side. In grander examples, a gabled porch was added to the front of the passage, along with a scullery or dairy at the back. The room over the porch was sometimes used as a wool store, keeping this valuable commodity secure. An example of a typical medieval longhouse modified thus is Jurston, which retains many of its original features.

The moorland farmsteads are sited in sheltered locations with 'their backs to the hill', out of the track of prevailing south-westerly winds. They often present a virtually blank 'weather wall', bereft of any but the smallest openings – characteristics easily seen at Higher Corndon or Jurston. In the Chagford district, these ancient longhouses are of massive solidity, often being built of huge blocks of granite, as at Stiniel or Lettaford. Generally, the more monolithic the construction, the older the structure – although it is interesting to speculate just how these big blocks of granite were moved to the site and then manipulated into place with the limited means then available. The rest of the structure is equally rugged, with heavy timberwork in oak and a thick roof, originally of heather thatch. Only comparatively recently – in the last 200 years – has the use of heather for thatch given way to long-straw or combed wheat-reed thatch, while re-roofing with slate (imported from Delabole in Cornwall or by sea from Wales) started in the nineteenth century. Very often such re-roofings followed a fire, to which thatched properties have always been somewhat prone. Many local farmhouses bear evidence of past fire damage, and accounts of farm fires occur regularly in written records.

Many Dartmoor farmsteads were completed by the later addition of a barn and 'linhay' or open-fronted shed. These were often added in the eighteenth or nineteenth century to form a U-shaped group or even a complete quadrangle of buildings giving all-round shelter from the driving winter weather. A good example of a fully-developed Dartmoor farmstead of the seventeenth century is Hole, on the 'back road' from Thorn to Yardworthy, about a mile and a half south-west of Chagford. Other additions might include a 'pound house', containing a horse-gin – a small circular track around which an ox, ass or horse would walk to turn a vertical shaft by means of a pole attached to a collar. Such gins were used to power machinery for apple crushing, chaff-cutting, milling or similar purposes. A typical example of such a building – usually a five-sided structure built against the side or end of a barn, with a hipped roof supported by monolithic granite or heavy timber pillars – can be seen at Nattadon Farm.

TRADITIONAL HUSBANDRY

On the typical Dartmoor farm the 'home fields' surrounded the farmstead. Here, stock was over-wintered in conditions somewhat more sheltered than the open moor, while crops of meadow hay were grown in the summer. Out on the moor, sheep husbandry demanded few facilities; pounds (rough stone-walled enclosures for herding or lambing) and simple shelter-huts for the shepherds are the only abiding signs. The spring grass was encouraged by 'swaling' – burning off rough, dead vegetation early in the season, a process which not only removed the top layer of dead vegetation but also returned nutrients to the impoverished moorland soils by way of the resulting ash. Unfortunately, the swaling process used over the past few centuries has also had the effect of encouraging the replacement of slower-growing heathers by the thick-growing Western Gorse and bracken; these alien, introduced plants have proved more vigorous than the native species.

The open moor provided many resources for the hill farm other than grazing. Furze (gorse) was cut as a valuable fuel and ferns or bracken were also harvested for bedding animals in the shippons. Most upland farms had turving rights on the moor peat, and each summer enough turves would be cut and dried for winter needs. Comparatively little wood was available for fuel, as it had to be carted up from the lower-lying areas. Wortleberries (bilberries) were a further resource widely exploited in earlier times, both as a useful addition to the farm diet and as a saleable crop. Doubtless the humble blackberry also figured in this way, along with sloes, hips and haws. The last great moorland bounty was the almost limitless availability of good building stone, found in easily accessible form scattered about the moorland surface.

Inset: Swaling is the tradition of burning off dead vegetation and unwanted overgrowth early in the spring to bring on the 'first bite' grass keep in early summer. As well as clearing the gorse or – as here – dead bracken, the ash resulting from swaling fires also fertilises the soil. This area is on the face of Meldon Hill below Buda Farm. (Thorn Collection)

LIVESTOCK

The upland commons of Dartmoor are suited only to sheep of hardy breeds, and over the centuries specific strains have evolved that are peculiarly suited to the rough grazing and even rougher climate. Locally, the most characteristic of these traditional breeds are the Dartmoor and Whiteface Dartmoor. The traditional Dartmoor is a stocky, heavy-fleeced animal with a long, thick, curled coat that extends to the legs and head; it is related to the ancient Devon Longwool breed. The wool produced, while relatively coarse, is long-stranded and thus readily spun into tough and hard-wearing yarns, and is suited to the production of worsteds as well as to the felting and serge-making processes. In spite of their name, these animals do not fare so well on the highest ground except in very favourable conditions, and are usually kept on the moor fringe and over-wintered in-by (in sheltered folds or fields close to the farmstead).

The Whiteface Dartmoor is a smaller but exceptionally tough beast with a shorter but denser coat, giving wool less coarse in texture and not quite so long, but very thick and compact. These are more agile animals than the longwool types, and use the steep, rocky and rough areas of grazing on the high moor to full advantage. The lambing ewes are over-wintered in-by, but the wethers remain on the sheepwalks throughout the year. The Whiteface is also noted for producing fine mutton, and has long been the staple breed on Dartmoor. Vancouver gives the typical yield of a five-year-old Whiteface wether as '16lbs (meat) per quarter, and 4–6½lbs unwashed wool'. In more recent times, upland breeds from other parts of the British Isles have been introduced to the moor,

Maurice Hill moving ewes and lambs on to pasture at Factory Cross, Chagford, about 1960 – the Dartmoor hill farmer complete with pony. The relaxed demeanour of the stock and the patient attitudes of the farmer and his dog provide a stark contrast with what is often seen today – harried beasts being rushed along the roadway ahead of a roaring tractor. (Courtesy of Maurice Hill Esq., East Coombe)

most notably the Scotch Blackface and the Cheviot. Nowadays, many sheep over-winter on the open moor except in the harshest conditions, but the older tradition was to shelter them in pounds.

All these Dartmoor sheep have that 'ranging' instinct that is so vital in hill breeds; an inherited knowledge of the area of moor on which they were raised and to which they belong. It is rare for a Dartmoor-bred sheep to stray far from their own 'range' or sheepwalk. Even if a flock changed ownership, their range on the moor remained the same – the grazing essentially went with the animals. The moor sheep are also very savvy as to the best

Above: *Sheep on summer pasture at East Coombe, Chagford. This wonderful picture encapsulates the essential relationship of true Dartmoor hill farming: the farmer, his stock, and his dog. The only missing element here is the pony traditionally used to reach the higher sheepwalks.*
(Courtesy Maurice Hill Esq., East Coombe)

Left: *Winters nowadays may not be as hard as they once were, but few years pass on Dartmoor without some snowfall – at least on the higher ground. Here, the Mortimore family are feeding sheep in the winter of 1996 on Hurston Ridge, Dartmoor.* (Courtesy of the Mortimore family, Shapley)

Right: *The high sheepwalks on the open moor are the basis of Dartmoor grazing and sheep-rearing, reached peaceably by pony before the invention of the quad bike. Maurice Hill on Shovel Down, Chagford.* (Courtesy of Maurice Hill Esq., East Coombe)

Above left: *Shearing at Higher Shapley, June 1946. Fred Hutchings, Harold, Albert and Cyril Wonnacott with dogs.* (Courtesy of the Mortimore family, Shapley)

Above right: *A shearing party at Higher Shapley Farm in June 1946. Left to right, the shearers are: Fred Hutchings of Yardworthy, Albert, Mary and Cyril Wonnacott, Joe Wonnacott, Harold Wonnacott and Will White. Note the two-wheeled farm 'tip cart' on the right in the background, typically used for liming, muck-carting and manure-spreading. This example was locally built by Drewes of Venton. Here it forms part of a temporary sheep pen.* (Courtesy of the Mortimore family, Shapley)

Albert Wonnacott and his dog 'Squig' at Shapley before the Second World War. (Courtesy of the Mortimore family, Shapley)

Ivan Mortimore feeding an orphan foal in the yard at Higher Shapley in September, 1973. (Courtesy of the Mortimore family, Shapley)

locations for resisting all types of adverse weather, using every scrap of shelter to best advantage. They thrive on the coarse Dartmoor grasses and sedges, and can also browse heather and some types of moss or lichen.

The traditional Dartmoor cattle are the upland or 'Widecombe' variant of the South Devon or South Hams breed; they are slightly stockier and with a rougher, darker coat than the smoother variant found south of Totnes. These are a hardy dual-purpose animal, well equipped to deal both with the poor grass keep – on which they fare surprisingly well – and with the climate. As such they are an ideal compromise for small mixed upland farms. Some sources derive these splendid beasts from thirteenth-century importations of the French Limousin breed, and they certainly have much in common with that strain. South Devons are good milkers, both in quantity and quality, coming close to the fabled Channel Islands breeds for butterfat levels, while they also fatten to a good weight; indeed, they are among the largest of our native breeds. A full-grown South Devon bull or steer will make a ton or more in weight. Traditionally, they are also good draft animals, being strong but amenable to the plough.

Again, the last 50 years or so have seen a number of other upland breeds successfully introduced on

the moor, including the black Aberdeen Angus, the wide-horned Highland and the characteristically marked Galloways. Some cross-breeds – often with Charolais – are also now seen, while the ubiquitous Friesian has largely displaced the South Devon for dairying on the lower ground. Despite this there are still a number of farms in the Chagford district that pride themselves on clinging to the 'Devon Reds', and there are several pedigree herds in the Dartmoor area, although one such was tragically lost in the 2001 foot-and-mouth disease outbreak.

DARTMOOR PONIES

The other main livestock run on the moor is, of course, the Dartmoor pony, descended from the wild native British hill pony first tamed in Celtic times. These ponies have adapted over the centuries to the Dartmoor conditions, producing a small breed that embodies exceptional hardiness. In former times, these sturdy beasts were used for all manner of draft work on the moor as well as for military purposes, such as drawing Celtic war chariots. Later, they became a base breeding stock which, crossed with imported strains, produced many of the other traditional British breeds. In the eighteenth and

Left: *A farming essential; the draught horse 'Prince' at Shapley, c.1950.* (Courtesy of the Mortimore family, Shapley)

Below: *The three Wonnacott sisters – Mary, 'Dar' and Vera on their pony, c.1930.* (Courtesy of the Mortimore family, Shapley)

Below left: *Ponies were an integral part of life on Dartmoor, and most farm children learnt to ride as naturally as they learnt to walk or speak. Here are Vera and Dar (Dorothy) Wonnacott on their ponies at Shapley in 1946. On the left is the end of the original Shapley farmhouse, unusually, given the moorland situation, built of cob. It became unsafe and was demolished in the early 1950s. It had been uninhabitable for a long time by then, being replaced by a new farmhouse in the 1920s.* (Courtesy of the Mortimore family, Shapley)

Below right: *The continuity of the Chagford farming tradition: a pen of blackface sheep at the Young Farmers' show at Exeter Market in 1988 entered by Gordon and Julie Mortimore – the generation of the family farming Higher Shapley at the time of writing.* (Courtesy of the Mortimore family, Shapley)

Ploughing with horses at West Coombe Farm, Chagford, before the Second World War. A youthful Ivan Mortimore assists his uncle, George Sprague.
(Courtesy of the Mortimore family, Shapley)

Right: *Horses were still being used for farm work in the Chagford area until well into the 1960s and even the early 1970s. Universal though the diesel tractor became, there were some aspects of Dartmoor farm topography that were just unsuited to mechanisation.* (Courtesy of Maurice Hill, East Coombe)

Below: *The Dartmoor pony is now firmly established as an excellent riding pony, especially for children. Here is Anne Thorn on her Dartmoor pony, c.1962.* (Thorn Collection)

Below right: *Dartmoor ponies grazing on the open moor. Contrary to widespread popular belief, these animals are not 'wild', but are farm livestock ranking with sheep and cattle in the moor's economy.* (Thorn Collection)

Harrowing by horse at East Coombe, using a chain harrow to break up the surface ley and aerate the soil. (Courtesy of Maurice Hill Esq., East Coombe)

nineteenth centuries, Dartmoor ponies were in great demand for draft work of all sorts – as pack ponies, to go between the shafts of light vehicles and to toil underground in the Victorian coal pits. In cases where small size was important, as with the pit ponies, Dartmoor mares were often run with a Shetland stallion.

In spite of their small size (generally 12.2 hands or less), Dartmoors also proved excellent riding ponies, particularly on difficult ground. To this day some of the moor farmers use them to get out onto the sheepwalks of the moor and for drifting (rounding-up) animals. More recently, the breed has found favour as a good, all-round children's mount, a role in which they are still popular. They even have their own 'Dartmoor Derby', run each year at the Chagford agricultural show! Not so long ago, there was a healthy export trade in Dartmoor ponies that covered most of Europe and North America. However, in the last 30 years or so of the twentieth century, the Dartmoor has suffered something of a decline; introduction of poor breeding-stock from off the moor has diluted the bloodline somewhat, producing an inconsistent and less-hardy animal that cannot cope so well with the harsh conditions. The market for ponies has also declined latterly, with many selling at annual pony sales for only a few pence, destined to finish up as canned pet food. Moves are now afoot to conserve and improve the traditional Dartmoor by a programme of selective culling and careful breeding to try and get back to the true bloodline.

The only other livestock to have contributed significantly to the economy of the Dartmoor farms is the rabbit, introduced in the twelfth century and extensively raised for meat and fur. This continued until the mixamatosis outbreak on the moor in 1954 wiped out most of the population. Rabbits were farmed in warrens – artificial mounds of soil raised to facilitate burrowing – and were trapped in large numbers, especially after the arrival of the railways made it possible to get them to distant markets swiftly. They were a significant traffic at many railway stations bordering Dartmoor, most notably Bridestowe, which annually despatched more rabbits to London than any other place in Britain. In the Chagford area, Headland Warren was a large rabbit farm on the higher commons that originated in the medieval period.

Cyril Wonnacott and Will White stooking corn to dry at Higher Shapley in 1946. Shapley, in spite of its elevated position – around 1,000 feet up on the moor shoulder – has quite a tract of good arable land stretching away below the farmstead towards the southern slopes of Meldon Hill at Corndon. (Courtesy of the Mortimore family, Shapley)

Above left: Haymaking by horsepower at Higher Shapley in 1962, with 'Prince' in the shafts and a full load. Although a four-wheeled wagon is in use here, it is a great deal smaller than the traditional pattern of four-wheeled farm wagons used on easier ground elsewhere in England – a reflection of Dartmoor's demanding combination of steep gradients and narrow ways. (Courtesy of the Mortimore family, Shapley)

Above right: Carting the hay by horsepower at East Coombe on a two-wheeled Dartmoor 'tumbril' cart, c.1960. Many Chagford hill farmers stuck to loose hay and traditional harvesting methods for some time after mechanical balers had been introduced. These may have been faster and – theoretically – more efficient, but they suffered acute indigestion when faced with the loose lumps of granite often encountered amid the grasses on a typical Dartmoor hay field. The writer well recalls the spectacular demise of an elderly Jones machine when he unwittingly attempted to bale one such boulder at Cranbrook in 1976. (Courtesy of Maurice Hill Esq., East Coombe)

CULTIVATION

On the hill farms, the small areas of arable land were cultivated for both animal and human foodstuffs, with crops of corn (wheat), barley and oats. Roots were also important, particularly after the introduction of the potato ('tiddy' in the local vernacular) in the seventeenth century. These became a subsistence crop and led to the development of the Dartmoor 'tiddy-pit', a tunnel excavated into a bank or in a convenient field-corner for the frost-free storage of potatoes. These are still in use on some farms in Chagford. Later, potatoes became a cash crop for many farms. Other root crops included mangels, turnips or beets, and were grown in rotation with the cereals.

Cultivation was generally undertaken using oxen, as these animals were easy to rear, hardy, adaptable, powerful and, at the end of their useful lives, edible! The draft horse did not really arrive on Dartmoor until the late-eighteenth or early-nineteenth century, and well into the latter century Chagford smithies were making and fitting the characteristic double-point ox-shoes that are still occasionally found on arable land.

The tillage was a three-stage process: the surface 'ley' was broken initially by a wide but shallow furrow cut with a single broad ploughshare which turned the turf but did not cut it free. The turf was allowed to lie and wither before being harrowed, a process which broke it up into soil particles and a mixture of dead grass and root fibre known as 'beat'. This was raked up and burned to produce an ash which – mixed with wood ash, dung, compost, soil recovered from hedgerows or roadways as run-off, hedgerow mosses and moulds and, later, slaked lime – was ploughed in, using a deeper share to produce a tilth, although rarely of any great depth.

The seed-corn was cast onto the ridges, then the soil harrowed and finally turned-in by hand. Oats were the first crop in the rotation, followed by wheat and barley. Summer weeding was done by hand using a mattock, 'thistle spudder' or dock-iron. Harvesting was also a manual task, the crop being cut with a sickle or reaping-hook, bound into sheaves and stooked to dry before being carted in for threshing. Carts or wains did not come into widespread use on Dartmoor until about 1820; the traditional methods of cartage being a packhorse with 'crooks' – a wide wooden framework set on the pack-saddle to carry light, loose loads such as hay, straw sheaves, furze or bracken – or by primitive ox-drawn sleds that essentially dated back to Celtic times.

At the end of this back-breaking toil the result was a yield that was rarely better than mediocre and, in bad seasons, could be negligible. With the contrast in conditions between the poor soils and exposed situations of the Dartmoor hill farms and the far better soils and more sheltered conditions in the Teign Valley and on the gentler land to the north of Chagford, the hill farmers soon came to rely little on their own arable activities, preferring to trade their staple produce – wool – and to purchase cereals from the valley farmers. A house cow or two might have been kept for milk and butter, but few of the hill farms could be regarded as self-sufficient and certainly none of them derived significant income by selling crops.

The Shapley sheepwalks extend up onto Chagford Commons and down to the parish boundary near Bennett's Cross. Here is Ivan Mortimore outside the nearby Warren House Inn, riding pony 'Daisy' and leading draught horse 'Prince'. The route back to the farm followed that of the ancient trackway over Hurston Ridge. (Courtesy of the Mortimore family, Shapley)

THE POTATO TRADE

The exception to this rule was the growing of potatoes on the moor edge, which came to the fore at the end of the eighteenth century and flourished greatly through the nineteenth. There were a number of factors that account for the emergence of potatoes as a cash crop in the Chagford district at this time. Of these the main ones were: firstly, the introduction of hardier potato varieties and simpler cultivation methods, probably from Scotland; and secondly, the advent of wheeled carts and the improvements of the byways (detailed in Chapter 6) which provided a ready means of moving such a relatively heavy crop to market.

Dartmoor potato-growers usually used the 'lazy-bed' system of cultivation that was popular in upland Scotland. This involved the potatoes being grown in raised beds of soil rather than in the ground. The soil was first roughly ploughed into ridges around a yard in width and separated by trenches. After manuring the beds, the setts were placed on top and the soil from the trenches thrown onto them. As the setts took root and grew, this last process was repeated (several times!) to protect the emerging plants. This was a laborious and labour-intensive activity, frequently calling upon all the labour the farms could muster. Chagford School's log-books are full of entries noting 'the absence of the older boys, kept home to help with the potato-tilling'.

The potatoes were harvested in the summer and autumn and either stored in pits or carted to Tavistock and Plymouth. They were originally sold at a market at Two Bridges, known to have been operating as early as 1765. It may be asked why Tavistock and Plymouth did not grow their own potatoes, given the similarity in conditions, but there

was a difference in the terms of the farm leases that gave the advantage to the northern and eastern quarters of the moor. It was a commercial opportunity fully exploited in the Chagford and Moretonhampstead districts for many years, especially after the coming of the railway to Moreton made it quicker and cheaper to despatch potatoes to market. They formed an important traffic on the railway until the motor lorry took it away in the years immediately preceding the Second World War. The potato trade also supported a number of merchants and kept the local carriers busy; among the invoices and receipts studied from the Great Tree, Yeo and Shapley Farm records are many for the cartage of potatoes to Moretonhampstead.

LATER FARMSTEADS & NEWTAKES

Although most of the farms in Chagford have their origins in the medieval period or earlier, farm settlement on the moor fringe continued into the nineteenth century, as at Teignhead, where the 'newtake' was reclaimed from open moorland in 1808. These newtakes were made under the ancient forest customs of Dartmoor, which allowed Duchy tenants of the moor tenements to reclaim and enclose up to eight acres of land each time a newcomer entered the holding. Newtakes are thus simply enclosed areas of moorland grazing, effectively large dry-walled rough fields tied to a particular farm or landholding, and attracting an annual rent to the Duchy of a penny-ha'penny an acre. These enclosures are characterised by their boundaries of true drystone walls rather than by the traditional Devon stone-and-thorn hedgebank. Many of the nineteenth-century newtake walls in the Chagford area were built by William Rogers, an Irish branch of the Perryman family, and are known locally as 'Irishman's walls'.

In some instances ancient farmsteads were replaced by completely new steadings, sometimes on a different site. Most of these rebuildings or relocations date from the mid-nineteenth century, as at Yeo, Great Weeke, Yellam, Great Tree and Monk's Withecombe, but the process went on well into the twentieth century. A notable example is Rushford Mill Farm, established in the 1890s on a site adjacent to the mill, with the original farmhouse at Rushford Barton eventually becoming solely a residence. This pattern recommenced towards the end of the twentieth century with new farmsteads established on old farmlands to allow the original buildings and a small area of land to be sold off for residential or equestrian purposes. At the time of writing, these old farms are greatly sought after as country homes by people moving from the affluent South East and

CULTIVATION

Above: *Liming in progress at Higher Shapley in January 1946, showing the tip-cart made by Drewe at Venton in use for its intended purpose. The lime – probably originating from quarries at Buckfastleigh – usually came by rail to Moretonhampstead and thence by cart or lorry.* (Courtesy of the Mortimore family, Shapley)

Right: *Fowls have always formed a part of the farm economy on Dartmoor. These geese are at Higher Shapley in 1930, below the new farmhouse. The young girl is Mary Wonnacott, who later married Ivan Mortimore and took over the farm when her father retired. Her son Gordon farms Shapley at the time of writing.* (Courtesy of the Mortimore family, Shapley)

Left: *Building the rick at Higher Shapley; Albert Wonnacott is on the top and his niece, Pearl, is pitching. Haymaking and harvest were labour-intensive operations often calling for the services of family members, neighbours or casual labourers.* (Courtesy of the Mortimore family, Shapley)

Inset: *Topping the rick was always a milestone in the farming year. Alfred Wonnacott and his wife Fanny rest atop the finished rick with daughters Vera and Mary just before the Second World War.* (Courtesy of the Mortimore family, Shapley)

Left: *Shapley in the snow, 1981. The faithful David Brown – Shapley's first tractor – in the farm lane just above Lower Shapley Farmhouse. Not much else on wheels could move in these conditions, but dogs and ponies managed well enough.* (Courtesy of the Mortimore family, Shapley)

Below: *Cyril and Arthur Wonnacott with horses in the yard at Higher Shapley, ready to leave for the first postwar Chagford Show on 15 August 1946. The end of Shapley Old Farmhouse just shows on the left, by this time used only as an outbuilding.* (Courtesy of the Mortimore family, Shapley)

Above left: Higher Shapley and Yardworthy are among Chagford's Duchy farms. Here the landlord – the Duke of Cornwall – inspects walling work at Yardworthy. (Courtesy of the Mortimore family, Shapley)

Above right: The Duchy farms are bastions of family tradition, both in terms of the individual families farming each holding and as part of the overall family of the Duchy's Dartmoor estate. HRH Prince Charles takes a keen personal interest in the moor farms and has made many informal visits as here, with several generations of the Hutchings family, at Yardworthy. (Courtesy of the Mortimore family, Shapley)

consequently command high prices in the property market. This trend has resulted in completely new farmsteads, as at Hillhead and Waye Cross.

Few of the farms in Chagford achieve any real size (in fact only four per cent of the farms in Britain exceeded 300 acres in 1970) and even today when several of the farmsteads have been divested of their land to augment neighbouring holdings, farms of more than a few hundred acres are uncommon. However, it has long been a tradition for Chagford farmers to rent or occasionally buy 'accommodation land' away from the moor, often several miles away in the rich red-clay country towards Crediton. Such land offers high-quality grazing to supplement the moor grasses, especially towards the beginning and end of the season when the moor is some way behind 'down country' in grass growth and nutrient value for 'first bite'.

This land is also used to take crops of hay, or more recently, silage, while some arable land is also rented to farmers to enable them to grow feed crops, such as barley, that are not possible on their moorland holdings. Accommodation land allows Chagford farmers to 'finish' stock to market weight (and hence to realise the maximum value for their beasts) rather than being forced to simply sell the animals to the lowland farms at store weight.

FARM TENURE IN CHAGFORD

The original basis of farm tenure throughout most of Britain was established in the wake of the Norman conquest and the Domesday survey. This gave rise to the feudal system under which all land was owned by the Crown but 'held' by lords under the manorial system, to whom all the lower orders owed allegiance. The basis of the system was the granting of land by the Crown in recognisance of military support – each lord made a commitment to provide a certain number of troops, supplies, horses and other necessities to support the King in times of war. These troops were drawn from the ranks of the villeins, or subservient classes: the peasantry, farm workers, foresters, tradesmen, smallholders and cottagers, all of whom worked on the lands of the manor in common bond.

The manor was thus essentially a communal structure, land being worked in common. The Manor of Chagford is centred on Waye, for many years the seat of the lord. Later, the lordship became split between Waye and Holly – or Holy – Street. In 1878 the Lords of the Manor were William Ellis at Waye and the Revd A. Whipton at Holy Street.

Above: *A family group at West Coombe Farm, Chagford, in the mid 1930s. The farmer is William Mortimer, and the young boy is his son Ivan, who later farmed Higher Shapley. (Courtesy of the Mortimore Family, Shapley)*

Left: *A handwritten lease for Great Tree Farm, the term being 14 years from 25 March 1916 (Quarter Day) at a rent of £160 per annum. The lease is a highly detailed document incorporating very specific requirements, such as the commitment to 'plough out the hedge-beds and spread the soil over any thin parts of the field; in the case of hilly fields, to carry the earth accumulated at the lower end of the field to the upper part thereof' – a process sometimes known as 'lynchetting', the old term used to describe terracing on steep ground. (Courtesy of Leonard Brommell Esq., Great Tree)*

However, the manors over which these worthies held lordship were but a shadow of their Norman predecessors. The true manorial system gradually broke down over the early-medieval period, and led to the division of the manor into individual farms or holdings, let by the lord to one individual or family on a tenancy. These tenancies often remained in the same family over a number of generations. In the Chagford area, few farms were actually sold to the men who farmed them under the 'yeomanry' system that sprung up elsewhere; the 'yeoman farmer' was associated far more with softer, richer arable land.

Farming in Chagford is rooted in the old style of manorial farm tenancy; much of Dartmoor and most of the moorland farms in the parish of Chagford form part of the Duchy of Cornwall. This situation arose from Dartmoor's early status as a Royal Forest, which meant it was a direct property of the Crown. The Duchy was granted the 'Forest of Dartmoor and Manor of Lydford' in 1239, so very few of the farms pre-date this acquisition. The ancient boundary of the forest coincides with that of Lydford, the largest parish in Devon, and abuts Chagford to the south. The moorland adjacent to the ancient forest was also claimed by the Duchy as 'the Commons of Devon', with a further boundary cutting across the upper valleys of both branches of the Teign. All the farms and holdings above this line are – or have been – Duchy property, including East and West Coombe, Thorn, Teigncombe, Northill, Southill, Batworthy-in-the-Moor, Frenchbeer, Teignworthy and Yardworthy.

The Duchy was anxious to exploit its holdings and to attract farmers to the harsh environment of the moor, so it offered tenancies on very favourable terms with low rents (for many years, only a ha'penny an acre) and an open form of tenure that allowed for succession. This was called a 'copyhold of inheritance', and relied on a central roll or register to record the entitlements of tenants and their successors to occupy farms. This unusual provision has meant that many Duchy farms have been farmed continuously by the same family over long periods. Such hereditary tenancies later became known as 'customary freeholds', and gave the farmers an unusually strong claim over their holdings; they were effectively freeholders in the wider sense. They could bequeath or even sell their rights under the tenancy. Indeed, when the Duchy bought out many of these tenants in the nineteenth century it dealt with them on the basis of purchasing their freeholds exactly as if they had been owners rather than tenants.

In addition to the Duchy tenants farming on the moor, there was a further class of tenancy on Dartmoor granted to farmers whose holdings lay outside the Duchy. This was the 'venville' tenancy which, for an annual rent, granted many of the rights of Duchy tenants proper to utilise the resources of the moor, including grazing and the taking of furze, turves, fruits (mainly wortleberries) and freestone. The only stipulation was that a venville tenant could not graze more head of stock on the moor commons than he could over-winter on his farmstead.

Away from the moor proper, the ownership of the land came to rest in relatively few hands, with a number of local proprietors – among them the Coniam, Ellis, Hames, Hayter, Hooper, Perryman and Whiddon families – accruing substantial estates. More recently, in the nineteenth and early-twentieth centuries, landowners such as the Rolle Estate, the Wills tobacco propriety and several other large commercial organisations, have built up substantial landholdings in the area. Most of these farms were historically let under the old 'free tenancy' system, which was very open and allowed a wide range of different types of lease to operate – although the landlord generally came out somewhat better under the law than did his tenant. These leases were normally annual and contained safeguards as to proper husbandry of the land, often going into considerable detail over the specifics of ploughing, cropping or grazing. The Great Tree lease, for instance, specified action to be taken to combat 'lynchetting' – the tendency of soil on sloping ground to migrate to the lower hedgebank; this was required to be 'ploughed out and carted' to the top of the field at least one season in three.

THE AGRICULTURE ACTS

This largely unregulated system of tenure existed right up until the Second World War, when three successive legal changes came about between 1940 and 1948. The first of these was the draconian imposition of the War Agricultural system, brought in under the provisions of the Emergency Powers Act of 1939. Under the 'War Ag', directives were made that all possible land – including permanent pasture, water meadows, hill and marsh land previously held to be unsuitable for ploughing – were to be brought under cultivation as quickly as possible.

The execution of this policy was entrusted to local War Agricultural Committees, which usually consisted of farmers that worked large areas of land and important landowners in a given area. The committee in the Chagford area was chaired by George (later Sir George) Hayter-Hames. These 'War Ags' had extensive powers to force compliance with their dictates, even to the point where farmers could be dispossessed of their holdings – leasehold or freehold – if they failed to comply. Across the country these provisions led to many old scores being settled and new enmities being fostered, and there is little doubt that many farmers were harshly and unjustly treated for failing to obey orders they knew were either impracticable or against the best interests of their farms. Fortunately, affairs in the Chagford district seem to have been conducted in a more amicable spirit, and there are no indications of enforcement measures being taken.

At the end of the war, such an unaccountable system could not be long tolerated. The election of a Labour government in 1945 was followed by two pieces of agricultural legislation which radically changed – some would say undermined – the whole system of farm tenure. The first of these Acts was the 1947 Agriculture Act, which essentially set out to define 'rules of good husbandry' to guide farmers, as well as regulating many aspects of their activity. This Act also established for the first time the principle of a guaranteed minimum price for farm produce, a scheme designed to avoid any repetition of the near-catastrophic decline in agriculture that had occurred during the 1930s. This decline resulted in many farms being neglected or even abandoned – a situation which greatly hindered the drive to increase home production during the war.

The following year, 1948, saw the introduction of the far-reaching 'Agricultural Holdings Act' which, for the first time, set down a precise legal frame-work for farm leases. The

effect of this legislation was to swing the balance of advantage very much in favour of the tenant, offering a wide range of protections and restricting both the level of rent and the frequency at which it could be reviewed. Only if the husbandry was sufficiently bad (which had to be proved before a court) could a landlord regain possession of his property. So long as the farmer kept the farm in a reasonable state, he had total security of tenure.

The 1948 Act essentially removed all a landlord's control over his property and made it very difficult for him to effect any change. Farms tenanted under these provisions lost much of their value, becoming almost unsaleable. Eventually, many landowners took the only option open to them to realise any capital value from their properties, which the imposition of Death Duties frequently forced them to do: they sold the farms to the tenants in possession – often on very favourable terms for the tenant! It was during this period – the 1950s and early 1960s – that many farms that had been tenanted for centuries became owner-occupied free-holds, previously a relatively rare type of landholding in this part of Devon. Thus did a new breed of yeoman farmer emerge in the modern period.

Harry Wonnacott, brother of Alfred Wonnacott, at Shapley.
(Courtesy of the Mortimore family, Shapley)

Above: *Miners outside the higher bothy, or living quarters, at Warren House, around 1890. They would have been working the Birch Tor and Vitifer mines at this date for tin, copper and iron. The garb is typical of West-country miners, with felt hats or helmets and well-padded knees; many of the 'stopes' of these mines were not high enough to stand in.* (Chapman Postcard)

Above: *A more general view of the mining area on the edge of Chagford Parish, with the Warren House Inn at the centre flanked by the bothys or 'barracks' that housed the miners during the week; they returned home for weekends.* (Chapman Postcard)

FOUR

INDUSTRY & MINING

THE CHAGFORD STANNARY

Chagford owes its eventual status as a stannary town to the original charters granted to the moor tinners by King John in 1201. This established the early tin industry on Dartmoor and in Cornwall. The rights granted under these charters included:

... digging of tin and of turfs for smelting it at all times, peaceably and without hindrance from any man, everywhere in moors and in the fees of bishops, abbots and counts.

The rights of tinners under the original charter were gradually eroded over the ensuing 100 years, to the point where they petitioned the Crown for a new charter to re-establish their position. Edward I granted the stannary charter in 1305, and this established the formal stannaries – with their parliaments and courts – and the stannary or 'coinage' towns. Chagford was chartered as such in 1328.

The various areas of tin-working in Devon and Cornwall were gathered into defined areas, the stannaries, each administered by a stannary court. These courts served to settle disputes over tinning rights, to try those accused under stannary law and to determine the tax payable on the metal – the 'coinage'. The location of these courts on Dartmoor were at Ashburton, Chagford and Tavistock – all of these places became coinage towns under the provisions of the 1305 charter. Later, a fourth stannary covering southern Dartmoor was set up at Plympton. Overall, the stannaries were governed by stannary parliaments, to which each stannary sent 24 'jurates' as elected representatives. The Dartmoor tinners met on Crockern Tor near Postbridge, or jointly with the Cornish tinners at Hingsdon Down near Tavistock.

The tinners were exempt from the common laws of the Kingdom, answering only to the jurisdiction of the stannaries. Stannary law was enacted by the stannary parliament and enforced (rigorously, it would seem) by the stannary courts. Tinners who broke these laws faced imprisonment in the stannary jail at Lydford Castle. The rights of tinners under the

1305 charter were extensive and superior to the rights of other users of the moor, be they tenants or freeholders. This not unnaturally led to friction between the farming and tinning communities, but the tinners' rights were derived directly from the Crown and were almost always upheld. The fact that the Crown derived a large income from the tax on tin probably had much to do with this somewhat unjust state of affairs!

The size of Chagford Stannary – in terms of the number of tinners working and the amount of metal produced – is quite hard to determine, although it was very small compared with the important Cornish stannaries. In his *English Tin Production and Trade before 1550*, mining historian John Hatcher notes that 'throughout the period the Devon Stannaries remain very much the province of the small-scale operator'. The tin taxed at each stannary was recorded on the Coinage Rolls, and these thus preserve an accurate record of the trade. There were usually two 'coinages' a year. In 1394 a total of 109 persons presented a production of just over 55 thousandweights (a thousandweight being the predecessor of the ton, 1200lbs in Devon) of tin for coinage at the three moor stannary towns of Ashburton, Chagford and Tavistock – an average annual production of only around 600lbs per man. A year's work to produce considerably less than half a ton of metal was no sinecure; the equivalent output for a Cornish tinner during the same period was between 6,500 and 7,500lbs. Further analysis of the Coinage Rolls suggest that many Dartmoor tinners produced on a very small scale indeed as, of the 109 tinners, only six were taxed on more than a single thousandweight of metal, and the total production was less than 30 tons.

From the best evidence, it appears that the Stannary Court building in Chagford was originally on the south side of the Square, adjacent to what is now the Three Crowns Hotel. It was presumably this building which, on 6 March 1617, collapsed while the court was in session, killing nine people including the steward, Master Nicholas Eveleigh, and his two clerks, John Cleake and Richard Beere. A further 17 people were 'grievously hurt and wounded'. The story goes that a defendant in the case being heard at the time, having expounded a defence verging on the fantastical and full of falsehoods, invoked the fates by asserting that if his claims were not just, the court house might fall about his ears. Unfortunately for him and the others within, it did just that! The building is described as being 'large, of timber', and the cause of the collapse has been suggested as an earth tremor – of which many have been recorded in the Chagford district. It is possible, however, that the collapse was due to overcrowding and overloading of the upper floor of the structure. A new court house was built on the 'low side' of the Square, while the story became the subject of a moral pamphlet published in 1618 to warn all others of the consequences of taking in vain an oath sworn before God.

STREAMWORKS & BLOWING HOUSES

Early tinning on Dartmoor was not mining in the usual sense, but rather involved the streaming of the tin-rich alluvial material in the Dartmoor water-courses or from surface diggings – a laborious method of extracting small quantities of what was then a precious metal. Tin was a principal compo-nent in both bronze and pewter, two of the most important alloyed metals in use during the period AD800–1800. Pure tin was also used for jewellery and coinage, and more prosaically, to make solders for joining other metals, including copper and iron.

There were two forms of stream workings: alluvial and eluvial. In the former, river gravel was crushed to a fine dust in a pound-mill or mortar, then 'panned' in settling troughs to separate the metal. However, this was a very limited form of production, and it soon became the custom to work the tin-bearing areas of 'eluvial' ground by cutting a series of trenches adjacent to the watercourse or leat. The spoil from the working was piled up at the rear of the trench as the tin-bearing soils were streamed, and a series of channels or 'tyes' were cut to bring a water supply through the working. This passed through the wooden settling-trough, called a 'buddle', where the lighter elements of the finely-crushed material were washed out and the heavier metal sank to the bottom of the trough.

At first, the rock and soil was pounded to a consistency suitable for streaming by hand, but the abundance of water-power soon led to the intro-duction of water-powered mortars or 'stamps', sited in purpose-built structures called 'stamp mills'. At their most primitive, these mortars were trip hammers made of granite, with the 'pestle' or hammer head being lifted by a cam on the wheel-shaft acting through a lever. Later, the multiple type of 'Cornish' stamps appeared, using iron hammer heads on a row of smaller, lighter pestles operated by a series of cams

on a shaft, arranged so that the stamps operated in sequence. Thus, the water-wheel was able to produce a series of blows per revolution rather than the one or two of the trip hammer. Cornish stamps were much faster acting and speeded up production.

As each tye was worked out, the working was carried on by cutting a new trench in advance of the original, with the spoil being backfilled onto the old working. This process was repeated many times over the centuries until the ground was worked out, giving the characteristic remains of such a stream works – a series of parallel ridges of spoil, now overgrown, together with traces of water-channels and perhaps the remains of the walls of a stamp house or the wheel-pit that held the stamp-wheel. Older, more primitive mortars can also be found and are large granite boulders with the characteristic bowl-shaped hollow in the centre.

The tin was then formed into crude ingots in primitive turf-and-faggot fired blast-furnaces known as 'blowing houses'. Again, these were water-powered, the wheel in this instance driving a bellows to provide blast for the furnace. The fuel was peat from the moor, probably mixed with furze (which burns very hot) to get the furnace quickly up to blast heat. Fortunately, no great temperature is required to smelt the moor tin, which was of high purity and melted at around 150–200°C. While many of the stream-works were remote on the high moor and temporary in nature – as at North Teign and Wallabrook – various works are also recorded in the vicinity of Chagford itself, including sites near Chagford Bridge, at Crosse Park and Doggamarsh.

For a full explanation of Dartmoor tinning processes and a gazetteer of sites, the reader is directed to the excellent Dartmoor tin industry field guide by Phil Newman and to Tom Greaves' book on Dartmoor's tin mines and miners – details can be found in the bibliography.

SHAFT & ADIT MINING

With the opening-up of deep shaft mining for tin in Cornwall and West Devon from the fifteenth century onwards, the Dartmoor stream works began to decline in importance, and the institutions of the stannary gradually fell into disuse, although the Chagford assay mark, the 'tinners' rabbits', contin-ued to be used and has become the town's unofficial badge and symbol. This first great period of mineral activity brought considerable wealth to the town and laid the foundations on which much of ancient Chagford was built. The legal framework of the stannary system survived until the end of the nine-teenth century, being abolished by the Stannaries Courts (Abolition) Act of 1896. Today, the most visible sign of the early prosperity brought to Chagford's stannary is the magnificent granite

The Warren House Inn was at the centre of the mining district on Chagford Commons, serving as a supply centre for the miners – many of whom slept in an adjacent 'barracks' during the week, returning to their homes in the villages surrounding the moor at weekends. (Courtesy of the Mortimore family, Shapley)

church of St Michael the Archangel, a large and accomplished building for so small a place.

Metal mining was not to return to Chagford Parish in any consequential way until the latter half of the nineteenth century, when a series of shafts were sunk and adits driven around the hamlet and farm of Great Weeke, to the south-east of the town. These culminated in the substantial mine at Great Weeke Consols, sunk by mine adventurers seeking tin in 1886. This mine had considerable facilities including a large water-wheel driving the de-watering pumps and a set of Cornish stamps, but it was never a commercial success. Some 55 tons of black (unrefined) tin ore were produced in the period up to 1890, but as with many Westcountry mines around this date, the opening up of major open-cast tinworks in Malaya, Indonesia and South America resulted in cheap imported metal with which the native product could not compete.

Desultory efforts were made to work the Great Weeke mine over the last decade of the nineteenth century under successive proprietors, but the workings were finally abandoned in 1904. It has been suggested that the whole Weeke Consols operation was almost a 'scam', and that the adventurers of the mine lured importunate investors into parting with cash against little real prospect of economic return. It also seems strange that so substantial a mine should have so small an output, giving rise to the suspicion that not all the metal produced was assayed, taxed and sold on the tin exchange. Today, a few traces of the mine remain – the count house, the wheel-pit and, most apparent, the mine captain's residence which passed to the Ellis family, whose fortune was a victim of the mine's failure. The remains of adits and spoil heaps can also be seen in fields at Footaway and adjacent to the trackway from there up on to Week Down.

There was also an extensive system of shaft and drift mines on the borders of the common lands of Chagford, North Bovey and Manaton parishes near the Warren House Inn, notably the two deep mines of Birch Tor and Vitifer. These were on the site of ancient stream works and the ground in the vicinity is scarred with a maze of spoil-heaps, ravines, trenches and pits, as well as the shafts and adits of the more recent mines. The underground works were extensive and reputedly linked with those of the Golden Dagger mine in Manaton parish, further down the West Webburn valley. The first adits were cut in the eighteenth century and the mines were worked, on a modest scale, until late in the nineteenth century. The mine machinery was again water-powered, the water being diverted from the East Dart by a leat some seven miles long – a considerable work in its own right.

These mines were sunk on the sites of older tin-workings and would appear to have been at least commenced quite early on. When the main workings were being sunk in the early-nineteenth century, much older shafts and tunnels were uncovered, although at no great depth. Vitifer was eventually the most important and successful of these mines, operating on quite a large scale between about 1820 and its closure in 1870. The mine lay dormant for over 30 years, but was re-opened early in the twentieth century when a new, deeper shaft was sunk and more modern machinery installed. The mine worked regularly until 1914, then spasmodically for a further 25 years. It was finally abandoned in 1939, and the machinery fell victim to the wartime scrap-metal drive.

The shaft mines on and around the moor produced, at one time or another, a number of different ores. As well as tin, Dartmoor was also a source of iron ores, copper and lead, as well as rarer metals such as wolfram (tungsten) and uranium. The Birch Tor/Vitifer/Golden Dagger mine complex also produced low-grade iron ore, although this was subject to only very limited commercial exploitation and much of it finished up in the spoil heaps, where it can still be found today. Other important mining sites not far from Chagford included the Ramsley copper mine at South Zeal and Pepperdon iron mine in Moretonhampstead.

THE WOOLLEN INDUSTRY

The other great generator of wealth throughout much of rural Britain from the middle ages onwards was the trade in woollen cloth. This is an industry that became well-established in West Devon from the fourteenth century onwards. The combination of plenty of hill and down grazing suited to sheep, together with ample supplies of soft water, which was ideal for washing the wool, and sufficient water power to drive the machinery led to the establishment of wool manufactures all around Dartmoor. The most notable of these were at Ashburton, Buckfastleigh and Ivybridge in the south, Tavistock to the west and at Chagford, North Tawton, Sticklepath and Okehampton in the north.

Spinning and weaving were essentially cottage industries well suited to the scattered settlement pattern of the area, while woollen cloth, felt and yarn were products that were relatively easy to transport by packhorse – the only practicable means of reaching markets until well into the nineteenth century. The invention of the tucking-mill in the early-thirteenth century gave an added boost to the Dartmoor woollen industry, as the swift-flowing streams were well suited to driving the water-wheels that powered this process. Fulling – bulking and cleaning the raw wool by abrading and washing it, and later, by treating it chemically with 'Fuller's Earth' – was another process facilitated by the pure, soft Dartmoor water.

The woollen trade around Chagford thrived in piecemeal fashion until around 1800, when there arrived in the town Mr Berry of Ashburton, a considerable entrepreneur who saw in Chagford the potential to rival the established woollen industry to the south of the moor, which had its origins in the pioneering work of the industrious monks at Buckfast. In Chagford, Berry found not only a suitable situation with good water supplies for both power and fulling, but also an under-employed labour force – in contrast to Ashburton, where workers were in short supply. Berry set about establishing a substantial woollen manufactory in Chagford, on several sites to the north and west of the Square. The first of these was the complex of fine early-nineteenth-century buildings that later became the Moorlands Hotel. These included 'Mr Berry's House', the original mill driven by a leat taken from the same source as the town water system (of which it came to form a part) as well as a drying-shed, warehouse and wool store. Also in this complex of buildings were weaving-lofts, several workers' houses and, at one stage, a chapel.

The second site, the fulling-mill and pond in the valley at the foot of Mill Street on the higher (Waye Hill) side of the road, was probably of medieval origin. This took its water supply from the Padley Brook, which joins the Teign a short distance below the road, and has every appearance of being an ancient mill site. It was probably the location of the original tucking-mill, although in the fifteenth century, a woollen mill was recorded on the river bank at the same location as the much later 'Lower Factory'. After a period of disuse, the fulling-mill was converted into living accommodation and was occupied during the war years by a farming family who had been displaced by military activity from Teignhead Farm, which was abandoned in 1940. More recently, this complex of buildings has been the subject of an award-winning conversion into a house, 'Millponds', designed by Chagford-based architect Allen van der Steen.

Mr Berry's main mill was on a site adjacent to Chagford Bridge – now the kennels of the mid-Devon hunt – fed by a substantial leat from a weir at Holy Street. This complex included a tucking-mill and power looms, all driven by a water-wheel of 14 feet diameter by 14 feet breast. There were two large structures on this site, housing the main looms and associated machinery, with a further large wooden drying shed or 'rack' in the field on the opposite side of the road, now known as Rack Park. This structure fell into disuse and finally collapsed in a gale in 1861. The products of this mill were yarn, felt and serges – tough, hard-wearing materials that used to best advantage the strong, wiry wool of the Dartmoor sheep. The finished goods from the Berry operations were taken by road to Ashburton for further finishing or for sale through the merchants based there. The military was an important customer, but much also went for export to the Low Countries and Northern

Germany. The returning carts brought lime from workings at Buckfast to improve or 'sweeten' the acid soils of the Chagford area.

The latest and largest of Chagford's woollen-mills was the Lower or Blanket Factory, built around 1820 on the site of the original riverside tucking-mill. It took water from the same leat as the main mill (subsequently known as Higher Factory) at Factory Cross. The new factory had a wide range of power-driven looms as well as felting tables and various finishing processes. Berry's mill complex was a very substantial enterprise in its day, and at busy times gave full employment to up to 120 local men and large numbers other part-time workers, both in the mill and as 'outworkers'. Many children were also employed in the mill until well into the 1870s. It was during the working life of these mills that Chagford's population peaked at just over 1,800. By this time the junior school regularly had between 160 and 180 children enrolled, including the 'half time' students who worked in the mill in the morning and received their education in the afternoons.

The decline of the Dartmoor woollen industry in the mid-nineteenth century was due to a number of factors, including war and political unrest, which affected several traditional export markets. However, the main death-knell was sounded by the establishment, on a far larger scale, of the Yorkshire woollen industry. The big new mills of Bradford and Huddersfield drew on a large working population and made use of modern high-speed power looms driven by steam machinery. Coal was abundantly at hand, as were copious supplies of suitable wools from the Pennine and Dale areas, and the trade was organised on a far more commercially-unified basis. The mills of the West Country, especially smaller enterprises such as Chagford, were undercut for price and delivery and were unable to compete. Only where the Devon mills were offering a unique or high-quality product, like fine broadcloth or the West of England cloth widely used for superior upholstery, did operations survive.

The Chagford operation closed for the first time in 1848 and lay dormant for a period until it was acquired by Mr Vicary of North Tawton. Over the ensuing 30 years, Mr Vicary was active in Chagford, not just in the wool trade but also in other areas. In conjunction with the ever-enterprising Revd Hayter-Hames, he established the Chagford Gasworks in 1869 on a site adjacent to the old fulling-mill. The coal that was used to fuel this small retort was brought by cart as a return load from the despatch of finished wool goods, which by that time went via the railway at Moretonhampstead. The gasworks originally provided light and power to the Lower Factory, but later gas was also supplied for street and domestic lighting; Chagford was one of the first country towns to possess this amenity. The factory as a whole finally ceased production of woollen goods

in about 1880 and lay dormant for a considerable period. The last military contract worked was reported to have been horse blankets for the British Army, then engaged in the Crimea.

NEW INDUSTRIES & USES

As with many mills, the decline of the woollen industry in Chagford caused great hardship and brought about efforts to diversify operations or to re-use the old mill buildings for other purposes. The original complex at Mill Street was extensively rebuilt and eventually became the Moorlands Hotel. The old fulling-mill on Padley Brook was abandoned and lay semi-derelict for a period before being converted to living accommodation.

The main mill site at Factory Cross was eventually taken over by Mr G.H. Reed who arrived in Chagford in about 1890 to set up as an agricultural merchant, threshing and haulage contractor, millwright and engineer. As well as the premises at Higher Factory, he also took over Rushford Mill, which was used for a while as a sawmill and works to produce agricultural implements, gates, farm machinery and the like. Mr Reed's business prospered greatly; he used a powerful traction engine in the early-twentieth century and became a main supplier of artificial manures or fertilisers, then being widely brought into use to improve the arable land. He was an agent for the Dublin & Wicklow Manure Company, as well as a representative for many major manufacturers of farm machinery. The Blanket Factory, which is a substantial structure on four and five floors, had a variety of subsidiary uses before being finally converted into houses at the start of the twentieth century. Even today, parts of this large building lie unused.

THE CHAGFORD BUILDING TRADE

Most places the size of Chagford might be expected to provide employment to a number of craftsmen skilled in the building trades – masons, carpenters and joiners, thatchers, glaziers, painters and plumbers. But building in Chagford became far more than just a group of tradesmen working individually in maintaining or renewing the fabric of the town. Building became an industry with several prominent firms undertaking what were major projects, including the construction of hotels and the erection of large and elaborate country houses commissioned by the new wealthy merchant class which found the Chagford district so much to its liking.

The largest of these building enterprises was the long-lived family firm of Stones, which originated in the mid-nineteenth century and only ceased trading in the 1980s. By the later nineteenth century, Stones had set themselves up to be in a position to under-

(Meldrum Collection)

Holy Street Manor, before (above) *and after* (right) *rebuilding in 1913–15; a somewhat radical transformation from the pleasantly ordinary eighteenth-century farmhouse to ersatz Tudor mansion, carried out by the Chagford building firm of Stone's.*

(Thorn Collection)

Left: *Typical of the sort of country houses being constructed by the builders in Chagford around the turn of the century was this home, Batworthy-in-the-Moor, burnt down in 1967 but seen here when nearly new.* (Thorn Collection)

take quite substantial building projects. They had a yard and works behind Nos. 18 and 20 New Street, where a long two-storey stone building housed their stores, joinery shop, coppersmithing and lead shop, cart shed and stable. By the early 1900s these works were powered by a single-cylinder gas engine that drove the machinery via flat belts and shafting, with timber seasoning racks along the rear of the building and gas lighting throughout. Here were made the staircases, windows, doors, panelling, joinery, mouldings, rainwater goods, plumbing fixtures and even some of the furniture for the extensive country-house building projects undertaken by Stones between about 1870 and the outbreak of the First World War. Most notable of these country houses were Outer Down, Holy Street and Teignworthy. Stones also built the New Rectory in 1872.

As well as Stones, who employed up to 50 men at busy times, other smaller traditional building firms flourished in Chagford from the end of the nineteenth century until the final decades of the twentieth. The family firm of Collins spanned more than a century and three generations, being started by James Collins in the 1870s and trading until his grandson R.G. (Dick) Collins retired in 1981. At its busiest period, during the 1930s, Collins employed 16 men and incorporated (by marriage) the other main old-established Chagford firm of W.H. Ellis, who were employing 12 men up to about 1930. Collins and Ellis were

responsible for buildings as diverse as the Parish Assembly Rooms (later the Rex cinema), Monte Rosa, Westcott House, Dial House, and many of the houses in Broomhill and Adley Lane. Collins' premises were in Store Street, off New Street; their 'store' was only redeveloped after the firm closed.

Other Chagford builders included the Weekes brothers, Fred and Will, who were joined by Fred's son Bert Weekes and then by John Pleace, who later carried on under his own name. Saunders, the agricultural engineers at Easton, built a number of houses in that area, while the Brimblecombe family were also active in the Chagford building trade. Building materials, including 'clean sharp gravel' and fine granite, were obtained from quarries at the foot of Meldon Hill below Knowles, worked until the Second World War.

IRONWORKING AND BELL HANGING

There were several smithy sites in Chagford, of which the main ones were the Vulcan Iron Works, sited in a number of buildings at what is now the rear of Bowden's shop; the Crown Iron Works at the lower end of the Square, now the Old Forge Café; a smaller general smithy in New Street, known as Blacksmith's Cottage; and on the corner of the Square adjacent to the building now occupied by Lloyds Bank. As well as the normal farm work of shoeing, making gate

An unusual form of competitive event was this smithing contest, held in Chagford Square in the early 1900s. All five Chagford smithies are represented.

71

hinges and other farm ironwork and implement repairs, the Chagford smithies undertook quite a lot of manufacture of new machinery. The remains of the iron-framed water-wheel at Lapford Mill in mid-Devon bear the mark of the Vulcan Iron Works, which suggests a foundry as well as a forge. The billhead of Frank Hill (RSS) of the Crown Iron Works lists him as a 'Shoeing and General Smith', that specialised in 'plain and ornamental' iron railings. It was probably Hill who was responsible for much of the architectural ironwork needed for the new country houses, such as the splendid gates at Holy Street. Several farms in the Chagford area also had quite extensive runs of iron field-railings, such as those that can still be seen at Highbury and Stiniel, which were probably also locally produced.

One of the less-usual aspects of the iron and carpentry trades that flourished in Chagford was that of bell hanging. Wm Aggett & Sons occupied a workshop in Southcombe Street (now the 'Courtyard' café and shop), where bell frames were constructed, along with other iron and wood work. It is not recorded whether Aggett's ironwork was actually cast in Chagford, but it is not unlikely. Certainly, Aggett's name and place of business were cast into the frameworks. Aggett was responsible for hanging many rings in the West Country, including Buckfast Abbey.

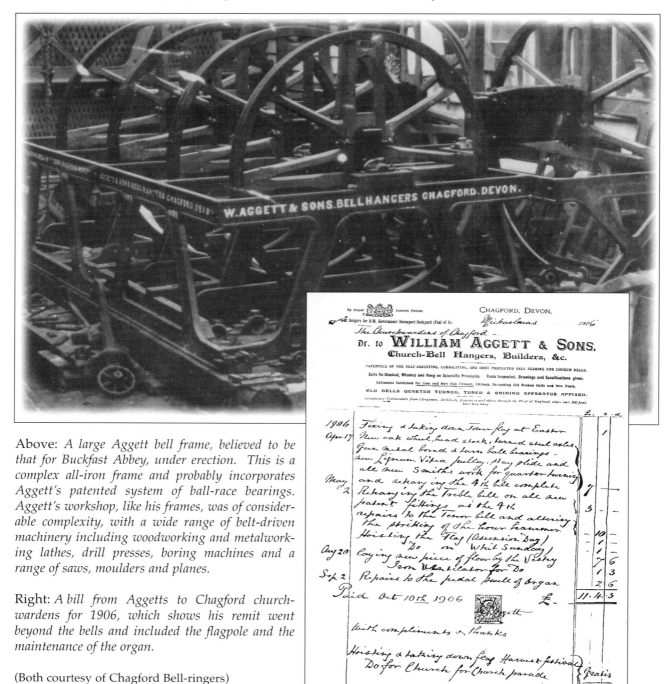

Above: *A large Aggett bell frame, believed to be that for Buckfast Abbey, under erection. This is a complex all-iron frame and probably incorporates Aggett's patented system of ball-race bearings. Aggett's workshop, like his frames, was of considerable complexity, with a wide range of belt-driven machinery including woodworking and metalworking lathes, drill presses, boring machines and a range of saws, moulders and planes.*

Right: *A bill from Aggetts to Chagford churchwardens for 1906, which shows his remit went beyond the bells and included the flagpole and the maintenance of the organ.*

(Both courtesy of Chagford Bell-ringers)

FIVE

✥

CHURCH & SCHOOL

CHAGFORD PARISH CHURCH
ST MICHAEL
THE ARCHANGEL

Chagford's fine parish church reflects its status as a stannary town, a market and a manufactory. It is also one of the few churches for which an exact consecration date is known – it was dedicated by Bishop Branscombe on 30 July 1261. At the time the church was founded, the town had yet to acquire stannary status and the resulting wealth and position. From all accounts the original building would appear to have been a much smaller and simpler structure without a tower. As well as the parish church, there were a number of early chapels in Chagford Parish, mostly connected with the larger houses. They are recorded as having existed at Teigncombe, Great Weeke (Wyke St Mary) and at Rushford, but all had fallen into disuse by the early-nineteenth century and few traces still remain.

It has been strongly suggested that the 1261 foundation replaced an even earlier Saxon church, a supposition based partly on the normal pattern of Saxon settlement and partly on Chagford's proximity to the major Christian centre, Crediton. From the eighth century, Crediton exercised a wide influence.

Although there are stone Saxon church buildings extant and recorded, most Saxon structures were of wood and it is likely that this was the case in Chagford. Such a building would leave few traces and is most probably overlaid by the later stone church. There is an ancient altar – usually called the 'Roman altar' – in Chagford churchyard (on the north side of the church). This pre-dates even the original 1261 building, as does a Norman font discovered in the rectory grounds. All this evidence supports the possibility of an ancient foundation preceding the present St Michael's Church.

As with most churches, St Michael's has a history of continual evolution. The present building dates for the most part from the fifteenth century, although elements of the earlier structure are incorporated. The tower was built at this time, almost certainly incorporating the thirteenth-century west window. It is a massive ashlar granite construction (69 feet high) and incorporates a niche with a statue of St Michael. Originally, it had the pinnacles that are a feature of many Westcountry churches, but the tower is now simply battlemented. The Lady Chapel, with its fine window tracery, was recorded as being added in 1482 and this date may give an indication of the time at which many of these major reconstructions were carried out.

Inset: *The only view so far found of Chagford church tower with the granite pinnacles intact. Not an original feature, these were added in the eighteenth century. Unfortunately, as with much of the stone of which the tower is built, the granite from which they were carved proved porous. In the case of the massive ashlar blocks of the tower, this porosity is not structurally significant, although it has been to the subsequent detriment of the internal timberwork and bell cage. Unfortunately, the same was not true of the slender, carved pinnacles which, under the action of wind, rain and frost over some 200 years, became thoroughly rotten; they were truncated in the 1890s and finally removed during the November 1914 tower works. The tower parapet as seen today is believed to follow the original form.* (Thorn Collection)

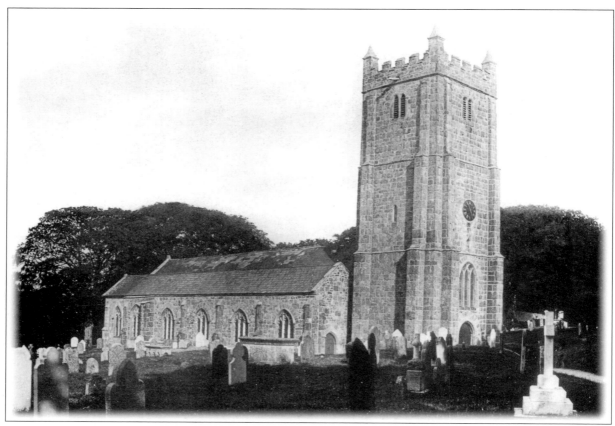

Above: The church of St Michael the Archangel, c.1905, seen from the north-west corner of the churchyard, a view now somewhat obscured by an avenue of yews on the north-east path and two birch trees. The pinnacles of the tower have been cut down but not yet removed. (Thorn Collection)

Below: *An early-twentieth-century postcard view of Chagford church, taken from the gateway to the High Street opposite the Three Crowns. The window seen here in the west face of the tower is believed to have been the west window of the original thirteenth-century building, relocated when the tower was added in the fifteenth century.* (Meldrum Collection)

Above: *The porch and south door of Chagford church, c.1900. There is a handsome sundial on the west corner of the porch — not always the most useful of fittings on Dartmoor!* (Thorn Collection)

A view of the interior of Chagford church, c.1900, after the removal of the high-backed Georgian pews and pulpit, and with the Pearson reworking of the chancel completed. The 1857 font carved in granite by Chagford stonemason John Aggett is seen here with its ornate Victorian-Gothic carved oak cover. (Meldrum Collection)

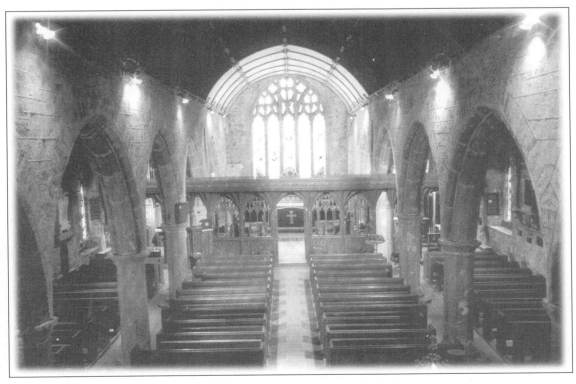

The most significant twentieth-century addition to Chagford church was the ornate carved oak rood-screen constructed, in a very traditional style, by Herbert Read of Exeter in 1925–7; it is similar to the much older screens in other Dartmoor churches, notably Bovey Tracey. Read also added the pulpit in 1928. This view was taken from the ringers' gallery, constructed to mark the church's septcentenary in 1961. (Courtesy Julia Endacott/Chagford Ringers)

There was a further chapel at the sanctuary end of the north aisle dedicated to St Katherine, the patron saint of tinners. A new altar was built here when the rood-loft was added in 1555, but the chapel was eventually removed to make way for the current organ-loft in the nineteenth century. The Guild of St Katherine was an association of tinners who supported the church foundation, the name also being associated with the ancient hall that abuts what is now the Three Crowns Hotel but was then the house of the Whyddon family.

Much of what exists in the interior of the church is of far more recent date. The original interior would have been richly and gaudily decorated with paintings and gilding, but it is recorded that the paintings were defaced in 1551 during the reign of Edward VI. The original medieval glass may well have been lost at the same time, the only surviving fragments being the two roundels in the upper part of the east window. The arms here are those of the Battershall and Ferrers families.

The fortunes and state of the church were allied closely to those of the town. For example, the prosperity generated from the tin and, later, wool trades financed the extensive works of the fifteenth and sixteenth centuries. This affluence gave way to a period of economic decline and agricultural depression in the eighteenth and early-nineteenth centuries. Little work appears to have been done at St Michael's at this time and it is probable that the fabric of the building fell into some disrepair – a common fate for many Devon country churches during this period.

The new prosperity of the Victorian age financed the revival of many such churches – or, in some cases, led to their destruction through over-zealous restoration. Chagford was among the more fortunate. Although much work was carried out on the building in the mid-nineteenth century, the work was generally sympathetic to the original structure. The massiveness and solidity of the ashlar granite masonry probably enabled St Michael's to survive the period of comparative neglect rather better than less durable structures. Many of the Victorian improvements date from the period 1857–65, when the modern organ-loft and sacristy were added and the remains of the original painted decorations removed from the aisles, walls and columns.

The church is recorded as having an organ of 82 pipes as long ago as 1592, and a Victorian instrument was given in 1853, probably occasioning the alterations to St Katherine's Chapel to provide the organ-loft. There are few details of this instrument, which was the gift of Mrs Hayter-Hames. The organ in 2002 is also of 82 pipes, a three-manual instrument built by Heles of Saltash in 1891 and re-cased and modernised in 1961.

The font dates to the Victorian era. It was carved from Dartmoor granite by Chagford stonemason John Aggett in 1857 to replace a Portland stone font dating from 1762. This was recorded as being disposed of in the rectory grounds, but it has never been found. However, an even earlier font, described as being of Norman date, was unearthed in the rectory garden in a damaged state. As St Michael's is ostensibly a post-Norman foundation, the origins of this relic are unclear.

The present east window – the Hayter-Hames memorial window – dates from 1860 and depicts scenes from the life of Christ. The sanctuary was redecorated to the designs of J.L. Pearson – architect of Truro cathedral – in 1887–8, and it is possible that he also designed the window, which was executed by Robert Beer of Exeter. Although Pevsner describes the Pearson redecoration as being carried out in a 'totally un-Devonian way', he admired the reredos with its 'crisply drawn Ascension and Saints'. This altarpiece was executed by Clayton and Bell of London and dedicated to the memory of the Revd Hayter George Hayter-Hames – the great improver of Chagford who died in 1886 – on Whit Sunday, 1888. The three windows in the north aisle also date from this period, being executed between 1884 and 1893 by Clayton and Bell.

CHAGFORD BELLS & RINGERS

Chagford's first ring of four bells was recorded as being in place in 1537, and the ring was later augmented to six. The dates of 1760 and 1766 are given for the new bells, although as six bells were said to have been added at this time it may well be that the originals were re-cast; it is difficult to envisage the bell chamber at Chagford housing a ring of ten! Certainly, when the whole ring was re-cast again in 1914 there were only six bells extant but a further two additions brought it up to a conventional 'full ring' of eight, which it remains at the time of writing. Chagford has a long tradition of campanology, and the present Captain of Bells, Julia Endacott, continues a family tradition by succeeding her father – the late Percy Rice – in the office.

A number of notable peals have been rung at Chagford, as well as the normal ringing before services and at weddings. The Queen's jubilee in 1977 led to a celebratory lengthy peal, as did the dawning of the new millennium. Each new year is also rung in with a 'goodly peal'. Other uses of the bells have been as a means of summoning the members of the old parish fire brigade and, more recently, as an invasion warning in time of war. The alarm was raised by 'clashing' several bells, causing them to ring discordantly. Nowadays, Chagford is a popular tower and attracts visiting teams of ringers, particularly in the long summer evenings when a lusty pull produces a goodly thirst to be slaked in the Globe or the Three Crowns.

Chagford ringers on the occasion of the church septcentenary in July 1961. The team included: *Hilda Flood, Will Bowles, Dick Stanbury, Percy Rice (Captain of the Tower), Jim Brimblecombe, Jago Endacott, Jack Rice, Mary Ainsley, John Collins, Ruth Lake and Tim Bennett.* (Thorn Collection)

Left: *The ringing tradition in Chagford is as strong as ever, with many young people taking up the ancient art. Here are the ringers in their gallery in March 1998.* Left to right, back row: *Mike Webber, Edward Haws, Richard Thomas, Ray Squire, Matthew Shields, John Collins;* centre: *Hannah Lester, Dave Barnett, Tony Judge, Jonathon Bint, Revd Louis Baycock (Rector), Evan Endacott, Andrew Lester, Laurence Bennie, Amy Lester;* front: *Diana Marriott, Ruth Bint, Janet Lammacraft, Julia Endacott (Tower Captain and Churchwarden), Karen Lammacraft and Helen McIntyre. For the second time in a century Chagford's bells were silenced when wet rot in the oak foundation beams of the bell cage (due, once again, to that porous granite) was uncovered at the end of 1999. Again, funds (more than £55,000 rather than the £750 that sufficed in 1914!) were raised very quickly to finance refurbishment of the whole tower and the underpinning of the defective beams with galvanised steelwork. The work was carried out in the summer of 2000 and the first peal rung on Advent Sunday that year – after an enforced silence of just ten months.* (Courtesy of Julia Endacott/ Chagford Ringers)

TWENTIETH-CENTURY ALTERATIONS

The early-twentieth century saw further work carried out on the church. The choir stalls were rebuilt in 1914 by Herbert Read of Exeter, a well-known ecclesiastical woodcarver and maker of church furnishings. He was to do much further work in Chagford church, which has seen several major twentieth-century alterations. Some of these, such as the removal of the old Market Cross from the Square to the churchyard and its re-dedication as a war memorial, date from the First World War. At the same time, in 1918, the lady chapel in the south aisle was reworked by Read and dedicated as a war memorial chapel in January of the following year. Another rather odd relic of this war found in the church is the processional cross, made of aluminium salvaged from the wreckage of a German 'Zeppelin' airship brought down at Cuffley, Hertfordshire, in 1916.

The 'Chagford Through the Ages' wall-hanging at the west end of the south aisle; the work of local people celebrating the town's rich history. The project was initiated and largely carried out by members of the Chagford Women's Institute under Phil Williams, but many people had a hand in the final result. (Rice Collection)

Read continued to work in Chagford over the next decade. His major opus is the magnificent and intricate rood-screen in oak. This is entirely traditional in design, echoing screens at other churches in the locality. The screen was another gift from the Hayter-Hames family, whose long association with the church and living of Chagford has been a profound influence. It was constructed in memory of Noel Hayter-Hames, who was tragically killed in a flying accident in India in 1925; the work was completed and dedicated in 1927. Read was also responsible for the pulpit, made in 1928 to accord with the screen and dedicated to the memory of Revd Colville Hayter-Hames in 1930. The previous pulpit, removed in about 1860, was described as being of the 'double decker' construction, popular in the early-Georgian period.

Also a common Georgian feature were the high-sided, high-back enclosed pews which the Victorians replaced with plain deal pews during their reworking of the interior around 1860. These pews were in turn replaced by Herbert Read's traditionally designed oak pews, while more modern additions were the work of the late Michael Gaillard-Bundy, a local woodcarver and craftsman. He also carved the arms of the Prouz family on the south wall of the nave and made the case for the Parish Memorial Book adjacent to the lectern.

To mark the septcentenary of the church in 1961, a range of works were carried out under the direction of Mr S. Dykes-Bower, one-time 'surveyor of the fabric' to Westminster Abbey. The work undertaken included the re-flooring of the nave and aisles with granite paving, the construction of a ringers' gallery in the tower, the provision of a new and colourful organ case and the re-gilding of the reredos and parclose screens. The choir screens were also re-gilded in 1963 and the carved roof-bosses, which include the Chagford tinning-mark of three conjoined rabbits, were repainted. These restorations revived much of the colour and splendour of the interior of the church, latterly further enhanced by the remarkable 'Chagford Through the Ages' wall-hanging executed by members of the Women's Institute, which hangs on the west wall of the south aisle.

CHAGFORD RECTORY

The living of Chagford was well-endowed, a reflection of the town's medieval importance and prosperity. In the mid-nineteenth century, it was described as 'one of the richest livings in Devon, with an annual income of £850'. According to Hoskins, the earliest surviving habitation of the incumbent was the Church House, the sixteenth-century thatched house, now called 'Bellacouch', on the south boundary of the churchyard. In around 1820, a new rectory, Chagford House, was built on a splendid elevated site to the south of the town, approached by an avenue that ends only a few yards from the south gate of the churchyard. Chagford House remains in the possession of the Hayter-Hames family, from whose ranks a succession of Chagford rectors were drawn.

In 1887 the Stones, a family of local builders, constructed a further large new rectory at the foot of Nattadon Hill, a little above and behind Chagford House. This rectory abutted a large area of glebe land, traditionally let as church allotments. The allotments still survive, albeit reduced in area. Part of this land formed a proposed early site for Chagford's Victorian 'elementary school', later built in New Street. The modest modern rectory was built in 1972 in a corner of the garden belonging to the Victorian building, now known as Nattadon House. After a spell as a hotel, this is now a private residence.

A view from the lawns at the rear of the new rectory, built on glebe land in 1872 by the Chagford building firm of Stones. The current modest rectory occupies a corner of this garden. (Thorn Collection)

NONCONFORMISM IN CHAGFORD

West Devon was an early stronghold of Methodism. John Wesley made the first of many visits to the area while on his journey to Cornwall in the summer of 1743. He preached at a number of localities close to Chagford, notably at Sticklepath and South Zeal. Between then and his death in 1791 Wesley made no less than 32 further visits to the far west, and his influence in West Devon and, especially, Cornwall was profound. However, it was the Baptists who opened the first Nonconformist meeting in Chagford in 1829. John Berry, the Chagford woolmaster, was a Wesleyan sympathiser, and in 1834 he leased them a chapel in his buildings for a nominal rent. This site is now included within the houses below Mr Berry's House – the chapel interior is still partly extant within the roof of Millaton. This chapel was succeeded by the new Methodist Chapel in Mill Street, built in 1861 and active until the early 1990s; it is now the offices of Helpful Holidays, a prominent Westcountry holiday letting company.

Chagford's oldest surviving Nonconformist place of worship is the Ebeneezer Gospel Hall of the Bible Christians (Plymouth Brethren) in Southcombe Street. This beautiful little chapel and the accompanying minister's house were built in 1844 and remained almost unchanged until the end of the twentieth century, when structural problems forced a renovation. The opportunity was taken to create a space which had social uses as well as being a place of worship. With a strong following and a lively youth club, the 'Ebeneezer' is still very much thriving today.

CHAGFORD PAROCHIAL SCHOOL

There are records of a school in Chagford in the seventeenth century. The schoolmaster in 1659 was a Mr David George, but the site of the school is obscure. It may well have been in the church or the church house. Most early schools in rural areas were run by the church, and the initial provision of public education in Chagford was no exception. The

The Ebeneezer Gospel Hall, Chagford, the meeting-place of the Plymouth Brethren in Southcombe Street, from a drawing by the author.

Chagford (Voluntary) Parochial School opened in 1799, with Mr William Short as its first master. He was succeeded by his son, Caleb Short, in 1845. Initially, the school was funded through the Parish Rate, overseen by the churchwardens, and by public subscription.

The curriculum was basic and very much based on the Scriptures and on rote, learning of 'ciphering' and reading, with a little arithmetic. The Parochial School taught pupils between the ages of seven and about 13. After this age, children were expected to start contributing to the family income. Children could stay on at school until they were 15 or older, often as monitors, and those who achieved the required standards could be entered for scholarship examinations at one of the grammar schools in the area – Exeter, Okehampton or Totnes were the usual possibilities. In 1853, the school acquired an infant department, started by Mrs Hayter-Hames, wife of the rector. This started in a small room at the rear of the main school.

The pupils of the Parochial School were divided into six 'standards' but initially all were taught in the same room. The staff at this time (around 1850) seems to have consisted of the schoolmaster, Mr Caleb Short (certificated teacher – first class) assisted by his daughter Eleanor, described as a pupil teacher. He was also assisted by monitors – older or brighter children appointed to oversee the work of their compatriots – and by various peripatetic teachers who taught specific subjects, such as sewing. This subject figured large in the girls' curriculum, while the older boys were expected to show proficiency in 'military drill'.

The school was administered by a Board of Managers chaired, ex-officio, by the rector. Many visits from the Revd Hayter G. Hayter-Hames and other leading school board members, which included Mr William Perryman and Mr William Ellis of Waye Barton, are recorded in the school log, which was started in 1863. The rector's initials and com-

Former Chagford Infants School scholars gather in 1986 for a reunion in the old schoolyard, now renovated as the courtyard of Endecott House. The location is identical to the one shown below – the window being that of the Victorian schoolroom built in the 1890s.
(Courtesy of the Mortimore family, Shapley)

ments at intervals show that he inspected the records regularly and took a close interest in the activities of the school.

CHAGFORD SCHOOL LOG

By the 1860s Chagford's school had been named the National School, No. 5197. It's log was a compulsory record that documents the school's activities for the 108 years from 1863 to 1971. Under the Revised Code of Regulations for 1862 the Principal Teacher was required to:

Above left: *The pupils of Chagford Infants' School photographed in 1925 with their schoolmistress.* (Thorn Collection)

Above right: *Junior schoolchildren on the same occasion. The photograph was taken in the yard at the rear of the Infants' School (St Katherine's Hall).* (Courtesy of the Mortimore family, Shapley)

... daily make in the log book the briefest entry which will suffice to specify either ordinary progress, or whatever other fact concerning the school or its teachers, such as the dates of withdrawals, commencements of duty, cautions, illness &c.

This requirement – amended to require only weekly entries from April 1871 – meant that the log recorded many factors affecting the town at large, such as fair days, public holidays, severe weather, epidemics, the state of farming, the occurrence of fires, floods or other disasters, the deaths of local and national figures, local elections, and even national and international events. It thus forms a valuable primary resource for Chagford historians and has been used for much of the research for this book.

The first entry, made by Caleb Short, is dated 2 March 1863 and reads: 'Examined first five classes in Catechism: about 15 children said it imperfectly – ordered to learn it during the week.' Other subjects included knowledge of the Bible and Church liturgy, ciphering (writing out letters neatly and legibly), writing from dictation, reading aloud from texts (usually Biblical), knowing by heart letters, numbers and multiplication tables, performing simple arithmetic and (for the girls) sewing.

Following a visit from Revd E.P. Arnold, the Diocesan Board of Education's Schools Inspector, on 17 April 1863 comment was made that 'of the 39 girls on the register above the age of seven, only 24 learn sewing.' This was deemed inadequate, and it was suggested that the school managers:

... consult some experienced Lady as to the age at which girls ought to begin to learn to sew, and then at that age make attendance at the sewing lessons a sine qua non of every girl's attendance at the school.

The inspector also stated that 'it would be a relief to the bareness and cheerless aspect of the room if some maps and prints were hung up on the walls.'

Even in 1908, needlework was still high on the school managers' agenda. Having resolved to increase the time devoted to this activity to at least three hours per week (one hour of which was to be spent knitting), the chairman, Revd G.H. Ley, commented in the log: 'I heartily welcome the additional time for "needlework" – the most important of girls' subjects of instruction.' One suspects that Mrs Pankhurst might have taken issue with the reverend gentleman! Other early log entries give a flavour of school life during this period:

Two boys playing the truant – cane them tomorrow...

... gave instructions... that the writing of sums on the boys' slates must be more carefully done...

Writing of sixth class poor – monitor admonished.

It was not all bad, however. Mr Short evidently also believed in the efficacy of the occasional carrot: 'Examined the Arithmetic Classes. Gave pence to the most proficient.'

Caleb Short died 'in post' at the end of 1879. His place as schoolmaster was taken by George Smith, 'late pupil of Culham College'. Caleb Short's daughter Eleanor stayed on for a while; she left the following Christmas after obtaining a 'First Class Queen's Scholarship' to receive formal teacher training at Truro.

Top and right: *Several pages taken from the school log dating from the late 1800s.*

The eleven volumes of Chagford's school log-books form a wonderful primary source for the town's history between their commencement in 1863 and the discontinuing of the system in the mid 1970s.

Reproduced here are a selection of entries covering the period 1863–1908, to give an idea both of the detailed content of the logs and of the meticulous way in which these records were kept by the schoolmasters of the day, Caleb Short and George Smith. (Chagford Primary School)

Left: *Douglas Thorn as a Chagford Infant School pupil, c.1933.* (Thorn Collection)

ATTENDANCE

School attendance was compulsory under the Universal Education Act of 1870, but the logs show that the numbers attending school were variable, as a result of three main factors: children (mostly the older boys) were kept home by their parents to assist with farm work; the influence of the weather; and ill health. The attendance figures are given frequently in the logs, and one of the duties of visiting members of the school's Board of Managers was to check the registers and attendances and record their findings. The needs of the smaller farmers for all the help they could get and the subsequent effect on school attendance is frequently noted, although in a carefully-written commentary, school-master George Smith demonstrated sympathy for the farmers 'who cannot afford or find adequate labour'. Farm work, where duly notified, was accepted by the Education Board as a valid reason for absence from school. Consequently, there was little Mr Smith could do about these periodic depletions of his school roll.

However, it was not only farm children that had to work. Many of the poorer children only attended the school part time – usually in the afternoons. In the morning they were employed in the Blanket Factory. Yet work was not the only thing that kept the eager pupils of Chagford National School from their desks. Almost anything was enough to divert some of them, as recorded in a series of exasperated entries overleaf. Additionally, the health of the children seems to have been relatively poor, and there are many entries relating to outbreaks and, on

occasions, epidemics of illness. Such conditions also extended to the teachers, who were similarly absent through ill health. The final major reason for absenteeism at school was severe weather.

Also recorded in the pages of the log, duly circumscribed by ruled black borders, are the deaths of both notable local and national figures, as well as, occasionally, those of pupils. The schoolmaster penned a brief and elegant obituary, and on occasions staff and pupils were given leave to attend funerals.

The First World War naturally had a considerable impact on the school. On 8 September 1914 the log includes the wry comment: 'I shall be without a teacher for Standard II pro tem, as Mr Bond has been accepted for military service.' Meanwhile, the pupils also did their bit for the war effort, as the log records: '...the senior boys have... cultivated a piece of land a mile distant from the school for potatoes.'

THE SCHOOL BUILDINGS

The school was originally housed in the old guildhall of St Katherine, which has been known latterly as the British Legion Hall and is, at the time of writing, Endacott House. This fine sixteenth-century thatched building was owned by the Church and was being let as a residence for the market overseer when the school first started – the school only occupied an upper room. The children were all taught in this one large room, apparently created by gutting the original second-storey interior. When the infant school opened in 1853, the younger children

Left: *Chagford Church of England Primary; a school group photograph taken in the hall in 1976 with Ralph Faulkener where he most liked to be – in the midst of his pupils. He retired in 1981.* (Courtesy of the Mortimore family, Shapley)

Above centre: *Ralph Faulkener was the last head teacher of Chagford Junior School and the first head of the combined Chagford Church of England Primary School which opened in 1971.* (Thorn Collection)

The original architect's drawing of Chagford Secondary School, designed by the Devon County Architect M.V.C. Hague and then very much 'state of the art'. These were excellent buildings and survive, largely unaltered, to this day. (Courtesy of Chagford Primary School)

occupied the lower floor and the market overseer went elsewhere. Later – after 1891 – a completely new schoolroom was added at the rear of the original building. At the same time, the children attending the infant school were provided with a row of splendid lavatories at the top of the rear courtyard – facilities now protected by a listing order!

The Parochial School rapidly outgrew this original accommodation and in 1859–60 the old Parish Almshouse in New Street was extensively rebuilt to provide a new school. The building comprised a single lofty classroom measuring 68 x 18 feet and was 15 feet 6 inches high. It was lit by two large windows and heated by two coal-burning iron-railed fireplaces. There were separate entrances for boys and for girls, with a small yard each side and a yard at the rear with lavatories along the back of the site. There was also a smaller room, built as a lean-to at the rear of the south end of the main schoolroom, which was originally used as the teacher's office, but soon became part of the school proper as numbers continued to swell. The New Street schoolroom was opened in September 1860 and the junior school moved there, leaving the infants in undisputed possession at St Katherine's Hall. A schoolmaster's house was also provided (No. 24 New Street).

In 1896 the New Street school was modernised and extended: a new rear wing was built at the north end of the main building, and the internal divisions were reorganised to give two main classrooms and a smaller room. Each classroom was lit by one large window and was provided with a cast-iron coke-fired stove. The playground facilities were extended, with a new toilet block being added to the south side of the yard. The school was now lit by gas, and was connected to the main drainage system, which had been installed in Chagford after 1880. Further modifications were carried out up to the 1930s: the rear wing was extended twice to provide further classroom space – up to four main classrooms – and indoor toilet

facilities. Electricity was eventually installed and the heating and other facilities improved.

CHAGFORD SECONDARY SCHOOL

In 1934 the Devon County Council Education Committee decided to establish a secondary modern school at Chagford to serve the whole north-east Dartmoor area, augmenting the grammar school provision at Okehampton, Exeter and Totnes. The new school opened in September 1936 in a fine building designed by the County Architect, Mr M.V.C. Hague. This was regarded in its day as something of a 'model school' with large, light, airy, centrally-heated classrooms, a barrel-roofed school hall and landscaped central quadrangle. It occupied a spacious site on the eastern edge of Chagford, with fine views across the Teign Valley and towards Whiddon Park. As well as the classroom and craft-teaching facilities, there were extensive playing-fields and, from 1939, an outside swimming pool. A house was provided for the head teacher, adjacent to which was an outside amphitheatre for the production of plays.

Chagford Secondary School was further developed and expanded in the postwar period, additional accommodation being provided firstly by a wartime prefabricated 'Horsa Hut' (designed for a ten-year life, and still in place and in use after more than 50 years!) and subsequently by the 'New Wing' built in the 1960s. This block of four classrooms under a monopitch roof has huge picture windows looking out over one of the finest views in Chagford. The swimming pool was also modernised, and changing rooms and showers added to the main school buildings. Chagford Secondary School had only one head teacher throughout its 35-year independent existence – Mr Ron Jewell, who retired when the secondary school provision passed to Okehampton in 1971.

Extracts from the school log, 1877–1918

Farm work

16 July 1877: The upper end of the room begins to get thin already; the hay harvest has begun and they are wanted home.

28 August 1882: Opened with a small school today; many of the children are kept home to assist in the ingathering of crops.

8 April 1892: A great deal of irregularity this week, especially among the boys; the old excuse at this time of the year – planting potatoes. (An entry repeated almost verbatim for most springtimes up until 1918.)

Factory work

7 July 1877: The attendance of the factory children and the pauper children has not been quite so good as I could wish during the last week or two. The attention of the Foreman of the Factory has been called to it and he has promptly sent them home from work.

Distractions

20 May 1884: The attendance is small today – many of the children having gone to Moretonhampstead, a large circus being there for the day.

21 June 1887: Slack school today and yesterday, many children having gone to the neighbouring parishes to witness the Jubilee celebrations. (Queen Victoria had been on the throne for 50 years.)

20 May 1892: Nearly all the First Class boys are absent this afternoon. During the dinner hour some cottages and the farmhouse at Westcott were reported on fire and the boys, attracted to the scene, evidently find this novelty a greater attraction than their school. One third of school absent.

9 Nov. 1892: The children from the country have been very late mornings during the past fortnight. I suppose it is due to the dark mornings. Many of them have two miles to come.

1 May 1911: 53 absent this afternoon – local attraction – Kestor races.

Sickness

15 Jan. 1900: Owing to the large amount of sickness (influenza principally) prevailing in the parish, the Managers, advised by our local doctor, decided that the schools should remained closed a further week...

16 March 1908: H.A. Smith (pupil teacher) absent through having a bad abscess in his face.

28 June 1909: All the children from the hamlet of Sandypark and from Parford have been ordered to remain at home for a period, three cases of scarlet fever having been notified in that locality.

17 Oct. 1911: Freda and Pearl Williams, by Medical Order, to cease attendance for a time; supposed diphtheria in the house...

7 March 1913: There are now seven children notified as absent through ringworm.

15 Sept. 1913: Reopened this day, the school having been closed a further fortnight by Medical Order owing to measles.

22 March 1918: Whooping cough outbreak. Close school today mid-day under Medical Order for three weeks.

Weather

16 March 1891: Since my last entry we have experienced such weather as the oldest inhabitant in the Parish cannot recollect. The snow in many places was from 15 to 25 feet deep. The roads for a few days were impassable not only for vehicular but pedestrian traffic... for a time it will be simply impossible for 50 of the country children to attend.

8 Jan. 1893: Attendance very poor – snowstorm. 87 present this morning, 99 this afternoon. Number on roll: 166.

12 July 1900: Severe thunderstorm during dinner hour. Water came into the room by the eastern door – no school this afternoon.

14 July 1911: A very hot week. Temperature in school this afternoon 84°. A class has been on forms in the schoolyard when possible. Have taken singing this week instead of physical exercises – the heat being too great for the latter lesson.

CHAGFORD CHURCH OF ENGLAND PRIMARY SCHOOL

The secondary school continued in being until the end of the summer term in 1970. In the autumn of the following year, after the buildings had been suitably adapted as a primary school, the children from both the Chagford infant and junior schools – combined with the pupils of the small village schools of Drewsteignton, Gidleigh, Throwleigh and Whiddon Down – moved onto the site. The new school became known as Chagford Church of England Primary School (Voluntary Aided). The secondary children now had to get up earlier to catch buses to the rapidly-expanding Okehampton College, itself reconstituted as a Comprehensive School. The village schoolrooms were closed and sold off, except for Throwleigh which was retained as a Field Study Centre. The bells of these old village schools are preserved in the quadrangle of the present Chagford school. Chagford Primary continues to thrive and grow, catering for some 200 children in 2002, with provision for children from the age of four upwards and a pre-school playgroup.

The New Street school and schoolhouse were sold off for residential purposes, and St Katherine's Hall was taken over and restored by the Chagford Combined Charity, a trust which also incorporated all the pre-existing church charities. Grant aid was sought and donations attracted from as far away as the USA. This was made possible as, in 1644, one John Endicott (contemporary spelling), a Chagford man and a prominent Puritan, became the first governor of the Colony of Massachusetts. A further famous member of the family was William Crowninshield Endicott, born in Salem, Massachusetts in 1826, who rose to become a Supreme Court Justice and Secretary for War under President Cleveland. The old St Katherine's guildhall was renamed Endicott (or Endecott or Endacott!) House in honour of these eminent sons of Chagford. There is also an Endicott House in Salem, which for a time was used as an almshouse. It stands next to the historic Custom House at the head of the quays.

CHAGFORD HEAD TEACHERS

In recent times, Chagford has continued the tradition of long-serving head teachers that dates back to the opening by William Short in 1799. In over 200 years the school has had only nine permanent head teachers, and some of them have served remarkable terms of office – over 45 years apiece, in the cases of William Short and George Smith.

Below: The Primary School celebrated its 25th anniversary in 1996, when this mosaic version of the tinners' rabbits was added to the school's courtyard at a ceremony attended by both former head teacher Ralph Faulkener and then-current head Graham Reynolds – second from right at rear. (Courtesy of Chagford Primary School)

CHAGFORD PRIMARY HEAD TEACHERS

William Short, 1799–1845
Caleb Short, 1845–79*
George Smith, 1880 –1925
William Alfred Bennett, 1925–38
Miss Eleanora Davy, 1939–55
J.C. Dunks, 1956–65*
Dennis Miller, 1966–68*
Ralph Faulkener, 1968–81
Graham Reynolds, 1982–2002.

(* = died in office)

NURSERY SCHOOLS

As well as the infant and junior schools, there has long been nursery provision – of a private nature – in Chagford. The 1857 *Billing's Directory* lists a 'day school' run by a Mary Dymond in Sidcombe (Southcombe) Street, while more recently the nursery run by Mrs Suzanne Egan at her bungalow 'Heather Cottage' at Yeo is fondly remembered by many native Chagfordians. Today, a Mother and Toddler group operates in conjunction with the pre-school playgroup and an independent Montessori School also offers nursery and pre-school education.

Left: The facilities of the modern Chagford Primary School include this wonderful wildlife study area.

Right: The schoolchildren of the old Parochial School – raised on the Scriptures, ciphering, arithmetic and sewing – would find much to wonder at in the richness and diversity of the curriculum offered to their modern-day counterparts, here seen examining the Devon Air Ambulance – another facility undreamed of even in the relatively recent past.

(Both courtesy Chagford Primary School)

An 'unimproved' section of one of Chagford's historic packhorse trackways. This is the lower section of what is now Northill Lane, on the route from Chagford to Kestor Down via Holy Street and Teigncombe. There are several other such trackways surviving in the parish. (Rice Collection)

SIX
TRAVEL & TRANSPORT

ANCIENT TRACKWAYS
& PACK ROADS

Chagford owes its foundation as a settlement to its position on one of the main ancient trade routes across Dartmoor – that from Ashburton to the North Devon ports. This gave access to Bristol and South Wales for the tin and woollen trades, and served as a main highway from around the seventh century. Most of the roads in the parish are at least equally ancient, although some date from prehistoric times. Although many of the original ways have been subsumed into the more recent road network of the past 200 years, enough sections of ancient trackway remain in the parish to give a clear idea of the nature of these 'old roads'.

One of the oldest and most important of these was the way from Chagford to Tavistock, which is shown in detail on maps drawn in the fifteenth century. The route was part of a 'high way' from Exeter into Cornwall, which approached the moor by way of Dunsford and the Teign Valley, passing through Chagford and over the shoulder of Meldon by Waye Hill, whence it continued around the hill to Tunnaford, Yardworthy and Metherall. It continued up over Hurston Ridge, before dropping down to join the route from Moretonhampstead near Bennett's Cross. The route to Tavistock passed by Postbridge (the famous clapper bridge there was on this track), Cherrybrook and Two Bridges. Here, the ancient route, known as the 'Lich Way', climbed steeply up towards Beardown Farm, thence over the open moor to Merrivale, and approached Tavistock via Whitchurch, well to the south of the later turnpike route.

These were all packhorse routes. Or rather, on Dartmoor, packhorse, pack pony and donkey routes, for the sturdy, thickset Dartmoor pony and humble ass also proved useful for draft work on this difficult terrain. The 'old roads' are thus of a primitive nature suited to small, sturdy and sure-footed animals. Typically, they are narrow – mostly 6–7 feet wide – winding and deep-set between primitive hedgebanks in the 'in country', or forming faintly-discernible trackways with perhaps direction stones, cairns or skyline 'ridge cuttings' on the open moor. In the farmland, the trackways follow field and clearance boundaries, which gave rise to otherwise inexplicably-tortuous routes. The road surfaces were rocky and miry by turns, deep-scoured by the winter rains and full of loose rock, silt and gravel, while gradients were frequently extraordinarily steep and quite unsuited to any form of wheeled traffic. Characteristically, these old lanes are banked by fieldstone walls topped by ancient hedgerows; the stones, many of them massive boulders, came from the initial farm settlement land clearances carried out in the seventh and eighth centuries.

One such ancient route up onto the moor was by way of Holy Street and Leigh, thence up Northill Lane to Teigncombe, continuing by the very steep and rocky 'Featherbed Lane' to the moorgate onto Brimstone Down. The sections of this route (from Leigh Bridge to Northill Farm gate, and from Teigncombe to Kestor) that were never 'improved' for vehicular traffic give a clear idea of what a traditional Dartmoor pack-trail looked like: rough. This road was used to bring cut peat 'turves', furze, bracken (for bedding) and 'freestone' off the moor, as well as providing access to the various farms along its route. These included Teigncombe, one of the five Chagford farmsteads recorded in the Domesday Book.

Other early trackways still retaining a ghost of their original character include the bridleway from Great Weeke up over the shoulder of Weeke Down, and the short section at Downes leading towards Corndon. The medieval 'Mariner's Way', an important link between the seaports of the Exe Estuary and those of West and North Devon, traverses the higher reaches of Chagford Parish – from the North Bovey boundary at Lettaford across Jurston and Shapley farms to the crossing of the South Teign below Yardworthy, thence by Frenchbeer and Teigncombe (where it intersects Featherbed Lane). The track enters Gidleigh Parish at the crossing of the North Teign River below Gidleigh Tor, now deep in woodland but originally on the open moor.

ROADSIDE CROSSES

One of the distinguishing features of many of these old routes was their marking by waymarkers or direction stones and, most characteristically, by roadside crosses. There are two fine surviving examples in Chagford, both in the area of Weeke Down and Middlecott, on the route from Chagford to North Bovey by way of Thorn and Youlden. Of these, the higher – on the crown of Weeke Down – was restored in the late-nineteenth century, having acquired a steep angle of lean over many years. There are also many of these crosses and stones on the open moor, some close to routes still used, but many are far away from any modern road. The 'Lich Way' route has a good number of both crosses and direction stones and there is an exceptional series of crosses on the Southern Moor between Holne and Walkhampton.

It is probable that there were many more such crosses and marker stones on the 'old roads' that were lost when the roads were widened and otherwise improved. The site of a former cross is recorded at Sandsgate, where the old route from Chagford over Chagford Bridge and up over the heights of Withecombe towards Exeter crossed the line of the new turnpike road from Whiddon Down to Moretonhampstead. It is also suggested that many of these ancient monuments were broken up as a convenient and easily accessible source of road stone, while other old crosses have been discovered serving as gate posts.

THE TURNPIKE

With the growth in road traffic, particularly wheeled road traffic, in the late-seventeenth and early-eighteenth centuries, the network of byways and packhorse trails that formed Britain's only continuous inland transport network came under a pressure of traffic that could not be sustained.

Byways within parishes were the responsibility of the parish authorities, that is to say, the church-wardens, who levied a Parish Rate to pay for upkeep and improvements. Ratepayers everywhere complained that they were now being asked to improve and maintain routes for trade and traffic that had its origins and destinations far beyond their locality. Hence road improvements were often opposed on these grounds, becoming the subject of bitter dispute.

The first major national infrastructure developments took place in the late-seventeenth and early-eighteenth centuries with the creation of Turnpike Trusts, statutory bodies authorised by Parliament to build and maintain highways and to charge a levy for their use. The first of these trusts was set up in 1663, to improve the Great North Road from London to York. From the last quarter of the eighteenth century, the inland waterway network also began its rapid phase of expansion, although in Devon there was little significant canal construction. A parallel development over the later part of this period was the tram road, where stone, wood or iron rails allowed horses to draw heavier loads. An outstanding example of such a tram road exists not far from Chagford, in the form of the Haytor Granite Railway. A number of other tram roads were laid down on Dartmoor in the early-nineteenth century, most notably Sir Thomas Tyrwhitt's Plymouth and Dartmoor Railway. However, the only tram roads constructed in Chagford were the limited and short-lived routes associated with the mining activity at Greet Weeke.

Many turnpike roads were constructed during the seventeenth and eighteenth centuries, but such developments did not really affect a remote neighbourhood like Chagford until well into the nineteenth century. With the tin and woollen industries both in decline, traffic to and within Chagford was still adequately served by the traditional pack-animals. It was as late as 1836 that the first turnpike penetrated the parish, and then only marginally, with the construction of the road from Whiddon Down to Moretonhampstead, via Sandsgate, Sandy Park, Doggamarsh and Easton. This was established by the Moretonhampstead Turnpike Trust, which was granted its Act

A fine example of a granite wayside cross, this being at Weeke Down. Once, there were many more of these crosses marking the old routes; a goodly few were lost to nineteenth-century road improvements.
(Meldrum Collection)

in 1826. The road led southward to Bovey via the Wray Valley and thence to Newton Abbot; it is now the A382. Chagford was thus bypassed by the main road – unlike neighbouring Moretonhampstead, which became an important highway centre where the Exeter to Tavistock turnpike (established in 1772) was crossed by the new road. This comparative isolation – not being on the road to anywhere else – has certainly contributed much to Chagford's distinctive character.

It is subsequent to the opening of the turnpike in the years 1836–40 that most of the Chagford Parish's road improvements date. The first and most important of these was the widening and easing of the route between Chagford and the new highway; the old route to Exeter via Drewsteignton met the new road at Sandy Park, and was greatly improved between there and Rushford. In addition, the road to Easton Cross was improved, with passing places for wheeled traffic being provided at several points.

A typical section of early-nineteenth-century 'improved byroad'; the road to Gidleigh from Holy Street at the entrance to Leigh Bridge Farm, looking towards Chagford. This is a macadam road of fine gravel over a rammed-stone foundation. (Meldrum Collection)

IMPROVED BYWAYS

The gradual replacement of the traditional Dartmoor packhorse or donkey by wheeled farm carts, together with the introduction of the heavier carriers' wagons, led to a programme of improvement to many of the old packhorse routes within the parish. These were widened and straightened and had their gradients eased by means of rock cuttings on the hillcrests. Some of these cuttings are quite deep, as at Eastholme on Mill Street, on the old Gidleigh road just above Holy Street, and between Great Weeke and Drewston Cross on the traditional route to Moretonhampstead. The widened roads also gained passing places, rudimentary paving on the wetter stretches, and crude drainage systems. The edges of the lanes were built up with the characteristic Devon hedge of a drystone bank topped by thorn or beech. A good example of this nineteenth-century road improvement is the section from Sandy Park to Crossways via Rushford, where the road was straightened and the grade eased by cutting and embanking. The stone banks on the side of the hill above Furlong were further braced by massive granite props. There is a hillcrest cutting at Rushford Barton, where a loop and sharp bend that originally took the road north of the orchard was eliminated. The old 'narrowbridge' between Rushford Mill and Chagford was also widened at this time.

These road improvements, most of them carried out in 1835–6, were paid for by the Parish Rate and regular meetings of the ratepayers were held to discuss the works and the increasing problem of road maintenance. This latter task brought into being the calling of roadman or 'waywarden', a workman appointed by the parish to repair potholes, clear the culverts and ditches and keep in repair the banks,

gates and stiles. The paving of the roads was gradually improved along the lines laid down by John MacAdam, with a foundation of large stones rammed into the subsoil, topped with smaller stones and then gravel to give a crowned road with drainage ditches cut either side. Many of these ditches were also paved with small river pebbles or even sea cobbles, to stop the swift run-off from the Dartmoor rains scouring and undercutting the road margins. Such paved drainage channels can still be discerned in a number of places, notably near Rushford Barton and on the section of Mill Street leading down through the deep cutting below Eastholme – although this large channel also served as an outfall for part of the town's water supply and drainage system.

Stone for this roadwork was obtained from a number of small quarries dotted about the parish, and, if some reports are to be believed, by the destruction of some ancient standing stones, wayside crosses and other antiquities. Road stone was broken by hand to the required sizes. The roadman's tools included a stout wooden wheelbarrow, a heavy pick and stone hammer, a lighter dressing hammer, a long-handled Devon shovel, a heavy rammer for consolidating the stone foundation and sub-surface and a sturdy gravel rake. The traditional road surfaces lasted in many places in Chagford well into the twentieth century, with gas-tar binding of the macadam gravel surface (hence tarmacadam) being gradually introduced from about 1910. Nationally, the responsibility for the upkeep of public highways passed to the county councils when these came into being. Devon County Council found itself responsible for the largest road mileage of any English shire county, with over 9,000 route-miles consisting for the greater part of narrow, twisted byways.

The County Council exercised its responsibility for local road maintenance through the appointment of lengthmen – each responsible for the secondary roads on his own 'patch'. The main roads were usually upgraded and maintained by a new breed of road contractor, working directly for the County Councils. The last traditional road lengthmen in Chagford was Sam Fishleigh, a local legend and a true fund of country lore. He had an intimate knowledge of the ways of wildlife and game, and his family always dined well. Sam was known on occasion to stop a conversation with a raised hand, cock an ear, then bring his spade down hard into the ground straight into a mole run whose denizen just happened to be passing at the time. 'That's dun fer the varmint,' he would say as he wiped the gory evidence from the blade. 'Now, what was yew sayin?'

More recently, the solitary roadman with his barrow has been replaced by the two or three-man road gang, with a pick-up truck and selection of tools. Although this usually still includes the traditional implements familiar to the nineteenth-century waywarden, the team often also has at its disposal a vibrating compactor or powered road drill as well. However, in truth, the job remains much the same, for while tar and chippings overlay the original macadam stone road surface, the ditches and drains, banks, hedges, stiles and culverts still call for the same skilled care they have always needed.

WAGONS, CARRIAGES & BRAKES

With the advent of roads suitable for the passage of wheeled traffic, trade in the Chagford district was greatly facilitated. 'Road wagons' operated by common carriers provided services to Exeter and Newton Abbot for both passengers and merchandise, and with the advent of the turnpikes these services grew to have substantial capacity. The payload of a nineteenth-century heavy road wagon was measured in tons rather than the couple of hundredweight that formed the limit for a pack pony, and on good roads they could make a speed of around five miles an hour between stops.

Swifter still were the mail coach post-chaise services operated along the Exeter to Okehampton turnpike, and quite probably down to Bovey and Ashburton as well. Inns were established at the main posting points, most notably the Post Inn at Whiddon Down and the White Hart at Moreton. For a while, this type of operation flourished for those that could afford it, while the spectacular growth and efficiency of the Royal Mail and the network of mail-coach routes meant that even Chagford was no longer considered remote from the centre of national commerce, London. By the mid 1820s, the swiftest mail coach made the Exeter–London run in just 16½ hours. Chagford Post Office was warranted in 1824, when a letter from the General Post Office in London could reach the town inside 36 hours – things are little faster today!

The improved roads also brought another type of vehicle to the Chagford district – one which was ultimately to have the greatest impact of all. These were the private carriages of the newly emerged mercantile elite, people whose wealth gave them the leisure to travel and who were drawn to Dartmoor by the beauty and romance of its scenery and associations. A number of these wealthy merchants found the district greatly to their liking, and from the 1860s onwards began that great spurt of country-house building that ultimately ringed Chagford, turning many a modest farmstead into a dwelling of near-baronial splendour as at Holy Street, Outer Down, Ford Park and Teignworthy.

The new roads also accommodated a more prole-tarian form of conveyance, the 'brake' – a large open vehicle that could carry upwards of a dozen passengers. These became popular as a means of visiting the moor for organised groups such as church outings, temperance societies or trade guilds. They were the progenitor of the modern 'coach trip', and the first manifestation of that essentially twentieth-century phenomenon, 'mass tourism'. Trade directories of the time were full of advertisements of 'conveyances for hire' and organised sightseeing tours to popular beauty spots on Dartmoor became popular.

THE RAILWAYS ARRIVE

In 1844, the Brunel-engineered Bristol and Exeter Railway was opened from Temple Meads Station in Bristol to the new Exeter Station on the Exe River bank at St Davids. As the B&E in Bristol made a direct junction with the Great Western line from Paddington via Reading, Swindon and Bath, Exeter was henceforth directly connected with the capital, now only a few hours away. Indeed, so speedy were the new broad-gauge flyers (capable of speeds of over 60 miles an hour, when previously the most rapid form of transport had been the 11 or 12 miles an hour of a post-chaise or swift mail coach) that Chagford found itself within a comfortable day's journey of London.

However, the railway did not stop at Exeter. Even before the B&E was open Brunel was surveying the line of the remarkable South Devon Railway, notable among other things for its spectacular sea-wall route from Starcross to Teignmouth, for some ferocious gradients west of Newton Abbot and, of course, for that most glorious failure, the Atmospheric Propulsion System. As with all Brunel's railways, the Bristol and Exeter and the South Devon were laid on the 'broad gauge' of 7 feet ¼ inch, compared to the 4 feet 8½ inches of Stephenson's 'standard' gauge (which was always referred to disparagingly as the 'Narrow' in the Brunel camp). The SDR opened to Newton Abbot on New Year's Eve 1846, went on to Totnes in July 1847 and then to Laira in Plymouth in

WAGONS, CARRIAGES & BRAKES

A very rakish lightweight horse-drawn 'brake' on Dartmoor (believed to be near Bennett's Cross). This is typical of the vehicles which opened up Dartmoor to road-borne tourism – several such conveyances operated from Chagford in the later nineteenth century. (Thorn Collection)

Above: *Private transport in the pre-motor age on Dartmoor was on horseback or, as here, by pony and trap. Lower Square, Chagford. (Thorn Collection)*

Right: *Another horse brake in Chagford – although this one is participating in a carnival procession, c.1960, passing the Post Office. (Thorn Collection)*

May 1848. The attempt at atmospheric working lasted only a few months before being finally abandoned in early 1847.

politicking was the construction of an isolated section of standard-gauge route in the lower Teign Valley from Heathfield to Christow in 1875.

THE TEIGN VALLEY RAILWAY PROPOSAL

With the main line through to Plymouth complete, attention turned to the making of branch lines. An early proposal was for the 'Teign Valley Railway', a broad-gauge line intended to link Chagford directly with Exeter by way of the Teign gorge and a tunnel through the ridge below Longdown. This scheme, of which Revd Hayter George Hayter-Hames was a director, dated from 1860 and was one of a flurry of similar railway proposals that would have linked 'just about everywhere of little consequence to just about anywhere else of no consequence at all', as a newspaper wag of the time put it.

In the context of the time, the Teign Valley was a bold undertaking, although an alternative South Devon Railway proposal had also envisaged a long tunnel below the Haldon Hills and a route via Ashburton rather than Newton Abbot. An Act was obtained in 1861 and surveys were made for a route from Exeter to Teign House, near Christow, via Steps Bridge, Fingle and Sandy Park to Chagford. Although a contractor was appointed and some earthworks commenced, the Chagford proposers failed to raise sufficient capital to complete their railway, even in part.

The original Teign Valley Railway scheme rumbled on, going through a number of iterations over the succeeding years, with further Acts granted in 1864, 1866 and finally in 1878. During this period the Teign Valley was drawn into much broader proposals that sought to link Newton Abbot with Launceston via the Teign Valley and Okehampton (The Devon Central Railway), and a later scheme that would have struck north from Dunsford via Tedburn to Crediton (The Mid-Devon Railway). The only concrete result from all this speculation and

THE MORETONHAMPSTEAD RAILWAY

Fortunately, the original proposal for a line to Moretonhampstead fared better, which at least brought the railway within easy reach of Chagford. The Moretonhampstead and South Devon Railway was constituted in 1862, gained its Act the following year, and was constructed rapidly in 1864–5. The broad-gauge line opened in July 1866 and it was worked from the outset by the South Devon Railway. In 1870, a horse omnibus began running from Moreton-hampstead Station to the Cross Tree in Chagford – the culmination of an exceedingly round-about rail and road route from Exeter that took in Starcross, Dawlish, Teignmouth, Newton Abbot, Heathfield, Bovey Tracey and Lustleigh.

However, in spite of its length this was at least a practical proposition and even before the Moretonhampstead line opened, consideration was being given to an extension onwards to Chagford. This railway, for which the plans were deposited in 1864, proposed a terminal station in the field at Narrowbridge (Rushford) between Teign View House and the river. However, the M&SDR and the SDR failed to promote the scheme before Parliament so the proposal never received an Act.

In truth, such a line was not an easy prospect as there would have been considerable engineering and some stiff gradients to overcome in order to get a railway up out of the Wray Valley, over the watershed and down into that of the Teign. A tunnel would almost certainly have been called for at the summit of the route below Meacombe, along with substantial earthworks on either approach. It would have been a very expensive four miles of railway, both to build and to operate, and although detailed surveys were conducted and the proposal

Left: *Brunel's broad-gauge railway reached Exeter in 1844, and here is one of Daniel Gooch's 'flyers' that sped trains westward at speeds of 60 miles an hour in the 1850s. The coming of the railway had a fundamental effect on the whole Dartmoor area – easily and swiftly accessible from the South East and the Midlands for the first time.* (Rice Collection)

(Rice Collection)

Left: *The Teign Valley train at Exeter, c.1910. Had the 1883 'Exeter, Chagford and Teign Valley' scheme come to full fruition, this is what the Chagford branch-line train would have looked like. As it was, only the Teign Valley section of the line was ever completed, with the Chagford part being abandoned in 1897.*

Below: *The railways promoted the Westcountry holiday trade throughout the 1930s and 1950s, running a number of specially named trains to the area in the summer months. None was grander than the Pullman 'Devon Belle' of the Southern, which served Exeter, Crediton, Barnstaple and Ilfracombe; the connection to Chagford was by bus from Queen Street.*

(Rice Collection)

was periodically revived, no serious move was ever made to commence construction. When it became apparent that the 1860 Teign Valley scheme was falling by the wayside, Revd Hayter-Hames pressed the SDR to proceed with the Chagford extension, and as late as 1875 procured a promise from the SDR that if the local landowners contributed the land free, they would be induced to build and work the line. However, this attempt also came to nothing, and led to further efforts to revive the original Teign Valley proposal.

THE EXETER & CHAGFORD RAILWAY

A further scheme was promoted in 1877: the Exeter and Chagford Railway. This abandoned the Teign Valley route in favour of one via Whitestone Valley and Tap House near Tedburn St Mary. From there it passed south of Cheriton Bishop and Crockernwell by way of Greystone and followed the Fingle Brook from East Fingle to Fingle Bridge. At this point it

rejoined the original Teign Valley route through the gorge to Sandy Park. The E&CR proposal was put up by Exeter interests – the diversion of Chagford and district trade to Newton Abbot by reason of the Moretonhampstead line having caused little consternation in the city.

Unfortunately, this Exeter scheme was promoted in direct opposition to the 1877 reorganisation of the Teign Valley company, which had already revived the proposal for a direct line from Exeter to Chagford via Dunsford, this time on the standard gauge. The original company had been re-financed, with further backing from the Fulford family at Dunsford and some Exeter interests. The reborn company proposed a series of bills in 1878 for a railway linking both with the GWR at Exeter St Davids and with the LSWR at Queen Street, and running via Longdown to Leigh Cross (near Bridford Mills), where the Chagford route would strike off north-westwards along the line of the 1875 route to Crediton, swinging west just south of Dunsford to follow the river through the Teign Gorge to Chagford. Again, this was a scheme which failed to attract capital.

This LSWR advertisement dates from 1915 and features Chagford prominently: 'The L & SW Railway Company's Motor Bus runs every weekday from Exeter to Chagford.' By this time, the LSWR Chagford agents were Webber & Sons in the Square. (Rice Collection)

THE EXETER, CHAGFORD & TEIGN VALLEY RAILWAY

The future of the Exeter and Chagford Railway and revived Teign Valley schemes soon came to a head, as they both failed to attract sufficient parliamentary support and finance. The collapse of these two schemes resulted in a third prospectus being issued, that of the Exeter, Chagford and Teign Valley Railway. This emerged in 1881 out of the wreckage of the various earlier proposals and envisaged a standard-gauge line from a junction with the GWR at Alphington, thence via Longdown, through a tunnel under the ridge to a junction at Teign House, just north of Christow. Here, the line was to split. The 'main line' led southward to join up with the existing but hitherto isolated section of the Teign Valley Railway, while the Chagford route diverged at Teign House on a trailing junction (no direct connection from the Exeter direction) and followed the previous surveys up through the Teign Gorge to Chagford. Under this proposal, Chagford Station would have been built beside the road to Easton Cross between Teign Marsh and Crosse Park, with an extension along the river bank to serve the Lower Factory and the gasworks.

The EC&TVR received an Act of Parliament in 1883, but the company experienced great difficulty in raising the necessary capital. In the event, construction did not finally start until 1894, when the section to Dunsford was commenced. This involved some very heavy work in driving the Perridge tunnel below the ridge at Longdown and costs spun out of control. Work slowed almost to a stop on several occasions due to lack of capital, and the enterprise was perpetually dogged by its adverse financial situation. Finally, in 1897, the struggling company applied to Parliament to abandon the Chagford line, of which earthworks for a scant 400 yards had been started. Permission for the abandonment was granted in 1898. Even then, the section through to Christow did not finally open until 1903, 20 years after the original Act.

The impoverished Teign Valley line was soon absorbed within the GWR fold, but was never of any more than local significance. It was used on occasions as a diversion when adverse weather affected the South Devon line along the sea wall and proved a valuable strategic route during the Second World War, but tight curves and light construction limited its usefulness. There was some mineral traffic from the mines and quarries of the Teign Valley area – a traffic upon which the promoters had pinned great hopes – but this was not enough to sustain the service. Passenger trains ceased in 1958 and the route closed to goods in 1960.

THE LONDON & SOUTH WESTERN RAILWAY

The other prospective rail approach to Chagford was from the north, via the metals of the standard-gauge London and South Western Railway. The LSWR had reached Exeter from Yeovil in 1860 having already acquired – by means of some dubious share-dealing – a controlling interest in the earlier Exeter and Crediton Railway, then broad gauge and leased to the Bristol and Exeter interests. From this foothold the LSWR commenced a bold push into the far west by extending the Exeter and Crediton line from Crediton to Barnstaple as the North Devon Railway, opened in August 1854. This was originally broad gauge, but narrow rails were soon in place as well, and by 1863 LSWR passenger trains were running from Exeter through to Barnstaple and on to Bideford.

Further expansion of the LSWR system came with the formation of the standard-gauge Okehampton, Lydford and North Cornwall Railway in 1862. This left the Barnstaple line at Coleford Junction and the first section, to North Tawton, which swung close to Chagford, opened in November 1865. In 1891, the LSWR appointed Webbers as its agent in Chagford. They handled the sale of tickets and the forwarding of parcels, taken by road carrier to Yeoford.

MID-DEVON LIGHT RAILWAY

The final proposal for a Chagford railway, made in 1897 under the provisions of the 1896 Light Railways Act, sought to exploit the proposed Chagford and Teign Valley route by linking this to the LSWR line at Fatherford, near Okehampton. This was put forward by Dicksons, an established contracting interest, with the objective of joining the North Cornish and North Devon resorts with those of Torbay. Dicksons also had ideas of reviving the direct link from Crediton to Newton Abbot via Tedburn, Dunsford and the lower part of the Teign Valley Railway. This Crediton scheme was soon abandoned, and replaced with a further revival, this time of the 1864 proposal for a line from Chagford to join the Moretonhampstead branch – which had by now been converted from broad to standard gauge. It is difficult to see that this last proposal would have done anything other than harm the prospects of the struggling Teign Valley Railway even further.

John Dickson carried out surveys for the proposals in 1897. The MDLR Okehampton–Chagford line was to run via Tongue End (for Belstone), thence by Sticklepath (for South Zeal), Wyke, Throwleigh (Ashe Bridge) and via the Blackaton Valley and Holy Street to Chagford, where it used the line of the proposed gasworks/Lower Factory extension to make an end-on junction with the Exeter, Chagford and Teign Valley Railway. The route on to Moretonhampstead followed the 1864 Moretonhampstead and Chagford survey. In the event, the 1898 abandonment of the Chagford part of the Exeter, Chagford and Teign Valley Railway effectively killed off the Mid-Devon Light Railway proposal as well, and with it any hope of Chagford getting its own railway. In the end, the buses had to suffice. The Moretonhampstead line closed to passengers in 1959, pre-dating even the infamous Beeching report which decimated Devon's rail network. Freight services lasted a further five years until, in 1964 the line was closed beyond Heathfield. It was dismantled shortly afterwards.

HORSE OMNIBUSES & 'ROAD MOTOR CARS'

Chagford's first omnibus service was the 1870 horse-bus route from Moretonhampstead Station. It was originally operated on behalf of the South Devon Railway, but after the GWR took over the SDR in 1876, it was run directly by the railway company. A further horse-bus link was established in about 1875 – from the Yeoford (Coleford) Junction on the LSWR route from Exeter to North Devon. This ran via Cheriton Bishop, Crockernwell and Drewsteignton, and offered an alternative if rather tenuous link to Exeter.

In 1906 the Moretonhampstead to Chagford route became one of the first two in the West Country to be operated by a GWR 'Road Motor Car' (the other was Helston to The Lizard, in Cornwall). These early buses were Milnes-Daimlers and had single-deck bodies, about 20 seats and a large luggage rack on the roof. The driver sat in the open without even the benefit of a windscreen. With their 15mph top-speed capability, the 4-mile run to Chagford took around 20 minutes. The LSWR responded by replacing their Yeoford horse-bus with a pair of Clarkson steam buses running from Exeter (Queen Street), which were much quieter and swifter than the GWR's Milnes-Daimlers, but considerably less reliable. It was often said of these vehicles that they ran more miles between Exeter and the LSWR locomotive depot at Exmouth Junction going to and from repair than they did carrying passengers and parcels to Chagford. By 1908, the LSWR had sold them and introduced conventional Thorneycroft motor buses.

THE MOTOR OMNIBUS

While Chagford never got its railway, the bus services continued and thrived. A somewhat rudimentary bus and lorry garage made of old railway sleepers and corrugated iron was erected by the GWR to stable the vehicles used on the Chagford services. This was situated behind Rock House, then occupied by Messrs H.J. Osborne (potato merchants, seedsmen and coal factors), who were the GWR's ticket and goods agents in Chagford. It still exists in 2002, and is the building where Rendell's stores its hurdles, trestle tables and other auction equipment. With the introduction of larger vehicles these premises, which had a very narrow, awkward entrance and a steep and confined yard, became inadequate. As a result, the Osbornes leased space in Steven's garage in New Street. This was a large stone structure with a corrugated-iron roof and doors high enough to take double-decker buses (although it is doubtful the garage was ever used for such vehicles). This building was redeveloped for housing (Stannary Close) in 1994. The GWR also built a garage in Moretonhampstead, to house the buses as well as the charabancs and coaches used on the various Dartmoor tourist services.

With the 'grouping' of the railways in 1923, there was a rapid expansion of railway interest in bus services at national level. There followed a series of amalgamations centred around the pre-existing National Steam Omnibus Company which led, in 1929, to the formation of a series of 'regional' transport undertakings. In Devon, Western National took over former GWR routes (of which there were more than 70 in Dorset, Devon and Cornwall) and Southern National took over those routes previously operated by the Southern Railway, the successor to the LSWR. The Moretonhampstead to Chagford route

Right: *The LSWR buses originally ran from Yeoford Junction, on the North Devon and North Cornwall lines. This route also started with horse-buses and is believed to have commenced as early as 1865 when the line from Yeoford to Okehampton opened. This photograph shows one of the Clarkson steam buses put on by the LSWR in 1906 to counter the GWR Daimlers in Chagford Square. By 1908 these unsuccessful vehicles had been replaced by Thorneycroft motor buses, and the route was later altered to run*

The Square, Chagford, Devon.

from Exeter (Queen Street) Station to Chagford (via Whitestone, Tedburn St Mary, Cheriton Bishop, Crockernwell and Drewsteignton). This route is still in operation under Devon General. (Thorn Collection)

Left: *The motor charabanc was the great leveller of tourism, allowing those of more modest means to reach all parts of Dartmoor. This is a typical 1920s 'chara', very possibly on a Lancia chassis of the type then popular for use in hilly districts in Devon. The occasion is not recorded on the photo, which was taken 'in the Chagford district', but it looks like a church outing or a similar event of comparable respectibility.* (Thorn Collection)

Right: *Chagford was served by horse-omnibus from Moretonhamstead railway station in 1870. In 1906 this route was one of the first railway-operated bus services to be motorised, using a pair of these single-deck Milnes-Daimler buses. In Chagford they were garaged in Mr Osborne's yard behind Rock House. Osborne was the GWR agent in Chagford, and the bus here stands outside his premises, which also housed a ticket and goods receiving office. The 'road motor' route actually terminated at Cross Tree.* (Thorn Collection)

Above: *Pictures of Chagford's buses proved hard to find, but a Devon General AEC in the much-missed 'cherries and cream' livery features in the background of this 1970s portrait of Lillian Thorn, taken in Chagford Square. Devon General took over the various ex-railway Chagford routes in a rationalisation scheme of 1933–4.*
(Thorn Collection)

Right: *Greatly daring for her day was this lady cyclist, pictured on Dartmoor around 1903. Her name is not recorded but she is believed to be a member of the Maddicott family.*
(Thorn Collection)

Top right and above: *Several Chagford firms set up in the motor carriage trade and provided a service to local people as well as to visitors. Jack Rice was an individual proprietor, but A.E. Thomas went into the business in quite a large way, running lorries, coach tours and a market bus service in addition to private hire work.*
(Courtesy of Leonard Brommell Esq., Great Tree)

thus became Route 121 of Western National W2 area, South Devon and East Cornwall. The old LSWR route to Yeoford Junction had been discontinued before the First World War when a direct service to Exeter was introduced, and this was taken over by what became the Devon General Omnibus Company. As such, this route was never operated by Southern National.

The Moretonhampstead–Chagford route was isolated from all other Western National Services, and rapidly became an operational headache. So, in March 1934, the Stage Carriage Licence for the route, together with the garaging facilities at Moreton and Chagford, were handed over to the Devon General Company, who were by then operating all other services in the area. They modernised and improved the Moreton garage as their operating base, although the arrangement to stable a bus at Chagford was continued, probably until the Second World War. The route number was changed, confusingly, to 120, and the service was eventually extended to Bovey Tracey and finally, with the closing of the railway, to Newton Abbot. At the time of writing this route is still running as service 173.

ROAD-BORNE TOURISM

With the exception of the Princetown line, which developed from the original horse-worked Plymouth and Dartmoor Railway, the railways ran around Dartmoor rather than penetrated it. So there was no scope for the sort of rail-borne tourism that developed in North Wales after about 1880. The alternative was road transport, initially by horse brake and later by motor charabanc. Bovey Tracey

Station on the Moretonhampstead line became a popular centre for exploring Dartmoor by road, with both the enterprising GWR and a host of private operators advertising a bewildering range of motor tours. In 1924 the GWR went regularly to Haytor or on a circular route that took in Haytor, Widecombe, Grimspound, Beetor Cross, Manaton and Becky Falls. Chagford, however, did not usually figure on these tours and seems to have been more the preserve of a wealthier clientele using private transport.

People really began touring Dartmoor in private motor cars in the 1920s, by which time they were reasonably comfortable, mechanically reliable, and able to cope with the considerable demands that Dartmoor's difficult roads made on engines, transmissions, steering and especially brakes. It is difficult to estimate how popular the area was with 'motor tourists' at this period. A view of Chagford Square taken in the summertime during the mid 1920s shows only two parked cars – a considerable contrast to the current situation! The same picture shows Webber's shop displaying a 'Pratt's Perfection Motor Spirit' sign, which reflects the fact that petrol was sold in 2-gallon tins over the counter by ironmongers rather than being safely dispensed at a pump. The petrol tax in those halcyon days was a mere 3d. (1.25 pence) per gallon!

MODERN TRANSPORT

The population of contemporary Chagford relies almost entirely upon the private motor car, augmented only by a rather meagre bus service, by which it is possible to reach Moretonhampstead, Exeter, Newton Abbot and Okehampton. It is not

This view of Chagford Square was taken in the summertime during the mid 1920s. In contrast to the number of vehicles in the Square today, this picture shows only two parked cars. A 'Pratt's Perfection Motor Spirit' sign is clearly displayed outside Webber's shop. (Rice Collection)

Left: *One deciding factor in local transport development was the growth in the reliability and capacity of the motor lorry, especially after the Second World War. This handsome Austin K4 dated from the late 1940s and belonged to Bovey Tracey coal merchants A. & W. Jeffrey, who supplied fuel in the Chagford district until quite recently. The vehicle is shown decorated for Chagford Carnival, where it conveyed the Carnival Queen.* (Courtesy of the Mortimore family, Shapley)

Left: *Latterday successor to Nathaniel Stone as Chagford's general carrier was William Denham, who operated from Dartmoor Lodge in the Lower Square as a haulier, contractor and fuel, seed and corn merchant.* (Courtesy of Leonard Brommell Esq., Great Tree)

Local shops made use of motor transport to enable them to serve a wider area. Here are the delivery vans of Chagford butcher C. Holmes & Sons in a picture taken outside their shop during the Second World War – hence the blacked-out headlights and white visibility stripes on the vans. The vehicles are an Austin 'Big 7' van of c.1938 vintage and what looks like a Morris 5cwt of about 1935. (Courtesy of A. L. Martin & Sons, Chagford)

always so easy to get back again! With the improvements to the A30 trunk road between Whiddon Down and Exeter and the increasing congestion of the old turnpike route to Bovey and Newton, Chagford's main trading links have reverted to being with Exeter. Okehampton has also become more important as it has developed as a commercial and cultural centre for West Devon. Chagford's secondary schoolchildren normally attend Okehampton College (a school bus route connects the two towns).

With the opening of the A30 trunk road from Whiddon Down in 1979, a direct high-speed road link to the national motorway network was established. As a result Chagford ceased to be remote from the rest of Britain. With the continuing upgrading of the old mail-coach route to London (the A30/A303), the metropolis is now only around four hours away by car, and even less by fast train from Exeter. This has had, and continues to have, a profound demographic effect on Chagford, making the district an even more desirable place of residence and attracting not only professional people working in Exeter, but also those needing to travel much further afield. Exeter Airport – now only half an hour distant – is increasingly offering direct flights to a range of UK and overseas destinations, further improving Chagford's links with the rest of the world. It is a sobering thought that the time once needed to drive to London during a busy period on the old A303 recently sufficed to get your author to Toronto!

Above: *Not many Chagford farms were motorised before the Second World War – but John Northway at Middlecott had a motorcyle in the late 1930s.* (Courtesy of the Northway family, Middlecott)

Left: *Private motoring – other than the visiting cars of tourists – did not become at all widespread in the Chagford area until after the Second World War. Typical of the vehicles used by local people around that time is this late 1930s Austin 7 that belonged to a member of the Thorn family.* (Thorn Collection)

Above left: *By the later 1970s, traffic congestion was becoming a real problem in Chagford Square. By the mid 1980s, it was a main item on the town's agenda.*

Above right: *Members of the Parish Council hold yet another site meeting with the Okehampton police inspector in 1984 – a proposal for the introduction of yellow lines followed shortly afterwards! It was rejected at a public consultation the following year. (Thorn Collection)*

Above: *Frank Pearse was Chagford's first motor engineer, setting up in premises in North Street in the early 1920s. He also handled the servicing of electrical goods and the recharging of accumulators for radios. (Courtesy of Leonard Brommell Esq., Great Tree)*

Right: *Learning to drive was a big adventure not so long ago, and for many Chagford families it was the younger generation that took to the 'new' form of transport – like Margaret Stanbury, here taking to the road around 1968. (Thorn Collection)*

Left: *The oldest surviving garage establishment is Northfield Garage, founded by Tom Fitzpatrick of Northfield House in 1936. Here is his son, Wilf Fitzpatrick, by the pumps, c.1967. The Lewis family took over the garage when Wilf died in November 1993, and the site was rebuilt to modern requirements for a service and MOT station in 1998. It still serves Chagford with motor fuel – a facility lost to many similar-sized places elsewhere in Devon. (Thorn Collection)*

Now the two best-known shops in Chagford – having a fame that extends far beyond the locality – Webber's and Bowden's have nestled cheek-by-jowl in amicable competition for well over a century. Bowden's started out as a smithy, through the archway seen on the right, in the mid-nineteenth century, and gradually grew to become not only a substantial ironworks but a large general ironmongery business, specialising in the needs of agriculture. Webber's commenced trading in 1891 and were also ironmongers, although in a more refined way than Bowden's. They also sold china, glassware and household goods. Webber's were the LSWR and subsequently the Southern Railway's Chagford agents. Note that Webber's sold Pratt's Perfection Motor Spirit. Bowden's were agents for British Petroleum, while Gray's supplied Shell.

SEVEN

MARKET & TRADE

In the days before effective and speedy communications – which did not really arrive in Chagford until well into the nineteenth century – transport (or the lack of it) was the main obstacle to trade. However, Chagford was relatively fortunate in that it was already on established and important trading routes and was a principal fording-place of the upper Teign. It was also relatively close to the coast and several thriving sea ports, of which Plymouth, Exeter, Topsham and Bideford were to become the most important. Additionally, by producing commodities of high value, such as tin ingots and finished woollen cloth, that could readily be transported by packhorse, Chagford was at less of a disadvantage in terms of trade than other outlying districts that had to rely upon less valuable or less portable produce.

CHAGFORD MARKET

The exact date of Chagford's market charter (granted by the Crown) is not known, but it is certainly ancient and probably dates from not long after the stannary charter. Unfortunately, the original market charter document is now lost, although various accounts of the conduct of the market at different periods do exist. What is evident is that two factors worked to promote the success of Chagford as a market town. Firstly, as the coinage town of the stannary, it also became the natural supply point for what was then a very considerable industry. This gave many local farms a ready outlet for produce without the need to transport it over anything but a local distance. Secondly, it was geographically well-placed to become a main mercantile centre for the woollen trade on this part of Dartmoor. Sheep markets and wool trading figured greatly in the town's economy from the middle of the fourteenth century until the early years of the twentieth.

Only with the arrival of a ready means of moving livestock to distant markets (other than by droving), in the form of the railway to nearby Moretonhampstead, did this aspect of the town's commerce start to decline. Chagford market also handled farm produce of all sorts as well as fatstock for slaughter. The 'shambles', which preceded the current Market House in the Square (built in 1862) incorporated a public slaughterhouse (a 'shambles' was a common term for such a facility). It also housed the toll office and such other facilities the market required. Animals were killed at several other locations around the Square, including slaughterhouses behind both the Three Crowns and Ring O' Bells Inns. (The latter operated as a butcher's shop as much as a pub until well into the 1950s.)

The other principal trade that developed through the market was the sale of moor ponies for various purposes. The true Dartmoor is a compact but sturdy animal, well-

Left: *Chagford market in operation in the Square. This is a sheep fair, c.1910, when a bowler hat was as de riguer for yeomen farmers and merchants as it was for city financiers. These quarterly fairs were in addition to the regular weekly Saturday public markets, and were public holidays in the town.* (Courtesy Pauline Spear)

Another sheep sale, one of the last conducted in the Square by Coe & Amery, probably around 1921–22. The auction market was moved shortly afterwards to a field behind the Globe. (Courtesy Tim Garrett, Rendells)

suited to a number of uses including as pack ponies, mounts (particularly for farmers and others needing to cross difficult ground), to work pony gins and for some types of light draught work. In the nineteenth century, Dartmoor was the source of many pit ponies that hauled coal in the mines of South Wales, the Midlands and the North East. The pony sales are still held each October, but the modern market for the ponies is poor. Some are sold as riding ponies, but most are bought cheaply for slaughter and end up as tinned pet food.

The original Chagford market was a weekly public gathering under royal charter; the Crown charged tolls on all trade. These tolls were originally in the gift of the church and remained in force until the cessation of public markets in the Square in 1923 – by which time the collecting authority was the Okehampton Rural District Council. The last set of public market tolls are displayed in St Katherine's Hall (Endacott House), which was once the residence of the market overseer. The facilities of the market were very basic and with the encroachment of building into the lower part of the Square from the eighteenth century onwards, space became quite restricted. The old shambles – a rather rambling and dilapidated structure – was removed in 1861–2, when the present octagonal Market House was built, the gift of the Hayter-Hames family. It is now Chagford's most instantly recognisable structure and was extensively restored in 1984.

The general market at Chagford declined in importance towards the end of the nineteenth century, when the greatly improved communications brought about by the opening of the railway and the upgrading of the roads opened up wider markets to local farmers and producers. Much of the trade was lost to Newton Abbot and, later, to Exeter, centres which developed not only as large livestock markets but also as general or 'pannier' markets; they opened new, covered market halls, often on a daily basis.

This period also saw the role of the agricultural merchants grow in importance, not only in terms of supply to the farms, but also as an outlet for produce. Many farms had direct contracts with dairies as well as cereal, wool or potato merchants who would offer price guarantees and an assured market. The late-nineteenth and early-twentieth century directories list literally scores of such merchants operating in the district.

THE AUCTION MARKET

Previous to 1923, the old and somewhat uncertain market system of direct bid or barter was commonly used. Under this arrangement, vendors paid the appropriate toll to allow them to display stock or goods for trade in the market. Buyers were then able to inspect what was on offer and to strike a direct deal with the vendor. Although well-suited to the relatively limited trade of earlier times, such a system is inherently incompatible with the volatile, mobile and competitive nature of modern livestock and produce dealing.

So with the abandonment of the weekly public market (held on Saturdays) the remaining livestock trade was moved to a private auction market established on a field belonging to the Webber family and situated behind the Three Crowns Hotel. This market was set up by the local firm of auctioneers and valuers, Arthur Coe & Amery, and was in operation until 1988. By this time the access via Store Street was too narrow for modern livestock trans-

Chagford's private auction market on Webber's Field was a small and somewhat cramped affair dealing with store cattle and ponies. It was one of the smallest markets operating in England and attracted occasional press coverage, as here. There was insufficient space on the site to conduct sheep sales (which had often overflowed into the Square), so these were usually held on fields at Bailey's Hey or, later, Rushford. (Courtesy Tim Garrett, Rendells)

porters, while the driving of beasts to market through the town's increasingly congested streets caused many problems. The market itself was also very cramped, but it was convenient for one important facility – the bar of the Globe Hotel, long the favoured market hostelry.

In 1989 Messrs Rendells, the successors in trade to Arthur Coe & Amery, established an entirely new market on a field at Crannafords, on the approach to the town from Easton Cross. The road access here is relatively good and the site is convenient, even if it lacks the intimate atmosphere of the old town market. It is also regrettable that a beer tent and a hot-dog trailer form a poor substitute for the solid comforts and roaring fires of the Globe! This market still operates in a limited way, mostly dealing in store cattle, although it also holds the annual pony sale. As with many small markets, it is threatened by the requirements of new regulations introduced in the wake of the 2001 outbreak of foot-and-mouth disease.

The recent trend, particularly with finished livestock ready for slaughter, has been to sell through specialist markets like Hatherleigh or through large regional markets such as Exeter or Newton Abbot, where sufficient stock is entered to interest the supermarkets and other large-scale buyers. The smaller markets are left with the intermediate sales of young stock or stock for finishing, and the trade of a few local butchers who prefer to buy direct rather than wholesale and who are thus interested in bidding for one or two beasts at a time. It remains to be seen how long this level of trade will sustain Chagford market, but many in the town would be very sorry to see it cease.

AUCTIONEERS & LAND AGENTS

Arthur Coe set up as a land agent, valuer and auctioneer in the early-twentieth century. He was joined in 1920 by Charles Amery, whose family were landowners and farmers in the district. The business operated from Amery's house, 'Hillsborough', at the upper end of Southcombe Street. The firm Coe & Amery acted as an agent to many of the landowners in the parish and handled auction sales of all sorts, such as the grass keep sale advertised in the poster reproduced below from the Great Tree Collection. The firm also acted as an insurance agent and tithe collector. After the public market ceased in 1923, Charles Amery rented the field behind the Globe Inn and established the small livestock market that continued to operate on this somewhat-restricted site until it was moved to the present location.

As Chagford's resident auctioneer and valuers, Messrs Coe & Amery found themselves drawn into the estate agency business, negotiating not only farm sales or tenancies but also the sale or lease of private houses and town cottages, many of which belonged to prominent landowners or local families. They also came to conduct probate valuations and to handle estate disposal, auctions of furniture, or similar non-farm sales. Indeed, the opening entry in the first Coe & Amery valuation book, in June 1920, was an inventory and valuation of the contents of the Three Crowns Hotel, then about to change hands. The sum valued was £320!

The partnership of Coe & Amery continued until the death of Arthur Coe, when Charles Amery carried on alone as a sole practitioner. After 1929 the business was moved from Amery's old house at

Arthur Coe, who later joined with Charles Amery as Arthur Coe & Amery, was Chagford's principal land and estate agent, although he wasn't the first auctioneer to practice in the town. The annual letting of grass keep was a fundamental activity of the Coe & Amery practice, as was agricultural valuation and the handling of livestock at auction. (Courtesy of Leonard Brommell, Great Tree)

Above: *Charles Amery of Coe & Amery, valuing a field of turnips in 1932. In the days when most farms were tenanted, such valuations were an essential facet of agricultural life.* (Thorn Collection)

Right: *The short-lived partnership of Rendell & Sawdye was eventually amalgamated with that of Coe & Amery to form the nucleus of the modern Rendell's, today one of the largest agricultural land and estate agency, valuation and auctioneering practices in Devon. They still operate from Coe & Amery's old premises at Rock House.* (Courtesy of Leonard Brommell, Great Tree)

Hillsborough to Rock House, still in Southcombe Street. These premises had by then been given up by H.J. Osborne & Son, the GWR agent and agricultural merchants, after the bus service based there passed to Western National. Here the business continued until the late 1930s, when Charles Amery was approached by Mr Charles Morgan of Rendell & Sawdye with a proposition of amalgamation.

Rendell's was an old-established firm of land agents dating back to 1816, and had hitherto operated in the Newton Abbot and Ashburton areas. The founder's son, Arthur Rendell, was a bachelor and on his death during the period of the First World War the firm passed by bequest to Charles Morgan,

his clerk. Morgan carried on the business alone until he was joined in a partnership with John Sawdye as Rendell & Sawdye (this was some time before the sale of the Manor House estate at North Bovey in 1927, one of Rendell and Sawdye's major coups). The partnership did not prove to be a happy one and things soon became very difficult, but it remained in being until the mid to late 1930s (it is difficult to be specific as to dates as many of the records of the old firm were unfortunately lost to an outbreak of dry rot at Rock House in the 1960s). Sawdye then left, firstly to practice alone and later to form a new partnership, Sawdye & Harris, with offices in Ashburton. This left both Charles Morgan and Charles Amery as sole practitioners, both of them approaching retirement. The logical solution was to unite the Coe & Amery and Rendell businesses and to bring in new partners, including Charles Morgan's son, Arthur. The Second World War brought a halt to development, but once it was over a lot of new people were brought in to the business which, with offices and markets in Ashburton, Chagford, Newton Abbot and Totnes, was well-placed to become the pre-eminent firm in the livestock marketing, auctioneering, land and estate agency business in the East Dartmoor area, a position it still holds at the time of writing. The Chagford partners in the postwar period were Percy Hughes and Fred Rhill, brother of Harry Rhill the chemist. The current Chagford partner, Tim Garrett, joined the firm in 1962 and became a partner in 1969.

CHAGFORD POST OFFICE & THE THORN FAMILY

The Royal Mail coaching route to Exeter was established in 1824, and soon had a 16½-hour service over the 171 miles from the GPO in London to the Red Lion Inn in South Street, Exeter. The mail service was rapidly extended to the surrounding areas, especially after the introduction of the universal postage stamp system in 1833. Postmasters were appointed by warrant and an office was established in Lower Street, Chagford in 1842. Shortly afterwards the name of the street was changed to Post-Office Street. The 1850 *White's Directory* does not list a postmaster as such, it merely notes that the Post Office was 'at Eliza Pratt's; letters via Moretonhampstead'. The 1857 directory lists Eliza Pratt as, simply, 'Shopkeeper; Post-Office Street'.

Chagford was initially home to a sub-office and was served by messenger from Moretonhampstead, which had a mail-cart connection with the Exeter–Falmouth stage at Crockernwell. With the opening of the railways and the transfer of the mail from coach to train, the postal town serving the area became Newton Abbot. This is still the case at the time of writing and is the reason why Chagford has a

Above left: *Chagford has had some notable and long-serving postmen. One of the best known was George Allen, on the right in this 1951 view, with Reg Border by the van.* (Thorn Collection)

Above right: *Chagford's Post Office was moved to this building – which it still occupies in 2002 – in 1892. Here is the Post Office in the early 1950s. The leftmost of these two chimneys was removed when the building was re-roofed in the mid 1950s.* (Thorn Collection)

Inset: *Chagford mail collection, c.1958. This is Sam Wilcocks of Newton Abbot – on the left – with a youthful Michael Sheriden, who recently retired after 39 years' service. The Post Office van is a Morris J-type, a larger vehicle used to collect the mail from the outlying districts for the Newton Abbot sorting office. The Post Office traditionally bought Morris vans, the last being Metros in the early 1980s.* (Thorn Collection)

Left and inset: *Being a Chagford postman was no sinecure. Here is George Burrows in a wintry Chagford church-yard in 1963. In these conditions, the outlying roads were impassable to the post vans, so alternative arrangements had to be made. The mail had to get through – and, by and large, it did.* (Thorn Collection)

TQ (Torquay) postcode rather than EX (Exeter). As an additional point of interest, it is worth noting how closely the modern postcode area boundaries link to the old turnpike system and the original mail coach and rail postal routes. The mail initially went from Newton Abbot railway station to Moretonhampstead by cart – a service extended on to Chagford in 1854. From 1866, the mail reached Moreton by train, while the cart completed the final four mile stretch.

In 1856, John Thorn, saddler and harness maker, became the first listed Chagford postmaster and the office was moved to his premises in the High Street (now Whiddons Tearoom). John Thorn was succeeded by his son, Robert Hole Thorn, in 1882 when the office was moved to its present location in the Square and gained a telegraph service. Robert Thorn in turn handed the office to his son, Reginald R. Thorn in 1922. Reginald Thorn died while in office in August 1931 at the early age of 46, and the title then passed to his wife Lillian Thorn, who lived until 1989. Lillian was succeeded by her youngest son Douglas and when he retired in 1994, he was succeeded by Anne Thorn – the daughter of his elder sister Betty and her husband Arthur Thorn (not related) of Ashburton. This remarkable tradition, extending over more than 150 years and six generations, is quite possibly unique in the history of the postal service.

It is not only postmasters or postmistresses that are long-serving at Chagford. A number of Chagford's postmen also put in working lifetimes delivering the mail to this corner of Dartmoor. Mark Hext retired as a Chagford postman after 46 years and 9 months of service and it was estimated that he walked 226,824 miles in that time, a feat which achieved national publicity. He was awarded the Imperial Service Medal in recognition of this achievement. Other notable Chagford postmen have included George Allen, who served from 1949 until 1984. He was the archetypal country postman, who appeared on television several times in stories relating to the Royal Mail on Dartmoor. He was a lifelong and staunch trade unionist and represented the postmen of the Newton Abbot area for the Post Office Workers Union before becoming a senior official of that union. Michael (Mick) Sheridan served the Post Office from 1958–96, although he was also a smallholder, stockdealer, horse-breeder and Chagford's best-known Irishman. Ray Butt switched from being a mason for Stone's the builders to serving as a postman; he delivered mail for 20 years between 1967 and 1988. He was also Officer-in-Charge of Chagford Fire Station until he retired in 1986.

CHAGFORD'S MERCHANTS

Chagford's early status as a market and trade centre for the tin and woollen industries introduced a merchant class to the town as early as the fourteenth century. Tin and wool were widely traded and wool merchants, in particular, exercised great influence in the district, not only in buying the raw commodity but also in organising the spinning of yarns and the weaving and finishing of cloth. The Chagford woollen industry in the sixteenth century had wide links, with finished cloth being traded extensively in Germany and the Low Countries as well as in Italy and Spain. This development of Chagford as a centre of trade as well as production continued throughout the seventeenth century and into the eighteenth, with the number of traders and shop-keepers increasing steadily over this period.

The woollen trade through Chagford was twofold. Firstly, there were livestock sales, which took place on the 'Fair Days' – the first Thursday in May and the last Thursdays in March, September and October. These fairs were a major feature of Chagford trade well into the twentieth century. Llatterly, they were held on fields behind Bailey's

Left: *Two well-known Chagford postmen in more recent times were the late George Allen and Jack Rice – both, coincidentally, keen exponents of the 'squeeze box'. They are seen outside the Post Office in 1979 with one of the Chagford mail vans (there are normally two stationed in the town) and the cycle used for the town round. By this date, Morris no longer had a monopoly on mail van supply, and Chagford's allocation was a pair of these Bedford HA types.* (Thorn Collection)

Inset: *Lillian Thorn was Chagford's postmistress from the death of her husband Reginal R. Thorn in 1931 until her son Douglas took on the job in 1964. She continued to help out until her death in 1989, and was one of the best-known figures in Chagford. Here she is in the mail room at the Post Office, c.1971.* (Thorn Collection)

Hey, as the livestock numbers had outgrown the capacity of the temporary penning set up in the Square. Due to the numbers of animals traded, it is likely that the fairs were conducted as auctions well before this became the normal practice for the market. In 1857 Chagford had a practicing auctioneer and surveyor – John Hooper, who was also a farmer at Withecombe.

The other aspect of the wool trade was the dealing in raw and finished wool, which was always controlled by powerful merchant interests. There was a certain amount of open market 'wool sale' by bid or auction, but most wool came to be traded by merchants dealing directly with the wool producers. These wool merchants also ran the 'outworking' trade in the local area for the spinning of yarns and worsteds and the weaving of woollen cloths. With the advent of the mechanised wool carding, spinning and weaving processes in the early-nineteenth century, the woollen industry soon became centralised in large, purpose-built mills, such as those belonging to Mr Berry in Chagford and Mr Viccary in North Tawton. These men came to dominate the trade in all its aspects, dealing in the raw wool, spun yarns, woven cloth, felts and serges.

After a brief period of prosperity in the first 30 years or so of the nineteenth century, the rapid growth of the large-scale, highly-mechanised woollen manufacturing industry in Yorkshire drastically reduced the value of the local trade, resulting in a depression in the Devon wool trade from which Chagford, in particular, never recovered.

AGRICULTURAL MERCHANTS & CONTRACTORS

With the dramatic improvements in communications and the development of farm mechanisation and 'artificial manures' towards the end of the nineteenth century, there arrived in the Chagford area a new class of entrepreneur: the agricultural merchant and contractor. None of the farms in Chagford were big enough or wealthy enough to invest in the new machinery directly. In order to capitalise on this situation, several firms in the district started to offer ploughing, threshing and cartage services using the newly developed steam traction engine and such machines as the cable plough, the wheat comber and the threshing box. By the turn of the twentieth century a number of such businesses were operating in the area, most notably those of Mr Reed at Rushford and Factory and Saunders & Rowe at Easton. Indeed, by about 1905 the Chagford area boasted at least four steam tractors, the most powerful being Mr Reed's 8-horsepower Marshall, together with at least three threshing boxes.

These businesses also dealt in the supply of smaller machines for use on farms or in workshops, notably the versatile oil and gas engines. These became prevalent after about 1880 as they powered all manner of farm operations, from chaff-cutters and beet-mills to sawmills, water pumps and, later, electricity-generating plants. Alongside the supply, installation and maintenance of such machinery, the merchants also began to supply seed, animal feed supplements and, most significantly, 'artificial manures'. The advent of naturally sourced phosphate fertilisers (usually guano), lime in bulk and, later, manufactured nitrate-based products, meant that for the first time it was economically and practically feasible for many Chagford farmers to dramatically increase their arable yields. In addition, they were able to improve their pasturage and hay crop, increase their stock levels and bring stock to a finished condition on their own farms without depending on accommodation land elsewhere.

NINETEENTH-CENTURY TRADESMEN & SHOPKEEPERS

Chagford has long been a main supply point for the northern moor fringe, a status reflected in the number and range of shops, tradesmen and other business enterprises found in the town. The various directories and gazetteers published throughout the nineteenth century reveal a bewildering array of trades operating in the town, which seems to have been self-sufficient in most instances. *Billing's* 1857 directory gives a fascinating listing of Chagford tradespeople that runs to over 100 entries. Predictably, there were a lot of farmers, many of whom operated from premises within the town, but craft trades and retailing were also well represented.

Many of the trades were to be expected. For example, in 1857 there were five smithies in the town: William Cann and William Stoneman in Mill Street, Samuel Hill in Post-Office (Lower) Street, George Murch in the High Street (where he also made wheels

An essential agricultural service in pre-mechanical days was the shoeing of horses and oxen for farm and draft work. Chagford had several smithies, one of them being Frank Hill's Crown Iron Works which was at the top of Southcombe Street, now the Old Forge Café. (Courtesy of Leonard Brommell Esq., Great Tree)

Left: This corner shop in the Lower Square was occupied by Gray's for many years – at one time or another, they dealt in everything from bicycles to jewellery and from motor spirit to spectacles. Gray's also became a newsagent, and this use came to predominate. After a spell as Hallets and then Hardings, the shop became Nichols newsagents. Thankfully, it remains much the same today as Youds, continuing independence having kept it from the corporate image makeovers that have despoiled so many traditional shop fronts. (Thorn Collection)

Right and below right: Chagford had a thriving agricultural contracting industry in the earlier part of the twentieth century, before the tractor became universal equipment on every farm (something that didn't happen in Chagford until the late 1960s). Saunders & Rowe and Chapples both offered steam threshing services, as did George Reed. Chagford was, at one period, home to at least four steam traction engines and three 'thrashing boxes'. (Courtesy of Leonard Brommell Esq., Great Tree)

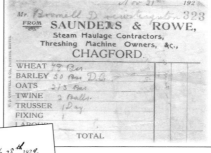

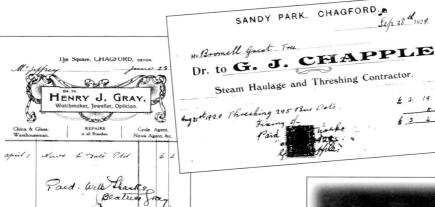

Above: Henry Gray used a very elegant billhead indeed, suited to the more refined aspects of his business. This 1918 invoice is receipted by his wife Beatrice. (Courtesy of Leonard Brommell Esq., Great Tree)

Right: 'The village blacksmith, Chagford' was a popular postcard in earlier times. It is not clear which forge is depicted although it is possibly Bowden's Vulcan Iron Works or Gregory's Forge in Mill Street, c.1900.

and dealt in glass and china) and John Stott in New Street. Mr Murch did not have the wheelwrighting or crockery supply business to himself, with wheelwrights William Burrows at Leach's Cottages in Sidcombe (Southcombe) Street and James Perrot just down the High Street, as well as Thomas Pearce – 'Grocer, draper, glass and china dealer' – in Mill Street. Some tradesmen, however, did not suffer such local competition. John Callard of North Street, who was an ironmonger, brazier and tin manufacturer (a maker of metal vessels such as buckets and churns) had the field to himself, as did agricultural implement makers J. & W. Dicker, in the High Street.

The hottest competition comes in unexpected areas. Still in 1857, Chagford (then with a population of 1,557) had seven boot- and shoemakers – James Aggett in the High Street, Robert Holmes in Post-Office Street, Joseph Gale (no address given), George Lewis in Mill Street, and no less than three members of the Lyddon family – Edward and George in Post-Office Street and John in Mill Street. There were also five tailors: Bartholomew Gidley, William Gilbert, John Jeffries, James Pike and John Scott, together with an astounding 14 'dressmakers and milliners', although many of these women were the wives of other tradesmen. Of these, two – Esther Thorn and Thirza Underhill – also made straw bonnets. There was even a 'stay maker' – Elizabeth Brock – in the Square. Harness and saddlery was the business of John Brely and of John Thorn (postmaster), both of whom at that time were based in the High Street.

Four corn-mills were active in Chagford Parish in 1857, with James Collins as the miller at Batworthy, William Curzon at picturesque Holy Street, John Perryman at Yeo and John Tarr at Rushford. There is no mention of the Sandy Park mills – Doggamarsh or Furlong – at this date. Furlong is technically in Drewsteignton Parish (by a yard or two) and Doggamarsh had yet to be built.

The town also had a number of hostelries, with George Chudleigh at the Three Crowns, where he was licensed as a 'victualler and armer' as well as to hire horses. William Flood kept the Ring O' Bells (although it suffered a fire four years later, in 1861) and Samuel Gregory had the Globe, also described as a 'boarding and lodging house'. Gregory was also listed as a farmer, as was John Hooper at the King's Arms in the Square (now 'Lydstone'). Also in the Square, on the corner opposite the Three Crowns, was the Royal Oak, kept by George Hatherleigh, while the Baker's (now Buller's) Arms in Mill Street had a landlady, Mary Holmes.

What was surprisingly thinly represented in Chagford in the 1850s were the building trades, suggesting that the boom in house building that characterised the latter years of the nineteenth century had yet to get under way. John Aggett, the stonemason who made the new church font in 1857, was working in the High Street, with fellow masons

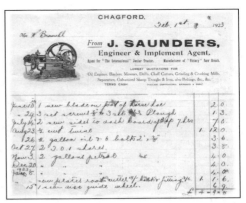

Saunders were also in the business of agricultural engineering and machinery supply from their premises at Easton Cross, Chagford. Oil or gas engines of the type shown on their billhead were popular for a wide range of on-farm uses in pre-tractor days, and now form popular exhibits at agricultural shows. (Courtesy of Leonard Brommell Esq., Great Tree)

Samuel Ellis and John Stone both in Post-Office Street. Local carpenters included John Aggett, Thomas Ball and William Brimblecombe in Sidcombe Street, James Collins in Post-Office Street and William Underhill in Mill Street, while John Collins the glazier was in Sidcombe Street. John Luscombe was simply described as a 'builder', with no address given. There are also a few less usual trades listed in the directories. Chagford had its own watch- and clockmaker, Thomas Miles, trading in North Street, while at Whiteabury Cottage there resided the very Cornish-sounding Thomas Penrose, mine agent. Oddest of all was James Palmer, 'Marine Store Dealer', operating in New Street – rather a long way from anything remotely maritime.

In terms of pure retailing, Chagford has also been well served for a long time, although some of these businesses combined shopkeeping with other enterprises. In 1850 the list of 'grocers, drapers & c.' included Joseph Gale (also a bootmaker), William Gibbons (also a wool comber), Mary-Anne Heard, and Eliza Pratt (Post Office). William Morrish, grocer, draper and druggist, was based in Mill Street (by the entrance to Gregory's Court), while Thomas Pearse, grocer, draper, glass and china dealer, was just down the way. James Pike was a shopkeeper and a tailor in the High Street. By 1857, there were several additional traders – William Harvey's butcher's shop had opened outside the Three Crowns in the High Street and Mary Knapman's shop was in New Street. John Middleton (butcher and farmer) was trading in Post-Office Street and shopkeeper John Walter, was working in Sidcombe Street. There were three bakeries – Mary-Ann Heard and Ann Stone in 1850, joined by Richard Northcote in 1857. Nathaniel Stone was Chagford's carrier, who ran a service of 'stage waggons' to Exeter on Tuesdays and Fridays, departing Chagford at 5.30am.

LATE-NINETEENTH-CENTURY TRADE

By the 1870s, Chagford's trade had expanded still further. Following the opening of the railway to Moretonhampstead, coal became available in the town, and the 'Devon Gas Association Ltd' began operating its small gas retort at the foot of Mill Street. James Knapman and George Lewis are both listed as 'coal merchants' in 1879, while the familiar name of Collins appears several times, with George Collins being described as 'plumber, gas-fitter and general metal worker'. All the smithies except that of Mr Murch were still operating, now joined by James Bowden as 'agricultural implement maker, machinist and ironmonger' at the Vulcan Iron Works off the Square. W. Longman was also in business as a 'millwright and engineer', although his premises are not listed. By this time the firm W. & J. Garrish was the town's carrier, running services to Moretonhampstead Station as well as to Exeter. It may have been this company that operated the horse-drawn bus and 'parcels break' service linking Moreton and Chagford after 1870 on behalf of the South Devon Railway Company.

The building trade had burgeoned somewhat. William Aggett was 'church bell hanger, builder & c.', while James Collins was building, as were Henry Ellis, William Stone and William Underhill. All these were building firms rather than individual craftsmen. James Collins (Monte Rosa) and William Stone (Meldon Hall) also offered 'superior apartments' for holidays or permanent let.

Other craft trades were also thriving. The wheelwrights William Burrows and Perrot & Sons were still in Sidcombe Street and High Street respectively, while most of the bootmaking brotherhood were still cobbling away – reduced slightly to six. One of their number, George Lewis, also dabbled in the coal trade. The town was well supplied with tailors (there were six of these). Of these, William Lyddon also traded as 'agent for the woollens manufactured in Chagford and at South Molton' and John Scott was 'lessee of the market and fairs', a privilege which cost him £10 per annum. However, the dressmakers and milliners had apparently suffered a drastic decline, as the 1879 *Harrod Directory* does not list any at all!

On the retail front, competition was as vigorous as ever and a wide range of goods, including many luxuries, were on offer. Richard Powning, family grocer, draper and provision merchant, had as his

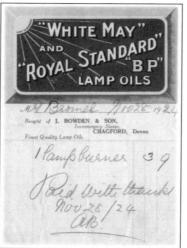

This 1920s Bowden's billhead advertised a vital commodity in the days before all homes and farms had electric power – lamp oil, or kerosene. (Courtesy of Leonard Brommell, Great Tree)

sideline the agency for the National Steam Packet Company, Liverpool – by means of whose ships more than a few Chagfordians emigrated to the New World. His premises were opposite the Moor Park Hotel. John Trick spread his retail net, if anything, even wider. His advertisement ran: 'grocer, draper, seed dealer and wine merchant. Funerals furnished'. Chagford, it seems, has a long tradition of wide-ranging emporia, which is still alive and well today.

Other innovations in the 1879 directory include Chagford's first apothecary, Philip F. Hanson: 'Family and dispensing chemist, physicians' prescriptions and family recipes accurately prepared'. Fruit and vegetables, hitherto home-grown, could now be bought in the town, either from 'Thomas Brewer, fruiterer', or John Osborne's market garden. Chagford could still boast a watch- and clockmaker, W. Early, who also traded as a 'sewing machine agent'. Insurance could be purchased in several places, most notably from Henry Cooper, 'agent to the London and Provincial Horse and Carriage Insurance Company, Tavistock House'. Henry Cooper was in partnership with John Hooper of Withecombe, 'surveyor, road surveyor and auctioneer'. Also appearing for the first time are two famous Chagford names – 'Morrish, William S., Artist', and William Perrot, 'fishing tackle maker, carriage proprietor, guide to Dartmoor. Fishing tickets issued. Enquiries for lodgings attended to'.

TWENTIETH-CENTURY TRADE

By the middle of the first half of the twentieth century, Chagford's trade had taken on a familiar look. For a start, both of Chagford's famous ironmongery businesses were by then established more or less in their current premises, although not to their current extent. 'Jas. Bowden & Son' had an ironmongery shop using the front part of the old Vulcan Iron Works, a complex which also included the smithy and the original Parish Fire Station. Two doors along (then; now they're cheek-by-jowl) was Webber's, the family ironmongery, glass and china retailing business, started in 1891. Collins the butcher was on the far side of Webber's at the head of the Square, next to the Ring O' Bells inn. The King's Arms had become the genteel Central Private Hotel while the Royal Oak had closed down; it was demolished and replaced around 1935 by the modern block

Above: Hallet's took over Gray's business in about 1930; they became agents for Pratts Perfection Motor Spirit, among other things. This picture was taken during an election campaign in the 1930s. (Courtesy of Pauline Spear)

Left: Another shop with an interesting past is that on the corner of the High Street and New Street, Chagford's corner shop and florist in recent years. It has previously served many purposes – as a cobbler's shop and harness maker in the last century, then as 'Collins' Penny Library', newsagency, confectioner's and toy shop (note the Meccano sign visible in the window in this 1930s view). Until the mid 1970s it was run as a sweet and toy shop by Ernie Hewitt – the mecca for Chagford children with money burning holes in their pockets. (Courtesy Laurette Rice)

of shops on the south-eastern corner of the Square opposite the Three Crowns. Another pub to close about this time was the Three Cannons, which was situated in the Lower Square opposite the present delicatessen.

The 1935 *Kelly's Directory* lists, among other craft trades still active, wheelwright William Burrows in Southcombe Street and four bootmakers (including Arthur Lyddon, whose tiny cobbler's shop at the lower end of the Square by the fountain latterly became quite famous). There were three tailors, including the Parsons brothers, Ernest and Mark, who occupied as a shop what is now the Post Office; the office was then in the other half of the same premises. Smithies, however, were in decline, with only Frank Hill's 'Crown Iron Works' at Lower Square (today's Old Forge Café) still listed. According to advertisements of the time, he was concerned as much with decorative ironwork and mechanical repairs as with traditional smithing work.

New ventures had arisen to take the place of the traditional trades in decline. In 1935, a considerable number of motor car and charabanc proprietors were listed, while William Denham of Dartmoor Lodge (now Chagford Galleries) was in the road haulage business. His advert ran: 'road transport & removal contractor; light haulage – any distance; coal merchant'. A.E. Thomas was also in the motor conveyancing business with buses, charabancs and conveyances for hire. He was based at Tregare, Mill Street, which remained a bus depot until the Arscott's and Moorland Heather coaching businesses were taken over by Mid Devon Coaches of Bow in the 1960s. Motor engineers were Goodings, Stevens Garage in New Street and F.G. Pearse in North Street. The wide doorway that at the time of writing serves the veterinary surgery and the adjoining shop once housed Chagford's first petrol pumps. There was also a range of workshops to the rear of this block of buildings. Northfield Garage had yet to be established in 1935 (it was operating by the war).

Both Lloyds and the National Provincial Bank were open in the Square by 1935, although both were sub-branches. Chagford had long enjoyed the services of a solicitor, originally Ormerod's, while Arthur Coe & Amery was still busy in the land agency, auctioneering, valuation and insurance businesses. By 1935 it traded from Rock House, the premises occupied in 2002 by Rendell's. Any oppo-

sition that might have been offered by Hoopers had ceased by this time, the family having reverted to farming. Other services on offer – besides the inevitable building – included gardening, clock and watch repairs and 'wireless engineering'.

The town's increasing popularity as a visitor centre was also evidenced by a large number of boarding and lodging-houses as well as private and public hotels. In addition there were still four inns open – the Globe, the Three Crowns, the Ring O' Bells and the Buller's Arms (the old 'Baker's Arms' having been renamed to honour Exeter Boer War hero, Sir Redvers Buller). There had also appeared a 'dealer in curiosities and souvenirs' – a Miss C.M. Hunt trading as 'Pixie Holt' – and an antique dealer, Reginald Middlewick. Those wishing to ride to hounds, hire ponies or to take lessons in equitation could do so from stables at Lower Weddicott, Murleigh, and Briarfield.

On the general retail front, the Chard family was by this time trading as a fruiterer against Mrs Morecambe in Lower Street, while the town's chemist was Arthur Merrifield. Chas Hill was baking in Lower Street and Harry Ball in the Square. Messrs Headon and Holmes competed in the butchery trade, also both in the Square. Henry Lewis was the dairyman and delivered milk throughout the district daily. Gerald Harding, a newsagent and tobacconist (who also dabbled in ironmongery) was also in business and there was even a penny library, as well as a toy and sweet shop. Collins' were reduced simply to 'Grocers and Tea Merchants, Tel. No. Chagford 7', while Victor Burgess junr ran a hairdressing salon in Southcombe Street and Arthur Kirtley one in the Square.

Above: *William Collins' 'Chagford Supply Stores' was the largest and most comprehensive of Chagford's shops in the early part of the twentieth century, dealing in a wide range of goods from premises in the Square. This shop, on the north-west side of the Square (now a chain grocer) was extensively rebuilt in the Edwardian period, being transformed from a modest thatched structure of two floors to an imposing three-storey building with double shop front and a large oriole bay at first-floor level. Mr Collins' billhead was of a flamboyance befitting his station among Chagford's shopkeepers.* (Courtesy Leonard Brommell Esq., Great Tree)

CHAGFORD TRADE TODAY

The history of Chagford's trade is one of vigour and enterprise. Even at the start of the twenty-first century, visitors to the town are surprised both by the range and quality of the goods offered in the shops as well as at the specialised services on offer. Of course, modern demographic and trading patterns have impinged on a small town centre like Chagford's; supermarkets have leached away some staple trade. However, the continued popularity of the place with visitors has led to an increase in the number of shops selling gifts, art and crafts, antiques and souvenirs. The staple services and shops are still intact and thriving, with a full range of professional, medical, legal and agricultural services still on tap. You can buy petrol, oil or a new tyre in the town, have your car serviced, and have a sick animal tended by a vet.

The two surviving 'emporia', Bowden's and Webber's, are famous in their own right, especially since the former was made the subject of a TV documentary by business guru Sir John Harvey-Jones. He concluded that Bowden's had no right to thrive in the modern world, breaking every tennet of contemporary retail wisdom – but he was jolly glad that it did as it was one of the most fascinating shops he'd ever struck, London notwithstanding!

On a basic level, Chagford is no longer quite so self-sufficient as it once was, when being cut off by a winter snow had surprisingly little impact. Bread is no longer baked in the town, but is delivered on a daily basis from Bovey Tracey or Okehampton. Similarly, the main grocery is part of a large chain supplied from a distant warehouse. The dairy, however, still sells a lot of local produce, including milk, cream, cheeses and excellent ice-cream made in Murchington. Chagford still has a greengrocer and fruiterer offering fresh produce that hasn't been trucked around half of Europe. It is also possible to purchase locally-killed meat from the butcher and even locally-made chocolates and patés from the delicatessen.

Today, you can find things in Chagford that were once solely the preserve of larger towns. Fine food and wines, floristry, hairdressing, upholstery, chair-caning, a wide range of holistic and alternative therapies, wholefoods, pioneering organic recycling schemes, translations into – or lessons in – a dozen languages and music tuition in a vast array of styles, to convey but a sample. And if you want something really obscure – like a packet of raddle to mark your sheep at tupping-time, an ounce or two of hobnails for your boots or a fibre washer and hemp packing for an old-fashioned tap – then Chagford may just be about the last place in England you'll find it still on the shelf!

Left: The north-west corner of Chagford Square has long been important in trading terms and is seen here, c.1930. The thatched building in the centre has been occupied by Lloyds Bank since just after the First World War. The elegant frontage of the rebuilt Collins' 'Chagford Supply Stores' is seen at right (inset: the original building) with a fine window display – which, under magnification of the original photo, can be seen to include jams, and preserves, sauces, cordials, tonics, pickles, spices, 'fancies' and Huntley & Palmer's biscuits in tins. This was the original projecting shop front which also supported the large oriole window of the first floor; this splendid frontage was unfortunately lost to renovations and widening of the pavement after the Second World War. Bowden's ironmongery shop was situated in the original, smaller premises (now the shoe shop) to the left of the archway that led to the Vulcan Iron Works and a range of further workshops and sheds – including the original fire station – behind the street frontage. Webber's had the shop next door to Bowden's, with Collins' the butcher's (no connection to the grocer or builder!) and the premises of Perrot's – fishing tackle maker and Dartmoor guides – adjoining. (Thorn Collection; inset, courtesy Pauline Spear)

The Market House is probably the building most closely associated with Chagford's civic administration, reflecting the central role of the market in the life of the town in former times and the importance of the market tolls to the economy of both the churchwardens and the council.

Built to replace the old shambles in 1861–2, the Market House became an asset of Chagford Parish Council when they took over the secular functions of the churchwardens in 1894. It was sold by them to the Okehampton Rural District Council in 1920s – a transaction which caused a considerable uproar at the time, the building having been at least partly financed by public subscription.

Today it falls within the remit of West Devon Borough Council and was extensively renovated by them in 1984. It now houses two lock-up shops, the public conveniences and a small office formerly used by the local Community Constable. (Meldrum Collection)

Left: *The oldest formal unit of administration in Chagford is the lordship of the manor. The manorial rights of 'Kagefort' eventually became vested at Waye Barton and Holy Street Manor, with the lordship split between them. The Ellis family held Waye for many years, and became the sole lords of the manor of Chagford in the late-nineteenth and early-twentieth centuries. The lordship subsequently passed to the Hayter-Hames family around the time of the Second World War. Here is an Ellis family group at Waye, taken c.1895.* (Courtesy Pauline Spear)

EIGHT
❦
ADMINISTRATION & AMENITIES

LORDSHIP
& ADMINISTRATION

The first administration to affect Chagford was its inclusion as a manor – Kagefort – in the Saxon hundred of Wonford, which was centred on Exe Bridge, just outside Exeter. The original site of the manor steading is obscure, although it almost certainly formed the nucleus of medieval Chagford. This Saxon manor of Chageford (as it became) was one of five that later came to be wholly included in the Parish of Chagford. The others were (sic) Rishford, Taincombe, Escapeleia and Middlecote. There was also the 'Royal Manor' of South Teign, which included that part of Chagford Parish that comprised Great Weeke and Easton, although it mostly lay in what became Moretonhampstead.

Each Saxon manor was the preserve of a lord, or thane, who had absolute rights of ownership and of feudal dues from those under him – the serfs, villeins and freemen. Serfs, the lowest order, were effectively slaves with almost no rights and no property, while villeins were feudal subjects who had the right to work a small parcel of land (a furlong) using oxen and chattels, as long as they also laboured on the common lands and the demesne (the lord's private lands). Bordars were dependants with a few acres of land held by grant, who farmed partly on their own account and were partly in the service of the lord. Freemen were those who had 'bought out' their feudal obligations and held land on tenure from the lord of the manor.

This Saxon manorial system was largely taken over by the Normans after their invasion in 1066. The main difference in the system at this time was that all manors were owned by the Crown and were 'granted' to the lords in return for allegiance and for military forfeits. Whereas Saxon lords had been known by their own names – Dodo, Alric, Edwi, Alwyn and Uluric in Domesday Chagford – the Normans commonly used the form of the Christian or forename of the lord followed by 'de' and the name of the manor. Thus, in 1261 at the foundation of the Church of St Michael, the lord of the manor of Chagford is recorded as Henry de Chageford. The manorial rights of the de Chageford line were amalgamated by marriage and sale with those of the de Wibberi family in 1299. Simon de Wibberi is the first recorded rector of Chagford, in 1315.

The maintenance of the manorial order was upheld, not just by established right and custom, but by a system of courts which served to determine the dues of subservients and their rights and to settle all disputes. These courts were the first recognisable form of local civil administration, and were presided over by the the lord or, if he was absent (many lords had several manors to oversee, which were often quite widely dispersed) then his steward would deputise. The different levels of the feudal system were regulated by separate civil courts – the Courts Baron for freemen, and the Courts Customary for villeins and serfs. Criminal justice was administered by the Court Leet – at first held individually on each manor but later held centrally for a group of manors. This was the predecessor for the divisions of the courts into 'petites sessions' (petty sessions), that for Chagford being based at Crockernwell. As well as their many rights, however, the lords had a range of obligations, not only of fealty to the Crown, but of civil duty to their dependants. Among these duties were the care of the sick, destitute or lame and the aid and protection of the manorial population in times of war or other peril.

THE PARISH TAKES
OVER

Chagford's lord of the manor also held the patronage of the church, and the close link between the lordship of the manor and the living of Chagford extended well into the twentieth century. Gradually, manorial rights and responsibilities – particularly civil duties – were devolved or linked to those of the Church, which included obligations of 'Christian Charity'. The wealth and influence of the Church as an institution increased dramatically in Chagford through the fourteenth and fifteenth centuries, and soon came to eclipse that of the individual lords of the various manors in the parish. The position of figurehead in the community gradually moved from the lordship of the manor of Chagford to the incumbent of the living – the rector. At various times, these two positions came to be effectively combined.

The church had a central role in medieval society. It was not only the centre of spiritual life, but also the main meeting-place of the town and hence the medium of consensus on local matters. It was also a place of refuge and of sanctuary, and the solidity and size of the church building reflects its importance as a haven for the townspeople in time of flood, fire or tempest. The chancel was sacred, but the 'body of the church' was a civil amenity, and would have been very much used as such, being by far the largest sheltered space in the town. The church thus became a natural forum in which to discuss matters of concern to all in the form of parishioners' meetings. Not unnaturally these gatherings soon became a de facto organ of local civil governance, for all that they had no statutory power as such. Such ad hoc local assemblies were termed 'Vestries', named after their habitual meeting-place.

The Church had its own system of administration at parish level and from the fifteenth century onwards it was the parish authorities who gradually became responsible for the upkeep of many of the secular institutions of the town as well as those of the Church. It was through the Church's duty of charity – the giving of alms – that the first vestiges of social welfare appeared, with provision for the aged, unemployed or infirm. This provision usually took the form of 'almshouses' for the deserving elderly, and the 'workhouse' for the unemployed or destitute. In some cases, 'infirmaries' or 'hospices' were also provided for the sick. All this was often a heavy burden on local church resources and the attention of the Vestries was often directed toward this problem. 'Vagrancy' – not having a place of residence or an occupation – became a criminal offence in the fourteenth century, which meant that anyone so classified could be housed (cheaply!) in the local gaol. However, that expedient did not remove those who, by ill luck or ill health, could not support themselves. In 1601, Parliament empowered the Vestries to raise a local tax, the Poor Rate, to provide basic services for these people. Chagford had already started to do this in 1558, following the Dissolution of the Monasteries which had previously met this need.

The 1601 Poor Act marked a transition of the unit of local administration from the manor to the Vestry of the parish, an entity which was collective rather than linked to an individual, and for which it was much simpler to legislate centrally. Successive Acts of Parliament subsequently placed many responsibilities on these parish authorities, from the upkeep of the highways and byways to the provision of fire precautions, the care of the destitute or sick (the old civil duty) and, later still, the provision of general education. Originally, the Vestries had been uncon-

stituted bodies and their size depended upon the number of people who wished to have a say in any particular matter. With the growth of population throughout the fifteenth and sixteenth centuries this soon resulted in an unwieldy and increasingly unworkable system. Thus, it became customary to elect or appoint a 'select Vestry', a committee of individuals who were deemed suitable custodians of the parish's affairs, usually through claims of rank or position. Members of this group became churchwardens, the trustees of the church's property and interests.

The churchwardens, being appointed or elected by their peers, were answerable only to the Church, Parliament and the Crown, and hence lacked the element of 'local accountability' that underpins modern democratic government. They came to be funded by a series of 'rates' or levies on land and property of the parish, established by Parliament and hence compulsory. The Poor Rate of 1601 was joined by the Church Rate and the Parish Rate – which should not be confused with the Tithe, which was a tax in kind on product or income that directly benefited the rector as part of his living. Works undertaken by churchwardens for the common good were paid for by the Parish Rate. These rates were paid by the occupiers of land and property rather than by the owners, and thus fell on those who, in theory at least, should have benefited from the services provided. Of course, the ratepayers of the parish didn't always see it that way, and many expenditures or rate calls were hotly disputed! The due collection of rates – Poor, Parish and Church – was the responsibility of the parish overseers, paid officials appointed from within the body of churchwardens.

The churchwardens discharged their responsibilities in a number of different ways. To look after the roads of the parish they appointed 'waywardens', each charged with the upkeep of a specific section of highway and provided with a barrow and tools. The 'fire precautions' required under the Act of 1707 that followed the fire of London amounted to little more than the provision of a few rudimentary appliances kept in the porch of the church. These consisted of 'leathern buckets, preventers (long-handled hooks like a military pike for pulling down burning thatch) and 'engines'. These last were hand-squirts, a sort of giant syringe capable of throwing two or three gallons of water at a time over a distance of around 10–15 feet.

The needs of the poor and the lame were met by the distribution of alms collected from parishioners and the proceeds of a number of Church and parish charities, together with the statutory 'Poor Rate'. It appears that the Parish and Poor Rates were levied on farmland right up until 1929, although by this time the sums levied did not generally amount to much, rateable values on farmland having been halved by statute in 1896.

Above and right: *The renovation of Chagford Market House in 1984 included a completely new roof structure in timber over a steel subframe. Even the cupola was replaced, the new version being swung into position by crane.*
(Thorn Collection)

Left: *Two of Chagford's best-known and longest-serving parish councillors, Robert Sampson and Peter Hill, inspecting progress on the Market House renovations, doubtless (given the huge cost involved) relieved that their predecessors had sold the building to the District Council!* (Thorn Collection)

CHAGFORD CHARITIES

In common with most ancient church foundations, St Michael's was entrusted with the administration of a number of charities – usually consisting of the interest of a sum of capital or a piece of property invested for the purpose. These funds were administered by the churchwardens as trustees. Most of the capital had been bequeathed or donated by the prominent landowners of the district at various dates from the sixteenth to the eighteenth centuries.

The John Hunt or Hunt's Charity was the gift of the Hooper family of Withecombe in December 1791, when the sum of £5 per annum was pledged 'for the relief of the poor not having received Parish or other relief'. The Bonamus or Bunamy's Bread Charity was in the gift of the churchwardens and allowed for the equivalent of £1.7s. in bread to be distributed to the poor of the parish every Good Friday, 'to be continued for ever'. The Endacott Blanket Charity was the gift of the Endacott family, and provided monies for the purchase of blankets to be provided to the poor, the sick, the aged or infirm. The John Weekes Charity provided 'education for poor children of the Parish', and crops up regularly in the school logs, when the

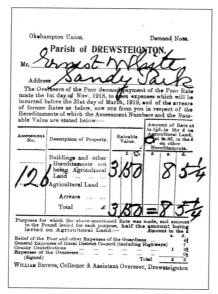

The Poor Act of 1601 was the first piece of State social welfare legislation, and empowered churchwardens to raise a 'Poor Rate', levied on the property of the parish, to finance care for the needy and destitute. It is not generally realised that this Act was only finally repealed in 1929, until which time the parishes were still collecting the rate. Above is a Poor Rate demand issued by Drewsteignton Parish Council for the year 1918–19, when eight shillings and fivepence-farthing was levied on 126 acres of land (the portion of Great Tree Farm lying within Drewsteignton Parish), rateable value £3.15s.0d. The rate collection was administered by the Parish Overseers and the money went to the Rural District. (Courtesy of Leonard Brommell Esq., Great Tree)

schoolmaster made reports and recommendations as to its application.

The Church Lands Charity was an anonymous annual gift, amounting to around £30 a year, bestowed on the rector and churchwardens, who kept two thirds for church purposes and distributed the balance. After the Parish Council assumed responsibility for the Chagford charities, the Charity Commissioners permitted this annual income to be split; two thirds went to the church as an ecclesiastical charity and the remaining third passed to the council as a parochial or non-ecclesiastical charity.

THE OKEHAMPTON POOR BOARD

Social provision for the sick and destitute was an ongoing issue for parish authorities, and methods of dealing with the problem varied very widely from place to place. Chagford is recorded as having a 'Parish Workhouse' in New Street, but there were no almshouses comparable to the well-known set at nearby Moretonhampstead. This unsatisfactory situation nationally was addressed by Parliament in a series of measures which culminated in the Poor Law Reform Act of 1834. This placed the responsibility of provision of relief services on district 'Poor Boards', charged with overseeing the activities of the various groups of churchwardens in their area. These boards effectively became the forerunners of the Rural District Councils, and Chagford, for the first time, found itself under the jurisdiction of Okehampton.

The poor boards looked at the needs of a whole district rather than an individual town, and effected economies by providing workhouses or other facilities serving a wider area. As so often has been the case, this made good economic but poor social sense, and many people came to dread being sent to the often distant 'poor house' when their own community could not offer them succour. The system of committal to the workhouse was compulsory under the Act, and in many instances was regarded as little different to being sent to prison.

COUNTY & PARISH COUNCILS

By the latter part of the nineteenth century, the administration of the parish was becoming both an onerous task, and one calling for a degree of scrutiny – given that the sums of public money involved by this time were substantial. Also, with the strong rise of Nonconformism in the area, many people in Chagford objected to the rates being levied by what, to them, was an alien church. The suspicion that church and secular funds mingled somewhat

An ancient tradition still maintained in Chagford is the seven-yearly 'beating of the bounds', in which the parish boundary is walked by a (usually large and festive) group of churchwardens, parish councillors and parishioners. Certain landmarks along the way are 'bumped', using the backside of the youngest parishioner present – presumably to impress on the rising generation the exact extent of the parish! It is also important to make sure that the 'CP' marking incised on the Langstone, Kestor – which is the meeting point of Chagford, Gidleigh and Lydford parishes – is clear and legible.

in the churchwarden's accounts was also hard to dispel! A further complicating factor was the series of disputes that arose over improvements that were to be funded by the Parish Rate, such as sanitation or water supply schemes, proposed by the church-wardens and led, no doubt, by the Revd Hayter George Hayter-Hames. Many residents were left feeling that the changes were of no direct benefit to them. At national level, there was an increasing realisation that many of the services and facilities being somewhat inadequately provided by parish authorities on a strictly local basis might be better and more efficiently administered by a broader-based and less partisan body.

The result was the enactment of a series of reforms that created, in 1884, the County Councils, and in 1894 the Rural District and Parish Councils. These new, elected, accountable bodies were to take over all the 'civil duties' and secular matters previously administered by the churchwardens. The first major area to come under these wider powers were the 'ordinary roads and highways'. The new Devon County Council took over from all the pre-existing turnpike trusts and parish authorities. The only exclusions were those 'footpaths and byways' deemed to be of purely local significance and thus best left under the authority of the parish. The other major area to fall to County Council control was education; Chagford Parochial School became DCC National School No. 5197. With this change, the two largest budgets were removed from the churchwarden's control. In 1894, with the passing of the Local Government Act, the remaining parish responsibilities for fire precautions, care of the town and social welfare became the remit of the new Parish Council. To look after the affairs of the church, a Parochial Church Council – in effect, a revival of the old Vestry – was instituted.

Parish councils were accountable to their electors in the parish – the ratepayers. The council had to report to them annually at a public meeting or series of meetings known as Parish Meetings, at which councillors could be challenged or resolutions passed. Parish councils were also overseen in their duties, especially those of social provision, by the Rural District Councils that had replaced the District Poor Boards, in Chagford's case the Okehampton RDC. The power to raise the Parish and Poor Rates passed to the new councils, the church being entitled only to a tithe to support the living. The old Church Rate, so hotly disputed by Nonconformists and other non-church interests, had been finally abolished in 1868, while agricultural land was devalued by 50 per cent for rating purposes in 1896, plunging many parish councils into early financial difficulty. The peculiarly British fondness for devolving administrative responsibility without the necessary fund-raising powers would seem to be nothing new!

CHAGFORD PARISH COUNCIL

The 1894 Local Government Act created strong opposition among the established ruling classes, who saw many of its provisions as an intrusion into their traditional spheres of influence. Many of the newly formed parish councils found themselves opposed and obstructed on every hand. Elsewhere, the new councils were simply hijacked by the existing dominant interests. At first glance, it would appear that this was the case in Chagford, where the first council of 1894 was littered with familiar names: Thomas Amery, T.T. Coniam, William Ellis, William Perryman and Richard Stanbury were all prominent landowners, with Colville George Hayter-Hames as the seemingly inevitable chairman. In fact, these appearances were deceptive, as of the 12 elected councillors a majority were in fact craft and tradespeople of the town: Thomas Ball, James Bowden the smith, Alf Jeffrey (the first clerk), with John Osborne, Alf Pearce, William Stone and Richard Dunning Underhill (the last four all being builders). The provisions of the Act allowed for a non-elected person to take the chair, having no ordinary vote but a casting vote, and C.G. Hayter-Hames was unanimously offered this position, which he retained for 33 years. William Perryman (noted as something of a radical in his day) became vice-chairman. The council appointed as treasurer the Postmaster, Robert Thorn.

The initial business of the new council was to 'ascertain the status of the parish'. Among the assets that were identified were the Market House, certain pieces of land, various parochial charities, the infrastructure of the water-supply system and the fire brigade. This last soon became a major item of business, being handed over lock, stock and engine by the Royal Insurance Office of Exeter. Other responsibilities that devolved included the collection and disposal of refuse, the cleaning of the streets, the amelioration of 'public nuisance' (sewage) and the provision of street lighting, paid for by a separate 'Street Lighting Rate' levied only on those who actually received the said illumination. This boon was provided by Mr Reed, who had made the original electrical installation three years before the council came into being. The provision of this service later passed to the West Devon Electricity Supply Company, his successors in trade.

CHAGFORD FIRE BRIGADE

The original churchwardens' 'fire precautions' having been found somewhat lacking, many small towns in Devon acquired some sort of organised fire brigade during the nineteenth century. This was a period when a succession of long, hot, dry summers saw serious conflagrations affecting a number of

Above: *The first brand new motor fire-engine to come to Chagford arrived in 1961, a Bedford J5 with Hampshire Car Bodies coachwork to the 'Devon rural water tender' design. It remained in service for 15 years.* (Chagford Fire Service)

Above: *Chagford's 1864 Shand Mason manual fire-engine remained in regular use until 1937, when it was replaced by a petrol-driven trailer pump. The Parish Council held on to the old manual engine, here seen at Chagford Show, c.1950. It is now in the museum of the Chartered Insurance Institute in London, although if Chagford ever establishes its own museum it may one day return to the town.*

Above: *Chagford became a retained station of the Devon County Fire Service in 1948. Stephen Lewtas, 12-year-old son of Chagford's long-serving GP, was made a junior fire-fighter in the 1960s, and is here seen at the retirement of Claude (Ginger) Cousins. The crew at that time were, left to right: Martin Stone, Norman Mallett, John Pleace, Charlie Rice, Ginger Cousins, George Bennett and Ivor Pidgeon. The officer with the shirt and tie was a supervisory Outposted Station Officer.* (Chagford Fire Service)

Above right: *The Chagford crew in 1986, this time marking the retirement of Alan Rice. Left to right: John Osborne, Jim Forsey, Anthony 'Jack' Paddon, Peter Stocks, Alan Rice, Ivor Pidgeon, Graham Stoodley, David James and Iain Rice. The fire-engine is the 'Multi-Purpose' appliance that came to Chagford in November 1976.* (Chagford Fire Service)

towns, notably – in the Chagford district – North Tawton (twice) and Moretonhampstead (three times). These old parish brigades were voluntary, ill-equipped, generally untrained and almost invariably ineffective. The only trained and organised fire brigades were those provided by the various insurance offices, which were restricted to places where those offices carried substantial risk – generally, the larger towns.

It is therefore somewhat surprising that a town as small as Chagford came to be blessed with a properly constituted, paid, trained and equipped insurance brigade. But just such a brigade was established in 1864 with a captain, 12 uniformed firemen and a nearly-new manual Shand Mason fire-engine, all provided by the Exeter office of the Royal Insurance Company. The reason why the Royal was so moved is unclear, although the beginning of the phase of extravagant country-house building in the Chagford district may have had something to do with it. There must have been a considerable insured risk in the area to warrant such comprehensive provision.

The fire-engine was kept in a shed next to Mr Bowden's forge – the fumes from which, from all accounts, did it no good whatsoever – and was drawn to the scene of operations by a pair of horses obtained locally when required. The alarm was originally raised, as was tradition, by 'clashing' the church bells (ringing two bells haphazardly) but the problems with the bell cage in 1895 that silenced the bells for a period brought about a change to the use of 'maroons', as used to summon the crews of lifeboats. The Chagford brigade attended around 20 fires annually for many years, mostly rick or barn fires or that common Devon bugbear, thatched roofs. Among notable premises to suffer fires during the life of the Chagford Parish Brigade were Huish, Rushford Barton, Waye Barton and Old Walls, together with cottages at Jurston and Sandy Park as well as at various places in the town.

The brigade continued virtually unchanged until 1937 when, following the report of the 1936 Riverdale inquiry into the state of Britain's fire-fighting capabilities in the face of the increasing threat of war, hurried steps were taken to abolish or update anachronisms such as the Chagford brigade. It was subsumed into the Okehampton Rural District Fire Brigade in 1937, and received a second-hand motor trailer pump. This was towed to fires by 'Mr Morecambe's lorry', previously used to transport the old manual engine. When the old Shand Mason was taken out of service, it was reported as being the oldest such machine 'in regular use by a public fire brigade in England and Wales'. It was preserved by Chagford Parish Council and, at the time of writing, is housed in the museum of the Chartered Insurance Institute in London.

In 1941, the erstwhile Chagford brigade became a very minor unit of the National Fire Service, being issued with a standard wartime utility trailer pump and, later, an Austin towing vehicle. The new equipment would not fit in the shed in Bowden's yard, so the fire station was moved to the ground floor of the former Assembly Rooms, beneath the Rex cinema. The Austin was kept in the yard of the Globe Hotel next door. After the war, a national review of the fire service proposed a wholly new arrangement of provision, and in the list of stations drawn up for Devon, Chagford was not mentioned. The NFS station was closed at the end of 1946 and the brigade disbanded, but a vigorous local campaign led by George Hayter-Hames (who was a member of Devon County Council, the new Fire Authority) saw this decision reversed and Chagford was reconstituted as a retained (paid part-time) station of the Devon County Fire Service in 1948.

A new fire station was converted out of an old farm building, used formerly as a piggery, in Manor Road, and the former Chagford NFS unit became Devon Station A4, issued with a second-hand 'water tender' converted from a wartime Ford V8 utility appliance. This remained in service until 1961, when it was replaced by a brand new J5 Bedford. In 1976, the Bedford was replaced by another new appliance, a Commer 'Commando' multi-purpose machine which was a real step forward. In 1987, a new fire station was built in Lower Street, opening the following year as Station 23 of the Devon Fire and Rescue Service. A more up-to-date, but basically similar, appliance was provided at the same time. In September 1995, Chagford received one of the first of Devon's new-generation 'fire rescue' vehicles, fully equipped for road-traffic accident and civil rescue. In 1998, the Chagford fire crew became one of the first in Devon to operate an emergency medical 'co-response' scheme in conjunction with Westcountry Ambulance – in this instance, a step behind Moretonhampstead, the very first!

CHAGFORD WATER SUPPLY

One of the other responsibilities taken over by the Chagford Parish and Okehampton Rural District Councils was the public water supply. By 1880, at the instigation of Hayter George Hayter-Hames, Chagford had quite a sophisticated system of leats, mains and pipes to supply fresh water for domestic purposes to most parts of the town. The main water supply was that originally provided around 1800 in connection with Mr Berry's woollen mill at Moorlands, which was later modified and extended. The supply was obtained from a series of springs that rise on the middle slopes of both Nattadon and Meldon hills, and came down through Quintatown to an intercept of the Padley Brook below Meldon House. From here, a leat led along the lower edge of Nattadon Common to an open reservoir above

The channels of the Chagford water-supply leats are precisely surveyed in the great tradition of Dartmoor leat-building, with an accuracy that enabled them to be engineered with falls of only a few inches in a mile. This maintains steady flow rates without scouring. The leats are also beautifully constructed, with dressed granite cills and a paved bed to the watercourse. Grooves in the stonework at intervals were for 'stop planks' to hold back or divert the water. Preservation of the surviving portions of the network is the remit of the new Turnlake Trust, set up to look after the system for posterity. (Rice Collection)

Dennis Park, and thence across the Glebe behind New Street to Long Park and Turnlake. The reservoir was not originally on the direct line of the leat, but off to one side, the leat channel acting as a 'by-wash' to allow the reservoir to be emptied for cleaning.

At Turnlake a branch split off and was led back by a culvert under New Street and ran thence along the lower side of the street, apparently as far as Fernleigh. A further channel ran into Hore Hill field, where it connected with the channel of the original supply leat that fed the mill, which can still be seen curving around the contour of the hill. This connection of the leat is believed to be a later arrangement; it is probable that the original leat fed the mill directly, the system being subsequently modified to provide the New Street supply as well as providing an overflow at times of flood. The New Street channel was subsequently altered to be a main water pipe below the pavement, its course marked by frequent fire hydrants or 'plugs' – literally, a pit containing a wooden bung forced into the iron water pipe. In case of fire, the nearest bung was drawn and the pit flooded, providing a convenient supply suited to the limited pumping arrangements of the old manual engine.

The main water-supply channel from Turnlake continues behind the cottages at the end of New Street, the occupiers of which have occasionally been on the receiving end of rather more water than they really wanted, and thence by a culvert under the lane at the foot of Nattadon Hill. Here there was a further junction at Cross Tree, where the branch serving the Square and Mill Street turned and ran along the western wall of the churchyard in a channel alongside the High Street. The main leat fell sharply along the southern boundary of the churchyard behind Bellacouch, then split again below the church, crossing what was then a paddock but which is now the lower churchyard to reach the head of Southcombe Street outside Mr Hill's forge. It then flowed down the side of the roadway in a deep gulley.

It is difficult to determine the exact arrangements of the lower part of the system from the records of the Water Committee, but it seems this gulley originally extended the whole length of Southcombe and Lower Streets and continued down the hill to Cross Park and Murleigh, where it flowed into the main outfall of the system which led back to the Teign. This deep, open channel in the narrow road evidently caused a lot of problems with carts getting caught and horses stumbling. The upper part of the channel was soon covered with granite slabs, and it would seem that by the time the Parish Council Water Committee took over in 1895 the lower part had already been piped as a water main which extended as far as Glendarah.

Gradually, the process of paving over the open channels or replacing them with iron water mains

A famous Chagford amenity was the 'Corporation Dustcart', subject of a popular postcard. It shows the donkey cart provided by the Sanitation Committee's contractor, Mr J. Ball, engaged on the daily sweeping of New Street. The sweeper is Bob Cann and the donkey was called 'Sweet'. The raised channel of the town leat at Turnlake is just visible at the left of the picture. (Thorn Collection)

was undertaken, with fire hydrants and stopcocks being provided at various points. By the beginning of the twentieth century the Square, Mill Street, New Street and the whole of Southcombe Street were connected to the water mains. The system was gradually extended to Lower Factory, which was by then converted into dwellings, and finally (after many requests) to Mr Reed's house at Teign View (now Narrowbridge House).

Connections to individual properties were by branch mains or standpipes, usually of half-inch bore, provided with stopcocks. The main system was finally connected directly to the reservoir which, being at a 'head' of some 20–30 feet over most parts of the town, provided a pressurised supply. The sections of the old open leat now remaining merely provide an overflow for the system, although allotment-holders find it useful for gardening purposes and Turnlake spout is commonly used by people washing their cars.

Latterly, the old Chagford main system was connected to the supply pipes of the North Devon Water Company, which used as its principal local source the upper River Taw at Taw Marsh, Belstone. The Chagford reservoir and supply leat are still functional, however, and – with the addition of a small filtering plant – are used to augment or even replace the pumped mains supply at times of drought. At the beginning of the twenty-first century, Chagford's water mains, which have recently been relined and refurbished, are connected to the modern South West Water high-pressure pumped supply system, and Chagford residents no longer have cause to complain about low water pressure.

The cost of the original system was met by a loan, the interest being born on a Water Rate. This charge was levied originally by the churchwardens but later taken over by the Rural District Council, although still administered by the Parish. The Parish Council – whose position in overseeing the water supply was always somewhat ambivalent as the Okehampton RDC refused to formally appoint them as a local Water Supply Committee – looked after the system on a daily basis, appointing a caretaker to keep the channels and pipes clear and carry out any necessary repairs or improvements. The water supply became a major preoccupation of the council, the minutes being full of references and resolutions concerning its upkeep. The overall direction of the system was, however, the remit of the Okehampton RDC surveyor, who did not always see eye-to-eye with the Water Committee of the Chagford Parish Council; indeed, he frequently omitted to consult or inform them, which gave rise to some testy correspondence!

Problems with the water supply included excessive demand in the summer season, frequent silting, particularly of the Long Park section, leaks and vegetation growth in the reservoir, and illegal extraction of water by unauthorised persons (notably builders). Other users included the London and South Western Railway's 'steam motor cars'.

The level of supply was a constant worry, and the Water Committee expended much time and energy trying to increase the water catchment. However, there were problems in reaching agreement with the landowners from whose estates the springs flowed and there were many site meetings and much correspondence on this subject. Mr Flood and Mr Blanchford, the landlord and tenant of Quintatown, were particularly obdurate in these matters. Even at the end of the twentieth century, the condition of the leat and works have given cause for concern, and the Turnlake once again figures regularly in the Parish Council minutes! Plus ça change!

SANITATION

The other side of the water-supply coin is the disposal of what are probably best termed 'waste waters'. Historically, this had not been a great concern in the town, and the primitive earth closet had sufficed for many generations of Chagfordians. However, it is evident that with the growth in population in the early-nineteenth century, there began the 'public nuisance' that inadequate sanitation begets; with some seven slaughterhouses and four farms also close to or within the boundaries of the Square, the less-than-fragrant effect of the combined 'nuisances' on a warm summer's day is best imagined.

The Revd H.G. Hayter-Hames obviously identified an improvement in the town's sanitary arrangements as a prerequisite for attracting the monied and refined visitors he sought and a sewerage scheme consequently formed the core of one of his most ambitious calls on the ratepayers of the town. The cost of a system of main sewers leading to remote cesspits on the outskirts of the town, together with an arrangement of 'flushing tanks' to clear the pipes on a regular basis, was obviously a heavy burden. Given that it would not benefit all the ratepayers equally, it was determined that it was not to be charged to the general Parish Rate. Instead, a one-off rate call and a loan was to provide initial funding, and an annual 'Sanitation Rate' was to be levied on the dwellings of the town connected to the new system. Even these proposals met with opposition, and it is evident that the Revd Hayter-Hames needed to deploy all his considerable powers of persuasion to get this far-sighted project under way in what were financially difficult times.

Fortunately, Chagford's siting on a hillside above a river valley made it relatively easy to lay out a simple gravity-worked sewerage system. Glazed clay pipes of 12 or 9 inches diameter were laid along New Street, the High Street and down Mill Street as far as the top of 'The Pit' – the deep cutting that starts at Eaglehurst. A further system of pipes led down both sides of the Square and along Southcombe and Lower Streets as far as Monte Rosa. Two large flushing-tanks fed by the water supply leat were located in the upper corner of the churchyard, controlled by stopcocks in a recess in the churchyard wall. One cesspit (euphemistically and, one suspects, optimistically referred to as a 'filtering tank' in the Sanitation Committee's minutes) was sited in Town

Left: *One of Chagford's greatest public amenities is the swimming pool at Rushford, built in 1934–6 and always popular. The pool is fed by the Rushford Mill leat, which runs behind the low wall at the rear of the pool that also forms a convenient seat.* (Thorn Collection)

Right: *Open fields and the new artisans' cottages at Dennis Park as viewed from the slopes of Meldon Hill, c.1930. The most distant of these fields – closest to the town centre – is Hore Hill, one proposed site for the troubled recreation-ground.* (Thorn Collection)

During the Second World War, Chagford was quick to form its own Home Guard platoon, one of the few such units to be mounted. They were led by Major W. Arden of Stiniel and carried out regular patrols. In the above picture the unit parades on the school field in front of the schoolhouse early in the war, while the second picture shows them patrolling on the moor, now fully armed with service rifles but not yet issued with uniforms, merely armbands.

Today it is easy to find these scenes somewhat humorous, but at the time these precautions were in deadly earnest and, had invasion occurred, there is no doubt that the Home Guard would have offered resistance every bit as tenacious as the Partisans in Yugoslavia or the Résistance in France. (Courtesy of the Mortimore family, Shapley)

Chagford gained its first resident constable, PC William Bray, in 1857. The Police House was for many years situated in New Street – number 20 – being replaced with a new purpose-built dwelling when Orchard Meadow was constructed in 1951–4. PC Cyril Tapper, seen here in Chagford churchyard in 1974, was the last of Chagford's resident policemen. When the 'unit beat' system came about in the late 1970s, Chagford was served by a Community Constable who also had responsibility for a number of other parishes, and relied on a car or motorcycle for mobility. Chagford's first Community Constable was John Dyke, who lived in the Police House at Whiddon Down and still does in 2002, although he is now retired. Nowadays, Chagford is policed from Okehampton.
(Thorn Collection)

Meadow at Padley, fed by main sewers that came down Hore Hill and Mill Street, with an overflow pipe discharging into the Padley Brook. A second tank was situated at Orchard Farm – in the field behind the current fire station, where the deep hollow that once contained it is still discernible. The sewer feeding this pit came across the paddock from Monte Rosa, and the discharge was into the lower outflow of the Town Leat.

This system proved remarkably effective and, with minor additions and modifications, served the town's sanitation needs for some 80 years, not being finally replaced until 1961. The system was never extended far beyond its original limits, as the necessary falls in the land were not extant to permit the gravity system to function properly. Properties built beyond the limits of the sewerage system, such as those in Broomhill, were provided with individual cesspits or septic tanks. The capacity of the system was in any event limited, both by the diameters of the pipes and by the size of the collection pits at Town Meadow and Orchard Meadow. These pits had

to be cleared out from time to time, an unenviable task in the days before vacuum gully-emptier lorries.

The sewerage system seems to have given less trouble than the water-supply network and features less frequently in the deliberations of the Parish Council who administered it through their Sanitation Committee. The only troublesome feature of the original system seems to have been the flushing tanks in the churchyard, which were apt to silt up and consequently needed fairly frequent cleansing. As most houses in the town gradually acquired flushing 'water closets' and more and more waste water outlets were connected to the 'foul drains', the flow rates in the sewers increased to the point where they became self-cleansing and the flushing-tanks became obsolete. A fair amount of storm water also found its way into the sewers (whatever the public health regulations might require to the contrary) and, given Chagford's healthy level of annual rainfall this was usually enough to ensure adequate flushing.

It was as much expansion pressures as environmental concerns that started to be felt in the late 1950s, which finally caused the system to be updated. With the addition of the Dennis Park houses – built as 'workmen's cottages' by the Okehampton Rural District Council in the early 1920s – at the New Street end of the system, and the completion of the postwar council-housing schemes at Orchard Meadow and Biera View at the opposite extremity, the capacity limit of the old system was reached. For further development to be contemplated, the decision was taken that a new rotating filter-bed treatment works was needed, together with large-capacity concrete pipes to 'intercept' and link the existing main sewers with the proposed works.

This new treatment plant was constructed by the South Western Water Board in 1960–1 on the banks of the River Teign at the foot of Grammar's Lane, and the cesspits were finally emptied for the last time in the summer of 1961. The old system, which by now was complemented by a proper storm-drain network to cope with surface water, was connected to the new large-diameter main sewers, although still functioning as a pure gravity system. When Broomhill was added to the mains drainage scheme in the late-twentieth century, a pumping facility had to be provided to transfer effluent to the treatment works. This modern addition appears to give more problems than the old system, for all its convolutions, ever did!

In 1900 the Sanitary Committee was also charged with the responsibility for street cleansing and refuse disposal. A man was to be employed for 'street cleaning in the summer months', while it was decided that refuse collection was to be effected by means of an annual contract, let by tender, for 'a man with horse and cart for the purpose of carting refuse once a month, to places as may be decided upon' (Parish Council minutes, 24th May 1900). For many years this place was an old quarry – known for some reason as 'The Guile' – which was situated on the old Moretonhampstead road opposite what is now Linden Spinney. Initially, no one came forward to tender for this less-than-savoury task, and councillors Underhill, Underhill and Brimblecombe had to arrange to do the work with their own resources. The following March, the two jobs – street cleaning and refuse carting – were combined, and put to tender. Mr J. Ball was awarded the contract, at 3s. (15p) per month for the refuse collection and 10s. (50p) per week for 'sweeping streets daily'. It was Mr Ball's donkey-cart that featured on a popular postcard, entitled 'The Chagford Corporation dust cart', depicting the 'daily sweeping' of New Street before the First World War. The sweeper for many years was Mr Bob Cann.

PADLEY COMMON, THE OPEN FIELDS & THE RECREATION-GROUND

The Parish Council's major 'new works' project was the creation of what eventually became the War Memorial Playing-Fields on Padley Common. The origins of this scheme go back, unbelievably, as far as 1897 when, on 28 January, a letter was received from 'Societies in London' suggesting that 'where necessary and practicable, open spaces or recreation-grounds should be secured, in celebration of the 60th year of Queen Victoria'. The council promptly formed a sub-committee to examine such a scheme which put forward a startling proposal for the 'enclosure and draining' of Padley Common as a recreation-ground. However, when the council held a site meeting the following month, they rapidly reached the conclusion that the cost of such a scheme would be too great for any funds likely to be raised.

At a Parish meeting held at the end of April 1897 to discuss the jubilee, various other proposals were mooted, including the creation of a 'bathing ground' at Padley, which presumably would have made a virtue of the marshy condition of the common. More ominously, however, there was raised the question of the Open Fields, a regular bone of contention in Chagford over many years. The Open Field system is a legal arrangement – many would say anachronism – peculiar to Chagford and the Padley, Meldon and Nattadon commoners, the origins of which are lost in the mists of 'custom and practice' extending back to medieval times. Under the system, a number of privately-owned pastures in the parish adjoining or communicating with Meldon and Padley commons are required to be thrown open as common grazing for three months of every year, from 4 August to 5 November. During this period, the gates onto the common must be unhung or secured open, and free access of livestock permitted between the commons

and all the fields. Enclosing the common would obviously fly directly in the face of this requirement.

The Open Fields question dogged the Parish Council's efforts to secure a recreation-ground for the better part of the next five decades. In 1902, Mr Amery offered the council part of Hore (or Hoar – the spelling is ever-variable) Hill Field as a recreation-ground, if he could retain unencumbered possession of the remainder. However, Hore Hill was an Open Field, and the commoners were having none of it. The council resorted to an appeal to the lady of the manor, Mrs Ellis of Waye, but she felt she had no authority in the matter. Hore Hill was also somewhat steep for any sporting purpose, having long been Chagford's favourite toboggan run! Fittingly, it is now owned by a charitable trust and has been added to the amenities of the town.

A lengthy negotiation was entered into involving landowners, the commoners, the council, the Charity Commissioners and the Rural District Council. A number of legal devices, including making the recreation-ground scheme a charitable trust, were tried to circumvent the Open Fields arrangement. Despite this, all efforts fell on the grounds that, when all was said and done the fields were, for the three months they were open, effectively common grazing and that such common rights were superior to all others. This called into question the legality of enclosing any or all of Padley Common. Eventually, the matter went to a Public Inquiry, which in December 1904 ruled in favour of the commoners and the status quo.

There matters rested until 1910 when the Okehampton Rural District Council stepped in to this troubled arena with a proposal, under the powers granted in the Housing and Town Planning Act of 1909, to build 'cottages and allotments for artisans' on the three open fields adjoining New Street. This caused further uproar, and drew in not only the Parish Council and the commoners, but the Board of Agriculture as well. Eventually a resolution was passed in November 1912 that Dennis Park – a field on the higher or Nattadon side of Meldon Road – should be compulsorily purchased for the erection of dwellings under the provisions of both the 1909 Act and the 'Housing and Working Classes Act. This resolution was carried 83–3, thus avoiding the need to resolve the Open Field question. The District Council duly acquired the field, which was used as allotments to grow food (potatoes) for the war effort during the First World War.

Matters rested again until the dust of war had settled in 1922, when the Parish Council tried another tack by attempting to buy the manorial rights on Padley Common from the lady of the manor, Mrs Ellis of Waye. This was a proposal made under the Commons Act of 1899, which empowered the council to make 'schemes of regulation and improvement' for commons lying in their jurisdiction. However, it transpired that Mrs Ellis was a 'life tenant' of the manor and did not actually own the manorial rights, which were in trust. The scheme sank once again into a seemingly bottomless mire of legal difficulties and opposing interests, which engaged the 'Commons Improvement Committee' for the next several years. Some drainage and footpath works were carried out by the Committee in 1926, but progress was otherwise imperceptible. The entrance to the common from the foot of Parely Hill (Manor Road) was improved in 1932–3, the brook being diverted and bridged.

The next attempt to establish a playing-field was mooted in connection with King George V's jubilee in 1935. This came to nothing, but was revived after the King's death in 1937. The council hoped that by renaming the project the 'King George V Memorial Playing-Field', patriotism would overcome petty opposition and the proposal would also attract a grant from the National Playing-Fields Association. In connection with this proposal alternative sites were also examined, at Bower's Park and in 'a field belonging to Mr Garrish'. Neither of these were found to be acceptable, so it was back once more to the intractable problems of Padley Common, before the outbreak of the Second World War put aside further consideration of the matter. The NFPA had, in any case, turned down the council's grant application; the site was 'not suitable'. Towards the end of the war Padley Common was used as a base by a US Army logistics (engineering and medical) unit preparing for D-Day, and for the first time commoners' rights were subjugated to the national interest.

The playing-field project did not surface again until April 1946, when the Devon County Council wrote to all its parishes suggesting they devote five per cent of the rate in that year for the establishment of local war memorials throughout the county. This, at last, gave the council a handle to grasp. The project became known as 'The War Memorial Playing Field', and this time patriotism and respect for those who had suffered in the conflict prevailed over petty local interests. At a parish meeting in May 1946, the opposition to the siting of the playing-field on Padley Common was finally defeated, and the meeting unanimously delegated to the Parish Council

'authority to proceed with a survey and lay-out of the playing-field on the common'. The lordship of the manor of Chagford had now passed to George Hayter-Hames, who at once gave his consent for the enclosure – although, in fact, he had no legal right to do so! In the climate of the times, however, such matters did not assume the importance they once had.

At last, work could start on the long-delayed facility. The five per cent rate, along with various other moneys, had produced a sum of £576.14s.2d., and with this behind them the council started drainage works. A War Memorial Playing-Field Fund was set up, and fund-raising started in earnest: sports days at the school, dances, whist drives and fêtes. It took a further five years of such efforts to fund a lengthy programme of drainage, levelling, access and other land improvement works before the chairman of the Playing-Field Fund, councillor Smardon, could report to the Parish Meeting of March 1954 that:

> ... the committee had reached the object that they had set themselves, in that they had developed the six-acre portion of the moorland into a playing field.

A children's play area was established, with swings and a sandpit, and football and cricket pitches were laid out by voluntary labour. A sports day was held on the new facility in August, but in typical Chagford style it rained heavily and the event made a loss of £36! However, the Chagford Football Club used its pitch for the following season and cricket was played on the new wicket for the first time in May 1955.

At the time of writing, of course, Padley is the site of state-of-the-art sports facilities representing the investment of hundreds of thousands of pounds; in this regard, Chagford must be one of the best-provided small towns in the whole of Britain. However, without the remarkable resolve of the Parish Council over some 50 years, none of these facilities would exist. That they do (and that the Open Fields are still open for three months from the fourth of August each year) reflects something of the character of Chagford – stubbornly persistent and never in too much of a hurry for change. Well, what other place do you know that finally commemorated Queen Victoria's diamond Jubilee in 1954?

Since 1918 and the end of the First World War, the Chagford Branch of the Royal British Legion has formed an important pillar of Chagford's civic establishment. After the Infants' School closed in 1970, they took over full use of St Katherine's Hall, which many Chagfordians still refer to as the Legion Hall. In this 1950s view, members of the Legion march down the High Street to mark Armistice Day, a tradition that is still very much upheld in the town.
(Thorn Collection)

Above: *A rare item is this novelty card dating from the First World War; a flap in the soldier's cap pulls out to reveal a folded strip containing miniature views of Chagford – a dozen of them on the original; some are shown above left.* (Meldrum Collection)

Left: *A five-view Chagford postcard dating from about 1905 and 1960 are typical of a great number issued over the years, featuring the quaintness of the town, the splendour of its setting against the backdrop of the moor and the antiquities to be found in the district. Fingle Bridge invariably gets a look in, too.* (Thorn Collection)

NINE

❧

TOURISM, LEISURE & THE ARTS

If there is one thing that can be said to characterise the major change that has taken place in Chagford since 1850, it must be the growth of the town as a centre for a gentle kind of tourism and as a haven for artists and the arts. In 1850, Chagford was a small-scale industrial town and a minor agricultural centre, experiencing a sorry decline in its fortunes in the face of vigorous competition from areas favoured with greater resources and, most importantly, better transport links. The main woollen mill closed in 1848, never to fully re-open, while the tin trade through Chagford was all but dead. Indeed, in 1790 the Chagford Stannary Court had been abolished and its few remaining functions transferred to Tavistock. With the decline in population and prosperity after 1840, the strong local market for farm produce also fell away; together with the slowing down of the raw wool trade, this was a serious blow to Chagford's farming community. Potato growing was the last resort of many.

The rocking stone at Sitaford Tor was just one of the antiquities and curiosities that attracted visitors to the Chagford district in the later nineteenth century; others delights included the scenery, the fishing, and the 'bracing' climate. (Thorn Collection)

By 1860, Chagford was in bad way. The population was in rapid decline, poverty and disease were on the increase, and the prospects of revival in the town's traditional trades were bleak. This was a state of affairs that greatly distressed the Revd Hayter George Hayter-Hames, the first in a long line of pragmatic parsons who have served not only Chagford's spiritual needs, but its more basic and practical ones as well. It was Hayter George who appreciated that Chagford's greatest asset in the climate of those times was its situation, scenery and associations. The Victorian romantic movement was just getting into its stride, expressed in art, architecture and literature, and the perceptive rector realised that Chagford's combination of rural charm, rich history and sublime scenic setting fitted exactly with these new romantic aspirations. As rector and principal landowner – and hence effectively leader of the community – Hayter George aimed to bring about a revival in Chagford's fortunes, by transforming the town into a mecca for the new class of cultured, leisured and wealthy visitors.

There is no doubt that Hayter George was a remarkable personality: vigorous, perceptive and practical. Everything written about him conjures up an image of a sympathetic but determined man who would spare no pains to achieve what were far-sighted and laudable ends. Everywhere one looks in the enterprise of Chagford in those later years of the nineteenth century, one discerns the hand of Hayter George – parson, educator, entrepreneur, railway promoter, builder, farmer, improver and philanthropist. Comparing the history of Chagford over the period between 1850 and the outbreak of the First World War with that of small country towns elsewhere in Devon facing similar decline and stagnation, one realised just what an impact Hayter George had and how successful he was in lifting Chagford from its slough of despond.

ROAD, RAIL & ROMANCE

Hayter George's analysis of the task was straightforward. Chagford needed to smarten itself up, move from being a sleepy and – if truth be known – somewhat run-down and shabby little town, to somewhere offering interest, fresh air and rustic charm, together with a unique atmosphere that might be characterised as 'rural romantic'. He also realised that charm and fresh air alone would not be enough; such practical facilities as good road and rail access, modern sewerage and gas systems, comfortable hotels and lodgings and even a degree of sophistication in the shops and services were equally necessary.

He started with the roads. The first round of road improvements aimed at accommodating the heavy-wheeled traffic of trade, carried out mostly in the 1840s, was followed by a programme of further upgrading of road surfaces, drainage and boundaries to provide an easy passage to the private carriages of the new class of visitors. The railway was also a key factor in Hayter George's plan, although it became the only aspect of his concept that was not entirely successful. He was, alternately, promoter of Chagford's own Teign Valley Railway and an enduring thorn in the side of the South Devon Railway's board, keeping up the pressure on the directors to extend the line from Moretonhampstead to Chagford. It was almost certainly Hayter George's lobbying that resulted in the South Devon Railway contract for the horse omnibus service to Chagford that started in 1870, and he continued to press for a proper rail link until his death in 1886.

Transport was only one side of Hayter George's vision. Publicity was another. He used his social connections extensively to get writers, artists, journalists and other influential figures to visit Chagford, where his hospitality was generous and his advocacy both charming and devastatingly effective. Hayter George was evidently an excellent public relations man, and articles about Chagford soon started to appear in the fashionable press, singing the praises not only of the scenery, interest and antiquities of the district, but also of the 'salubrious climate, excellent for consumptives'.

However, Hayter George was also aware that it was no good attracting people to the town if the facilities to receive them, to make them welcome and comfortable (and thus to relieve them of the money so badly needed to help the local economy) were not in place. The 1850 *White's Directory* lists only the traditional inns as places to stay. By 1879, the picture had been totally transformed: the Moor Park Hotel had been built, together with large, luxurious private apartment villas at Meldon Hall and Monte Rosa. The King's Arms was now styling itself as a 'family and commercial hotel', offering 'hacks and hunters for hire, fine wines, good fishing and shooting'. The Three Crowns, too, claimed all these benefits and facilities with 'good stabling and lock-up coach houses'. James Perrot, the Dartmoor guide and fishing-tackle maker, was in business in the Square, while the range of shops had increased significantly and many luxury goods were on offer. 'Ladies kid boots' were hardly the everyday wear of Dartmoor farmers' wives! Coal and coke for heating could be freely obtained, the streets and the principal houses were lit by gas, and a wide range of 'conveyances' could be hired.

CHAGFORD THE SPA

By the time Hayter George Hayter-Hames died in 1886, Chagford was firmly established as a fashionable resort for the tourist of means, with an appreciation of country pursuits, fine scenery, art and antiquities. Everything about the town, from the pure, soft Dartmoor spring water to the clear, clean air and the 'bracing' climate, was seen as beneficial and desirable. The district abounded in antiquities attractive to a new breed of wealthy amateur, fashionably dabbling in archaeology and the restoration of historic sites. Artists flocked to paint Chagford scenes, Eden Philpotts commenced his series of popular Dartmoor romances by basing the first of them here, and William Crossing's *Amid Devonia's Alps* raised still further the fervour of Victorian enthusiasm for the wild country and rustic charm offered by the whole Dartmoor region.

The Chagford seen in the postcards of the last two decades of the nineteenth century is a smart, attractive town possessed of remarkably sophisticated facilities and some fine new buildings. This development continued until the outbreak of the First World War, by which time the town was lit by electricity, Moorlands had become a large and fashionable hotel, further large 'villas' had been built at Ferndale (Greenacres) and Beverly, and the ring of fine new private country houses around Chagford that included Meldon Hill House, Greenbanks, Outer Down, Ford Park, Teignworthy, Thornworthy, Holy Street Manor, Puggiestones, Denshams, Gidleigh Park, Saint John's and Furlong were complete. In the adjoining parish of Drewsteignton, less than two miles from Chagford Square, the largest and grandest of all these romantic Victorian/Edwardian country houses, Lutyen's unique Castle Drogo, was slowly taking shape.

All these developments brought renewed prosperity to Chagford, revitalising both the town and the surrounding countryside. The building trade bloomed and burgeoned as never before, and Chagford soon came to possess a wide range of skilled building craftsmen and tradesmen. The wool trade also recovered somewhat, particularly when improved transport opened up wider markets. The farms found a ready outlet in the local hotels for high-quality dairy produce, beef and lamb, while the broadening of tourism to include the middle classes also created a demand for more down-to-earth accommodation. Many farmers' wives began to take in guests or to offer refreshments to passing cyclists and walkers, while in the town 'boarding houses' soon abounded. Also being felt were the first impacts of that great leveller of the twentieth century, the internal combustion engine. Chagford was, in 1906, one of the first country towns to be served by motor omnibus (a breed of vehicle that had only originated in practicable form in 1903) while the first private motor cars popped and stuttered their

Top: *Chagford was very proud of its swimming pool at Rushford, opened in 1936 on the river bank. Before the pool opened, the mill-pounds on the river formed a somewhat more rustic alternative.*

Above: *Hilary Thorn taking a dip, date unknown.*
(Thorn Collection)

way into the Square before the new century was five years old.

The First World War brought only a temporary lull in this development. Chagford contributed a surprising number of men to the war effort, while many young Chagford women became auxiliary nurses staffing the recuperation centres for wounded soldiers set up in several large houses in the district. The number of Chagfordians who gave their lives in that bloody and futile conflict, most of them farm workers or skilled tradesmen, makes a depressing list, and it is perhaps owing to the impact of this loss on the town that things were never quite the same in the building trade after 1918. However, the expectations of a wide range of people were raised following the war and visitor numbers to Dartmoor continued to rise – aided by vigorous promotion of the area by the railway companies, especially the GWR.

POPULAR TOURISM ARRIVES

In Hayter George's day, tourism was essentially the preserve of the wealthy, so these were the people he set out to attract. The facilities needed were thus biased towards quality rather than quantity, and it is probably this 'top down' development of the local tourist business that has spared Chagford many of the denigrations so often associated with mass tourism. However, the improving transport links and prosperity of the immediate postwar period inevitably led to a broadening of the social groups able and wanting to take country holidays in Devon in general and on Dartmoor in particular. Chagford adapted accordingly and by 1935 the town offered a wide range of accommodation, from grand hotels through lodging-houses and 'cottages to rent' down to 'chambers', or as they are now known, 'B & Bs'.

The charabanc and the motor coach were the means to this opening-up of the Chagford area to a more numerous but less prosperous class of tourist. By that same date of 1935, Chagford was being served by the Devon General Omnibus Company with a number of routes linking the town directly to Exeter, Newton Abbot and Okehampton, as well as by the associated 'Grey Cars' tours based in Torquay. The fondly remembered Royal Blue line was also offering a through express coach service from London, connecting at Crockernwell with the Devon General services to Chagford. The fares were highly competitive and, for the first time, 'all in' package holidays were being offered. The popularity of cycling, which grew rapidly throughout the 1920s and early 1930s, also helped Chagford. These cycling tourists (the author's father was one such) were made of stern stuff, and were undeterred by the rugged terrain or the lack of smooth main roads.

Left and below: *One of the chief visitor attractions of the Chagford district has always been the well-known beauty spot at Fingle Bridge in the Teign Gorge, which is, of course, in Drewsteignton Parish. The walk along the river bank from Rushford to Fingle via one of the two paths through the Teign Gorge (the riverside Fishermans Path or the precipitous Hunters Path) features in almost all the guides and directories covering Chagford, and is still popular today. What is now hard to appreciate was how wild and open this part of the Teign Valley was before the present woodlands were established, as these two cards, from c.1900 and c.1910, clearly show.* (Meldrum Collection)

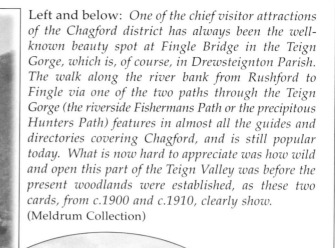

Above: *Dartmoor's Tors form a great attraction to visitors and are geological features shared only with Bodmin Moor. This is Kestor, Chagford, seen in the 1920s. It is a prominent landmark visible from the town and a popular destination for a ramble by way of Holy Street, Leigh Bridge, Teigncombe and Featherbed Lane.*

Left: *The tearooms and accommodation at the Angler's Rest, Fingle Bridge, were erected in their current form after the First Word War, replacing an earlier and by all accounts rather ramshackle wooden structure. The building has since been extended several times and is now a popular venue for many local functions. It is seen here being visited by a party from Chagford out for a Sunday-afternoon stroll in 1926.* (Both Thorn Collection)

Rambling, too, was a popular and economical way of taking a vacation during this period, and was another sphere in which Chagford had much to offer. The youth hostel movement was thriving, and although there was never a hostel in Chagford itself there were two close by – at Step's Bridge in the Teign Gorge and at Gidleigh. To accommodate the needs of this new class of tourist, Chagford soon boasted a number of cafés and tearooms, while almost all the shops sold a wide range of souvenirs. Local coach operators offered Chagford-based tours on Dartmoor and day-trips to a range of destinations. Thomas' (later Arscott's) ran several such coach routes, as did the Moorland Heather company after the Second World War. Chagford also featured as a stop on tours based elsewhere in the Dartmoor and South Devon area, and coaches would regularly arrive from Bovey Tracey, Newton Abbot, Ashburton, Torquay and Exeter – although never in the numbers or to the extent in which they besieged such popular destination points as Widecombe, Haytor or Dartmeet.

The popular conception of Chagford in the interwar period is neatly summed up by the entry in the 1924 GWR *Holiday Haunts* guide:

A thriving, up-to-date little town on Dartmoor. It is within easy reach of Moretonhampstead, with which place it is linked up by a service of GWR Road Motor Cars. The golf course is situated in an exceedingly beautiful and salubrious position. Drewsteignton Cromlech on Shilstone Farm, the sole perfect specimen of the kind remaining in the county, and once but a single member in a series of very remarkable monuments, is in the Chagford District. The famous Teign Gorge and Fingle Bridge are within easy walking distance. Excellent fishing in the River Teign.

That is probably as neat a summary of Chagford's traditional attractions as might be found: the tiny, bustling Dartmoor town; the 'exceedingly beautiful and salubrious position' of the golf course (opened in 1906, of nine holes only and, situated as it was atop Meldon Hill, just about the highest in England); the proliferation of antiquities in the area; the fine walking and fishing and, of course, the scenery, the pure, fresh air, the delicious local produce and the tranquillity of this still-remote countryside. From 1936, Chagford possessed a fine open-air swimming pool, claimed to be one of the best-situated in the Kingdom. In addition, after the opening of the Jubilee Hall in 1937 and the subsequent conversion of the old Parish Assembly Rooms behind the Globe into the Rex cinema, Chagford also offered the up-to-date glamour of the silver screen and the 'talkies' to while away the odd rainy afternoon.

THE SECOND WORLD WAR & BEYOND – THE MOTOR CAR ARRIVES

The Second World War affected Chagford in a number of ways. The young men went once more to fight, farming was under the control of the 'War Ag' and Land Girls worked the farms. The town received evacuees from large cities including Bristol, London and Plymouth, while Holy Street Manor and Scorhill House in Gidleigh both became home to boarding-schools that had been evacuated from risk areas. Anti-aircraft guns were sited on Nattadon Hill to protect the south-western approach to Exeter, and various military units were billeted in the area, especially in the later stages of the war when there was an American encampment on Padley Common. A Home Guard unit was formed, Chagford girls were once more nursing wounded soldiers and several of the large country houses in the vicinity again became recuperation centres. Some architectural ironwork and other 'non-essential' metal artefacts were also lost to the wartime scrap drive.

Nevertheless, people continued to visit Chagford throughout this difficult wartime period, coming to escape the pressures and dangers of life in the cities. Walking and cycling holidays became more popular than ever, as they needed no scarce petrol coupons

Above: *A family picnic on Dartmoor in the 1920s – in this case, the Thorn and Maddicott families.*
(Thorn Collection)

Top: *Rambling in the countryside was not an occupation reserved solely for visitors; many local people also made use of the many footpaths around the town, and local family albums contain many delightful snaps like this one – Anne Thorn wearing her best bonnet and climbing the stile on the riverside path opposite Lower Factory, c.1957.*
(Thorn Collection)

and cost very little. Farmhouse accommodation offered not only shelter and tranquillity, but a far better diet than was available in most large towns. And lending a hand with the haymaking or harvest was as patriotic as it was enjoyable for city folk. The war changed many things, but it did not change the essence of what Chagford had become – a place that represented the ideal of a rural, tranquil and beautiful Britain, a Britain worth fighting for.

At the end of the war, life took some time to return to normal. Agricultural production was still at the increased wartime level but many other supplies were unobtainable, transport was difficult and money was short. In the 1940s, Chagford was still, relatively speaking, remote and off the 'beaten track'. The main means of access for visitors was by rail and bus via Newton Abbot or Exeter, and once in the district people walked, rode or cycled. Holidays at this time were a real adventure, and only the more determined of tourists managed to reach areas as remote as north-east Dartmoor. Even so there were enough of them to ensure the gradual emergence of the 'visitor trade', which in turn led to the revival of the town's economy.

Gradually, the situation eased. The period of austerity drew to a close, new cars became available on the home market and, as the 'New Elizabethan' age dawned in the early 1950s, prosperity returned to many people. The motor coach was now a swift and comfortable mode of transport offering real competition to the railways, with the advantage that almost any destination was within its scope. Ownership of private cars was also on the increase, with a wide choice of popular, affordable models coming on to the market in the mid 1950s. The conditions were in place for more people than ever before to gain access to the 'holiday areas' of Britain, and resorts such as Exmouth and Torbay commenced a period of rapid growth. Foreign holidays and 'continental tours' were not yet a threat to the domestic tourist industry, and so visitor numbers boomed throughout the popular South West.

Chagford was at, or perhaps a little beyond, the northern limit of the hinterland of the popular coastal resorts of Dawlish and Torquay, and consequently was never so popular a destination for 'day-trippers' as the more obvious Dartmoor beauty spots. This helped the town regain its position as an alternative to the crowded and bustling popular resorts; it was perfect for people seeking either a healthy and active open-air holiday or a quieter, more contemplative retreat of the kind favoured by fishermen and artists. So Chagford was once again spared the trappings of mass tourism – the car parks and the ice-cream parlours that were seen as essential to the well-being of 'The Man on the Clapham Omnibus' and his family when on holiday.

The hotels continued to offer quiet comforts as before, the boarding-houses and farmhouse accommodation remained the resort of the walkers and artists, and the shops regained much of their pre-war sophistication. There was now an established art gallery in the town together with several antique and curio dealers, while the needs of walkers, riders and fishermen were also well catered for. Alongside these new businesses, Arthur Lyddon was still making and mending boots in his little shop by the fountain, and Lillian Thorn remained in charge of the Post Office. The Rex was still showing films in its upstairs room, not yet killed off by television. Chagford at this time was was still very much the town it had been during the interwar years.

However, access to Chagford was changing. By the late 1950s it was increasingly by means of the private car, although it was still a long and tortuous journey. The queues that stretched for miles around the Exeter bypass and the slow, 40mph jog across Salisbury Plain on the A30 or the A303 meant that Londoners visiting the region in the summer often faced an eight-hour drive to reach Chagford. The A38 from Bristol was also a notorious road, with a bad reputation for accidents and heavy congestion. In spite of this, the advantages of the car in terms of flexibility and freedom brought a new class of visitor to Dartmoor, a visitor who had no need for the railway (the Moretonhampstead branch closed to passengers in 1959) or for buses. The roads around Chagford became busier and busier throughout the 1960s, as did the local garages. The Square started to fill with the parked cars from which it has never since been free.

The Globe Hotel and Chagford High Street in 1931.

CHAGFORD HOTELS

Left: *For a town of such modest size, Chagford has always been well provided with inns and hotels. The largest of these was the Moorlands Hotel, formerly the house and mill of Mr Berry. Latterly, it was a retirement home and is now being converted to appartments.* (Courtesy Pauline Spear)

Right: *One of Chagford's ancient inns was the King's Arms, which ceased to be a public house before the First World War, trading then as the Central Private Hotel, as seen in this view dating from around 1920. It is now 'Lydstone', a private house.* (Thorn Collection)

Left: *The longest-established surviving hotel is the Three Crowns. This nineteenth-century view shows the prominent porch heavily overgrown with ivy. The picture was taken from churchyard, and clearly shows the church stile beside the iron gate opposite the inn.* (Meldrum Collection)

Right: *The Mill End Hotel opened in 1917, but is here seen in the early 1950s in the age of motor tourism. The cars include a 1950 Austin 'Devon', a 1937 Alvis, a Morris tourer of about 1930 and a rare HRG sports car of 1949–50. The large saloon in the distance is a wartime Humber.* (Thorn Collection)

Most glamorous and probably best-known of Chagford's current hotels is Gidleigh Park, now an internationally renowned country-house hotel with a worldwide clientele and a Michelin rosette for its cuisine. It is superbly sited on the banks of the North Teign River, on the boundaries of Chagford and Gidleigh Parishes. (Thorn Collection)

MODERN TOURISM IN CHAGFORD

With the opening of the trunk roads into the area – the M5 in stages throughout the early 1970s, and the first section of the new A30 to Whiddon Down in 1978 – Chagford was no longer anything like so remote. By 1974, following the commencement of the Intercity 125 service, the fastest trains from Paddington to Exeter made the trip in a scant two hours. By road, the journey time had been cut to around twice this by means of the M4 and M5 motorways, even if the A303 route was still often a six-hour slog. The story subsequently has been one of dramatically-improved road links, a process that still continues. At the time of writing, Chagford is only around 3–4 hours distant by road from the major population centres of Birmingham and London.

This accessibility has fundamentally changed the nature of Chagford's tourist trade. The number of casual visitors – people who stumble across the place by chance while touring around the Dartmoor area by car – has dramatically increased, leading to the chronic traffic congestion that now often characterises the town in high summer. The pressure this places on car parking and access has had to be balanced with the benefit these visitors bring to the local economy. The best way to accommodate this type of tourist, both to the benefit of local trade and to the enjoyment of the visitor, is an ongoing problem that has increasingly engaged the attention of the Parish

and County Councils, the National Park Authority and local amenity groups.

The easy access, from London in particular, has also made Chagford a very popular 'weekend break' destination with the more traditional type of discerning visitor – people who appreciate the town's particular combination of qualities. It is also popular with those who may seek a main holiday in some exotic foreign destination, but find Chagford ideal for a brief respite from a hectic city lifestyle. This 'quality' trade has helped sustain the local hotels, of which Chagford still has a good number, although fewer than in the town's pre-war heyday when it was

A Chagford Sunday school seaside treat to Paignton in about 1933. Teignmouth was another popular destination. (Thorn collection)

Right: *Chagford is the home of the Mid-Devon Hunt, founded by Mr Spiller of Eaglehurst in the 1920s. The hunt kennels occupy part of the site of the original Factory – Mr Berry's large woollen mill by Chagford Bridge. Here are the hounds in the High Street, c.1930. The hunt is still active today although it faces an uncertain future.*

Below: *The Boxing Day Meet in Chagford Square has always been popular and attracts a large following of visitors as well as locals. This is the meet in about 1972.*

A more recent meet of the Mid-Devon Hunt was at Southill in 1998, this being the last occasion when they rode out with Bernard Parker as Huntsman. (Courtesy of Maurice Hill Esq., East Coombe)

Riding was always an important aspect of leisure in Chagford, and still is. **Above:** *The Ellis family stand with their ponies by the lake at Waye, c.1895.* (Courtesy Pauline Spear)

Right: *Anne Thorn sitting rather self-consciously on Jumbo in Chagford Square, 1954. The rear corner of one of Moorland Heather's distinctive cream-and-blue coaches is just visible on the right.* (Thorn Collection)

Left: *Point-to-point races, cross-country and hunter trials are popular equestrian events throughout the Dartmoor area, and horses for these sports have long been bred in Chagford. This is Joyce Mortimore on 'Oakey' at Higher Shapley, c.1970 – the horse being so named because he was born on Okehampton Show day.* (Courtesy the Mortimore family, Shapley)

Chagford Agricultural and Horticultural show originated in 1898. The first shows were held on the sheep sale fields at Bayley's Hey, but after the First World War the show was moved to a wonderful riverside location on meadows at Rushford. The pictue shows Mary Wonnacott with her parents at the show in about 1932. (Courtesy of the Motimore Family, Shapley)

holiday homes are often regarded as something of a mixed blessing by residents, especially by young Chagford families seeking their first home. Nevertheless their presence also contributes to the local economy; as always, the problem is in striking an equitable balance between the needs of all those who are attracted to Chagford.

CHAGFORD AT PLAY

It is ironic that other people's leisure has become the main business of Chagford, as it is evident from such sources as the school log that the ordinary people of the district had relatively little opportunity to relax and take time off from toil throughout much of the last 200 years. Market days and fair days were prime opportunities for farming people to socialise and they were certainly enjoyed as such. School attendance on fair days was 'negligible', and after a few years the school was closed on such occasions. Communal events such as the autumn pony drifts also assumed something of a festive air, as did the various high points of the farming year including haymaking and harvest. Public holidays as such, however, were far fewer than is the case in the early-twenty-first century. Many of them seem to have been unofficial, occasioned by such events as markets or other celebrations in neighbouring towns, the visits of circuses and similar travelling entertainments to the district, or local sporting events.

That is not to say that the Chagford of the last two centuries has been a dour and dull place to live. Far from it; the photographic archive assembled during the production of this book shows Chagfordians from all walks of life enjoying a wide range of entertainments and pursuits – from picnics, rides and rambles on the moor to carnivals, concerts, amateur dramatics and 'dramatic readings'. Chagford people also went on a variety of trips, often to the seaside. Teignmouth, Dawlish and Paignton were popular destinations, and such expeditions were organised by the local churches, school and Sunday school.

Sport was also a popular diversion: from horse-racing at Kestor or Rushford to football (particularly against age-old rivals Moretonhampstead), and from angling to archery. Even before the swimming pool was built in 1936, swimming in the mill-pounds of the river and at such favourite moorland spots as Teignever or Shilley Pool was popular.

Cricket is another sport that has thrived in Chagford; again, the cricket field on Padley Common has a wonderful setting, even if the original wicket was usually a bit 'green'. Short bowling rarely troubled Chagford batsmen of old, and the outfield was best described as 'lush'! In 2002 the town possesses state-of-the-art sporting facilities provided under the auspices of a highly-professional Recreational Trust, with all-weather football pitches, a first-class wicket

a thriving rural and sporting resort. In particular, demand has grown at the luxury end of the market, and in the Gidleigh Park Hotel Chagford has one of the most exclusive retreats in Europe, popular with the rich and famous from both Britain and, particularly, the USA.

By the end of the twentieth century Chagford had also become popular with European visitors, especially from the Low Countries and Germany. French visitors also find much to admire in Chagford and the town consequently acquires something of a cosmopolitan air in the holiday season. Several local guest houses and hotels now pride themselves on being able to offer a proper welcome to overseas tourists, the traditional 'B & B' sign being quite likely to also bear the wording 'Chambres d'hôte', 'Übernachtung mit Früstück' or 'Kammer met ontbijt' and increasingly 'French (or German, Dutch, Italian or Spanish) spoken'.

As is the case in many Westcountry towns, there are also a goodly number of second homes and holiday cottages in Chagford, although the number declined slightly towards the end of the twentieth century. This was probably as a result of changes in local taxation laws and the rapid escalation of property values in the locality. Like the summer swamping of the roads by tourist traffic, these

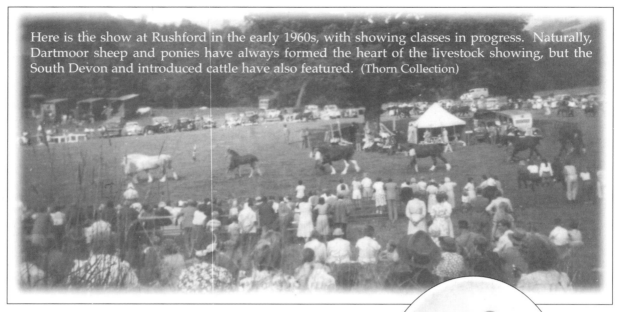

Here is the show at Rushford in the early 1960s, with showing classes in progress. Naturally, Dartmoor sheep and ponies have always formed the heart of the livestock showing, but the South Devon and introduced cattle have also featured. (Thorn Collection)

Below: *Judging from the hats and the motor cars, this shot of the show in progess dates from the early 1930s. On this occasion, the event is apparently being staged on the meadows on the Withecombe side of the river. The fields on the Chagford side were more often used, although as the show expanded it soon came to occupy the whole site.*
(Thorn Collection)

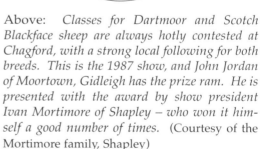

Above: *Classes for Dartmoor and Scotch Blackface sheep are always hotly contested at Chagford, with a strong local following for both breeds. This is the 1987 show, and John Jordan of Moortown, Gidleigh has the prize ram. He is presented with the award by show president Ivan Mortimore of Shapley – who won it himself a good number of times.* (Courtesy of the Mortimore family, Shapley)

Right: *Show President Ivan Mortimore and his wife Mary with Tony Beard, the 'Widecombe Wag', at the 1987 show. Chagford is a very popular show in the summer season and has continued to grow and thrive. The relatively poor road access to the Rushford location led to a move to fields at Doggamarsh, also superbly situated on the banks of the river below Castle Drogo – although much further from the town; indeed, most of it strays into Drewsteignton parish! The new site has the advantage of a greater area of level land and direct access from the main A382 Whiddon Down–Moretonhampstead road.* (Courtesy of the Mortimore family, Shapley)

Above: *Chagford Carnival, which had lapsed since 1962, was revived in 1977 for the Queen's Silver Jubilee, when the band of the Brigade of Coldstream Guards were the stars of the celebraions.* (Thorn Collection)

Above: *These morris dancers were taking part in the Jubilee Carnival, but Chagford Square is nowadays a popular venue for touring morris dancers throughout the summer.* (Thorn Collection)

Centre: *Chagford has always been a patriotic and festive place, likely to break out in swathes of bunting at the least excuse. A Royal jubilee is an ideal occasion for celebration. Here are Coe & Amery's offices at Rock House be-flagged for the 1935 Jubilee of King George V.* (Thorn Collection)

Above left and right: *The 1977 Jubilee celebrations in Chagford. The Jubilee Pageant in the grounds of Chagford House featured a range of floats and tableaux, including youthful maypole dancers, a Ferguson T20 tractor masquerading as Stephenson's Rocket, and schoolchildren in a variety of traditional British costumes.* (Courtesy of the Northway Family, Middlecott)

Left: *Carnival week in Chagford is a relaxed and festive affair, featuring a wide range of events and attractions from Chagford Show through Darts tournaments, pram races and treasure hunts to concerts dances and discotheques. Here, in a quieter interlude, two of Chagford's resident exponents of 'squeeze' – George Allen on accordion and Les Rice on concertina – entertain outside the Market House.*
(Thorn Collection)

Below: *The Chagford Town Band were a feature of carnivals or other celebrations until they were wound up. Here they are in the Square before the Second World War.*

Left: *Chagford carnival has, over the years, seen some extraordinarily ambitious and effective floats, such as this Land Rover-mounted dragon in 1960.* (Thorn Collection)

Right: *The highlight of the carnival is, of course, the procession itself, usually held on the last Saturday in August. After the war, the carnival was held each year until 1962, when it lapsed. It was revived for the 1977 Jubilee celebrations and was then held regularly for a further 20 years. In recent times, with increasing regulation and a steep bill for compulsory insurance, it has not proved possible to hold a carnival every year; but it still happens on occassion. Here is an early postwar carnival parade in the Lower Square, with a rather sepulchural float carried on a Ford AA lorry of pre-war vintage.* (Courtesy of the Northway Family, Middlecott)

Right: *The carnival route takes in all parts of the town, and in this 1950s view the Royalty float takes the corner from the High Steet into New Street, with the Chagford Town Band in attendance. When the band ceased to function in the 1960s, the instruments passed to the junior school, which is why Chagford is now one of the few primary schools in Devon with its own brass band.* (Courtesy of the Northway family, Middlecott)

Left: *Many of the floats are based on farm trailers, such as this early 1950s example pictured passing the Jubilee Hall with Bellacouch in the background.* (Thorn Collection)

Captain Pugwash in the 1977 Jubilee carnival was Nick Daymond; the float is in the old mason's yard below Bellacouch. (Thorn Collection)

Above: *As well as elaborate mobile floats, there has always been a strong equestrian, juvenile and walking entry in the Chagford carnival. Here is a junior prizewinner at the event in the mid 1930s.* (Thorn Collection)

Below: *Chagford always does its carnival royalty proud. Here are three of the carnival queen's floats. One is from the 1950s (below), another from 1960 (inset) and the third from the following year (bottom left).*

(Both Thorn Collection)

(Courtesy of the Mortimore family, Shapley)

Right: *One of the keenest supporters of the carnival is ex-Postmaster Douglas Thorn who, over the years, entertained with an astounding range of individual entries. Here he is in patriotic vogue in 1977 as a bicycling Britannia, complete with 'trident'.* (Thorn Collection)

and practice nets for cricket and a palatial pavilion, all sited at Padley. There are also hard tennis courts in the Jubilee Field, and the outdoor swimming pool has been subject to major renovations.

The 1937 Jubilee Hall has, from the outset, been a centre of the social life of the town and the scene of many a notable dramatic production, concert or dance. In the twentieth century, many organisations have thrived in Chagford, from such formal institutions as the Loyal Order of Buffalos (the 'Buffs' in the local vernacular), the Royal British Legion, the Women's Institute and the Lions, to all manner of ad-hoc and special-interest clubs. These include those who gather to play bridge or chess, people who participate in sport of all kinds, as well as groups interested in conservation, natural history, flower arranging, allotment-holding, local history and model railways.

SHOWS & CARNIVAL

Gardening and horticulture have always been popular in Chagford. The Chagford Horticultural Show started in 1898 and became a Horticultural and Agricultural Show a couple of years later. It has since become an institution and a highly popular fixture in the summer show calendar, normally held on the third Thursday in August. Prince Charles was Show President in the centenary year of 1998, by which time the show had grown to a considerable size. It was originally held on the fields below and behind Mill Street, stretching toward Southcombe and Lower Streets (a site also used for sheep and pony sales when the capacity of the street market was insufficient). The show later moved to the meadows on the river bank at Rushford, a setting that many regarded as incomparable, but the difficult access here led to the show being moved to another riverside site at Doggamarsh, below Castle Drogo, where there is more space and better road access. The show continues to thrive and grow in popularity, and has been held almost every year since 1898.

Another long-lived Chagford institution has been the carnival, usually held on the bank holiday weekend following the Show. The fortunes of the Carnival have waxed and waned somewhat since it was first held in 1887 (the year of Queen Victoria's Golden Jubilee). There was even a 15-year interval – from 1962 to 1977 – when no Carnival was held. The event was revived for Queen Elizabeth II's Silver Jubilee, and has been held in one form or another in most years since. Latterly, increasing red tape has made it more difficult to stage, and insurance and public liability worries have curtailed some of the more ambitious presentations seen in previous years.

Amateur dramatics of all kinds have long been popular in Chagford, right back to the Dramatic Readings held in Victorian times. The construction of the Jubilee Hall in 1935–6 provided a stage with good facilities, still used today for a range of events. The exact nature of the production featuring in these snaps from one of Douglas Thorn's albums isn't recorded, but it was evidently of a highly dramatic nature! (Thorn Collection)

Chagford has long had both a Cub pack and troops of Guides and Brownies. Above: The Cubs c.1970, saluting Scoutmaster Douglas Thorn in the Jubilee Field. (Thorn Collection)

Above and below: Farms in the Chagford area have long proved popular venues for Scout and Guide camps. They were held at Rushford in the early 1970s. (Thorn Collection)

Above: Douglas is seen with four of his charges. (Thorn Collection)

Above: Jamborees and other scouting events were popular. Here, a Chagford Cubs team is ready for the start of a novelty race involving what appears to be potatoes on sticks at a jamboree at Okehampton in the 1960s. It was a serious business in those days... (Thorn Collection)

CHAGFORD LITERATURE & ART

Dartmoor has long aroused a response from artists of all sorts including painters, poets, sculptors and storytellers. Since the middle of the nineteenth century, Chagford has been associated with many novelists that are within the 'rural romantic' school of writing, as well as with the school of Dartmoor landscape painters dominated by F.J. Widgery and William Morrish. The moor around Chagford is particularly picturesque and mountainous – more so with a spot of melodramatic exaggeration – and was a popular subject with Victorian and Edwardian artists, amateur or academician alike. Among the latter, Walter Sickert visited Chagford in 1915, staying at 'Teign View' where Mr Reed let rooms. He painted several subjects in the town, including the churchyard and, more prosaically, the Post Office.

The wild scenery also inspired a number of writers to use the district as a setting for novels, ranging from the homely to the macabre. Undoubtedly, the most famous cycle of novels set on Dartmoor were the 18 books written between 1898 and 1923 by Eden Philpotts, of which the first, *The Children of the Mist*, is set around Chagford and Fernworthy. Among the local places featured in this dark romance are the town itself, together with Rushford Mill, Farm and Bridge (called 'Monk's Barton' by Philpotts; presumably from *Monks* Withecombe and Rushford *Barton*); Coombe Farm (the Drewsteignton Coombe that lies to the north side of the entrance of the Teign Gorge); Whiddon Park (The Deer Park), Cranbrook, Nattadon and Middledown (Meldon) Hills; Batworthy and 'Newtake' (Metherall) Farms, Scorhill and the Wallabrook. Apart from the warmth and romance of the story, the book's vivid descriptive passages paint an appealing picture of Chagford and Dartmoor as they were when the whole area seemed far more remote and mysterious than it does today. The passages describing the area around 'Newtake' are the best portrait we have of the South Teign Valley and Fernworthy before it was all drowned beneath a dam.

Probably the *worst* book to feature Chagford was a laughably improbable spy story concocted – in a moment of mental aberration, one trusts – by the well-known travel writer S.P.B. Mais (author of, among other classics of the genre, *Glorious Devon*). Mais' effort, the *Three-coloured Pencil*, is the sort of tale that only a John Buchan or a Rider Haggard could bring off; in Mais' hands, the only bits that chime true are the topographical details of Dartmoor. Sir Arthur Conan Doyle was much more successful in combining acute topographical observation with fantasy and a touch of horror in the immortal *Hound of the Baskervilles*.

As well as those writers directly inspired by the moorland setting, others have found the peace of this quiet corner of England a fitting place in which to work. One of the most famous literary sojourns was probably that of Evelyn Waugh, who wrote a portion of *Vile Bodies* whilst staying at the Easton Court Hotel.

In more recent times, other artists have made their homes here. How many people realise that many of the mythical and fantastical 'faery' creatures in the 'Star Wars' films have as their birthplace a farmhouse a mile outside Chagford? Wendy and Brian Froud are model makers, illustrators and designers known worldwide, with a long string of major film successes. Working in a not-dissimilar vein is Alan Lee, also an illustrator of the fantastical, who, among other things, has brought to life important texts such as the great Welsh legend, *The Mabinogion*, and J.R.R. Tolkein's *Lord of the Rings*.

Chagford Galleries, established by June des Clayes in 1967 at Dartmoor Lodge, which was Mr Densham's old house in the Square, has a long history of presenting exhibitions of contemporary work by local as well as nationally- and internationally-known artists, sculptors and potters. Many an artist now well-known received their first exposure here, and the gallery attracted some of the best modern artists working around Dartmoor, including Lawson Rudge, Francis Goodchild, Robin Armstrong and Mary Martin. In 2002, there are several art galleries in the town, although fewer artists or craftsmen now live here, as they have been displaced by the relatively high cost of living in modern Chagford.

Chagford people have always been fond of outings, often organised by Douglas Thorn. Shown here are Jack and Hetty Rice at Brentor on one of Douglas' less-ambitious trips, which are known to extend to foreign parts – such as Petticoat Lane market, in East London. (Thorn Collection)

Left: *Doreen Hutchings of Yardworthy Farm and Joyce Mortimore of Higher Shapley with their entry for Belstone Show in 1967. The donkey had been borrowed from Collihole.* (Courtesy of the Mortimore family)

Below: *Brothers John and Ernest Northway on John's motorcycle at Higher Middlecott, 1930s.* (Courtesy of the Northway family)

Below centre: *Maurice Hill, Dartmoor farmer from East Coombe, Chagford, with his sheep, 1970s.* (Maurice Hill)

Bottom right: *A very young Ivan Mortimore at West Coombe with his cousin Jack Hutchings and the farm collie in the early 1930s.* (Mortimore family)

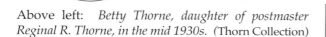

Above left: *Betty Thorne, daughter of postmaster Reginal R. Thorne, in the mid 1930s.* (Thorn Collection)

Above right: *Reginald R. Thorn – Postmaster and pillar of the Plymouth Brethren.* (Thorn Collection)

Below: *Miss Pryor, Sunday school teacher, c.1950.* (Thorn Collection)

Left: *Northway family group in the yard at Higher Middlecott, c.1930. Ernest Northway is on the left with his sister Edith standing on the wagon rave. Their mother, Mrs Northway, is in the centre and on the right with the terrier is her cousin John Coleridge.* (Courtesy of the Northway family, Middlecott)

Below right: *Albert and Fanny Wonnacott of Shapley, at their golden wedding in 1961.* (Courtesy of the Mortimore family, Shapley)

Below: *Two Chagford schoolboys (Freddy Berry and Douglas Thorn) on the top of the church tower in 1937.* (Thorn Collection)

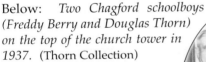

Above: *A meeting at the lane end. The Hutchings and Mortimore families at the Shapley gateway in 1980.* (Mortimore family)

Below: *Miss Ruth Lake of Crosse Park, Chagford – lifelong Chagfordian, bell-ringer, and cashier at Collins' store for many years.* (Thorn Collection)

Below left: *A formally-attired Douglas Thorn with Bill Chard and Bill's lorry, c.1960. The occasion was believed to have been a jumble sale for the Scouts.* (Thorn Collection)

BIBLIOGRAPHY

General Sources

A History of Chagford, Jane Hayter-Hames. Phillimore Books, 1981.

Crossing's Guide to Dartmoor (various editions).

Crossing's Dartmoor Worker (Facsimile). Peninsula Press, 1992.

Dartmoor – a New Study, Crispin Gill (Ed.). David & Charles, 1970.

Dartmoor in the Old Days, James Mildren. Bossiney Books, 1984.

A New Survey of England – Devon, W.G. Hoskins. Collins, 1959.

Unknown Devon, L. du Garde Peach. John Lane/Bodley Head, 1926.

The Making of the English Landscape, W.G. Hoskins.

The Buildings of England – Devon (2nd combined edition), Bridget Cherry with Nikolaus Pevsner. Penguin, 1989.

Old Devon Bridges, by C. Henderson. Wheatons, Exeter, 1938*.

The West in English History (transcripts of BBC radio broadcasts), A.L. Rowse (Ed.). Hodder & Stoughton, 1949.

Historical Geography of England before 1800, H.C. Darby (Ed.). Cambridge University Press, 1969.

The Old Series OS Maps of England and Wales, Volume II: Devon, Cornwall and Somerset. Margary, 1977.

OS Sheet 181 Okehampton (various editions).

White's Directory of Devon, 1850.

Billing's Directory and Gazeteer of the County of Devon, 1857.

Harrods Royal County Directory of Devonshire, 1878.

Kelly's Directory of Devonshire, 1935.

Transactions of the Devonshire Association (various)*.

Farming and Agriculture

General View of the Agriculture of the County of Devon, Charles Vancouver. Pub. 1808. Reprint by David & Charles, 1969.

History from the Farm, by W.G. Hoskins. Faber & Faber, 1970.

Farm records from Great Tree, Shapley and Yeo** farms.

Archives of Rendell's, auctioneers, Chagford.

Mining and Industry

Industrial Archaeology of Dartmoor, Helen Harris. David & Charles, 1972.

Metal Mining, J.B. Richardson. Allen Lane, 1974.

Tin Working in the Eastern District of the Parish of Chagford, Devon, (pamphlet), D. Broughton. Extract from proceedings of the Geologists' Association, 1967.*

English Tin Production & Trade Before 1550, John Hatcher. Clarendon Press, 1973*.

The Dartmoor Tin Industry – a Field Guide, Phil Newman. Chercombe Press, 1998.

Church and School

Church of St Michael the Archangel, Chagford – Official church guide.

John Wesley 1703–1791, Revd John Pollock. Hodder and Stoughton, 1989.

Chagford Parochial and National School Log Books, 1863–1971.

The Buildings of England – Devon (op cit)

Transport and Travel

History of the GWR, by E. MacDermott. GWR, 1927.

The London and South Western Railway, O.S. Nock. Ian Allan, 1965.

BIBLIOGRAPHY

The Teign Valley Railway, Peter Kay. Wild Swan Publications, 2002.
Regional History of the Railways of Britain, Vol I: West Country, David St John Thomas. David & Charles. Fourth Ed., 1973.
Newton Abbot – 150 Years a Railway Town, Iain Rice. Hawkshill, 1997.
Bradshaw's Railway Guide (April 1910 and August 1922 editions).
A History of the National Omnibus Company – the years between 1909–1969, Vol III: Western National and Southern National from 1929. Crawley & Simpson, Calton Promotions, 1990.
The Devon General Omnibus Company – History and Fleet List (various editions). Ian Allan.
Road Vehicles of The GWR, Philip J. Kelly. OPC 1979.

Town and Institutions
Local Council Administration (general introduction), Charles Arnold-Baker. Fourth Ed., 1994.
The Shearers and the Shorn – A Study of Life in a Devon Community, E.W. Martin. Dartington Hall, 1965.
Chagford Parish Council minute books, 1894 – present. Transcripts by Peter Hill, Chagford Parish Council.
Devon Fire-fighter – A Century of Courage and Service, Iain Rice. Halsgrove, 2000.

Leisure and Tourism
The GWR 'Holiday Haunts' guide (various editions, notably 1924).
Dartmoor Inns, Tom Quick. Devon Books, 1992.
The Ward Locke Red Guide to Dartmoor (various editions).
The AA Handbook (various editions).
The RAC Handbook (various editions).
Glorious Devon, S.P.B. Mais. GWR, 1930.

*   = In West Country Studies Library, Exeter.
**   = In Devon County Record Office, Exeter.

An old Chagford tradition was that of electing a May Queen and attendants (lots of attendants!). This custom was kept alive at the school, as seen here in about 1960. (Mortimore family, Higher Shapley)

SUBSCRIBERS

Chris and Lynda Addison, Chagford

Audrey and Edwin Ames

Stewart J. Andrews, Chagford

E.M. Andrews, Chagford

Sylvia Auliffe (née Underhill)

Mrs Peter Barker, Gloucestershire (Chagford connections)

Stuart Barnes, Meldon Hall, Chagford

Mr and Mrs N.A. Beer, Thorn, Chagford

Mrs Leonora Benny, Plymouth, Devon

Mr A.J. Berry, Horrabridge, Devon

Barbara M. Bexon, Allestree, Derby

Jonathan and Ruth Bint, Rushford, Chagford

Paul Boardman and Judith Llewellyn, Chagford

The Bonfield Family, Chagford

Gwen and Dennis Bowles, Exminster, Devon

John L. Boyd

James S.M. Boyd, Perth, Australia

Gladys Kathleen Brewer (Jeffery family), Torquay, Devon

K.J. Burrow, Bucks Cross, Devon

Anna and Simon Butler, Manaton, Devon

Sue Butterfield, Chagford

Ros and Steven Carr, Barne, Moretonhampstead, Devon

Dale A. Chadwick, Chagford

Nicola J. Chadwick, Chagford

Chagford Parish Council

Anne E. Clement (née Morrish), Woodmancote, Cheltenham, Gloucestershire

Richard Colman, Chagford

J. Colpoys Wood, Highbury, Chagford

Marcia Coombe, Chagford

Penny Corke, Chagford

David Cornford, Murchington, Devon

Philip Court, Chagford

Sandra Coventry, Chagford

Joshua Coyne, Chagford

Ian and Tina Coyne, Chagford

Jason Crisp, Teddington, Middx

Ann M. Darlington, Merriott, Somerset

Dartmoor National Park Authority

Lesley Davies, Chagford

Philip Davies, Chagford

Miss Sheila Denham, Torquay, Devon

Basil and Mavis Denham, Chagford

Barry Denham, Chagford

Timothy Dudman, Chagford

Alex, Karen, Jack, Charlotte Duxbury-Watkinson, Chagford

Catherine Endacott, Chagford

The Etheridge Family, Sanderstead, Surrey

Mr R.W. Evans, Boscombe, Dorset

Peter and Cindy Farrington, Chagford

David and Jacqui Floyd-Walker, Chagford

Edward and Josephine Foster, Chagford

Dr James Garratt, Enviresearch Ltd, Newcastle-upon-Tyne

Elise Gaudion and Dean Gardiner, Chagford

Godolphin Fine Art, Chagford

Roberta Greenslade (née Thomas), Taunton, Somerset

Mrs Joyce Haines, Falkenham, Suffolk

Margaret and Philip Halliwell, Chagford

Richard Hammocks, Crockernwell, Devon

Mr and Mrs Hancox, Brean, Somerset

Mike and Lyn Hanrahan, Texas

John and Elizabeth Haws, Chagford

David and Susan Hill, Chagford

Nigel Hill, Cheshire

Peter Hill, Lower Street, Chagford

Margaret R. Hill (née Peardon), Moretonhampstead, Devon

Sarah Howard, Chagford

Amanda A. Howard, Chagford

Peter and Dagmar Huggett

Mr Christopher P. Humphries, Launceston, Cornwall

Stefan Hunt, Chagford

Ricky and Isabel James, Lamb Park, Chagford

Barry Jarvis, Bovey Tracey, Devon

Maurice and Margaret Jeffreys, Chagford

David S. John, Chagford

Colin C. Kilvington, Stoke, Plymouth, Devon

Joy King, Chagford

D. Kingsland, Chagford

M. Komaromy, Chagford

Marjorie Lawrence (née Denham)

Brian Le Messurier, Exeter, Devon

Tim Leaman, Glasgow, Scotland

Marja Lee, Chagford

Alan Lee, Chagford

Linda Lemieux and Peter Montanez, Basketmaker and Woodturner, Chagford

Joe and Mary Lindsay, Chagford

Elizabeth Lockley (née Rowe), Lichfield, Staffordshire

Lydgate House, Postbridge, Devon

Nora E. Lynch, Norton, Gloucester

Mr and Mrs Bruce MacEacharn

J. and Y. Mackegg, Chagford

Gyula Makk, Iskola, Hungary

Jim Manchester, Chagford

Douglas Marsh, Peter Tavy, Devon

Douglas Marsh, Mary Tavy, Devon

Sally R. Massey (née Morrish), Lewes, East Sussex

Patrick McCormack, Chagford

John McCormack

Sonia and Brian Meaden

David Meldrum, Chagford

Gilbert J.C. Molland, Chagford

Gwen and Arthur Mortimore

David I. Neeson, Chagford

Mr and Mrs Nicholson, Henham, Essex

S. Nicholson and J. Hancox, Kestor Glen, Chagford

Barry J. Northcott, North Beer, Launceston, Cornwall

Peter Northway, Chagford

Michael Northway, Chagford

Robert Nowell, Chagford

Mr N.J. Osborne, Westbury, Wiltshire

Roma Painter

Chris and Fiona Pamplin, Symondsbury, Dorset

Mr and Mrs A.J. Parrott, Old Walls, Chagford,

Lucy C. Peck (née Weeks), Tucson, Arizona

Mr and Mrs P.M. Perry, Plymouth, Devon

Mr and Mrs M. Perryman, Drewston, Chagford

Judith Pool, Ring 'O' Bells, The Square, Chagford

Mr and Mrs D.W. Puttick, Eastbourne, East Sussex

Mr and Mrs M.J. Rice

Eric Rice "Jed", Chagford

Ken Rickard, Lydford, Devon

Alan J. Roberton, Berrydown, Gidleigh

Mr and Mrs Rolfe, Tamerton Foliot, Plymouth, Devon

Mr and Mrs Rolfe, Lower Dimson, Cornwall

Edna Rowe, Linden Spinnery, Chagford

Bryce Rundle, Chagford

Robert F.D. Sampson, Chagford

Annie G.M. Sampson, Chagford

Nick and Virginia Sandon, Dunsford

Ian Satow, Week Brook, Chagford

Julie Scoines (née Long), Bovey Tracey, Devon

Sir David Serpell, Dartmouth, Devon

Mrs J. Shephard, Plymouth, Devon

John F. Sheridan

Aubrey M. Slater, Middlecott, Chagford

Carol A. Slaven, Chagford

Mrs Hazel Smith, Easton Cross, Chagford

Frank Smyth, Chagford

Mrs Jane Somers Cocks, Abbotskerswell

Mrs Pauline Spear (née Ellis), Chagford

Norah F. Stocks, Chagford

Sarah E. Stone, Chagford

Alan Stone, Chagford

Greg and Elizabeth Stone, Chagford

Andrew Stone, Chagford

Richard C. Stone, Chagford

Angela M. Stone, Long Ashton, Bristol

Martin C.G. Stone, Chagford

Charles G. Stone, Chagford

Mrs Raymond Stone, Chagford

Mr Leslie James Stoneman

David and Sandra Swetman, Nattadon Farm, Chagford

Eric Thompson, Chagford

Douglas Thorn, Chagford

Arthur Thorn, Moretonhampstead

Anne Thorn, Chagford Post Office

Three Crowns Hotel, Chagford – John Giles

A.J. and E.S. Trott, Reading, Berkshire

Mr G. Waldron, Plymouth, Devon

Louise Walker, Chagford

John and Helen Wallace, Tavistock, Devon

John F.W. Walling, Newton Abbot, Devon

Bob Waburgh, Mendocino, California

Jane Walton, Chagford

Linda A.E. Warne (née Sampson), Manaton, Devon

K.M. Warry, Moretonhampstead, Devon

Miss Sylvia J. Webber

Margaret L. Weeks-Talbott, Santa Barbara,
California

John, Margaret, Darren and Rachel, Weir-Everitt,
Meacombe Cottage, Moretonhampstead

Michael L. Wheeler, Chagford

Agnes Williams, Chagford

Carl, Diane and Alice Wills, Manaton, Devon

Kenneth J. Willsher-Chadwick, Chagford

Terri Windling, Chagford

Ann Winsor, Chagford

David and Sally Wonnacott, Chagford

V.M. Wotton

CONTENTS

On the remote Piggy Island, a group of rare birds are always being annoyed by the local pigs' attempts to steal their last three eggs before they hatch. It's no wonder that they've become...

ANGRY BIRDS™

FOLLOWERZ CALL HIM:
Boss Red, Wood Breaker

KNOWN ALIAS:
The RED BIRD

FORMIDABLE

POWERZ:
Strong leader

MOST DANGEROUZ:
All the time!

STRENGTH:
Average

RED

WARNING!
Red will do anything to protect the eggs!

FEARLESS

LEADER OF THE BIRDZ

PIGGIE PATROL!
WHERE DID THE PIGGIES LAST SPOT RED?

CHUCK

PIGGIE PATROL!
WHERE DID THE PIGGIES LAST SPOT CHUCK?

WARNING!
He's fast as lightning!

HYPERACTIVE

KNOWN ALIAS:
The YELLOW BIRD

EXCITABLE

POWERZ:
In-Flight Acceleration

MOST DANGEROUZ:
At high speed!

PRACTICAL JOKER

STRENGTH:
Normal

FOLLOWERZ CALL HIM: *Lazer Bird, Speedy Bird*

MATILDA

FOLLOWERZ CALL HER:
Egg Master, Chicken Bird

KNOWN ALIAS:
The WHITE BIRD

SENSITIVE

KIND

WARNING!
Once she loses her temper, there's no stopping this protective bird!

PEACE-LOVING

POWERZ:
Drops Egg Bombs

MOST DANGEROUZ:
When she's laying an egg bomb!

STRENGTH:
Weak (before egg drop)
Average (after egg drop)

PIGGIE PATROL!
WHERE DID THE PIGGIES LAST SPOT MATILDA?

BOMB

WARNING!
His explosions can incinerate most obstacles.

SHORT-TEMPERED

KNOWN ALIAS:
The BOMB BIRD

TENSE

POWERZ:
Exploding!

MOST DANGEROUZ:
When he turns red!

EXPLOSIVE

STRENGTH:
Tough

ORGANIZED

FOLLOWERZ CALL HIM:
Stone Smasher

PIGGIE PATROL!
WHERE DID THE PIGGIES LAST SPOT BOMB?

5

WARNING!
Launch as one
but split into
three to attack.

THE BLUES

KNOWN
ALIAS:
JIM, JAKE, JAY

FOLLOWERZ
CALL THEM:
Cluster Birds

STRENGTH:
AVERAGE

NAÏVE

MISCHIEVOUS   SILLY

BUBBLES

STELLA

CUTE

MYSTERIOUS

PRETTY

FIESTY

CHEERFUL

DRAMATIC

WARNING!
May expand massively on impact.

WARNING!
Can trap
objects in
bubbles!

PIGGIE
PATROL!
WHERE DID THE PIGGIES
LAST SPOT STELLA?

KING PIG

ALSO KNOWN AS:
SMOOTH CHEEKS

SELFISH

ROLE:
Ruler of the
Pig Kingdom.

OINKFUL INFO:
Hopes to one day rocket into
snouter space!

GREEDY

PIGGY SECRET:
He's never
actually
tasted
an egg!

ARROGANT

BIRD WATCH!
WHO IS THIS TERRIBLE,
AQUATIC, PIG-MONSTER!?

FOREMAN PIG

SULKY

HAIRY

ALSO KNOWN AS:
BOSS PIG

ROLE:
Leader of the minion pigs.

OINKFUL INFO:
His favourite film is 'Harry Trotter and the piglet of fire!'

STUBBORN

PIGGY SECRET:
His engineering skills are severely lacking, and finished structures are usually on the verge of collapse.

CHEF PIG

NEW PIG!

PIGGY SECRET:
Thinks he could overthrow King Pig and rule with an iron spatula.

ROLE:
Chef for the pigs.

OINKFUL INFO:
Trained to cater for posh swine and cheese parties.

MAVERICK

CALM

OBSERVANT

PROTECT THE EGGS!

An army of piggies is coming!
Use your stickers to help Red
and his fellow birds defend
those precious eggs.

LET'S CRACK SOME YOLKS!

What's the fastest type of egg?

ONE THAT'S RUNNY!

What's an egg's favourite fizzy drink?

YOLK-A COLA!

Who is an egg's favourite cartoon super hero?

HEN 10!

How does an egg speak to its friends?

BY USING A SHELL PHONE!

What did the egg say to the chef?

"I'M BEATEN!"

What's an egg's favourite TV sports programme?

HATCH OF THE DAY.

Did you hear about the egg who went crazy?

DOCTORS SAID IT CRACKED!

What do you call a stolen egg?

POACHED!

What did the hot egg say when it had to leave?

"MUST FRY!"

ON THE WING!

Help Red find his way back to the eggs!

START HERE!

ANGRY BIRDS GO!

The race is on! Use your stickers to decide who'll take pole position and who'll come in dead last!

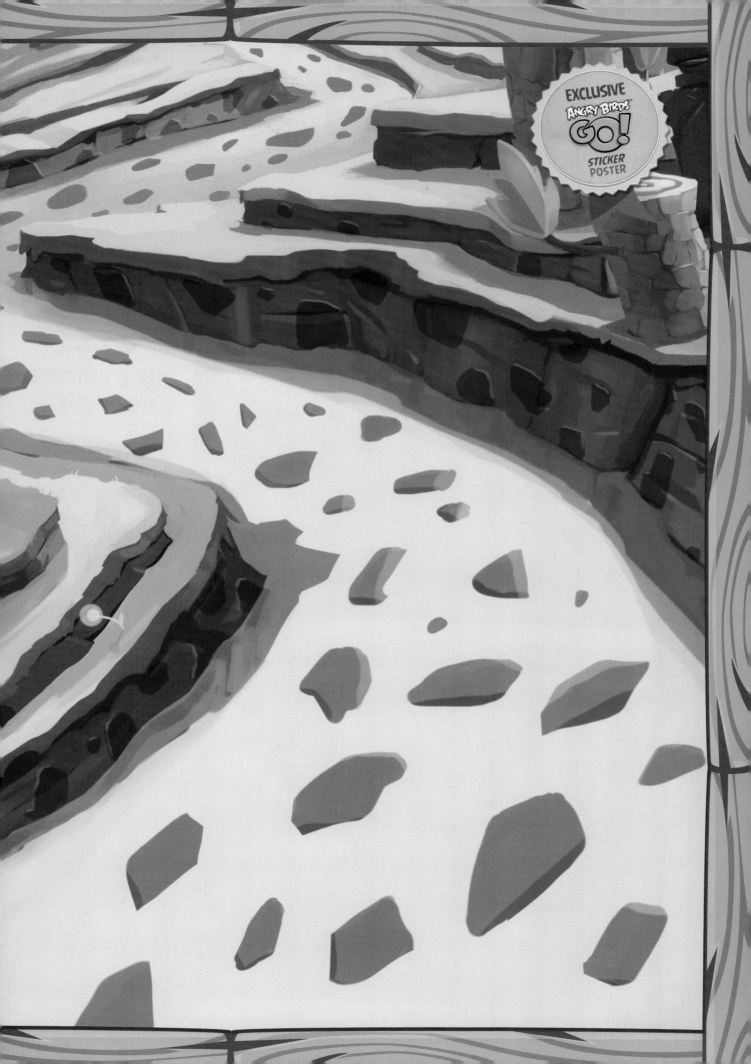

EAGLE EYES!

This race was a photo finish and the camera never lies... or does it? There are in fact six differences in these pictures- see if you can find them all.

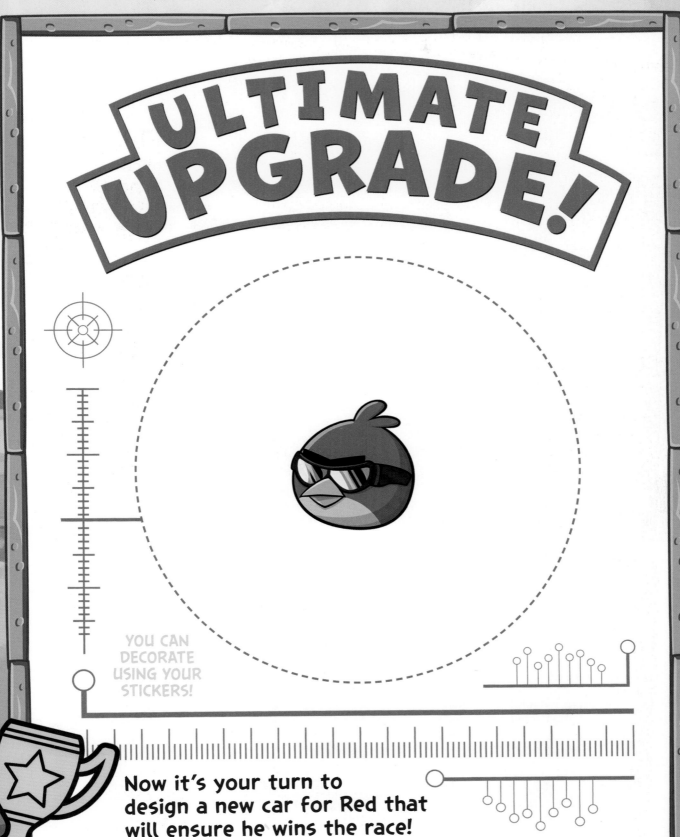

ULTIMATE UPGRADE!

YOU CAN DECORATE USING YOUR STICKERS!

Now it's your turn to design a new car for Red that will ensure he wins the race!

DOWNFALL!

Can you help the Angry Birds crash through these enemy towers? Work out the clues to figure out who can knock down which tower! Use your stickers to match the bird to the tower!

1. Chuck can knock down a tower that's twice as tall as the one the Blue Birds can knock down.

2 Stella can knock over a tower that's one block high.

3. Red can knock down a tower that's one block taller than Chuck's, but two blocks shorter than the one Bomb Bird can destroy.

4. Bomb can knock down the tallest tower.

5. The Blues can knock down a tower that's one block higher than the one Stella can knock down.

EXCLUSIVE ANGRY BIRDS STICKER POSTER

BIRD SEARCH

So you think you know the Angry Birds? You'll need to know their names if you're going to find them in the bubble below.

Look closely– there's also a piggy hiding in the middle!

```
P D M T A T I G
R A E B G L C K J D
D I N E J F A E B H I G P C
R H A E K D M C I E O M L I M B
I D L F O B P A N K H C Q J E D O
C S G E A I H M B E C N E R E T G
B E L C H U C K T D E P M I C L N H
G K L E I J S B M C G S A O D M F C J
A P B N H F K I N G P I G H G H K G E
N I B C A P D O T M F A D Q Y J B P M
P O U Q K G T F K A B H R Y E C O T D
L H B J I B G B L T O N A N S L M P S
L M C F O Z L P I K J N E G A B M
D E I T E C L L H R B I F P J A
K G T N I M D I F O J Y F K
S H B E C A G J A K E R
I A D B E F C H G
```

ANGRY BIRDS™

FLY ANG

EXCLUSIVE ANGRY BIRDS POSTER

THE PIG PICTURE

CAPTURING EGGZ TAKES SKILL, CUNNING N QUICK THINKIN'. THESE R ALL THINGS PIGZ DON'T HAVE! JUST LOOK AT THESE DISASTROUS INVENTIONS THAT FAILED!

INVENTION 1:
Yo-Yolk!

THE PLAN:
Launch captured egg on a string.

WHAT HAPPENED:
Pig got tangled in string and launched himself to the other side of the island.

INVENTION 2:
PositiveEggative!

THE PLAN:
Electrify egg to power it back to King Pig.

WHAT HAPPENED:
Minion Pig caught in power lines and now glows in the dark.

INVENTION 3:
Under-eggchiever!

THE PLAN:
Hide egg underground.

WHAT HAPPENED:
Pig buried himself by mistake!

TROTTER ROTTERS!

Now it's your turn. Use all your inventive skills to create a foolproof way to steal an egg!

Good luck!

INVENTION 4:

Use your stickers to construct a ramp so that the eggs can safely roll from 1 to 2 to 3. Don't make it too steep or the eggs could roll away!

1

2

3

Help the pig steal these eggs away by drawing a boat before he sinks!

INVENTION 5:

INVENTION 6:

....

Use your stickers to help the pigs hide the eggs from the Angry Birds!

INVENTION 7:

....

Now's your chance to devise a super trap for the eggs. It could be a cage or a mechanical arm to hold them or maybe a giant pig robot! It's up to you!

ARE YOU A GREEDY PIGGY?

WHAT KIND OF PIGGY WOULD YOU BE? ANSWER THESE QUESTIONS TO FIND OUT WHETHER YOU'D BE KING OF THE HEAP OR BOTTOM OF THE TROUGH!

1. WHAT IS YOUR FAVOURITE SNACK?

A. FRUIT.
B. CRISPS.
C. SWEETS.

2. DO YOUR FRIENDS THINK YOU ARE....?

A. EASY-GOING.
B. A TERRIBLE PLANNER.
C. THEIR LEADER.

3. WHAT IS 5 + 6?

A. ERM... I DON'T HAVE ENOUGH FINGERS TO ANSWER THAT BUT IT'S MORE THAN 10!
B. 100. EASY!
C. I DON'T HAVE TIME FOR SUMS– ASK ONE OF MY MINIONS.

4. THERE'S AN EXTRA PIECE OF CAKE LEFT OVER AFTER TEA. WHAT WOULD YOU DO?

A. SHARE IT WITH ALL MY BUDDIES.
B. CUT IT UP IN FRONT OF MY EMPLOYEES AND SHARE IT THROUGH ALL MY BREAKS.
C. EAT IT YOURSELF. YUMMY!

MOSTLY A'S
YOU'RE A MINION PIG! YOU ARE A GOOD FRIEND TO HAVE AND YOU'RE HAPPY TO GO WITH THE FLOW.

5. WHAT IS YOUR FAVOURITE TYPE OF HAT?

A. A BASEBALL CAP.
B. A CYCLING HELMET.
C. A CROWN.

6. DO YOU PREFER YOUR EGGS...?

A. SCRAMBLED.
B. BOILED WITH TOAST SOLDIERS.
C. HIDDEN AWAY SO NO ONE ELSE CAN TOUCH THEM.

7. WHICH TYPE OF SEAT DO YOU PREFER?

A. A SOFA TO SIT WITH MY FRIENDS.
B. SOMETHING COZY SO THAT I CAN HAVE A GOOD NAP.
C. A GOLDEN THRONE LOOKING DOWN ON EVERYONE ELSE.

8. HOW DO YOU LIKE TO TRAVEL?

A. ON FOOT.
B. WITH MY HENCHMEN.
C. WITH FRIENDS CARRYING ME ON THEIR SHOULDERS!

9. DO YOUR DREAMS SEEM...?

A. POSSIBLE.
B. AMBITIOUS.
C. COPIED FROM SOMEBODY ELSE'S DREAMS.

10. WHAT IS YOUR FAVOURITE WAY TO CONTACT FRIENDS?

A. PHONE, IT HAS A MORE PERSONAL TOUCH.
B. E-MAIL, SO THAT I CAN REACH MY SUBORDINATES AT THE SAME TIME.
C. LETTER USING A STAMP WITH MY PICTURE ON IT. OH, AND I'LL DICTATE THE LETTER.

11. DO YOU THINK A GOOD LEADER SHOULD...?

A. BE WISE.
B. AVOID WORKING.
C. EAT ALL THE PIES.

MOSTLY B'S

YOU ARE DEFINITELY FOREMAN PIG! YOU'RE SO STUBBORN THAT YOU USUALLY GET YOUR WAY AT THE END OF THE DAY.

MOSTLY C'S

YOU'RE KING PIG! NO ONE KNOWS IF YOU'RE A GOOD LEADER OR NOT, BUT THEY CAN GUESS WHERE ALL THE CAKES WENT, YOU GREEDY PIG!

SPLIT RESULT
(THE SAME NUMBER OF TWO OR MORE LETTERS)

YOU'RE CHEF PIG! YOU HAVE PLENTY OF IDEAS AND YOU'RE YOUR OWN BOSS!

THE SPACE RACE!

The Angry Birds must keep their eggs safe—even in outer space! Add your stickers to the scene to make sure they stay out of the reach of those greedy piggies!

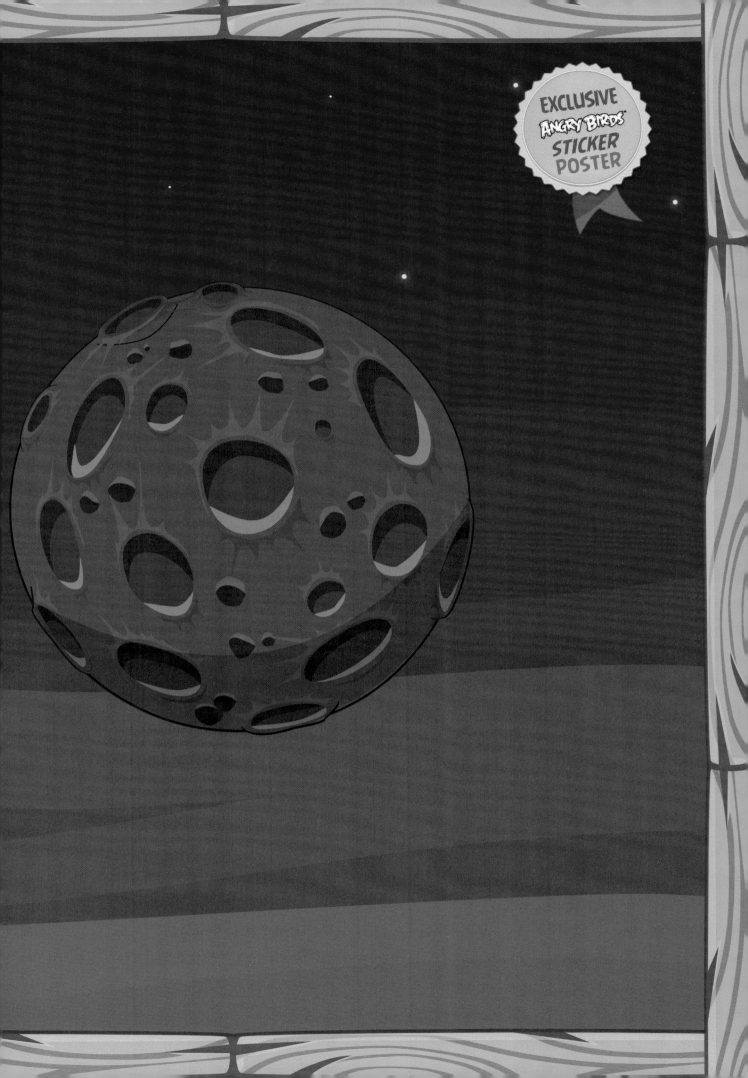

SPACE COLOURING!

USE YOUR BRIGHTEST PENS TO ADD SOME COLOUR TO THE COLD VACUUM OF SPACE!

CA-CAW!

34

THE USS OINKTEPRISE!

Now it's your turn! Design a brilliant new space weapon which the pigs could use to steal the eggsteroids. You could add some pig stickers to show how the weapon is operated, too!

SPACE MOBILE

YOU WILL NEED:

- A sheet of cardboard, such as the back of a cereal or frozen pizza box.
- Two drinking straws (you can get these from a fast food restaurant)
- A reel of cotton thread.
- String.
- Scissors (always ask an adult to help).
- Paper glue and sticky tape.

INSTRUCTIONS:

1. To make your mobile, start by carefully cutting out the characters from this page. If you don't want to spoil the Annual, you can make a copy of this page and use that.

2. Using glue, stick one half of each character to the cardboard—use the dotted line to guide you.

3. Use glue or sticky tape to attach a length of cotton to the reverse side so that it sticks up to a length of about 8 cm will do.

TOP TIP: You don't need to be too neat about this because you'll cover up the glue in a moment!

4. Fold the character down the line, and stick that half to the other side, hiding the thread.

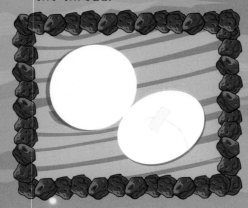

5. Cut out the characters—now they should look the same on both sides.

You now have the hanging characters for your mobile! Now you need to make the mobile structure to hold them.

6. Create a cross-shape using the two straws so that they meet in the centre. You can stick the straws using glue or sticky tape.

7. Next, stick or tie some string to the centre so that it hangs to about 15 cm—you may need an adult to help you. A simple knot works best.

8. Now take your characters and fix the ends of the strings to the ends of the straws—one for each end, so that the mobile is balanced. Use sticky tape. You may need to test the balance a few times to get it just right.

9. Now, take the long end of string that's in the centre of the mobile and tie it wherever you want to hang your mobile! You'll probably need an adult or a taller brother or sister to help!

Hang your mobile somewhere the breeze will catch it, so that it spins around.

TOP TIP: To really bring your mobile to life, add some glow stars to the wall behind it —these are available in most toy and craft shops and they glow in the dark!

CATCH THE EGG!

HOW TO PLAY:

1. First, place the angry bird and greedy pig counters on the starting square in row 1, and place the egg on its own starting square in row 2.

2. Both players roll the dice to see who will be the bird and who will be the pig. The angry bird is the player who rolls the highest number. (If you get the same number, just roll again)

3. First the greedy pig player rolls for the egg and moves it that number of squares. If the egg lands on a blue circle it gets another go!

4. The angry bird player rolls next, followed by the pig.

5. Once both players have had their turn the egg rolls again. That means that every round, the egg gets a turn too!

6. Take it in turns to chase after the egg, following whatever instructions are on the squares that you land on.

7. The egg never follows instructions-except when it lands on a blue circle.

8. Players don't get to roll again if they land on a blue circle-that's only for the egg!

YOU WILL NEED:

- Two players
- Three counters (which you can make from the stickers inside this Annual)
- 1 Dice

START HERE

BAD START. ROLL AGAIN!

14

FACE OFF! WHOEVER THROWS THE HIGHEST MOVES NEXT.

12

15   16

KING PIG'S GETTING HUNGRY- BIRDS ROLL AN EVEN NUMBER, PIGS GO AGAIN!

36   35   34   33

PATH BLOCKED! ROLL AN ODD NUMBER TO MOVE.

37

TOLD A GREAT JOKE! ROLL AGAIN!

39

CAUGHT PLAYING FANCY DRESS MISS A TURN WHILE YOU GET CHANGED.

42   43

HERE'S A GREAT GAME FOR TWO PLAYERS.

THOSE GREEDY PIGS HAVE GOT THEIR HANDS ON AN EGG...
BUT CAN THEY KEEP IT? THE EGG'S ROLLING AWAY AND ONLY
YOU CAN CATCH IT! BUT WILL YOU BE A HEROIC BIRD OR A
GREEDY PIG?

THE OBJECT OF
THE GAME:

BOTH PLAYERS
ARE TRYING TO
CATCH THE EGG.
THE WINNER IS
THE PLAYER WHO
EITHER LANDS ON
OR OVERTAKES
THE EGG!

HOWEVER, IF
NEITHER PLAYER
CATCHES THE EGG
BY THE FINAL
LEVEL, FOLLOW
THE SLIDE BACK
TO THE TOP AND
KEEP CHASING!

NOW—LET'S
SCRAMBLE!

3

4

HEY, HEY,
SLOW
DOWN!

MISS A GO!

6

10

SLIP ON
SOME YOLK...

SLIDE
AHEAD TWO
SQUARES.

8

EGG
START
HERE

SPEED-
BOOST!
DOUBLE THE
NUMBER
YOU ROLL.

20

21

22

LOST YOUR
WAY...

GO BACK
THREE
SQUARES.

24

30

29

28

SURROUNDED
BY ANGRY
BIRDS

PIGS SKIP A GO.
BIRDS ROLL
AGAIN!

26

25

NOW YOU'RE
REALLY
ANGRY!

ROLL AGAIN
AND MAKE
IT COUNT!

45

46

47

48

49

END
NO EGG?
FOLLOW THE
PATH BACK TO
THE START!

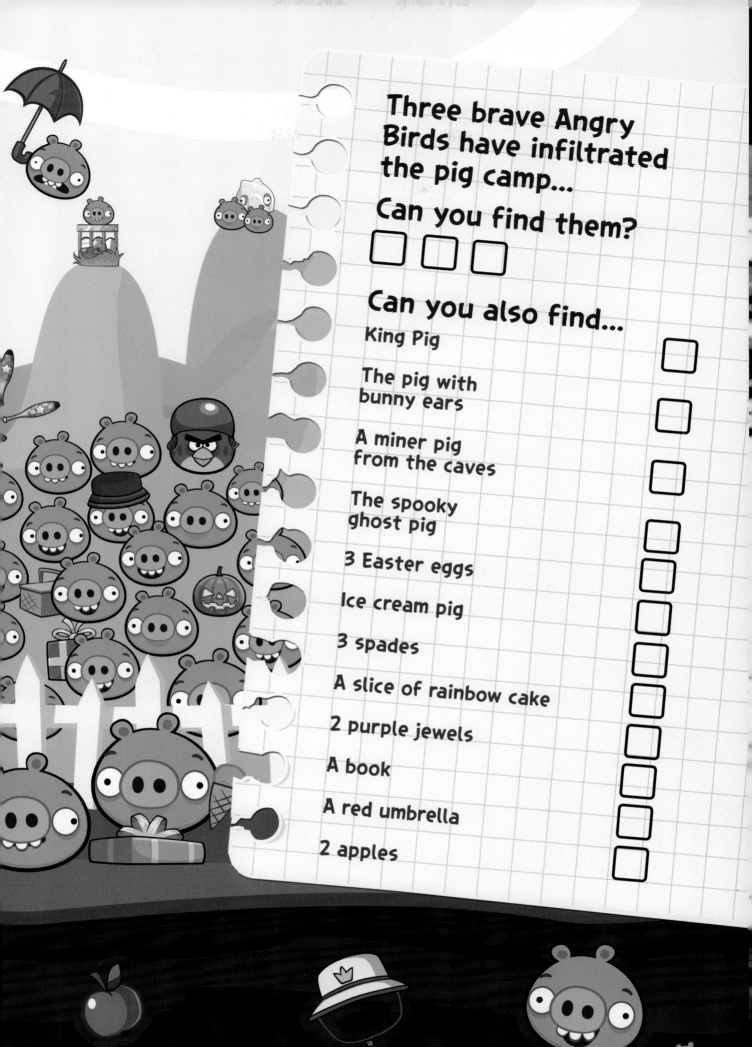

Three brave Angry Birds have infiltrated the pig camp...
Can you find them?

☐ ☐ ☐

Can you also find...

King Pig ☐

The pig with bunny ears ☐

A miner pig from the caves ☐

The spooky ghost pig ☐

3 Easter eggs ☐

Ice cream pig ☐

3 spades ☐

A slice of rainbow cake ☐

2 purple jewels ☐

A book ☐

A red umbrella ☐

2 apples ☐

FRIEND OR FOE?

TERENCE HAS SUNK UNDERGROUND AND NEEDS YOUR HELP TO SPOT THE SILHOUETTES OF HIS PALS... AND KNOW WHO TO AVOID!

CAN YOU NAME ALL EIGHT?

1

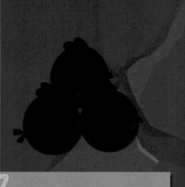

2

3

4

5

6

7

8

QUIZ TIME

So you think you know the Angry Birds! See if you can answer these tricky questions...

EASY:

1. Who is the born leader of the Angry Birds?

2. Name this bird.

3. Who is the fastest bird?

4. Which bird lays egg bombs?

5. How many Blue Birds are there in all?

MEDIUM:

6. What is the name of the island where the Angry Birds live?

7. What's the first thing that happens when Terence gets angry?

8. How many eggs does King Pig have in his secret egg stash?

9. What are the names of the three blue birds?

10. What is Chuck known as in Angry Birds Space?

HARD:

11. Who drives this car?

Fill in the blanks to make the names of some Angry Birds game levels. *(Clue-they're all piggy related words)*

12. _ _ _ O'ween

13. Seasons _ _ _ _ _ings.

14. Summer _ _ _nic.

15. Who is the biggest pig in Angry Birds Space?

EXCLUSIVE
ANGRY BIRDS
STICKER
POSTER

ANSWERS

PAGE 15...ON THE WING!

PAGE 18...EAGLE EYES!

PAGE 20...DOWNFALL!

01. Chuck - 4 blocks
02. The Blues - 2 blocks
03. Red - 5 blocks
04. Stella - 1 block
05. Bomb - 7 blocks

PAGE 22...BIRD SEARCH

PAGE 42...UNDERCOVER MISSION

PAGE 44...FRIEND OR FOE?

01. Minion Pig
02. The Blues
03. Chuck
04. Red
05. Bomb
06. Matilda
07. Egg
08. Foreman Pig

PAGE 45...QUIZ TIME

01. Red
02. Stella
03. Chuck
04. Matilda
05. 3
06. Piggy Island
07. He sinks into the ground
08. None!
09. Jim, Jake, Jay
10. Lazer Bird
11. Bomb
12. HAM O'ween
13. GREEDings
14. Summer PIGnic
15. Big Bork

W hen the Second World War began in 1939, despite the many signs that conflict was imminent, no nation was truly ready for it – including the Germans. Yet German forces surprised even themselves by steamrollering their way through Europe, the Luftwaffe's advanced fighters largely able to overcome their less able opponents.

The only nation able to withstand the Nazi ground assault was Great Britain – in large part due to the protective barrier formed by the English Channel. In the air, it was a different story however. Thanks to its own advanced fighters and the skill and heroism of its pilots, the RAF alone was able to hold its own against the full and growing might of the Luftwaffe for more than a year – with the rest of Europe defeated, neutral or siding with the Germans, and the Soviets and the USA remaining neutral.

During this time, neither of these latter two nations possessed fighter aircraft capable of tackling the Luftwaffe's best on equal terms. However, as Britain continued to resist, they both ploughed massive resources into improving their fighters – resulting in many of the types included in this publication.

When the Soviets were forced into the war by the German invasion commencing on Sunday, June 22, 1941, their next generation aircraft were and huge problems were encounte development of types such as the Yak-1. The German war machine c and unreliable Soviet aircraft in the the tide was finally turned.

The USA, for its part, was able combat experience and some of its best late-war fighters were derived directly from interaction with the British – the Mustang was originally designed for use by the RAF. By the time the USA was dragged into the war by the attack on Pearl Harbor on Sunday, December 7, 1941, it had the beginnings of a fighter force to be reckoned with.

During the final year of the war, all three of these Allies were operating hugely powerful and capable fighters that could not only take on the Luftwaffe's best but overmatch them.

Allied Fighters examines the fighter aircraft flown by the RAF, Soviet VVS and US Army Air Force during that time and presents detailed illustrations of notable individual machines.

Dan Sharp

ABOUT CLAES SUNDIN

I llustrator and author Claes was born in 1957 and lives in the southern part of Sweden. Since finishing four years of studies at the University of Uppsala, he has been active as a teacher, marketer, photographer and art director, among other occupations.

Since childhood, Claes has had a strong interest in everything concerning the combat aircraft of the Second World War and later. This interest stems from the time when he, as a boy of seven, started building and collecting plastic scale models. Simultaneously, he has been a keen draftsman for as long as he can remember, as well as an accomplished CGI artist in more recent years. At present, Claes is producing books, writing articles and lecturing. Up to now he has produced more than 2000 CGI profiles, mostly of aircraft, but also of Second World War armour.

His previously published books include: Luftwaffe Fighter Aircraft in Profile (1997), Deutsche Jagdflugzeuge (1998), More Luftwaffe Fighter Aircraft in Profile (2002), Luftwaffe Fighter Aircraft, Limited Edition (2011), Luftwaffe Fighter Aircraft, Profile Book No 1 (2013), Allied Fighter Aircraft, Profile Book No 2 (2013), Tiger and Panther Tanks (2014), Luftwaffe Fighter Aircraft, Profile Book No 3 (2014), Luftwaffe Attack Aircraft, Profile Book No 4 (2015), Profiles of German Tanks (2015), Luftwaffe Night Fighters, Profile Book No 5 (2016) and Luftwaffe Fighter Aircraft, Profile Book No 6 (2016). In addition, he has provided aircraft and tank profiles, photo refinement, and artwork for many other books and papers.

Claes says: "As a long time profile artist, I am well aware that a few of the profiles included in this publication will be the subject of some criticism. The reader however, must acknowledge that all the profiles included are based on solid photographic documentation. I will always use at least one reference photo, more if available, of the subject. I seek the best photos available for the related close-up details as well.

"However, misinterpretations could naturally occur, especially regarding the colours I've chosen for the different profiles. One has to appreciate the difficulty of interpreting the colours from dated black and white photographs. But know that I have, together with my colleagues, made the utmost effort to determine the actual appearance and colouring of the individual aircraft profiles presented here."

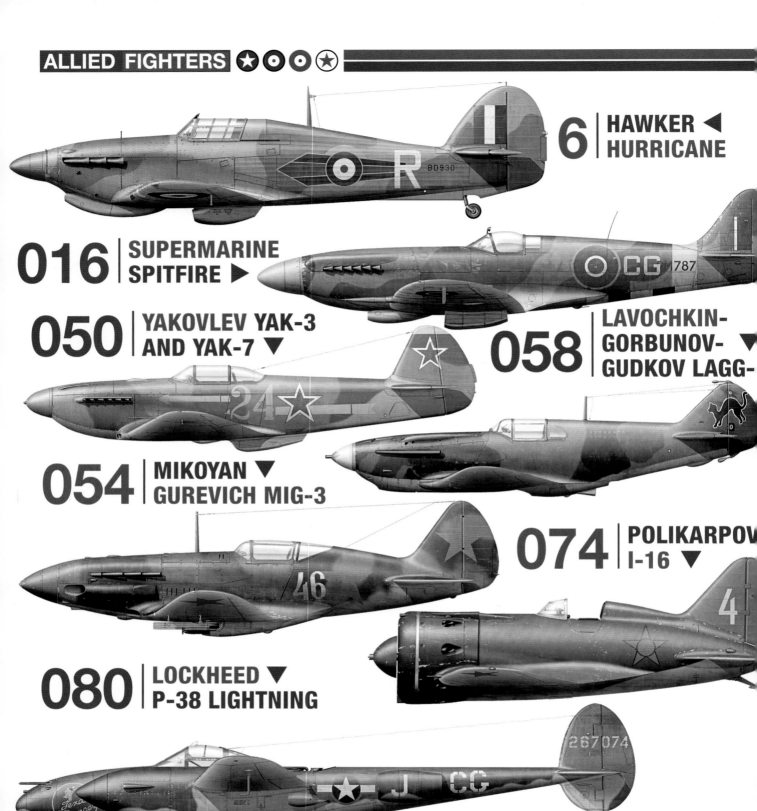

6 | **HAWKER ◄ HURRICANE**

016 | **SUPERMARINE SPITFIRE ►**

050 | **YAKOVLEV YAK-3 AND YAK-7 ▼**

058 | **LAVOCHKIN-GORBUNOV-GUDKOV LAGG- ▼**

054 | **MIKOYAN ▼ GUREVICH MIG-3**

074 | **POLIKARPOV I-16 ▼**

080 | **LOCKHEED ▼ P-38 LIGHTNING**

All illustrations:
CLAES SUNDIN

Design:
ATG-MEDIA.COM

Publishing director:
DAN SAVAGE

Publisher:
STEVE O'HARA

Reprographics:
JONATHAN SCHOFIELD & PAUL FINCHAM

Production editor:
DAN SHARP

Marketing manager:
CHARLOTTE PARK

Commercial director:
NIGEL HOLE

Published by:
MORTONS MEDIA GROUP LTD, MEDIA CENTRE, MORTON WAY, HORNCASTLE, LINCOLNSHIRE LN9 6JR.

Tel. 01507 529529

MORTONS MEDIA GROUP LTD

Printed by: **WILLIAM GIBBONS AND SONS, WOLVERHAMPTON**

ISBN: 978-1-911276-40-1

032 | **HAWKER** ▶
TYPHOON

038 | **HAWKER** ◀
TEMPEST

044 | **YAKOVLEV**
YAK-1 ▶

062 | **LAVOCHKIN**
LA-5 ◀

068 | **LAVOCHKIN**
LA-7 ▶

086 | **BELL P-39/P-400**
AIRACOBRA ▼

096 | **REPUBLIC P-47**
THUNDERBOLT ▶

090 | **CURTISS** ▼
P-40 WARHAWK

130 | **ALLIED AIR**
FORCES
RANKS CHART

114 | **NORTH AMERICAN**
P-51 MUSTANG ▲

HAWKER HUR

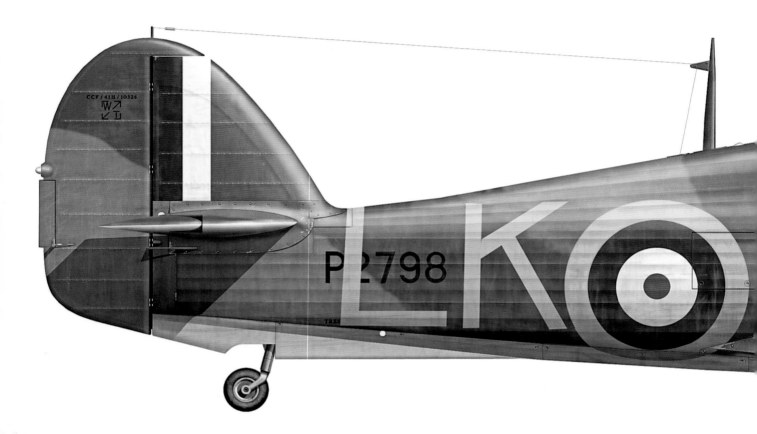

1935–1944

Hawker's legendary Hurricane must be in the running for most highly regarded British combat aircraft of all time and its vital importance to the RAF during the early years of the war cannot be overstated.

The Hurricane that first appeared in 1935 was the ultimate product of a successful evolutionary line, beginning nearly a decade earlier with the Hawker Hart – a two-seater biplane light bomber.

Designed during peacetime when defence budgets were small, the Hart nevertheless attracted substantial interest. Hawker capitalised on this by developing a wide range of variants based around the same winning features – an aerodynamic airframe and powerful Rolls-Royce V12 engine – and among these was a single-seat fighter, the Hawker Fury.

Fitted with a Rolls-Royce Kestrel engine, the Fury became the first British fighter to exceed 200mph in level flight. Its aerobatic performance and rate of climb were exceptional too, but relatively few examples were ordered as

the country struggled through the ravages of the Great Depression.

With the economy turning a corner, in 1933 Hawker entered into discussions with the Air Ministry concerning a proposal to develop the Fury as a new monoplane fighter. The company's chief designer, Sydney Camm, had come up with a suitable design by January 1934 but revisions were required by the ministry including an enclosed cockpit and retractable undercarriage. With these added, a new specification was drawn up around the design in August 1934. Six months later, Hawker was awarded a contract to build a prototype of the new single-seater and the firm's engineers set to work.

Construction was completed within nine months and the resulting aircraft, serial K5083, first flew on November 6, 1935,

RICANE

Hurricane Mk.I

This aircraft, P2798, was flown by Pilot Officer Ian R Gleed of 87 Squadron, based at Lille-Seclin in France during mid- to late-May 1940. Gleed joined the unit as a replacement on May 17 and quickly became an ace, destroying a pair of Messerschmitt Bf 110Cs the following day, then two Dornier Do 17Zs and a Bf 109E the day after – also sharing in an He 111 and with another Bf 109E claimed as a probable. He was killed in action on April 16, 1943, aged 26, having achieved 13 victories in air combat plus three shared.

powered by a Rolls-Royce PV-12 – the earliest version of what would later be renamed Merlin. The aircraft had a metal cross-braced fabric-covered fuselage, fabric-covered wings and a tailplane supported by struts. Armament was to be four .303in Browning machine guns in each wing, though a version with four 20mm cannon had been proposed and rejected.

In early 1936, after company tests, K5083 was sent to the Aircraft and Armament Experimental Establishment at Martlesham Heath for handling trials. Finally, in mid-1936 the aircraft was given the name Hurricane and put into full scale production with an order for 600 examples on the company's books.

But even as production lines were being prepared, the

Hurricane was undergoing a redesign. Its engine controls were revised, its engine mountings were altered and its nose cowlings were changed to accommodate a new powerplant – the 1030hp Merlin II.

This resulted in further delay and it would be over a year from the production order being placed to the first production model aircraft being flown, on October 12, 1937. Once the design was frozen, however, the experienced Hawker workshop crews were able to turn out Hurricanes more rapidly than expected. They made 40 in the first three months and 111 Squadron, stationed at Northolt, received enough machines to equip a flight before Christmas 1937.

Spin trials necessitated an on-the-run modification at this point and a larger rudder was fitted in addition to an under-fin. These began to appear on

Hurricanes reaching squadrons from February 1938 onwards. Some 200 Hurricanes had reached units by the end of 1938 and the British government had placed a second order, for another 1000, in the meantime.

The aircraft was proving to be such a success that several foreign governments ordered it too, including Romania, Yugoslavia and Belgium. Hawker had by now completed a new factory at Langley to help build it and a deal was signed on January 4, 1939, for the Canadian Car and Foundry Company to build it under licence in Canada.

The first Canadian Hurricane, a Mk.I, flew in January 1940 and at the end of that year a new Canadian-exclusive variant was created, the Mk.X, which was powered by a Packard-built Merlin 28 engine and had 12 Browning

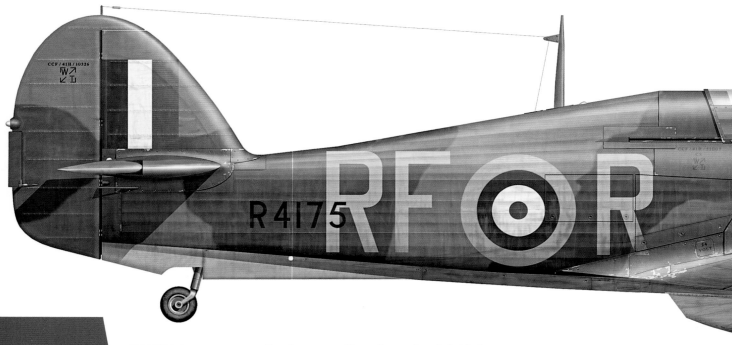

machine guns corresponding to the Hurricane Mk.IIB in England. A Mk.XI was made in small numbers as a trainer with a modified throttle system but the major Canadian production model was the Mk.XII, first flown in November 1941. A later version with only eight guns was designated the Mk.XIIA.

Meanwhile, further design changes up to the beginning of 1939 in England included the replacement of the Merlin II with the 1310hp Merlin III, standardisation of triple ejector exhaust manifolds and the adoption of a three-bladed de Havilland two-pitch propeller. There was a move towards replacing the fabric wing covering

with a stressed metal skin too.

Experimental trials were conducted with tropical filters and sand guards, in the increasingly likely event that the Hurricane would be required to fly in the Middle East, and one machine was tested with a 20mm Oerlikon autocannon fitted in a pod under each wing. Later in the year another new engine, the Merlin XII, was trialled.

When the Second World War began, on September 3, 1939, there were 19 RAF squadrons flying a full complement of Hurricanes. It was one of these aircraft, a 1 Squadron

Hurricane Mk.I

Having joined the RAF in 1935, Robert S Tuck of 257 Squadron was promoted to squadron leader in September 1940. V6864 was his Hurricane while based at Coltishall, England, during December 1940. On January 28, 1942, he was hit by anti-aircraft fire, forced to land in occupied France and taken prisoner. By that time he had achieved 29 victories plus two shared. He later escaped from Stalag Luft III on February 1, 1945, and spent time fighting alongside Russian troops before returning home via the British embassy in Moscow.

▼

◀ Hurricane Mk.I

The highest scoring RAF pilot during the Battle of Britain was Sergeant Josef Frantisek of 303 (Polish) Squadron. He flew R4175 while based at Northolt, Ealing, England, during August 1940. Frantisek, who was actually a Czech, had escaped to Poland in 1938 when the Nazis occupied Czechoslovakia. He was killed in a flying accident on October 8, 1940, with a total of 17 air combat victories to his name.

Hurricane Mk.I

Flying Officer William L 'Willie' McKnight, of 242 Squadron based at Duxford, England, flew P2961 with its distinctive half skeleton and boot-kicking-Hitler artwork during September 1940. McKnight was the second Canadian ace of the war and had 17 victories in air combat plus two shared when he was shot down and killed, aged 22, on January 12, 1941, while taking part in a fighter sweep over Calais.

▼

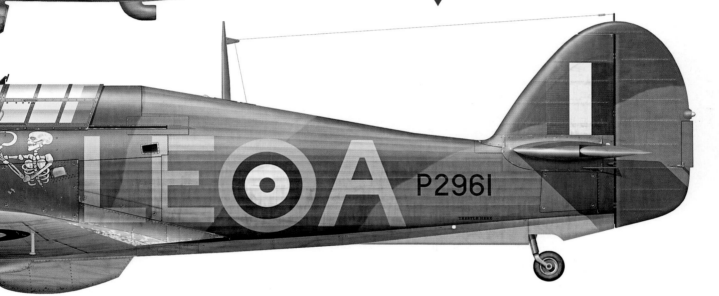

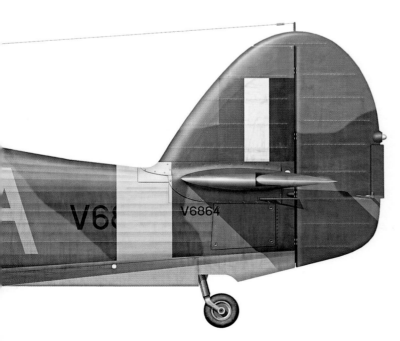

Hurricane flown by Pilot Officer Peter 'Boy' Mould, that would score the RAF's first air-to-air victory of the war – shooting down a German Dornier Do 17 P reconnaissance aircraft near Toul in France on October 30, 1939.

During the invasion of Norway in 1940, it became evident that the RAF lacked fighters equipped for long-range operations, particularly over water, and Hawker began working on the provision of new underwing fuel tanks, floats and ski undercarriages for the Hurricane. The firm also continued to ramp up production – the RAF's Fighter Command had an average of 1326 Hurricanes on strength between July 10 and October 31, 1940.

Another Rolls-Royce Merlin, the XX, became standard equipment from August 1940 – resulting in the Hurricane Mk.IIA. Front line units began to receive these from September, but the design continued to evolve with

A HURRICANE SCORED THE RAF'S FIRST AERIAL VICTORY OF THE WAR ON OCTOBER 30, 1939

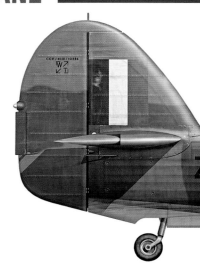

the Mk.IIA Series 2 featuring a slightly lengthened nose.

Armament was improved with the addition of yet another four .303 Browning machine guns, for a total of 12. This resulted in another variant – the Mk.IIB. The Mk.IIC had an even more potent armament of four 20mm cannon, with production commencing on January 20, 1941.

The Battle of Britain, between August and October 1940, had seen the air war become one of attrition with Hurricane losses mounting rapidly. Yet by March 1941 Hawker was able to produce 12 Hurricanes every day. And the output of the Kingston, Brooklands, Langley and Hucclecote

factories was supplemented by the arrival of 10 Hurricanes a week by ship from Canada.

During August 1941, an initial batch of 39 Mk.IIA Series 2 and Mk.IIB Hurricanes were sent to Russia to help Britain's ally fight off the German invasion, which had begun five months earlier. Shipments continued as the war progressed and a grand total of 2952 Hurricanes were sent – though the number that actually arrived is uncertain since many were lost when the vessels carrying them were sunk. Hurricane deliveries made up the largest part of all aid sent to Russia by Britain.

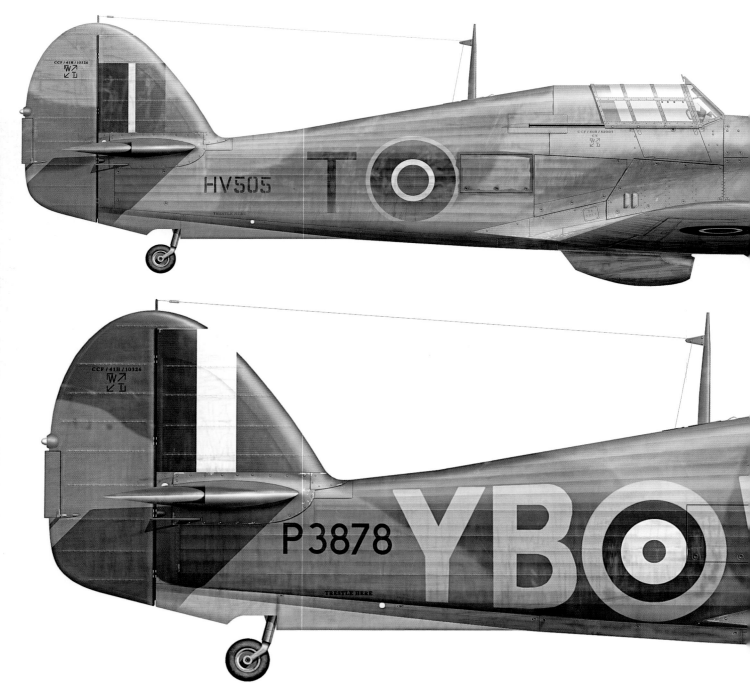

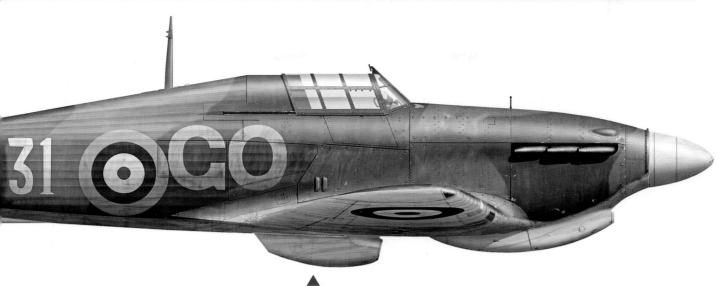

Hurricane Mk.IIB

Flying Officer John F D 'Tim' Elkington joined 134 Squadron in July 1941 when it was forming up at Leconfield for service in Russia. He flew this aircraft while based in Vayenga, USSR, on September 17, 1941. During the Battle of Britain, Elkington shot down a Messerschmitt Bf 109 on August 15, 1940, only to be shot down and wounded himself the following day by German ace Helmut Wick. He ended the war with that one victory plus two shared and at the time of writing was still alive aged 96.

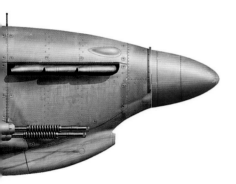

Hurricane Mk.IIC ◀

Hawker Hurricane Mk.IIC HV505 saw service with 336 (Greek) Squadron, stationed at Sidi Barani in Egypt during May 1943.

Hurricane Mk.I ▼

On September 24, 1940, flying Hurricane P3878, Flying Officer Harold Bird-Wilson of 17 Squadron, based at Debden, England, had the dubious distinction of becoming the 40th 'kill' of German ace Adolf Galland of JG 26. He bailed out, landed in the Thames and was picked up by a navy vessel. He went on to serve throughout the war and afterwards, rising to the rank of air vice marshal. Bird-Wilson died in 2000 aged 81.

BY MARCH 1941, MORE THAN A DOZEN HURRICANES WERE BEING BUILT EVERY DAY

Production of an even more powerfully-armed Hurricane, the Mk.IID, commenced in 1942. This had a pair of 40mm cannon in underwing pods plus a pair of wing-mounted Brownings loaded with tracers for aiming purposes. Its primary role was ground-attack against tanks and other armoured fighting vehicles.

A handful of Mk.IIDs were used in Europe, fitted with Rolls-Royce BF cannon, while the majority of them were sent to the Middle East fitted with Vickers 'S' Class cannon. The former had just 12 rounds per gun while the latter had 15.

With a variety of different Hurricane marks now in use, Hawker decided that a universal wing should be produced which could mount a variety of different loads – particularly for ground-attack. This, combined with fitment of a 1620hp Merlin 24/27, became the basis for the new Mk.IV. The Mk.III, which was to have been a Hurricane powered by an American Packard-produced

Hurricane Mk.I ▶

P3059 was flown by Pilot Officer Kenneth 'Hawkeye' Lee, 501 Squadron, based at Hawkinge, England, on August 18, 1940. He was on a patrol at 17,000ft over Canterbury when Luftwaffe ace Oberleutnant Gerhard Schöpfel shot down his machine and three others in a single pass. The attack was so sudden that even though Lee was the last to fall, he had no warning until a bullet hit his leg and another hit his seat from behind and filled his shoulder with metal fragments. He bailed out and survived, continuing to fly and fight until he was shot down over Crete and taken prisoner by the Germans, finally being liberated in 1945. He died aged 92 in 2008.

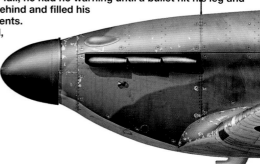

Hurricane Mk.I Trop

Flying Officer Roger 'Jock' Hilton-Barber of 261 Squadron, stationed at Hal Far on Malta, had been flying Gloster Gladiators until his unit received tropicalized Hurricanes in August 1940. Even then, most of Hilton-Barber's missions for the rest of the year were flown in Gladiators.

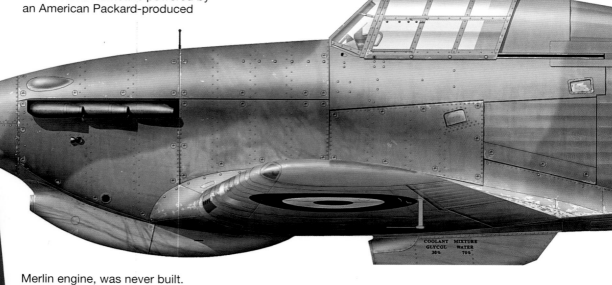

THE CANNON-ARMED HURRICANE MK.IID'S MAIN ROLE WAS GROUND-ATTACK

Merlin engine, was never built.

Entering production in 1943, the Mk.IV was built in relatively low numbers – 524 compared to, for example, 4711 Mk.IICs. However, it was the first Hawker aircraft to make widespread use of 3in rockets for ground-attack ahead of their more well-known use with the Typhoon during 1944.

Just two Hurricane Mk.Vs were made. They were essentially Mk.IVs fitted with ground-boosted Merlin 32 engines and four-bladed Rotol propellers. Thorough trials determined that there was no real advantage to this configuration and both Mk.Vs – KZ193 and NL255 – were returned to their original Mk.IV form.

The other major variant of the type was the Sea Hurricane.

Hurricane Mk.I

The wasp emblem on the nose of Pilot Officer Arthur Victor 'Taffy' Clowes was intended to record his victories – one stripe for each enemy aircraft shot down. The aircraft in shown as it was in September 1940 when Clowes' unit, 1 Squadron, was based at RAF Wittering in England. Clowes scored 10 victories plus one shared.

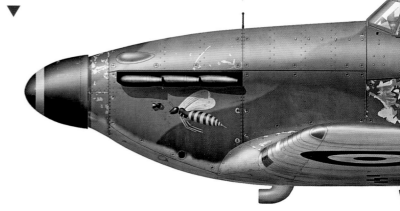

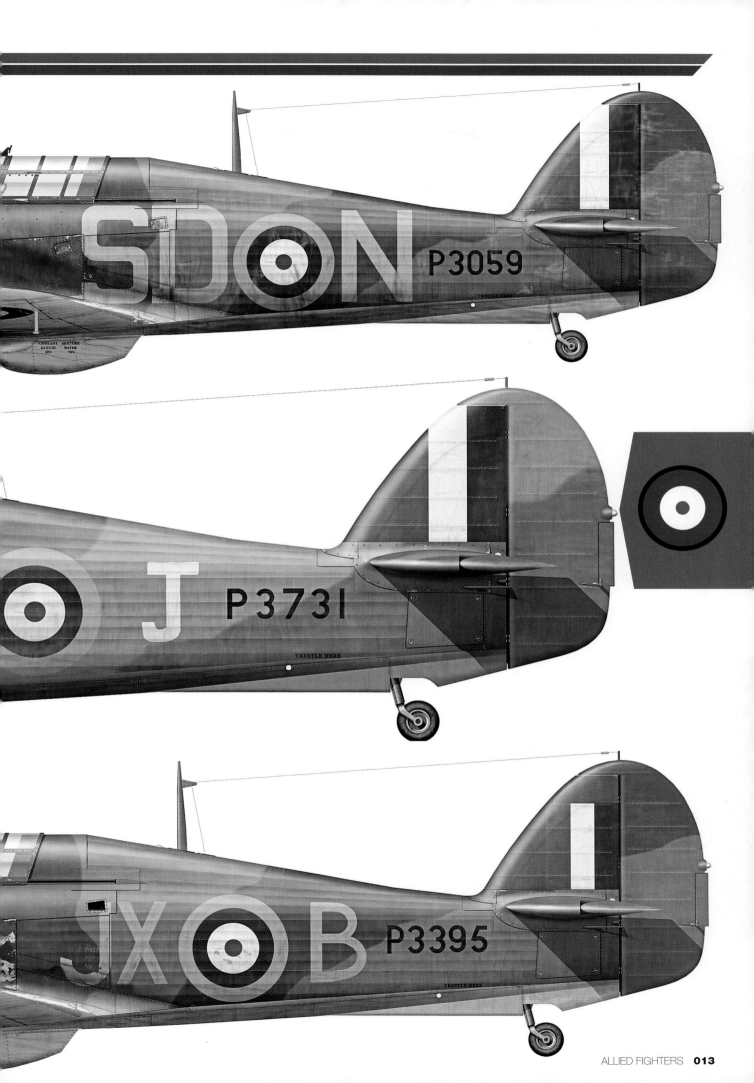

SD N
P3059

J
P3731

JX B
P3395

HURRICANE MK.IIC

Canadian Pilot Officer Albert U 'Bert' Houle Jr, who had previously been a boxer and wrestling champion, and worked as a miner, enlisted in 1940 before training as a pilot and eventually being stationed at Edku, Egypt, with 213 Squadron, during the spring of 1942. He ended the war with three victories plus one shared and died in 2008.

▼

HURRICANE MK.IIB

The distinctively marked BD930 as it looked when serving with 73 Squadron, based in Gambut Main, Libya, during Apil 1942.

▼

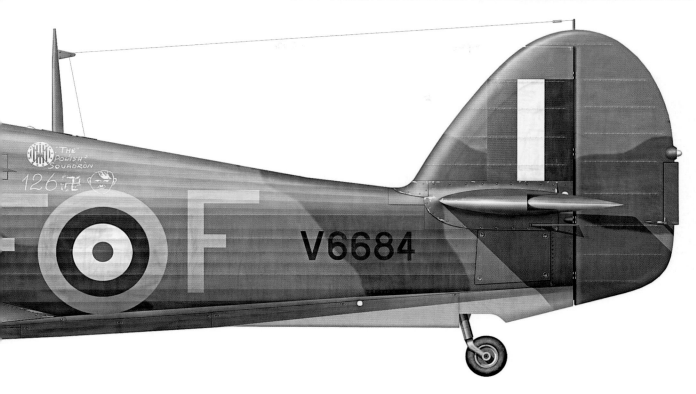

HURRICANE MK.I ▲

Polish ace Squadron Leader Witold Urbanowicz flew with 303 (Polish) Squadron, based at Northolt, England, during September 1940. On the 27th, he shot down four enemy aircraft – two Ju 88s, a Bf 109 and a Bf 110. Three days later, he shot down another three Bf 109s and a Do 17. He achieved 18 victories overall plus three shared. During the war none of the aircraft he flew was ever hit by an enemy bullet and he died in 1996 aged 88.

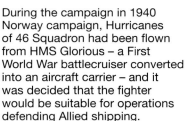

During the campaign in 1940 Norway campaign, Hurricanes of 46 Squadron had been flown from HMS Glorious – a First World War battlecruiser converted into an aircraft carrier – and it was decided that the fighter would be suitable for operations defending Allied shipping.

Early Sea Hurricanes were created by modifying existing Mk.Is with catapult gear. The first example also featured an arrester hook but this was deleted from the remainder of the initial batch of 50, known as Sea Hurricane Mk.IAs. Rather than being launched from aircraft carriers, single Sea Hurricanes were to be launched individually from catapults fitted to merchant vessels.

These ships did not possess any means of recovering their Hurricane, once it had been launched, so the pilot was usually required to either bale out or ditch their machine in the sea and hope for rescue.

The success of these aircraft in shooting down Focke-Wulf Fw 200 Condor long-range maritime patrol aircraft – five by the end of 1941 – resulted in an order being placed for another 300. These were again

converted from existing Mk.Is but this time with arrestor hooks fitted, making them Sea Hurricane Mk.IBs. Twenty-five Mk.IIA Series 2s were also converted, also becoming Sea Hurricane Mk.IBs.

Rather than being launched from single one-shot catapults, the hooked aircraft were embarked upon converted merchantmen known as MAC-ships which had short flight decks fitted. These too enjoyed considerable success, paving the way for the Sea Hurricane Mk.IC, which was converted from the Hurricane IIC. The final Sea Hurricane was the Mk.IIC, a variant fitted with both an arrester hook and a naval radio.

A limited number of Canadian-built Hurricane XIIAs were also converted to Sea Hurricane configuration.

Overall, 14,533 Hurricanes had been built by the end of July 1944, when production finally ceased with PZ865, a Mark IIC known as 'The Last of the Many'. This aircraft was bought by Hawkers and kept in storage at Langley. Today it continues to fly with the Battle of Britain Memorial Flight in Lincolnshire. ●

SUPERMARINE

Note: Only the main wartime land-based fighter versions of the Spitfire are covered in this account.

1936–1961

The iconic Supermarine Spitfire became a symbol of British resistance in the face of the Luftwaffe onslaught during the Battle of Britain. The subject of continual evolution and enhancement, it remained at the forefront of the action throughout the war.

Having previously concentrated almost entirely on flying boats and seaplanes, Supermarine's chief designer R J Mitchell first began to consider working on land-based fighter aircraft in February 1931. The Air Ministry had been discussing the specification for a new single-seat night and day fighter since 1929 but had yet to release a formal set of requirements.

Drawing on the company's experience with building metal wings and stressed skin structures for its Schneider Cup racers, Mitchell prepared two designs

under the designation Type 178 – one a biplane and the other a monoplane. Apart from their wing layout, they had many features in common, such as a fixed undercarriage and the use of a Rolls-Royce Kestrel 'S' engine.

Finally, Specification F.7/30 for a single-seat fighter was issued in October 1931 and Mitchell submitted the monoplane to meet it in February 1932 while development work continued, with the design being redesignated Type 224. A contract was awarded for a prototype in August and after much redrafting and many alterations the aircraft

SPITFIRE

Spitfire Mk.IA ▼

At the height of the Battle of Britain, 74 Squadron was led by Adolph Gysbert 'Sailor' Malan. During the fierce fighting over Dunkirk in June 1940 he flew this Spitfire Mk.I while stationed at Hornchurch, England. A South African, Malan was nicknamed 'sailor' for having previously been a naval officer cadet. He ended the war with 27 victories in air combat plus seven shared and died from Parkinson's disease in 1963.

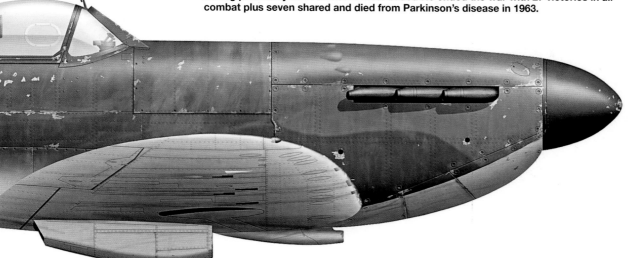

Spitfire Mk.IA ◄

Flight Lieutenant Alan C Deere of 54 Squadron, stationed at Hornchurch, England, shot down a Bf 109 while flying this aircraft on August 11, 1940. He shot down two more, plus a Bf 110, the following day. Deere survived the war with 17 victories in air combat plus one shared and died in 1995 aged 77.

was completed, except for its engine, in November 1933. Rolls-Royce managed to supply an example of what was now known as the Goshawk on December 8 and it was duly installed, the work not being finished until February 10, 1934, due to the aircraft's complicated evaporative cooling system.

The Type 224's first flight took place on February 19. It had an inverted gullwing arrangement, a fixed undercarriage and an open cockpit. Its performance, though not poor, was still a disappointment, particularly given the years of work that had already been put into it. The cooling system failed to operate as expected and the engine suffered from overheating.

Eventually the F.7/30 competition was won by the Gloster Gladiator but Supermarine did not give up on the Type 224. Instead, its development continued under the new designation Type 300. Supermarine offered this to the Air Ministry as two options – the first an upgrade of the existing Type 224 prototype,

the second incorporating the same features but as part of an entirely new design.

Type 300 replaced the inverted gullwings with conventional straight ones housing machine guns. It also had a retractable undercarriage and featured a fully enclosed cockpit. By mid-1934 the Type 300 was being worked on outside the usual specification structure as an experimental aircraft. The Air Ministry asked for a cost estimate to build it as a prototype in September 1934. By this point the cockpit had been lowered and aerodynamically shaped wing fillets had been added, the wings themselves becoming thinner and more elliptical in shape. The undercarriage had been further modified too, and the type now carried four Vickers .303in machine guns – two in each wing outboard of the propeller.

A new specification, F.37/34, was drafted specifically for the Type 300 and on January 3, 1935, Supermarine received a contract to build a prototype. It would be powered by a new Rolls-Royce engine, the PV-12, rather than the Goshawk, which had proven to be unreliable. A new Air Staff Requirement for an eight-gun fighter, F.10/35, was issued in April 1935 but withdrawn when it became clear that both the Supermarine design and another being developed by Hawker could meet its specification.

The Type 300's armament was changed to eight Browning .303s, four in each wing and detail design and construction of the first prototype began. The prototype, serial K5054, was rolled out in early 1936 and made its first flight on March 5. A new two-bladed wooden propeller was then fitted and the aircraft flew again on March 10. Tests revealed that the aircraft could reach a top speed of 330mph but this was improved to 348mph with the addition of another new propeller in May 1936.

Reports from pilots were universally positive, with only minor requests for alterations – such as the addition of an undercarriage position indicator. The Air Ministry therefore placed an order for 310 production models on June 3, 1936. It was around this time that the name 'Spitfire' was formally applied.

Work on setting up production lines for the Spitfire progressed

THE SUPERMARINE TYPE 300 FORMALLY BECAME THE SPITFIRE DURING THE SUMMER OF 1936

Spitfire Mk.IA ▼

On September 3, 1940, having just achieved his fifth aerial victory, becoming an 'ace', Pilot Officer Richard H Hillary of 603 Squadron, stationed at Hornchurch, England, was shot down himself. He struggled to get the canopy of his crippled Spitfire open and suffered extensive burns to his face and hands. Having undergone extensive plastic surgery and still suffering from his injuries, he returned to active service but was killed when his Bristol Blenheim crashed during a night flight on January 8, 1943. He was 23.

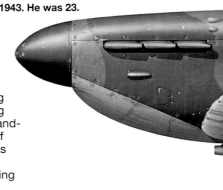

more slowly than expected, primarily because Supermarine was a relatively small company with only 500 employees – and was already engaged in fulfilling orders for other types, including the Walrus. Reproducing the hand-made stressed-skin structure of the prototype machine on series production jigs also created serious difficulties, as did building all-metal elliptical wings.

In practice, this amounted to each Spitfire taking twice as long as a Messerschmitt Bf 109E to build and two and a half times longer than a Hawker Hurricane. With Supermarine still struggling to get its act together, parent company Vickers was forced to bring in sub-contractors including General Aircraft, Westland, Folland and General Electric.

In the meantime, the lone prototype was the subject of continual improvements. Its eight machine guns were fitted in August 1936 along with a reflector gunsight and its radio kit. Its engine, actually a prototype for the Merlin C, produced 990hp and had six flush-fitting exhaust ports on either side.

Spitfire Mk.IA ▶

This aircraft was flown by Flying Officer John Colin Mungo-Park, 74 Squadron, Hornchurch, England, on October 29, 1940. Mungo-Park was flying a Spitfire VB when he was shot down and killed near Dunkirk on June 27, 1941, aged 23. In all he had claimed 11 aircraft destroyed and two shared, five probables, and four damaged enemy aircraft.

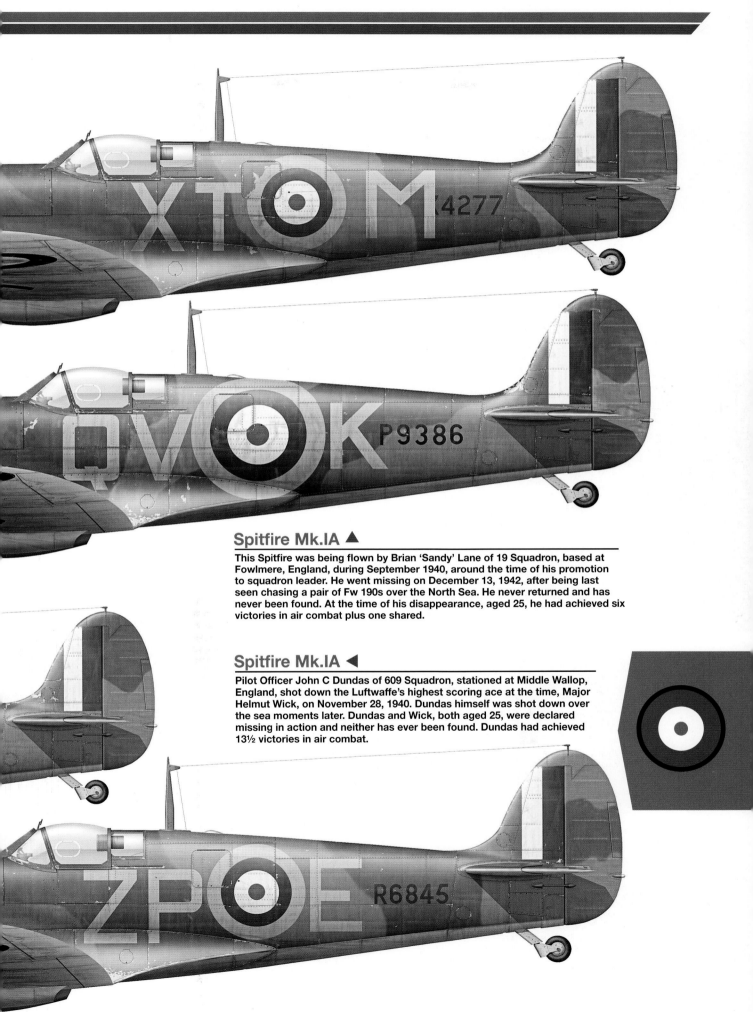

Spitfire Mk.IA ▲

This Spitfire was being flown by Brian 'Sandy' Lane of 19 Squadron, based at Fowlmere, England, during September 1940, around the time of his promotion to squadron leader. He went missing on December 13, 1942, after being last seen chasing a pair of Fw 190s over the North Sea. He never returned and has never been found. At the time of his disappearance, aged 25, he had achieved six victories in air combat plus one shared.

Spitfire Mk.IA ◄

Pilot Officer John C Dundas of 609 Squadron, stationed at Middle Wallop, England, shot down the Luftwaffe's highest scoring ace at the time, Major Helmut Wick, on November 28, 1940. Dundas himself was shot down over the sea moments later. Dundas and Wick, both aged 25, were declared missing in action and neither has ever been found. Dundas had achieved 13½ victories in air combat.

As testing continued, it became evident that there was a problem with the wing guns freezing up. This first happened during firing trials in March 1937 and was eventually resolved by installing ducting which diverted hot air from the underwing radiators to the interior of the wings. It was not until July 1938, around a year later than scheduled, that deliveries of the first full production Spitfire Mk.Is were finally being made to Fighter Command.

From late 1938 a Barr and Stroud GM 2 reflector gunsight was fitted to Spitfire Mk.Is. Now an order for another 1000 Spitfires was placed, with a new factory being built at Castle Bromwich expressly for this purpose. Further orders followed in 1939 for first another 200, then another 450 – a grand total of 2160.

With the 1030hp Merlin Mk.III engine fitted as standard, driving a 10ft 8in diameter Aero Products two-bladed wooden propeller, the earliest production Spitfires were able to achieve a top speed of 362mph at 18,500ft with a maximum climb rate of 2490ft per minute at 10,000ft. Service ceiling was 31,900ft.

However, from the 78th Spitfire, a three-bladed 9ft 8in diameter two-position metal de Havilland propeller was installed which improved service ceiling, up to 34,400ft, and top speed – up to 367mph. In addition, the 'flat' canopy of the earliest Spitfires was soon replaced

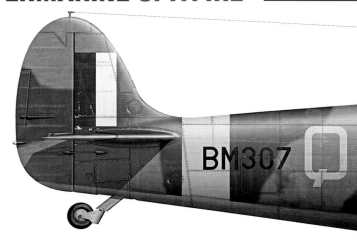

Spitfire Mk.VB ▼

Despite his short stature, Flight Lieutenant Eric S 'Sawn off Lockie' Lock of 611 Squadron was one of the RAF's finest aces. He flew this Spitfire Mk.VB while stationed at Hornchurch in England on July 14, 1941. That day he shot down his third Bf 109 in just over a week. Three weeks later, on August 3, 1941, he peeled off from his formation to strafe a column on infantry on the ground near the Pas-de-Calais. He is believed to have been hit by ground fire during the attack but neither Lock nor W3257 were ever seen again. He was 22 years old and had achieved 26 victories in air combat plus one shared.

Spitfire Mk.VC ▼

This Spitfire Mk.VC was flown by members of 603 Squadron from their base at Takali on Malta, during April 1942.

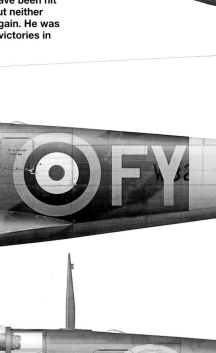

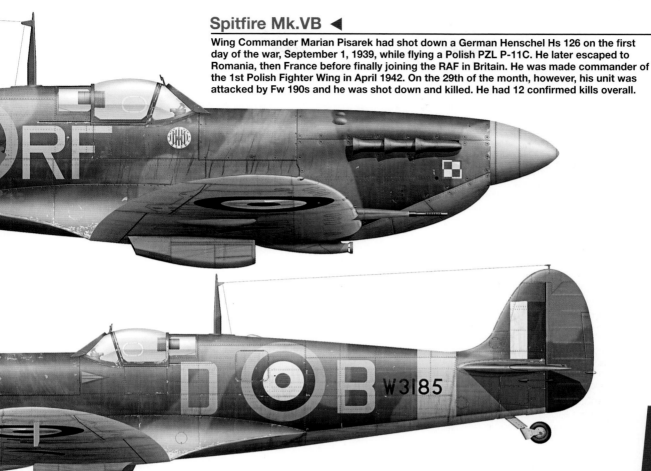

Spitfire Mk.VB ◄

Wing Commander Marian Pisarek had shot down a German Henschel Hs 126 on the first day of the war, September 1, 1939, while flying a Polish PZL P-11C. He later escaped to Romania, then France before finally joining the RAF in Britain. He was made commander of the 1st Polish Fighter Wing in April 1942. On the 29th of the month, however, his unit was attacked by Fw 190s and he was shot down and killed. He had 12 confirmed kills overall.

Spitfire Mk.VA ▲

Famous amputee ace Wing Commander Douglas R S Bader flew this Spitfire Mk.VA while stationed at Tangmere in England during July 1941. That month he shot down five Bf 109s and damaged or shared in several others, but the following month he was shot down and spent the rest of the war as a prisoner. He achieve 20 victories in air combat plus four shared.

with a 'blown' version which provided more headroom and better visibility, particularly to the rear. The handpump-operated undercarriage retraction system was also replaced with a hydraulic pump.

It was this version of the Spitfire that went to war in September 1939. From mid-1940, the Mk.I also received 73lb of steel armour plating for the pilot's seat and headrest, plus the front of the glycol header tank. An improved propeller from de Havilland – constant speed rather than two-position – was introduced from late June 1940 and Identification Friend or Foe (IFF) equipment for radar was installed from September 1940. This was

outwardly visible as wires which ran from the tips of the tailplanes to the sides of the rear fuselage.

All of these changes resulted in substantially increased weight and the Spitfires that fought the Battle of Britain had a top speed on normal power of only 353mph at 20,000ft as a result. However, the constant speed propeller provided a significantly improved rate of climb to compensate – 2895ft per minute at 10,000ft. In addition, thanks to the availability of 100 octane fuel, Spitfire pilots could apply an 'emergency boost' for up to five minutes during combat. This effectively increase power to 1310hp at 9000ft and increased top speed by 34mph at 10,000ft.

During June 1940, the RAF received its first Spitfire Mk.IBs. These were fitted with a single Hispano 20mm cannon in each wing, in place of the Browning machine guns. However, due to jamming problems with the cannon, it was decided that a compromise – two cannon and four machine guns – would work best. A total of 1567 Mk.Is were built.

SPITFIRE MK.II
During the summer of 1939, a production model Spitfire was tested with the new 1175hp Rolls-

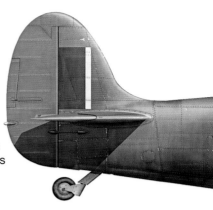

Royce Merlin XII. It was decided that this new version, the Mk.II would be built at Castle Bromwich and would feature a new Rotol-made 10ft 9in propeller which had already been fitted to some Mk.Is. Performance was improved at lower altitudes, though the Mk.II's absolute top speed was lower than that of the Mk.I due to weight increases. The Mk.II was available in both IIA eight machine gun and IIB cannon weapons configurations and fast deliveries from the factory meant that all Mk.Is had been replaced with Mk.IIs in front line units by April 1941. Several Mk.IIs were converted for long range bomber escort duties with the fitment of a fixed 40 gallon fuel tank under the port wing. In all, 921 Mk.IIs were built.

SPITFIRE MK.III
For the Mk.III, which started out as the Supermarine Type 330, the Spitfire underwent a significant redesign. The new Rolls-Royce RM2SM engine, later redesignated Merlin XX, was installed producing 1390hp thanks to its two-speed supercharger. The aircraft's wingspan was significantly shortened from 36ft 10in to just 30ft 6in, and the fuselage was lengthened from 29ft 11in to 30ft 6in.

The undercarriage main legs were made stronger and raked forward slightly for added stability when the aircraft was on the ground and the tailwheel was

Spitfire Mk.VB ▲
More than 100 Spitfires Mk.VBs were shipped to the Soviet Union as war aid and this brightly coloured example was flown by 57 GIAP on the Kuban Front during April 1943. In this area of the Eastern Front, the Germans initially tried to gain control of the Caspian oil fields but ended up being forced to evacuate through the bridgehead they had earlier created.

A SIGNIFICANT REDESIGN OF THE SPITFIRE RESULTED IN THE MK.III

Spitfire Mk.VC ▲
Major Robert Levine of the 4th FG, 52nd FS, flew this desert camouflaged Spitfire Mk.VC Trop with its dagger-in-skull logo from La Sebala in Tunisia during June 1943.

Spitfire Mk.VC ▶
This Spitfire Mk.VC Trop was flown by Lieutenant Ronald H Brown of the 31st FG, 307th FS, based at Licata, Italy, during July 1943.

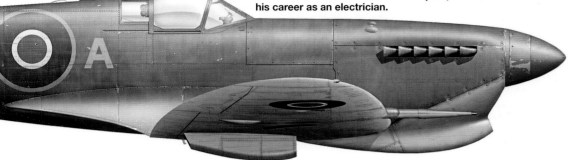

Spitfire Mk.VC ▼

Squadron Leader Evan D 'Rosie' Mackie of 243 Squadron flew this tropicalized Spitfire from Hal Far on Malta during June 1943 – the month when his unit moved to the island in readiness for the invasion of Sicily. He survived the war having achieved 20 victories, six and a half of them in a Hawker Tempest, and went back home to New Zealand to resume his career as an electrician.

now completely retractable. The cockpit was improved too, the windscreen being fitted with a new bulletproof panel, plus optically flat quarter panels made of glass.

While the Mk.III was flown as a prototype on March 16, going on to achieve a top speed of 400mph at 21,000ft, a shortage of Merlin XXs meant that it never went into production.

SPITFIRE MK.IV / MK.XII

As early as December 1939, Supermarine had been considering the single-stage supercharged 1735hp 36.7 litre V12 Rolls-Royce Griffon as a new engine for the Spitfire. Unfortunately, the powerplant's development was delayed and the first flight of a Griffon Spitfire prototype, the Mk.IV, did not take place until November 27, 1941.

The shape of the Griffon meant that the Mk.IV was visually distinct from its predecessors, with large bulges on the cowling over the cylinder heads and a teardrop fairing on the upper forward cowling over the magneto. The lower cowling had a shallower curve up to the spinner, and the spinner itself was much larger than those of earlier marks. The propeller itself was a four-bladed 10ft 5in Rotol type and as seen from the cockpit it

rotated to the left, rather than to the right as with the Merlin.

The remainder of the Mk.IV was similar to the Mk.III. Pilots found that the Mk.IV prototype, DP845, had much more power on take-off than the Merlin Spitfire and tended to swing to the right – which had to be counteracted by moving the rudder to the left. The Mk.IV was fitted with mock-up installations for three cannon in each wing and then redesignated Mk.XX to prevent it being confused with the reconnaissance type Spitfire PR Mk.IV. It was redesignated again to Mk.XII.

SPITFIRE MK.V

The next major production version of the Spitfire after the Mk.II was the Mk.V – which was essentially the same aircraft but fitted with the new Merlin 45 engine, which produced 1440hp with a single-speed single-stage supercharger. Work began on the new design immediately after the Battle of Britain, in late 1940. Changes to the carburettor at this point meant that the Spitfire was able to perform any manoeuvre without causing fuel flow problems. Previously, certain negative G aerobatic moves could result in the engine cutting out due to fuel starvation.

A number of Mk.I and Mk.II Spitfires were upgraded to Mk.V with the new powerplant but the majority were newly built at Castle Bromwich. The first version of the

Mk.V, introduced in 1941, was the Mk.VA (Supermarine Type 331), with four .303 Brownings per wing. Its top speed was 375mph at 20,800ft and the climb up to that altitude could be accomplished in a little over seven minutes.

The second, and production standard version was the Spitfire Mk.VB (Supermarine Type 349), which featured a continuous flow of modifications throughout its relatively lengthy production lifespan. These included an improved windscreen like that of the Mk.III, a range of different propellers and spinners, a system for increasing the flow of hot air into the gun bays, the option to have 'clipped' wingtips to increase roll-rate and airspeed at low altitude – reducing wingspan to 32ft 2in – and the option to use 'slipper' drop tanks fitted beneath the wing centre section.

A variety of different versions of the Merlin 45 were fitted to Spitfire Mk.VBs too, such as the Merlin 45M with a smaller supercharger impeller.

A less numerous but more visually distinctive version was the Mk.VB (trop). A sizeable Vokes air filter was installed under the aircraft's nose to prevent dust, dirt and sand from tropical or desert environments entering the engine. This cut top speed by 8mph and reduced climb rate by 600ft per minute but enabled the Spitfire to operate in harsh conditions around the world.

The second revision of the type was the Mk.VC (Supermarine Type 349). This featured a strengthened fuselage, new windscreen, a revised undercarriage, a deeper radiator fairing under the starboard wing, a larger oil cooler with kinked air outlet under the port wing, C-type wings and armour for the bottom of the pilot's seat and wing ammunition boxes. With the appropriate gear, it was also able to carry a single 250lb bomb under each wing – a first for a Spitfire.

The C-type wing was designed to be easier and faster to manufacture and could be reconfigured for a number of different weapons arrangements – most commonly two cannon and four machine guns.

A tropicalized version of the Mk.VC was sent overseas in large numbers to be used in the Mediterranean and Pacific theatres.

Overall Spitfire Mk.V production totalled 6479. Just 94 of these

Spitfire HF Mk.VII ▼

Pilots of 131 Squadron, stationed at Culmhead in Somerset, England, flew this invasion-striped Spitfire Mk.VII during August 1944.

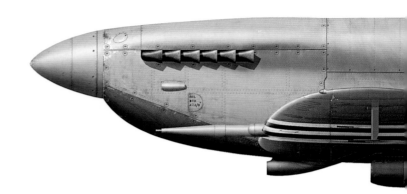

Spitfire HF Mk.VIII ▼

A Spitfire Mk.VIII that served with 417 (Canadian) Squadron when it was stationed at Pachino, Sicily, in July 1943.

were Mk.VAs, 3911 were Mk.VBs and 2467 were Mk.VCs.

SPITFIRE MK.VI
Work on designing the Mk.VI (Supermarine Type 351) took place in parallel to work on the Mk.V. It was to be the first Spitfire equipped with a pressurised cockpit for combating German high-altitude bombers if they appeared. The pressurisation was to be carried out using a Marshall compressor and the forward and rear cockpit bulkheads were sealed, with rubber grommets for all the cables, wires and tubes that needed to pass into the cabin.

A new non-sliding canopy was introduced which had to be locked into position over the pilot once he had climbed aboard, then sealed by inflating a rubber tube inside the cockpit. By comparison to modern pressurised aircraft, the pressurisation was only slight and made 37,000ft feel more like 28,000ft for the pilot.

The Mk.VI was powered by

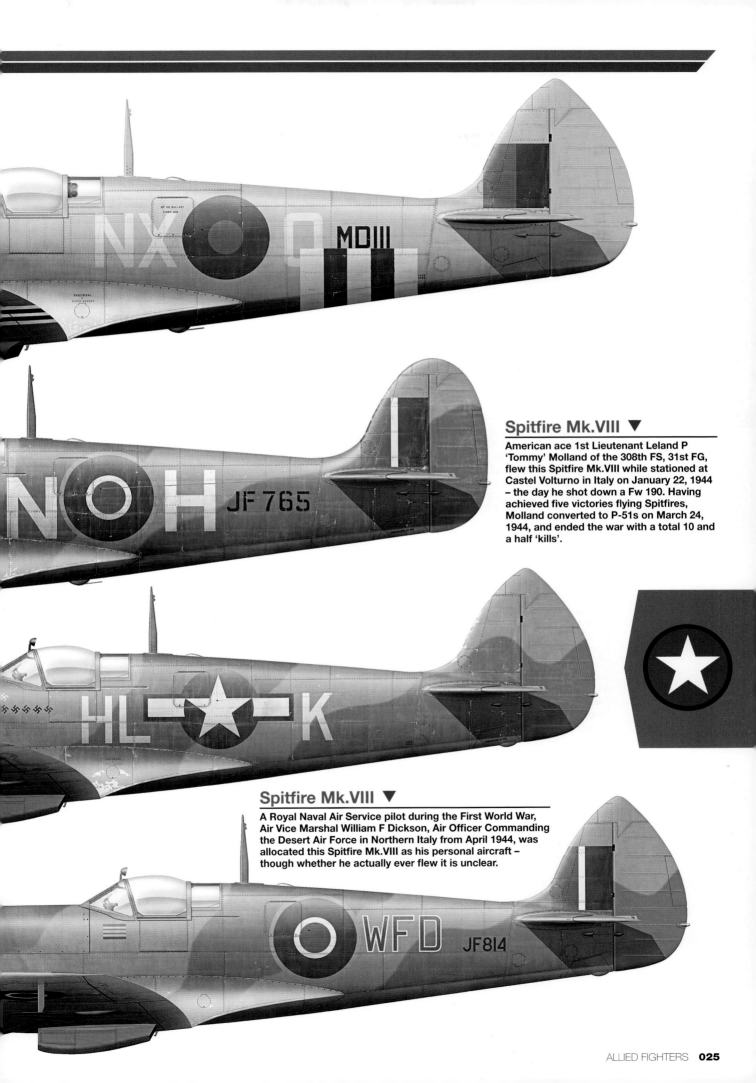

Spitfire Mk.VIII ▼

American ace 1st Lieutenant Leland P 'Tommy' Molland of the 308th FS, 31st FG, flew this Spitfire Mk.VIII while stationed at Castel Volturno in Italy on January 22, 1944 – the day he shot down a Fw 190. Having achieved five victories flying Spitfires, Molland converted to P-51s on March 24, 1944, and ended the war with a total 10 and a half 'kills'.

Spitfire Mk.VIII ▼

A Royal Naval Air Service pilot during the First World War, Air Vice Marshal William F Dickson, Air Officer Commanding the Desert Air Force in Northern Italy from April 1944, was allocated this Spitfire Mk.VIII as his personal aircraft – though whether he actually ever flew it is unclear.

Spitfire Mk.IXC ▼

Canadian Flying Officer Ian Keltie of 402 (Canadian) Squadron, stationed at Kenley in England during March 1943, flew EN398 emblazoned with a Popeye design and the maple leaf. The following month this same aircraft was allocated to Wing Commander James E 'Johnnie' Johnson.

a Merlin 47 and fitted with a Rotol propeller with four wide blades designed to improve performance in the thinner air at higher altitudes. The standard B-type wings were modified to incorporate pointed tips, which resulted in a wingspan of 40ft 2in.

Top speed was just 356mph at 21,800ft but service ceiling was 39,200ft, compared to 35,000ft for the Mk.VB. Only 100 Mk.VIs were made because the Germans never put a high-altitude bomber into full series production, let alone front line service.

SPITFIRE MK.VII

The performance of the Mk.VI had been disappointing so the Mk.VII represented an attempt to make improvements. With a similar pressurised cockpit to that of the Mk.VI, it was now powered by a Merlin 64 with a two-stage two-speed supercharger. It had pointed-tip wings like the Mk.VI, but derived from the C-type rather than the B-type. Although early versions had the same jettisonable hood as the Mk.VI, this was later replaced with a more conventional sliding version – albeit double glazed.

The new engine meant the Mk.VII's performance was significantly improved over that of the Mk.VI, with a service ceiling of 45,100ft. A total of 140 were built.

SPITFIRE MK.VIII

With the Luftwaffe's introduction of the Focke-Wulf Fw 190, the Spitfire Mk.VB was outclassed and an improved version was urgently needed. This was intended to be the Mk.VIII (Supermarine Type 360). It was very similar to the Mk.VII but without the pressurised cockpit. Some even featured the same pointed wingtips but most had standard wings.

> **WHEN THE FW 190 APPEARED THE SPITFIRE MK.VB WAS OUTCLASSED AT LAST AND A REPLACEMENT WAS URGENTLY NEEDED**

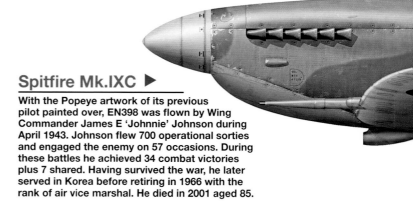

Spitfire Mk.IXC ▶

With the Popeye artwork of its previous pilot painted over, EN398 was flown by Wing Commander James E 'Johnnie' Johnson during April 1943. Johnson flew 700 operational sorties and engaged the enemy on 57 occasions. During these battles he achieved 34 combat victories plus 7 shared. Having survived the war, he later served in Korea before retiring in 1966 with the rank of air vice marshal. He died in 2001 aged 85.

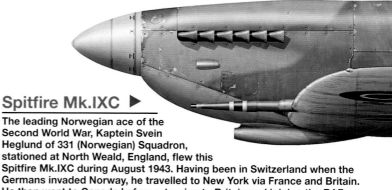

Spitfire Mk.IXC ▶

The leading Norwegian ace of the Second World War, Kaptein Svein Heglund of 331 (Norwegian) Squadron, stationed at North Weald, England, flew this Spitfire Mk.IXC during August 1943. Having been in Switzerland when the Germans invaded Norway, he travelled to New York via France and Britain. He then went to Canada before returning to Britain and joining the RAF, initially flying Hurricanes. His unit later received Spitfires. Finally, in May 1943, he joined 331 (Norwegian) Squadron and went on to shoot down 12 enemy aircraft with five probables up to November. He then transferred to RAF Ferry Command. Heglund ended the war with 16 victories and died in 1998 aged 79.

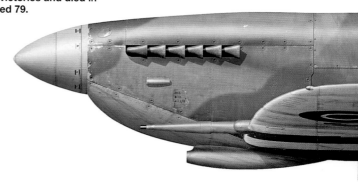

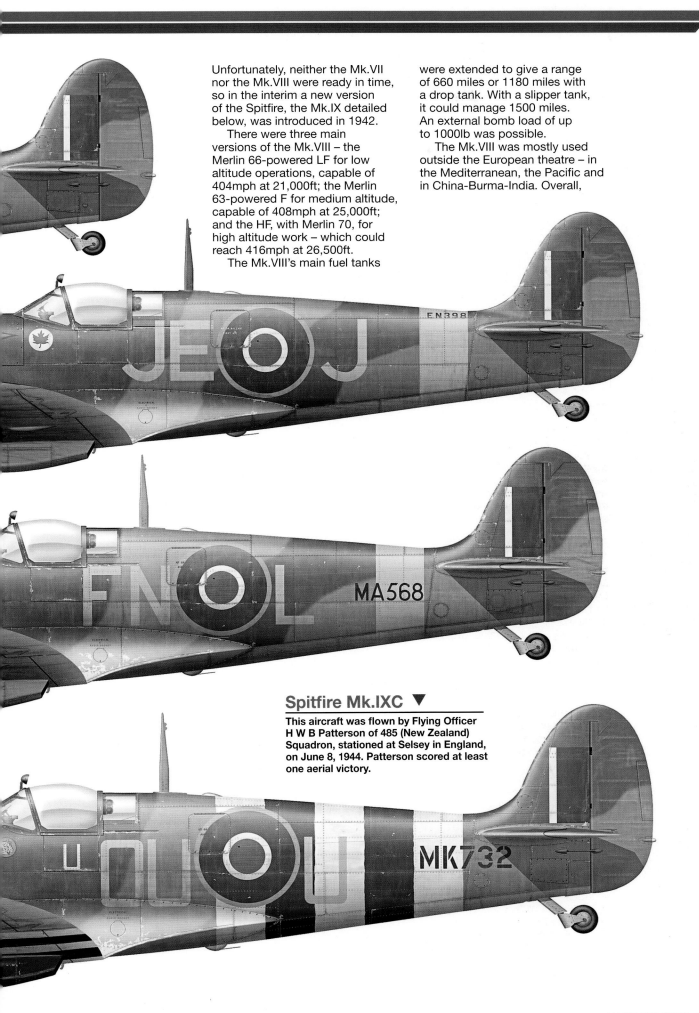

Unfortunately, neither the Mk.VII nor the Mk.VIII were ready in time, so in the interim a new version of the Spitfire, the Mk.IX detailed below, was introduced in 1942.

There were three main versions of the Mk.VIII – the Merlin 66-powered LF for low altitude operations, capable of 404mph at 21,000ft; the Merlin 63-powered F for medium altitude, capable of 408mph at 25,000ft; and the HF, with Merlin 70, for high altitude work – which could reach 416mph at 26,500ft.

The Mk.VIII's main fuel tanks were extended to give a range of 660 miles or 1180 miles with a drop tank. With a slipper tank, it could manage 1500 miles. An external bomb load of up to 1000lb was possible.

The Mk.VIII was mostly used outside the European theatre – in the Mediterranean, the Pacific and in China-Burma-India. Overall,

Spitfire Mk.IXC ▼

This aircraft was flown by Flying Officer H W B Patterson of 485 (New Zealand) Squadron, stationed at Selsey in England, on June 8, 1944. Patterson scored at least one aerial victory.

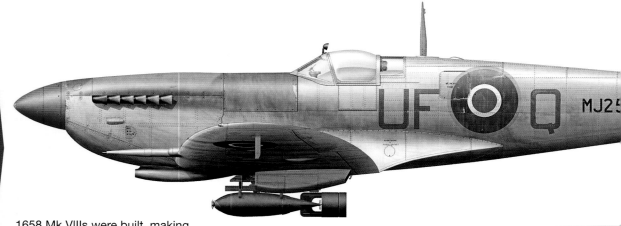

EVEN BY THE END OF THE WAR, THE SPITFIRE MK.IX COULD STILL OUT-CLIMB AND FLY HIGHER THAN MOST OF ITS OPPONENTS

1658 Mk.VIIIs were built, making it the third most numerous Spitfire type after the Mk.IX and Mk.V.

SPITFIRE MK.IX / MK.XVI

With the next generation Spitfire Mk.VII and Mk.VIII taking time to prepare, a stopgap was needed to combat the Fw 190. A Mk.III had been tested with the new Merlin 61 – originally designed for the Wellington Mk.VI high-altitude bomber – in September 1941 and the results had been impressive.

It was therefore decided that Mk.VC airframes should be modified to take the Merlin 61, resulting in the Mk.IX. Full production of bespoke Mk.IXs then commenced.

During early 1943, the Merlin 61 was replaced with the improved Merlin 63 and 63A. In the latter half of 1943 these too were superseded by the 1720hp Merlin 66. The Merlin 66-powered LF Mk.IX, with a top speed of 404mph at 21,000ft, became the workhorse of the RAF's fighter squadrons from its introduction through to the end of the war.

Compared against a captured Bf 109G-6/U2 with GM-1 nitrous oxide injection by the Central Fighter Establishment in late 1944, the LF Mk.IX was found to be superior in every respect except acceleration in a dive. Manoeuvrability was found to be "greatly superior" and it was noted that the LF.IX "easily out-turns the Bf 109 in either direction at

all speeds". Even by the end of the war, it could still out-climb and fly higher than most of its opponents, out-performing many of the most advanced German piston-engined types.

In early 1944, LF Mk.IXs were fitted with a new Mark II Gyro gunsight which calculated the correct angle of deflection to use when leading a target, hugely increasing the accuracy of RAF pilots' fire.

Late production models featured a new 'bulged' upper engine cowling and very late models had a cut-down rear fuselage and bubble canopy for improved visibility.

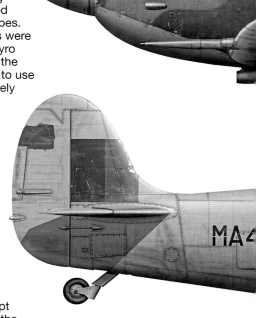

A grand total of 5656 Mk.IXs were made, with production only ending in April 1945. It was the most produced of all Spitfire marks.

The Spitfire Mk.XVI was identical to the Mk.IX except for the fact that its engine, the Merlin 266, was a licence-built version of the Merlin 66 produced by Packard in America. A total of 1054 Spitfire Mk.XVIs were built at Castle Bromwich.

SPITFIRE MK.XII

The Spitfire Mk.X and Mk.XI were both photo-reconnaissance versions and therefore fall outside the scope of this study. The Mk.XII, on the other hand, was

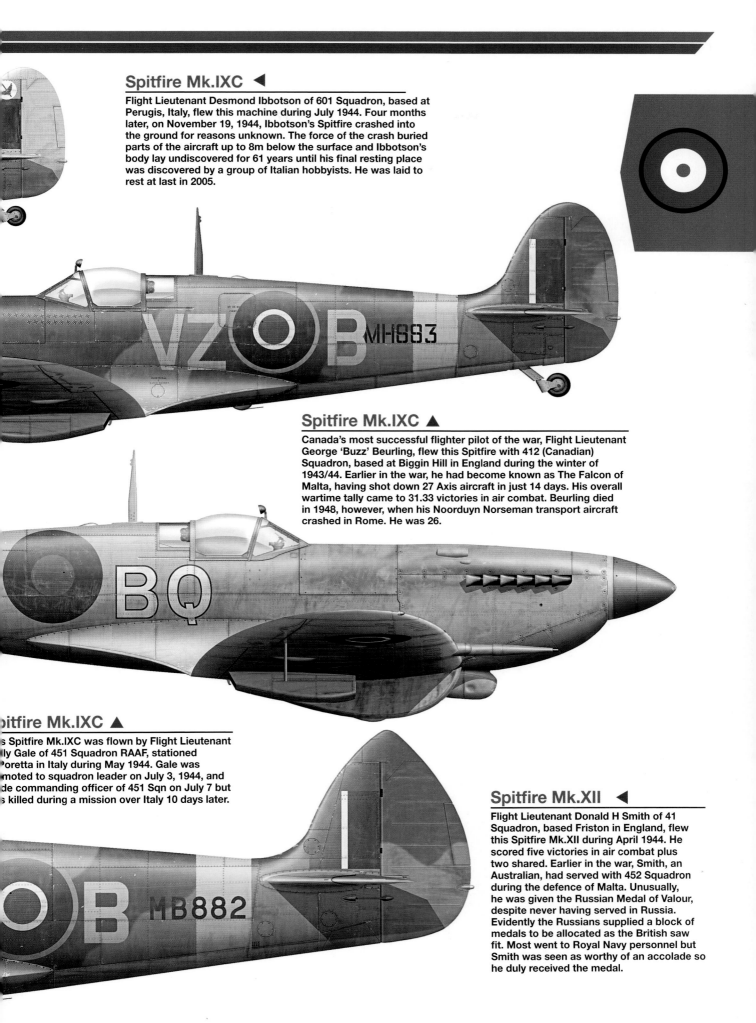

Spitfire Mk.IXC ◀

Flight Lieutenant Desmond Ibbotson of 601 Squadron, based at Perugis, Italy, flew this machine during July 1944. Four months later, on November 19, 1944, Ibbotson's Spitfire crashed into the ground for reasons unknown. The force of the crash buried parts of the aircraft up to 8m below the surface and Ibbotson's body lay undiscovered for 61 years until his final resting place was discovered by a group of Italian hobbyists. He was laid to rest at last in 2005.

Spitfire Mk.IXC ▲

Canada's most successful flighter pilot of the war, Flight Lieutenant George 'Buzz' Beurling, flew this Spitfire with 412 (Canadian) Squadron, based at Biggin Hill in England during the winter of 1943/44. Earlier in the war, he had become known as The Falcon of Malta, having shot down 27 Axis aircraft in just 14 days. His overall wartime tally came to 31.33 victories in air combat. Beurling died in 1948, however, when his Noorduyn Norseman transport aircraft crashed in Rome. He was 26.

pitfire Mk.IXC ▲

s Spitfire Mk.IXC was flown by Flight Lieutenant
lly Gale of 451 Squadron RAAF, stationed
oretta in Italy during May 1944. Gale was
moted to squadron leader on July 3, 1944, and
de commanding officer of 451 Sqn on July 7 but
s killed during a mission over Italy 10 days later.

Spitfire Mk.XII ◀

Flight Lieutenant Donald H Smith of 41 Squadron, based Friston in England, flew this Spitfire Mk.XII during April 1944. He scored five victories in air combat plus two shared. Earlier in the war, Smith, an Australian, had served with 452 Squadron during the defence of Malta. Unusually, he was given the Russian Medal of Valour, despite never having served in Russia. Evidently the Russians supplied a block of medals to be allocated as the British saw fit. Most went to Royal Navy personnel but Smith was seen as worthy of an accolade so he duly received the medal.

the first Rolls-Royce Griffon-engined variant to enter full production. They were initially built using Mk.VC airframes and had fixed tail-wheels with longer pointed-tip rudders.

Part-way through, production switched to using Mk.VIII airframes though with the longer rudder and retractable tail-wheels. A new type of IFF was introduced, with the older tailplane aerials being replaced by a rod aerial protruding from the underside of the starboard wing. In addition, the Mk.XII was given a flush-riveted finish which was later rolled out across all Spitfires. All Mk.XIIs had clipped wings and only 100 were made, those that survived being retired from service in September 1944.

SPITFIRE MK.XIV
The Spitfire Mk.XIV (Supermarine Type 379) was the last major production version to see combat during the Second World War, the Mk.XIII having been another photo-reconnaissance variant.

The Mk.XII had been powered by the Griffon III or IV, which had only a single-stage supercharger, blunting high-altitude performance. Rolls-Royce therefore worked to improve the Griffon by introducing a two-stage unit. The result, via the Mk.61 series, was the lengthy Griffon 65 and this was installed in the Spitfire Mk.XIV. It produced 2050hp and had to be mounted 10in further forward in the airframe. Its ejector exhaust stubs were of circular section and due to the massive powerplant's cooling needs all its radiators had to be significantly enlarged, with deeper underwing housings that those of any previous Spitfire. It drove a large five-bladed Rotol propeller.

A bigger oil tank – containing 10 gallons rather than six – was required and at the rear of the aircraft a new tail unit was installed to help provide balance. This featured a new taller and much broader fin and larger rudder. During early tests, the new design managed an incredible 445mph at 25,000ft and a climb rate of more than 5000ft per minute.

The only problem was range. With 109.5 gallons in two main tanks and a tank in the leading edge of each wing, it could manage just over 460 miles.

JUST 100 SPITFIRE MK.XIIS WERE MADE AND THEY WERE RETIRED IN SEPTEMBER 1944

Spitfire Mk.XIV ▼

The top New Zealand fighter ace of the Second World War was Wing Commander Colin F Gray. He flew this aircraft with the Lympne Wing from Lympne in England during October 1944 but had already scored his last two victories – a pair of Junkers Ju 52 transports – on July 25, 1943. He ended the war with 27 and a half victories plus two shared. He died in 1995 aged 80.

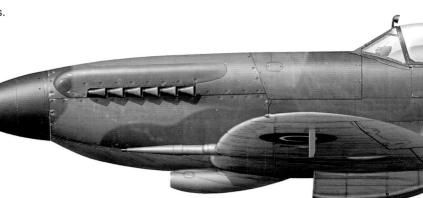

Spitfire Mk.XIVE ▲

Just a week from the end of the Second World War in Europe, on May 1, 1945, Flying Officer Eric 'Ricky' Gray of 41 Squadron stationed at Celle, Germany, flew this Spitfire Mk.XIV. Gray achieved four victories in aerial combat plus one shared.

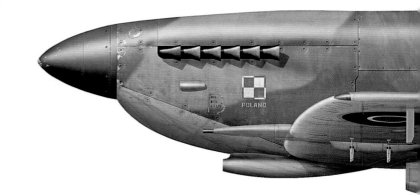

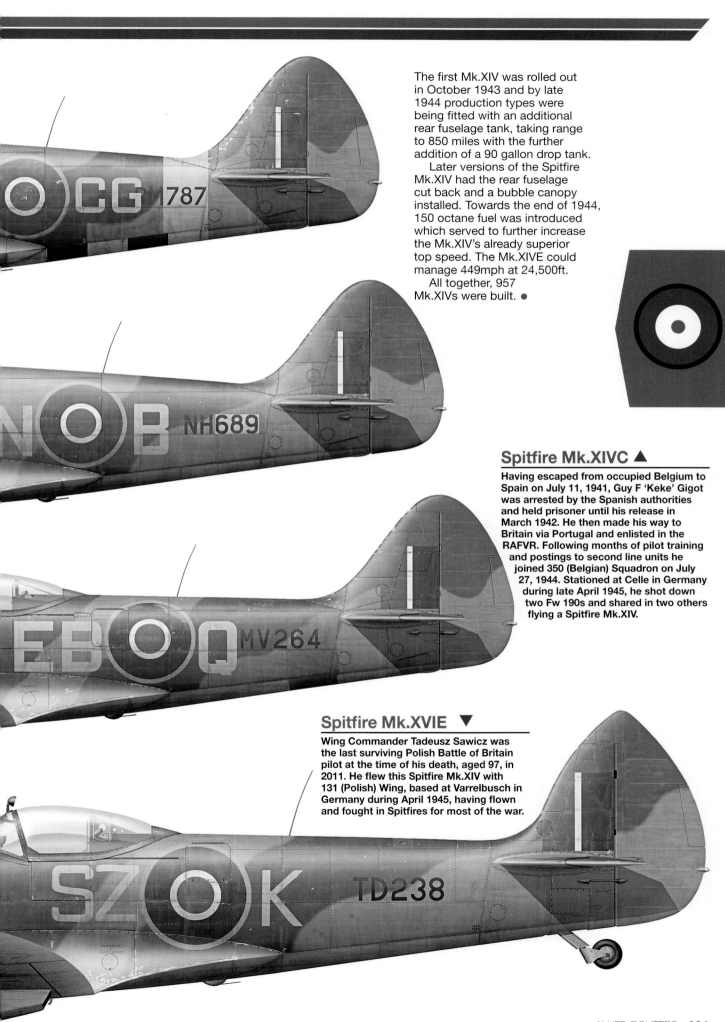

The first Mk.XIV was rolled out in October 1943 and by late 1944 production types were being fitted with an additional rear fuselage tank, taking range to 850 miles with the further addition of a 90 gallon drop tank.

Later versions of the Spitfire Mk.XIV had the rear fuselage cut back and a bubble canopy installed. Towards the end of 1944, 150 octane fuel was introduced which served to further increase the Mk.XIV's already superior top speed. The Mk.XIVE could manage 449mph at 24,500ft.

All together, 957 Mk.XIVs were built. ●

Spitfire Mk.XIVC ▲

Having escaped from occupied Belgium to Spain on July 11, 1941, Guy F 'Keke' Gigot was arrested by the Spanish authorities and held prisoner until his release in March 1942. He then made his way to Britain via Portugal and enlisted in the RAFVR. Following months of pilot training and postings to second line units he joined 350 (Belgian) Squadron on July 27, 1944. Stationed at Celle in Germany during late April 1945, he shot down two Fw 190s and shared in two others flying a Spitfire Mk.XIV.

Spitfire Mk.XVIE ▼

Wing Commander Tadeusz Sawicz was the last surviving Polish Battle of Britain pilot at the time of his death, aged 97, in 2011. He flew this Spitfire Mk.XIV with 131 (Polish) Wing, based at Varrelbusch in Germany during April 1945, having flown and fought in Spitfires for most of the war.

Typhoon Mk.IB ▼

The postwar fame of Squadron Leader Roland 'Bee' Beamont as a test pilot flying the Canberra, Lightning and TSR2 has tended to eclipse his wartime career – but in front line combat he was no less impressive. His operational career began in 1939 flying Hurricanes but by May 1943 he was flying this early model Typhoon with 609 Squadron stationed at Duxford in Cambridgeshire, England. Beamont was one of the Typhoon's strongest advocates, even as it was gaining a reputation for structural problems. Overall, he flew 492 combat sorties and achieved nine victories in air combat plus 36 V-1 flying bombs and 25 locomotives destroyed. He died in 2001 aged 81.

HAWKER TYPHOON

Striking fear into the hearts of German tank crews as the original rocket-firing 'jabo' earned the Typhoon its place in history. It was anything but an overnight success, however.

1940-1945

Once an order had been placed for the Hurricane, though before it had reached full production, Hawker chief designer Sydney Camm and his team began work on its successor. It was uncertain at this stage, however, which of the new 2000hp 24-cylinder engines then in development would be available to power the fighter.

Hawker therefore worked up two designs in parallel during 1937 – one to be fitted with the Rolls-Royce Vulture and the other the Napier Sabre. An Air Ministry specification, F.18/37, was issued in March 1938 which outlined a fighter capable of 400mph at 15,000ft powered by a British engine with a two-speed supercharger. It was to have 12 Browning machine guns with 500 rounds per gun but had to be capable of accepting alternative weapon loads.

Hawker was well prepared for this. The first engine to reach a state of readiness was the Vulture – which meant that the

Hawker design intended for this, the Tornado, was built and flew first, on October 6, 1939. The Sabre design, the Typhoon, was not ready for its maiden flight until February 24, 1940, due to delays in completing its Sabre engine.

While the Typhoon was similar in size to the Hurricane, being slightly shorter in the fuselage but slightly longer in wingspan, it was built differently. The forward fuselage was made of bolted and welded duralumin or steel tubes covered with skin panels. The rear portion, aft of the cockpit, was a semi-monocoque structure.

The thick 41ft 7in span wings

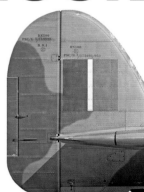

Typhoon Mk.IB

During June 1944 this rocket-armed Typhoon was flown by Flight Lieutenant Eric H A Vernon-Jarvis of 175 Squadron from St Croix in France. Having achieved one victory in air combat – a Bf 109 shot down on January 22, 1945, Vernon-Jarvis was himself shot down and killed by German flak near Dorenthe on February 3, 1945.

had a slight inverted gullwing bend and were extremely strong with sufficient space for fuel tanks, heavy weapons and the inward-retracting landing gear. A side effect of these capacious wings was high drag, which served to prevent the Typhoon from flying faster than 410mph. Its rate of climb was also disappointing.

After some uneventful early flights, the first prototype P5212 suffered a structural failure in mid-air during a test on May 9, 1940. A large crack appeared behind the pilot's seat at the point where the forward and rear fuselage sections were joined. The pilot, Philip Lucas, managed to land the aircraft nevertheless.

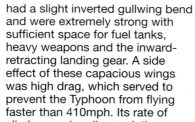

Typhoon Mk.IB

Squadron Leader Leon O J Prévot was appointed the commander of newly formed Typhoon unit 197 Squadron on November 21, 1942, having already achieved his three aerial victories of the war. Stationed at Tangmere in England, he was flying this aircraft on ground-attack missions in June 1943 shortly before he was rested from active duty and became a Typhoon instructor. He died in 1994.

▼

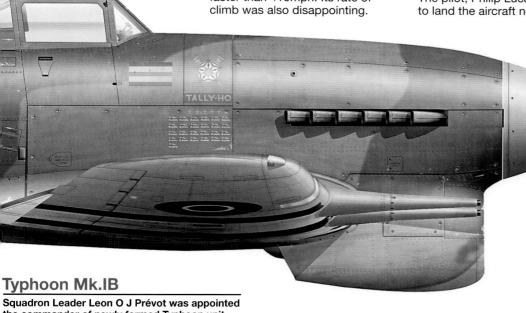

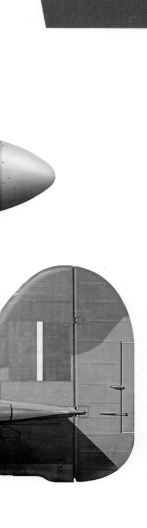

Typhoon Mk.IB ▼

Scrambled to intercept a formation of B-26 medium bombers 5km north of Amiens, France, on March 6, 1944, JG 26 pilot Hauptmann Klaus Meitusch instead shot down one of the Typhoons escorting them. The aircraft was flown by Pilot Officer Charles A Tidy of 3 Squadron, based at Swanton Morley in England. Tidy not only managed to escape his stricken Typhoon but also evaded capture by the Germans on the ground until September when France was liberated and he was able to return to his unit. There is no known photo of Tidy's Typhoon so this profile is based on other Typhoons from his unit during this period.

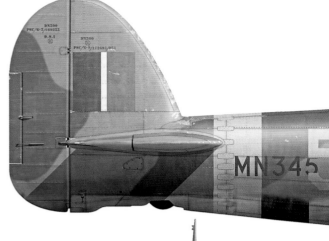

Six days later, the Government decided to concentrate production on just five aircraft types – the Spitfire, Hurricane, Whitley, Wellington and Blenheim – at the expense of everything else. The Typhoon's development priority was lowered and progress slowed. A second prototype was not flown until May 3, 1941, and in the meantime, armament had been changed to four 20mm Hispano Mk.II cannon with 140 rounds per gun. This aircraft, P5216, served as the prototype for the production model Typhoon Mk.IB.

However, engine development had now progressed to a point where the Vulture seemed much more promising than the Sabre. As a result, Hawker was ordered to proceed with building 500 Tornados but only 250 Typhoons. Since Hawker itself was fully committed to

Typhoon Mk.IB

The commander of 181 Squadron, Squadron Leader Denis Crowley-Milling, flew this aircraft from Duxford in England during the spring of 1943. Crowley-Milling was promoted to acting wing commander of 121 Wing in June 1943 but developed eyesight problems in October of that year which saw him removed from operational flying. He ended the war with four victories and two shared and afterwards rose to the rank of air marshal. He died in 1996 aged 77. ▶

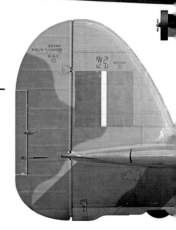

Typhoon Mk.IB ▼

Flying at extremely low level in this Typhoon on June 2, 1943, Flight Sergeant W H Ramsey of 1 Squadron clipped a telegraph pole. Nevertheless, he was able to coax the damaged aircraft back to his unit's base at Lympne in England before crash-landing in a nearby field.

Typhoon Mk.IB ▼

This Typhoon, MN345, nicknamed 'Peace River' was flown by Flying Officer James A Brown of 438 (RCAF) Squadron, based at Eindhoven in Holland, on November 6, 1944.

Hurricane production, it was decided that Hawker subsidiaries Avro and Gloster would build these aircraft respectively.

Being less occupied with other work than Avro, Gloster managed to put together the first production Typhoon just three weeks after the prototype had first flown – its first flight being on May 27, 1941. At the same time, it was becoming evident to Avro that the Rolls-

fumes tended to seep into the cockpit, necessitating the use of an oxygen mask at all times, even when taxiing on the ground. The huge Sabre engine also caused the cockpit to become stiflingly hot after prolonged use.

An unusual feature of the Typhoon was the 'car doors' which opened onto its cockpit in place of a conventional hinged or sliding canopy. They even had wind-down windows. There was also a dorsal fairing attached to the rear of the cockpit, which severely hampered rearward visibility.

The aircraft's greatest vice had yet to make itself known,

Royce Vulture was significantly less reliable than expected. The Vulture was cancelled in July and with it the Tornado.

Typhoon production was rapidly stepped up and the first machines off the line were rushed into service with 56 and 609 Squadrons. Their role was to be that of interceptor, to combat the new threat posed by the Focke-Wulf Fw 190.

Pilots soon discovered that the Typhoon was by no means a comfortable aircraft to fly however. Carbon monoxide

however. Several Typhoons were lost in mysterious circumstances and questions began to be asked about the type's airworthiness.

Then on August 11, 1942, Hawker test pilot Kenneth Seth-Smith was killed when his Typhoon R7692 broke apart and crashed during a straight and level test flight from Langley while over Thorpe in Surrey. The tailplane had detached mid-flight as a result of fatigue failure. An investigation determined that the elevator mass-balance bell-crank linkage had

Typhoon Mk.IB ▶

Wing Commander William Pitt-Brown started the war in India, flying Westland Wapiti and Vickers Valentia biplanes, before being posted to the Far East to fly Curtiss P-36 Mohawks in Assam against the Japanese. He returned to Britain in 1944 and led 174 Squadron throughout the Normandy invasion. In August he was made wing leader of 121 Wing and, stationed at Vitry-en-Artois, France, he flew this aircraft during September 1944. During a ground-attack mission over Belgium on the 10th he was hit by flak and bailed out. Later in the war, he served in the Far East once again as a Spitfire pilot.

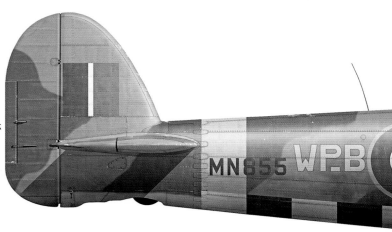

Typhoon Mk.IB ▲

This aircraft was flown by Canadian Wing Commander R T P 'Bob' Davidson, commander of 143 Wing, stationed at Hurn in England, during May 1944. Davidson had joined the RAF in 1937 and seen combat in Greece during 1940 before flying a Hurricane in Ceylon against the Japanese in 1941. On May 8, 1944, he made a forced landing in France and managed to evade capture, fighting with the Maquis until meeting up with Allied forces following the D-Day invasion.

Typhoon Mk.IB ▲

Canadian pilot Flight Lieutenant Harry Hardy flew this Typhoon with 440 (RCAF) Squadron, stationed at Eindhoven, Holland, on April 2, 1944. Hardy flew Typhoons on 96 missions from August 10, 1944, to March 24, 1945, and was hit by enemy fire six times. He survived the war and was still alive at the time of writing aged 95.

Typhoon Mk.IB ▶

Squadron Leader Thomas Henry Vincent Pheloung, commanding officer of 56 Squadron, stationed at Matlaske, England, flew this Typhoon during January 1943. He was killed in action on June 20, 1943, after being hit by flak during a low-level attack on enemy shipping off the coast of the Netherlands. His men watched EK183 flip onto its back and crash into the sea.

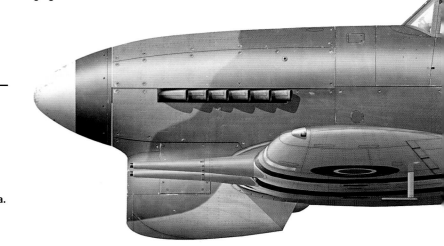

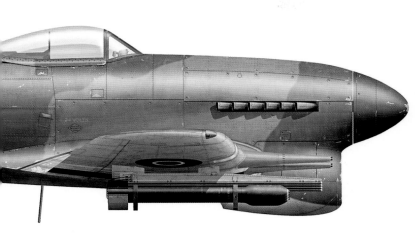

failed, causing severe vibration and the eventual catastrophic loss of the aircraft – an entirely different problem to that which had afflicted Lucas's machine.

The fitment of reinforcing plates partially cured the problem but it was never wholly solved.

Longer exhaust stubs were fitted in an attempt to fix the CO_2 problem in November 1941, and port cockpit doors were sealed over. In addition, a ventilation tube was installed to try and keep cockpit temperatures down and two vents were fitted below the port side radio hatch for the same purpose. The dorsal fairing was replaced with a transparent blister nicknamed the 'coffin hood' to improve visibility.

Finally, towards the end of 1942 and after numerous further tests, the Typhoon was able to demonstrate an acceptable level of reliability and continued to be used to counter Luftwaffe nuisance raids on the south coast of England. Meanwhile, bomb racks were

designed which would allow the Typhoon to carry 500lb bombs.

A few months later, in early 1943, new Typhoons had plumbing installed in their wings which allowed them to use 45-gallon drop tanks – improving range dramatically from 690 miles to 1090 miles. Larger solid rubber tailwheels were introduced in March 1943 to prevent shimmying and by mid-1943 every Typhoon was built with the attachment points needed to carry the new bomb racks. This also made small extensions to the cannon shell case ejector slots necessary so they would drop clear of any bombs or tanks fitted.

In addition, around 780lb of armour was added to protect the cockpit, engine and radiator bath from ground fire. Larger brake discs were eventually fitted too, to cope with the extra weight.

Experiments with fitting launch rails for 60lb RP-3 rockets were conducted in June 1943 and these were fitted to Typhoons operated by specialist fighter-bomber unit 181 Squadron from October 1943.

Beginning in November 1943, all new Typhoons rolling off the Gloster production line had a new one-piece sliding 'bubble' canopy fitted in place of the old 'car door' structure and a programme of recall and replacement was

instituted for older machines.

Early in 1944, it was decided that a four-bladed propeller should replace the original three-bladed type and that the larger tailplane of the Hawker Tempest should be fitted to improve stability – but both of these modifications took some time to introduce.

By the time of the D-Day landings and the subsequent Normandy campaign, the RAF had 18 operational Typhoon Mk.IB squadrons as part of the 2nd Tactical Air Force and a further nine as part of Air Defence of Great Britain. The dust and dirt whipped up by the powerful Sabre when the Typhoon was operating from hastily prepared forward landing grounds on the Continent necessitated the fitment of air filters and at the end of June 1944 it was decided that all Typhoons should have tropical filter kits installed as standard.

While the Typhoon came increasingly to be regarded as a developmental dead end, several unusual versions were contemplated – R8694 was experimentally fitted with the more powerful Sabre IV by Napier, achieving a maximum speed of 452mph; R7881 became a prototype night fighter fitted with an AI (Airborne Interception) radar and a few examples of the Typhoon FR IB reconnaissance version were built. The latter had three F24 cameras fitted in place of its port inner cannon, one facing forward and two pointing straight down. Unfortunately, the Typhoon's characteristic strong vibrations often meant that the resulting photographs were too blurry to be of any use.

A total of 3317 Typhoons were built, nearly all of them by Gloster. Twenty-five were lost to structural failure with the death of 23 pilots. ●

US○A   EK183

HAWKER TEMPEST

Tempest Mk.V ▲

Norwegian Lieutenant Johan Bernard Gilhuus of 80 Squadron, stationed at Volkel in Holland, flew this Tempest on October 11, 1944. Gilhuus was killed in action just over two months later on December 17 when his fighter was hit by flak in the cockpit area. He had achieved one aerial victory the year before – a Fw 190 – and was the first and only Norwegian to die while flying a Tempest.

Conceived simply as the Typhoon Mk.II, the Tempest earned itself a new name and went on to become one of the most powerful and deadly piston-engined fighters ever flown.

1942-1953

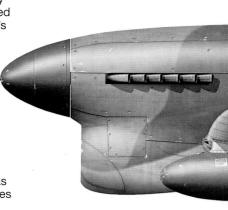

Urgently needed on the front line yet beset by technical maladies and hampered by its too-thick wing, the Typhoon quickly became Hawker's problem child. Stung by the type's embarrassing flaws, the company's design team set about devising a new version that would be superior in every respect to the Mk.I.

The first step was to improve the Typhoon's high-speed performance by fitting it with a thinner wing. This would improve airflow and therefore performance at higher altitudes and speeds. In addition, an elliptical shape was adopted which would allow the aircraft's four 20mm Hispano cannon to be set further back where the extra space available would allow for 200 rounds of ammunition apiece.

Drag would be further reduced by providing the aircraft with radiators set into the wing leading edges inboard of the landing gear for the type's chosen engine – the Napier Sabre IV. A four-bladed propeller would help to ease the seemingly incurable vibrations which afflicted the Typhoon Mark I and the pilot's visibility would be improved with a new sliding bubble canopy.

Tendering for Air Ministry Specification F.10/41 in November 1941, Hawker was awarded a contract for two prototype Typhoon Mk.IIs. Since the Typhoon's sibling, the Tornado, had been cancelled a few months earlier due to the non-availability of its proposed Rolls-Royce Vulture engine, it was decided that Typhoon II prototypes should be fitted with a range of under-development engines.

The contract was expanded

to six prototypes and given the ever-widening gulf between the design of the original Typhoon and the new aircraft it was given its own name on February 28, 1942 – the Tempest.

One Tempest was to be powered by the Sabre IV (Tempest I), as previously planned, two by the Bristol Centaurus (Tempest II), two by different Rolls-Royce Griffons (Tempest III and IV) and one by the Sabre II (Tempest V).

Good progress was made and in August 1942 the Air Ministry ordered 100 Tempest Vs and 300 Tempest Is, the latter to be built by Gloster in place of a planned batch of 300 Typhoons.

The Tempest I embodied the key design features planned for the Typhoon II – the new wings, radiators, canopy and propeller – but problems with the Sabre IV delayed its development. The first prototype to fly was therefore the Tempest V, HM595, on September 2. This featured a longer fuselage than that of the Typhoon, 33ft 8in compared to the 31ft 11½in of the latter, plus the new wings but without the new radiators or cockpit canopy. The tail unit was also very similar to that of the Typhoon.

The undercarriage main legs were longer than those of the Typhoon with a wider track to improve stability during landing and to provide better clearance for the propeller. Fitted with trunnions, the legs were shortened as they retracted to fit within their housings. The tailwheels was also retractable and fully enclosed.

In November it was fitted with the new cockpit design, which had a centre panel comprising a 1½in thick outer layer and a ¼in thick inner layer to make it bullet-resistant. The frame was carefully positioned to provide maximum visibility.

A tail fin fairing which served to almost double the fin's vertical surface area was also added

Tempest Mk.V

Two Bf 109s were shot down on February 25, 1945, by Flight Lieutenant L C Luckhoff of 33 Squadron, based Gilze-Rijen, Holland, flying EJ880. While chasing down his second victim at low level, Luckhoff's machine suffered heavy flak damage and he was forced to land at the nearest Allied airfield – Volkel.

Tempest Mk.V ▲

Having converted from Spitfires, Squadron Leader Evan D 'Rosie' Mackie flew Tempests as the commander of 80 Squadron, stationed at Volkel in Holland. This is his aircraft, NV700, as it looked in March 1945.

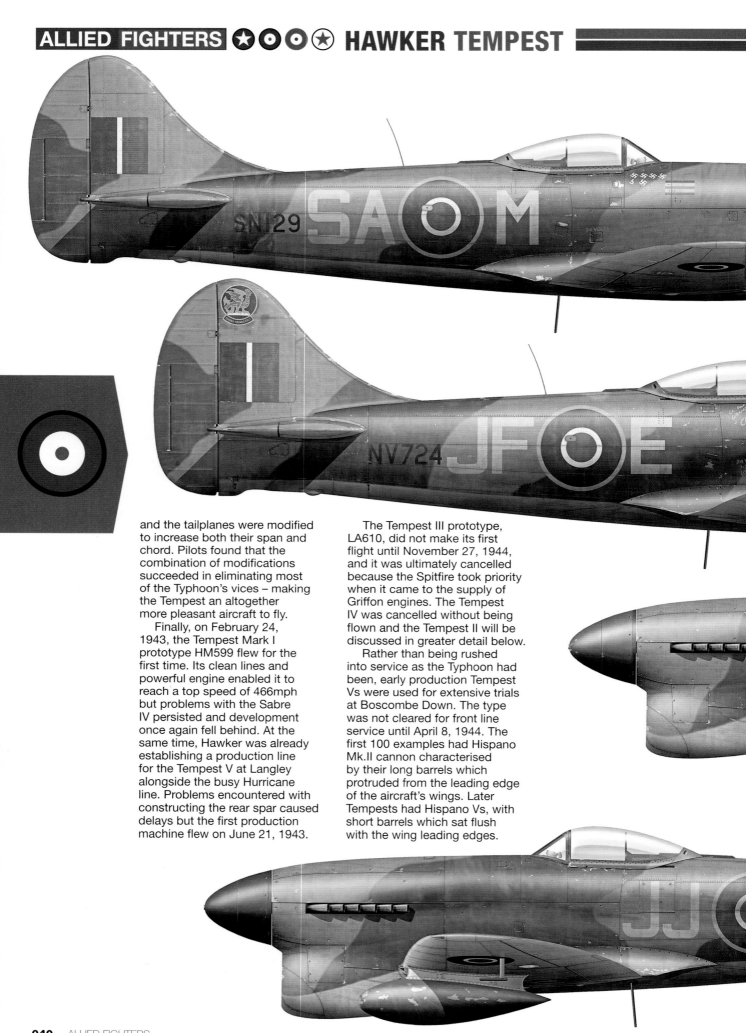

and the tailplanes were modified to increase both their span and chord. Pilots found that the combination of modifications succeeded in eliminating most of the Typhoon's vices – making the Tempest an altogether more pleasant aircraft to fly.

Finally, on February 24, 1943, the Tempest Mark I prototype HM599 flew for the first time. Its clean lines and powerful engine enabled it to reach a top speed of 466mph but problems with the Sabre IV persisted and development once again fell behind. At the same time, Hawker was already establishing a production line for the Tempest V at Langley alongside the busy Hurricane line. Problems encountered with constructing the rear spar caused delays but the first production machine flew on June 21, 1943.

The Tempest III prototype, LA610, did not make its first flight until November 27, 1944, and it was ultimately cancelled because the Spitfire took priority when it came to the supply of Griffon engines. The Tempest IV was cancelled without being flown and the Tempest II will be discussed in greater detail below.

Rather than being rushed into service as the Typhoon had been, early production Tempest Vs were used for extensive trials at Boscombe Down. The type was not cleared for front line service until April 8, 1944. The first 100 examples had Hispano Mk.II cannon characterised by their long barrels which protruded from the leading edge of the aircraft's wings. Later Tempests had Hispano Vs, with short barrels which sat flush with the wing leading edges.

◄ Tempest Mk.V

During April 1945, New Zealander Flight Lieutenant James C 'Jimmy' Sheddan of 486 Squadron shot down two Junkers Ju 87 dive bombers and a Fw 190. He had previously shot down a Fw 190 on January 1 that year but most of his early missions were flown to intercept V-1 flying bombs. On July 5, 1944, his Tempest crashed into the sea after an attempted V-1 interception and Sheddan survived 19 hours adrift in a dinghy. He died in 2010 aged 92.

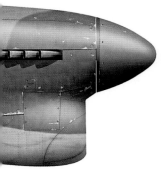

Tempest Mk.V

Flight Lieutenant Pierre H Clostermann, a Frenchman, served with 3 Squadron as the war drew to a close. After the war ended he flew this aircraft, NV724, while stationed at Lübeck in Germany in July 1945. He had joined the Free French Air Force in Britain in March 1942 and scored his first two victories, both Fw 190s, on July 27, 1943, while flying a Spitfire. He ended the war having flown 432 combat sorties and achieved 19 victories plus 14 shared, 72 Locomotives, 225 motor vehicles, five tanks and two torpedo boats. He died in March 2006 aged 85.

▼

As the number of Tempests being delivered to squadrons increased, further features were added and others altered. New aircraft came fitted with a Rebecca transponder from mid-to-late 1944, which required the addition of an aerial under the port side centre section.

On active service, the Tempest performed best when operating at low to medium altitude and was found to be well-suited to long-range armed reconnaissance operations thanks to its ability to carry a pair of 45-gallon drop tanks and the excellent field of vision afforded by its bubble canopy.

When German forces began launching V-1 flying bombs at London during June 1944, the Tempest demonstrated its ability to both catch and destroy the 'robot' invaders. It was also able to remain in the air for extended periods on patrol while waiting for V-1s to appear.

Beginning on September 21, 1944, Tempests were operated from forward airfields on the Continent by the 2nd Tactical Air Force. Between late October and mid-December, most were withdrawn for

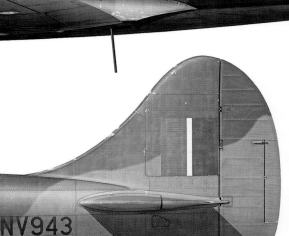

Tempest Mk V ▲

Bounced by Fw 190Ds on March 28, 1945, Staff Sergeant Stanley A Shepherd's Tempest was shot down. The 56 Squadron pilot crashed near Schoonrewoerd in the Netherlands but survived. He was approached by two locals who wanted to get him under cover and hide him but Shepherd decided that he first needed to return to his wrecked aircraft to retrieve his gun. This delay meant he was captured by German soldiers who had rushed to the crash site, and he was later shot.

Tempest Mk V

Nicknamed the 'Terror of the Rheine', Squadron Leader David 'Foob' Fairbanks, an American who joined the RAF via Canada, was the highest scoring Tempest ace with 11 victories. Serving with 274 Squadron on February 24, 1945, he scored his final 'kill': a Fw 190 over Plantlunne, Germany. Four days later, he led six Tempests into an attack on a formation of 40 Fw 190s and Bf 109s, eventually being shot down by one of the Fw 190s. He spent the rest of the war as a PoW.

◄

WHEN THE GERMANS BEGAN LAUNCHING V-1 FLYING BOMBS AT BRITAIN, TEMPESTS WERE USED TO CATCH AND SHOOT THEM DOWN

Tempest Mk.V ▶

Having been a 'millionaire playboy' on the Greek island of Chios, Basilios Michael 'Vass' Vassiliades joined the RAF in 1942. By March 1945 he was serving with 3 Squadron based at Volkel in the Netherlands. He scored his 10th and last victory flying this aircraft on March 7, shooting down Fw 190D-9 'Yellow 15'. On March 25, he attacked a convoy of trucks well behind enemy lines which was protected by a concentration of flak batteries. His wingman was shot down almost immediately and the two other Tempest pilots refused to continue the attack, but Vassiliades got in and out without a scratch. Having surveyed the damage caused, he went in for a second pass and was shot down and killed.

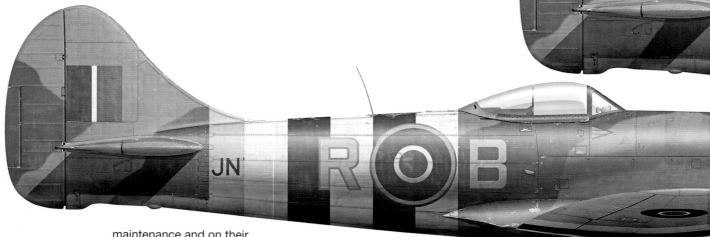

maintenance and on their return they were flown as an air superiority fighter, seeking out and destroying Luftwaffe combat aircraft at low level – sometimes with medium to high altitude cover from Spitfire Mk.XIVs.

During the final months of the war, the Tempest achieved an estimated 6:1 success rate against enemy single-seat fighters, even shooting down a number of Messerschmitt Me 262 jet fighters.

TEMPEST II AND VI

The quick success of the Tempest V led to an unusual situation where the Mk.V was in service long before any of the earlier marks. However, the Mk.II did eventually reach full series production.

Powered by a Bristol Centaurus IV engine, the Tempest II looked significantly different from both the original Typhoon and its sibling the Tempest V. The 18-cylinder Centaurus was radial in shape, rather than inline like the 24-cylinder Sabre, and air- rather than liquid-cooled. It therefore

featured a tight cylindrical cowl with its exhausts stacked on either side. Its air intakes were positioned on the leading edges of both wings and another air intake along with the oil cooler were installed on the inner starboard wing.

The first Tempest II prototype, LA602, had made its first flight as early as June 28, 1943, and the second flew for the first time on September 18, 1943. Severe engine vibration was experienced early on but was largely cured with the replacement of the usual rigid eight-point engine mountings with six-point rubber insulated shock mounts. In addition, the four-bladed propeller was briefly replaced with a five-bladed unit until a rebalanced version of the original was adopted.

Tempest Mk.V ▼

A handful of Messerschmitt Me 262 jet fighters were shot down by Tempests and among them were two destroyed by Wing Commander John Basil Wray, of 122 Wing, flying this machine.

> **UNUSUALLY, THE TEMPEST MK.V ENTERED SERVICE BEFORE ANY OF THE EARLIER MARKS**

◀ Tempest Mk.V

Wing Commander Roland P Beaumont commanded the first Tempest wing, 150 Wing, stationed at Newchurch, England, during June 1944. This was his aircraft at the time. Four months later, he was shot down while flying a Tempest near Nijmegen and became a prisoner of war until he was released by Soviet forces in May 1945.

Tempest Mk.V

Flying this Tempest with 3 Squadron, Belgian ace Flight Lieutenant Remy Van Lierde shot down up to 44 V-1 flying bombs. He ended the war with six air-to-air combat victories and died in 1990 aged 74.

▼

Longer than the Tempest V at 34ft 5in, the Tempest II was only slightly heavier even though the Centaurus weighed 2695lb compared to the Sabre's 2360lb. This was because the former did not require the heavy radiator unit of the latter – the overall difference amounting to just 20lb in the Tempest V's favour. The Tempest II was also 10mph faster at a top speed of 442mph.

The first production Tempest II, powered by the Centaurus V, was rolled out on October 4, 1944, but the first six off the line were removed for further trials rather than being allocated to front line units. The type was earmarked for the fight against Japan in the Far East but the war ended before it could enter service.

The last Tempest was the Mark VI, powered by the Sabre V. The original Tempest V prototype, HM595, was heavily modified to become the Tempest VI prototype, first flying in its new configuration on May 9, 1944. Two more Tempest Vs, EJ841 and JN750, were also converted to Tempest VI standard in 1945 and the type enjoyed a brief production run of 142 aircraft – eventually making it the last piston-engined fighter in operational service with the RAF. A total of 1702 Tempests of all types were produced. ●

YAKOVLEV

Yak-1 ▼

This rocket-armed tail-ski Yak-1 was flown by Kapitan Boris Nikolayevich Yeryomin, commander of the 2nd Eskadrilya, 296 IAP, stationed at Brigadirovka Airfield in Izyum, USSR, during March 1942. He flew 342 combat sorties and achieved eight victories in air combat plus 15 shared.

The first fighter from the soon-to-be-famous Yakovlev aviation bureau, the Yak-1 was a landmark design that would pave the way for some of the Soviet Air Force's best Second World War aircraft.

1940-1950

A t the end of the 1930s the Soviet government realised that the fighter aircraft equipping its air force were becoming increasingly outdated compared to the latest types being produced in Western Europe and instigated a programme of development that would redress the balance.

The Soviet Union's best and brightest young designers were handed this task and given enormous resources with which to see it through. Among them was Aleksandr Sergeyevich Yakovlev, aged 33 in 1939. He had designed his first powered aircraft in 1927 and graduated from the Zhukovsky Air Force Military Engineering Academy in 1931.

He was then assigned to Moscow Aviation Plant No. 39 and established his first design office there, working on

lightweight aircraft, the following year. He became the head of the Yakovlev Design Bureau in 1935.

When a competition was held in 1939 to produce the next standard Soviet single-seat fighter, he submitted four designs based on essentially the same airframe – a basic fighter (designated I-26), trainer (I-27), high-altitude fighter (I-28) and heavy fighter (I-30). Work on these concepts had begun in May and the basic fighter design, a sleek low-wing monoplane with fully enclosed cockpit and retractable undercarriage, was approved for first mock-up and then prototype production in October.

The I-26-1 prototype was rolled out in January 1940, making its first flight on the 13th equipped with a ski undercarriage due to the icy ground conditions at that time of year. The fuselage structure

was made of welded steel tubing and the forward fuselage had skin made from duralumin. The rear fuselage, however, had a fabric skin supported by wooden planks. The wings were wooden too. Although it had been hoped that a supercharged version of the Klimov M-105 engine could power it, this was unavailable so a standard M-105P had to do instead.

This produced 1050hp, driving a metal variable-pitch

YAK-1

Yak-1B

Starshiy Leytenant Pavel Pavlov, an ace who achieved 12 victories in air combat plus five shared, flew this aircraft while serving with 21st IAP, stationed in the Leningrad area, USSR, during the summer of 1942.

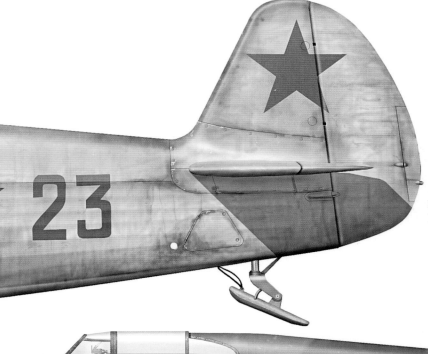

Yak-1

During the early stages of the Battle of Stalingrad, Starshiy Leytenant Mikhail Dmitrievich Baranov of 183 IAP became the leading Soviet ace with 24 combat victories. The inscription on the side of his aircraft reads 'Mikhail Baranov the Menace for the Fascists'. On August 6, 1942, Baranov and two wingmen were escorting Il-2 ground-attack aircraft when they happened upon 24 Ju 87s being escorted by four Bf 109s. In running battles he shot down three Bf 109s – the first four had been joined by more – before finally ramming a fourth. He died on January 15, 1943, while testing a new factory fresh Yak-1. It suffered a technical problem and rolled over before plunging into the ground.

Yak-1

Female fighter ace Serzhant Lydia Vladimirovna Litvyak, also known as Lilya, of the 586 IAP, flew this aircraft on the Stalingrad front on September 27, 1942. This was the day when she achieved what some regard as her first 'kill' – a Ju 88. Press reports referred to Litvyak as the 'White Lily of Stalingrad' and she reportedly did pick flowers and put bouquets in her cockpit, which would inevitably be thrown out by the male pilots who shared the aircraft.

▼

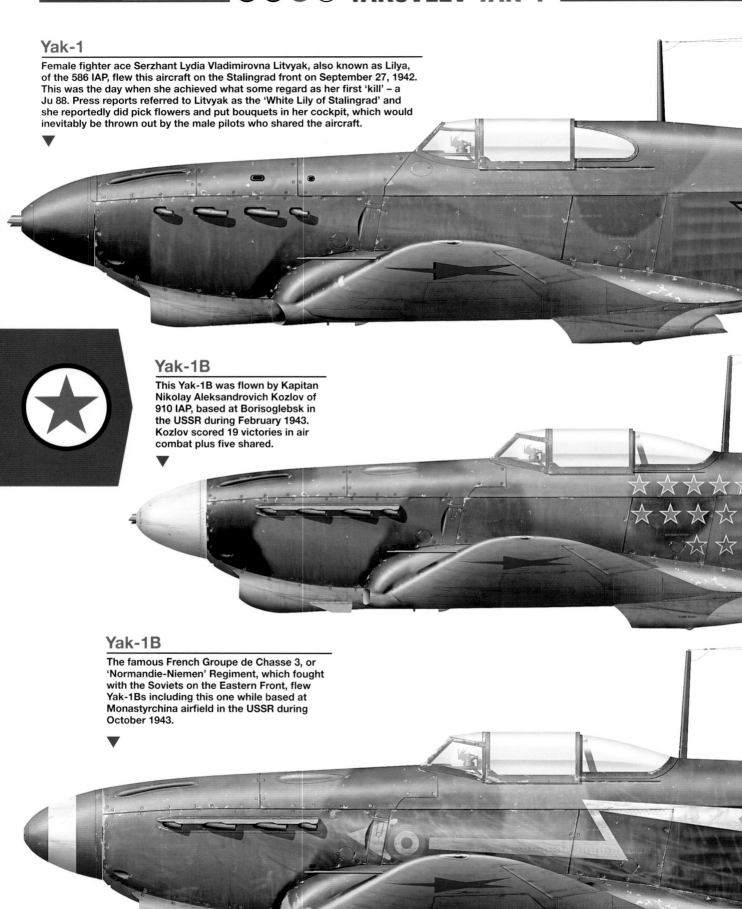

Yak-1B

This Yak-1B was flown by Kapitan Nikolay Aleksandrovich Kozlov of 910 IAP, based at Borisoglebsk in the USSR during February 1943. Kozlov scored 19 victories in air combat plus five shared.

▼

Yak-1B

The famous French Groupe de Chasse 3, or 'Normandie-Niemen' Regiment, which fought with the Soviets on the Eastern Front, flew Yak-1Bs including this one while based at Monastyrchina airfield in the USSR during October 1943.

▼

three-bladed propeller. By way of comparison its contemporary, the Supermarine Spitfire Mk.I, was powered by a Rolls-Royce Merlin that produced 1030hp. The 'P' in M-105P, meant that an engine-mounted cannon could be fitted, firing through the centre of the propeller. For this installation, a 20mm ShVAK cannon was chosen. Four additional weapons, 7.62mm machine guns, were to be fitted around the engine – two above it and two below. However, no weapons were actually added to the I-26-1 prototype.

While the original design had called for a fighter weighing 5070lb fully loaded, the I-26-1 actually weighed 5730lb when it was built, apparently because many of the manufacturers responsible for producing its components and equipment had given rather optimistic projections of how much their products would weigh.

The I-26-1 flew 26 times between January 13 and March 19, 1940. Test pilots found that it handled easily and could reach a top speed of 360mph on a good day – comparing well to the Spitfire I's 367mph. Unlike the Spitfire, however, the I-26-1 was let down by shoddy workmanship. The engine was prone to serious oil leaks and could suffer from critical overheating just a few minutes into a flight.

The leading edges of its wings began to break away far short of the design's intended maximum load and structural integrity in general was poor. The undercarriage could not be retracted if the aircraft accelerated too quickly after take-off and even when the wheels were retracted they would seldom lock in place correctly.

Incredibly, series production of the I-26 was by now already under way. The first production machine rolling off the line on March 22, 1940. At this point the second prototype, I-26-2, had not even flown yet. This featured a stronger airframe but although several advanced engines were considered it was again equipped with an M-105P because none of them were ready. In addition, it was decided that the two machine guns due to be fitted below the engine would have to be deleted due to the engine's oil system being extensively modified. Loaded weight rose to 5887lb.

The I-26-2 first flew the day after the first production machine, on March 23, 1940, and during trials which lasted less than two

Yak-1B ▼

By 1943, Serzhant Lydia Litvyak was flying Yak-1Bs with the 73rd GvIAP, based at Krasnyy Luch in the USSR. She was flying this particular example on August 1, 1943, when she failed to return from a mission. She is believed to have been shot down and killed, though rumours persisted for years that she had survived a crash landing and had been held in a German prisoner of war camp. At the time of her disappearance she had achieved 12 victories plus four shared.

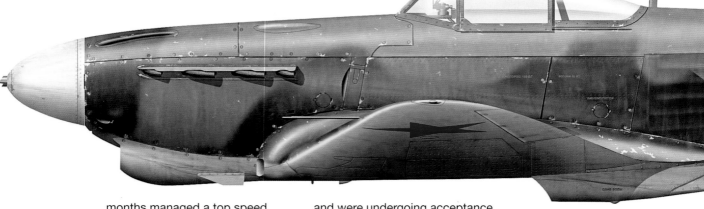

months managed a top speed of 374mph. No diving or spin trials were conducted and the armament was not tested.

The I-26-1 was destroyed in a fatal crash on April 27, 1940, when a sharp manoeuvre resulted in the undercarriage locks coming loose, the main wheels being deployed at just the wrong moment and the pilot losing control. It had only been airborne for a total of 13 hours and nine minutes up to that point.

On June 1 the I-26-2 was handed over to the Soviet Air Force for acceptance trials. These determined that the aircraft offered high performance but was structurally weak and the engine continued to overheat – so rpm could not be raised too high. Most aerobatic manoeuvres were banned too for fear of structural failure.

It was also noted that the aircraft had no communications equipment whatsoever, no generator and no vertical speed indicator. Its gunsight was woefully inadequate as well. By now though, a dozen production versions based on the first prototype had already been built

and were undergoing acceptance trials with the Soviet Air Force.

The third prototype, unsurprisingly designated I-26-3, was completed on September 17, 1940, and featured cockpit ventilation, more airframe strengthening, capacity for more ammunition and numerous further detail changes. Flight testing commenced immediately and it was determined that most of the earlier faults plaguing the type had been resolved – though

Yak-1M ▼

This aircraft was flown by Starshiy Leytenant Aleksandr Alekseyevich Shokurov of the 156th IAP while stationed in Czestochowa, Poland, during the summer of 1944. Shokurov achieved 19 aerial victories.

RELIABILITY AND BUILD QUALITY IMPROVED AS PRODUCTION SWITCHED TO THE YAK-1B

all-up weight had now reached 6175lb and a host of new defects were now picked up.

The production versions were modified on the fly as the prototypes trialled different fixes and new components – these continual revisions, some 300 of them between February 1 and October 1, 1940, serving to hamper the overall numbers being built. Finally, in December 1940, the I-26 was officially designated the Yak-1 in honour of its originator.

By the middle of 1941, two aircraft plants were engaged in building the Yak-1, No. 303 and No. 292, each apparently working to a slightly different set of drawings – resulting in aircraft that varied in performance.

The revisions kept coming, with the aircraft's equipment and engine being continually upgraded and improved. The upgraded Yak-1B had completely replaced the Yak-1 by October 1942. This boasted an improved oil cooler, 'bubble' canopy for improved pilot visibility, a single 12.7mm UBS offset to port in place of the two 7.62mm machine guns and slightly more power (1180hp) from the improved M-105PF.

Reliability and build quality also continued to get better as production progressed. Weight continued to be a problem, however, and by the time the last Yak-1Bs were completed in 1944 top speed was only 326mph.

Overall, a total of 8667 were produced with the last one being accepted in October 1944. ●

Yak-1B ▼

Leytenant Ivan V Fedorov of the 812th IAP, stationed at Kuban in the USSR, flew this aircraft on May 10, 1943. He is believed to have scored 36 victories in air combat plus one shared.

YAKOVLEV YAK-7 AND YAK-3

Yak-7B ▶

Starshiy Leytenant Vladimir Aleksandrovich Orekhov of the 434 IAP, based at Pichuga Airdrome, Leningrad, flew this aircraft during September 1942 when he returned to his unit after recovering from arm and leg injuries he suffered at the beginning of the year. He flew throughout 1943 and was promoted to major in early 1944. By the end of the war in Europe he had flown 420 combat sorties and achieved 19 victories in air combat plus two shared victories.

Originally designed as a two-seat trainer for pilots learning to fly the Yak-1, the Yak-7 was converted into a superior single-seater. The Yak-3 was quite simply the ultimate Yakovlev fighter of the war.

1940-1947

T he second design that made up Yakovlev's entry to the 1939 Soviet fighter competition was the I-27 trainer. As proposed this shared a great deal with the I-26 basic fighter, so when the I-26 began to progress through the development process it made sense to bring forward the I-27 too.

Detail work on it started in January 1940 and the government approved the programme two months later. Rather than retaining its original designation, the first prototype became the UTI-26-1. It was essentially an I-26, with the same M-105P engine and propeller, but with two cockpits. Each had its own sliding canopy hood and a set of flight instruments and controls.

There was no intercom however, the instructor and his student could only speak to one another by means of a crude rubber tube. In order to install the second cockpit, the I-26's wings had to be moved 100mm to the rear while the radiator went forward. Two 7.62mm ShKAS machine guns were fitted with 500 rounds apiece.

The prototype was flown for the first time on July 23, 1940, and tests continued until August when the undercarriage failed. Unsurprisingly, it suffered from all the same faults as the I-26,

particularly the failing undercarriage locks and the overheating engine oil. The second prototype, completed on September 17, 1940 featured a revised undercarriage and smaller elevators to make it easier for a trainee to fly safely.

There were numerous other alterations and the centre of gravity was shifting forwards which improved stability. After Soviet Air Force acceptance trials from January 1 to February 14, 1941, the type entered full production on March 4, 1941, powered by the M-105PA, under the new designation Yak-7UTI.

Five months later, a production model Yak-7UTI was withdrawn from the assembly line to have self-sealing fuel tanks, an armoured seat, and a 20mm ShVAK engine-mounted cannon fitted. It also received six under-wing launch rails for unguided RS-82 rockets. This was the first Yak-7.

The type was quickly put into production and then into service, reports on the prototype having been extremely positive. It was easier to fly than the Yak-1, the unoccupied rear cockpit could be used for the installation of a long-range fuel tank and it was easier to repair thanks to design changes around the engine.

While its performance differed

little from that of the Yak-1, the Yak-7 able to reach an unremarkable top speed of 348mph at 16,400ft, and its turning performance was marginally inferior, it was a much more stable and forgiving machine. This meant attacks on ground targets could be made with greater accuracy and it could be recovered from extreme manoeuvres with far greater ease.

Significant changes were made during 1942, the second year of Yak-7 manufacture – including the installation of a two-way radio complete with aerial mast, a semi-retractable tailwheel (it had been non-retractable before), fully enclosing main wheel doors, a plywood hinged hood in place of the rear cockpit canopy and ammunition belt link collectors. The latter was so that the links could be reused.

With these modifications in place, the standard Yak-7 became the Yak-7A and a total of 277 were built.

But the aircraft remained inferior to its opponents, chiefly the Messerschmitt Bf 109, in combat and further improvements were urgently needed. Work was now undertaken on aerodynamic

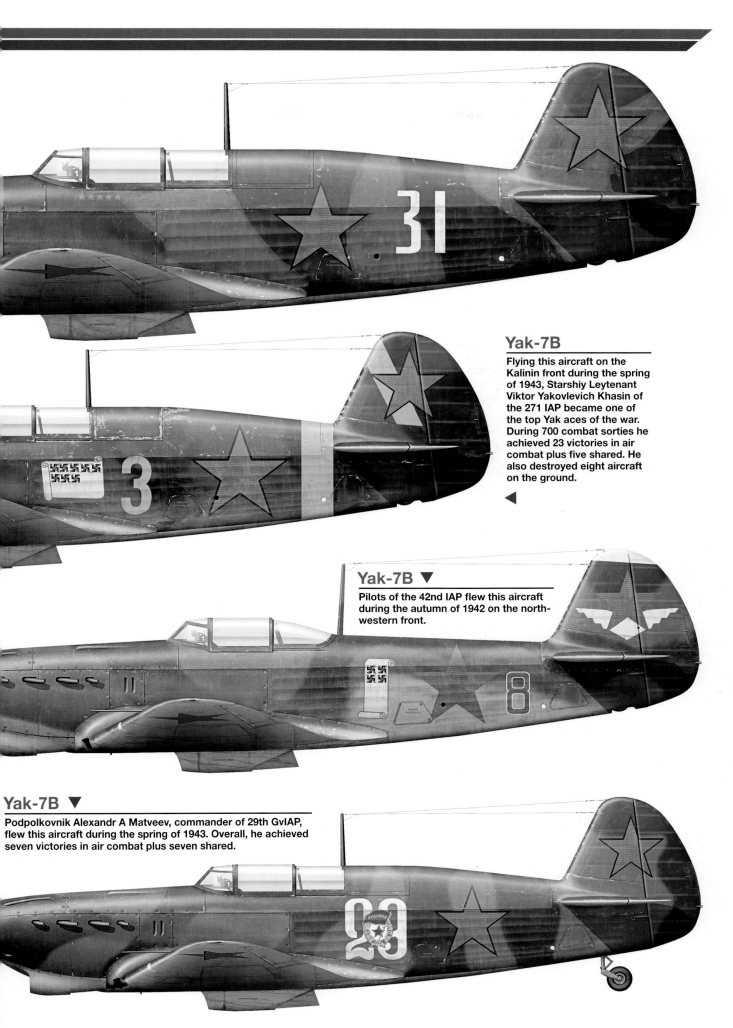

Yak-7B

Flying this aircraft on the Kalinin front during the spring of 1943, Starshiy Leytenant Viktor Yakovlevich Khasin of the 271 IAP became one of the top Yak aces of the war. During 700 combat sorties he achieved 23 victories in air combat plus five shared. He also destroyed eight aircraft on the ground.

Yak-7B ▼

Pilots of the 42nd IAP flew this aircraft during the autumn of 1942 on the north-western front.

Yak-7B ▼

Podpolkovnik Alexandr A Matveev, commander of 29th GvIAP, flew this aircraft during the spring of 1943. Overall, he achieved seven victories in air combat plus seven shared.

Yak-3 ▼

Already an experienced combat pilot when the Germans invaded, Podpolkovnik Anton Dmitrievich Yakimenko continued to fly combat missions until the summer of 1944 when he suffered a serious head would during the Jassy-Kishinev operation. He returned to the front during the final weeks of that year. This is his aircraft while he was stationed in Austria during 1945. The inscriptions reads: "Back to Motherland with Victory!" He is believed to have achieved about 30 victories during the war but no one is certain because he refused to keep count himself.

Yak-3 ▼

This aircraft was flown by Leytenant Dmitriy Karpenko of the 66th GvIAP, 4th GvIAD, while based in Šiauliai, Lithuania, during February 1945.

Yak-3 ▶

Though he was born in Russia, Léon Ougloff moved to France with his parents when he was just one year old in 1919. He eventually became a French citizen in 1933. Having become a trained fighter pilot in 1940, he joined the Free French Air Force in early 1943 and then volunteered for the GC 3 Normandie-Niemen Regiment, 303rd IAD, on May 22, 1944. He spoke fluent Russian so had no problem fitting in with the unit's Soviet comrades. This was his aircraft during April 1945 in East Prussia. By that point he had one confirmed victory plus another four shared. Having survived the war, he was killed only two years later in an air accident at Rabat.

Yak-3 ▲

The commander of 6th GvIAD, Podpolkovnik Boris Nikolaevich Yeryomin, flew this aircraft during May 1945 while based in Prague, Czechoslovakia. He completed 534 combat sorties, with 19 confirmed victories plus another three shared.

Yak-3 ▶

Pilots of the 7th GvIAP, 303rd IAD, flew this aircraft in East Prussia, Germany, during April 1945.

refinements such as reshaping the carburettor air inlets and oil cooler fairing, making the tailwheel fully retractable and improving the overall surface finish.

Armament was upgraded with the replacement of the two 7.62mm machine guns with two 12.7mm machine guns and the pilot's control stick was replaced with one modelled on that of the Bf 109. With all these alterations, the aircraft was designated Yak-7B – and its weight was now three and a half times that of a Bf 109.

Production began switching from Yak-7A to Yak-7B during April 1942 and from May 1942 an extra fuel tank was fitted as standard where the rear cockpit had originally been. However front line units, apparently appalled at the positioning of so much fuel in a non-self-sealing tank right behind the pilot, began to remove this feature.

That summer, a more powerful engine began to be fitted, the M-105PF. In addition, the production model Yak-7B featured alterations to lighten its structure and the back seat fuel tank was deleted.

As production of the Yak-7B progressed, the performance of new-built aircraft improved. The specification remained the same but build quality refinements allowed the basic design to realise more of its potential. During early 1943, a new bubble top cockpit canopy was introduced, finally removing all evidence of the Yak-7's origins as a trainer.

Despite the production improvements though, there were still problems. The use of new low-grade adhesives meant the wing skin had a disturbing tendency to come off in flight and there were problems with the cockpit canopy ejection system which could cause the canopy to warp or come off during a dive.

Efforts to resolve these and other issues would be taken up with the next sequential developments of the family – the Yak-9 and the Yak-3.

The Yak-3 was a successful attempt to take all the very best features of preceding models – the Yak-1, Yak-7 and Yak-9 – and put them all together in a single aircraft.

During September 1942, efforts began to create a lightened version of the Yak-1 – the Yak-1M. This incorporated all of the improvements that had been made to the Yak-1 up to this point, including a bubble canopy, and weight was indeed reduced significantly. The Yak-1M's wing had a smaller surface area and the oil cooler was moved from the aircraft's chin to the wing roots.

A prototype was built and tested 1943 with this configuration, then a second was constructed with plywood rather than fabric covering the rear fuselage. It also had a mastless radio antenna, a reflector gunsight and improved engine cooling. It was shown that the Yak-1Ms had exceptional performance – particularly their climb rate – and the type was ordered into series production as the Yak-3 in October 1943. It was to take the place of the Yak-1 on production lines.

Each Yak-3 took significantly longer to build than a Yak-1,

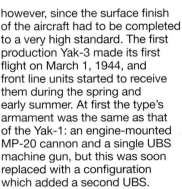

however, since the surface finish of the aircraft had to be completed to a very high standard. The first production Yak-3 made its first flight on March 1, 1944, and front line units started to receive them during the spring and early summer. At first the type's armament was the same as that of the Yak-1: an engine-mounted MP-20 cannon and a single UBS machine gun, but this was soon replaced with a configuration which added a second UBS.

Pilots responded well to the Yak-3 – despite the usual Soviet fighter teething problems its superior build quality allowed its latent performance to shine through. It was very small, agile and very fast at low altitude and this combination of attributes made it superior even to the best of the Luftwaffe's fighters on the Eastern Front.

A total of 4848 Yak-3s were built overall. ●

THE LAST WARTIME DEVELOPMENT OF THE YAK-1 FAMILY, THE YAK-3, FINALLY REALISED THE TYPE'S POTENTIAL

MIKOYAN-GUREVICH
MIG-3

ЗА Сталина!

MiG-3 ▶

Muscovite Kapitan Sergey Nikolayevich Polyakov, commander of the 7 IAP, flew this MiG-3 in defence of Leningrad during September 1941. He converted to the Il-2 ground-attack aircraft shortly afterwards and had flown 42 combat missions all together when, on Christmas Eve 1941, he flew a U-2 liaison biplane right into an ongoing German air raid. He was shot down and killed.

1940-1945

Looks to die for and a decent turn of speed at the right altitude were not enough to make the MiG-3 a successful fighter. It was available in numbers when the German invasion of the Soviet Union began but proved to be no match for the Messerschmitt Bf 109.

Soviet fighter designer Nikolai Polikarpov had been largely responsible for the successful I-16 design in 1931, despite having nearly been executed as a traitor to the people less than two years earlier, but the type's most advanced development, the I-180, was an abysmal failure.

The first prototype crashed during its maiden flight on December 15, 1938, with famous test pilot and Hero of the Soviet Union Valery Chkalov at the controls. He was killed and Polikarpov was held at least partially responsible.

Even so, a few months later Polikarpov was able to commence work on a new monoplane fighter with a liquid-cooled inline engine, as opposed to the I-16's air-cooled radial. This was codenamed Samolyot 'Kh' and good progress was made until the designer was sent to Germany as part of a trade delegation. Returning home in November 1939, he found that he had been displaced as head of his own design bureau by well-connected young engineer Artyom Mikoyan.

Shortly thereafter, Polikarpov was effectively ousted entirely but work continued on the Samolyot 'Kh' in the hands of Mikoyan and some of Polikarpov's former staff

MiG-3 (late series)

The slogan 'For Stalin!' appeared on many Soviet aircraft during the war, including this one flown by Lieutenant A V Shlopov of the 6th IAK, Moscow air defence, Moscow, during the winter of 1941-1942. Shlopov scored three victories in air combat plus five shared.

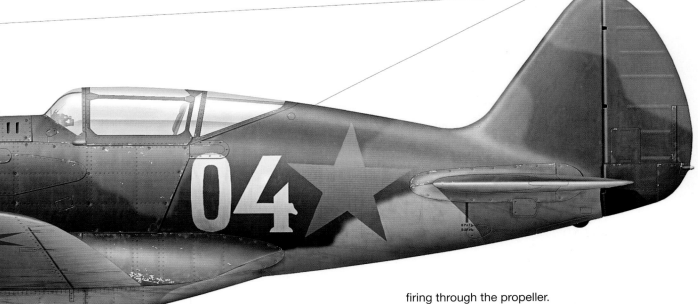

including Mikhail Gurevich and Vadim Aleksandrovich Romodin.

The Samolyot 'Kh' was submitted for the Soviet government's 1939 fighter competition under a new name, the I-200, and construction of a mock-up was ordered on Christmas Day 1939. Once built, this met with immediate approval and construction of three prototypes began in early March 1940.

The aircraft boasted exceptionally clean lines, looking more like a high powered racer than a fighter, though its engine

was the 1200hp AM-35A rather than the still-in-development 1400hp AM-37 that it had been designed for. Most of the I-200 was made of wood, though the wing centre section was metal and the forward fuselage was made of welded steel tubes covered with a duralumin skin. The water radiator was positioned beneath the cockpit, well towards the rear of the aircraft, and there were three exhaust pipes on either side.

The main gear and tailwheel were pneumatically retractable and armament was two .303 machine guns and a .50 calibre machine gun all above the engine,

firing through the propeller.

Early tests demonstrated the I-200's stunning potential – it achieved a top speed of 404mph on May 24, 1940 – and after all three prototypes had been constructed, series production began on May 31, 1940.

Unfortunately, the type's high performance came at a price: it was hard for even experienced pilots to fly. Taxying visibility was poor, the cockpit became very hot very quickly, the canopy was hard to open, the controls were very heavy and it suffered from longitudinal instability in flight – not to mention a tendency to enter unrecoverable spins.

Efforts to correct these issues

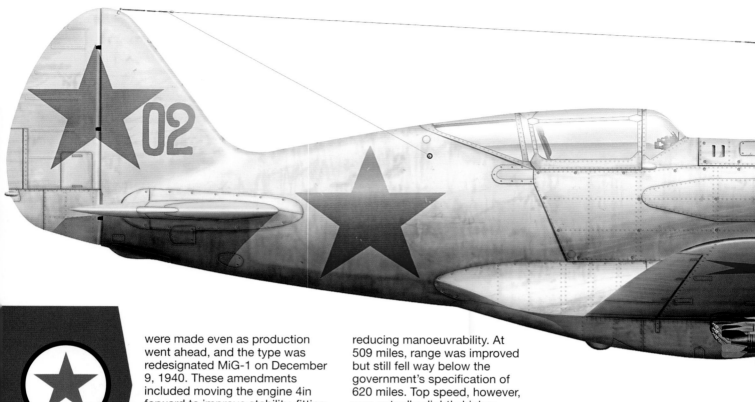

were made even as production went ahead, and the type was redesignated MiG-1 on December 9, 1940. These amendments included moving the engine 4in forward to improve stability, fitting a new water radiator, adding extra fuel and oil tanks, armouring the pilot's seat back, streamlining the engine's supercharger air intakes, strengthening the undercarriage, fitting a better propeller, providing more ammunition for the guns and installing a better gunsight.

With all of these changes in place, a new aircraft was born – the MiG-3. The first production example was finished on December 20, 1940, the type now being built in parallel with the unmodified MiG-1 rather than replacing it. State acceptance trials quickly indicated that curing some of the design's ills had also served to add weight,

reducing manoeuvrability. At 509 miles, range was improved but still fell way below the government's specification of 620 miles. Top speed, however, was actually slightly higher than that of the MiG-1.

As the MiG-3 entered service with the Soviet Air Force during early 1941, numerous complaints about defects and poor quality workmanship arose. When the German invasion began, it became painfully obvious that three machine guns was inadequate when compared with the Bf 109's two machine guns and one 20mm cannon. An attempt to fix this involved installing an additional pair of .303 machine guns in underwing pods – but this caused

MiG-3 (late series)

Painted in green/black camouflage, this MiG-3 belonged to the 162nd IAP, 43rd IAD, and was flown on the Leningrad front during the summer of 1942.

▼

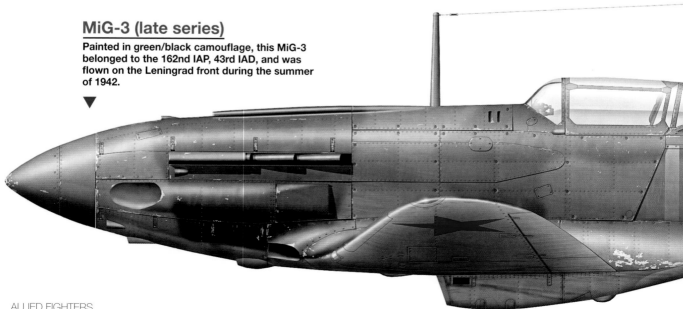

◀ MiG-3 (late series)

Pilots of the 12 GIAP/6 IAK flew this aircraft from Moscow PVO during March 1942. Note that the outer wing panels have been exchanged with green camouflaged wings without slots taken from an earlier MiG-3 version.

MiG-3

This MiG-3 was flown by members of 6 IAK from Moscow PVO during the spring of 1942.

▼

a marked drop in performance, further reducing pilots' chances of success in combat.

While the MiG-3's speed was roughly on a par with its contemporaries at high altitude, this parity disappeared at low level – where most aerial combat took place on the eastern front – and it proved inferior to German Bf 109Fs. Its high wing loading reduced its manoeuvrability too, and combat experience highlighted a degree of instability around the horizontal plane which in practice meant that it had a tendency to 'wander' when its pilot was trying to line up a shot.

A total of 3172 MiG-3s were built, with production coming to a halt at the end of 1941. However, some continued in service until the end of the war. After this less-than-promising start, Mikoyan-Gurevich would not design another fighter that reached full production until the MiG-9 of 1946. ●

HEAVY AND HARD TO FLY, THE MiG-3 WAS PLAGUED BY POOR WORKMANSHIP AND DEFECTS

LAVOCHKIN-GORE
LAGG-3

The single-seat LaGG-3 showed early promise but was let down by technical problems. It did, however, lay the foundations for a successful family of high-performance fighters that was to follow.

1940-1945

The head of the People's Commissariat of Aircraft Industry's technical department, Vladimir Petrovich Gorboonov, decided in early 1939 that what the Soviet Union really needed was a fighter made largely out of wood.

After having the idea for this aircraft, he directed engineer Semyon Lavochkin, who had studied under Andrei Tupolev, to actually design it. He was soon joined by another People's Commissariat of Aircraft Industry engineer Mikhail Ivanovich Goodkov and together Gorboonov, Lavochkin and Goodkov presented their project to the actual People's Commissar of Aircraft Industry, who gave them leave to set up their own design bureau together in May 1939.

The wooden design, dubbed 'Project K', was then submitted for the government's next generation fighter competition alongside the designs that would lead to the Yak-1 and MiG-3. In late June, the government ordered two prototypes and the Lavochkin-Gorboonov-Goodkov bureau was swiftly relocated a former furniture factory, Plant No. 301, which had originally been repurposed to licence-build French-designed aircraft.

After a mock-up had been approved, work on the first Project K prototype began in January 1940. It was redesignated I-301 in reference to the factory's number. Unfortunately, the factory only had 93 inexperienced staff and the three bureau leaders quarrelled so the People's Commissariat of Aircraft Industry decided to give overall leadership to Lavochkin, the I-301's original designer.

Within three months, the prototype was ready – although

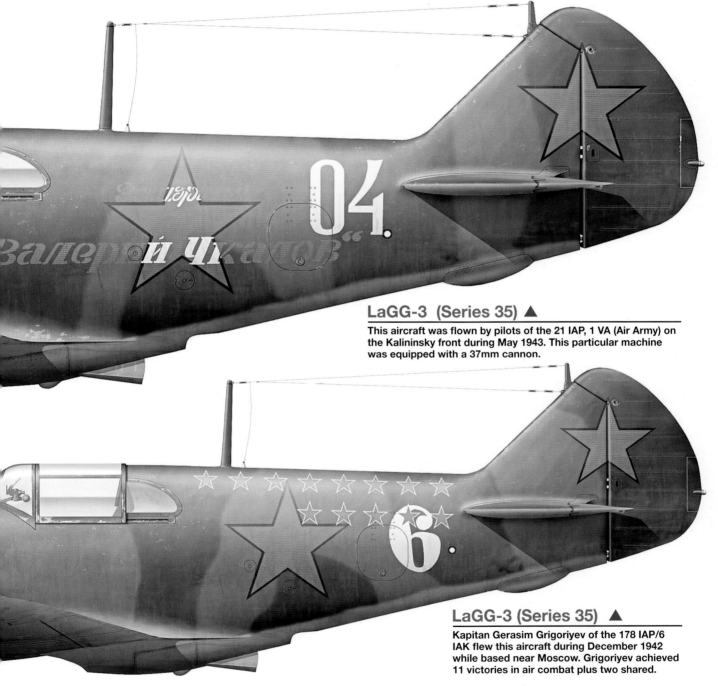

LaGG-3 (Series 35) ▲

This aircraft was flown by pilots of the 21 IAP, 1 VA (Air Army) on the Kalininsky front during May 1943. This particular machine was equipped with a 37mm cannon.

LaGG-3 (Series 35) ▲

Kapitan Gerasim Grigoriyev of the 178 IAP/6 IAK flew this aircraft during December 1942 while based near Moscow. Grigoriyev achieved 11 victories in air combat plus two shared.

the workers had discovered in the meantime that the chemicals needed to bond its wooden structure caused severe irritation when they came into contact with human skin.

The monoplane fighter was powered by a Klimov M-105 liquid-cooled V12 engine and the fuselage was made primarily of birch. It was armed with a single .90 calibre MP-6 cannon firing through the propeller hub plus a pair of .50 calibre heavy machine guns.

The aircraft's first flight was on March 30, 1940, and its performance was rated as satisfactory. After two months of in-house testing, state acceptance trials began on June 14. These revealed an all-up weight of 6543lb and a top speed of 363mph at 15,420ft. Modifications to the carburettor air scoop and with the radiator air flaps fully closed the type was able to achieve 375mph.

Besides this promising performance, as with the other new Soviet fighters then in development, a whole host of defects were also identified – including the cabin overheating badly and weakness in the undercarriage. Range was also insufficient and this resulted

LAGG-3 (SERIES 2/3) ▼

One of the LaGG-3's few supporters was Mayor Leonid Galchenko, commander of the 609 IAP. This was his aircraft while stationed at Afrikanda Airdrome in the USSR during late 1942. He had started out flying the I-16 until converting towards the end of 1941. Once the supply of LaGG-3s had been exhausted he switched to the La-5F but even when the La-5FN and La-7 became available he stuck with the La-5F, fighting on the Karelian front and in the arctic. Overall, he achieved 24 victories in air combat plus 12 shared.

LAGG-3 SERIES 11 ▼

Featuring a distinctive black lightning bolt with red edging, this aircraft was flown by Kapitan Victor Petrovich Mironov, commander of the 609th IAP during the summer of 1942. Mironov achieved 15 victories in air combat and was later made a Hero of the Soviet Union.

LAGG-3 (SERIES 29) ▼

Naval flying ace Kapitan Igor Aleksandrovich Kaberov, of the 3 GIAP/KBF, flew this aircraft while stationed at Lake Ladoga near Leningrad during the winter of 1942/43. He began the war flying I-16s with the air force of the Soviet Baltic Fleet – shooting down a Bf 109 on August 4, 1941, before ramming a Junkers Ju 88 later that month. He began flying LaGG-3s towards the end of the year. Before being withdrawn from front line combat during the summer of 1943, he achieved eight victories in air combat plus 18 shared.

a design change whereby additional fuel tanks would be fitted within the wings of the production version. When series construction was approved, the I-301 prototype without the extra tanks was designated LaGG-1, while the full production version became the LaGG-3. The first of these was flown for the first time in December 1940. With so little time for proper testing, many of the defects previously identified had gone uncorrected and front line units issued with the new type soon began to complain about engines overheating, hydraulics failing and radiators leaking.

There were problems with the LaGG-3's weaponry too. The mighty MP-6 cannon worked but its recoil was shattering, so in the earliest production model aircraft it was replaced with a third .50 cal machine gun. By

February 1941, an incredible 2228 design changes had been made on the fly as LaGG-3s continued to roll off production lines. Even then, the type's weak undercarriage remained a problem.

As late as July 1941, not a single unit equipped with the LaGG-3 was in a state of combat readiness due to the persistence of seemingly uncurable defects. To make matters worse, the poor build quality of the production models also hampered their performance. Far from doing 375mph, they could only manage 341mph on average. Climb rate and range also suffered.

Gradually, these problems were tackled and combat operations commenced in August 1941. However, like the earliest MiGs and Yaks, the LaGG-3 proved to be generally inferior to the Luftwaffe's Messerschmitt Bf 109s. Its cooling system was extremely vulnerable and it lacked the acceleration to properly defend itself, let alone protect ground-attack aircraft such as the Il-2. It had a good rate of turn but this alone was not enough to save it. In some situations, LaGG-3 units had to be protected by other units flying Yaks.

Devastating losses were incurred and the Soviet High Command ruled in August 1942 that the LaGG-3 was not to be operated in areas where Luftwaffe activity was high. Production continued into 1943 before the last plant building the LaGG-3 was switched to production of the Yak-3. Overall 6528 LaGG-3s were built. ●

LAVOCHKIN LA-5

Efforts to overcome the LaGG-3's manifold flaws along with the installation of a more powerful new engine resulted in a heavily modified version of the original that could hold its own against even the best of the Luftwaffe's mid-war fighters – the La-5FN.

With the LaGG-3 plagued by defects and suffering badly against the Luftwaffe's Bf 109s in front line combat, Lavochkin needed to come up with a replacement fast.

Part of the LaGG-3's problem was its weight. Apart from all the other concerns, it was badly in need of more power and there was no obvious way of providing it. Elsewhere, and at the same time, engine maker Shvetsov was struggling with its M-82 air-cooled two-row 14-cylinder unit.

The M-82 was a development of the M-62 nine-cylinder engine, which was itself a development of the M-25 – the licence-built copy of the Wright Cyclone which had powered the earlier Polikarpov I-16s. By mid-1941 both Mikoyan/Gurevich and Yakovlev had built prototype versions of their main line fighters around the M-82 but neither had been sufficiently impressed to put it into production.

Only Sukhoi had made use of it, on some later examples of its Su-2 bomber, but that type's limited production run meant Shvetsov's new engines were ending up stockpiled in a warehouse. With cancellation of LaGG-3 production imminent, Lavochkin made contact with Shvetsov and the two

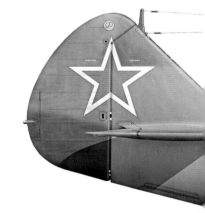

La-5F ▼

This aircraft was flown by pilots of the 5 GIAP on the 1st Ukrainian front during the spring of 1943.

La-5 FN

A trio of La-5FNs, one of them this one flown by Leytenant Sergei Makarovich Kramarenko of the 19th IAP, intercepted a group of Ju 88s escorted by six Bf 110s on March 19, 1944. The leader of the trio, Pavel Maslyakov, shot down one of the 88s but was then attacked by one of the Messerschmitts. Kramarenko in turn attacked the Messerschmitt but was then hit by his wingman. With his La-5FN burning, Kramarenko bailed out. He survived but suffered severe burns to his face and hands. Captured by the Germans, he was about to be executed by the SS when a German general ordered that be taken to hospital instead – where he was liberated by Soviet troops two weeks later. Having ended the war with two confirmed victories in air combat, Kramarenko was still alive at the time of writing, aged 93.

▼

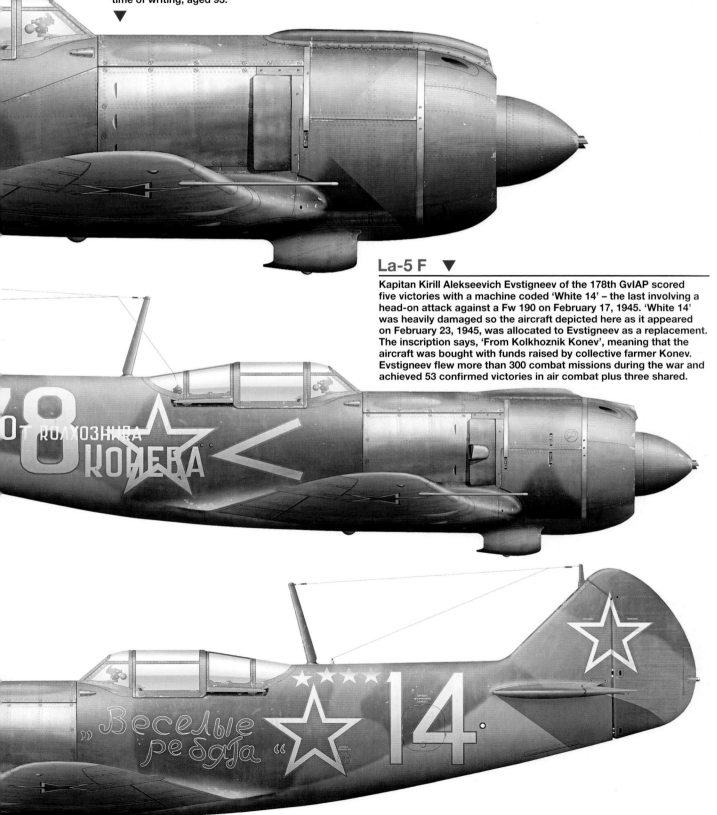

La-5 F ▼

Kapitan Kirill Alekseevich Evstigneev of the 178th GvIAP scored five victories with a machine coded 'White 14' – the last involving a head-on attack against a Fw 190 on February 17, 1945. 'White 14' was heavily damaged so the aircraft depicted here as it appeared on February 23, 1945, was allocated to Evstigneev as a replacement. The inscription says, 'From Kolkhoznik Konev', meaning that the aircraft was bought with funds raised by collective farmer Konev. Evstigneev flew more than 300 combat missions during the war and achieved 53 confirmed victories in air combat plus three shared.

parties resolved to work together to overcome their respective problems – by creating a new version of the LaGG-3 which used the Shvetsov powerplant.

Three serious problems stood in their way however. The M-82 was 18in wider in diameter than the LaGG-3's fuselage, it was unable to accommodate any engine-mounted weaponry and it was also substantially heavier than the fighter's original engine, the M-105P, causing the aircraft's centre of gravity to shift.

The first problem was solved by fitting a new fairing or skirt around the existing fuselage which joined it to the rear of the engine, the second meant the fitment of a pair of 20mm cannon above the engine, and the third was tackled by strengthening the engine mounts. Variable outlet flaps on the fuselage sides provided the engine with its air-cooling.

A rough-built flying prototype, known as the Gu-82, was ready by September 1941 and proved to be so impressive that series production was approved before any tests had even been undertaken. The first LaGG-3 M-82 was completed in February 1942 and when tests were finally carried out it was determined to be a full 10% faster than a production LaGG-3 with M-105P.

The aircraft was not burdened by field equipment such as a radio mast or bomb racks but this still represented a substantial improvement. The order to cancel production of the original LaGG-3 was given in April 1942 – though it continued for some time nevertheless – but the LaGG-3 M-82 required further development.

Heat from the engine made the cockpit very hot and oil temperature rose quickly to

▲

La-5FN

One of the La-5's more vocal supporters was Starshiy Leytenant Vladimir Aleksandrovich Orekhov, who fought on the Kursk Front during July 1943. He flew 420 combat sorties and achieved 19 victories in air combat plus two shared. He is also credited with four aircraft destroyed on the ground plus two balloons.

La-5 ▶

Controversial ace Kapitan Georgiy D Kostylev of the 4 GIAP/KBF flew this aircraft on the Leningrad front during October 1943 – and was very lucky to have been able to do so. During the winter of 1941 he was invited to a banquet but when he saw all the splendid food and drink laid out in front of him he became furious, smashing his glass and shoving a major from the supply train who tried to stop him. In a matter of days he was demoted to private, stripped of awards he had earned up to that point including Hero of the Soviet Union, expelled from the Community Party and ordered to serve in a penal battalion. When his sentence was up, his unit refused to have him back. However, an old friend got him into a unit flying the La-5 and by August 1943 he was deemed to have been 'rehabilitated'. During 418 combat missions he scored at least 22 victories in air combat plus 34 shared.

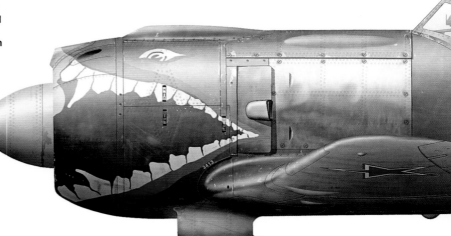

La-5 ▼

Kapitan Pavel Timofeyevich Tarasov of the 159 IAP flew this aircraft on the Kuban front during May 1943. Tarasov achieved 22 individual and three shared victories but was killed in 1944.

unacceptable levels. It was also harder for a pilot to handle than its predecessor and required considerable physical strength to exert sufficient stick force for more extreme manoeuvring.

Production model LaGG-3 M-82s began to reach squadrons in June 1942 and the type was redesignated La-5 in September 1942.

New problems had cropped up in the meantime – poorly fitted engine cowlings added drag and reduced performance, oil pumps struggled, sparkplugs failed after between five and 10 hours' operation, exhaust pipes overheated and burned through, cockpit visibility was limited and the fighter was too heavy.

Development work therefore continued and production line modifications were made even

as the defect-laden models were being delivered to Soviet Air Force units. Cockpit visibility was improved in November 1942 with a fuselage modification which saw the section immediately behind the canopy cut away and replaced with a new bulletproof glass panel.

Further changes included sealing the joints on the engine cowling to prevent drag-inducing airflow, reshaping of the duct for the oil cooler, increasing the cross-section of the exhaust pipes and strengthening the doors for the retractable tailwheel. The design of the trim tabs was altered several times, the control column was revised and the area of the control surfaces was reduced to offer a better balance of handling and manoeuvrability.

In January 1943, La-5s were fitted with the new M-82F engine,

> **HUGE EFFORTS WERE MADE TO ELIMINATE PRODUCTION DEFECTS FROM THE LA-5**

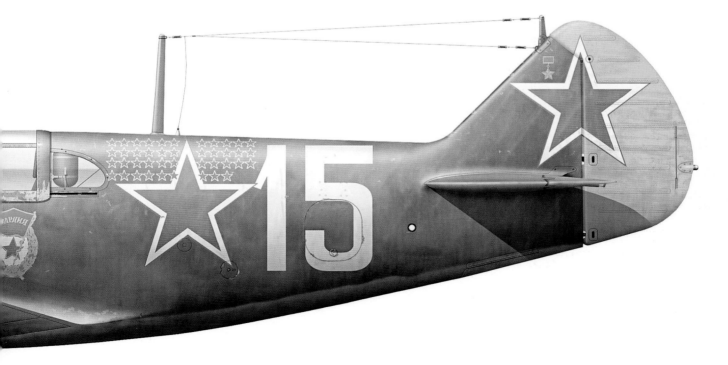

which had been altered to cure the oil pump and sparkplug problems – increasing engine life from 100 hours to over 150. With the cockpit and engine modifications, the La-5 became the La-5F. During the spring of 1943, another new engine was introduced, the M-82NV. This replaced the carburettors of the M-82 and M-82F with direct fuel injection into the cylinder heads and gave a very respectable top speed of 384.6mph at 18,400ft.

With the engine redesignated ASh-82FN, the aircraft became the La-5FN and designers next attempted to address its weight problem. The centre section of the wings, the cockpit hood, the engine's attachments and the undercarriage were all assessed and replaced with lighter components. In addition, weight was saved by replacing the original five small fuel tanks with three larger ones, the structure of the wing spars was altered to further shave off weight and surface finish was improved to create a more aerodynamic shape.

Even with all these alterations made, however, pilots continued

La-5F ▼

This aircraft was flown by pilots of the 3 GIAP, based at Lavansaari in the USSR during June 1944.

La-5FN

Two-times Hero of the Soviet Union Kapitan Vitaliy Ivanovich Popkov of the 5 GIAP flew this aircraft while based in the Lvov area during the autumn of 1944. He flew 478 combat missions and achieved 41 victories in air combat plus one shared.
▼

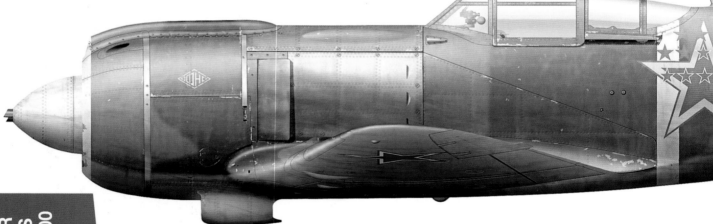

THE LA-5FN WAS ON A PAR WITH THE LATEST FW 190S AND BF 109S BUT ONLY 1500 WERE MADE

to complain about the cockpit being overly hot and inadequately sealed against the ingress of engine fumes. Consequently, they often flew with the canopy open – introducing more drag which again reduced performance. The raw power supplied by the ASh-82FN, particularly at low to medium altitude, and the aircraft's reduced weight put its performance on a par with that of the Bf 109s and Fw 190s it was now facing in combat. Full series production of the La-5FN continued throughout 1943 but the ASh-82FN proved more difficult to manufacture than its forebears and La-5FN production was severely hampered by a lack of powerplants.

Not only that, the ASh-82FN

La-5 ▼

The inscription on the side of this famous La-5 reads 'For the Motherland!' It was flown by Kapitan Ivan P Laveikin, commander of the 2nd AE, 5th GvIAP on the Stalingrad front during the winter of 1942-1943. Laveikin achieved 24 victories in air combat plus 15 shared.

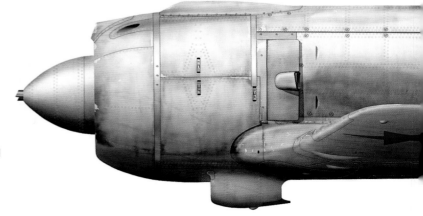

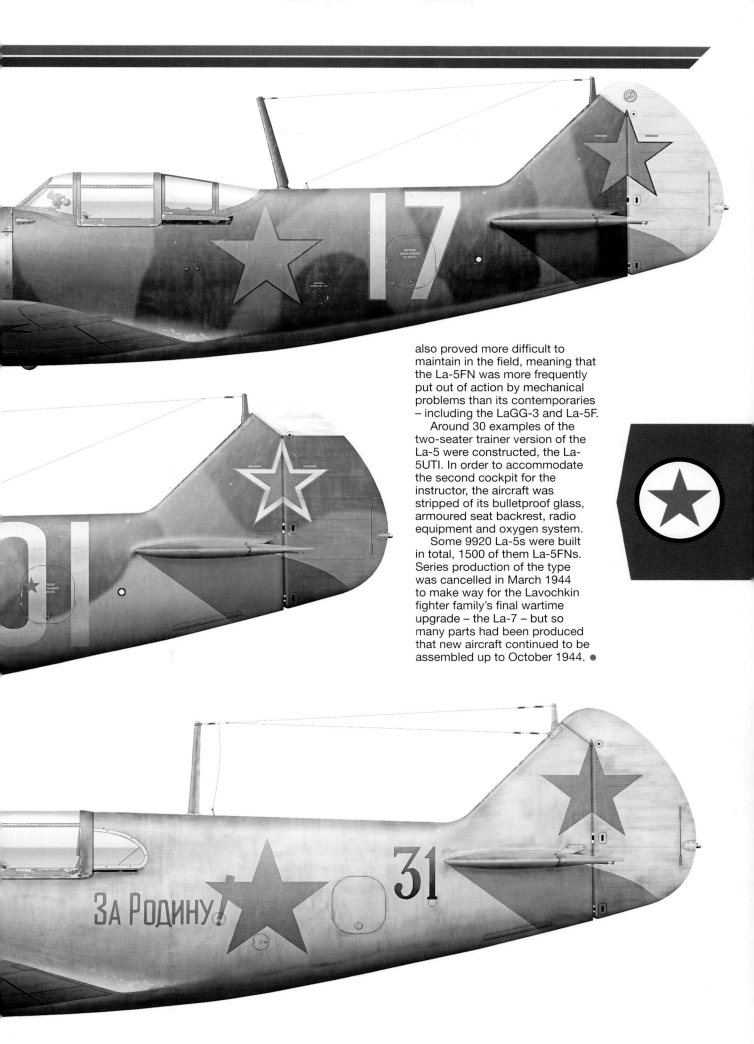

also proved more difficult to maintain in the field, meaning that the La-5FN was more frequently put out of action by mechanical problems than its contemporaries – including the LaGG-3 and La-5F.

Around 30 examples of the two-seater trainer version of the La-5 were constructed, the La-5UTI. In order to accommodate the second cockpit for the instructor, the aircraft was stripped of its bulletproof glass, armoured seat backrest, radio equipment and oxygen system.

Some 9920 La-5s were built in total, 1500 of them La-5FNs. Series production of the type was cancelled in March 1944 to make way for the Lavochkin fighter family's final wartime upgrade – the La-7 – but so many parts had been produced that new aircraft continued to be assembled up to October 1944. ●

LAVOCHKIN LA-7

The wartime evolution of the LaGG-3 reached its zenith with the La-7. It embodied countless hours of intensive development work and like the La-5 before it proved to be a match for the Luftwaffe's last crop of high performance fighters.

1944-1950

With production of the LaGG-3 winding down and production of the La-5FN in full flow, Lavochkin began working towards the type's next phase of development. The La-5's aerodynamic form had already been the subject of extensive wind tunnel testing to create the La-5FN but this now progressed further, as did work on lightening the aircraft.

Wooden wing spars were replaced with metal ones and further measures were taken to seal gaps in the engine cowling and fuselage panelwork – particularly by reducing the overall number of individual panels. The oil cooler, previously installed in the lower section of the engine cowling, was moved back to the underside of the centre fuselage, just below and to the rear of the cockpit.

While the La-5FN's ASh-82FN engine was retained, each cylinder was now given its own exhaust pipe, the propeller was reshaped to perform more efficiently at higher speeds and a larger spinner was installed. The fillets at the points where the wings joined the fuselage were also redesigned, the main landing gear was fitted with longer shock struts and the tailwheel strut was shortened. It was recommended that a metal roll bar, to protect the pilot in the event of a nose-over, be fitted to the rear of the cockpit but this modification was omitted, as was a proposal to fit a trio of B-20 cannon in place of the La-5's twin cannon.

The first La-5 to embody these features was completed in January 1944 and tested from February to March. Although work was suspended after just nine flights due to engine failure, the

La-7

The top Allied ace of the Second World War, Kapitan Ivan Mikitovich Kozhedub of the 176 GIAP, flew this aircraft on the 1st Belorussian front in Germany during February 1945. During 330 combat sorties, Kozhedub scored 62 victories in air combat – including the destruction of a Me 262 jet fighter. Forty-six of his victories were achieved while flying a La-5 and the rest after he converted to the La-7 during August 1944.

La-7

Some of the fiercest fighting of the final stages of the Second World War took place at Königsberg – a Prussian fortress city that was besieged by the Red Army for three months, beginning towards the end of January 1945. This La-7 was flown by Mayor Aleksey Alelyukhin of the 9 GIAP in the Königsberg area during March 1945, the height of the siege. Alelyukhin flew 600 combat missions during the war and achieved 40 victories in air combat plus 17 shared. The inscription on the fuselage reads: "To Aleksey Alelyukhin from the collective of factory No. 41 of the People's Commissariat of Aviation Industry."

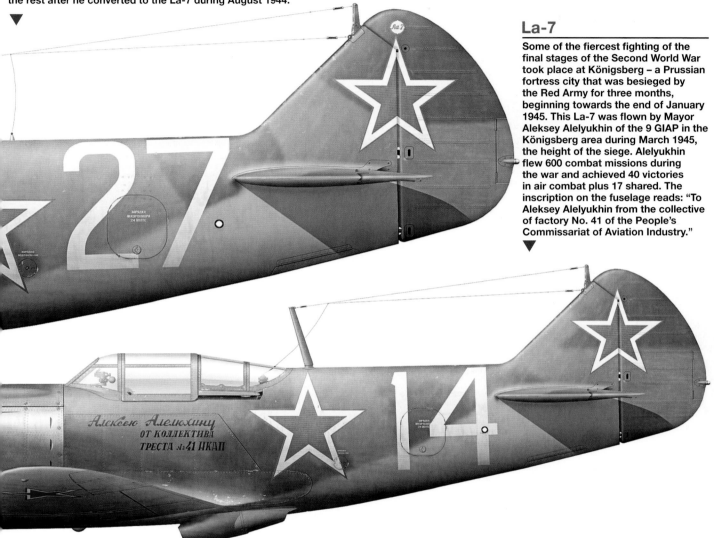

La-7

Mayor Amet-Khan Sultan achieved his first combat victory by ramming his Hawker Hurricane into a Junkers Ju 88 on May 31, 1942. By April 1945 he was serving with 9 GIAP during the siege of Berlin. This is how is aircraft appeared when it was housed in a hangar at Tempelhof Airport, Berlin, in May 1945. Sultan flew a total of 603 combat sorties, scoring 30 victories in air combat plus 19 shared.

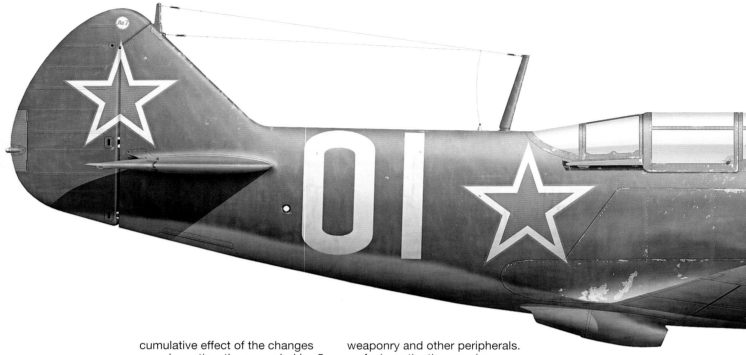

cumulative effect of the changes was dramatic – the upgraded La-5 could now manage 422mph at 20,000ft. This made it some 30-40mph faster even than the La-5FN.

The new version was given the designation La-7 and approved for production. The early war Soviet fighters – the LaGG-3, MiG-3 and Yak-1 had suffered from poor supply infrastructure, appalling factory workmanship and hasty design but by 1944 most of these problems had been overcome. The lines producing the La-7 were more efficient and better supplied. While the finished aircraft retained the no-frills character of their forebears, there had been huge improvements in quality.

As had become customary, the performance of the full production model La-7 could not quite manage the sparkling performance of the prototype, with a top speed of 397mph at 20,000ft. This puzzled the Lavochkin engineers, since the original machine had managed to reach its top speed complete with

weaponry and other peripherals.

An investigation was begun to work out why performance had dipped so significantly. This determined that the cowling was still being inadequately sealed, causing drag, and the propeller's new form had not been made properly. In addition, the ASh-82FN was found to be performing below the manufacturer's specification – which resulted in Shvetsov being required to improve the standard of its production output.

With all of these problems resolved, production La-7s were capable of a top speed of 418mph at 20,000ft. At the same altitude, the Bf 109 G-6 could only manage 404mph and the Fw 190 A-8 only 400mph. The Bf 109 K-4, however, deliveries of which began in October 1944, could reach 441mph. The Fw 190 D-9's top speed was 424mph.

Unfortunately, it proved

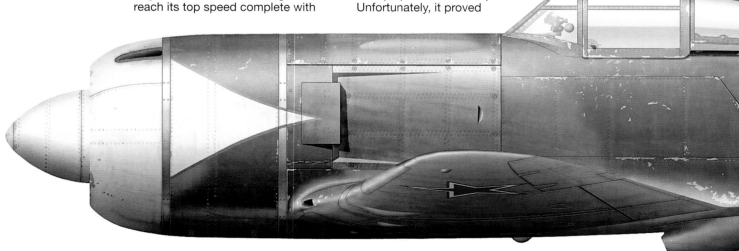

La-7 176 ▼

This aircraft was flown by pilots of the 176 GIAP during the siege of Berlin, April 1945.

La-7

'White 93' was flown by Podpolkovnik Sergey Fedorovich Dolgushin, commander of the 156 IAP, during April/May 1945. Dolgushin scored 17 victories in air combat plus 11 shared, which puts him just outside the top 100 Soviet aces of the Second World War. Nevertheless, this aircraft has subsequently become more famous than many of those flown by the top 100 scorers.

▼

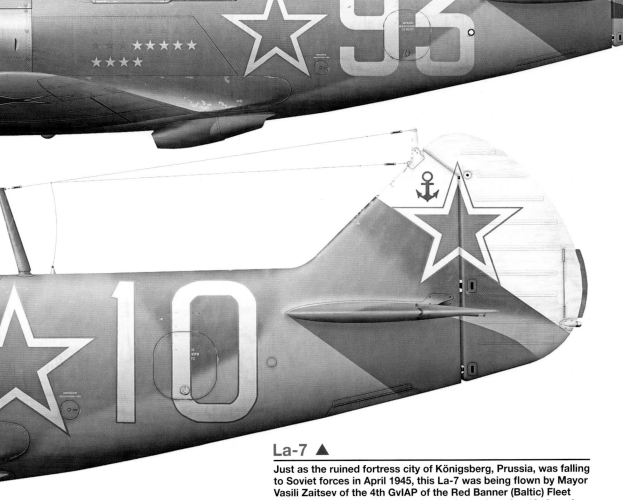

La-7 ▲

Just as the ruined fortress city of Königsberg, Prussia, was falling to Soviet forces in April 1945, this La-7 was being flown by Mayor Vasili Zaitsev of the 4th GvIAP of the Red Banner (Baltic) Fleet (KBF). Zaitsev scored 34 victories in air combat plus 19 shared.

THE LA-7 WAS AMONG THE MOST POWERFUL FIGHTERS OF THE WAR - ABLE TO BEST EVEN THE LATEST GERMAN MACHINES IN COMBAT

extremely difficult to bring production aircraft up to this standard. Sample aircraft were pulled from production lines in September 1944 and spot tested. This revealed that the typical La-7 still lagged well behind its target performance, at between 407 and 408mph at 20,000ft. However, the aircraft's rate of climb was better than expected, and comparative tests rated its performance in this regard as better than that of the Bf 109 G-6.

A handful of La-7s from the first production batches suffered from structural failure due to a weakness

La-7

This aircraft was flown by Kapitan Vitaly Ivanovich Korolev of the 482nd IAP, based at Prague, Czechoslovakia, during the spring of 1945. He achieved 21 victories in air combat plus 10 shared.

▼

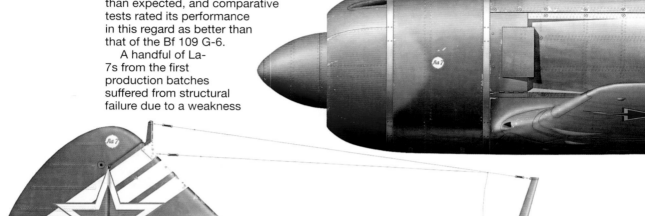

of the main spar. This was fault was traced and resolved – but not before six aircraft and four pilots had been lost.

The type's major vice in front line service was a propensity for engine failure. The aircraft was typically operated from rough forward airstrips and as a result the ASh-82FN's air intakes tended to ingest dirt, dust and sand whipped up by the propeller at an alarming rate. In addition, by the final phase of the war, the aircraft's two cannon provided an insufficient weight of fire against more heavily armoured targets.

A total of 5753 La-7s were built up to the end of the war. A handful of examples built at the end of the production run were fitted with the trio of B-20 cannon originally envisioned for the type.

Another development of the La-7 was the trainer version – the La-7UTI. Rather than rush it into production, Lavochkin took its time to perfect the aircraft's design. The inclusion of a direction finder and gun camera plus numerous

THE MAIN PROBLEM FACING LA-7 UNITS WAS THE DIRE AIRFIELDS THEY WERE REQUIRED TO OPERATE FROM

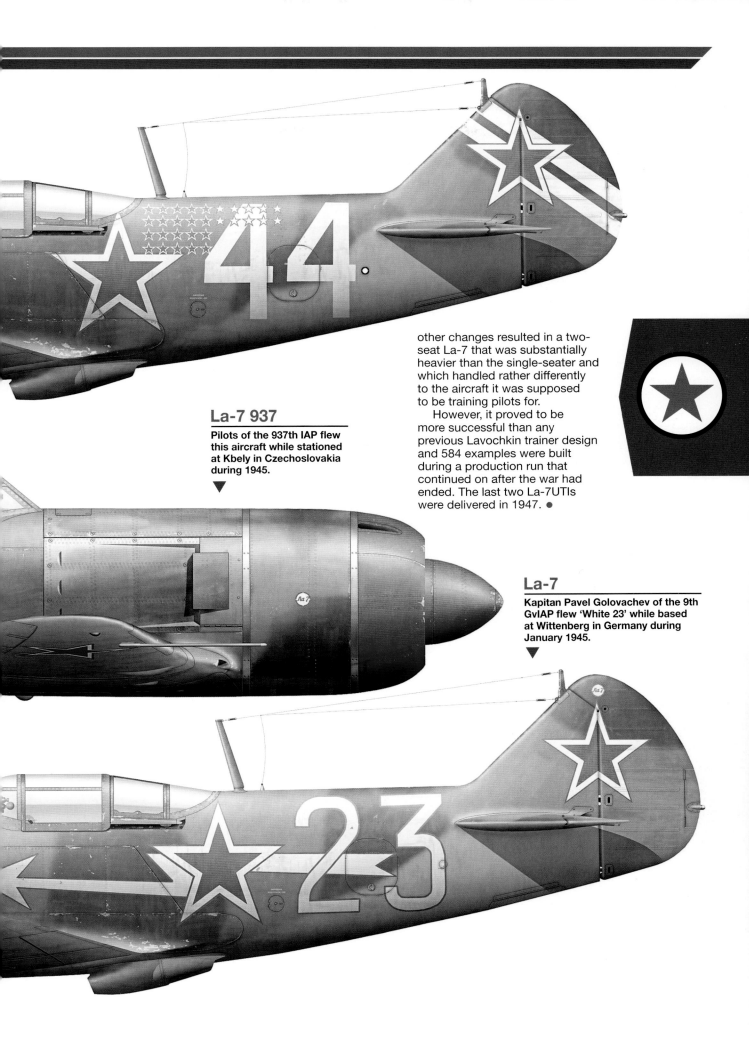

other changes resulted in a two-seat La-7 that was substantially heavier than the single-seater and which handled rather differently to the aircraft it was supposed to be training pilots for.

However, it proved to be more successful than any previous Lavochkin trainer design and 584 examples were built during a production run that continued on after the war had ended. The last two La-7UTIs were delivered in 1947. ●

La-7 937

Pilots of the 937th IAP flew this aircraft while stationed at Kbely in Czechoslovakia during 1945.

▼

La-7

Kapitan Pavel Golovachev of the 9th GvIAP flew 'White 23' while based at Wittenberg in Germany during January 1945.

▼

POLIKARPOV

I-16 ▼

Commonly shown in photographs standing beside someone else's I-16 bearing the slogan 'For Stalin!' this is the aircraft actually flown by Kapitan Boris Feoktistovich Safonov, commander of the 72 SAP/SF, based at Polyarnoye, Murmansk, USSR during September 1941. The slogan reads 'Death to Fascism!' Safonov flew 224 combat sorties and achieved 25 victories in air combat plus 14 shared. He later flew Hawker Hurricanes and Curtiss P-40s. His P-40E was shot down on May 30, 1942, and he was killed.

1933–1943

The diminutive Polikarpov I-16 had faced the Messerschmitt Bf 109 on almost equal terms during the Spanish Civil War and was still the Soviet Union's main fighter when the German army invaded in 1941. But where the Bf 109's development was just beginning, the I-16's was almost over.

Nikolai Polikarpov became the head of technical development at the Dux Aircraft Factory in 1923, having previously been part of the team who developed the Sikorsky Ilya Muromets heavy bomber for the Imperial Russian Air Service.

He then designed some of the Soviet Union's first biplane fighters – the I-1 and I-3 – before being tasked with the design of the more advanced I-6. When this took longer than expected and proved ultimately unsuccessful Polikarpov, along with 450 of his designers and engineers, was arrested in October 1929 and charged with industrial sabotage. He was then sentenced to death.

Two months later this was commuted to 10 years' hard

I-16

I-16

This grubby white rocket-armed aircraft was flown by Starshiy Leytenant Grigoriy Grigoriyevich Guryakov of the 4 GIAP/KBF on the Leningrad Front during the winter of 1941/42.
▼

wings, outboard of the main gear.

Construction of the prototype began in June 1933 but licensing arrangements for the Cyclone engine had not yet been completed so a 480hp Shvetsov M-22, itself a licence-built version of the Gnome Rhône Jupiter, a derivative of the Bristol Jupiter, had to be fitted instead.

The design was so promising that it was scheduled for production on November 22, 1933, and the prototype made its first flight on December 30, 1933.

It was followed by the second prototype, this being fitted with an American-built Cyclone and a three-bladed propeller, in January. Pilots found that the type was highly manoeuvrable but early flight experience suggested that moving the controls too abruptly could result in a spin from which it was almost impossible to recover. It was therefore decided that aerobatics should be forbidden

labour and he was then required to complete work he had previously begun on the I-5 fighter trainer. In July 1931 his sentence was suspended and he was released to work with Pavel Sukhoi on designing the I-15 biplane fighter. At the same time, Polikarpov began to work on a monoplane version dubbed the TsKB-12.

Powered by an American 710hp Wright SR-1820-F-3 Cyclone nine-cylinder radial engine, this was designed to be small and light with a hand-crank retractable undercarriage plus a fully enclosed 16in wide cockpit with an Aldis-type gunsight and armour protection for the pilot.

The fuselage was a wooden monocoque and the wings were built around a steel alloy spar and dural ribs with an aluminium skin on the centre and leading edges with the rest being fabric. Directly in front of the cockpit was a 59.4 gallon fuel tank and two 0.30in machine guns were installed in the

during the trials phase.

The tests also revealed that the more powerful Cyclone produced unwelcome vibrations, which resulted in pilot fatigue. Another complaint was how difficult it could be to climb into the very narrow cockpit aperture, and the manually cranked landing gear required a strong pilot – it was prone to jamming too.

During early 1934, an intensive programme of wind tunnel testing was undertaken to assess the type's tendency

I-16 ▼

During the spring of 1942 Starshiy Leytenant Mikhail Vasiliyev, commander of the 1st Eskadrilya 4 GIAP/VVS-KBF, flew this aircraft in the Leningrad area while based at Lake Ladoga, USSR. He achieved six victories in air combat plus 16 shared. He was made a Hero of the Soviet Union on June 14, 1942, but was shot down and killed on May 5, 1943.

to spin and work out what preventative measures might be necessary. It was determined that the type's short fuselage could result in an unrecoverable flat spin in certain conditions but this was impossible to prove conclusively – flight testing was the only way to proceed.

Since the Cyclone fitted to the second prototype was far rarer and more valuable than the M-22, it was decided that the first prototype should be used, and if necessary sacrificed, to continue the programme of spin testing.

Between March 1 and March 2, 1934, test pilot Valery Chkalov induced 75 spins and found that the much-feared flat spin simply never occurred. In reality, the TsKB-12 could be easily

I-16 ▶

The famous 'White 16' flown by Starshiy Leytenant Anatoliy G Lomakin of the 21 IAP/KBF. Lomakin was heavily involved in the defence of Leningrad during the summer of 1942 and flew 452 combat sorties in total, with seven victories in air combat plus 19 shared. 'White 16' later went on display at the Museum of the Defence of Leningrad.

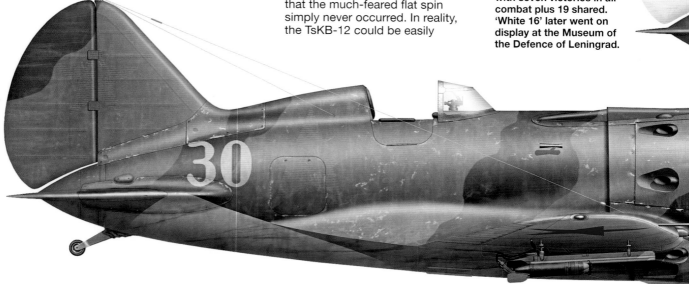

I-16 ▶

This I-16 Mark 10 was flown by Leytenant A Brazovets of the 7th IAP on the Finnish Front during the Winter War of 1939. The Soviet Union invaded Finland on November 28, 1939, but suffered heavy losses due to the determined Finnish defence. Eventually, however, Finland was forced to accept territorial losses in the Moscow Peace Treaty of March 1940. 'Yellow 4' is unusual in having the 'circle type' Soviet star and also in having its number on its fin, rather than the rudder.

recovered from an intentional spin simply by returning the controls to their neutral position and the type's stall behaviour was far more benign than expected.

With safety concerns now allayed, the TsKB-12 was redesignated I-16 and service trials began on March 22, 1934. With its relatively puny M-22 engine, the first prototype could reach a top speed of 223mph – the same as the Hawker Fury then in service with the RAF.

By now some 30 production examples of the I-16 had been made with the M-22 installed, but these were not delivered to Soviet Air Force units. In the meantime, licensing arrangements for the Wright Cyclone had been concluded and a Soviet-made version, the M-25, became available for use with the third prototype.

This new version of the design incorporated a number of improvements including a slightly smaller engine cowling with nine shuttered openings to control the flow of cool air into the unit and an exhaust that was redesigned to have eight individual outlet stubs. Government tests, which commenced on September 7, 1934, determined that it had a top speed of 270mph.

The production version fitted with the M-25, known as the I-16 Type 5, usually had low grade canopy glazing installed – which meant pilots often flew with it open or even had the rear section entirely removed. Even so, capable of reaching a top speed of 282mph at altitude it was the world's fastest production fighter.

During its early development, the I-16 was nicknamed Ishak or 'Little Donkey' but when it entered service with the Republican forces during the Spanish Civil War it was nicknamed Mosca or 'Fly'. The Nationalist enemy gave it their own

◀ I-16

Mladshiy Leytenant Ivan K Bratushko flew this aircraft on the Leningrad front while stationed at Lake Ladoga during the summer of 1942.

nickname however – Rata or 'Rat'.

Combat experience during the war resulted in the I-16 Type 10 with two more .303in machine guns installed in the upper fuselage to supplement the wing-mounted armament, firing through the propeller. Power was increased with the addition of the 750hp M-25V engine and a reflector gunsight replaced the original tubular type. Rather than allow the field modification of canopies to continue, the aircraft was now factory fitted with an open canopy and a fixed windscreen.

A two-seat trainer version, the UTI-4 or I-16 UTI, was developed in parallel with the Type 10 – a second cockpit being added

in front of the fuselage fuel tank. Early versions came with their undercarriage fixed in the down position but this was later replaced with the fully retractable system.

During the German invasion of the Soviet Union the I-16 was still the Soviet Air Force's most numerous fighter. It earned praise for its simple and rugged construction, which allowed it to be used for ramming attacks against German aircraft when the pilot ran out of ammunition, but it was obsolete by 1941 and when set against the latest versions of the Messerschmitt Bf 109 in dogfighting combat it suffered badly.

It struggled on in service until 1943 and it is believed that some 8644 were built overall. ●

I-16 ▲

Pilots of the 45th Division, based on the southern front near Odessa in the USSR, flew this aircraft during June 1941.

I-16 ▲

The inscription on the side of this aircraft, flown by General-Mayor Ivan Lakeev of the VVS KOVO (Kiev District HQ) from Vasilkov, USSR, during June 1941, says 'For the VKP(b)!' – the VKP(b) being the All-Union Communist Party (Bolshevik). The inscription on the spine says 'Named after Lenin!' 18 victories in air combat plus 20 shared. Lakeev had flown the I-16 Type 5 and Type 10 in Spain before participating in the Khalkin-Gol conflict against the Japanese. He was promoted to general after the Winter War against Finland.

I-16 ▲

More famous for flying LaGG-3s, this I-16 was flown by Leytenant Leonid A Galchenko of the 145th IAP, based at Shogui, Mongolia, during September 1939. He achieved seven victories in air combat overall, plus 23 shared.

I-16

This aircraft was flown by Starshiy Leytenant Gennadiy Tsokolayev, of the 4 GvIAP, from the Leningrad area on January 18, 1942. He achieved six victories in air combat plus 11 shared.

> THE I-16'S RUGGED CONSTRUCTION GAVE PILOTS A CHANCE OF SURVIVAL IF IT WAS USED FOR RAMMING

LOCKHEED P-38 LIGHTNING

An unusual twin-boom design set the Lightning apart from the beginning but the type overcame early scepticism and teething problems to become one of the most powerful Allied fighters of the war.

1935-1944

Lockheed and Vultee were among the companies that responded to a new US Army Air Corps requirement, Circular Proposal X-608, calling for a twin-engine high-altitude interceptor in 1937.

The aircraft was to carry at least 1000lb of weaponry, have a top speed of at least 360mph and climb to 20,000ft in less than six minutes powered by a pair of turbo-supercharged Allison V-1710 V12 engines. Lastly, it was to be fitted with a tricycle undercarriage.

The requirement was nearly the same as that which led to the Bell P-39 Airacobra, Circular Proposal X-609, except for the stipulation of two engines rather than one.

Vultee's proposal, the XP-1015, had a conventional single fuselage design with an Allison V-1710 V12 engine on each wing. It appeared solid and unremarkable.

Lockheed's Model 22 design, on the other hand, was radical. It had roughly the same dimensions as the XP-1015 and even a similar wing shape but that was where the similarities ended.

In coming up with the Model 22, Lockheed's engineers had studied a wide range of layouts, eventually settling on a twin-boom arrangement, with an engine on the forward end of each boom and a central nacelle housing both the pilot and the aircraft's main armament. This was planned to consist of two .50 cal Browning machine guns, two .30 cal Brownings and a T1 Army Ordnance .90in autocannon with a rotary magazine.

The cockpit featured a bubble canopy, a tricycle undercarriage was fitted as specified, and the aircraft's structure was largely

P-38J-10 ▼

'Journey's End' was flown by Captain Joseph Myers Jr. of the 38th FS, 55th FG, stationed at Nuthampstead in Hertfordshire, England, in January 1944. He achieved four and a half victories in air combat. The 55th Fighter Group was the first Lightning Group to become fully operational in England, flying long-range escort missions for bombers. They converted to the P-51 in July 1944.

made from stainless steel covered with smooth flush-riveted aluminium skin panels.

Despite, or perhaps because of, this unusual form Lockheed's fighter won the competition and the firm received a contract to construct a prototype under the designation XP-38. Work began in July 1938 and the XP-38 made its first flight on January 27, 1939.

Its performance was promising, though it was wrecked in a crash resulting from carburetor icing just over two weeks later, and the Army Air Corps placed an order for 13 YP-38s on April 27, 1939.

The joint Anglo-French Purchasing Commission ordered a total of 667 P-38s in March 1940. These were given the designations Model 322B for the British and Model 322F for the French but following the capitulation of France in June 1940 the British took up the whole order and decided that the type should be named Lightning in RAF service, rather than the name that Lockheed had given it – Atalanta, after a fierce virgin huntress from Greek mythology.

Work on building the YP-38s was slower than expected at Lockheed due to the massive growth that the company was experiencing, and the difficulties it encountered in translating the hand-finished one-off XP-38 prototype into a mass production model that could be rapidly assembled with minimal effort.

As a result, the first YP-38 that rolled off the line in early September 1940 differed somewhat from the original – being lighter and having different engine mountings. In addition, the propellers span the opposite way round. On the XP-38, they span inwards towards the cockpit – the left one spinning to the right, and the right one spinning to the left. On the YP-38, they span outwards, each turning away from the cockpit.

This aircraft made its first flight on September 17, 1940, but the 13th and last example was not ready to fly until June 1941. Testing revealed that when the aircraft reached a flight speed approaching Mach 0.68 during a dive, it began to shake uncontrollably and the controls would lock up. This was recoverable at low altitude if the pilot stayed with the aircraft but it was more

P-38J-10

Lieutenant Loren R Wilson of the 383rd FS, 364th FG, flew 'Betty A II' out of Honington, England, during May 1944.

P-38 H-10 ▼

Texas-born Major Jack S Jenkins, commanding officer of the 38th FS, 55th FG, flew this aircraft, the first of four he named 'Texas Ranger', while based in Nuthampstead during November 1943. On November 3, he shot down a Bf 109 over Wilhelmshaven and scored a 'probable' against a Fw 190 over La Bassee. He was shot down himself by flak while strafing the airfield at Coulommiers, France, during his 70th combat mission on April 10, 1944, and became a prisoner of war.

THE FRENCH PLACED AN ORDER FOR THE LIGHTNING BUT WHEN FRANCE WAS DEFEATED THE BRITISH AGREED TO TAKE IT UP IN THEIR STEAD

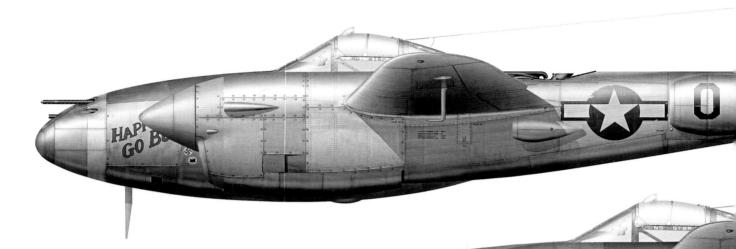

P-38J ▶

Major James T 'Jim' Tucker, commanding officer of the 402nd FS, 370th FG, based at Andover in England, flew this Lightning during June 1944. The logo on the nose depicts an outhouse being struck by lightning. Tucker was killed in action on a mission to Chateaudun on August 10, 1944.

P-38J-15 ▼

This aircraft, Scat II, was flown by Captain Robin Olds of the 434th FS, 479th FG, stationed at Wattisham in England during July 1944 – before he had achieved a single 'kill'. His first victories came on August 14 when he shot down a pair of Fw 190s and overall he claimed eight victories while flying the Lightning and was credited as the top-scoring P-38 ace of the European theatre. He later converted to P-51s and ended the war with 12 aerial combat victories. Flying the F-4 Phantom during the Vietnam War he added four more to his tally.

EARLY LIGHTNINGS SUFFERED FROM SEVERE VIBRATIONS IN A STEEP DIVE

likely that they would bail out rather than take the chance.

In spite of this known problem, the aircraft was rushed into full production to meet the demands of Lockheed's increasingly impatient customers. Following combat experience with other types during the Battle of Britain, the British realised that the Lightnings they had ordered during the war's first few months would be outdated and unfit for combat by the time they were delivered and on August 5, 1941, they attempted to have the contract amended so that only 143 aircraft would be built to the original specification, and the remaining 524 would be produced to the latest US spec as the Lightning Mk.II.

A few weeks later an RAF test pilot encountered the same vibration problem that the Americans had experienced previously but not yet resolved and reported it to his superiors as 'tail flutter'. This caused the British to cancel all but three of the 143 Lightning Mk.Is – resulting in a loss of $15 million for Lockheed. The company then launched a legal challenge, trying to hold the British government to

the terms of its original order.

By September 1941 a total of 66 first run P-38Ds had been built for the newly renamed US Army Air Force. Armament was four .50 cal machine guns with a single .79in Hispano autocannon. The 'D' was the first production model Lightning, with no 'B' or 'C'. The 'A' was a single experimental aircraft fitted

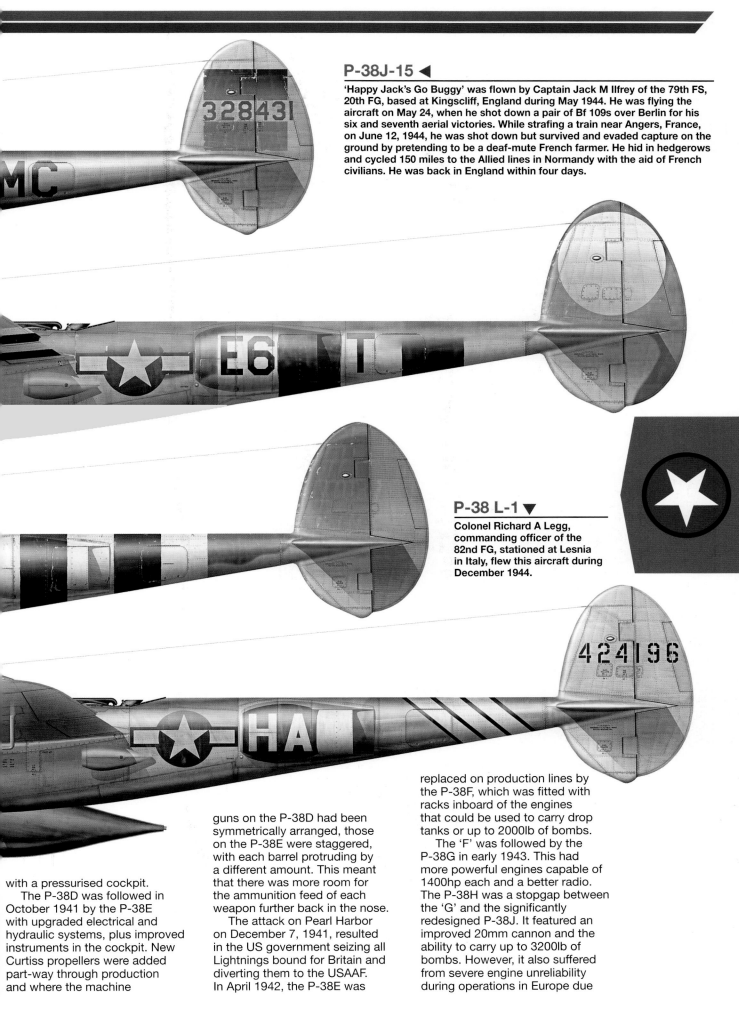

P-38J-15 ◀

'Happy Jack's Go Buggy' was flown by Captain Jack M Ilfrey of the 79th FS, 20th FG, based at Kingscliff, England during May 1944. He was flying the aircraft on May 24, when he shot down a pair of Bf 109s over Berlin for his six and seventh aerial victories. While strafing a train near Angers, France, on June 12, 1944, he was shot down but survived and evaded capture on the ground by pretending to be a deaf-mute French farmer. He hid in hedgerows and cycled 150 miles to the Allied lines in Normandy with the aid of French civilians. He was back in England within four days.

P-38 L-1 ▼

Colonel Richard A Legg, commanding officer of the 82nd FG, stationed at Lesnia in Italy, flew this aircraft during December 1944.

with a pressurised cockpit.

The P-38D was followed in October 1941 by the P-38E with upgraded electrical and hydraulic systems, plus improved instruments in the cockpit. New Curtiss propellers were added part-way through production and where the machine

guns on the P-38D had been symmetrically arranged, those on the P-38E were staggered, with each barrel protruding by a different amount. This meant that there was more room for the ammunition feed of each weapon further back in the nose.

The attack on Pearl Harbor on December 7, 1941, resulted in the US government seizing all Lightnings bound for Britain and diverting them to the USAAF. In April 1942, the P-38E was

replaced on production lines by the P-38F, which was fitted with racks inboard of the engines that could be used to carry drop tanks or up to 2000lb of bombs.

The 'F' was followed by the P-38G in early 1943. This had more powerful engines capable of 1400hp each and a better radio. The P-38H was a stopgap between the 'G' and the significantly redesigned P-38J. It featured an improved 20mm cannon and the ability to carry up to 3200lb of bombs. However, it also suffered from severe engine unreliability during operations in Europe due

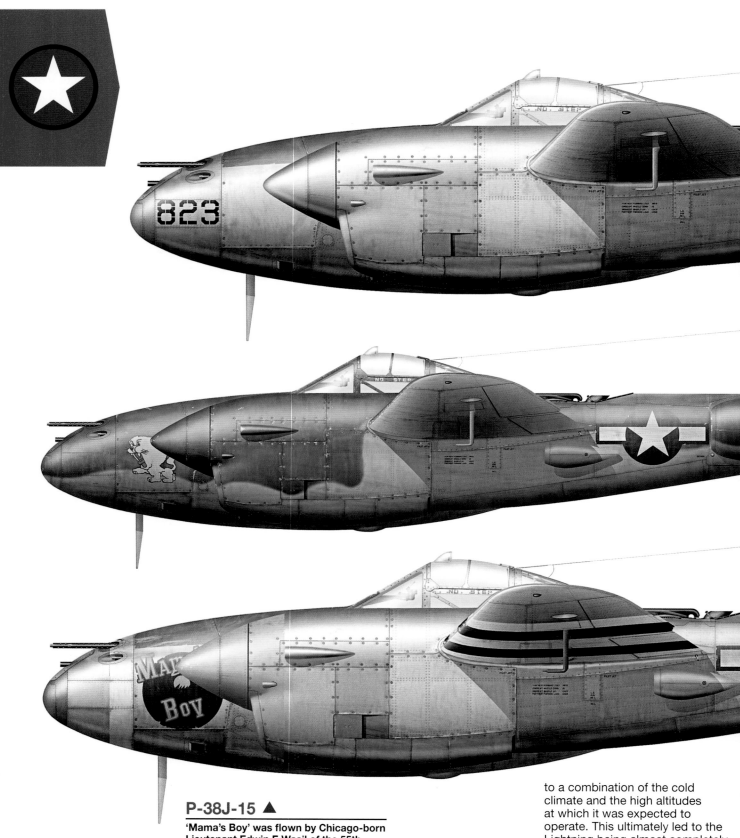

P-38J-15 ▲

'Mama's Boy' was flown by Chicago-born Lieutenant Edwin E Wasil of the 55th FS, 20th FG, while he was stationed at Kingcliffe in England during June 1944.

to a combination of the cold climate and the high altitudes at which it was expected to operate. This ultimately led to the Lightning being almost completely withdrawn from the European theatre by September 1944.

Introduced in August 1943, the P-38J had a new turbo-supercharger intercooler system fitted to the streamlined nacelles of its engines themselves – giving

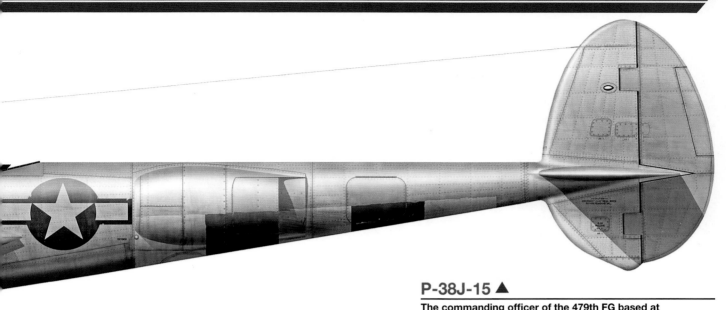

P-38J-15 ▲

The commanding officer of the 479th FG based at Wattisham, England, Colonel Hubert Zemke, flew this aircraft during August 1944. Zemke had previously led the highly experienced 56th FG, which became known as 'Zemke's Wolfpack' and claimed more than 500 German aircraft shot down during the period when he was in charge. Shortly after he joined the inexperienced 479th, the unit converted to P-51s and Zemke made one of the first probable shoot-downs of a Me 262. During a mission on October 30, 1944, the wing of his Mustang was torn off by turbulence and he was captured on the ground after bailing out. He spent the rest of the war as a PoW.

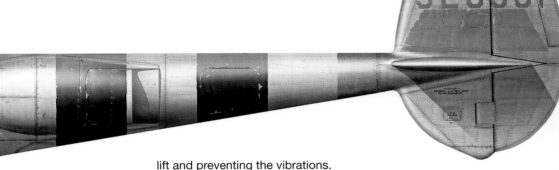

P-38J-10 ▲

It is not difficult to discern the inspiration for the lion that adorned the nose of this P-38J, flown by Captain Carl H Leo of the 384th FS, 364th FG based at Honington, England, during April 1944.

them a very visible 'chin'. This replaced the old system when had been positioned in the aircraft's wing leading edges and not only provided a power boost but also cured the engine problems which had plagued earlier Lightnings.

The 'J' also incorporated a feature which finally alleviated the Lightning's diving vibration problem. Electrically-actuated dive recovery flaps just outboard of the engines changed the geometry of the wing underside during a dive – providing more

lift and preventing the vibrations. Hydraulically boosted ailerons were also introduced with the P-38J-25 which dramatically improved the aircraft's roll rate and made its controls lighter.

Only one P-38K was built and used for experimental engine tests. The P-38L on the other hand was the most produced version of the fighter. Its most common sub-variant, the P-38L-5 had an improved cockpit heating system and uprated Allison V-1710-112/113 engines.

While most late-model P-38s were delivered unpainted, since

the aircraft's extremely smooth metal outer skin offered a small performance advantage, 75 P-38Ls were modified to become night fighters as the P-38M. These were painted matt black and had cone-shaped flash-hiders on their guns plus an AN/APS-6 radar pod positioned beneath the nose. Perhaps the biggest change, though, was the addition of a second cockpit behind the pilot for a radar operator.

A total of 10,037 Lightnings were built all together. ●

BELL P-39 /
P-400 AIRACOBRA

Design compromises limited its performance from the outset but nevertheless the P-39 Airacobra was heavily armed and saw front-line service with Allied forces around the world.

1938-1945

The need for a high-altitude interceptor was identified by the United States Army Air Corps towards the end of 1936 and in February 1937 a new specification was issued to manufacturers.

The new aircraft would need to be armed with cannon, feature a tricycle undercarriage and be powered by a single liquid-cooled Allison engine with a General Electric turbo-supercharger. Level airspeed at altitude needed to be at least 360mph and the climb to 20,000ft had to be achieved in less than six minutes.

Bell had relatively little experience in fighter design but still managed to come up with an innovative configuration, designated Model 12, which appeared to have a good chance of meeting the spec.

The Model 12's Allison V-1710 V12 engine was to be positioned centrally in the fuselage, with the propeller shaft passing under the pilot's feet and into a gearbox, which then drove the propeller. The gearbox was provided with its own lubrication system and later its own armour protection.

Directly beneath the engine, in the wing centre section, was its radiator and on either side was an oil cooler. On the upper side of the fuselage, immediately aft of the cockpit, was an oval air intake for the engine's carburetor.

This engine arrangement allowed sufficient space to be freed up in the nose for the powerful but temperamental 1.46in Oldsmobile T9 cannon to be fitted, firing through the centre of the propeller.

Having a centrally positioned main armament allowed for greater accuracy and stability during combat, even though the amount of ammunition that could be carried was severely limited.

Moving the engine away from the nose also improved the aircraft's aerodynamic profile, allowing the Model 12's projected performance to edge closer to the specification's ambitious requirements. A further aerodynamic improvement was the lack of a sliding cockpit canopy, with the pilot entering through one of the two side doors instead. Only the right hand door had an internal handle however, so this was the usual way of entering and leaving the cockpit.

Bell was given the go-ahead to proceed with prototype construction and the XP-39 made its first flight on April 6, 1938, at Wright Field in Ohio. It

P-400 ▼

Kapitan Ivan Dmitrievich Gaydayenko of the 19 GIAP flew this ex-RAF P-400 while based at Shongay in the USSR during the autumn of 1942. He achieved seven aerial victories plus 23 shared.

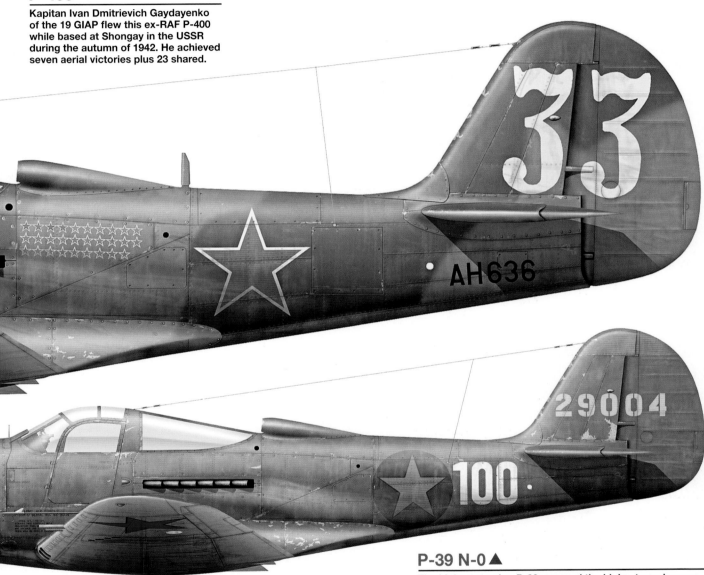

P-39 N-0 ▲

The highest scoring P-39 ace, and the highest scoring ace flying any American fighter design, was Mayor Aleksandr Ivanovich Pokryshkin of the 16 GIAP. This was the aircraft he flew on the Ukrainian Front during August 1943. Pokryshkin was the first person ever to be made a Hero of the Soviet Union three times over and towards the end of the war he spent most of his time training other pilots, having been made a famous hero by the Soviet propaganda machine. During 560 combat sorties he scored 59 victories in air combat plus six shared.

managed to reach 20,000ft in just five minutes and reportedly achieved a top speed of 390mph, albeit without weapons, armour or self-sealing fuel tanks – which would make it the fastest landplane in the world at that point.

The key to this stunning performance was the engine's turbo-supercharger, which was fed cooling air by a scoop on the left side of the fuselage.

However, it was decided that the type's top speed could be improved still further if the scoop was removed to reduce drag. Therefore, the turbo-supercharged V-1710 was swapped for a

V-1710 with only a single-stage single-speed supercharger.

A total of 13 YP-39s were ordered for evaluation by the Army in the latter configuration. These were later modified to include a pair of .30in machine guns in addition to the two .50 cal guns already fitted. Losing the turbo meant the aircraft was simpler and cheaper to build but its performance suffered dramatically as a result. It could no longer perform high-altitude operations and speed was reduced. Even so, an order for 80 full production P-39 Airacobras was placed on August 10, 1939.

The first 20 examples,

designated P-39C, were assessed without armour or self-sealing fuel tanks and found to be unsuitable for combat operations. The other 60 machines, the P-39D, had the armour and improved tanks.

Britain placed an order for 386 P-39Ds in September 1940, fitted with a .79in Hispano-Suiza HS.404 cannon and six .303 machine guns. This was export version was known as the P-400 and the order was later increased to 675 aircraft. However, testing with the RAF's 601 Squadron a year later revealed that the type's performance, particularly at altitude, was inadequate and only 80 examples entered service with the unit, these being used for only one combat mission before 601 was re-equipped with Spitfires. All RAF Airacobras were shipped as aid to the Soviet Union, except one which was retained for testing purposes.

The USAAF requisitioned another 200 P-400s from the RAF

order after the attack on Pearl Harbor and sent them to the Fifth Air Force stationed in Australia. However, the main user of the Airacobra during the Second World War was the Soviet Union.

By December 1941, some 600 had been produced and this number had grown to 9558 by the time production ceased in August 1944. Of these, 4773 were sent to the Soviets under the Lend-Lease programme. Most of these were P-39Ns and P-39Qs sent via Alaska and then on through Siberia.

The P-39/P-400 proved to be more successful on the Eastern Front where most air-to-air combat took place at low level and the aircraft's virtues of strong construction, good visibility, decent armour protection, powerful radio gear and heavy armament counted for more than raw speed. ●

THE P-39 WAS MOST SUCCESSFUL ON THE EASTERN FRONT WHERE MOST AIR-TO-AIR COMBAT WAS AT LOW LEVEL

P-400 601 ▶

No 601 Squadron, RAF, flew just one combat mission with their P-400s – a strafing run over France – on October 9, 1941. This is how the type looked during its brief stint in service with the unit, stationed at Manston in England. As with most other US fighter types, the British ordered very early examples of the P-39 (as the P-400) and found their performance disappointing – only for the US to then improve them later in the war.

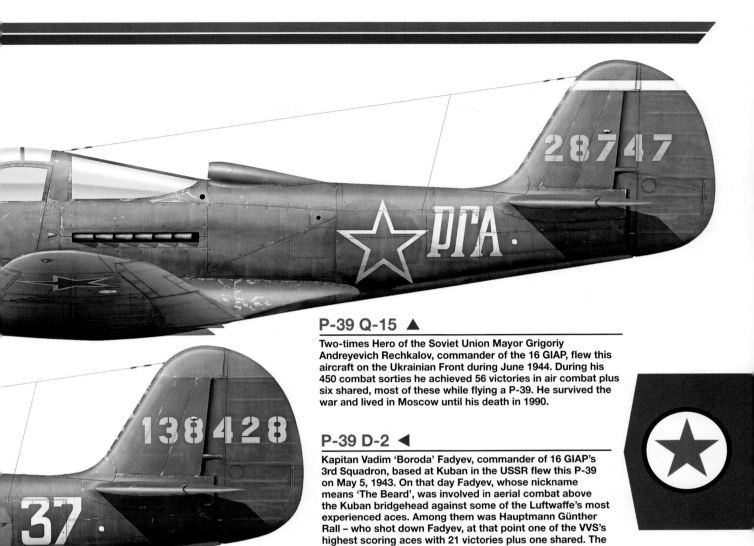

P-39 Q-15 ▲

Two-times Hero of the Soviet Union Mayor Grigoriy Andreyevich Rechkalov, commander of the 16 GIAP, flew this aircraft on the Ukrainian Front during June 1944. During his 450 combat sorties he achieved 56 victories in air combat plus six shared, most of these while flying a P-39. He survived the war and lived in Moscow until his death in 1990.

P-39 D-2 ◄

Kapitan Vadim 'Boroda' Fadyev, commander of 16 GIAP's 3rd Squadron, based at Kuban in the USSR flew this P-39 on May 5, 1943. On that day Fadyev, whose nickname means 'The Beard', was involved in aerial combat above the Kuban bridgehead against some of the Luftwaffe's most experienced aces. Among them was Hauptmann Günther Rall – who shot down Fadyev, at that point one of the VVS's highest scoring aces with 21 victories plus one shared. The Soviet pilot managed to bring his Airacobra down intact in a swamp but he had suffered fatal wounds and died in his cockpit before help could reach him.

P-400 ◄

This ex-RAF Airacobra was flown by Leytenant Yefim Krivosheyev of the 19 GIAP, stationed at Shonguy in the USSR during September 1942. On September 9, Krivosheyev took part in a battle where 11 Soviet fighters took on 17 Messerschmitt Bf 109s. Having shot down one Bf 109, he noticed another lining up to attack his unit commander Pavel Kutakhov. Having run out of ammunition, he rammed the Bf 109 instead and was killed in the process. Overall, Krivosheyev achieved five victories in air combat plus another 15 shared.

CURTISS P-40
TOMAHAWK/KITTY

1938-1958

It might have lacked the glamour of the Spitfire or the macho charisma of the Mustang but the Curtiss P-40 was just as vital to the Allied war effort. It served around the world and proved to be both rugged and adaptable.

Like many of the war's most successful fighters, the development history of the P-40 began during the mid-1930s. The US Army Air Corps launched a competition in early 1935 to decide on a replacement for the Boeing P-26 Peashooter and four designs were put forward.

All four of the contenders, from Curtiss-Wright, Seversky, Vought and Consolidated, were modern-looking low-wing monoplanes. All featured retractable undercarriages, all had fully enclosed cockpits and all were to be made of metal with using a stressed-skin construction.

The Curtiss entry was the Model 75, nicknamed the 'Hawk 75' since every Curtiss fighter since 1923 had been named 'Hawk' no matter how different they were from one another. With a promising

design in prospect, the Army handed Curtiss a contract to build a prototype powered by a 900hp Wright air-cooled radial engine.

While the competition was not announced until 1935, both the Model 75 and the Seversky entry, the two-seater SEV-2XP, had been largely completed in 1934 and so were ready almost from the word go – the Curtiss machine as a private venture and the Seversky as an offshoot from an earlier project.

HAWK/WARHAWK

P-40 Kittyhawk Mk.I ◀

The famous 'shark mouth' design came to be associated with the P-40 after being applied by 112 Squadron, RAF, fighting in Libya. This example was flown by Sergeant Henry G Burney from Gambut in March 13, 1942. Burney had 'London Pride' painted in small white letters above the 'Y' of GA-Y and scored five victories in air combat.

P-40 E ▼

The 154 IAP was one of the first Soviet units to be equipped with the P-40 Tomahawk and during early 1942 received its first P-40E Warhawks. This was the personal aircraft of Mayor Petr Afanasevich Pokryshev while he was stationed at Plekhanovo in the USSR during the summer of 1942. In June 1942 his score of victories stood at 11 with seven shared – within two months he had doubled it. His flying career was ended in September 1943 when he suffered crippling injuries in a crash following a training flight. From a total of 282 combat sorties, he achieved 38 kills with eight shared.

The Vought and Consolidated machines were further behind in their development.

First flown on May 6, 1935, the Model 75 was finished in time to compete in a series of fly-offs planned for June. The SEV-2XP prototype, however, was damaged in transit to the trials and Seversky seized upon the opportunity to quickly reconfigure it as a single-seater – the SEV-1XP. Curtiss protested and the formal head-to-head event

was delayed until April 1936.

Both companies now worked to improve their aircraft and in the meantime the other two competitors had the opportunity to get their prototypes completed – Vought's V-141 and Consolidated's single-seat version of the PB-2.

The Curtiss aircraft that competed in the April 1936 fly-offs was the Model 75B, which featured a reworked fuselage with scalloped rear windows for better visibility and most importantly a new

engine – the 950hp XR-1820-39 Cyclone. Unfortunately, this proved to be an error since the engine failed to perform as planned and a top speed of 285mph was all that could be managed.

The V-141 and PB-2 did even worse and the SEV-1XP, though it scarcely managed to outperform the Model 75B, was declared the winner. Seversky received an order for 77 production models as the P-35 on June 16, 1936, but at the same time Curtiss

received an order for three more prototypes of the Model 75B under the new official designation Y1P-36, as a backup in case of problems with the P-35.

A further Army Air Corps fighter competition was held in 1937 and this time the Curtiss design won, primarily thanks to its remarkable manoeuvrability, with a new order being placed for 210 P-36A fighters. Curtiss was also asked to work on a version of the P-36 that could be powered by the new turbo-supercharged V12 Allison V-1710 engine. The company modified the original Model 75B airframe to accept the engine and the new variant was designated XP-37. Its performance was exceptional but the engine's supercharger proved unreliable and its bulk meant the cockpit had to be moved further to the rear, reducing the pilot's visibility.

The compromises necessary to fit the turbo-supercharged engine were not outweighed by

the performance benefits and the project was about to be shelved when Curtiss offered a new proposal – why not fit the Allison V-1710 with a mechanically driven supercharger? This would make the powerplant less bulky and more reliable, and would not necessitate the extreme configuration changes that had made the XP-37 a failure.

This new design was the Curtiss Model 81, the Army giving it the designation XP-40. The prototype made its first flight on October 14, 1938, with a sharply pointed spinner and its radiator positioned aft of the wings under the fuselage. It was not as fast as expected initially but a series of modifications eventually saw it achieve 366mph at 15,000ft. Among these changes was the relocation of the radiator to the underside of the nose, giving the P-40 its characteristic look.

A full production order for 524

P-40s was placed by the Army on April 26, 1939. The production model was armed with two .50 cal machine guns but when France ordered a batch of 140 it specified a single .50 cal in the fuselage and four .303in machine guns in the wings. These were never delivered to the original customer, France having capitulated before they were ready, so they were diverted to Britain instead. In RAF service they were known as Curtiss Tomahawk Mk.Is.

The Tomahawk had several

P-40 F-1 ▲

French pilot Sergent Chef Jean Gisclon of Groupe de Chasse II/5 flew this P-40F-1 while stationed at Sidi Ahmed in Tunisia during January 1943. Gisclon claimed six victories from 300 sorties but recently historical research has revised this down to two.

P-40 F-15 ▶

'Sweet Bets', a P-40F-15, was piloted by 1st Lieutenant Charles 'Jazz' Jaslow of the 87th FS, 79th FG, based at Causeway LG in Tunisia during April 1943. Jaslow scored one confirmed victory from 80 combat sorties.

◀ P-40 E

Starshiy Leytenant Nikolay Andriyanovich Zelenov of the 154 IAP flew this P-40E while based at Plekhanovo, USSR, during the summer of 1942. He was killed in action on June 29, 1944 having scored 31 victories in air combat plus 10 shared.

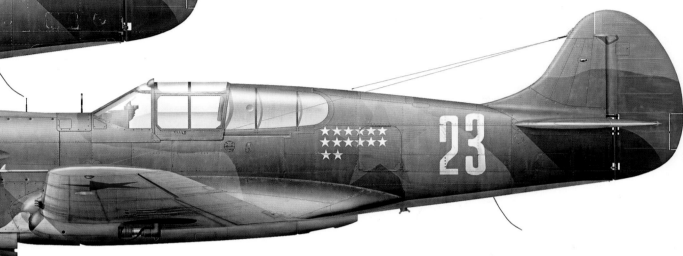

P-40 K ▲

This P-40K was flown by Starshiy Leytenant Nikolai Kuznetsov of the 436 IAP, based at Lake Seliger, USSR, on December 26, 1942. That day his was one of six P-40Ks sent to escort Il-2s in a bombing run on surrounded German forces at Velikiye Luki. The formation was attacked first by Bf 109s then Fw 190s, with Kuznetsov rescuing one of the Il-2s that was in trouble by shooting down a Bf 109 that was on its tail for his 26th and final aerial victory. It was the 26th of the month and Kuznetsov's 26th birthday too. That evening in the unit's mess, he was presented with a chocolate cake with '26-26' on top.

problems which made it unsuitable for combat duties in the RAF however. Metric instruments had been installed for the French pilots and French throttle control levers worked the opposite way around to the British and American versions. In addition, the Tomahawk had neither self-sealing fuel tanks nor armour. As a result, they were used mainly for tactical reconnaissance.

When Curtiss was made aware of this, it set about improving the design with armour protection and heavier weaponry – an extra .303 in each wing. The result was the P-40B. Fitting yet another .303 in each wing and adding

self-sealing fuel tanks resulted in the P-40C. The US Army Air Corps ordered both. The British government ordered 930 of the latter as the Tomahawk Mk.IIa (with British radio gear) and Mk.IIb (with American radio gear).

Making these improvements had dramatically increased the aircraft's weight however – from 7215lb to 8058lb – and top speed fell to 340mph, some 20mph slower than the Bf 109 E. The RAF flew the Tomahawk Mk.II in the Middle East and sent 195 of them to the Soviet Union as aid. No. 112 Squadron was equipped with Tomahawks during the summer of 1941 and it was

THE FIRST RAF UNIT TO OPERATE THE TOMAHAWK, 112 SQUADRON, BEGAN TO RECEIVE IT DURING THE SUMMER OF 1941

decided that the aircraft would be given snarling shark mouths based on those they had seen painted on the noses of German Bf 110s flown by ZG 76 in that theatre.

The resulting British designs were then featured in a colour magazine and read about by members of the American Volunteer Group in Burma, the Flying Tigers, who then painted up their own P-40s with shark mouths. These became so famous that the design was adopted by numerous units operating the P-40 elsewhere.

Curtiss attempted to come up with a replacement for the overweight P-40C with a version incorporating and upgraded Allison engine and five machine guns in each wing – the XP-46 – but instead the US Army Air Corps decided that the upgraded engine should simply be installed in the P-40 instead. The British had already ordered the XP-46 and allocated it the name 'Kittyhawk' but on its cancellation they ordered the re-engined P-40 instead and reapplied the name.

The P-40D was therefore known as Kittyhawk Mk.I to the British, although the Americans gave it their own name – Warhawk – and it first flew in May 1941 and had four .50 cal machine guns in its wings. A second version with six .50 cal machine guns was known as the P-40E or Kittyhawk Mk.Ia to the British.

Although the performance of these Allison-engined updates was an improvement on that of the P-40C, Curtiss wanted to improve the P-40's speed and rate of climb above 15,000ft so it installed a Rolls-Royce Merlin engine into the P-40D to create the XP-40F. Owing to concerns about the ability of Rolls-Royce to meet this new additional demand for engines, Packard in the US was given a contract to build 9000 Merlins under licence – 6000 for the RAF and 3000 for the Army Air Corps.

P-40 E ▶

On January 8, 1942, Flight Sergeant Ronald 'Ron' Henry Simes of 3 Squadron RAAF shot down a trio of Italian fighters in a single engagement while flying this aircraft – making him an ace. The following day his unit was bounced by Oberleutnant Gerhard Homuth of I/JG 27 – one of the top scoring German aces of the North African campaign. Simes was shot down and killed.

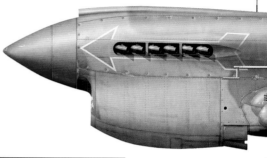

P-40 E ▼

Flight Sergeant Graham G Buckland of 250 Squadron flew this aircraft while stationed at LG 91 in Egypt during the spring of 1942. On May 30 his formation was attacked by Luftwaffe ace Hans-Joachim Marseille and his P-40E was crippled. Buckland bailed out but his parachute failed to open and he was killed on impact. Marseille personally travelled out into the desert and recovered his body before dropping a note over LG91 to explain what had happened.

P-40 E ▶

Having been asked to fly a damaged Kittyhawk to another air base for repair, Flight Sergeant Dennis Copping of 260 Squadron, took off from LG 115 in Egypt on June 28, 1942, and disappeared. Seventy years later, Polish oil workers discovered his near-perfectly preserved aircraft crash-landed in the desert. After an intensive search of the surrounding area, Copping's remains were discovered three miles away on a rocky outcrop. He had evidently taken the aircraft's radio and batteries out and tried to get them working before setting off into the desert on foot.

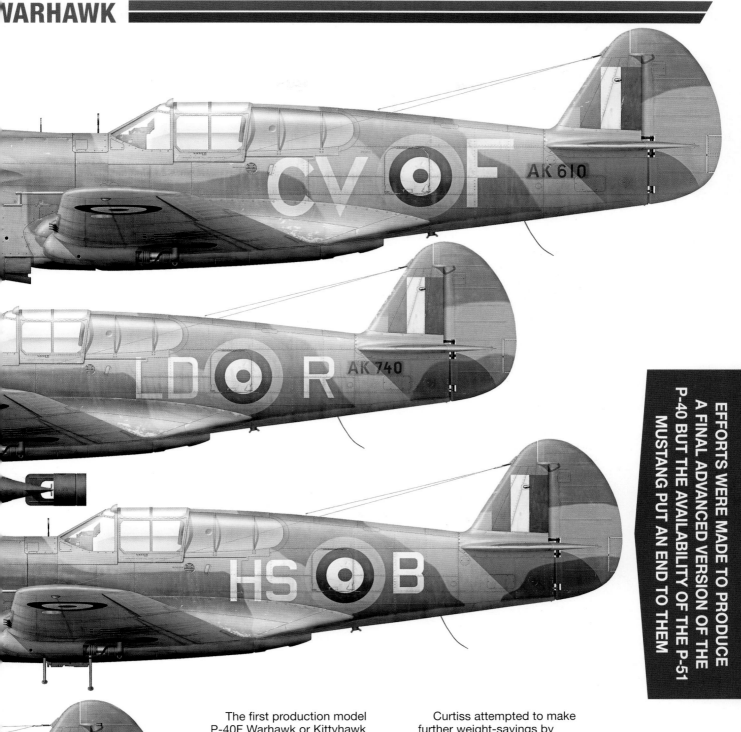

AK 610

AK 740

P-40 L ◄

This P-40L with its distinctive winged skull nose art was flown by pilots of the 85th FS, 79th FG, based at Causeway LG in Tunisia during March 1943.

EFFORTS WERE MADE TO PRODUCE A FINAL ADVANCED VERSION OF THE P-40 BUT THE AVAILABILITY OF THE P-51 MUSTANG PUT AN END TO THEM

The first production model P-40F Warhawk or Kittyhawk Mk.II flew for the first time in October 1941 and achieved a top speed of 364mph. A lightened version of the 'F' was also built, known as the P-40L.

When the supply of Packard Merlins finally dried up there were still a large number of P-40F airframes available, so these were completed with Allison powerplants and designated P-40R.

Another Allison engine upgrade – to the 1325hp V-1710-73 resulted in the P-40K and a lightened version, the P-40M. Despite their differences, both of these were known as the Kittyhawk Mk.III by the RAF.

Curtiss attempted to make further weight-savings by reducing the P-40's fuel tankage and deleting two machine guns to create the P-40N. This also featured more glazing behind the cockpit to improve visibility. The British naturally called it the Kittyhawk Mk.IV.

The last attempt to upgrade the P-40 resulted in the XP-40Q – which featured a 1425hp Allison V-1710-121 engine with a two-stage supercharger. It also had a bubble canopy and clipped wings and was good for 422mph at 20,000ft, but by this point, in 1944, the P-51D was available and only three XP-40Qs were built.

A total of 13,738 P-40s were built all together. ●

REPUBLIC P-47 THUNDERBOLT

1941-1966

Heavy and brutally powerful, the P-47 Thunderbolt was one of the USAAF's two main front line fighters alongside the P-51. Able to soak up considerable combat damage and capable of carrying a hefty weapons load, the P-47 became a legend in its own time.

The origin of the Republic P-47 Thunderbolt can be traced back to the same 1935 fighter competition which ultimately resulted in the Curtiss P-40.

Ranged against Curtiss were three other firms – Vought, Consolidated and Seversky. The latter's entry was the two-seat SEV-2XP, a development of the earlier SEV-3 amphibian, which was almost ready to fly by the end of 1934. After the SEV-2XP was damaged in a crash before competition fly-offs could take place, it was rebuilt as the single-seat SEV-1XP. Further delays saw this re-engined with a Pratt & Whitney R-1830-9 Twin Wasp and fitted with a new vertical stabiliser to become the SEV-7. This successfully won the competition

in April 1936 and 77 production models were ordered as the Seversky P-35.

Preparing the SEV-7 for full production entailed further modifications, including the replacement of full mainwheel fairings with partial fairings and seven degrees of dihedral to the outer wing panels. The Army Air Corps received its first full production P-35 in May 1937

THE ANCESTORS OF THE P-47 INCLUDED A SUCCESSFUL SERIES OF 1930S RACING AIRCRAFT

P-47C-5 ▼

'My Comrade' was flown by Colonel Hubert Zemke, commanding officer of the 56th FG. During his stint as leader during the summer of 1943, the unit became known as 'Zemke's Wolfpack'. This is 'My Comrade' as seen at Horsham St Faith in England. Later in the war Zemke would transfer to a P-38 Lightning unit, which then converted to the P-51 – but the P-47 was the aircraft in which Zemke make his name. Unimpressed by the aircraft's slow rate of climb and poor acceleration when he first flew it, he set about developing tactics that would allow pilots to make the best of its positive attributes – its ability to dive extremely quickly and its exceptional roll rate. As a result, during a 10-day period between October 4 and October 14 the 'Wolfpack' claimed 39 aerial victories for only one loss. Zemke himself flew 154 combat sorties and achieved 17.75 victories in air combat.

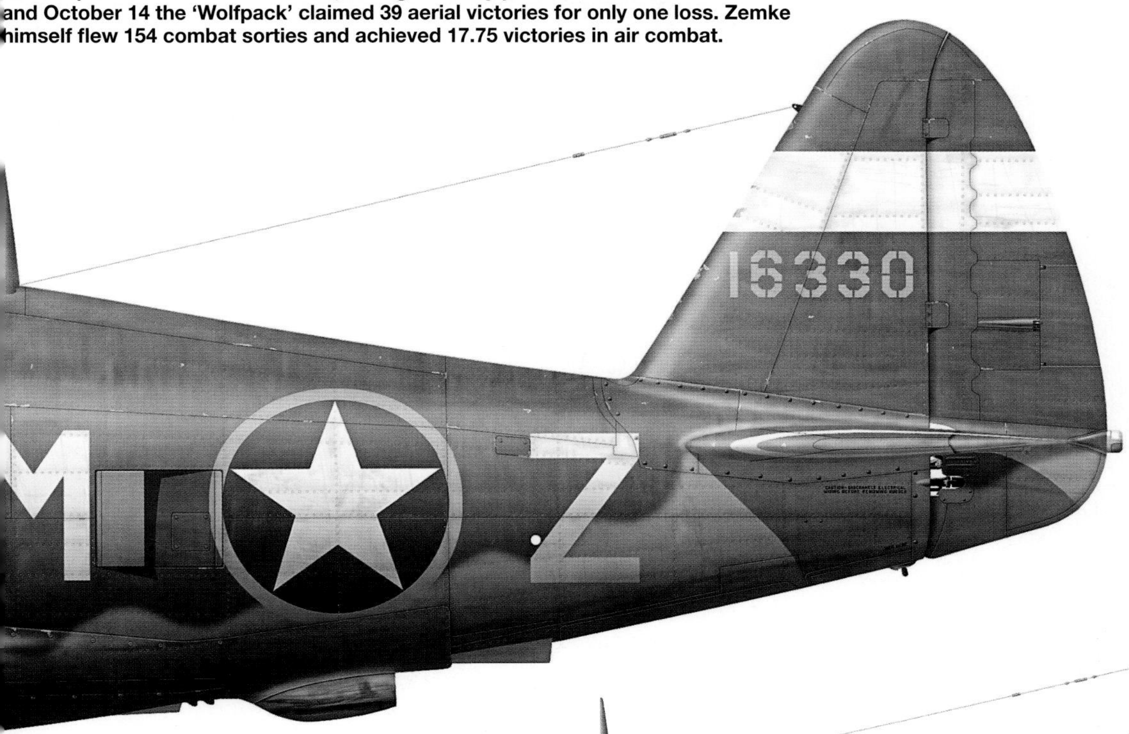

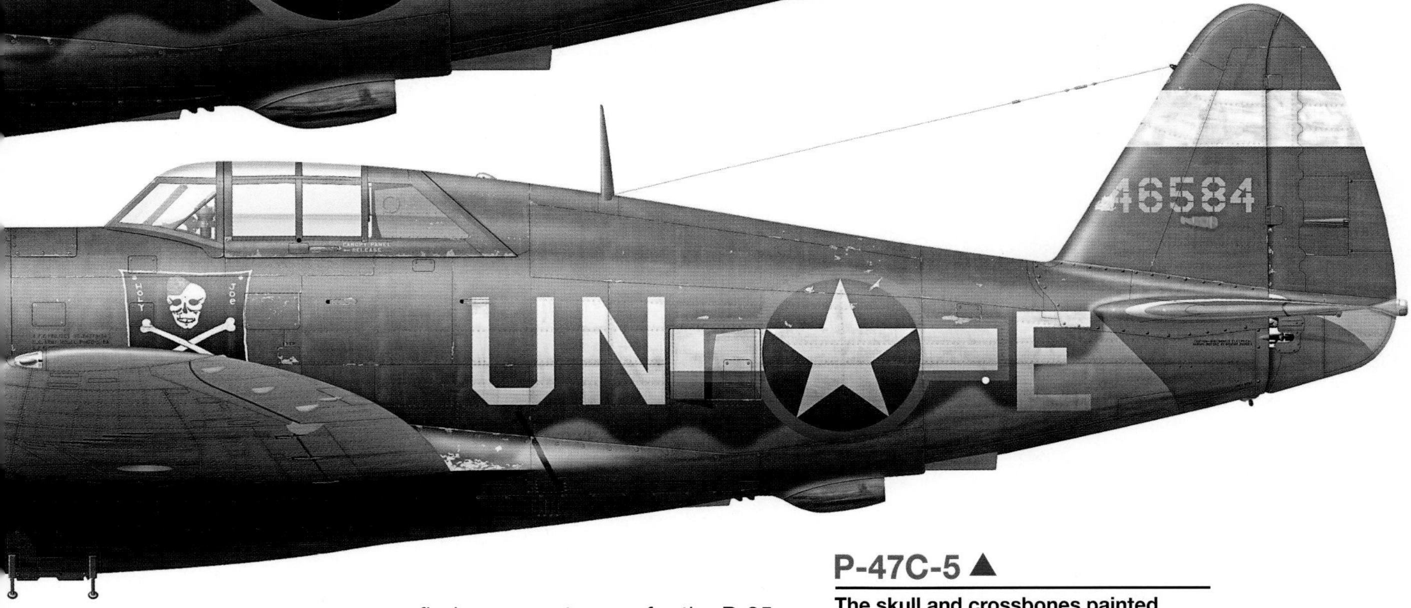

P-47C-5 ▲

The skull and crossbones painted on the side of Captain Joseph L Egan Jr's machine, shown here during September 1943, proved to be prophetic. The 63rd FS, 56th FG pilot was killed on July 19, 1944, when his P-47 crashed near St Avolt. He had five victories in air combat.

and the last in August 1938. Concerned by the very slow delivery of its order, not to mention the fact that Seversky had agreed to sell the very similar two-seater SEV-2PA-B3 fighter-bomber to the Imperial Japanese Navy, the Army placed a much larger order with Curtiss for its P-36.

Seversky was determined to find more customers for the P-35, however, and converted the SEV-7 prototype into a single seat racer, the S-1, which it entered for the 1937 Bendix Trophy – finishing in fourth place. The competition was actually won by another P-35 derived racer built for a private customer, the S-2 made for Frank Fuller of the Fuller Paint Company. The S-2 came second in the 1938 Bendix Trophy and won it again in 1939. Further P-35 based racers were built for James Doolittle and the Shell Oil Company – the latter beating the S-2 to win the 1938 Bendix Trophy.

Buoyed by these successes, Seversky also built a range of private venture one-off P-35 variants with different engines and other modifications to try and attract more military customers: the AP-2, AP-4, AP-4D, AP-7 and AP-9.

The AP-4 and AP-4D were the designs that initially caught the attention of the Air Corps, the AP-4D first being flown in March 1939. It had been modified from the last production model P-35 with the addition of a long streamlined glazed canopy and a Pratt & Whitney R-1830-19 engine with two-speed supercharger. The landing gear was also revised. The Army gave it the provisional designation XP-41.

The AP-4 was another P-35 derivative but had been built from scratch. It was powered by a Pratt & Whitney R-1830-SC2G, fitted with a belly-mounted turbo-supercharger and a new tight-fitting cowl. This gave the type good altitude performance but the cowling causing engine overheating. On March 22, 1939, the AP-4 prototype caught fire and the pilot was forced to bail out. Nevertheless, its performance had been sufficient to convince the Army to order another 13 in May 1939 under the designation YP-43 Lancer. Work on the parallel XP-41 development was stopped.

The YP-43 differed from the XP-41 in having a smaller cockpit which melded into a tall fuselage spine or 'razorback'. The engine's air intake was repositioned from beneath the port wing to directly under the engine, giving

P-47C-5 ▼

Notorious for failing to maintain radio discipline, 1st Lieutenant Ralph K 'The Kid' Hofer flew with the 334th FS, 4th FG, based at Debden in England. This was his aircraft circa October 1943. Hofer was shot down during a battle with Bf 109s over Budapest on July 2, 1944. His body was found amid the wreckage of the P-51B he had been flying. Hofer achieved 15 victories in air combat plus 10 on the ground.

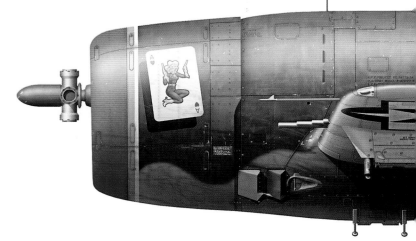

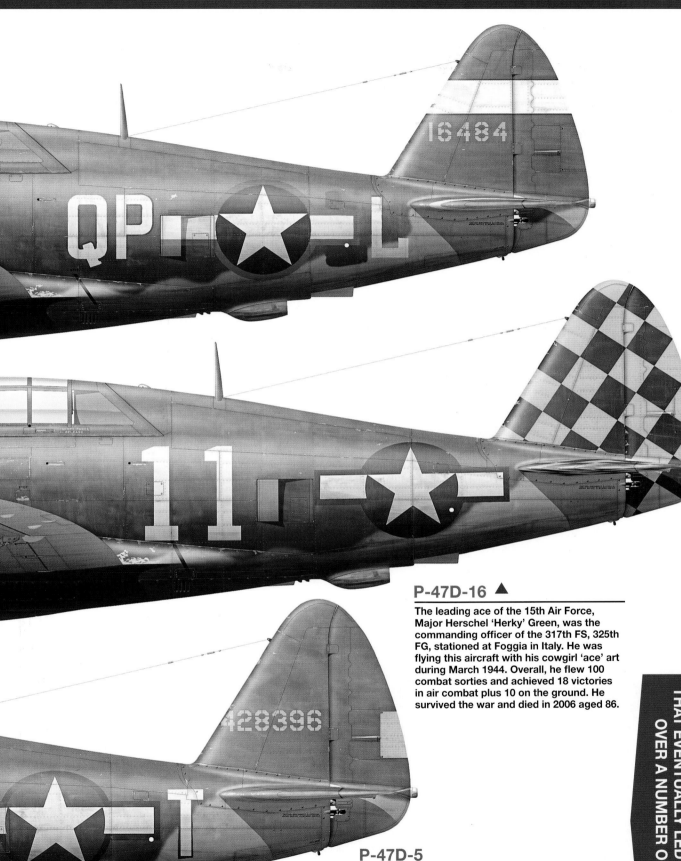

P-47D-16 ▲

The leading ace of the 15th Air Force, Major Herschel 'Herky' Green, was the commanding officer of the 317th FS, 325th FG, stationed at Foggia in Italy. He was flying this aircraft with his cowgirl 'ace' art during March 1944. Overall, he flew 100 combat sorties and achieved 18 victories in air combat plus 10 on the ground. He survived the war and died in 2006 aged 86.

P-47D-5

His aircraft had 'Lucky' on its nose and 1st Lieutenant William J Jordan of the 352nd FS, 353rd FG, proved to be exactly that. He completed his tour of duty then did a second, this time flying the P-51. He eventually went home safely with one and a half aerial victories. The aircraft is show as it appear at Raydon in England during April 1944. ◄

SEVERSKY, LATER RENAMED REPUBLIC, DEVELOPED THE DESIGNS THAT EVENTUALLY LED TO THE P-47 OVER A NUMBER OF YEARS

it a distinctively ovoid cowling. Its turbo-supercharged R-1830-35 radial engine drove a three-bladed variable pitch propeller and it had two .50 cal machine guns positioned above the engine plus a .30 cal in each wing.

In October 1939, the Seversky Aircraft Company was reorganised as the Republic Aviation Corporation and its charismatic founder, Alexander de Seversky was effectively ousted while he was away on a business trip in Europe.

As preparations were being made to produce the short-run YP-43, Republic was working up yet another P-35 derivative – the AP-10. This was to be a lightweight version, powered by a V12 Allison V-1710-39 and armed with eight .50 cal Browning machine guns. The Army was interested enough to give this new development the designation XP-47 and to order a prototype in November 1939, plus a prototype of a further lightened design, the XP-47A.

However, as the Battle of Britain unfolded in Europe during the summer of 1940 and combat reports made their way back to the US, it became evident that the XP-47 and XP-47A would lack the necessary armour, performance and weaponry to survive in a dogfight and both were cancelled. Therefore, Republic designer Alexander Kartveli came up with a larger, heavier version of the

P-47D-21 ▶

Major Robert S Johnson of the 62nd FS, 56th FG was the top-scoring P-47 ace of the Second World War with 27 victories in air combat from 89 sorties. This is his last aircraft, 'Penrod and Sam', at Boxted in England during May 1944. A boys' novel about best friends penned by Booth Tarkington in 1916, Penrod and Sam was made into a film in 1937; and it happened that Johnson's own middle name was Samuel while his crew chief's surname was Penrod. Johnson's final victories were scored on May 8 when he shot down a Bf 109 and a Fw 190 over Celle in Germany. He returned to the US on June 6, 1944 – D-Day.

P-47D-22 ▶

'Joan the Happy Hopper' was flown by 1st Lieutenant Russel S Fredendall of the 507th FS, 404th FG, based at Wington, England, during early June 1944.

P-47D-25 ▼

Captain Fred J Christensen Jr of the 62nd FS, 56th FG, based at Boxted, England, gave his aircraft two names – 'Miss Fire' complete with raunchy nude, and 'Rozzie Geth II' as a short form of his college sweetheart's name, Rosamund Gethro. He was flying it on July 5, 1944, when he made his last fighter kill of the war, a Fw 190 over Beziers in France. He rounded off his score at 21.5 overall with the addition of no fewer than six Ju 52 transports over Gardelegen, Germany two days later. He died in 2006 aged 84.

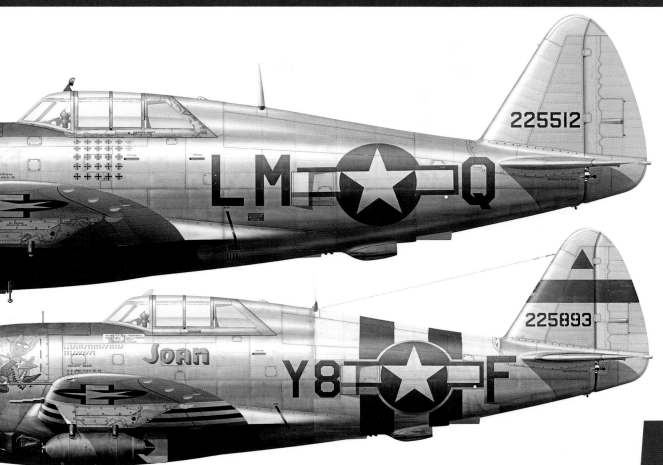

design that could carry all the necessary armour and armament to meet the challenge. This increase in weight was only made possible by the inclusion in the design of the new Pratt & Whitney R-2800 Double Wasp two-row 18-cylinder radial engine, which produced an incredible 2000hp.

Delivery of the 13 Republic YP-43s began in September 1940 and production was eventually extended to 272 examples but Republic now focussed much more of its attention on the new Double Wasp-powered design, which had been given the designation XP-47B even though it actually had little in common with the XP-47A.

The XP-47B was all-metal except for fabric coverings on its tail control surfaces. Its wings were elliptical in shape with a slightly swept leading edge. The cockpit was air-conditioned and spacious with a comfortable seat and canopy doors that hinged upwards. Self-sealing

P-47D-25 ◀

'Honey II' was flown by Captain James N Poindexter of the 352nd FS, 353rd FG, based at Raydon in England during August 1944. Poindexter was killed when his personal aircraft at the time, 'Honey IV', a P-51, crashed at Capel St Mary, Suffolk, on January 3, 1945. He achieved seven victories in air combat plus four on the ground.

fuel tanks beneath the cockpit could hold 305 US gallons.

The R-2800 engine drove a four-bladed propeller and was housed within a broad cowling which admitted air for the engine itself, the oil coolers and the turbo-supercharger intercooler system. This involved engine exhaust gases entering a pair of wastegate-fitted pipes which ran along the sides of the cockpit to drive the turbo-supercharger turbine about halfway between the cockpit and the tail at the bottom of the fuselage. This ducting resulted in the XP-47B having a very deep fuselage and the wings needing to be mounted relatively high up. Consequently, the aircraft needed long undercarriage legs.

It was armed with eight .50 cal machine guns – four per wing, staggered so that their ammunition boxes would have sufficient space. The XP-47B's first flight was on May 6, 1941, and after initial tests the type managed an impressive top speed of 412mph at 25,800ft.

As with most new designs, the type threw up a number of teething problems – it needed a long runway to take off, the tightly packed machine guns in the wings often jammed, control loads were excessive at high speed, the cockpit covers had a disturbing tendency to jam and the aircraft lacked the manoeuvrability of contemporary types such as the Bf 109 or Spitfire.

Even so, the USAAF ordered 171 P-47Bs and the first production example was delivered in May 1942. The canopy problem was cured with the introduction of a rearwards-sliding version which could be ejected in an emergency and the fabric covered control surfaces were replaced with all-metal construction.

As Republic reworked its design and continued to make improvements, the USAAF's confidence in the P-47 Thunderbolt grew and an order for a further 602 examples was placed. Embodying numerous detail changes, such as an upgraded General Electric turbo-supercharger regulator and a short vertical radio mast, these were designated P-47C and deliveries commenced in September 1942.

With the 58th P-47C, the production line was altered to include an 8in fuselage extension forward of the cockpit to alter the type's centre of gravity and allow improved access for engine maintenance. The oil cooler exhausts were changed and the brakes, undercarriage and electrical systems were improved. Aircraft with these features were designated P-47C-1 and 55 were made. The next 128 aircraft off the line became the P-47C-2, featuring a centreline fuselage hardpoint for carrying either a 500lb bomb or a 200 US gallon drop tank. The main production version was the P-47C-5, which featured a whip aerial.

Most of the P-47's early difficulties had been eliminated by the beginning of 1943 and a batch was sent to England to be operated by the 56th FG as part of the Eighth Air Force.

P-47D-27

Scoring one victory in air combat from 154 combat sorties, Captain Michael C McCarthy of the 64th FS, 57th FG, was based at Grossetto in Italy during September 1944 when he flew 'Maggie Hogan'. His air-to-air record belies the fact that most of his missions were flown against ground targets during the Italian campaign.

▼

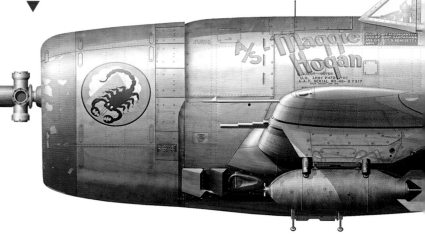

THE FIRST P-47S SENT TO THE EIGHTH AIR FORCE IN ENGLAND ARRIVED DURING EARLY 1943

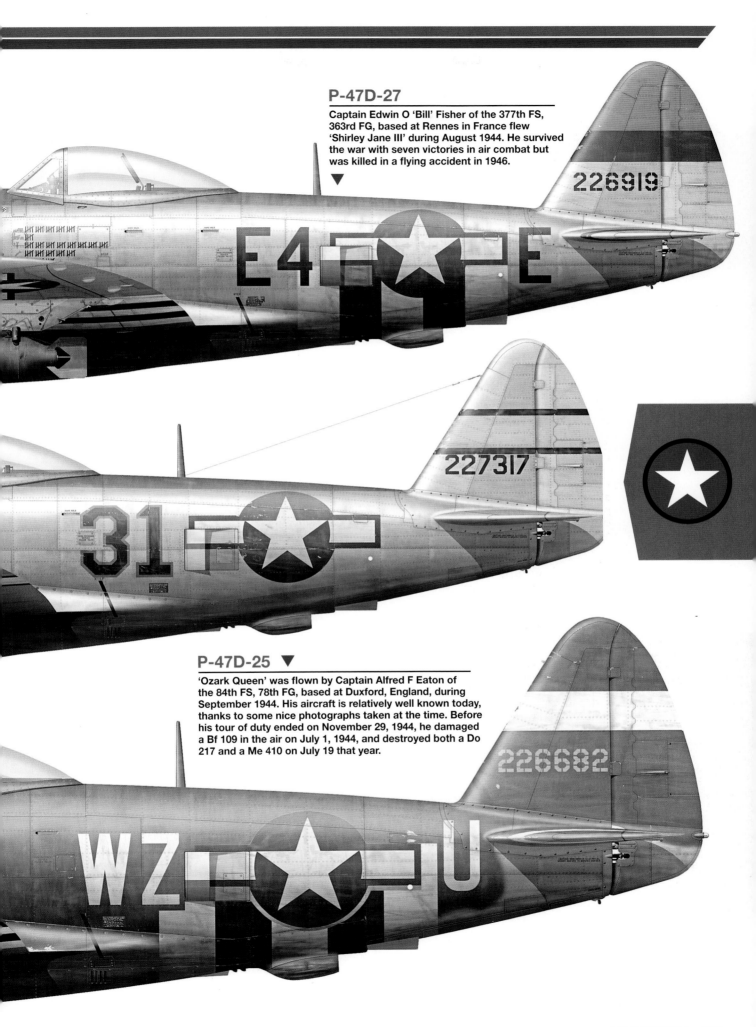

P-47D-27

Captain Edwin O 'Bill' Fisher of the 377th FS, 363rd FG, based at Rennes in France flew 'Shirley Jane III' during August 1944. He survived the war with seven victories in air combat but was killed in a flying accident in 1946.

▼

226919

E4 ★ E

227317

31 ★

P-47D-25 ▼

'Ozark Queen' was flown by Captain Alfred F Eaton of the 84th FS, 78th FG, based at Duxford, England, during September 1944. His aircraft is relatively well known today, thanks to some nice photographs taken at the time. Before his tour of duty ended on November 29, 1944, he damaged a Bf 109 in the air on July 1, 1944, and destroyed both a Do 217 and a Me 410 on July 19 that year.

226682

WZ ★ U

P-47D-26 ▶

This is how 'Toots', flown by Lieutenant Joseph Angelone of the 66th FS, 57th FG, based at Grosseto, Italy, looked on October 6, 1944. The following day, while setting out on his next mission, one of the aircraft's tyres blew out at 100mph on take-off. The fully-laden 'Toots' wasn't moving fast enough to get airborne and slewed into a mound of earth beside the runway. The right main undercarriage leg snapped and the wingtip hit the ground, causing the aircraft to be upended. Angelone jumped from the cockpit and ran just in time as the fuel leaking from its full fuel tanks ignited – resulting in a fireball that consumed 'Toots' completely. Angelone suffered only bruises.

P-47D-25

When Hubert Zemke left the 56th FG, his replacement as commanding officer was Lieutenant Colonel David C Schilling. This is his aircraft 'Hairless Joe' at Leavenworth, England, during October 1944. Schilling flew 132 combat sorties and scored 22.5 victories in air combat. He remained with the air force after the war and by 1956 was inspector general in Strategic Air Command's Seventh Air Division. He was also a fast car enthusiast and owned an open-topped Cadillac/Allard machine like his friend General Curtis LeMay and others who formed a group for Sports Car Club of America events. On August 14, 1956, Schilling was driving at high speed down a narrow two lane country road in Suffolk, approaching the rear of a slower vehicle he intended to overtake. At this point, his cap began to blow off. He reached up a hand to grab hold of it and lost control of the car, which skidded sideways and crashed into the side-railing of a bridge. The car was sliced in half at the driver's seat and Schilling died instantly.

▼

P-47D-27 ▲

During his tour of duty, 1st Lieutenant Walker A Diamanti of the 512th FS, 406th FG, flew 'Angie' from Mourmelon-le-Grand in France. This is how the aircraft looked in December 1944. Less than a month later, Diamanti was on his way back to the US and 'Angie' was assigned a new pilot – 2nd Lieutenant Fred V Brandt. At around this time, a huge pinup painting was added to the aircraft's engine cowling. Later in the war, 'Angie' was damaged and fitted with replacement parts plus a new name: 'Patty'.

P-47D-28 ▶

Another aircraft bearing a striking pinup portrait was 'Dottie Mae' flown by Lieutenant Larry A Kuhl of the 511th FS, 405th FG, stationed at Saint-Dizier, France, during December 1944. He flew a total of 90 combat sorties and destroyed three enemy aircraft on the ground. 'Dottie Mae' crashed shortly after the war while being flown by another pilot, Lieutenant Henry Mohr. Mohr was performing a celebratory flight over a lake in Austria but came in too low and hit the water. Mohr was rescued but 'Dottie Mae' sank – only to be recovered and restored 60 years later.

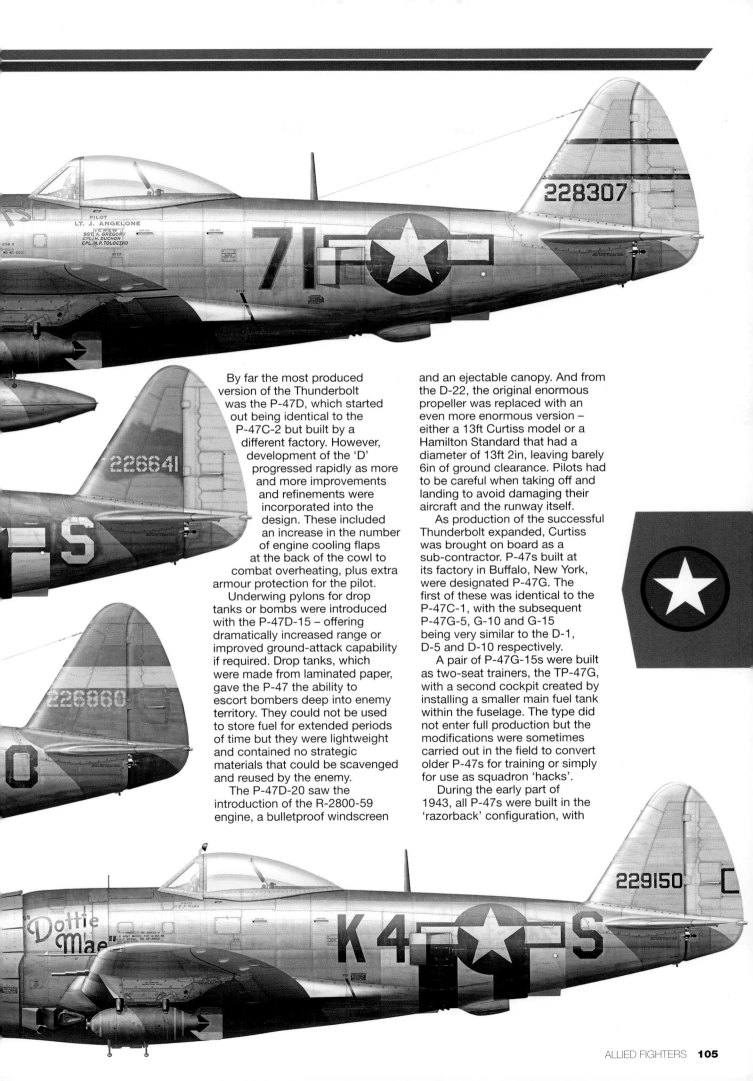

By far the most produced version of the Thunderbolt was the P-47D, which started out being identical to the P-47C-2 but built by a different factory. However, development of the 'D' progressed rapidly as more and more improvements and refinements were incorporated into the design. These included an increase in the number of engine cooling flaps at the back of the cowl to combat overheating, plus extra armour protection for the pilot.

Underwing pylons for drop tanks or bombs were introduced with the P-47D-15 – offering dramatically increased range or improved ground-attack capability if required. Drop tanks, which were made from laminated paper, gave the P-47 the ability to escort bombers deep into enemy territory. They could not be used to store fuel for extended periods of time but they were lightweight and contained no strategic materials that could be scavenged and reused by the enemy.

The P-47D-20 saw the introduction of the R-2800-59 engine, a bulletproof windscreen

and an ejectable canopy. And from the D-22, the original enormous propeller was replaced with an even more enormous version – either a 13ft Curtiss model or a Hamilton Standard that had a diameter of 13ft 2in, leaving barely 6in of ground clearance. Pilots had to be careful when taking off and landing to avoid damaging their aircraft and the runway itself.

As production of the successful Thunderbolt expanded, Curtiss was brought on board as a sub-contractor. P-47s built at its factory in Buffalo, New York, were designated P-47G. The first of these was identical to the P-47C-1, with the subsequent P-47G-5, G-10 and G-15 being very similar to the D-1, D-5 and D-10 respectively.

A pair of P-47G-15s were built as two-seat trainers, the TP-47G, with a second cockpit created by installing a smaller main fuel tank within the fuselage. The type did not enter full production but the modifications were sometimes carried out in the field to convert older P-47s for training or simply for use as squadron 'hacks'.

During the early part of 1943, all P-47s were built in the 'razorback' configuration, with

P-47D-28 ▶

During the final months of the Second World War, the nose art that appeared on American fighters became increasingly raunchy. 'Miss Caesar – the Greenpoint Gladiator', featuring a full nude wearing a little hat and tutu but holding a two-handed sword, was flown by Captain Stanley L Koslow of the 510th FS, 405th FG, based at Saint-Dizier in France during January 1945. He scored one confirmed victory.

the consequent poor rearward visibility. A number were fitted with a bulged canopy by the British but then Hawker came up with a full 'bubble' canopy for the Typhoon. The Americans were quick to seize upon this development and introduce it to both the P-47 and the P-51 Mustang.

A single P-47D-5 was modified to incorporate a prototype bubble canopy during the summer of 1943, being redesignated the XP-47K. A second older P-47 was also modified but this time to incorporate a larger internal fuel capacity of 370 US gallons, under the designation XP-47L. Both of these innovations were brought into production together for the P-47D-25 and first deliveries of the new type were made to front line units in May 1944.

All future P-47s incorporated the new 'bubbletop' and the D-26, D-27, D-28 and D-30 saw the introduction of further engine improvements and new dive recovery flaps. Experience with the

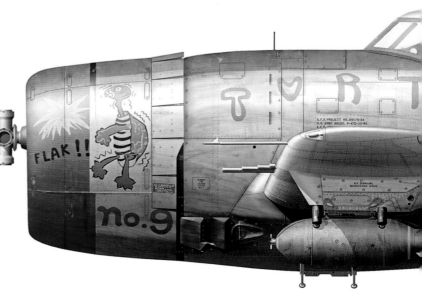

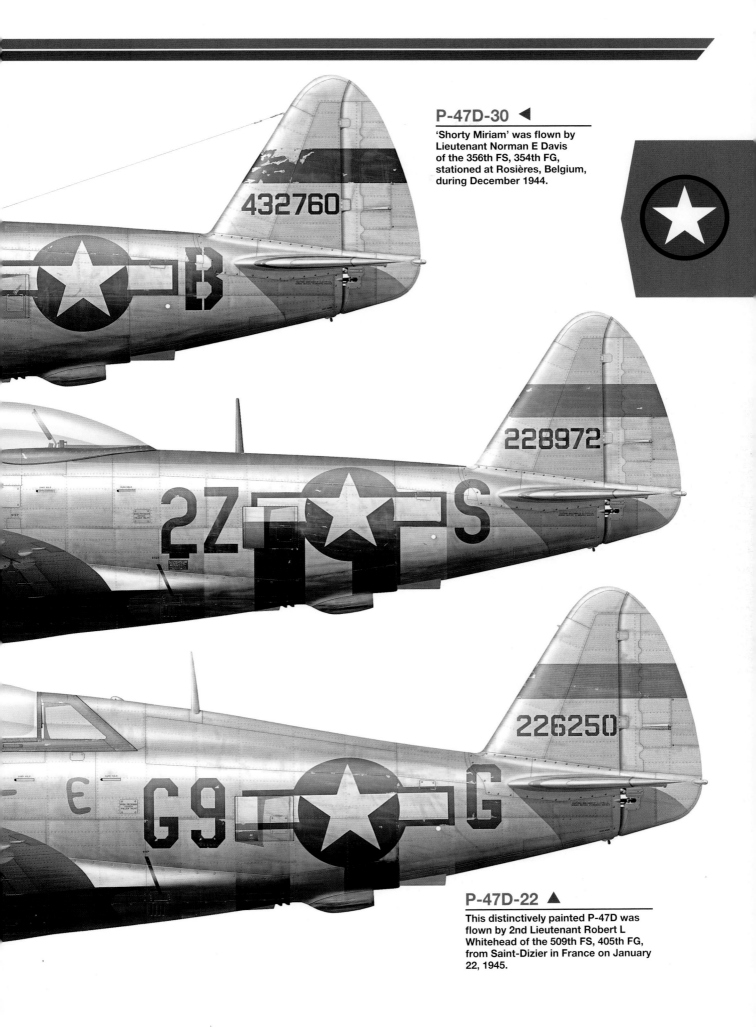

P-47D-30 ◄
'Shorty Miriam' was flown by Lieutenant Norman E Davis of the 356th FS, 354th FG, stationed at Rosières, Belgium, during December 1944.

432760

228972

226250

P-47D-22 ▲
This distinctively painted P-47D was flown by 2nd Lieutenant Robert L Whitehead of the 509th FS, 405th FG, from Saint-Dizier in France on January 22, 1945.

AN EXPERIMENTAL P-47, THE XP-47H, FEATURED A 2300HP ENGINE AND A COMPLETELY REDESIGNED NOSE

P-47M-1 ▶

'Teddy' was flown by Major Michael J Jackson of the 62nd FS, 56th FG, based at Boxted, England, during February 1945. After flying 86 combat sorties, Jackson finished the war with eight victories in air combat plus five and a half on the ground.

bubbletop showed that reducing the height of the rear fuselage served to produce yaw instability so a new 'fin fillet' was introduced to correct it which ran from the tailfin to a point just behind the radio aerial. Older bubbletops had the fin fillet retrofitted.

The P-47D-40 had provision for the fitment of 10 HVAR rocket launchers plus the new K-14 computing gunsight – a licence-built version of the British Ferranti GGS Mark IID sight. It enabled the pilot to input the target's wingspan and the range, which would then position the gunsight's reticle to allow for the necessary deflection.

Another experiment with the P-47, this time with a pair of D-15 airframes, was to fit them

with 2300hp Chrysler XIV-2220-1 16-cylinder inverted V liquid-cooled engine under the designation XP-47H. This engine, which featured a substantial radiator mounted beneath its fuselage, resulted in a transformation of the P-47's looks. Not only did it give the aircraft's nose a completely different shape, but it also increased its length from 36ft 1in to 39ft 2in. Initially, it was believed that this radical alteration of the original design would result in a top speed of 490mph.

Work on the conversion was begun in August 1943 but was not completed until 1945. The first

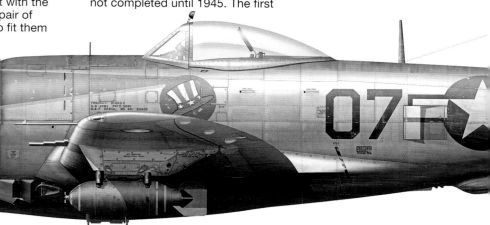

P-47D-30 ▲

'My Baby' was flown by Lieutenant J G Barber of the 514th FS, 406th FG, based at Asch in Belgium, during March 1945.

P-47D-30 ▶

Lieutenant Richard W Orth of the 513th FS, 406th FG, flew 'Diane' while based at Asch, Belgium, during March 1945.

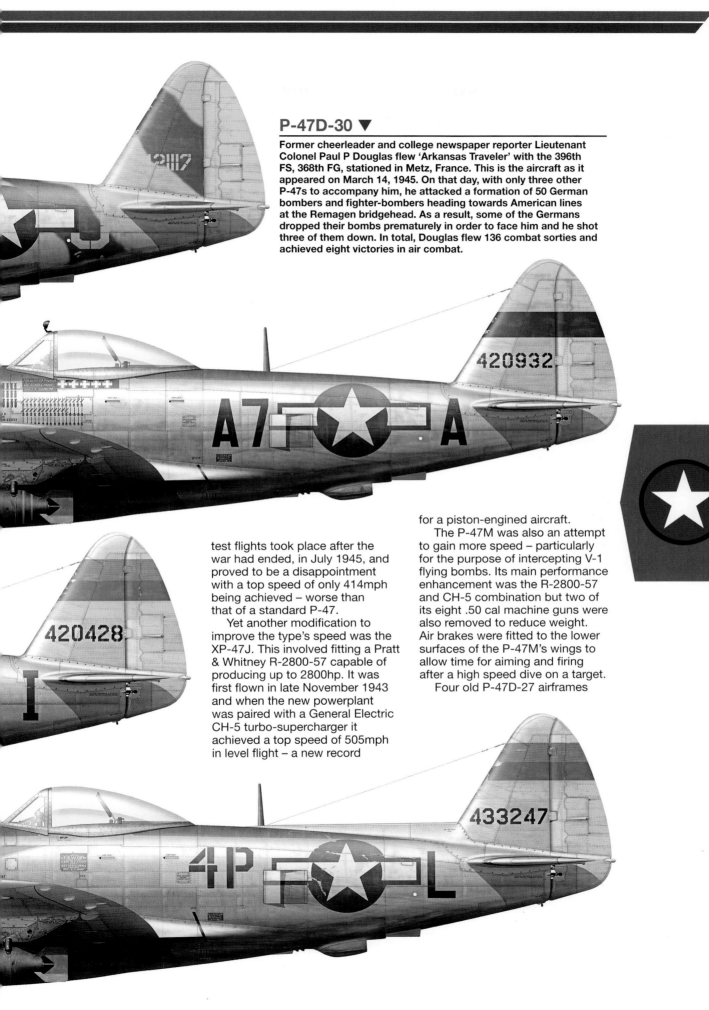

P-47D-30 ▼

Former cheerleader and college newspaper reporter Lieutenant Colonel Paul P Douglas flew 'Arkansas Traveler' with the 396th FS, 368th FG, stationed in Metz, France. This is the aircraft as it appeared on March 14, 1945. On that day, with only three other P-47s to accompany him, he attacked a formation of 50 German bombers and fighter-bombers heading towards American lines at the Remagen bridgehead. As a result, some of the Germans dropped their bombs prematurely in order to face him and he shot three of them down. In total, Douglas flew 136 combat sorties and achieved eight victories in air combat.

test flights took place after the war had ended, in July 1945, and proved to be a disappointment with a top speed of only 414mph being achieved – worse than that of a standard P-47.

Yet another modification to improve the type's speed was the XP-47J. This involved fitting a Pratt & Whitney R-2800-57 capable of producing up to 2800hp. It was first flown in late November 1943 and when the new powerplant was paired with a General Electric CH-5 turbo-supercharger it achieved a top speed of 505mph in level flight – a new record

for a piston-engined aircraft.

The P-47M was also an attempt to gain more speed – particularly for the purpose of intercepting V-1 flying bombs. Its main performance enhancement was the R-2800-57 and CH-5 combination but two of its eight .50 cal machine guns were also removed to reduce weight. Air brakes were fitted to the lower surfaces of the P-47M's wings to allow time for aiming and firing after a high speed dive on a target.

Four old P-47D-27 airframes

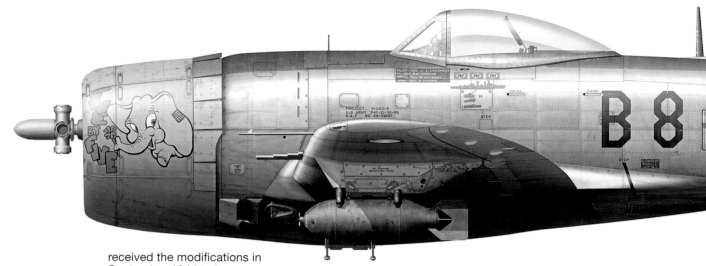

received the modifications in September 1944 to become YP-47Ms. These were able to achieve a top speed of 473mph and the type was put into limited production – just 133 examples being produced.

Unfortunately, the R-2800-57's high state of tune caused serious problems with the P-47M. Engine failure became common due to cracked ignition harnesses at high altitude, electrical problems, and carburettor valve diaphragm failures. Oil tanks frequently ruptured due to poor protection against salt water corrosion resulting from the aircrafts' shipment from the US to Europe.

The war was nearly over by the time the P-47M's problems had been overcome and it was fit to enter service. Even so, P-47Ms were still responsible for the destruction of 15 enemy aircraft in aerial combat between March and May 1945 – including seven German jets. Out of the total production run of 130 P-47Ms, 12 were lost in crashes with 11 pilots being killed.

The final Thunderbolt variant,

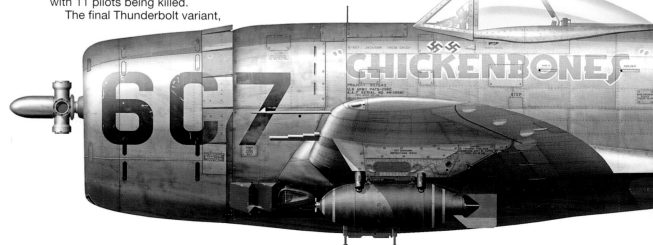

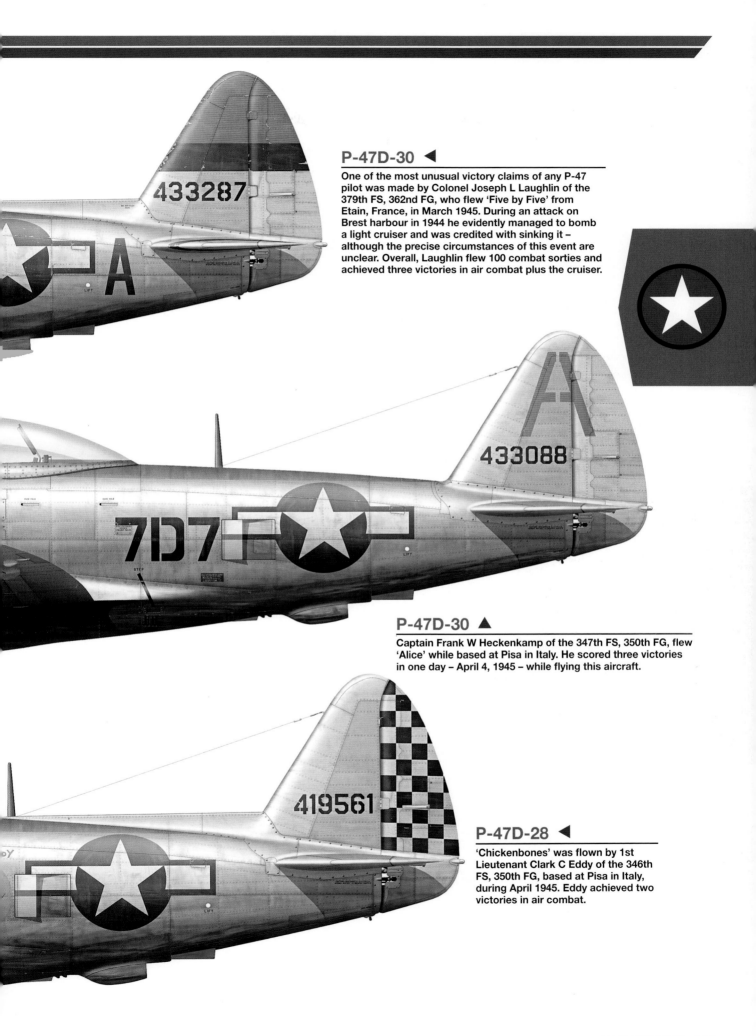

P-47D-30 ◄

One of the most unusual victory claims of any P-47 pilot was made by Colonel Joseph L Laughlin of the 379th FS, 362nd FG, who flew 'Five by Five' from Etain, France, in March 1945. During an attack on Brest harbour in 1944 he evidently managed to bomb a light cruiser and was credited with sinking it – although the precise circumstances of this event are unclear. Overall, Laughlin flew 100 combat sorties and achieved three victories in air combat plus the cruiser.

P-47D-30 ▲

Captain Frank W Heckenkamp of the 347th FS, 350th FG, flew 'Alice' while based at Pisa in Italy. He scored three victories in one day – April 4, 1945 – while flying this aircraft.

P-47D-28 ◄

'Chickenbones' was flown by 1st Lieutenant Clark C Eddy of the 346th FS, 350th FG, based at Pisa in Italy, during April 1945. Eddy achieved two victories in air combat.

P-47D-30 ▼

The original 'Tarheel Hal' was written off due to damage sustained during a ground-attack mission, so this is its replacement, flown by Lieutenant 'Ike' Davis of the 366th FS, 358th FG, stationed at Toul in France, during March 1945. Davis was from North Carolina, the 'Tarheel State' and Hal was his brother. The original meaning of 'tar heel' came from the American Civil War when the North Carolina troops were said to stick to their ranks like they had tar on their heels.

the P-47N, was designed specifically for escorting B-29 bombers on raids over the Japanese home islands. Therefore, its range was increased with new fuel tanks being built into its wings. It also had squared-off wingtips to improve its roll rate. The first experimental version, the XP-47N, was first flown in July 1944 and it was determined that the type's range could be boosted to around 2000 miles. Initially powered by the R-2800-57, later production was switched to the R-2800-73 or -77. The last P-47N was completed in October 1945.

The Thunderbolt's chief rival for the title of top wartime American fighter was the North American Mustang. On paper, the Thunderbolt seemed to have the edge over the Mustang, but pilots

told a different story. The Mustang was simply more agile – it handled better and was easier to fly well. Against German fighters, the Thunderbolt seems to have been just as effective at all altitudes. In the end, the Thunderbolt lost out simply because fewer were used in situations where they were likely to enter aerial combat with German fighters.

One source gives the total number of enemy aircraft shot down by the P-47 as 3662 compared to the P-51's 5944. General der Jagdflieger Adolf Galland's Me 262 was shot

P-47D-23 ▲

Lieutenant Colonel Gilbert O 'Gil' Wymond commander of the 65th FS, 57th FG, was the driving force behind efforts to redevelop the P-47 into an effective ground-attack aircraft. He called for modification which increased the accuracy of its weapons delivery during bombing and strafing missions and also to increase its overall bomb load. He flew 'Hun Hunter XIV' while based at Alto, Corsica, during August 1944. Wymond had three confirmed aerial victories plus two probables.

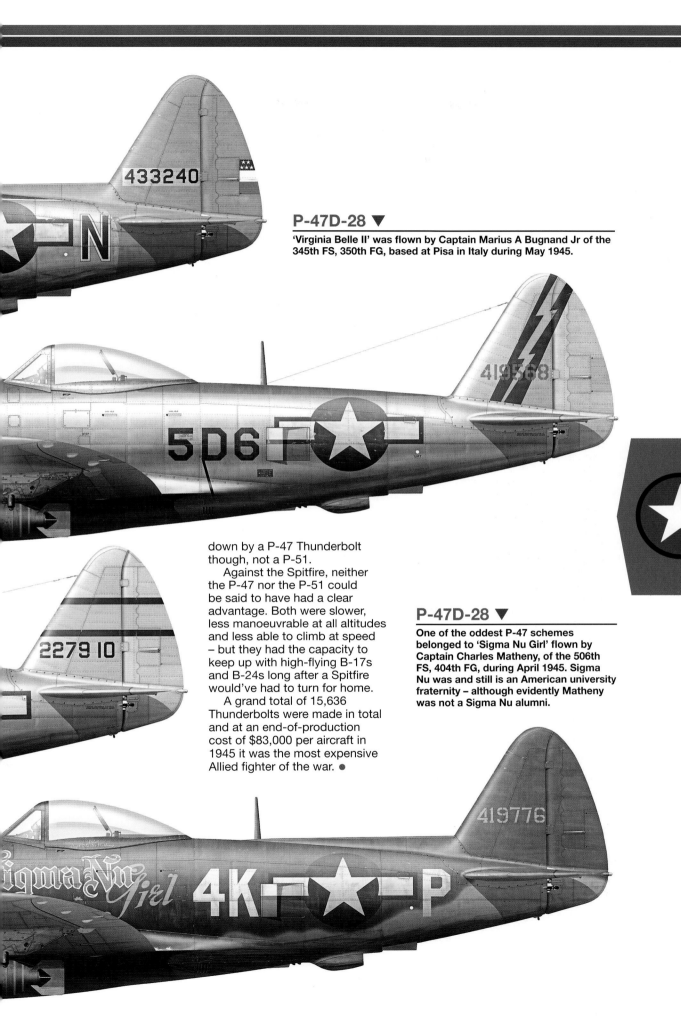

P-47D-28 ▼

'Virginia Belle II' was flown by Captain Marius A Bugnand Jr of the 345th FS, 350th FG, based at Pisa in Italy during May 1945.

down by a P-47 Thunderbolt though, not a P-51.

Against the Spitfire, neither the P-47 nor the P-51 could be said to have had a clear advantage. Both were slower, less manoeuvrable at all altitudes and less able to climb at speed – but they had the capacity to keep up with high-flying B-17s and B-24s long after a Spitfire would've had to turn for home.

A grand total of 15,636 Thunderbolts were made in total and at an end-of-production cost of $83,000 per aircraft in 1945 it was the most expensive Allied fighter of the war. ●

P-47D-28 ▼

One of the oddest P-47 schemes belonged to 'Sigma Nu Girl' flown by Captain Charles Matheny, of the 506th FS, 404th FG, during April 1945. Sigma Nu was and still is an American university fraternity – although evidently Matheny was not a Sigma Nu alumni.

NORTH AMERICAN P-51 MUSTANG

1940-1984

The P-51 Mustang was most famous American fighter of the Second World War and with good reason. Particularly in its late model form it was extremely fast, highly manoeuvrable and able to fly for huge distances. In combat it earned the admiration of its pilots and inspired fear in their opponents.

During 1939, the newly formed aircraft design team at North American Aviation – founded as a holding company in 1928 and only becoming a genuine manufacturing concern 10 years later – quietly began work on a new fighter aircraft.

At around the same time, the US Neutrality Act of 1939 featured a 'cash and carry' clause which effectively allowed the British and French, for the first time, to buy American arms as long as they could provide their own ships to take them away. As a result in early 1940 an Anglo-French purchasing commission was established in the US to work out what the two nations should buy.

Attention soon focused on the Curtiss P-40 and Lockheed's P-38, although the former fell some way short of the state-of-the-art in fighter design at that time and the latter would not be ready to 'carry' for months or even years. The Bell P-39 was also a strong contender for sales.

North American Aviation was able to sell its NA-16 trainer design to the British, who

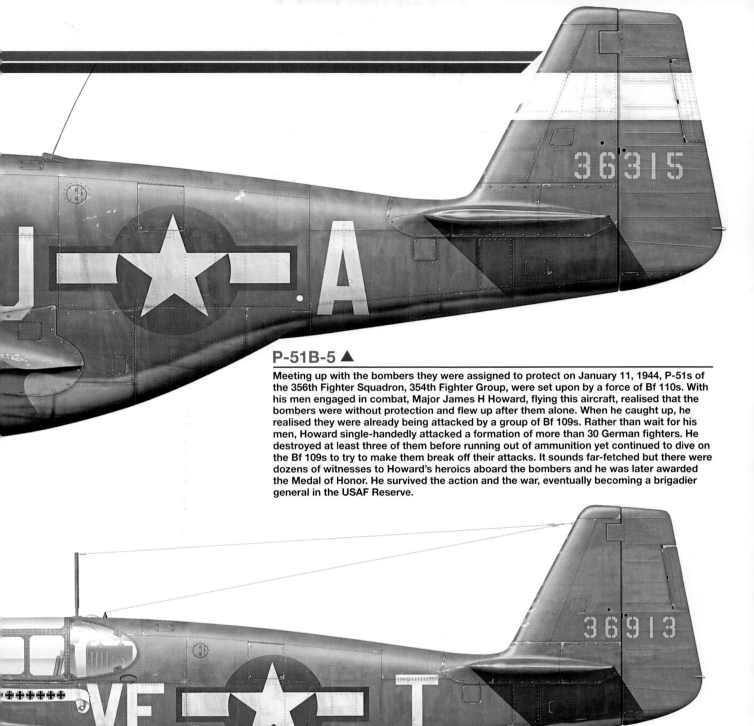

P-51B-5 ▲

Meeting up with the bombers they were assigned to protect on January 11, 1944, P-51s of the 356th Fighter Squadron, 354th Fighter Group, were set upon by a force of Bf 110s. With his men engaged in combat, Major James H Howard, flying this aircraft, realised that the bombers were without protection and flew up after them alone. When he caught up, he realised they were already being attacked by a group of Bf 109s. Rather than wait for his men, Howard single-handedly attacked a formation of more than 30 German fighters. He destroyed at least three of them before running out of ammunition yet continued to dive on the Bf 109s to try to make them break off their attacks. It sounds far-fetched but there were dozens of witnesses to Howard's heroics aboard the bombers and he was later awarded the Medal of Honor. He survived the action and the war, eventually becoming a brigadier general in the USAF Reserve.

P-51B-5 ▲

After becoming the 8th Air Force's top scoring ace by shooting down three Fw 190s on April 8, 1944, Captain Dominic Salvatore 'Don' Gentile of the 336th FS, 4th FG, was in the mood to celebrate. On April 13, 1944, he took off in his personal P-51 'Shangri La' to perform some stunts over his unit's base at Debden in England. Unfortunately, he crashed in front of a pack of press reporters and a firm crew and was grounded by his unit commander. During the war he achieved a total of 21.83 victories in air combat plus six on the ground. Afterwards, he became a test pilot but died on January 28, 1951, aged 30, when his T-33 Shooting Star trainer crashed.

renamed it the Harvard, but could not persuade them to buy its B-25 bomber. With the other firms landing contracts worth millions of dollars in a veritable sales bonanza, North American decided it was time to put its earlier fighter work to good use.

Knowing that the British were interested in the P-40 but were struggling to buy it due to Curtiss's production lines being over-stretched, North American offered what it described as a better fighter, the NA-73, which could be ready as early as January 1941. Having seen the company's designs, the British placed an order for a prototype on May 23, 1940. Six days later, an order for 320 full production examples was placed but only on condition that the prototype proved to be satisfactory during testing.

Despite the pressing timescale, the North American team incorporated a number of

advanced features into the NA-73. Firstly, it was to have a very thin laminar flow wing developed by the National Advisory Committee for Aeronautics or NACA, which generated very little drag at high speed. Secondly, it was to have a novel cooling system which was positioned towards the rear of the fuselage and used a single duct for both water and oil radiators – again reducing drag.

The design was also drawn up specifically with mass production in mind, the airframe divided up into five sections which would each be almost completed in their own right before being married up at final assembly. The more usual production method was simply to build an airframe in situ from the ground up.

With an all-aluminium fuselage, the NA-73 was to be armed with four .303 machine guns, two in each wing, plus two .50 cal machine guns mounted below the engine which fired through the propeller.

One hundred and two days after the order was placed, the prototype NA-73 was rolled out as the NA-73X, ready for engine installation and final assembly. With a non-supercharged 1100hp Allison V-1710-39 installed it made its first flight on October 26, 1940, receiving praise for its easy handling and low-altitude performance.

A member of the British purchasing commission named the aircraft Mustang Mk.I and a second additional contract was awarded for another 300 Mustang Mk.Is, now designated NA-83 by North American. The company began the process of establishing production and supply lines for the new fighter.

As part of the contractual arrangement that allowed the British to actually commission a new fighter from scratch, the US Army Air Corps was entitled to a pair of production model examples for assessment. These received the designation XP-51 and were duly delivered to Wright

THE MUSTANG WAS DESIGNED AT THE BEHEST OF THE BRITISH AND SPECIFICALLY WITH MASS PRODUCTION IN MIND

P-51B-1 ▼

This aircraft was flown by Captain Richard E Turner, commanding officer of the 356th FS, 354th FG, stationed at Lashenden, England, during May 1944 – shortly before his promotion to major. Turner flew 96 combat sorties and achieved 11 victories in air combat, plus two V-1 flying bombs destroyed. He later flew 13 combat missions during the Korean War while attached to the 4th FIW. Later in life he suffered from Alzheimer's Disease and died on November 15, 1986.

P-51 Mustang III ▼

A Fw 190 was shot down by Squadron Leader Eugeniusz 'Dziubek' Horbaczewski of 315 (Polish) Squadron, stationed at Coolham in England, on June 12, 1944, while flying this Mustang Mk.III. On August 18 that year, despite suffering from the flu, Horbaczewski led a 'Rodeo' mission with 11 other aircraft and attacked a formation of 60 Fw 190s near Beauvais, northern France. Horbaczewski shot down three enemy aircraft but then went missing. His body, still in his crashed Mustang, was finally discovered near Velennes in 1947. He had achieved 16.5 'kills'.

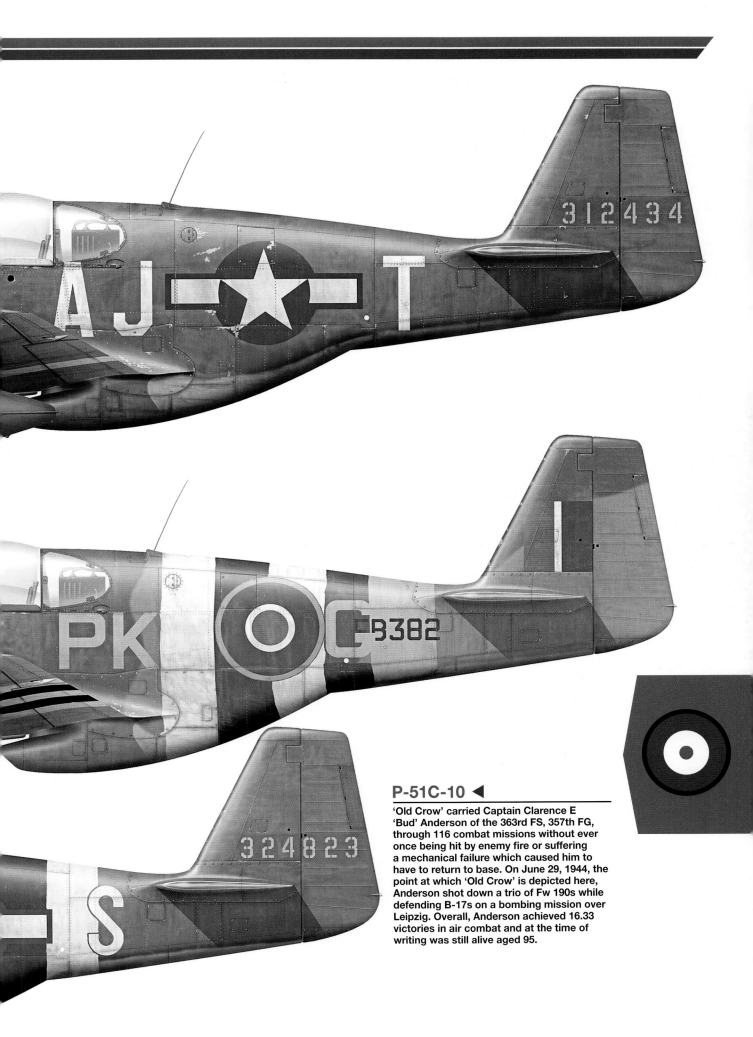

P-51C-10 ◀

'Old Crow' carried Captain Clarence E 'Bud' Anderson of the 363rd FS, 357th FG, through 116 combat missions without ever once being hit by enemy fire or suffering a mechanical failure which caused him to have to return to base. On June 29, 1944, the point at which 'Old Crow' is depicted here, Anderson shot down a trio of Fw 190s while defending B-17s on a bombing mission over Leipzig. Overall, Anderson achieved 16.33 victories in air combat and at the time of writing was still alive aged 95.

Field in May 1941 for testing. This was slow to begin since the centre was already working on the P-38, P-39 and P-47, but when it did get under way pilots gave very favourable reports on the new type. No production orders were forthcoming, however, until April 1942.

In the meantime, the Mustangs bought by the British entered service in January 1941 with 26 Squadron. Despite having not ordered any, the Americans received their first Mustangs in December 1941 shortly after the attack on Pearl Harbor when newly-made RAF Mustang Mk.IAs that were still waiting to be delivered were seized for use by the USAAC. Earmarked for tactical reconnaissance duties, they were fitted with a pair of K-24 cameras in their fuselages and designated F-6A, although this was soon dropped in favour of P-51.

When the Army finally did place an order for the Mustang, it was for 500 examples of the NA-97 ground-attack version, which was designated A-36A. This was given the name Apache at first, then attempts were evidently made to change it to Invader before the Army finally settled on simply calling it by its British name, the Mustang. Unlike the earlier models, however, the A-36A had hydraulically-operated perforated dive brakes on both its upper and lower wing surfaces

P-51B-5 ▶

This P-51B was flown by 1st Lieutenant Wilson K Baker Jr. of the 370th FS, 359th FG, stationed at East Wretham, in England, on August 4, 1944. Baker achieved two victories in air combat.

P-51D-10 ▶

The only P-51 pilot ever to shoot down two Me 262s in a single mission was Lieutenant Urban L 'Ben' Drew of the 373rd FS, 361st FG, based at Little Walden, England. This is how his aircraft appeared on the day he attacked the jet fighters – October 7, 1944. Although Drew reported his victories, his gun camera jammed and his wingman was shot down so the authorities denied his claims. It was only 40 years later, when they were fully investigated and corroborated, that he finally received credit and the Air Force Cross. Overall he flew 76 combat sorties with six victories in air combat plus one on the ground. He also destroyed 11 locomotives. He died on April 3, 2013, aged 89.

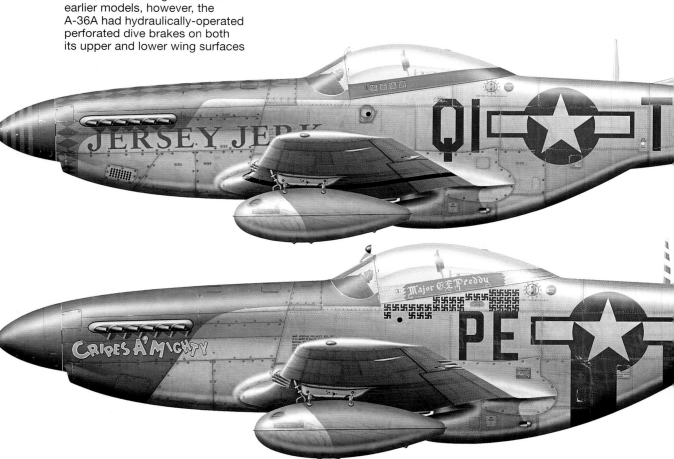

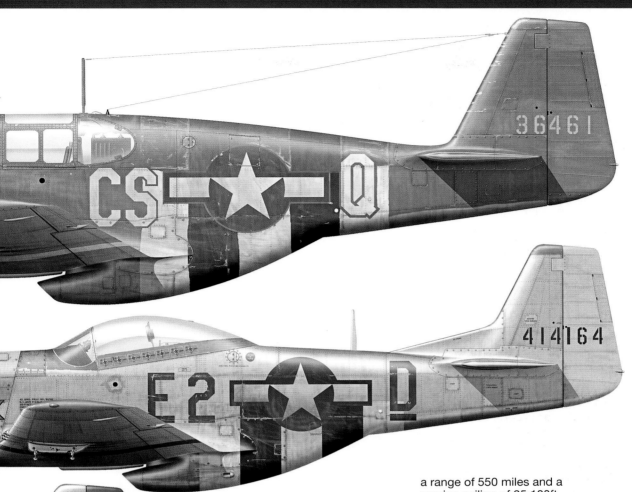

P-51D-15 ◄

Hailing from Verona, New Jersey, Captain Donald J Strait of the 361st FS, 356th FG, stationed at Martlesham Heath, England, named his aircraft in honour of his home town. It is depicted as it appeared on December 5, 1944, a day when Strait scored two victories. He ended the war with 13.5 in total.

outboard of the two .50in guns. These opened via a hydraulic jack to keep dive speeds down to 250mph and in keeping with the type's ground-attack specification a rack was fitted under each wing for a 500lb bomb, a 75 gallon drop tank or equipment for emitting a smoke curtain.

In addition to the four wing guns, there were another two .50in guns mounted in the lower fuselage nose although these were often removed in the field.

The engine was a 1325hp Allison V-1710-87 and with a full payload the A-36A had

a range of 550 miles and a service ceiling of 25,100ft.

On July 25, 1942, North American fitted a pair of Mustangs from the 'seized' British batch with Rolls-Royce Merlin 65 engines shipped over from England as the NA-101. These were then given the new designation XP-78. The revised design saw the aircraft's carburettor intake repositioned beneath the nose to better suit the Merlin and the intercooler radiator added to the radiator group already fed by the scoop under the rear fuselage. The airframe was strengthened too, new ailerons were installed and the underwing racks were upgraded to take either a 1000lb bomb each or the equivalent weight drop tank. A new four-bladed Hamilton Standard hydromatic propeller was also fitted and the full production version of the XP-78 was to be redesignated P-51B.

With the first A-36As approaching completion, on August 24, 1942, the Army placed an order for 1200 North American NA-99s – the P-51A. It also placed

P-51D-15 ◄

The highest scoring P-51 ace of the war, Major George E Preddy, commanding officer of the 328th FS, 352nd FG, stationed at Asch in Belgium, flew this aircraft on the morning of Christmas Day 1944. Attacking a Fw 190 that had been strafing Allied lines, Preddy's P-51 was hit by fire from a US Army anti-aircraft battery while flying at treetop height. He managed to release the canopy, despite suffering severe injuries from .50 cal bullets, but had no time to bail out and was killed in the ensuing crash. He achieved 26.83 victories in air combat.

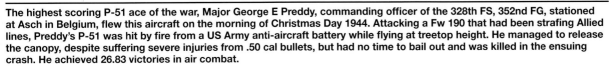

an order for 400 P-51Bs based on North American's performance estimates. The first A-36A flew the following month and on November 30, 1942, the first XP-78 flew for the first time. Its performance, albeit without armament, was a revelation with 441mph being achieved in level flight at 29,800ft. Rate of climb had doubled.

As 1943 began, the production of Merlins at Packard in Detroit and Continental in Muskegon increased dramatically, as did Mustang production. North American's ever-growing factory at Inglewood, California, ceased to build B-25 Mitchells and concentrated solely on the P-51. At the same time, the company's Dallas facility opened a second Mustang production line. Those made at Inglewood retained the P-51B designation but those built at Dallas became the P-51C even though they were identical in almost every respect.

As both factories began gearing up to build the new aircraft, a lend-lease deal was signed with the British for 274 P-51Bs and 626 P-51Cs to see service with the RAF as the Mustang Mk.III.

In fact, in early January 1943, the British government held discussions with North American about a possible successor to the original Mustang. The British felt that the P-51, as delivered, was too heavy and might perform better if its weight was similar to that of a Spitfire. North American took up the challenge and set to work on a lightweight version. The aircraft, designated NA-105, would be a complete redesign with every component and system assessed with an eye to simplification and reducing weight while retaining strength. Two prototypes were ordered as the XP-51F.

Meanwhile, it was clear that despite their outstanding

P-51D-10 ▼

Captain William T Whisner Jr. of the 487th FS, 352nd FG, was just about to take off from his unit's based at Asch, Belgium, on January 1, 1945, when a large formation of Fw 190s and Bf 109s appeared overhead and started attacking the airfield. This was the German Operation Bodenplatte – a last ditch attempt by the Luftwaffe to knock out the Allies' fighter forces on the ground. Whisner managed to get airborne and shoot down a Fw 190 before he was hit by 20mm cannon fire – resulting in his windscreen and canopy being cover with oil and one aileron being damaged. Nevertheless, he continued to fight and shot down another Fw 190 and two Bf 109s. He ended the war with 15.5 victories, adding another six during the Korean War flying F-86 Sabres.

P-51D-10 ▼

'Katydid' was the aircraft of Lieutenant Colonel Elwyn C Righetti, commanding officer of the 55nd FG, stationed at Nuthampstead, England, and this is how it appeared in February 1945. Two months later, on April 17, 1945, Righetti was shot down while strafing a German airfield – but not in Katydid since that was being repaired. He radioed his men to say that he had survived the crash-landing but he was never seen again. It has been speculated that he was killed by angry civilians but this has never been confirmed and his body was never found. Righetti had 7.5 victories in air combat plus 27 on the ground.

P-51D-20 ▼

Texan Lieutenant Colonel John D Landers, commanding officer of 78th FG, stationed at Wormingford, in England, began his third combat tour in March 1945 and added four and a half victories to the 10 he already had up to that point. He therefore ended the war with 14.5 victories in air combat plus 20 on the ground.

performance, the early versions of the P-51 suffered from poor cockpit visibility. One attempt to resolve this issue involved fitting a 'bulged' canopy Malcolm hood similar to those of Supermarine Spitfires but a better solution was arrived at in January 1943 when Wright Field representative Colonel Mark Bradley saw 'bubble' or 'teardrop' canopies fitted to the Hawker Typhoon and the latest Spitfires. He resolved to take the idea back to American companies and did so later in the year.

The first Allison-engined P-51A made its first flight on February 3, 1943, and deliveries of the 500 A-36As to the 27th and 86th Fighter Bomber Groups in Sicily and Italy were completed in March 1943. At the same time deliveries of the first P-51A got started. These had no dive brakes or fuselage guns – just the four wing-mounted .50 cal machine guns – and were powered by the 1200hp supercharged Allison V-1710-81, which performed far better at high altitude than the British version with its V-1710-39. They also

P-51D-10 ▼

Specialising in ground-attack strafling missions, Captain Edwin L Heller of the 486th FS, 352nd FG, flew this aircraft while stationed at Chievres in Belgium during March 1945. His Second World War tally reached 5.5 victories in air combat plus 16.5 on the ground. As a major in the USAF, during the Korean War, he was shot down on January 23, 1953, and captured. He was eventually released by the Chinese on May 30, 1955.

P-51D-20 ▼

Sporting a massive painting of a reclining nude, Captain Charles E Weaver's unnamed P-51D also carries 11 marks to indicate his eight aerial victories and three strafing 'kills'. Weaver served with the 362nd FS, 357th FG, stationed at Leiston in England during April, 1945. He survived the war and died in November 2008 aged 85.

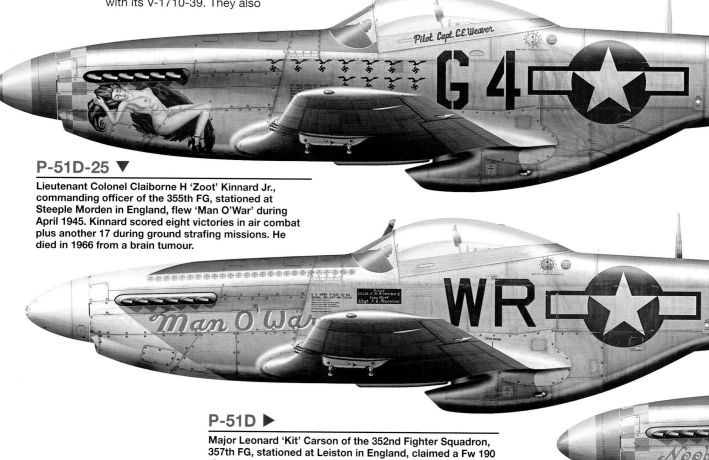

P-51D-25 ▼

Lieutenant Colonel Claiborne H 'Zoot' Kinnard Jr., commanding officer of the 355th FG, stationed at Steeple Morden in England, flew 'Man O'War' during April 1945. Kinnard scored eight victories in air combat plus another 17 during ground strafing missions. He died in 1966 from a brain tumour.

P-51D ▶

Major Leonard 'Kit' Carson of the 352nd Fighter Squadron, 357th FG, stationed at Leiston in England, claimed a Fw 190 shot down on Christmas Eve 1944 while flying 'Nooky Booky IV'. The German fighter is believed to have been flown by Oberleutnant Klaus Bretschneider, Staffelkapitän of 5./JG 300. Carson scored a total of 18.5 victories in air combat.

featured larger diameter propellers than their predecessors and had a top speed of 409mph at 11,000ft. Only 310 Allison-engined P-51As were built, however, before production switched to the Merlin-engined P-51B and 50 of them were sent to Britain for service with the RAF as the Mustang Mk.II in late 1942.

During production of the P-51B, a new self-sealing fuel tank was added behind the pilot's seat to offer a further boost to range. However, this tended to alter the aircraft's centre of gravity, which could make it difficult to keep the aircraft pointed in a straight line until the tank was almost empty. In addition, the olive drab livery of the early Mustangs was dropped in favour of a natural metal finish part way through the P-51B/C production runs.

In June 1943, North American's order for lightweight XP-51Fs was expanded to five examples – the original two for the British plus three more for the USAAF. The Army had wanted 25 examples but this request was denied since no prototype had yet flown and the type was as yet an unknown quantity.

As P-51Bs rapidly rolled off the Inglewood line, Colonel Mark Bradley was busily persuading the American manufacturers to adopt a bubble canopy for their fighters. Republic quickly came up with a design for the P-47D and North American decided to test a full bubble canopy on a P-51B. This machine, with the upper fuselage behind the cockpit cut away and reshaped to accommodate the new canopy was given the new designation XP-51D. The shape of the canopy was the result of wind tunnel testing to determine the best combination of improved visibility and reduced drag.

When work on the XP-51D was completed, it made its first flight on November 17, 1943, and the result was exactly as hoped – the pilot Bob Chilton reported that the canopy did indeed dramatically improve visibility without any drawbacks to speak of. With the concept proven, North American pulled two P-51Bs from the Inglewood production line and had them finished as NA-106s, with the remodelled rear fuselage and bubble canopy. These were the first P-51Ds. While the Inglewood plant built the 'D', the same machine but for a few small

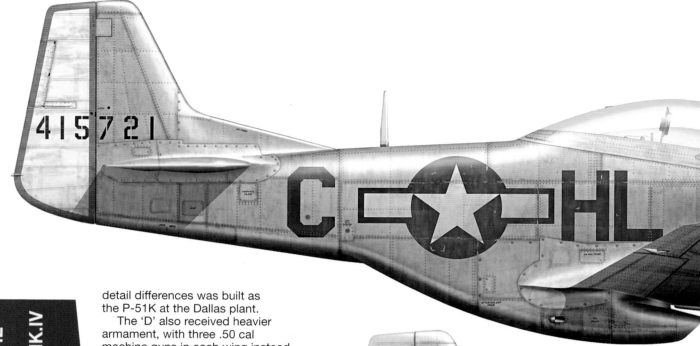

detail differences was built as the P-51K at the Dallas plant.

The 'D' also received heavier armament, with three .50 cal machine guns in each wing instead of two. The guns of the P-51B had been mounted at an angle within the wing due to the lack of space, which caused ammunition feed problems, but the P-51D's guns were all mounted upright – eliminating the issue. There was an increase in the P-51D's wing-root chord too, the landing gear was strengthened and a dorsal fin was added ahead of the rudder part-way into the production run to provide better directional stability.

The P-51D was the first variant to be fitted with the K-14 gyro gunsight, which dramatically increased P-51 pilots' chances of making a 'kill'. Later examples of the P-51D also had underwing hard points so they could carry bombs, drop tanks and a variety of different rocket launchers.

In addition to a large number of Ds and Ks being produced for the USAAF, the RAF received 281 Ds and 594 Ks, which it designated Mustang Mk.IV and Mustang Mk.IVA respectively.

In January 1944, it was decided that while three of the lightweight XP-51Fs should be built as planned, the remaining two would be fitted with Rolls-Royce Merlin 145M engines from England as the XP-51G.

The following month, the first XP-51F was completed and test flown. It did indeed represent a complete redesign and shared almost no parts in common with earlier Mustangs: the landing gear main legs were lightened, the wheels were made smaller, the wings were slightly larger with

THE RAF VERSION OF THE P-51D/P-51K WAS DESIGNATED MUSTANG MK.IV

P-51K MUSTANG MK.IVA ▼

Top scoring RAF Mustang Mk.IV pilot Flight Lieutenant Graham Pearson, of 65 Squadron, based at Peterhead in Scotland, was flying this aircraft on April 19, 1945, when he suffered engine failure and had to make a forced landing at Getteron, on the west coast of Sweden. He was interned for a short time before being returned to the UK. When the war ended he had four air combat victories.

P-51D ▼

On Sunday, March 19, 1945, 1st Lieutenant Elmer K Nieland of the 83rd FS, 78th FG, stationed at Duxford in Cambridgeshire, England, was flying as part of a group of 47 Mustangs tasked with attacking airfields around Osnabrück. They initially had some success in attacking Bf 109s of IV/JG 27 and Fw 190 D-9s of II/JG 26 before Fw 190 D-9s from IV/JG 26, returning from a patrol, saw what was happening and caught the Americans unawares. Nieland's was among a number of P-51s shot down but he managed to bail out and survived, albeit with burns to his neck.

P-51 B ▼

Flying this P-51B on September 17, 1944, near Geldern, Germany, Texan 1st Lieutenant Woodrow W Glover of the 376th FS, 361st FG, stationed at Bottisham, England, was shot down and killed by a Bf 109.

a straight leading edge and the inboard guns were deleted. The wing tanks were made smaller and the fuselage tank was also deleted but the cockpit canopy was substantially enlarged. The mounting for the engine, the radiators and the hydraulic system were all simplified to save weight and the oil cooler was removed from the rear fuselage radiator group – eliminating long oil lines and saving even more weight.

In the cockpit, a standard British layout was adopted and the pilot's seat was made from armour, rather than being made then having armour added to it. Improvements were made to the aerodynamic control surfaces and the tail fin was enlarged. Many parts were made from moulded plastic rather than metal and finally, a three-bladed hollow steel propeller saved even more weight.

It had the same engine as the P-51D, the 1695hp Packard Merlin V-1650-7, but it managed to achieve a top speed of 466mph at 29,000ft. The second and third XP-51Fs were finished on May 20 and 22.

The first XP-51G, which apart from its engine only differed from the XP-51Fs in having a five-

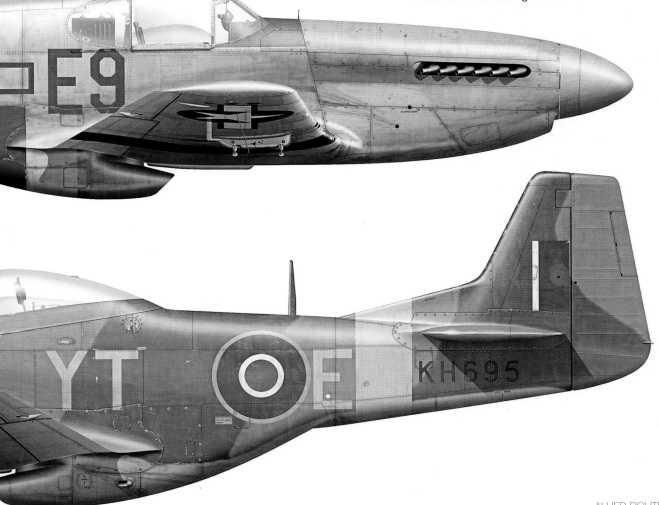

bladed propeller, was first flown in August 1944. Testing showed that it could reach an astonishing 472mph at 20,750ft. The second XP-51G, finished in November 1944, was sent to Britain where it managed to hit 495mph during tests at Boscombe Down.

Neither the XP-51F or XP-51G entered full production though two more prototypes were later ordered as the XP-51J, which did not enter production either. This had an Allison V-1710-119 engine with a two-stage gear-driven supercharger and was expected to achieve 491mph in level flight. The war ended and development halted before it got the chance.

The P-51H was the final wartime production version of the Mustang and had the North American company designation NA-126. Many of its features were taken directly from the XP-51F/G programme, although its engine was an uprated Packard Merlin V-1659-9 rather than a V-1650-7 or a Merlin 145M.

The V-1659-9 featured a Simmons automatic boost control for maintaining constant manifold pressure and was also equipped with a water injection system which allowed the pilot to briefly overboost the

P-51D ▼

During his 49th and last combat mission on April 10, 1945, Lieutenant Joseph A Peterburs of the 55th FS, 20th FG, based at Kingscliff, England, shot down a Me 262 piloted by Oberleutnant Walter Schuck. Later that same day, Peterburs himself was shot down by flak while strafing an airfield. He was captured but managed to escape and ended up fighting with a Russian tank unit during the Battle of Wittenberg on the Elbe. He later fought in both the Korean and Vietnam wars and in 2005 met up with Schuck in person.

P-51D ▼

This aircraft with its cheerful 'Hubert' pig logo was flown by Captain Rene L Burtner of the 369th FS, 359th FG, stationed at East Wretham in England. Burtner continued to fly with the 359th Fighter Group until his tour ended in September 1945.

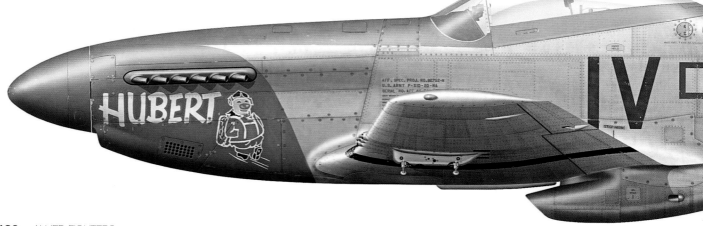

P-51C ▼

Tuskegee airman Lieutenant Charles McGee, of the 302nd FS, 332nd FG, flew the red-tailed 'Kitten' on October 4, 1944. His only victory of the war came on August 23, 1944, when he shot down a Fw 190. Afterwards, he flew P-51s during the Korean War then later F-80 Shooting Stars and F-89 Scorpions. During the Vietnam War, now a lieutenant colonel, he flew 172 combat missions in a McDonnell RF-4 photo-reconnaissance aircraft. At the time of writing he was still alive, aged 97.

engine up to a war-emergency power of more than 2000hp.

Compared to the P-51D, the H had a taller fin and rudder. The fuselage's overall length was increased too, up to 33ft 4in against the D's 32ft 3in. It had a shallower carburettor air intake under its nose, a modified engine cowl that included and integral engine mount and a simpler undercarriage with disc brakes and smaller wheels, like those of the P-51F. The radiator was deepened and the forward edge of the inlet duct was vertical.

The huge canopy of the two experimental designs was not carried over, however, with the P-51H featuring a hood that was closer in its dimensions to that of the P-51, but with the 'hump' further forwards, directly over the pilot's head. In fact, the pilot's position was raised slightly to provide a better view through the gunsight. The

P-51D ▼

Swedish American Captain William Y Anderson of the 353rd FS, 354th FG, flew this aircraft while based at Orconte in France during the autumn of 1944 after he had achieved the last two of his seven aerial victories – a pair of Bf 109s on August 7, 1944. Anderson survived the war and died in May 2011 aged 89.

fuselage fuel tank was still fitted behind the pilot but its capacity was reduced to 50 gallons.

Six machine guns were fitted, although there was also an option to fit only four, and the usual underwing hard points featured on the P-51D were included. However, the wing doors were redesigned to provide easier access to the guns and ammunition feed system to make reloading and maintenance easier.

Production lines for the P-51H were being established as early as June 1944 but the first full production example was not flown until February 3, 1945. The USAAF placed orders for a total of 2000 P-51Hs, since alongside the P-47N it was to be used during the projected invasion of the Japanese home islands. All of these were to be built at Inglewood, while a further 1629 were to be built at Dallas under the designation P-51M. The latter differed a little more than earlier Dallas version in having the V-1650-9A engine,

THE ADVANCED P-51H WAS INTENDED FOR USE DURING THE PLANNED INVASION OF THE JAPANESE HOME ISLANDS TOWARDS THE END OF 1945 BUT IT ARRIVED TOO LATE TO SEE ACTION

P-51D ▼

The 'Flying Dutchman' was piloted by Lieutenant Robert 'Bob' Goebel of the 308th FS, 31st FG. During a 91-day period, between May 29 and August 28, 1944, he shot down 11 enemy fighters.

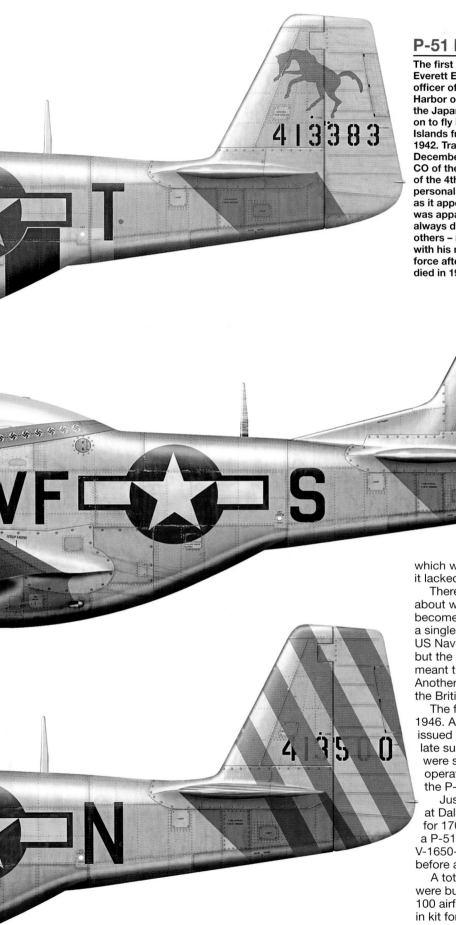

P-51 D ▼

The first mission flown by Colonel Everett E W Stewart, commanding officer of 4th FG, had been at Pearl Harbor on December 7, 1941, when the Japanese attacked. He then went on to fly P-40s from Wake and Midway Islands from February to September 1942. Transferred to Europe in December 1943, he was first made CO of the 355th FG then took charge of the 4th from February 1945. His personal aircraft, 'Sunny VIII' is shown as it appeared in April 1945. Stewart was apparently softly spoken and always did his best to get along with others – making him a firm favourite with his men. He remained with the air force after the war, retired in 1966, and died in 1982.

which was less powerful since it lacked water injection.

There was some discussion about whether the P-51H should become a carrier-borne fighter and a single example was sent to the US Navy in August 1945 for trials but the advent of new jet fighters meant that the idea was dropped. Another P-51H was evaluated by the British at Boscombe Down.

The final P-51H was built in 1946. Although some units were issued with P-51Hs during the late summer of 1945, these were still being worked up to operational status and in the end the P-51H never saw combat.

Just one P-51M was built at Dallas and another order for 1700 P-51Ls, effectively a P-51H but with a 2270hp V-1650-11 fitted, was cancelled before any could be built.

A total of 15,586 Mustangs were built overall, including 100 airframes that were sent in kit form to Australia, though only 80 of these were ever actually assembled. ●

AIR FORCE RANKS

RAF	USAAF	VVS
Marshal of the Royal Air Force (MRAF)	General of the Army (5-Star) (GA)	Glavn yy Marshal Aviatsiyi (Supreme Air Marshal)
Air Chief Marshal (ACM)	General (4-Star) (Gen.)	Marshal Aviatsiyi (Air Marshal)
Air Marshal (AM)	Lieutenant General (3-Star) Lt.Gen.)	General-Polkovnik (Colonel-General)
Air Vice-Marshal (AVM)	Major General (2-Star) (Maj.Gen.)	General-Leytenant (Lieutenant-General)
Air Commodore (A/Cdre.)	Brigadier General (1-Star) (Brig.Gen.)	Mayor-General (Major-General)
Group Captain (G/Capt.)	Colonel (Col.)	Polkovnik (Colonel)
Wing Commander (W/Cdr.)	Lieutenant Colonel (Lt. Col.)	Podpolkovnik (Lieutenant-Colonel)
Squadron Leader (S/Ldr.)	Major	Mayor (Major)
Flight Lieutenant (F/Lt.)	Captain (Capt.)	Kapitan (Captain)
Flying Officer (F/O)	First Lieutenant (1/Lt.)	Starshiyi Leytenant (Senior Lieutenant)
Pilot Officer (P/O)	Second Lieutenant (2/Lt.)	Leytenant (Lieutenant)
Warrant Officer (W/O.)	Flight Officer (F/O)	Miadshiy Leytenant (Junior Lieutenant)
Flight Sergeant (F/Sgt.)		
	Master Sergeant (M/Sgt.)	
	First Sergeant (1/Sgt.)	Starshiy Serzhant (Senior Sergeant)
Sergeant (Sgt.)	Technical Sergeant (T/Sgt.)	Serzhant (Sergeant)
Corporal (Cpl.)	Staff Sergeant (S/Sgt.)	Miadshiy Serzhant (Junior Sergeant)
	Sergeant (Sgt.)	
Leading Aircraftman (LAC)	Corporal (Cpl.)	Yefreyto (Corporal)
Aircraftman First Class	Private First Class (Pfc.)	
Aircraftman Second Class	Private (Pvt.)	Krasnoarmeyets (Red Army Man)

THRILLS

NASHVILLE

TERRORISE YOUR FANS THE PISTOL WAY

GOSH, BLIMEY, what's going on 'ere?
Relax, it's just a friendly Friday night down
at the local — the Nashville, Kensington to
be precise — and them there's the 'Sex
Pistols getting frisky with their audience.
Seems this particular fracas broke out in the
front row when two young ladies had a disagreement over just which of them was occupying a
seat. Reader Neil Tennant of London SW1 was
there and writes:

"As you know, the Pistols are composed of
three nice, clean, middle-class art students, and a
real live dementoid, Johnny Rotten. Now on
Friday night El Dementoid wasn't really on top
form, although the rest of the band were doing
their best to compensate. Johnny's heart wasn't in
the music. His lack of interest was naturally
reflected by the audience who, disappointed,
weren't reacting sufficiently to the band. So how
do the Pistols create their atmosphere when their
music has failed? By beating up a member of the
audience. How else?

One of their coterie of fag hags picks a fight
with the girl sitting next to her. The girl isn't
interested but the fag hag succeeds in getting a
reaction from her boyfriend. He ain't really an
aggressive type, but Ms. Hag perseveres . . . and
seven or eight of the band's chums leap over to the
scene of the crime from all over the Nashville and
proceed to beat the shit out of this bloke. Fists
aren't the only weapons.

Johnny Rotten comes alive.

While the reaction of the rest of the band is a
little confused, Mr Rotten joins in the fight and
has a few kicks at the victim. He cackles, he leers,
the amps are turned up. He's pleased. The Pistols
finish another unforgettable act."

Also, on the spot was Lieutenant ("I used to
be Captain") Joe Stevens, who braved injury to
both person and camera to take this candid shot,
over and above the call of duty. Pictured left to
right on stage are bass player Glenn Matlock,
singer Johnny Rotten, and guitarist Steve Jones.
Paul Cook, the quiet one, seems to have sat tight
on his drum stool and kept out of trouble.
Sensible lad.

It's interesting how so many people (promoters, press, etc.)
became so obsessed with the Sex Pistols violence myth.
There were a couple of over exaggerated fights which Malcolm
capitalized on.
Nobody noticed that the Bay City Rollers, who had been on
the road for years and years suddenly made it big when
directly or indirectly they started KILLING people.

May 1976 was a very hard period. The band, Nils, all the instruments and 400W P.A. travelled in the cheapest available four wheel transit and would leave London with enough petrol money to get to the first gig. That made life very difficult when promoters insisted on paying by cheque.

Sweetie stealing was not good for the bands' complexion and Steve would get withdrawal symptoms if he didn't have his daily baked beans........ But it did become necessary!

Sex Pistols banned

THE SEX PISTOLS have run into trouble with promoters and club owners. They have been pulled out of the French European Punk Rock Festival on August 21 at Mont de Morsan by the promoters who think they have gone 'too far'.

They have also been banned from appearing at London's Dingwalls after the management alleged they were responsible for an incident during the recent Flaming Groovies and Ramones concert when a door was broken and a bottle thrown at Joey Ramone on stage.

They have also been banned from London's Rock Garden.

When there was sufficient money Nils would comb his hair and put on his special respectable jacket to book two rooms at cheap bed and breakfast joints. The band wouldn't come in until he actually paid.

"The Doctors of Madness wouldn't let us use their equipment, so I went through their pockets while they were onstage."

Malcolm and Nils went to see John Curd at his office in Kings Road, Chelsea, to try to get the Pistols on at the Roundhouse with the Ramones.
"He's out," said his wife.
"No he's not..." said a young kid, "he's having dinner."
"He's seen your band and he doesn't like them," explained Mrs. Curd.
Malcolm: "It's not a matter of what he likes, it's what the kids want, he can't be an arsehole all his life!"
Nils: "Yes he can. Let's go."
As Malcolm was halfway down the stairs the door behind him burst open emitting what can only be described as a very angry Mr. Curd. He charged down the stairs fists flying and saved Malcolm the trouble of walking the last flight. Nils dashed to the rescue and proceded to get strangled and have his T-shirt fashionably ripped............................
..........The Sex Pistols did not support the Ramones at the Roundhouse.

The Sex Pistols are four months old, so tuned in to the present that it's hard to find a place to play. Yet they already have a large, fanatical following. So their manager, who runs a rubber and leather shop called Sex, hired a strip club where the two sides could meet...

By Jonh Ingham

THE SMALL, sleazoid El Paradise Club in Soho is not one of the more obvious places for English rock to finally get to grips with the Seventies, but when you're trying to create the atmosphere of anarchy, rebellion and exclusiveness that's necessary as a breeding ground, what better place? Name a kid who will tell their parents they'll be home really late this Sunday because they're going to a strip club to see the Sex Pistols.

The front is the customary facade of garish, flourescent lit plastic and enticing tit pix, gold flocked wallpaper and a life-size gold framed lovely beckoning you within.

Conditioning expects one to go down a hall or some stairs, but the minute you turn the corner you're there. A small room 20 to 30 feet long, bare concrete floor, a bar at one end, three and a half rows of broken down cinema seats. (The other half seems to have been bodily ripped out.) It's an unexpected shocking sight at first, but after it gets comfortable the thought occurs that perhaps it's not sleazy enough. It needs more black paint peeling from the sweating walls, a stickier floor . . .

With luck, the second gathering occurred there last Sunday (the Maltese landlords can be a little difficult to unearth). The first such gathering accumulated entirely by word of mouth, and by midnight the joint was *jumping:*

Flared jeans were *out.* Leather helped. All black was better. Folks in their late twenties, chopped and channelled teenagers, people who frequent Sex, King's Road avant leather, rubber and bondage clothing shop. People sick of nostalgia. People wanting forward motion. People wanting rock and roll that is relevant to 1976.

At the moment, that criteria is best embodied in the Sex Pistols. They fill the miniscule, mirror backed stage, barely able to move in front of their amps. They are loud, they are fast, they are energetic. They are great.

Coming on like a Lockheed Starfighter is more important to them than virtuosity and sounding immaculate. This quartet has no time for a pretty song with a nice melody.

Guitarist Steve Jones doesn't bother much with solos, preferring to just pick another chord and power on through. ("There's two reasons for that — I can't play solos, and I hate them anyway." As he said that 'I'm Mandy, Fly Me' came on the juke box and we agreed the only good thing in it was the solo.)

But imitating the roar of the Industrial Age doesn't mean they're sloppy. Although earlier reports reckoned their timekeeping somewhat off, to the point of cultivating an ethic of them being so bad they were good, Glen Matlock (bass) and Paul Cook (drums) seem to have

the beast on the rails, and in this stripped down form the beat is where it's at. One also has to remember that the Sex Pistols has only existed professionally since Christmas and that Steve has only played guitar for five months.

With inaudible lyrics the music is very similar from song to song, but a cranial trigger says that song is great (applaud), but that one is just okay (don't applaud). Everyone else seems to think similarly. Which annoys singer John Rotten endlessly. "Clap, you fuckers. Because I'm wasting my time not hearing myself." he begins a slow handclap; about three people join in.

John is a man who likes to confront his audience, not to mention the rest of the band. It's this Stooges like aura of complete unpredictability and violence that gives the Sex Pistols that extra edge. Paul reckons the broken glass attitude will only disappear when they get as old as Pete Townsend and just do it for the money.

The Pistols' roots lie with Paul and Steve, who left school with a healthy desire to avoid work. The obvious alternative was rock, even though neither could play an instrument. Their musical models were the Stones and the Who and the early Small Faces, which doesn't say much for Seventies rock, and was a reason for starting a band.

Out of the last six years Steve rates the Stooges. Paul admits to being fooled by Roxy Music for three albums. Later he added Todd Rundgren. "Yeah, there's what acid does to you," retorted Steve, adding proudly, "There's no drugs in this group."

Glen joined and they staggered on for a year, learning a Who/Small Faces repertoire (but that didn't get us anywhere"), buying their threads from Sex and bugging Malcolm, the owner, to manage them. Having already spent seven months in New York handling the New York Dolls he wasn't too interested, but he helped them a bit and they kept bugging and, well, London could do with a Seventies rock band.

Malcolm decided that Steve was hopeless as a singer, got him to learn guitar and the search was on. Into Sex walks John, who couldn't sing but looked the part. They tried to audition in the conventional manner, but finally settled on standing him in front of the shop's juke box, telling him to pretend he was on stage.

John had never even considered joining a band.

We're sitting in a tacky pub in Charing Cross Road. Until now John has been sitting politely, looking a bit bored while I talk to the others. He's wearing the ripped up red sweater he wears on stage, a safety pin dangles from a thin gold ring in his right ear lobe. So how come you're doing it John?

The intensity level *immediately* leaps about 300 percent, He looks manic. "I hate shit. I hate hippies and what they stand for. I hate long hair. I hate pub bands. I want to change it so there are rock bands like us."

This is delivered at full tirade, with a sneer to match the voice. He clocks my tortoise shell earring, the five weeks laziness straggling across my cheeks and chin and the sneer and the direct-eye blitz never stops. I'm inadvertently thinking 'Gosh, I'm not a hippie now — that was a childhood error,' and I never was one in the first place. The kid's got style.

You know what end of a switchblade he would have been on in 1956. I'd love to be present when the middle aged boogers who pass for rock critics on the nationals finally confront him.

But John's just winding up.

"I'm against people who just complain about Top Of The Pops and don't do anything. I want people to go out and start something, to see us and start something, or else I'm just wasting my time."

This last phrase is a favourite. He says it with just the right amount of studied boredom.

The Pistols found their first public by gatecrashing gigs, pulling up and posing as the support band. At the North East London Poly they succeeded in emptying the room, the same stylish feat being Shep Gordon's reason for signing up Alice Cooper. At St. Albans, where they supposedly played one of their worst gigs, they were asked back again. St. Albans was also the first place to recognise the Doctors of Madness.

In London they rapidly depleted themselves of potential venues. For a start they wouldn't play pubs.

Malcolm: "The trouble with pubs is that they're bigger than the bands. They're all full of people playing what a crowd wants rather than what they want because they can make a reasonable living from it' If you want to change things you can't play pubs. You don't have the freedom."

Paul: "The trouble with pubs is you have to please everybody. If we wanted to please everybody we'd end up sounding like the Beatles."

That left the Marquee, 100 Club, and the Nashville. Eddie and the Hot Rods asked them to support at the Marquee. It was the first time they had ever used monitors, and hearing themselves caused a slight o.d. John leaping into the audience and the others kicking the monitors about.

In the light of what the Pistols consider the Hot Rods' over reaction to the incident, the group insist they did little damage to anything that wasn't theirs. They've also written a song on the matter.

I think the photos speak for the particular violence of the 100 Club gig, but the band and the Nashville seemed to enjoy each other. Allan Jones of the *Melody Maker* described it: 'Their dreadfully inept attempts to zero in on the kind of viciously blank intensity previously epitomised by the Stooges was rather endearing at first . . . The guitarist, another surrogate punk suffering from a surfeit of Sterling Morrison, played with a determined disregard for taste and intelligence.' Taste. Intelligence.

"Who's Sterling Morrison?" asked Steve.

When last heard of he was a university professor in Santa Fe.

"Oh. That's alright then. What's 'surrogate' mean?"

They are going to play the Nashville again, but their problem, apart from finding it impossible to find a band they're compatible with musically, is that it's still not the right environment.

Malcolm decided early that France would understand much better and envisioned a couple of weeks or more in Paris. The French promoter saw the Marquee gig, and fired with visions of Gene Vincent and Vince Taylor has booked them across France and Switzerland for May. Meanwhile, El Paradise . . .

If things work out, Malcolm will obtain the old UFO premises. Apart from the difficulty of finding the landlords, the police arrived about 2 am the first night, what with

the noise of the steel rolling door going up and down all the time as people left, and it's not really the right thing to have Arrows spreadeagled against the wall being frisked as a nightcap to the evening's frivolities.

Basically, what Malcolm wants is a rumbling, anarchic, noisy energetic rock scene, the likes of which haven't been seen in this country since the mid 1960s. Any comparisons with the New York rock/club scene are briskly brushed aside.

"Maybe it's because they're so close to the media, but they're all so scared by them. I used to talk to Lisa Robinson and David Johanssen would pull me into the toilet and say, 'Don't you know who you're talking to? Don't say these things!' My God, if you worry about what you say to her . . .

"The trouble with the Dolls was that their hype was so much bigger than they were. They really had an opportunity to change it all around, but instead of ignoring all that bullshit about signing up with a company and a big advance they got sucked in.

"They get dazzled by the process. Every time the Ramones have a picture of them published it lessens their mystique. There's no mystery about the New York scene. Pretty soon Richard Hell is going to leave the Heartbreakers and Sire Records will dangle a contract in front of him and he knows it won't help and won't do any good, but he'll sign it because it's what's expected of him.

"The thing to do is just ignore all that. No-one came to sign up the Stones, no-one wanted to know. But when they saw a lot of bands sounding like that with a huge following they had to sign them. Create a scene and a lot of bands — because people want to hear it — and they'll have to sign them even though they don't understand it.

"The trouble with the pubs is that they're free, and people come for that reason. If you're at a Sex Pistols gig you wanted to go, because you spent money to get in. I opened the shop because I wanted people to make a certain statement if they wore my clothes. The Sex Pistols are another extension of that."

As for what the band think of comparisons . . .

"The New York scene has absolutely nothing to do with us," sneers John.

"Its a total waste of time. All anyone talks about is the image. No-one's ever mentioned the music."

But there's a remote connection with the aesthetic and their seeming to try and get on with the future.

"I like that word, 'remote'," he says real blankly.

(Is he always like this?

"No, he was rather polite tonight.")

Steve and Paul deliver the fatal blows.

"They're not like us. They all have long hair."

"Yeah, Anglophiles with Brian Jones mop heads."

So there they sit, waiting for a scene to build up around them, for the appearance of bands they can play with. They look rather glum at the prospect, and when you consider it, we can at least go and see the Sex Pistols.

"Yeah," sighs Steve, "I wish I could see us."

SEX PISTOLS: another peaceful evening at the 100 Club.

'*I hate hippies and what they stand for. I hate long hair. I hate pub bands. I want to change it so there are rock bands like us.*'

'*I'm against people who just complain about Top Of The Pops and don't do anything. I want people to go out and start something, to see us and start something, or else I'm just wasting my time.*'

ANARCHY IN THE U.K.

OUT SOON

Spedding's finger on Sex Pistols' trigger

THE SEX PISTOLS sneaked into Majestic Recording Studios recently with Chris Spedding (that's him second from right trying to out-punk the rest of the lads) as producer and managed to lay down three tracks, all of which were self written. Their precise future has not yet been determined but it is likely that at least one of them will find its way into your local record store in some form or other.

LETTERS

Pistols get the bullet
July 17, 1976

LAST NIGHT I went to see the Sex Pistols and Clash (formerly 101'ers) for the first time. I was very, very disappointed. Both bands were crap. It's enough to turn you on to Demis Roussos.

There is currently far too much publicity being given to pub bands by the music press. Clash were just a cacophonous barrage of noise. The bass guitarist had no idea how to play the instrument and even had to get another member of the band to tune in for him. They tried to play early '60's r'n'b and failed dismally. Dr. Feelgood are not one of my favourite bands, but I know that they could have wiped the floor with Clash.

The Sex Pistols despite having the wierdest bunch of followers in the audience, (and what a set of freaks they were) were even worse. John Rotten really lived up to his name. I've heard Mickey Mouse sing better. The rest of the band are average musicians, but all the material they played was the same.

At the end, Rotten stayed on the stage and shouted at the audience. One of his comments summed it all up:— "We were great, and you know it. We must have been; we're from London and any band from London is great."

Pathetic, just pathetic...
Yours sincerely — A real music lover, Sheffield.

And Now, the Sex Pistols controversy

SCREW YOU critics, it's your fault entirely and you'll never be fogiven.

What's with this trecking across the Atlantic every time you need a new cult band to discover? Ever try looking at your own backyard? Or course not.

Sure the Ramones were a lot of fun — but so are the Sex Pistols, so why the 'here they come, here they come — don't miss them' publicity for the New York foursome, whilst the Pistols only get a mench if some punter gets his face modified during their set?

Sounds Playlist

Alan Lewis
BLITZKRIEG BOP, Ramones, Sire (single)
LIVE AT THE MARQUEE, Eddie And The Hot Rods, Island (E...
...TE AND ANNA McGARRIGLE. Warner Bros.

John Ingham
PROBLEMS, Sex Pistols, (tape)
NO FEELINGS, Sex Pistols, (tape)
PRETTY VACANT, Sex Pistols, (tape)

Phil Sutcliffe
LET 'EM IN, Wings...
...AN ARM...NDING...
LIAR, Cas...

Sex Pistols secretly recording with Chris Spedding recently, an enthused Spedding producing three of their own numbers ('I'm Pretty Vacant", "No Feelings", "Problems") and we bet it makes him feel his age (vide famous refusal by John Rotten of Star Rock Journalist's request to jam with the band: "You're too old and you're hair's too long") . . .

'The Sex Pistols, dismissed as support bar to Eddie and the Hot Rods on the Rods current tour after only one gig.'

Weekend Plus

10CC are offering £100 reward for two...
...eir...ert at the Hammer...
New London last Tuesday...
Pistols startling the audience at the Marquee Club with mi-nude girls and tunes like I'm Pretty Vacant...
recordin... shortly fro...
manic Alber...
Paranoid...

THERE'S a startling teenage rock revolution beginning here in London.
The Rolling Stones and Elton John still pack them in at Earls Court. But down in the dimly-lit clubs and the smoky cellars the kids are turning on to a new, violent and ugly pop phenomenon. It's called punk rock.
JOHN BLAKE,

At last — rock 'n' roll!

I ATTENDED the Sex Pistols onslaught at the Manchester Lesser Free Trade Hall out of curiosity, and although they have no manners and don't use their instruments in the traditional way, they should make it for their enthusiasm alone. Their concert terminated after two encores and over an hour of dancing in the aisles. Musically, like many newcomers to this field, they owe a lot to the New York Dolls and, of course, the Stooges.

I have waited a long time

I RECENTLY saw Sex Pistols, and I'm afraid I have to say that they were not even indicative of what's wrong with the youth of today.

If this generation can't illustrate what is wrong with it, through the medium of music, then there must be something wrong with it — MARTIN FIEBER, London SW6.

P.S. They weren't even the worst band I've ever seen.

I PEN this epistle after witnessing the infamous Sex Pistols 'in concert' at the Manchester Lesser Free Trade Hall. The bumptious Pistols in jumble sale attire had those few that attended dancing in the aisles despite their discordant music and barely audible audacious lyrics, and they were called back for two encores. The Pistols boast having no inspiration from the New York / Manhattan rock scene, yet their set includes "I'm Not Your Steppin' Stone" a number believed to be done almost to perfection by the Heartbreakers on any sleazy New York night, and the Pistols' vocalist/exhibitionist Johnny Rotten's attitude and self-asserted "love us or leave us" approach can be compared to both Iggy Pop and David JoHansen in their heyday.

Not to mention the fact that the Pistols' manager is the legendary Malcolm MacClaren who has had close connections with the New York Dolls. The Sex Pistols are very New York and it's nice to see that the British have produced a band capable of producing atmosphere created by the N.Y. Dolls and their many imitators, even though it may be too late. I'd love to see the Pistols make it. Maybe then they will be able to afford some clothes which don't look as though they've been slept in.— STEVE MORRISEY, Stretford, Manchester.
● No comment — S. POKESMAN

...ey've got sewn up w... Springsteen. The Ramones are one such outfit — a hot little five-piece who f... unpleasant in ...ly, wasted sort of way and ...y play very loud filling-station roc...ey are another band in the same ...nd and a group evidently much fav...ous) Sex Pistols (The Pistols' singer openly abuses the audience sometimes walking off in the middle of a number ...cause he's "bored").

August bike

Melody Maker
LYCEUM

So tedious were the Pretty Things, in fact, that for the first ten minutes of their set the Sex Pistols, who followed and closed the event, were almost tolerable. They've improved since I saw them last, but their stance as Dead End Kids of the Terminal Zone is really quite wearisome.

New Musical Express, Nick Kent; Shepherds Bush answer to New York.

We walked to the Serpentine taking pictures on the way. The band were in the process of removing a coat of arms from above a shop doorway when a couple of special duty police introduced themselves.

MALCOLM

D.S.?

GLEN

JOHN

PAUL

D.C.?

STEVE

"Do you know what this is?"
Det. Sgt. (?) asked flashing an official looking pair of cards in a plastic wallet.
JOHN: "Yes. It's a British Rail season ticket!"
(?) : "The other one, smart arse."

YOU NAME IT— —WE MAKE IT!

'Mutiny on the Bounty' was on the T.V. the night before.

"How's this for 'Honey?'"

In the early pre-craze days, the only promoter prepared to support and nurture the New Wave was RON WATTS, who was running the 100 Club. How come he was first on the case? "Because, as you know, I am incredible. Not only am I an immensely likeable chap, very attractive to women..... I also have great vision. I was fed up with putting on the same old trying-to-make-it or didn't-make-it bands.... it was just a boring circle, going nowhere — but I wasn't in a position to do much about it. But then — weeks before they got into the papers — I happened to see the Sex Pistols. They came along to the High Wycombe College of Art Valentines Dance, at the end of their rag week in the middle of February 1976. They weren't booked or invited..... they just arrived, said they were the support band (Screaming Lord Sutch was topping), set up

their gear, and played..... and I thought they were great. So I found out who their manager was, and he came down the 100 Club to see me the following week. The outcome was that I began to book them consistently, whereas other promoters and venues wouldn't have anything to do with them. They played the 100 Club for the first time on 30th March 1976, then the 11th, 18th and 25th May, when they were resident band. They came back on the 15th and 29th June, and again on 6th July......and I always regard 6th July 1976 as the night that the New Wave actually started — because the Damned were on too, as support. It was their first gig, but you could see they were going to make it too. Not long after that, the papers got hold of it, and by Christmas I doubt if there was a single person in Britain who wasn't familiar with the word PUNK"

SEX PISTOLS PARTY
TUESDAY MAY 25
100 OXFORD ST.
LATE BAR, TIL MIDNIGHT
Dogwatch, PROBLEMS, + NITE Party
+ SUPPORT   TED CARROLL'S rock on disco
Creation, Stooges, Dolls, Teenage

But the latest pop phenomenon called Punk Rock makes all the rest look like nursery rhymes.

It's the sickest, seediest step in a rock world that thought it had seen it all.

Leading the cult is the group Sex Pistols — a bizarre band preaching the new rock religion of violence and anarchy.

100 CLUB

100 CLUB

Sid Vicious debut appearance as drummer for Siouxie and the Banshees.

"You mean old Jew Bernie"
(Bernie wouldn't allow the Banshees to use Clash's amps because of Sid's Swastika.)

SuB·Mission

Participation is the operative word. The audiences are revelling in the idea that any one of them could get up on stage and do just as well, if not better, than the bands already up there. Which is, after all, what rock and roll is all about.

When, for months, you've been feeling that it would take ten years to play as well as Hendrix, Clapton, Richard (insert favourite rock star's name), there's nothing more gratifying than the thought: Jesus, I could get a band together and blow this lot off the stage!

"I hate beer"

Gay Advert and Captain Sensible 'before'

SEX PISTOLS

100 CLUB
TUESDAY'S IN M
11, 18 & 25
100 OXFORD S

TUES 15th

100 CLUB
100 OXFORD ST, W1

sartorial
correctness

Sex Pistols

and a CAST (PLAStER)
7.30 till LAtE. bars

100 CLUB
100 OXFORD ST W.1
8 - 12 pm
LATE BAR

TUESDAY JUNE 29

SEX PISTOLS
TUESDAY
JULY 6

After several gigs at the 100 Club there was sufficient impetus and energy to
organise the 100 Club Punk Festival. It featured ALL of the new wave bands
over two evenings. Half of them debut gigs: Damned, Clash, Siouxie and the
Banshees, Buzzcocks, Subway Sect, and the Stinky Toys.

Steve and Glen were jumping about Paul was sweating away on drums, Johnny was deliberatley lazy. He spent much of the set crouching or sitting on the floor reflecting the apathy of the audience. "Clap, you fuckers!"

When Steve felt he'd had enough he grabbed a fistful of strings and yanked 'til they snapped. "WE'RE FINISHED!"

SEVENTEEN

He singled out cliques or individuals, stared straight at them and provoked and needled them beyond belief. Just at the point when everything went quiet and one knew there would be trouble, Paul gave the nod and 500W of submission would fill the club until it was some other sods turn to be abused.

Steve demonstrates the strength of the guitar he sold to Eater.

A girl lost her eye after a beer glass shattered against a column next to her on the second night. The Pistols were of course blamed even though they were in Wales at the time. Consequently the 100 Club banned all punk bands. Ironicly, Sid Vicious was blamed by the police.

100 Club 'I'll give them another gig.' not

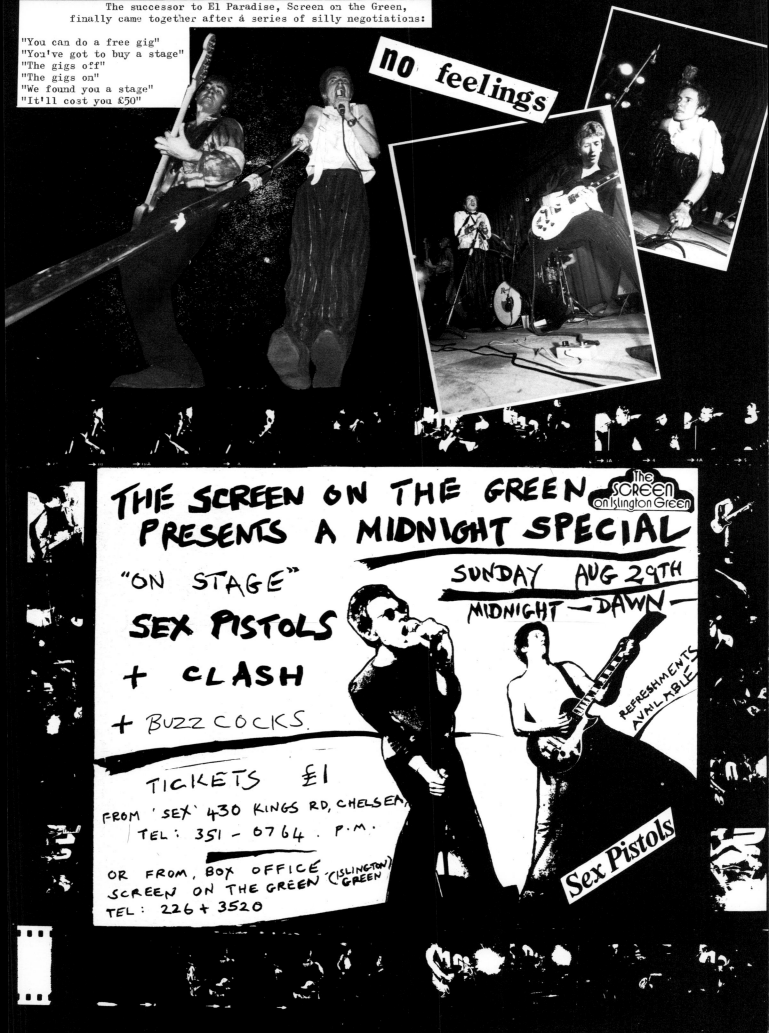

The successor to El Paradise, Screen on the Green,
finally came together after a series of silly negotiations:

"You can do a free gig"
"You've got to buy a stage"
"The gigs off"
"The gigs on"
"We found you a stage"
"It'll cost you £50"

no feelings

THE SCREEN ON THE GREEN
PRESENTS A MIDNIGHT SPECIAL

The SCREEN on Islington Green

"ON STAGE"
SEX PISTOLS
+ CLASH
+ BUZZ COCKS.

SUNDAY AUG 29TH
MIDNIGHT — DAWN
REFRESHMENTS AVAILABLE

TICKETS £1
FROM 'SEX' 430 KINGS RD, CHELSEA
TEL: 351 - 0764. P.M.

OR FROM, BOX OFFICE
SCREEN ON THE GREEN (ISLINGTON GREEN)
TEL: 226 + 3520

Sex Pistols

"If we pay your expenses will you come to Paris
with the band?"
Malcolm arrived at the airport at 9:45, a.m.
"Got any money?" he asked,
"Thirty quid"
"That'll do...Thanks."
He then went off to buy my ticket.
Dave and Kim (the sound crew) arrived at 10:00
"Just got our duty free!" They shouted as they
ran across the departure lounge.

WE MISSED THE PLANE!

HEATHROW 10:10.

Don't look over your shoulder, but the Sex Pistols are coming

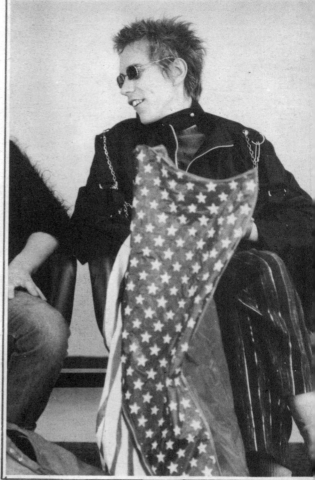

"NO!"

"Do you think I look like Marlon Brando"

"NON!"

"WHO?"

Steve told the air hostess it was his 21st birthday
But all he got was a glass of Champagne

"Where's my Brandy?"

PARIS

Steve getting into the doors.

"It's cold!"

PARIS

"What's French for 'squelch?!"

What did Malcolm buy Steve for his birthday
that made them an hour late?

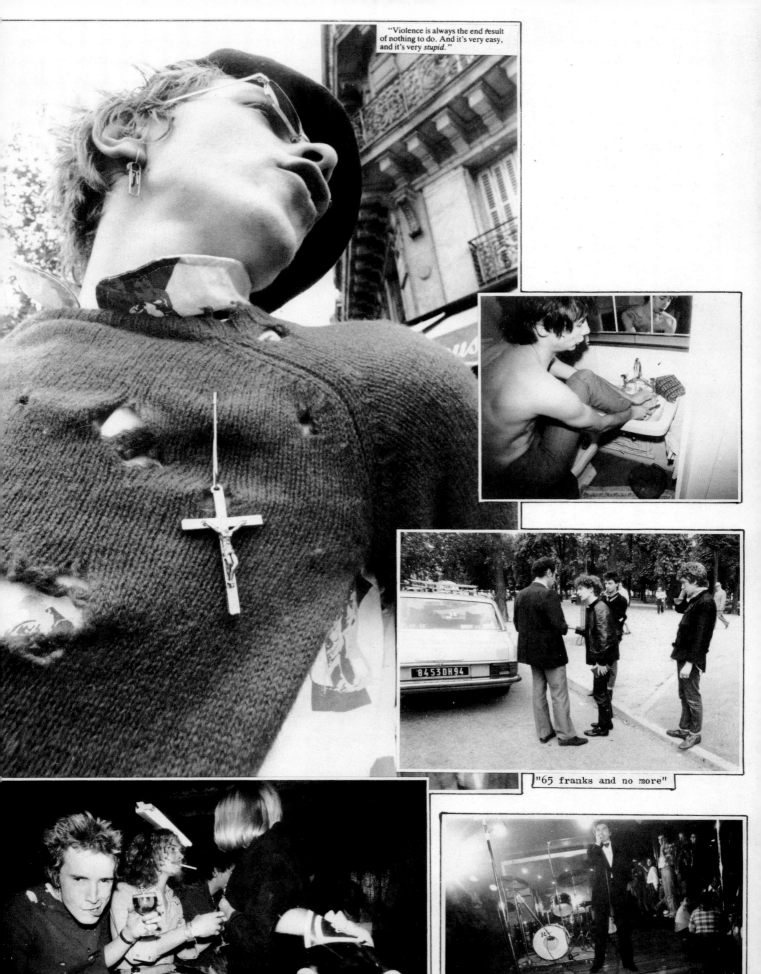

"Violence is always the end result of nothing to do. And it's very easy, and it's very *stupid*."

"65 franks and no more"

"I hate France."

"Mesdames et Messieurs, Voici les Sex Pistols"

The 1.00 pm Paris to Heathrow

Paris 1.15 pm

Welcome to the

"I didn't even know the Summer Of Love was happening. I was too busy playing with my Action Man." — *Sid Vicious*

THE AUDIENCE

YOU SEE them on Kings Road on Saturday afternoons. They look *different*. Longhaired youths in their flares and platforms turn and stare; tourists laugh and jabber among themselves, aiming expensive cameras for the folks back home; local residents of several decades standing look bemused or shocked and shake their heads with resignation.

Could their attention be focussed on the bright pink hair? Or the blue hair? Or green, mauve or yellow hair? Perhaps it's the rubber stockings or seamed fishnet stockings, or the shiny black stilettos with bondage overtones. Perhaps it's the sheets of PVC rubber safety-pinned into t-shirts, or is it the ripped t-shirts, the baggy pants ending in tight cuffs, the winkle-pickers, the wierd shades?

Maybe the "couture" look favoured by some of the more steadily employed has stopped them short. At Sex one can choose from trousers with vinyl pockets and zips on the arse, outrageously oversized fall-apart sweaters, studded belts and wrist straps, anarchy shirts with hand painted stripes and Marx and swastika patches and CHAOS arm bands, and the Sex staple, t-shirts — printed with everything from the Cambridge rapist's mask to the naked young boy that is the Sex Pistols' logo — and of course, out and out bondage apparel.

Up the road, Acme Attractions are denuding any warehouse still possessing early 60s fashion — you want an original Beatles suit? Look no further — the only thing out of step with Swinging London the booming reggae on the sound system and the perennial dreadlocked yout's grooving to the beat.

Between the two emporiums, Retro caters to all decades.

These people, this technicolour parade that owes no allegiance to any fashion or trend except that which they create themselves, this group that has uncompromisingly treated the 70s as the 70s, are the ones variously described as "folks in Bizarre Costumes" (Charles Shaar Murray) and "garishly designed night creatures" (Giovanni Dadomo). But as Bo Diddley said some eons ago, you can't judge a book by the cover.

On a recent Saturday Steve celebrated his 21st birthday. He and his 19 year old friend Siouxsie had spent the afternoon shopping and now, as midnight approached, picked their way through the Soho puddles towards Louise's, treating the staggering, pissing drunks with the same indifference as the rain.

The drunks laughed and tried to think of insults, but that was normal for straights. Steve *hated* them, because they refused to accept him for what he was. He didn't try to do anything about the funny way they looked, but they were always going on about the super-hero peroxide flashes gracing the sides of his jet black hair or his choice or sartorial correctness. Especially in Bromley, where he lived. Especially schoolgirls.

It was a good thing, probably, that Siouxsie was wearing her polka-dot plastic mac.

Louise's used to be an almost exclusively lesbian club but has graciously expanded to accommodate the leading edge of 70s youth and their pansexual tastes. In the reception Siouxsie removed her mac, revealing a simple black dress with a plunging V neckline, black net loosely covering her pert breasts. A home-made swastika flash was safety-pinned to a red armband. Black strap stilettos, studs gleaming, bound her feet; fishnet tights and black vinyl stockings her legs. Her short black hair was flecked with red flames.

Steve was still wearing the same clothes — white shirt daubed with paint and a Union Jack pinned over the right breast, black drainpipe slacks and winklepickers — he had worn on stage at the 100 Club the previous Monday night when he had played bass with Siouxsie, Sid Vicious and Marco, also known as Siouxsie and the Banshees. He had first picked up a guitar the previous afternoon.

"I don't know why I did it, I just knew I wanted to before I was 21."

It was also Siouxsie's first stage appearance.

"I'd always wanted to be on a stage . . . I was a bit nervous at first but when I saw everybody enjoying it, I enjoyed doing it. I think they considered it a joke.

"I've always gone around being looked at so I thought perhaps I should go on a stage and exploit it.

"I also had singing lessons," she added archly. "When I was about 16. I really wanted to do singing and I practised a lot and made cassettes and I dunno . . . I went to some interviews from *Melody Maker* ads, record producers looking for singers, and it really put me off. They made me think I'd have to become a classical type singer to be popular —."

"Dana," smirked Steve.

"—So that the general public would like you.They gave me the impression that everyone who makes it has to sleep around . . . The fact that I could get work by that and be paid for it and nothing be expected of me (professionally), that was, you know . . ."

They moved inside. Downstairs was non-stop dance-arama. Upstairs, in the fire-engine red room flanked by the bar and a wall of great posing mirrors, the party got underway. Most of Steve's friends — known for convenience's sake as the Bromley contingent — were there, all Sex Pistols fans of long persuasion, all looking just as much a part of the present as the Pistols, who were also there.

Most of the Bromley contingent owe their discovery of the Pistols to Simon (age, 19), who witnesed an early gig at Ravensbourne College of Art last December — "I was almost the only person applauding". Simon looks like the one established rock star he, or anyone else present for that matter, still rates — Bowie, Siouxsie, in fact, was inspired to perform because of Ziggy Stardust.

"He's the only singer who's managed to keep up by changing and not stay the same . . . get old."

Their other tastes are what you would expect: Lou Reed, the Velvets, the Stooges — in many instances discovered through Bowie's involvement — and old Stones and Who And Small Faces and offbeat soul tracks. They took to the Pistols because of the energy, and "they had guts to them, in the music and by being on stage" (Steve), and "they were different" (Simon), and "they were young" (Siouxsie). The only other 70s artists to so far make the grade are the Ramones and Jonathan Richman, who Siouxsie credits with a new concept of love songs — "They're not mushy, they're more fair" — though some of the new, post-Pistols English bands are viewed favourably.

Simon has definite ideas about the icons the Pistols are smashing, as well as the ones they're establishing.

"It's really funny all those kids shouting out anarchy and half of them don't know what it is. I agree with

Just good friends

Siouxsie of the Banshees

In love with the modern world

I WAS hoping to avoid mentioning the bloody word at all, but since *SOUNDS* has so adamantly advertised this shebang as a Punk Rock Special, I guess there's no avoiding it. In the context of the band and people mentioned in the following pages, I hate the word as much as they do. For a start it's (rock) historically inaccurate. Punk rock as a genre in the mid-60s, composed of American garage bands trying to duplicate or better their English fave raves like the Yardbirds and Them, has no correlation with the viciously original music of the Sex Pistols or the Clash or the Damned.

As an attitude there's basis for discussion, but consider Mark P in *Sniffin' Glue 3:*

"You get the feeling at Pistols gigs that everyone's posing so they can't really be punks can they? Punks are carefree, and I mean completely . . . you know, like a football who kicks in someone's head and don't care a shit. Yer, the Pistols crowd are not punks, they're too vain. But what's wrong with that so am I."

John Rotten half-seriously favours "anarchy rock".

Paul Morley in his fanzine *Out There* **wants "s rock". That's 's' as in 'surge'.**

The Jam mentioned the "punk rock (?) scene".

Siouxsie from the Banshees reckoned that should have been "(?) rock".

And so it shall.

Welcome to the (?) Rock Special.

In April, John Rotten wanted "more bands like us" — well now he's got them. Each week during their residency at the 100 Club more and more of the audience have felt the urge to create their own excitement, live out their rock and roll fantasies, get on that stage, have an audience looking at them. Each week sees new requests for satisfactory bassists and drummers (of which there is a sore need), cheap instruments and cheap or free rehearsal rooms. It has to be cheap or free because most of them are unemployed, and living on £11.10 a week doesn't leave much spare change for guitar and amp payments. But that doesn't lower the buzz of world-be rock stars organising themselves for action.

The bands in the following pages aren't necessarily inspired or influenced by the Pistols, but they do share (with one exception) youth, the belief that old farts like the Stones, Beatles, Yes — in fact, the entire pantheon or rock aristocracy — should have been carted off to the euthanasia centre years ago, and, for the first time in rock, a background that is 99% working class.

It's gratifying and exciting that the Damned and the Clash share almost no musical similarities either with the Pistols or each other — the more experimentation the better — and it's equally exciting that while the groups jibe about each other's demerits, the audience is judging and accepting each new group on its own terms. (It should be mentioned that the jibes are seldom in earnest. When did you last see or hear of the Stones et al loaning their equipment to other bands or tuning the guitars for musicians so fresh they can't do it themselves? Yet that attitude of help and cooperation was commonplace among the bands at the 100 Club Punk Festival.)

On the other side is the music industry. As the Sex Pistols gigs have changed from private party to public celebration, the A&R men, agents, and even managing directors have walked into the 100 Club to weigh the band and their prospective future. I keep saying the 100 Club because no other London club (with the initial exception of the Nashville) has wanted to give them the chance to develop what is obviously a departure from the past. (You need only look at the audience to begin seeing that.).

That repressive attitude permeates most of the industry boffins. Ten and 12 years ago they were telling the old farts in power to take their Dennis Lotises and Lita Rosas and slope off into the sunset; now they're the old farts, unwilling to give any time or encouragement to youth who want to do things that might threaten their power and position. Even though it is those same youths who will be providing the record industry with its means of survival and profit over the next 10 years.

The comments of some of these influential industry people can be found further on. It is worth remembering that these people with their fingers on the pulse are evaluating the Sex Pistols and the whole scene in the context of record sales being 40% lower than last year. Most of them prefaced their comments with variations of, 'Oh — hmmm . . . How can I put this?'

But while the industry stands by the bar and tries to determine the minimum amount they could spend on the band in the hope that it took off without the company having to actually commit itself, the audience leaps and bounces and doesn't give a shit about commerciality or whether 'Anarchy In The UK' has chart potential. They're present for excitement and a good time, and they can tell you why in highly articulate terms.

Interestingly, as the audience continues to grow, the new fans assume the trappings of the original audience. In the Ladies toilet, for instance, three immaculate Pistols fans of three weeks standing are applying makeup and grooming their newly short hair. Leaning against the wall in brogues and a Dannimac, is long haired, 18 year old Mary from Plumstead. She has been trying to make a gig for ages and she is watching the other three girls with open admiration. When Mary goes to her next Sex Pistols gig, you know exactly how she will look.

JONH INGHAM

?) Rock Special

*ohnny Rotten, the Clash, the Damned and a
ommitted cast of hundreds of new music
iakers give the finger to the old farts*

thing was moving so fast in the 50s and 60s that it just couldn't go on, but instead of slowing down it ground to a halt.

"I never took that much notice of hippies. I liked things that really took the piss out of it, like Frank Zappa, but then he went all serious . . . As people get older they just act older, don't they? Want to be taken seriously. Stupid."

"Flowah powah," mocked Debbie, sitting next to him. Debbie is 15. "I don't remember that long ago," she laughed. "I remember Woodstock . . ."

"It was so weak and stupid," continued Simon, "And they believed it. To try and change things with flowers; if you get beaten up you've got to retaliate. I really think that violence is the only way. If you're going to change the world you've got to use violence — not beating people up, but destroying property. It doesn't matter if you protest — it's property that really counts. As soon as there's damage they take notice. If the IRA had only done buildings and not people . . . There was a really good feeling at first, people wanting a united Ireland, but the minute they did people . . . They're not opponents

any more, they're murdere

"I want to stop older peo telling young people what do. I'm young and everythi I do there's some arseho telling me I'm wrong. The are a few exceptions . . they're alright.

"But I don't think anyo will bother, will they? To violence. They're too la aren't they?"

Steve's view is far mo succinct. "There'll only e be anarchy in the 100 Clul he laughed. He also believ in love. "But I don't believe devotion, thinking that son one or something is the o thing there. I'm interested marriage, but not in t traditions and the possessi ness. It's just for a laugh.'

They drained the cha pagne. Vivien Westwoo seditionary and Sex mast mind, bought another bot for the birthday man. Debb changed into a black leota and red leggings, went dow stairs and danced. Her h was cut in a modern int pretation of a 50s flat-top. the past it had been spray every colour of the rainbo now it was blonde. Since the other girls at her sch

> "I go home once a week to have dinner with my mother."
> — Sid Vicious

were starting to crop t hair, her's was growing ou

But she isn't what demographics experts call opinion-former among mostly Jewish, middle-c teenage femininity that

archy, but I was like that fore the Pistols. People are ways telling you what to do d it's always old people lling young people. If you're ing to be told what to do it ould be from young people. here's no way old people are ing to just sit back, they're st going to tell young people do too much. It's like all ose old people trying to stop e Pistols thing. They're like rents."

He sneered, and took a sip champagne.

"This nostalgia thing, I n't like it. First the 40s, en the 50s, then the 60s. hy no 70s? I think every-

> "I did like the New York Dolls a lot — their ambiguity and also the racket they churned out. I was very impressed by their ordinariness and how bad they were."
> — Sid Vicious

> "I don't believe in sexuality at all. People are very unsexy. I don't enjoy that side of life. Being sexy is just a fat arse and tits that will do anything you want. I personally look upon myself as one of the most sexless monsters ever."
> — Sid Vicious

didn't even know the mmer Of Love was appening. I was too busy playing with my Action Man."
— Sid Vicious

stitutes her peer group suburban Burnt Oak, wh she lives.

"You're joking?!? At f they really had someth against me. Now they sor take it. Laugh.

They're into what I was three years ago. Clumpy sh . . . What gets me something will come out a if one person gets it, then t all get it. They're just clockwork.

"I bought some pla sandals a couple of years a

and they *really* laughed at but now everyone's gett them and they turned arou to me and said, 'Why do you get a pair?' They for that they used to laugh at y . . . You get used to it." The party carried on.

(?) Rock Special

playing in the provinces. Record three tracks with Chris Spedding.

John Curd, promoter, refused to give a quote, not wanting to sully his mouth with the name Sex Pistols. He had seen the band at their first 100 Club gig and thought them awful. His wife confirmed that he had thrown Pistols manager Malcolm McLaren out when the latter asked Curd to book the band at Roundhouse.

Betcha thought you had it all
worked out
Betcha thought you knew what
I was about
Betcha thought you solved all
my problems
Fuck you — all my problems
Problems, got a problem,
The problem is you
What you gonna do?
('Problems')

July: Get a decent p.a. Play the Midnight Court at the Lyceum, the largest stage they have encountered, in the largest venue. They deal with a bad case of nervousness, but as Steve relaxes he takes off in shuddering, blasting experimentation, face screwed up in concentration as he searches for unheard notes. Afterwards, a young girl in denim twinset comes up and appropriates his attentions.

Two weeks later in Manchester the experience is repeated, Glen suddenly launching into the bass explosions that are now a staple of their sound. 'Anarchy In The UK' is unveiled.

A week later, Steve relaxes in Louise's. Suddenly, he is no longer just another young man playing guitar, but basks in the self-assurance of one who accepts attention as a matter of course.

John: "I can't see much future in this country . . . Ten years . . . I dunno, I'm not a prophet like Richard Williams — ask him. He's the problem — complacent cynics, they've seen it all before, they've been through it, man, they've experienced it. They're just yapping the way bloody parents do.

"What do I care about the end, I'm having fun now. I don't want to die an old fool on a pension."

August: The crowd at the 100 Club continues to grow. Music biz figures start turning up en masse. The band record seven tracks on a four track deck in their own studio, over-dubbing and mixing on 16 track facilities. Malcolm starts shopping for a recording contract. In the middle of what is the music biz's "dead" period, the band work continually.

On Bank Holiday Weekend play a midnight concert at the Screen on the Green cinema. Launched in a blaze of smoke bombs, it is their best gig yet, Steve raging away in simultaneous feedback, noise and ringing, crystal clear rhythms, Paul and Glen thundering like a stampeding herd of cattle. John knocks a capped tooth out with the mike during the second song. The blinding pain provokes an unbelievable performance.

"As a musical thing I found them very unmusical — perhaps the fact that it wasn't disciplined prevented me from liking it. I could see it was valid; you can't knock anything that has an audience.

"It's right for now because they have an image but I can't see it going anywhere further than where it is right now, and when you sign someone you have to think in terms of five years.

We had a meeting today and we'd be interested in signing them for a single or an EP and see what happens. If their manager is sensible and didn't want the world." — Dave Dee, A&R Manager, Atlantic Records.

September: The Pistols play in in Paris — their first gig outside Britain — inaugurating a new, 2,000 capacity disco. The promoters haven't advertised them due to nervousness — most of the capacity crowd have no knowledge of them. John wears a black bondage suit dripping with pins, swastikas, crucifixes and chains. Half the crowd love them and dance wildly, half hate them and take it out on the outrageously dressed English fans, punching and pawing them.

After a short Northern tour they play Chelmsford maximum security prison. Steve draws a few wolf whistles, John — in his homemade anarchy shirt — draws a lot. The band play clean and precise, John taunting the prisoners mercilessly. They love it, returning the ripostes with gusto. By the end the prison hippie breaks the rules and starts dancing — he isn't stopped.

At the 100 Club Punk Festival the audience stretches around the block. As the band hit the stage there is a mass epidemic of pogo-dancing. John looks at the seething crowd with a satisfied grin: "Great." As the evening progresses the band tread a thinner and thinner line between order and chaos. The encore of 'Anarchy' is a blazing carnage of feedback, noise and head crushing rhythm. It is great.

John: "There'll always be something to fight — apathy's the main thing. All those silly bastards . . . The *Melody Maker* telling us what bands to like every week, and they go off like sheep and rabied dogs and do. The brainless generation."

"When I saw them at the Nashville my first impression was that they were too unattractive, but I went back as the press built up. I went up to Barbarellas and that impressed me. They looked and sounded so new, which was a major criterion in my interest.

"They have a very good mainstream rock appeal overlaid with their own uniqueness. The guitar is very fresh and Johnny's singing is very unique. They've improved one hell of a lot — the improvement ratio is enormous — and that's what music needs." — Chris Parry, A&R Manager, Polydor Records.

Paul: It's great the way all this is getting up the old farts' noses."
I wanna be an anarchist.
Get pissed.
('Anarchy In The UK')

All songs copyright 1976 Sex Pistols/ Glitterbest

"The great ignorant public don't know why we're in a band — It's because we're bored with all that old crap. Like every decent human being should be."
— John Rotten

SEX PISTOLS

John Rotten (vocals), Steve Jones (guitar), Glen Matlock (bass), Paul Cook (drums).
I am an anti-Christ
I am an anarchist
Know what I want and I know
where to get it
I wanna destroy the passer-by
I wanna be anarchy
No dogsbody
('Anarchy In The UK')

1975: Paul, Steve and Glen rehearse every night in a warehouse in Hammersmith, playing a repetoire of Small Faces and Who. Paul played guitar, Steve sang, there was a second guitarist and a variety of drummers.

Paul: "We were a good band — really tight and solid, but we never played publicly because it wasn't going anywhere."

November 1975: Play first gig at St. Martins Art College. The plugs are pulled after 10 minutes. Play Central School Of Art the next night. They are allowed to finish their 30 minute set.

December: Get gigs around outskirts of London by gate-crashing colleges, posing as the support band. Alienate most people. A small group, mostly young, suddenly find a band to be excited about again.

John: "The great ignorant public don't know why we're in a band — it's because we're bored with all that old crap. Like every decent human being should be."

1976

January: Get first real boost playing at Andrew Logan's party.

February: Play the 100 Club on new band night. Glen decides mid-set he's had enough of John's out of tune singing and tells him in no uncertain terms. John retaliates by pulling over Paul's cymbals. Paul rushes off and demolishes the dressing room. Steve breaks all his strings. John storms offstage and out the exit. Booker Ron Watts is impressed enough, and by their audience, to start booking them regularly.

March: Play the Marquee supporting Eddie and the Hot Rods. The first time they have

monitors, they go a bit wild. John throws some chairs. They are banned.

"I heard about them through friends quite early on. They looked and sounded good — most groups are pretty boring, they weren't boring. I find it very weird all that about them not playing music. If they're notable for one thing it's that. They're always in time and in tune. I can't understand why some of the *Melody Maker* have chosen to attack them on the very thing that is their strength, Obviously, they've got cloth ears." — Chris Spedding, musician.

April: Promote their own gig at the El Paradise strip club in Soho. Support at the Nashville several times. Get heckled a lot.

May/June: Residency at the 100 Club, now the only place in London they can play. The audience slowly grows; with headline gigs the hecklers vanish. When it's time to play the band just step onstage out of the audience. New songs are constantly being introduced. Start

Polydor were paying for studio
time to record 'Anarchy In The
U.K.' when..............

Page 2 SOUNDS   October 16, 1976

Pistols sign EMI deal

RECORDING

THE SEX PISTOLS, the leading British 'new wave' group, have been signed to EMI Records.

The two-year contract, with two one-year options was signed last Friday night and the Pistols spent the weekend recording a single, 'Anarchy In The UK', at the Lansdowne studios. No release date has yet been fixed but it is thought that EMI will release the single next month.

The battle between the major British record companies to sign the Sex Pistols had hotted up over the past fortnight. Every company had seen the band and Polydor, RAK and Chrysalis had all made offers.

EMI scooped the others by drawing up the fastest contract in their history — it was done in a single day — and by offering an advance believed to be in the region of £40,000, the largest amount ever offered to an 'unknown' band.

The A&R manager of EMI, Nick Mobbs, told SOUNDS this week: "Here at last is a group with a bit of guts for younger people to identify with; a group that parents actually won't tolerate. And it's not just parents that need a little shaking up; it's the music business itself.

"That's why a lot of A&R men wouldn't sign the group; they took it all too personally. But what other group at a comparable point in their career has created so much excitement both on stage and off.

"For me the Sex Pistols are a backlash against the 'nice little band' syndrome and the general stagnation of the music industry. They've got to happen for all our sakes."

The Sex Pistols begin a month-long European tour next week which will take them to Holland, Belgium, France and Germany.

They will embark on a major UK tour when they return which will open at Manchester Palace Theatre on November 20 and will include their first appearance at a major London venue.

● The Sex Pistols, Britain's leading punk-rock band, have been signed by EMI. And the band's first single will be released in three weeks' time. The Pistols, the first of the new-wave punk bands to sign with a major record company, were the biggest success of the recent punk-rock festival at London's 100 Club.
● Commented Nick Mobbs, EMI's A and R director: "They are a band who are shaking up the music business. They've got to happen. I don't think there'll be any problems with their lyrics because I've got more than a little sympathy with what they're doing."

EMI photo

ANARCHY meets Establishment (left to right): Paul Watts (general manager EMI group pop repertoire division), Johnny Rotten, drummer Paul Cook, manager Malcolm McLaren, bassist Glen Matlock, guitarist Steve Jones, Laurie Hall (EMI business affairs manager) Nick Mobbs (A&R manager), Roger Drage (EMI solicitor), Steve Fisher (Sex Pistols' lawyer). Note copy of SOUNDS in the corner, open to our Pistols feature. Remember where you read about 'em first!

The piano track was not used

Look what Spedding showed me

ANARCHY IN THE U.K.

SUNDAY
The Sex Pistols are at Lansdowne Studios, a few blocks from home, recording their first single. The mood is relaxed. The sound is good. John, recovering from nodes on the throat, sits catatonically while the rhythm track to 'Anarchy In The UK' is recorded. Malcolm sprays ANARCHY in shaving cream on the interconnecting window to inspire them.
Jonh Ingham.

"It is!" ...."It isn't!"

Caroline  Coon
reviews the new singles

Anarchy, venom, outrage, fury!

SEX PISTOLS: "Anarchy In The UK" (EMI). The first time the Pistols performed this number the audience surged in front of the stage, ripping at each other's jackets and T-shirts, throwing themselves at each other and bouncing off again — a seething, gleeful mass of bodies forming a trampoline of human flesh.

It was obvious that if ever there was to be a single then this should be it. But it was difficult to imagine how the band could capture all that excitement on vinyl. They HAVE done it, though.

The single is an epitome of their sound, at the band's most furious, venomous best. The song is a threat, a malediction. In the last bar Johnny Rotten (19), with the feel of an urban desperado, yells "D-E-S-T-R-O-Y!"

Earlier on he asks, "Is this the UK or just another country, a council tenancy?" He seems outraged, surprised, betrayed perhaps. As if he still can't believe how utterly without hope his childhood was and how callously (or so he believes) he and his friends, aged 11, were written off as factory fodder.

They scrapped the first try at recording the single after an abortive weekend where good fun and liquid refreshment flowed to the detriment of music. They re-recorded it with Chris Thomas producing.

This time they were meticulous and their care and attention pays dividends, totally destroying the myth that UK punk rock revels in untuned instruments and sloppiness.

All through the track bassist Glen Matlock and drummer Paul Cook grind out a demon rhythm which is, compared with other numbers like "No Feelings" or "Submission," laidback for them! Guitarist Steve Jones, in two sparse breaks, kicks the track to new levels of white hot power with the strength of a Chieftain tank. Rotten enunciates every word with the clarity of a branding iron.

It's great. It's startlingly harsh, loaded with cynical irony and too concerned with urban reality to appeal to those settled into the thrill of romance.

But for restless young renegades bored with sugar and spice images, which are about as far removed from the life they know as Venus and Mars, it will be an instant hit.

One of the rumours is that Spedding was on the record. Cook: Spedding can't play as good as that (laughs).

100 hours later. The final mix.

SINGLES
SOUNDS Star Single

SEX PISTOLS: 'Anarchy In The UK' (EMI). *Thrashing guitars, a maniacal chuckle from Johnny Rotten, and we're into the most eagerly-awaited single in ages. Single Of The Week? Has to be, and not just because Sounds was the first to feature the Pistols/Punk phenomenon. It explodes out of the pre-Christmas product pile, and by any standards it's a great rock record.*

In fact it has so many of the traditional ingredients of high-energy rock that it makes nonsense of all those hysterical letter-writers who see the Pistols as a threat to Music As We Know It. Conversely, it also makes nonsense of any claims that the Pistols are revolutionaries: they may want to push the old farts aside, but they've borrowed a lot from 'em.

Far from being bizarre, it's really a simple, basic record: so basic in fact that even fans of Hawkwind would feel at home with the relentlessly hammering rhythm section (shades of 'Silver Machine').

Pistols fans, I suspect, will be surprised (disappointed?) that the record isn't faster and nastier. It's just a little too smoothly produced by Chris Thomas of Roxy Music fame. Will the Beeb ban it? Hard to see why: the opening line, 'I am an anti-Christ' is intended to shock, but in these irreligous times who can it offend?

No, this ain't revolution, it's the same old rock and roll — but YOUNGER and more intense than we've heard it for a long while. And as an old fart who loved the early Who, I welcome the Pistols.

ALAN LEWIS

"Jimi Hendrix"

"Don't shoot, it's me!"

"Marc Bolan"

"Chuck Berry"

I wanna Be ME

Nils expresses an opinion during the sound check.

Melody Maker

JOHNNY Rotten looks bored. The emphasis is on the word 'looks', rather than, as Johnny would have you believe, the word 'bored'. His clothes, held together by safety pins, fall around his slack body in calculated disarray. His face is an undernourished grey. Not a muscle moves. His lips echo the downward slope of his wiry, coathanger shoulders. Only his eyes register the faintest trace of life.

SATELLITE

pretty vacant

problems

Malcolm: "But it's our only legitimate bit of equipment"

Vive La Résistance

ANARCHY IN THE U.K.

20p

Sex PISTOLS

THE SUBWAY

PRETTY VACANT

AND WE DON'T CARE!

'Anarchy in the U.K.' was the Sex Pistols fanzine. It featured photos of the band, but mostly people around the band. Its main purpose was to outline a visual identity for the fans.
Anarchy No. 2 was to feature information Malcolm said he found in some E.M.I. files relating to electronic component supplies to Russia, and to demonstrate why only E.M.I. artistes get to play the

Malcolms comments to me on the mag.
"Paid! What do you mean you want to be paid?"
"But you're a photographer, what do you want credit for?"

NEW MUSICAL EXPRESS

THE INTERVIEW that started the controversy took place on Wednesday December 1, on Thames TV early current affairs programme, *Today*. The actual interview lasted one minute 40 seconds, after a short introduction by Bill Grundy and a 44 second film clip of the Pistols on stage.

Grundy: ". . . chains round the neck. And that's just it fellas, yeah, innit? Eh? I mean, it is just the fellas? Yeah? They are Punk rockers. The new craze, they tell me. They are heroes, not the nice, clean Rolling Stones. You see, they are as drunk as I am. They are clean by comparison. They are a group called the Sex Pistols. And I'm surrounded now by *all* of them . . .

Sex Pistol: In action!

Grundy: . . . just let us see the Sex Pistols in action. Come on chicks . .

(A film clip, taken from the London Weekend Show's documentary on punk broadcast the previous Sunday, came on screen.)

Grundy: I'm told that *that* group *(he hit his leg with a sheaf of papers)* have received £40,000 from a record company. Doesn't that seem . . . err . . . to be slightly opposed to their *(deep breath)* anti-materialistic . view of life?

Glen : No. The more the merrier.

BG: Really?

Glen : Oh yeah.

BG: Well, tell me more then.

Steve : We've fuckin' spent it, ain't we?

BG: I don't know. Have you?

Glen : Yeah. It's all gone.

BG: Really?

Glen : Down the boozer.

BG: *Really?* Good *Lord!* Now, I want to know one thing . . .

Glen : What?

BG: . . . are you serious or are you just making me, trying to make me laugh?

Glen : No. It's gone. Gone.

BG: *Really?*

Glen : Yeah.

BG: No, but I mean about what you're doing.

Glen : Oh yeah.

BG: You are serious?

Glen : Mmm.

BG: Beethoven, Mozart, Bach and Brahms have all died . . .

Glen : They're all heroes of ours, ain't they?

BG: Really? Wh-aat. What were you saying sir?

John : They're *wonderful* people.

BG: Are they?

John : Oh *yesss!* They really turn us on.

SP 2: Well, they're very . . .

BG: Well, suppose they turn other people on?

John : (whispered) That's just their tough shit.

BG: It's what?

John : Nothing. A rude word. Next question.

BG: No, no. What was the rude . word?

John : Shit.

BG: Was it really? Good heavens, you frighten me to death.

John : Oh, alright Seigfried . . . *(The last word was mumbled and unclear. Grundy then turned his attention to one of the girls standing behind the band.)*

BG: What about you girls behind . . .?

Glen : He's like yer Dad, in' he, this geezer. Or your grandad.

BG: . . . are you err, are you worried, or are you just enjoying yourself?

Siouxsie : Enjoying myself.

BG: Are you?

Siouxsie : Yeah.

BG: Ah, that's what I thought you were doing.

Siouxsie : I've always wanted to meet you.

BG: Did you really?

Siouxsie : Yeah.

BG: We'll meet afterwards, shall we? *(Laughter)*

Steve : You dirty sod. You dirty old man.

BG: Well, keep going chief, keep going. *(Pause)* Go on, you've got another five seconds. Say something outragious.

Steve : You dirty bastard.

BG: Go on, again.

Steve : You dirty *fucker!*

BG: *Whaat* a clever boy.

Steve : What a fucking rotter.

(More laughter from the band and fans)

Grundy, *turning to face the camera, then closed the show:*

Well that's it for tonight. The other rocker Eamonn, I'm saying nothing else about him, will be back tomorrow. I'll be seeing you soon. I hope I'm not seeing you *(to the band)* again. From me though, goodnight. *Today theme. Closing credits.*

'I DID IT TO SHOW THEY ARE JUST FOUL MOUTHED YOBS'

TV's Bill Grundy in rock outrage

Last night Thames repeated a public apology for the obscene language.

Grundy slams back at critics

THE

The Great Punk Rock Storm

DAILY MIRROR, Thursday, December 2, 1976

FILTH

"Go on. Again," said Grundy. "You dirty f---er."
"What?"

AND THE

Yet the rewards are enormous. If, as the result of the group's behaviour, a record made the Top Ten it would sell 10,000 copies a day and gross £30,000 a week, with the company clearing two per cent on every single.

The Sex Pistols claim they are striking a blow against the superstar rock establishment, who, they say, have grown out of touch with the so-called "blank generation," the 1976 breed of youth brought up on frustration and unemployment.

FURY!

Lorry driver James Holmes, 47, was outraged that his eight-year-old son Lee heard the swearing . . . and kicked in the screen of his T.V.

"It blew up and I was knocked backwards," he said. "But I was so angry and disgusted with this filth that I took a swing with my boot.

Uproar as viewers jam phones

Punk Rock is the craziest pop cult of them all

■ EVERY generation of teenagers finds something that it can call its own

What The Sun said on October 15.

Four-letter words guarantee gold for the punk rockers

By David May

The Sex Pistols, led by a one-time sewage worker who styles himself Johnny Rotten, were launched last April by Malcolm McLaren, 29-year-old owner of a London clothes shop called "Sex." Rotten—real name Lydon—and Glen Matlock, Steve Jones, and Paul Cook, are all 19 years old and were unemployed before Mr. McLaren gave them guitars and billed them as leaders of the teen craze "Punk Rock," describ...

At this critical time the strength and influence of E.M.I.'s promotion and marketing ensured a series of remarkable appearances for a brand-new group—on London Weekend's "London Programme," B.B.C. TV's "Nationwide," B.B.C. Radio Four and "Newsbeat," and finally Thames TV, in which E.M.I. has a 50 per cent share.

The bizarre face of Punk Rock

Sex Pistols record 'blacked' by packers

DAILY TELEGRAPH REPORTER

THE Sex Pistols, the leading exponents of the punk rock cult, who used obscene language on television earlier this week are being banned from appearing at concerts on their first nationwide tour.

At least seven engagements have been withdrawn, there are doubts about others, and women packers at EMI's Hayes record factory have refused to handle their latest record, "Anarchy in the U K."

Thames Television was inundated with protests following an interview with Bill Grundy on the "Today" programme, in which obscenities were used.

Mr Grundy was later suspended from appearing on any Thames programme for two weeks.

Worth £750

Yesterday the Sex Pistols, whose lead singer rejoices in the name of Johnny Rotten, found that their television outburst had left them out in the cold.

Major concerts on their Christmas tour were cancelled at Norwich, Lancaster University, Preston, Torquay, Guildford, Newcastle, Bournemouth, and, possibly, Bristol.

At the University of Norwich the decision to cancel the Sex Pistols concert was taken after a meeting of the Students' Union and university authorities. A spokesman said the university was responsible for the "safety and security" of people

Mr Leslie Hill, managing director of E M I Records, said yesterday that the group's record "had commercial potential.

"I do not think there is anything objectionable about it. The record industry is often a controversial business."

The Sex Pistols have a £44,000 contract with E M I, which owns 50 per cent of Thames Television. E M I is releasing "Anarchy in the U.K." to coincide with the group's seasonal tour.

The record, which begins with the words "I am an antichrist, I am an anarchist" goes on to exhort listeners to "destroy." But it has now been banned by the B B C and many record shops are believed to have sent back the record to their **head** offices.

Asked later about the swearing on the programme Grundy said : 'You'll get nothing from me, so you can ——— off. I'm saying nothing.'

The Sex Pistols are leaders of the "punk rock" pop cult. They hurled four-letter words at Grundy during an interview on Thames TV's tea-time programme Today on Wednesday. The filthy language brought a

2-week TV ban on Bill Grundy

A POP group shocked millions of viewers last night with the filthiest language heard on British television.

The Sex Pistols, leaders of the new "punk rock" cult, hurled a string of four-letter obscenities at interviewer Bill Grundy on Thames T V's family teatime programme "Today".

THEY wear torn and ragged clothes held together with safety pins.

They are boorish, ill-mannered, foul-mouthed, dirty, obnoxious and arrogant. They like to be disliked. They use names like Johnny Rotten, Steve Havoc, Sid Vicious, Rat Scabies

WHO ARE THESE PUNKS?

Obnoxious, arrogant, outrageous.. the new pop kings

BRITAIN'S notorious new punk rock group, the Sex Pistols, were sent packing yesterday.

Their foul-mouthed performance on TV backfired on them with a vengeance.

For the publicity they had counted on to promote sales of their new record led instead to its rejection.

Angry women workers at EMI Records, the company which has sponsored the Sex Pistols to the tune of £40,000, refused to handle orders for the disc, Anarchy in the U.K.

And as the fury grew, the group's planned concert tour was hit by a spate of cancellations.

Bookings made for Bournemouth, Preston, Lancaster and Newcastle were scrubbed by anxious organisers. A spokesman for Rank Leisure Services, who had arranged the Bournemouth show said: "It is not the type of presentation with which we wish to be associated."

Preston entertainments chief Mike Smith said : "If anything like the TV programme happened here parents would be up in arms."

Lancaster Students Union president Maggie Gallagher said they had cancelled the show because the movement was "sexist."

Meanwhile, at the EMI factory at Hayes, Middlesex, one woman claimed that key workers on two shifts had refused to handle the disc.

Three thousand records which should have been sent out had been marked "out of stock," she said.

tut!! tut!!!

"Don't over-react when children turn to Punk Rock," is their advice to parents. "If you ignore Punk Rock it will eventually go away."

Tomorrow, the three leading punk bands—Sex Pistols, Clash and The Damned—begin a nationwide tour.

"It is very likely there will be violence at some of the gigs," says tour organiser Malcolm McClaren, "because it is violent music.

"We don't necessarily think violence is a bad thing because you have to destroy to create."

ANARCHY IN THE U.K. TOUR

SEX PISTOLS

FIRST MAJOR U.K. TOUR WITH SPECIAL GUESTS

THE DAMNED

JOHNNY THUNDER'S HEART BREAKERS

(Ex New York Dolls from USA)

THE CLASH

TOUR DATES

		Tickets From
FRI 3 DEC	**NORWICH** University	Students Union, U.E.A.
SAT 4 DEC	**DERBY** Kings Hall	Kings Hall, Derby
		R.E. Cords, Derby, Burton Slect a Dis
		Nottingham Record Centre. Long Eat
SUN 5 DEC	**NEWCASTLE** City Hall	City Hall
MON 6 DEC	**LEEDS** Polytechnic	Village Bowl
TUE 7 DEC	**BOURNEMOUTH** Village Bowl	Students Union, Leeds Poly
THU 9 DEC	**MANCHESTER** Electric Circus	Hime & Adamson, Manchester
		Virgin Records, Manchester
FRI 10 DEC	**LANCASTER** University	Students Union, Lancaster University
SAT 11 DEC	**LIVERPOOL** Stadium	Virgin Records
MON 13 DEC	**BRISTOL** Colston Hall	Top Rank, Cardiff
TUE 14 DEC	**CARDIFF** Top Rank	Buffalo Records
		Colston Hall
WED 15 DEC	**GLASGOW** Apollo	Apollo, Glasgow
THU 16 DEC	**DUNDEE** Caird Hall	Caird Hall
		Students Union, Technical College
FRI 17 DEC	**SHEFFIELD** City Hall	City Hall — Wilson Peck Records
SAT 18 DEC	**SOUTHEND** Kursaal	Usual Agents
SUN 19 DEC	**GUILDFORD** Civic Hall	Usual Agents
MON 20 DEC	**BIRMINGHAM** Town Hall	Town Hall
TUE 21 DEC	**PLYMOUTH** Woods Centre	Virgin Records
		Woods Centre
WED 22 DEC	**TORQUAY** 400 Ballroom	400 Club
SUN 26 DEC	**LONDON** Roxy Theatre Harlesden	Roxy Theatre

SINGLES AVAILABLE

THE DAMNED. NEW ROSE   HELP   (BUY 6)
Available from even your dumbest dealer
SEX PISTOLS. ANARCHY IN THE U.K. (EMI 2566)
Available from your cleverest

TOUR PRESENTED BY ENDALE ASSOCIATES IN ARRANGEMENT WITH MALCOLM MACLAREN

"No publicity"

The Norwich gig was cancelled so we went straight to Derby where we hoped to escape the "press". By next morning a few reporters had found us and were hanging round the lobby asking the receptionists if the band were behaving themselves.

By the afternoon we were surrounded by photographers and reporters and the News of the World were offering large amounts of money for one of their exclusives. Malcolm was really shaking by now. He had confined the band to their rooms and warned me, "If I see you taking any pictures I'll smash your camera!"

Chaos on the U.K. tour '76

A message came from Derby Kings Hall to the effect that 'The show will only be allowed to go on with the approval of local dignitaries (including a lady who had the distinction of successfully bringing about a by-law limiting the number of shirt-buttons holiday-makers may undo.

These people insisted on a special performance at 3:00 p.m. 'behind locked doors.' Malcolm sent down the sound and lighting crews to set up and all preparations were made.

At 3:15 Nils called up 'We are all ready here but the place is swarming with reporters." At 3:40 Nils called again. "Where are you? We're all waiting."

Malcolm then took the band into his room, locked the door and had a very secret meeting. Twenty minutes later they all emerged. "O.K. get all your stuff together. We're leaving."

"For the gig?" "No! We're not going to encourage censorship. If we perform for these idiots we'll end up doing matinees for every council in the country. No!" It was not until we were all aboard the coach that Malcolm told us and the coach-driver, "We're going to Leeds."

"I hate eating!"

In the foyer of the Draganora Hotel, Leeds, a Yorkshire T.V. interviewer asked me if I was anything to do with the Sex Pistols.
"I have been waiting here for over an hour. How can I get to speak to the group or Mr. McClaren?" he asked.
"Very unlikely."
"We cover a much greater area than Thames T.V.," he remarked with a knowing little smile.
"I'll tell Malcolm you're here. Shall I tell him you want some swearing?"
He smiled again.

"what can I say...boys will be boys!!!"

"My mummy knitted it"

Rotton glares at them. "Your not wrecking the place", he says. "The *News Of the World* will be REALLY disappointed."

This gets a laugh, but the crowd don't seem to realize that the two things Rotten hates most are apathy and complacency, both of which are rife tonight at Leeds Poly.

"'ope you 'ate it!" he screams. "You don't like it then your know where the EXIT door is!"

Earlier he had been taking a sip from a can of beer and then handing the can to the crowd. Now he spits at them . . .

Even with numbers that the crowd know, like the Who's "Substitute" or the Monkees' "Stepping Stone", the punters never really get into it. Rotton's going crazy with angry frustration. A token object thrown from the audience hits him in the face. "You just stand there, you don't know whether you like it or not!"

The band eventually returns for a few more numbers. The Small Faces' "What'cha Gonna Do 'Bout It" has its lyrics changed to Want you to know that I hate you baby, want you know I don't care," and then it's the last number, with the audience finally putting some effort into lifting the band. It's Iggy's "No Fun", arguably the definitive Pistols live number — even more so than "Anarchy".

Then they were gone and I felt for them. A string of cancelled gigs, the press labelling them Public Enemies No. 1, and a frightened element of the rock press saying they can't play (obviously a lie) — and when they finally get a chance to play the kids *ain't* all right. What a choker.

"This song will be over soon, then you can go back to yer mushy peas and chip butties."

'Punks' in hotel row

Lord Shawcross, the former Attorney General and a director of the E.M.I. recording company, last night promised an investigation into the latest activities of punk rock group the Sex Pistols.

Soon after the group arrived at a new, four-star hotel in Leeds yesterday they caused havoc in the foyer by destroying a rubber plant and throwing earth on the carpet.

They shouted, "Send the bill to E.M.I."—with whom they have a contract. Lord Shawcross said : "I think we are being taken for a ride."

Johnny Rotten is a perplexing performer.

He has an extraordinary ability to enrage his audience.

At the most basic level it's his insults and his bad behaviour, but Rotten has something deeper. It goes deeper, too, than his contempt for society in songs like "I'm A Lazy Sod". And surely it goes beyond his looks, his fleabitten hunchbacked reptilian cadaver.

Somehow this guy repels virtually everybody, and somehow his power reaches through the taunts to the sensibilities of thousands, maybe even millions, of people who have only ever heard his name and seen his picture.

Yet he is mesmerising. He can't be ignored. He's not just some hooligan who swore on TV, he drags the most casual observer into, usually, a love-hate relationship: probably the most charismatic rock star to emerge since Bowie.

Steve Jones has improved immensely both as a guitar player and a stage presence since the last time I saw him. He slashes chiv-artist chords as he leaps, struts and swaggers across the stage, his new axe rammed into his groin and aiming at the front row chicklets. His performance very often outdoes that of Rotten himself, the well-mannered boy spastic-dancing and looking like a week-old corpse still shaking with the shock of the red-hot piece of wire that a sadistic undertaker shoved up his anal passage on the very instant of death.

"I don't know what all the fuss is about"

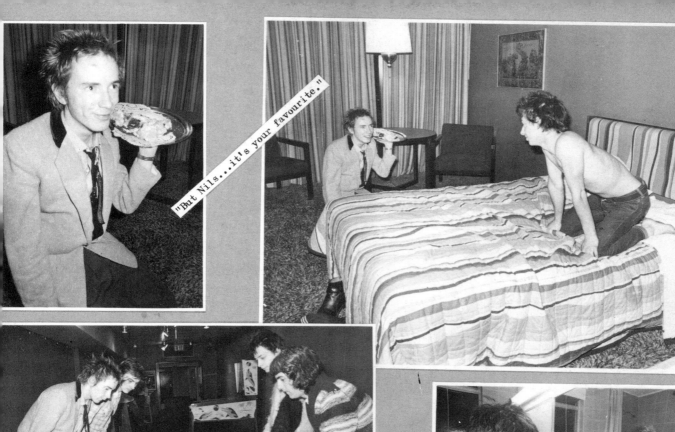

"But Nils...it's your favourite."

Glen prepares for the gig

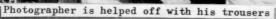
Photographer is helped off with his trousers

Steve makes his room more comfortable

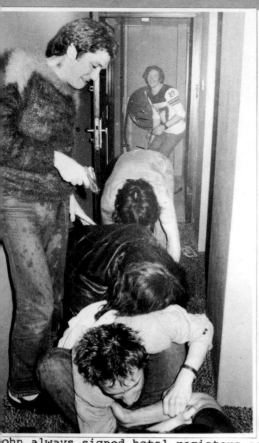

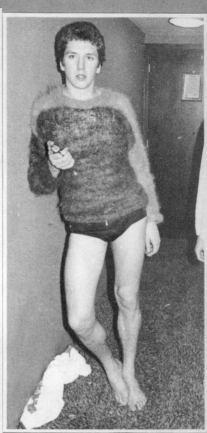

ohn always signed hotel registers as 'Nick Kent'. Just in case.

The furniture was all 'rearranged' by 3.00 am
and the only thing left to do was break into
the hotel swimming pool. Twenty minutes later
the night manager and a few porters asked us
to leave, in no uncertain terms.

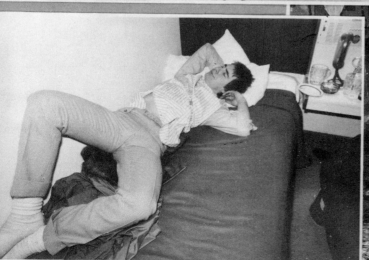

"I demand to see the manager!"

Self Portrait by J. Rotten

Back in London .... SKINT.

'I feel sorry for people who stand up for what they believe and get kicked in the teeth. That's what would have happened to me if I hadn't joined the Pistols. I would have been locked up, put quietly away, classified as insane'

Johnny knows he's not mad. Can you say that?

THE SEX PISTOLS are about as subtle as a sawn-off shotgun.

Like hit men they have come out of the night to shoot the legs off a tired music industry that has relied on crutches far too long.

They are a great fat threat to complacency in a cocksure, candid and utterly contemptible way.

The single 'Anarchy In the UK' is the most vital, electric record to be released in a long time. It craves attention . . . and gets it.

But are Mr Rotten and co dedicated anarchists · or just grimy kids let loose in an ice cream factory and liable to get so sick to do anything constructive?

Ready, aim, fire!

"We are totally against apathy of any kind," says self-styled prince of punk Johnny Rotten.

"We have got to fight the entire super band system. Groups like the Who and the Stones are revolting. They have nothing to offer the kids anymore.

"All they're good for is making money. You just read the balance sheets of any of these. Life has really become safe for them. They are just so pathetic."

He spits out the words, and when they land on target they spread out like phlegm. Reminiscent of the time he used to bowl down the Kings Road and gob on the posters.

"When the Pistols first started we found it impossible to get gigs. The business bends over backwards to help the big bands. If you're not established you've got no chance.

"But by hook or crook we forced gigs onto people. And now we're established. All the big bosses think they've got us sussed — no way. They only took us on because they could see something was going on. But now we're fighting from the INSIDE."

Dragged up in Islington council flats. Kicked out of Catholic school "because they thought I was a rocker". Squatter. Dole queue Johnny.

The Pistols were spawned in the famous 'Sex' shop in Kings Road, Chelsea, owned by Malcolm McLaren, now the band's manager.

Sex sells everything from PVC strides to rubber gloves. "I only went to the Kings Road for sex. I used to despise the fading posers that walked up and down.

"London is supposed to be one of the most entertaining capitals in the world. It's full of nothing clubs where people can spend their money to see so called new' bands.

"Why doesn't just one guy who's made a lot of money out of the music business plough some of it back into rock? It's just take, take, take. All they're interested in is buying a country house. It's just greed. Life is such easier if you let things over-ride you rather than fight against

"And we don't want things easy."

Cries of "Anarchy!" have always been associated with bored, middle class students who follow each other like sheep. But the Pistols are spearheading, or hoping to, a backstreet backlash of working class kids who have never really had it hard, but are still put down.

STEVE JONES

PAUL COOK

GLEN MATLOCK

JOHNNY ROTTEN

Barry Cain talks to the band everyone's talking about, the Sex Pistols

'The only constructive thing left for Surbiton bores to do is kill themselves'

"They try to ruin you from the start. They take away your soul. They destroy you. 'Be a bank clerk' or 'join the Army' is what they give you at school.

"And if you do what they say you'll end up like the moron they want you to be. You have got to fight back, or die.

"You have no future, nothing. You are made unequal. Most of the time the kids who fight back

don't use their brains and it's wasted. Join a band is one way, or teach yourself is another. It doesn't take very much.

"Every kid who gets to a comprehensive school isn't worth bothering about half the time. They are taken as mugs, and don't realise until it's too late."

Bassist Glen Matlock is the only member of the band who went to a grammar school.

"You're never told what you should be told. They fill you up with so much sh- — you soon find out that Keats was a disgusting old fart.

"That way you can only expect to think like a fool for the rest of your life. I look at my old man as he's watching television and think 'God, what a mug you've been'. He's never tumbled.

"I don't see what's good about working in a

'We have got to fight the entire super band system. Groups like the Who and the Stones are revolting'

factory. It's not hard enough and the more problems you have the better.

"Me, I never stop complaining. Everyone should question things and that's unheard of these days.

"The Pistols are sticking their necks out all right. I don't know why it should be us and I don't really care. And we ain't in it for lining our pockets either."

"So many of my old mates from school come up to me now and say they're married," says drummer Paul Cook. "That's very frightening. I mean, none of us is older than 20."

"I don't believe in marriage, mortgage or houses in the country," says Johnny.

"It's awful. It's disgusting. All these bores who have crawled out of their little Surbiton huts. The only constructive thing left for them to do is kill themselves.

"You've met one — you've met them all. Their personality is

governed by what they do . . . and they do nothing worth talking about. They don't like people to have notions because they accept how they live.

"They're the ones who make it so much harder for us. But don't ever tell me I'm the same. The Pistols are presenting one alternative to the apathy and if you don't like it that's just too bad.

"I just get so f—— off with those little b———who love to put you into slots. Anything you're supposed to say these days is a hype to those sort of people.

"Oh that's all happened before in the sixties and fifties. You're not any different.' I am being myself and that's all I ask of anyone. Anarchy is self-rule and that's better than anything else.

"If everyone accepts everything in the same quantities, that's meaningless. But that's what happens now. People wear clothes very similar to those of their friends. They're just not thinking.

It's the attitude that matters, not the established kind of form.''

Is their anyone he feels compassion for?

"I feel sorry for people who stand up for what they believe and get kicked in the teeth. And that's what would have happened to me if I hadn't joined the Pistols. I would have been locked up, put quietly away, classified as insane.

"I know I'm not mad. Can you say that?''

Does he think that blacks could play punk rock?

"There hasn't been a very 'white' thing in music for years. It's pretty bad when whites have come to accept themselves as nothing, but it's all so easy when the music is done by someone else.

"And it's done by blacks for whites. I hate disco music. I don't like to think that whites are going there to hear their music.

"But I guess blacks could play punk rock. It doesn't matter what colour your skin is.

There is a pause. Then Glen speaks. "I like people to surprise me. To come out with shocking things like the Bay City Rollers have got spotty arses. But don't quote me because I wasn't passing comment then.''

What does he think of the Bay City Rollers?

"They've got spotty arses."

The band refuse to look into the future. People won't accept things for what they are now," says Johnny.

"They want to know what it will be like 10 years from now. Why can't they live for today? At 30 it's too late. Most people are clapped out with beer guts. Just look at Michael Jagger. I don't think of getting old — it doesn't bother me.

"Look, we really want to do something for our own sakes as much as anyone else's. We want to be people, people with a mind of our own. We are just doing our bit to punch the rest of 1976 away.

"Our songs are ideas. Just spend one night in London and you'll become f-—-off with the old ways. You're bound to get ideas from that.

"And soon this whole country will be just one city. What'll happen then?''

POSTSCRIPT. This was the last interview with the Pistols before the Bill Grundy controversy. Because of that their new tour with The Damned and Clash lies in shreds.

Production of their single has ground to a halt because the people involved are too disgusted to package it.

And our national press has cut the band to ribbons with articles boasting such headlines as 'PUNK JUNK SKUNKS!'

OK, so punk at times does smack of contrived lunacy, wasted violence and heavy shock tactics. But it's young, fresh and very much alive. There are many more obscenities in this country today that people close their eyes to — just look at the Government.

Most important of all, punk rock is a threat to the music establishment. And if that doesn't deserve to be threatened I don't know what does.

Daily Mail, Friday, December 17,

My Paul the punk, by his mother

By JENNY REES

PUNK ROCK drummer Paul Cook may be in for a rotten surprise next week.

When he returns home from a somewhat disrupted tour, he is likely to find he's no longer welcome.

For his mother, 44-year-old Mrs Sylvia Cook, is heartily fed up with Punk Rock in general and The Sex Pistols pop group in particular.

'For four years my bedroom has been full of drums,' she said yesterday at her two-up, two-down council house in Hammersmith.

'I wouldn't mind if he played tunes, but it's just bang, bang, bang.

'My hall is full of Sex Pistols' dirty washing and my husband has temporarily left home because he can't stand the row. It's rotten.

'The Sex Pistols don't believe in anyone giving them advice, especially mothers and fathers.

'I'm going to make a very nice little dining-room out of Paul's bedroom. I don't think I really want him back.'

Loutish

Mrs Cook is not surprised The Sex Pistols' swearing loutishness on TV caused such storm and led to the cancell of many tour bookings.

In fact, after finding the gr singer, Johnny Rotten, in her one day, nothing surprises her

❝ I found him sleeping in wrong end of Paul's bed. I d quite know what I'd found, bec his hair was multi-coloured, m ginger.

When he got dressed he smothered with safety pins, w dummy round his neck and a blade.

After he'd been around a used to tell my husband th wasn't surprising he couldn't any pins to eat his winkles because Johnny Rotten had t them all.

We all had a say in calling Johnny Rotten, because h teeth were all green and decayed

Mind you, says Mrs Cook, Johnny Rotten never swore at her.

'He was a very quiet boy . . . depressing looking. He never ate much and used to sit on the step in the back kitchen.'

As for 20-year-old Paul, she thinks he takes his musical talent from her side of the family.

'His great-grandmother, who's now 85, plays the piano and I'm quite a singer myself round in the pub.'

Even when he was very small he used to play the biscuit tins.

'I've asked the band to play for me at parties, but they refuse. They say I'm old fashioned.

Now Mrs Cook is off to Ramsgate with her 12-year-old daughter, Margaret, to spend a quiet Christmas away from the pressures of Punk Rock.

Had she bought a present for her son perhaps?

Mrs Cook was not amused.

'What I feel like giving him for Christmas is a punch on the nose,' she said.

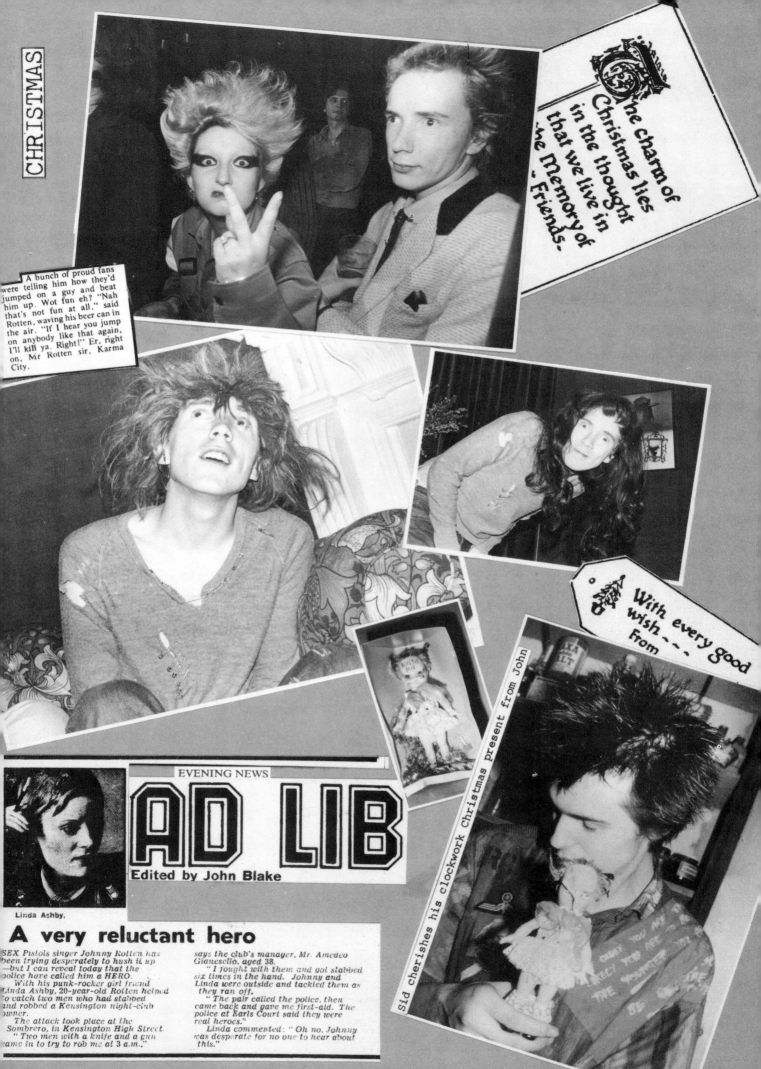

The charm of Christmas lies in the thought that we live in the Memory of our Friends.

A bunch of proud fans were telling him how they'd jumped on a guy and beat him up. Wot fun eh? "Nah that's not fun at all," said Rotten, waving his beer can in the air. "If I hear you jump on anybody like that again, I'll kill ya. Right!" Er, right on, Mr Rotten sir, Karma City.

With every good wish . . . from

Sid cherishes his clockwork Christmas present from John

EVENING NEWS

AD LIB

Edited by John Blake

Linda Ashby,

A very reluctant hero

SEX Pistols singer Johnny Rotten has been trying desperately to hush it up —but I can reveal today that the police have called him a HERO.

With his punk-rocker girl friend Linda Ashby, 20-year-old Rotten helped to catch two men who had stabbed and robbed a Kensington night-club owner.

The attack took place at the Sombrero, in Kensington High Street.

"Two men with a knife and a gun came in to try to rob me at 3 a.m.,"

says the club's manager, Mr. Amedeo Gianescelio, aged 38.

"I fought with them and got stabbed six times in the hand. Johnny and Linda were outside and tackled them as they ran off.

"The pair called the police, then came back and gave me first-aid. The police at Earls Court said they were real heroes."

Linda commented: "Oh no, Johnny was desperate for no one to hear about this."

Paul has a way with girls

Malcolm having fun

PISTOLS ROCK THE AIRPORT

By KENELM JENOUR

THE Sex Pistols punk rock group shocked passengers and airline staff at Heathrow Airport yesterday by swearing, spitting—and vomiting.

Four-letter words flew as they checked in for a KLM flight to Amsterdam.

Later, a KLM ground hostess said: "They are the most revolting people I have ever seen. They called us filthy names and insulted everyone in sight. One of them was sick in a corridor leading to the aircraft.

"While this was going on the three others were spitting on the floor and at one another."

Last Tuesday the Pistols flew out to Amsterdam for a five-day tour and apparently spat, vomited and swore their way through London's Heathrow Airport en route.

Conservative MP Robert Adley took this to heart and sent a blistering letter to Sir John Read, chairman of EMI, the same day. He told Read: "The fact is that your company is providing funds for a bunch of ill-mannered louts who seem to cause offence wherever they go. Surely a group of your size and reputation could forego the doubtful privilege of sponsoring trash like the Sex Pistols."

On Thursday, EMI announced they and the Sex Pistols had agreed to drop the contract.

£50,000 pay-off for Pistols

PUNK rock group the Sex Pistols have been given a £50,000 payoff by EMI two weeks after being sacked by the company.

The controversial band's manager, Malcolm McLaren, said last night: 'We came to a mutual agreement, but we have not neither a penny more nor less than we were due.'

The four-man group who shocked TV viewers with obscenities during a tea-time interview recently, were signed by EMI last October. McLaren said: 'We received £30,000 then and the balance was due in the next two years. It makes a total of £50,000 but that can't be called compensation.

'There hasn't been a settlement. There has been a fulfilment of obligations by EMI.'

Vulgar

The group was sacked a fortnight ago after reports that they had vomited, spat and swore at Heathrow Airport before leaving for Holland.

EMI chairman, Sir John Read, said then: 'This was the last straw. They have been vulgar and outrageous and an embarrassment to us as well as themselves.'

He said that sacking the Pistols would amount to a breach of contract but that EMI would be prepared to honour its side of the deal.

The group leaves next month on a tour to Holland, Denmark, Sweden and Finland. 'We are going to end up with a little holiday in Leningrad,' McLaren said. 'Then we come back to consider any other recording contracts and to make some more British appearances in March.'

Evening News

LONDON: TUESDAY JANUARY 4 1977

THESE REVOLTING VIPs!

ex Pistols n rumpus t airport

THE controversial Sex Pistols punk rock group caused an uproar at Heathrow today.

They shocked and revolted passengers and airline staff as they vomited and spat their way to an Amsterdam flight.

And their behaviour earned them a VIP send-off — but only because it was so bad.

An official of the KLM airline who normally tends to VIP passengers rushed to the No. 2 terminal where the group were waiting for their plane.

"They were behaving so disgustingly that he put them aboard the plane himself," said another official.

"We had been keeping an eye on them in the departure lounge because we thought they were thoroughly unsavoury.

"But he saw something that made him take action.

"It must have been pretty bad — he wouldn't even tell women staff what it was."

January 29th, 1977

News Desk

Pistols pocket £30,000 as EMI settle

THE SEX PISTOLS are still waiting to hear if another record company is prepared to sign them, but in the meantime they can console themselves on three different counts:

● Manager Malcolm McLaren has been attending the Midem Festival in Cannes during the past few days, and has had discussions with various recording executives, which could well lead to a new contract in the near future.

● They resume live work next week, by way of a 24-day European tour starting on February 1 and visiting Holland, Denmark, Norway, Sweden and Finland.

● They are £30,000 better off, as the result of compensation paid to them by EMI in an out-of-court settlement, following their sacking by that company.

They were originally signed by EMI on a £40,000 guarantee, half of which was paid to them immediately. This first half has already been spent in setting up their ill-fated autumn tour, but they have now been paid the other half of the guaranteed sum, plus a further £10,000 from their publishing contract with EMI.

Sex Pistols give EMI chief a four-letter reply

Steve: "There's no way we will ever regret what we have done."

McLaren told the MM that pressure to dump the Pistols had been put on EMI's executive by "the Sir John Reads and the Lord Delfonts — the seventh-floor guys who you can never see. They just don't want their reputation tarnished by being associated with us."

"Absolute nonsense" retorted Rachel Nelson. "Personal opinions do not come into it. It was a company decision made by the executives."

Cook: Like that thing at the airport. I'm not kidding, straight up, we couldn't believe it when we got over here. Someone phoned up, said this that and the other — we just couldn't believe it. There was a press bloke waiting I suppose, just waiting at the airport for something to 'appen. We just acted our natural selves. It just beats me.

Wasn't there anything at all?

Cook: Nothing. Really. The bloke from EMI was with us all the time. He would have said if there was, but he didn't.

Pistols sack bassist

"Leaving the Sex Pistols!!!!!!!!!!"

POST OFFICE

TELEGRAM

Charges to pay
Tariff £
V.A.T. £
Total £

RECEIVED
From

B 183 1747 LONDON T 86

DEREK JOHNSON NEW MUSICAL EXPRESS KINGSREACH TOWER
STAMFORD ST SE1

YES, DEREK GLEN MATLOCK WAS THROWN OUT OF THE SEX
PISTOLS SO IM TOLD BECAUSE HE WENT ON TOO LONG
ABOUT PAUL MCCARTNEY STOP EMI WAS ENOUGH STOP THE
BEATLES WAS TOO MUCH STOP SID VICIOUS THEIR BEST
FRIEND AND ALWAYS A MEMBER OF THE GROUP BUT
UNHEARD AS YET WAS ENLISTED STOP HIS BEST
CREDENTIAL WAS HE GAVE NICK KENT WHAT HE DESERVED
MANY MONTHS AGO AT THE HUNDRED CLUB   LOVE AND PEACE
            MALCOLM MCLAREN

        TSO TGMS LNAU

SE1 SEX PISTOLS

I just wanna make my music, get a band together. Maybe we'll call it The Rich Kids — with my mate Jimmy

Rich Kids (see ... but his former employees haven't, so it appears, totally dispensed with his services. Despite getting a new bassist in the shape of the very lovely **Sid Vicious**, it seems Her Majestys favourite band had to call Mattress back to — errum — help them out with their new single, "God Save the Queen". Certainly adds fuel rumours that Matlock was responsible for more of the Pistols music than the quarter share he got on the label

Fired Pistol reloads...

SEX PISTOLS SIGN FOR £150,000

Pic: CHALKIE DAVIES

SEEMS YOU have to do more than stick up two fingers and shout "Bollocks" — even if it is in front of Buckingham Palace and you're The Sex Pistols — to merit substantial coverage in the daily press these days.

For last Thursday the Malcolm McLaren masterminded stunt whereby those lovable spike tops he manages, The Sex Pistols, "signed" their new recording contract with A&M outside the Queen's prime pad, was greeted with indifference by the press.

And not one of the stream of four-letter words the lads let fly at the subsequent press conference was even hinted at in the pages of Fleet Street the following day.

Perhaps reporters would have had a more profitable time if they'd attended the proper signing which had taken place the previous afternoon (Wednesday) at Rondor Music, where the group's newest member, Sid Viscious, tried his darndest to vomit and one of the other members, on finding the wine that A&M had thoughtfully provided not to his taste, spat it out on the floor.

And there was always Johnny Rotten's custom-made jump-suit, featuring padlocks instead of buttons and a strap tying the knees together, to raise the odd eyebrow or two.

Wednesday's signing was the first time A&M's British boss Derek Green had actually met the latest addition to his roster. This was itself an unprecedented event; Green normally insists on meeting new artists before putting pen to paper.

But as he says, "It's an exceptional case," adding, "I don't think they liked me very much."

McLaren himself says the feeling is mutual. "We don't have a fantastic rapport with A&M. I would say that a lot of people there probably don't like us. A&M are a very middle of the road company and I think they probably thought we could change their image."

Negotiations with A&M started on January 9 when McLaren first met Green at the former's instigation. Green was played eight Pistols tracks, including three versions of "Anarchy In The UK", "Submission", "No Feelings", "No Future" and "Pretty Vacant".

Naturally McLaren had other irons in the fire — the reason, he says, why he didn't inform the band with whom they were signing until the very last minute.

At one time or another RCA, WEA and CBS were all involved around the negotiating table with McLaren — who ultimately had to settle for £50,000 less than the initial £200,000 price he wanted for the Pistols' signature.

Although Green refused to give details of the sum he'd paid for the Pistols, McLaren wasted no time in informing the music press and Fleet Street's pop writers, sending them a telegram the next day telling them he'd signed for £150,000. A&M will neither confirm nor deny that this was the actual figure.

Both American CBS and American WEA were keen to have the Pistols on their labels, but the British part of each operation was less enamoured of the *enfants terribles.*

While WEA's British chief John Fruin "hated the band", his second in command Derek Taylor wanted them on the roster.

Under pressure from the States, from whence the majority of the company's acts emanate, WEA decided to leave it to the company's grass roots to make the decision for them. After contacting the shop floor and not eliciting so much as one vote in favour of the Pistols, WEA dropped out of the race (according to McLaren).

Which still left CBS.

Says McLaren: "In America CBS's president was very heavily for the band, and in fact offered a quarter of a million. But Loggins (Dan Loggins, CBS's British A&R chief) said we sucked. And Oberstein — the managing director, said he got depressed every time he heard "Anarchy In The UK'."

McLaren is highly critical of other new wave bands' involvement in the music industry.

"I think bands like The Damned and The Clash and The Stranglers have been taken over by the industry.

"The Damned are into the custard pie paper bag thing, going through to *Magpie* and being the nice new wave band . . . a little bit of horror rock, a little bit of fun and games and they'll work very well on TV.

"The Stranglers will work pretty well on the college circuit. They'll be taken as a reasonably serious rock act, and The Clash, well, they're the intellectuals of the punk rock movement and they'll be taken seriously.

"The Sex Pistols don't work within any of those spheres. Their spontaneity is something people feel a little threatened by."

Such was the Pistols' spontaneity at their press reception that they immediately zeroed in on the bar, Viscious himself taking hits on a litre bottle of vodka throughout the questioning, which was punctuated by belches from the podium.

Sounds reporter Vivienne Goldman was unjustly abused by the group's new bassist. And when asked why Viscious had joined the group, they replied that it was because he beat up our own Nick Kent whom Rotten proceeded to call a hypocrite. And as events drew to a close the band sprayed the Fleet Street mob with soda syphons.

Asked about Glenn Matlock's leaving the line-up, McLaren has this to say: "We always knew Glenn was into The Beatles and at first we lived with it.

"It was all right Johnny Rotten having a go at him because of it, but when it became three of the band against one the pressure was to much and I had to deal with it.

"I felt he would be better off with another group because he had his own problems and his own attitudes, rather than staying with people who didn't want to accept them.

"The Pistols are heavily into chaos and not music. They didn't want to get involved in harmonising and they didn't want to get involved in . . . Glenn was involved in rhythm and blues and things like this.

"They thought Glenn had become a pain in the neck 'cause they hate The Beatles. They hated EMI. They didn't want to stand for The Beatles as well. They were a provincial idea to start with. It wasn't something they could relate to."

But wasn't Matlock the band's most accomplished musician?

"I would deny that. I would say Steve Jones is the most accomplished right now. Originally he may well have been 'cause Steve couldn't play guitar.

"But Glenn stayed as he was. Steve has become a great guitarist. The playing is not the big deal. That comes afterwards. It's the attitude that counts."

The Pistols did, however, hit the headlines on Friday when all of Fleet Street reported Johnny Rotten being busted £40 for possession of amphetamine sulphate (speed). A policeman giving evidence told the court that of the £25 per week Rotten is paid by McLaren, he gives £15 to his mother for board.

Pistols: another golden bullet

SOUNDS March 26, 1977

£75,000 pay-off after less than a week

SEX PISTOLS seem in r of isolating themselves the rock business after fired by their latest company after less than k.

Thursday A&M issued a tatement which read: "A&M ls wishes to announce that its ing agreement with the Sex has been cancelled with liate effect. The company ore will not be releasing any ct from the group and has no r association with them."

record company spokesman d to comment on the reason e Pistols had been fired. It ave something to do with the s behaviour after they signed ntract outside Buckingham and then went to the A&M where, according to reports, roke a window, were sick on loor, broke wine glasses, ed the ladies toilet and ted one of the company's employees.

re were also stories that the s new bassist, Sid Vicious, ysically assaulted a member M's A&R department and the staff of BBC2's 'Old Whistle Test' (who was red to have been given a stitches in his face) in two te incidents at London's easy last week.

At all events the company were alleged to have paid the band off to the tune of £75,000, half their original contract value.

It means the Pistols have now collected £125,000 in three months from two record companies and during this time they have had one single, 'Anarchy In The UK', released by EMI for less than a month and they played only a handful of dates on their abortive pre-Christmas tour and have played no live British dates this year.

Despite Johnny Rotten's claims that other companies are still interested in signing the band, it seems unlikely that any major company will sign the group without demanding assurances as to the band's behaviour.

RCA, who were strongly tipped to sign the band before A&M stepped in, replied with a firm 'no comment' when asked about the prospects of signing the band. And Jake Riviera, boss of Stiff, the leading new wave record label, told *SOUNDS*: "I love their attitude, I admire their temperament but I don't think they can play well enough".

The widespread ban on Pistols live gigs around the country remains and seems unlikely to be lifted following the latest events.

Pistols guitarist Steve Jones told *SOUNDS* that A&M had dropped the band "because they were scared". A&M had already pressed 25,000 copies of the group's new single, 'God Save The Queen' which will now be destroyed. All tapes, including 'Anarchy In The UK' have been returned to the group.

Even before the contract with A&M was cancelled the company had redused to p6t out an advertisement designed in the band's office which depicted a picture of the Queen with her eyes masked out by the song title and her mouth covered by the group's name.

The record included the lyrics: 'God save the Queen, a fascist regime/It made you a moron, a potential H-Bomb/God save the Queen/She ain't no human being/There is no future in England's dream'.

Pistols manager Malcolm MacLaren told *SOUNDS* this week that he was "extremely hopeful" of getting another recording deal in the near future, "I've talked with two major companies in the last two days and we shall be getting our new single out shortly," he said.

Asked about the settlement with A&M, MacLaren said that he had received £75,000 from the company but talk of the Pistols being "filthy rich" were "rediculous". "All that's happened is that the taxman has won the pools".

"It's another kick in the face by the record business. We have no problems from the kids in the street but it looks as if the industry is trying to blackmail us."

But he was still in favour of finding another recording deal rather than setting up his own company. "It's just what the industry is looking for. It would break us," he said.

MacLaren said that the reasons given to him by A&M for terminating the contract were "dissent in the music industry, the staff of A&M and the artists on the label."

But he added that A&M's lawyers told him at the meeting to end the contract last week that the real reasons would probably never be discovered. "The lawyers told us that we will not get the real truth so we might as well not ask any more questions and get our release from them. If we remained the company would not have released any product from us."

Was the Speakeasy incident involving Bob Harris last week a factor in their dismissal? "It was mentioned but not seriously. Maybe the band should have been carpeted for that incident." He dismissed as "hogwash" reports that one of A&M's A&R staff had been attacked later last week.

"None of the rumours going around so far have held up. After all is our behaviour really worse than othe groups? What about Les McKeown of the Bay City Rollers being fined for running someone over, or Keith Richard for his drug offences, or Keith Moon for throwing televisions out of his hotel room?"

We haven't killed the Prime Minister . . . yet! We'll fight back and get the record out."

The advert which A and M rejected

MacLaren said that A&M's lawyers had been upset by the lyrics of 'God Save The Queen' but added that he had played the record to CBS, who were among the companies still interested in signing the band, and there had been no objections.

The incident involving Bob Harris' friend record engineer George Nicholson at the Speakeasy received considerable publicity in the Sunday papers at the weekend and brought forth a statement from Harris' manager Phillip Roberge who said that Bob, who was with George and three other friends at the Speakeasy early on Saturday morning, was approached by a tall blond man who pushed his way through to Bob and asked when the new Pistols single would be played on the 'Old Grey Whistle Test'.

The statement said that Bob tried to avoid the blond who continued pushing and fighting broke out nearby, at which point the blond who was not a member of the Pistols, started assaulting and punching Bob. Bob did not see what was happening until someone told him George was in the lobb covered with blood. Bob got aw from the blond to find George wh told him he was standing by whi Rotten was fighting with someor George didn't know. Sudden Rotten grabbed two glasses an started punching wildly into th crowd, slamming one of the glass into George's forehead.

When the blond saw Bob helpin George in the lobby he came ov and threatened to kill Bob when h didn't have friends around to hel him. Bob did not have time consider the threat as he was in volved in getting George to hospit where he had 14 stitches in h head. Bob did not require trea ment although he was bruised an had a cut back. The matter is no in the hands of Bob and George solicitors.

A&M would neither confirm no deny the second alleged incident a the Speakeasy last week when Si Viscous was reported to have at tacked one of A&M's A&R staff.

As *SOUNDS* went to press it wa learnt that the Pistols were playin their first live gig this year a London's Notre Dame club o Monday. The concert was bein filmed by the American NB Television Company for possibl screening in the States.

SEX PISTOLS SEX PISTOLS SEX PISTOL
SEX PISTOLS SEX PISTOLS SEX PISTOL
SEX PISTOLS SEX PISTOL SEX
SEX PISTOLS SEX
SEX PISTOL SEX
SEX PISTOLS SE
SEX PIS

"What they did on TV was something that was quite genuine. They were goaded into it, and being working class kids and boys being boys they said what they felt was . . . O.K. They don't regret it.

"The KLM situation at the airport was fabricated up to a point. Yeah, the band might have looked a little bit extraordinary, they may have spat at each other. Big deal. And someone may have appeared a little drunk. But they weren't flying the plane, they don't need to be that sober.

"There are these bands now that have some sort of petition, like Mud, Tina Charles, all these other Top Twenty acts, and sent round this petition to all the record companies saying that they do not support this kind of music."

(NME talked to Mud's manager, Barry Dunning, on Monday. He denied Mud had signed any petition, nor would they ever do so.)

"My lawyer asked: We'd like a meeting with John Read or the rest of the money. They'd rather give us the rest of the money than have a meeting. John Read speaks on behalf of all the shareholders, he controls the whole of EMI Ltd., which covers far more than just a record company. He wouldn't meet us. He sent Hill instead; every time you just get to speak to Hill. Hill has his orders and he can't move from that point."

How much money have you had of the £40,000?

"Half. The first year. But that has been spent on supporting a tour.

They end but don't go. "You're boring," drones Rotten. This weird challenge to the audience to respond. I look round at McLaren — and see that he is standing there gesticulating to Rotten, the upswept arms of the "Get Up" movement and the hands clapping overhead . . . and Rotten is mimicking McLaren. This show ends when Malcolm says so.

Malcolm McLaren, 28-year-old manager of the Sex Pistols, has been in the forefront of the movement in this country. A former Goldsmiths College fine are student, he started in business selling old records in Oxford Street. He moved to a shop at the World's End, Chelsea, at the beginning of the seventies and since then has been involved in reviving teddy-boy clothes and promoting an American college look.

In 1975 he renamed his shop SEX and started a bizarre style of sexual clothing adapted by many teenagers. "I was bored," he said. "I thought of sexual clothing . . . clothing for people who engaged in various sexual perversions, if you like."

"Hello boy...no, not much. Just sitting in the office counting my money."

"Record companies are always ripping off artistes. They just can't understand what's happening."

"Well, Nils. I'm prepared to pay you £300 for your years work."

"Boys will be boys."

"Yes, I know it says that in the contract, but it's not what it means."

"I said, 'What happens if we're on another label and the distribution is through EMI? Are EMI gonna distribute the record?' They can't really answer that. It's very difficult, it really is. I feel pretty bad about it.

"Hill's now saying, 'Can't you go to Virgin Records, I hear that's an interesting company.' Bollocks man, we went to Virgin Records before we went to EMI and they didn't wanna know.

It's been very nice. Someone's decided behind our back to 'mutually terminate' our contract.

— MALCOLM McLAREN

The manager of the Sex Pistols and the man credited with masterminding the whole Punk Rock scene is Malcolm MacLaren, 28. "He's fast asleep. Can't you call back later?" said a girl at his Balham home.

Pistols: new label, new row

Pistols line up distribution deal

THE SEX PISTOLS are likely to set up their own record label to release their own material following their short-lived recording contracts with EMI and A&M.

The band are currently negotiating an independent pressing and distribution deal with Virgin.

Virgin are also known to be interested in signing other new wave acts, notably Roogalator and the Motors.

A Virgin spokesperson told SOUNDS this week: "We haven't signed any of these people . . . but we might."

a 55c   15p

new MUSICAL EXPRESS

SPECIAL GRATUITOUS SEX PISTOLS OVERKILL ISSUE

PAGES 1, 3, 7, 8, 12, 23, 58, 59, 60.

THE SEX PISTOLS have signed their third record contract, this time with Virgin Records, who will release their controversial single, 'God Save The Queen' on May 27.

But with the ink barely dry on the contract, the band have already run into more of the censorship troubles that have plagued them throughout their career.

Virgin were to announce the signing of the Pistols on Thursday in a seven-second ad on Thames Television's Bill Grundy show, the programme which outraged the media after the band swore on the air.

But Thames refused to show the ad within half an hour of the show. Attempts were made to reschedule the ad for Friday evening on London Weekend Television, but this was also refused.

The ad showed Johnny Rotten sitting down and saying, "You thought you'd got rid of us but you haven't. The Sex Pistols are back."

Despite the censure — which follows the banning of the Pistols by practically every local council in Britain, rejection by American distribution outlets, and the non-appearance of ads in the music press due to objections by printers — the single has gathered massive advance orders and will be the subject of Virgin Records' biggest ever promotion campaign.

Pistol's manager Malcolm McLaren said, We feel really lousy about this. We are still being used as some form of scapegoat. I can't see any reason why the ad should have been turned down but I can't comment further until I get to the truth of the matter.

"But we're happy to have a contract with Virgin. Other contracts we had offered to us contained certain paranoiac clauses which we couldn't accept."

Virgin Records responded to the LWT action with "barely surpressed anger" and said that the Pistols "must now be the most hated and potentially most successful band in England."

London Weekend claim the advert was not shown because there was not the necessary authorisation from the Independent Television Companies Association.

But Virgin Records maintain that the ad was approved by both the Independent Broadcasting Authority and ITCA and that it was London Weekend alone who were unwilling to advertise the record.

A spokesman for ITCA said that as far as he knew it was London Weekend who took the decision.

To test this thesis, we a snatch of the lyrics of "God Save The Queen" to the National Association For Freedom, and asked if they were likely to take any action when the single is released.

A spokesman, confiding that he had never personally found the Pistols "very impressive", and adding, "Even I could write lyrics on those lines", said that putting out a record which would certainly outrage so many people struck him as a "desperate gimmick", and that being sued or otherwise publicly opposed by his organisation was "probably exactly what The Sex Pistols and their manager would like."

Regular air-play for the single is certainly out of the question (although John Peel has already played it twice on his late-night Radio 1 programme), and many retail outlets might refuse to handle it at all (Woolworths have already told NME that they will not be selling Pistols' product).

It is nevertheless likely that, when the lyrics become publicly known, some organisations will attempt to take out an injunction to prevent the sale of the single at all – especially it being Jubilee time.

But. If The Sex Pistols are so anti-establishmentarian, why should they even need to bother with bourgeois outfits like A&M or EMI — why don't they just do like half the other young bands in the world today and put out their own records, completely uncensored, on some underground label? I mean, if it's all just chaos then who gives a shit, right?

Derek Green insists that the band left A&M was merely because he changed his mind. "It was as simple as that, and it was nothing to do with pressure from any other quarter," he said. "I just didn't want to be involved in their music." Rumour has it, in fact, that Capitol involved in outside their music." Radio head Aidan Day stated (after the Speakeasy incident between the BBC's Bob Harris and his friends and some friends of the Pistols), that he would blacklist all A&M artists if the band remained with the label.

"I don't know happened with A&M you have a fight. But what's a fight got to do with selling records? Sure Sid was involved in a fight with Bob Harris and his mate. But if a fight has got to do with records how come we had to take the brunt of the blame and not the DJ?"

JOHNNY'S ROTTEN GNASHERS!

THE spitting, swearing Sex Pistols singer, Johnny Rotten, is foul-mouthed in more ways than one.

By DAVID ALFORD

SUNDAY PEOPLE, June 26, 1977

May 28th, 1977

SINGLES OF THE WEEK

SEX PISTOLS: God Save The Queen (Virgin). Ramalamafa fa fa! Just in case there was any danger of forgetting that the Pistols are a rock band instead of just a media hoax/guaranteed talk-show laff-getter / all - purpose scapegoat or whatever, here's a record which actually managed to squeak its way past the official guardians of our morality and may well be in your shops any minute now. It may even stay there long enough for you to buy it. It comes out on Saturday and it'll probably be banned by Monday, so move f-a-s-t.

The "real" title of this song is "No Future", but it's received so much notoriety as "God Save The Queen" that now it's called "God Save The Queen" so that you can get what you ask for when you ask for it, and what you will get when you ask for it (and you will ask for it) is a remorseless, streamless crusher of a single that establishes the Pistols'

THE SEX PISTOLS looked set this week to become the first band to reach number one in the singles charts with a record that has been banned by both BBC radio and television and commercial radio and television stations.

The Pistol's single, 'God Save The Queen' leapt straight into the singles charts at Number 11 on the strength of just one day's release.

In the five days that it has been on sale (although not at Boots, Woolworths and Smiths who have banned it) the record has sold 100,000 copies, which means that it will almost certainly be number one next week, unless a number of the record shops used for compiling the charts are refusing to stock it.

MEANWHILE the Sex Pistols are planning to make a film written by Johnny Speight — creator of Alf Garnett — and produced by Russ Meyer. Virgin told RM, "There are certain plans in that direction, but I'm not

PISTOLS PROFIT WITH QUEEN 'INSULT'

THE Sex Pistols are shooting up the pop charts with a record calling the Queen "a moron."

A&M. The lyrics go something like:

God save the Queen, a fascist regime
It made you a moron, a potential H-bomb
God save the Queen.
She ain't no human being.
There is no future in England's dream.

Shot down

THE Sex Pistols record calling the Queen a "moron" was yesterday banned from commercial TV and radio. The BBC had already banned the disc.

about it for he record, said: "The objections appear to revolve principally around the phrase 'fascist regime'. If this country isn't one, which is clearly the case for most people, then one of the first principles of democracy is that the band should be free to sing that line on radio and TV.

"I think they are just suffering from the traditional response to anyone who steps out of line, particularly at a time like Jubilee week when everyone becomes monarchist.

"It is not an offensive record but one in a long line of socially outspoken records."

Meanwhile, there was no firm news of any live dates in the immediate future by the Sex Pistols, although they could well be appearing at London's Rainbow Theatre later this month.

A spokesperson for Virgin Records, who are distributing the

The Sex Pistols wouldn't talk to us this week (sob!), so instead we bring you this heart-warming exclusive interview from the Islington Gazette...

JAWS

ISLINGTON GAZETTE   FRIDAY MAY 27 1977 - THIR

Why the X-certificate superstar is still mother's pride

Johnny's top of the pops with me says Mrs Rotten

By Robert Eddison

THE SEX PISTOLS could have no stauncher ally than Johnny Rotten's mum.

Which is just as well because, with punk rock storming back into the news again, they're going to need all the support they can get against the growing army of "Disgusteds."

"I wanna riot! Fans smash 200 seats at Punk Show" screamed a recent Evening Standard headline after London's largest-ever new wave punk rock concert.

It was The Clash group that night. The Sex Pistols have been in limbo for a while, following the bans provoked by their earthy language on television.

For months now, Eileen Lydon's anger at her son's treatment has been simmering just below the surface. But in an exclusive interview with the Gazette at her home on the Six Acres Estate, Finsbury Park, Johnny's sharp-shooting mum fired off enough verbal salvoes to bring down a whole army of punk-stopping councillors.

"Surely it's better to let out your anger with a few swear words than with violence?" blazed this Irish-born mother of four.

"On that 'Today' programme, if they'd wrecked the studios and everyone in them, they could hardly have been worse treated.

"It's true I've brought up my children to be plain-speaking. OK, so Johnny will sometimes say things straight from the shoulder, but he's not the violent type at all.

"Yet, he seems to bring out violence in others. One viewer got so worked up at their language that he swore back at them and kicked in his colour TV set, the stupid nut.

"'I hate those punk rockers,' people say to me. 'They're so violent.' Yet, they're NOT violent. It's the anti-punks who are the real troublemakers. There wasn't any trouble at the Screen On The Green concert; they were all our own followers in that audience."

She handed me a steaming mug of tea with HANDS OFF! painted round the side. There was an ominous silence. After the scatter fire, you could almost hear the big guns being mobilised.

"I can understand people being shocked at something new. But that's no reason, sod it, for the press to invent stories about my son's group vomiting all over Heathrow airport and spitting at the air staff. They were even supposed to have done something the press 'couldn't write about.' Can you imagine?

"'How disgusting!', people say, 'to stick pins through their ears and nose.' What the hell has it got to do with them? It's THEIR nose and ears, isn't it?

"In fact," confided Eileen, leaning forward on the divan, "they don't stick them right through. It just looks that way."

The phone rang. For Johnny, of course. From some girl in Manchester who wouldn't leave her name. With him out so much, mum fielded the calls on automatic, like a human answering machine.

"People take them so seriously," she went on, ignoring the interruption.

Many's the laugh Johnny and I have over it. Being both Aquarius, we have the same sense of humour.

"There was this vicar, I remember, marching up and down in the snow outside the Welsh Hall they'd booked for a concert. 'Keep out of there!', he shouted. 'They're the Devil's Children!'

"There are more nutters outside than in, if you ask me. He must have heard their banned single: 'Anarchy In The UK,' where Johnny sings 'I'm An Anti-Christ.' Fancy him believing it was true! He's the Anti-Christ if anyone is. His job, after all, is to save everyone."

And that little matter of the drugs charge?

"Pop stars get handed all sorts of things after concerts. They can't examine everything their fans give them. Besides, it was only Speed: it wasn't a hard drug. When I went along to the West End Central police station to bail him out, I went mad at the way they treated him — like a common criminal.

"My boy is doing his own thing. He's not going around murdering people," she shot out. "In fact, groups like Johnny's help society by bringing kids in off the streets. A friend of ours thinks the Sex Pistols are doing more good for the country than Jim Callaghan."

A budgie flew past and landed on the teapot. The cage door stayed open. The Lydon family believes in freedom.

"Some parents are too quick to condemn their children. After my own mum stopped me having a dancing career, I swore I'd even allow my kids to become roadsweepers if that's what made them happy.

"Life's hard enough today without pushing your children into something they don't want to do. That's how parents lose their children. Take religion. We're Roman Catholics. Johnnie used to be a churchgoer. If he comes back to it, he'll return on his own. Not because I've pushed him."

And marriage? Despite all the outward rebellion, she believes in marriage — for herself. For Johnny, she's not so sure. "What with all the travelling, it might be better not."

While her son reaches for the stars, Eileen Lydon's feet remain firmly on the ground. For her, the Finsbury Park flat is home.

"'Now that Johnny's on the up,' the neighbours say, 'I suppose he'll soon be buying you a grand house in the country.' What they don't understand is that I'm quite happy here.

"And, with all the money in the world, I'd still go to work. Being house-proud, I found myself getting over-fussy and annoying the children. So the answer was to get out of the house."

Johnny Rotten could hardly wish for a better mum. Not only is she his best ally, but she's the Sex Pistols' No 1 fan. "I'd do anything for music. If it wasn't for keeping home, I'd go everywhere with them."

SEX PISTOLS

● JOHNNY ROTTEN . . . . not the monster he's made out to be says his mother who lives in a council flat on Finsbury Park's Six Acres Estate.

● We're the only honest band that's hit this planet in about two thousand million years ●

'A friend of ours

Vicious has caused everybody a
...ve amount of relief by returning
...London with the news that he
...he assault rap completely and
...ed a mere (?) £125 fine for the

...w'd you dress for court, Sid?
...h, I wore this real corny shirt my
...got me about five years ago and
...eels. I must've looked a right
...y cunt."

...yeah, we haven't really met Sid
...e got the name "Sid" when he
...amed after an allegedly really
...ooking albino hamster of that
...that he and Rotten used to

...ate the name Sid, it's a right
...name, it's really vile. I stayed in
...out two weeks because
...ne kept calling me Sid, but they
...ouldn't stop. Rotten started.
...orrible like that, he's always
...g on me..."
...ten: "Sid's the philosopher of
...nd."
...ious: "I'm an intellectual."
...ten: "He's also an oaf. He
...to what everybody else says
...inks, 'How can I get in on

...ious: "No I don't! I'm a highly
...l thinker, man, he's just
...s because I'm really the brains
...group. I've written all the
...even right from the beginning
...wasn't even in the group. They
...useless they had to come to me
...e of they couldn't think of
...ng by themselves..."

**COMMENT FROM Johnny
Rotten's** Mum after last wek's
stabbing
"You don't go out on a
Saturday night with knives
unless you're looking for
trouble. It was ten against
three. What cowards they
were, not to dare fight man to
man and use their fists".

"A balding old hippy with a big pair
of platforms on," sneers Vicious.
"That's what you were. I went to the
same college as him..."
"... to get O-levels," Rotten
finishes the sentence for him. "I
waited a year and a bit because I went
on building sites working, and then I
went to get some O-levels because I
still had it in me that *O-levels were the
way to heaven*... plus I didn't want
to work no more. I got a grant. It was
very easy. For some reason I always
liked Technical Drawing and
Geography. At college, I did maths,
English, physics, technical drawing
and chemistry..."
Cook: "I've got an O-level in
woodwork."
Vicious: "I've got two O-levels..
English and English Literature...
and I'm very intelligent."
Rotten: "English Literature was a
joke. I passed that with flying colours
without even trying. It was stupid
fucking Keats poetry, because I did
my English in my Catholic school.
They kicked me out halfway through
the course because they said I'd never
pass, but they'd already entered me,
so I went and took the exam privately
because I was still entitled to down at
County Hall.
"And I passed with an A... and I
went down there with the certificate
and showed it to 'em."

"When we went to Jersey the Customs bloke wanted to look
up my arse, so I farted in his face!"

VIRGIN information

CONFIDENTIAL. FOR INTERNAL USE ONLY.

SEX PISTOLS RIVER PARTY ... NOTES.

TOTAL BUDGET ... £1500. Virgin contribution £750.

Cost of boat .. £500.

Cost of food £3 per head.

Boat capacity 175. Suggested invitations limited to 60 for Sex Pistols, management, friends and 60 for Virgin, journalists, staff, etc.

Guest list (strictly by invite only) to be drawn up tomorrow (Thursday) and invites/passes printed.

Programme as follows

Board - ~~5~~ 5.30 p.m. (Westminster Pier at High Tide, Charing X at low tide)

Leave at ~~7.~~ 6.15 pm.

From Westminster, down to TOWER BRIDGE
back to LONDON BRIDGE
WESTMINSTER BRIDGE
LAMBETH/VAUXHALL/CHELSEA
ALBERT BRIDGE
PUTNEY BRIDGE
HAMMERSMITH BRIDGE ... then back to Westminster Bridge.

Under each bridge play cassette of National Anthem and follow by the band live.

Party at Andrew Logan's Warehouse, A Block, 7th floor, Butler's Wharf. (403 0813) opposite South side of Tower Bridge.
Film to be shown in disco continuously

No advertising as the boat will be cancelled. IF wrong people informed. No press release until after the event.

Keith to arrange for projector and screen

Warren Mitchell as disc jockey ?

Malcolm to provide PA

Cooke-Key working on 50 foot flag for boat

Security - Dave and Kevin (+ mates)

Fireworks at each bridge to be provided by rocket man.

Virgin press office and Sex Pistols office to exchange guest lists by Friday mid-day. Discretion essential.

What did you do on the Jubilee?

Sounds 18th June 1977

Jon Savage sailed with the Pistols on the Queen Elizabeth

Before the police came, it was a great party. Make that a capital G.

Let's take all this sequentially: after an hour of waiting, the 'Queen Elizabeth' left Charing Cross Pier at 6.30, and, after a moment's hesitation, decided to head downstream. If you aren't on the List, you aren't on. Nobody jumps . . . not even Palmolive. Bye bye.

Begins very restrained — too too 'vousetes', but come Rotherhithe, some booze and more food, and everyone gets mellow, if such a thing is possible. I mean it's a nice evening (albeit a bit chilly) and there's space all around instead of tower-blocks, so why be surprised?

The disparate crowd mixes surprisingly well — the only jarring note in fact is the refusal of the bar to serve doubles . . . never know what these notorious punk-rockers might get up to. Downstream away, we turn as a banner is unfurled along the length of the boat — red on yellow, it proclaims proudly 'Queen Elizabeth — the new single by the Sex Pistols 'God Save The Queen', or something similar. Really low profile.

Inside, the conversation's covering some pretty recherché territory, but, hey, upstairs, in the covered area, the tapes start rolling. Dance. Great selection — moving from arcane dub to the Ramones, thru Paul Revere and the Raiders. More boozing/dancing/yammering — general party patter — but expectation is heightened. They have to start playing outside the Houses of Parliament.

We repass under Tower Bridge, picking up a police boat on the way — sniff sniff sussy sussy — but it falls behind: meanwhile Jordan's telling me about this group she's managing called the Ants. Upstream it gets chillier — most take refuge in the downstairs bar (big boat this), ostensibly for a film that never happens. There's no pretence now: we're waiting.

More turns (Battersea funfair — for the detail-obsessed) and it's home run time.

The Pistols take the 'stage' — at the back of the raised covered area: the conditions are appalling, and it's amazing that any sort of sound comes out. The main one is feedback — this delays their start, and is never fully resolved. Any blasé traces are swept away — pulses race/everyone rushed to be at the front. Pure mania.

Rotten gives up on losing the feedback, and the band slams into 'Anarchy', right on cue with the Houses of Parliament. A great moment. It's like they've been uncaged — the frustration in not being

see is a snarling mouth and wild eyes, framed by red spikes. Can't shake that feedback: he complains, won't sing for the first verse of 'No Feelings' but the others carry on. More frustration to explode.

By now the atmosphere is electric/heart thumps too hard/people pressing, swaying — it's like they have to play to blast them away. They're also playing for their/our lives — during 'Pretty Vacant' and the next song two police boats start moving around in earnest.

Now all adrenalin is flat out do it do it do it now now now NOW — suddenly in 'I Wanna Be Me' they get inspired and take off / 'No Fun' SCREAMED out as the police boats move in for the kill is one of the rock 'n' roll moments EVER. I mean EVER. (Think about that).

What/shit suddenly we're in the dock 'n' the power's off and Paul Cook's beating the hell out of the drums 'n' there are all those police and WHAT'S HAPPENING and what the fuck IS this . . .

Fax. We dock. The power is off. The bar is closed. Suddenly no more party. Suddenly a lot of police on the quay. Altercations begin. Nobody wants to leave. The police want us to leave. So does the owner. The owner can terminate the contract of hire at any time. Small print, baby.

Richard Branson loses his £500. Richard Branson doesn't want to leave. Tension. Indecision. People trickle off, slowly, after a half-an-hour. Most stay on. More police. The police move on the boat. People move off. Nothing happens, bar a bit of pushing and shoving on either side.

Someone gets nicked. Now things start getting crazy. People are *aided* up the long gangway. Explosion of movement. Fear. Confusion. Flash/people running/Ted restrains/'Get 'Im'/crying faces/spin around/black marias/no objectivity/each for himself/quick spurts of movement/hate/'You're shit'. And there's 11 people in the marias and we're on the pavement wondering what's been happening. Very quick.

We leave. We go to Bow Street police station, via the Zanzibar (whose cutesy-poo decadence is sickening). No message. No bail. No press. No, not an IPC card. 'There are people we'd like to arrest

but we don't know who they are'. A direct hint. Buzz off. And don't wait on the pavement. No help.

And then the seven of us REALLY slip into 1984: we move to this pub where everybody is enacting this weird ritual which involves the wearing of red/white/blue hats and 'singing' arcane folk-lore. They want us to join in/we can only make silly jokes out of pain. Zoom zoom/'I don't wanna grow up: there's too much contradiction'.

Chickens come home to roost baby, you'd best believe.

Some jubilee. But look: I mean McLaren's brilliant at the Theatre of Provocation, didn't he set all this up? To an extent. Provocation, yes, incitement, no. OK, I mean all of us were expecting SOME interference, let's be frank — but not such emotional overreaction.

WHATEVER the rights and wrongs of the individual cases, objectively, yeah, Responsibly, that's what it was. You know — nothing doing in the centre of town and these allegedly 'notorious-foul-mouthed-punk-rock-Sex-Pistols' . . . Image vs. reality.

The charges run like this (approximately): Malcolm McLaren/'Using Insulting words likely to provoke a breach of the peace': Vivien Westwood/'Obstructing a policeman': Sophie Richmond and Alex McDowell/'Assault': Debbie and Tracy/'Obstruction': Ben Kelly and Chris Walsh/'Obstruction': José Esquibel/'Threatening behaviour': Jamie Reid/'Assault'. All have denied the alleged charges, and have been released on bail/surety until their case will be heard.

No future, eh? Feelings are bound to run high. But wait. Neither 'side' is blameless, but there are a few things left to say: To a certain extent the barriers are down a bit more. That means if you look anything like a Sex Pistol, or a 'punk-rocker', you're likely to get pulled in. Right: that means — No martyrs, No victims, No heroes, No stereotypes. No games on this score, No provocation. Things have gotten more serious. No escalation. . . . . ?

Uuuh. Um. Is it too late for me to say that it was a Great party and that the Pistols were amazing? Oh, it is, but it's a shame, because that's a part of the evening too. . . . .

SEX PISTOLS JUBILEE BOAT TRIAL RESULT

WHILE MASTER PHILLIPS gurgles snugly in his cot at Buck House and a nation drools, Jubilee year is climaxing in a different way for a select coterie of New Wave royalty.

Remember the Pistols' Jubilee boat-trip back on the Queen's big day?

The party ended badly for several people — particularly for Pistols manager Malcolm McLaren and his girlfriend Vivienne Westwood, who were among those arrested when the police 'persuaded' the revellers to break things up and come ashore.

Last Thursday both were called to Bow St. Magistrates Court for the continuation of their respective trials; McLaren's, however, was postponed, to hang over his head until February 3, so *Thrills* own court-hack sidled into No. 3 Court instead, to observe the end of Ms Westwood's trial on a charge of obstructing the police.

Two policemen had told the court that the defendant, having already been restrained from trying to pull a cop off McLaren whilst he was being arrested, had become violent, kicking and punching other policemen who were gathered round the van into which McLaren had been put away. A third was now corroborating their evidence down to the last detail.

He told the court that he and a colleague put Ms Westwood into the van, told her she was being arrested, and cautioned her. He was unable to say definitely how she might have incurred bruising on her right hip, left leg and ankle: it might have been as a result of her struggling as she was lifted into the van.

Ms Westwood, dressed in a sea-green mohair sweater and black leather trousers, told the court that she was McLaren's "common-law wife" and that he was the father of her second child. She claimed that her first contact with the police that night had come when they had dragged her off the boat and down the gangplank, pulling her by both legs.

She denied assaulting any police officer, claiming that she had simply tried to keep McLaren in sight as he was led away, because she was afraid he would be taken to a police station and beaten up.

"I was not cautioned till I reached the police station," she claimed. Asked if she had not been "very angry with the police", and so upset that it would have been "reasonable" for her to grab the arm of the police officer arresting McLaren, she replied: "I don't get angry at the police any more. I know they behave like that to people like us."

She was found guilty of obstructing a police officer and fined £15 with £15 costs. As we all left the court, I heard one policeman remark to another: "It's amazing how these people can transform themselves, isn't it?"

AMY PROSSER

THRILLS

OFF ON THE ROAD

Sex Pistols
BBC1

"OOH, careful with the plate mother. It's hot," said Dad. Mum ignored him and went back into the kitchen. Dad looked down at the plate of spam and chips on his lap and grinned. Peeping out from under the plate was a pert nipple belonging to today's Page Three Girl. He slid out the copy of the brightest daily paper in Britain and folded it up, taking one last glance at those graceful curves.

"I see those filthy Sex Pistols are on the telly again," said Dad as he placed the neatly folded 'Sun' under his bum.

"Gnf," said Mum as she brought in more spam and chips. The inch of ash on the end of her cigarette was dislodged by this assenting mumble and sailed gracefully down to land in the tangle of chips on the plate in her left hand. She handed the plate to Grandma, who began to eat ravenously, her false teeth clicking together from time to time.

Mum went back for more food as the programme started. The camera panned up the chart to show two Sex Pistols records in the chart, 'God Save The Queen' at 27, 'Pretty Vacant' at 7.'

"Oughta be shot. Dirty little buglurk!" said Granma, her sentence cut short by her upper plate's having shot out of her mouth just as Rita Coolidge appeared on screen. Miss Coolidge wore a woolly jumper and sang 'We're All Alone' as Gran and Rover (a dog) struggled under the table for ownership of Gran's teeth.

"Ooh, I don't like the look of them," said Mum, looking up from her knitting as The Saints thundered through 'This Perfect Day'. "Is that the Sexy Pissers, Dad?" Dad ignored her, as usual.

There was an unearthly scream from under the table. Gran's final solution to the problem of extricating her teeth from Rover's jaw had been to strike the brute a hefty blow on the testicles with a poker. Seconds later she emerged triumphant accompanied by Rover's agonised whimpering.

Kid Jensen grinned his way through another link. "Belt up now," said Dad as Legs & Co. appeared on screen. The six nymphets undulated jerkily in approximate time with a slushy number from Tamla's Commodores. Dad's jaw was slack for the entire two minutes they were on. A trickle of saliva coursed down his chin.

"Tsk!" said Mum, returning to her knitting.

Soon Jensen was back. He appeared to have a couple of boiled sweets stuck on his jumper. Dave Edmunds and Rockpile came on and everyone ate quietly again. Jensen returned. "If you've been wondering what happened to Jigsaw, puzzle yourself no more," grinned Jensen. "Who?" said people all over the country.

Seconds later an elegant young gentleman came on and did a pained impression of Frankie Valli. "I like this," said Mum. "Lovely tune." Rover started whining again but relapsed into silence when Gran made to get up. Supertramp came and went with all the excitement of a flea farting, quickly followed by Cilla Black. "I liked her better before the nose job", was Dad's only comment. In between close-ups of Cilla and her nose the screen showed several miserable teenagers moving sluggishly about, obviously drugged with tranquilisers to keep them docile.

Finally The Sex Pistols came on. Johnny Rotten wore dark glasses and sang 'Pretty Vacant', Steve Jones played guitar with a handkerchief knotted on his head. From time to time one saw close-ups of Sid Vicious or Paul Cook.

It was at this precise moment that Rover took his revenge. Leaping on Gran from behind he ripped a large piece from her throat. Blood spurted from the wound and spattered Mum's half-finished jumper. "Really," said mum.

Rover had Gran on the floor now and was trying to rip her left cheek off. Mum's wool got caught up in the struggle and she was pulled into the fight. Gran bit Mum's calf.

"THAT'S IT, THAT'S ENOUGH. I'M NOT HAVING THIS FILTH IN MY HOUSE!"

Dad put down his plate, picked up the bloody tangle that was Mum, Rover and Gran and hurled them out the window. There was a faint thud as the bodies hit the ground, fifteen floors below.

Dad didn't notice. He'd switched channels and was watching 'Charley's Angels' contentedly. His hands were in his lap. He was smiling. An ambulance bell sounded miles away. — GIOVANNI DADOMO.

THE SEX Pistols punk rock group, banned by ITV, are to appear in BBC's Top of the Pops tonight.

"I think the Sex Pistols are absolutely bloody revolting"

Pistols on TV: 'no shocks' shock

"I felt unclean for 48 hours after I saw them"

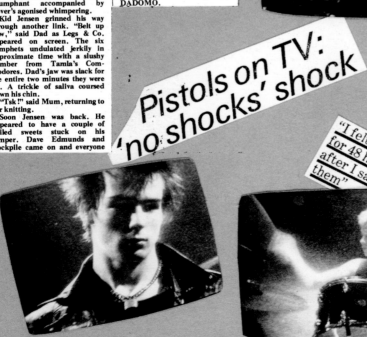

Pistols make it

The BBC is to screen the Sex Pistols punk rock group for the first time since ITV banned them over the four-letter word interview. Scores of viewers protested when the group was interviewed by Bill Grundy on Thames Television's Today programme nine months ago. There has since been a near nationwide ban on public appearances for the group. But its records continue to be best sellers—and the BBC will feature it today on the Top of the Pops show, which has more than eight million viewers.

Pics: *PHOTOFEATURES*

Pistols LP set at last

THE SEX PISTOLS' long-awaited debut album is finally confirmed by Virgin for November 4 release. Titled "Never Mind The Bollocks, Here's The Sex Pistols", it has already qualified for a Gold Disc on the strength of 125,000 advance orders.

Police move in on punk disc shops

THE REASON we were all in Nottingham was to see justice take its course. Because up for grabs last Thursday was the question of whether the word bollocks is indecent or not (when associated with The Sex Pistols, one should add).

Rotten wasn't required to give evidence so his presence was really a question of moral support more than anything else. The rest of The Sex Pistols were due to arrive from London that morning. Rotten was taken to Nottingham the night before the case to ensure he actually made it. Predictably enough, the others didn't.

Perhaps it didn't seem as important to them to fly the flag in court, but J R himself was keenly aware of what was at stake. It wasn't really an Anglo-Saxon word that would be on trial in Nottingham, it really was The Sex Pistols and the foulness and evil they seem to represent in the eyes of the authorities.

And when the Crown went to work on the Pistols' album "Never Mind The Bollocks Here's The Sex Pistols" the Crown would no doubt have the silent support of a goodly number of concerned authorities.

"Never Mind The Bollocks" was released on Friday, October 28, the most eagerly-awaited album this year or any other year you care to mention since the hey-day of The Beatles.

Release day saw The Sun splashing its arrival with bold headlines proclaiming— SEX PISTOLS IN A NEW FOUR LETTER WORD STORM. The story was really a storm in a tea-cup, but Tory shadow education Minister Norman St John Stevas felt sufficiently incensed to pontificate to The Sun that the album "has been produced deliberately to offend" (clever isn't he?). "It is the kind of music that is a symptom of the way society is declining. It could have a shocking effect on young people."

He was, of course, talking about "Bodies".

CAPITAL Radio started the ball rolling when it banned the Pistols' current single, "Holidays In The Sun", on the basis that the song likens Belsen to a holiday camp. The ban was imposed despite the fact that it had already been played intermittently, had actually made the Capital hit-line, and that they had accepted 10 advertising spots for it.

EMI also got their oar in. Mr D. C. C. Pick, the group's trade marks executive, dispatched a letter to Virgin Records chairman, Richard Branson, on November 2, warning that the company considered the track "EMI" to be a possible breach of their trade mark copyright.

Bearing in mind the Pistols' previous involvement with EMI, the letter smacks more than a bit of spoilsports.

On November 5, in Nottingham, policewoman Julie Dawn Storey looked in the window of a Virgin Record shop in King Street and saw the album sleeve "with the word bollocks not obscured in any way". She spoke to shop manager Christopher Seale, told him she thought the word bollocks contravened the Indecent Advertising Act, and informed him he might be prosecuted.

Nottingham Magistrates Court was told last week, when Seale faced four charges under the Indecency Act, that Seale replied to policewoman Storey: "Is that all? What about free speech?"

It was inevitable. The Pistols' album shot straight to the top of the charts and the band have earned an estimated £250,000 in their two years together.

interesting point that two newspapers, the Evening Standard and The Guardian, had seen fit to use the album title in front page stories and that The Guardian had actually ran a photo of the offending sleeve with its story.

If the sleeve upset the police, he asked, why did they not perform similar arrests with Nottingham newsagents who displayed The Guardian?

The defence case was really won with the introduction of Professor James Kingsley, head of English Studies at Nottingham University — an accepted expert on the derivations of the word bollocks . . . and also a former Anglican priest. Touché!

Prof. Kingsley told the court that bollocks had been used in records (the written kind . . .) from the year 1000, and that in Anglo Saxon times it mean a small ball. It also appeared in Medieval bibles and veterinary books. In the bible it was used to describe small things of an appropriate shape. It had also appeared in place names without proving difficult for local residents.

"Much as those who now live in Maidenhead?" Mr Mortimer chimed in.

The Professor also raised a laugh when he said that bollocks was used to denote a clergyman in the last century.

"The word has been used as a nickname for clergymen. Clergymen are known to talk a great deal of rubbish, and so the word later developed the meaning of nonsense. They became known for talking a great deal of bollocks, just as 'old balls' or 'baloney' also come to mean testicles, so it has its twin uses in the dictionary. I would take the album title to mean 'Never Mind The Nonsense Here's The Sex Pistols'."

IT WAS then left to Mortimer to deliver his summing up for the defence, and he attacked the whole case as a judicial fiasco, stating that it didn't just raise sinister suggestions of possible police conspiracy against the Sex Pistols, but the whole question of free speech. "One wonders what the world is to think about a judicial system which has to spend its time to consider a word that is used to describe a load of nonsense, balderdash," he told the court.

The Chairman: "Much as my colleagues and I wholeheartedly deplore the vulgar exploitation of the worst instincts of human nature for the purchase of commercial profits by both you (Seale) and your company, we must reluctantly find you not guilty on each of the four charges." Choke!

McLaren knows the score. "Christ," he says, "if people bought the records for the music, this thing would have died the death long since." He knows the kids buy the records for what he calls "the attitude".

"Great!" laughs Johnny. "Bollocks is legal. Bollocks! Bollocks! Bollocks!"

BOLLOCKS

YANKS SPIKE SEX PISTOLS' GUNS

DAILY MIRROR, Thursday, December 29.

PUNK Rockers Johnny Rotten and the Sex Pistols may be banned from America. Britain's most controversial group were due to fly out yesterday to start a nineteen-day tour of the States.

But the American embassy has refused to grant them visas until they have answered questions on any previous criminal convictions. Rotten, above, was fined £40 last March for possessing a small amount of "speed" — amphetamine sulphate.

A spokesman for the group said: "Our solicitor is trying to contact everyone and we hope that by tomorrow we will have all the answers."

Their manager, Malcolm McLaren, said last night: "Steve used to be a brilliant cat burglar before he joined the band.

the quantity of the drug Sid and Nancy are accused of possessing is the smallest anyone in Britain has yet been charged with. It's claimed it was not visible to the naked eye.

JOHN LYDON IE JOHN ROTTEN

DATE	OFFENCE	FINE
11.3.77	POSSESSION OF AMPHETAMINE SULPHATE	£40

HE HAS NO MORE OFFENCES

JOHN BEVERLEY IE SID VICIOUS

DATE	OFFENCE	FINE
27.5.74	ASSAULT OF TWO POLICEMEN CRIMINAL DAMAGE	ABSOLUTE DISCHARGE
26.7.77	POSSESSION OF OFFENSIVE WEAPON (FLICK KNIFE)	£10. FORFEIT WEAPON
26.7.77	ASSAULT OF POLICEMAN	£50 FINE £25 COMPENSATION
17.8.76	TAKING OF FORD TRANSIT DESTROYING POLICEMANS HAND SET	£20 FINE £10 FINE. £4 COMP.

SID HAS NO MORE OFFENCES

PAUL COOK

DATE	OFFENCE	FINE
22.5.77	STEALING PROPERTY WORTH £900	£60 FINE

MORE TO COME MONDAY - SMALL THEFT. NO DRUGS OR OFFENSIVE WEAPONS

STEVE JONES

DATE	OFFENCE	FINE
10.10.68	BREAKING AND ENTERING STORE £143 STOLEN	ONE YEAR PROBATION (£1 FINE FOR BREACH OF PROBRATION)
27.9.71	STEALING 8 IGNITION KEYS	£6 FINE
27.9.71	TAKING AND DRIVING AWAY VEHICLE	£6 FINE
27.9.71	USE OF MOTOR VEHICLE WHEN UNDER AGE, NO INSURANCE OR LICENCE	£8 FINE IN TOTAL
19.1.76	DAMAGING PLATE GLASS WINDOW	£15 FINE £7,20 COMPENSATION
19.1.76	DRUNK AND DISORDERLY	£7 FINE
16.1.74	VAGRANCEY ACT CHARGE	£30 FINE

PISTOLS SHOCK USA!

JANUARY 14, 1978, BILLBOARD

Sex Pistols Shoot Blank On First Atlanta U.S. Gig

NEW YORK—The much delayed and detoured American debut of the Sex Pistols finally took place in Atlanta Thursday night (5). So far in the U.S. the group has generated more interest in the media than with the fans.

The tour had been scheduled to open in Pittsburgh a week earlier, but was delayed when the U.S. Embassy in London refused to grant the musicians visas because of the arrest records (Billboard, Jan. 7, 1978).

However, after appeals by lawyers from Warner Bros., the band's U.S. label, the State Dept. permitted the group to enter the U.S. The flap over the visas received heavy publicity in the U.S. When the band arrived from London there were more reporters and camera crews to greet the young punks than fans.

The Pistols played before about 600 fans and media people when the band debuted at the Great Southeast Music Hall in Atlanta. The crowd reportedly included vice squad officers from Memphis, next stop on the band's tour of secondary markets. No dates are planned for New York or Los Angeles.

The band has refused all interviews with the media and so far has created no untoward incidents, much to the published chagrin of reporters covering the tour.

RADIO PHONE IN SHOW, ATLANTA.

Listener — Say, Ah've hearrd them Pistols even crack hamsters in hairf on stage.

DJ — Yep, seems like Ah've hearrd that too.

Listener — Ah jest want them suckers back in London.

DJ — Ah was a little disappointed with them lest night, y'know. The worrst thing thrown was a plastic football. Why, up therre on that stage the worrst thing them boys did was to blow theirr noses.

Lieutenant Ronald Howell of Memphis said, "We have heard a lot about these boys and if they behave themselves we'll give them a right friendly welcome. Memphis is a clean city. We aim to keep it that way. We will not tolerate any real, or simulated, sex on stage. No sir. They can be nude if they like." (Thrills advises against full-frontals due to the growing obesity of Steve 'The Beer-Belly That Ate Atlanta' Jones!) "They can spit! They can even vomit!" (If Steve is allowed to appear in the naughty-naked-nude, they probably will!) "No law against that! But there must be no lewd or indecent behaviour ..."

"op throwing things at me."

Rotten, as usual, has taken it upon himself to be spokesman of the group, spouting forth eminently quotable jibes at each audience he's encountered. At Memphis, he yelped: "I'm not here for your amusement, You're here for mine!"

screamed at the audience: "You cowboys are all faggots!" — and retaliated as the audience threw beer cans by beating a heckler in the front row over the head with his unstrapped bass guitar.

"You bleedin' bunch of statues. I've never seen an audience stand like you bleedin' rotters."

The safety pins, the self-mutilation, the practice of vomiting and spitting are much in the minds of confirmed citizens like E. Winslow Chapman, director of Memphis police, who has said: "Ah doan 'low no masturbation on stage. They kin spit and vomit as much as they lahk, but no masturbation."

concerning Steve Jones trying to pick up a local wench who turned out to be a transvestite.

"Funny place, America," Steve said.

"The worst thing about them is their music," the police were quoted as saying

Barry Cain reports on the start of the Sex Pistols' American tour

Record Mirror, January 14, 1978

Johnny leaves his heart in Finsbury Park

SEX PISTOLS
Atlanta, Georgia

"HULLO MY name's John and this is the Sex Pistols."

Atlanta, Georgia. The Great South-East Music Hall.

Redneck City welcomes punk city slobs.

The opening night of the Pistols' American tour and the southern weirdos are out in force along with vice-squad.

Nobody quite knows what to expect. There are queues of people outside in the rain taking shelter in the shopping precinct doorways.

There's no way they're gonna get in. Curiosity, fried chicken style, sold out the tickets weeks in advance.

About the best these southern zeroes can hope for is a raid.

"Hullo, my name's John and this is the Sex Pistols" and into 'God Save The Queen'.

And so the band belly-flopped into one of the worst gigs they have ever played.

It was bad, I mean crapola. Rotten, in tails (minus top hat) left his heart in Finsbury Park. His voice has never been so flat.

Steve Jones' guitar is mercilessly out of tune. The timing on nearly every song is hopelessly out.

'I Wanna Be Me' follows which Rotten claims is the "new British National Anthem."

"Forget about staring at us and just start dancing. Have some fun, we're all ugly. We know that.'' Rotten book of quotes number 134.

By the third number, 'I'm A Lazy Sod', Vicious slips out of his leather jacket revealing his Bullworker body. America doesn't seem to agree with him.

Hell, life doesn't seem to agree with him.

'See the fine up-standing young men Britain's chucking out these days." Quote number 289.

The men from Atlanta reserve spitting. For special occasions — like baccy chewing. So they're content to throw plastic cups and — rolled up bits of paper?

And a lot of them are too drunk to appreciate the sheer amateurism of the band. It's impossible to gauge reaction from this crowd — too full of journalists.

"Aren't we the worst thing you've ever seen?" queries Rotten. The Atlantans cheer — though they can't understand what he's saying anyway.

The band fumble through the rest of the set finishing on song number 12 — 'Anarchy In The UK' or US of A as Rotten's trashcan intonation dwells on the A-A-A.

There was no encore. Sid Vicious in airport waiting lounge next day — "We were terrible last night." Point taken.

Now if y'all wanna hear some more of this, toon in next week. Same grime, same flannel. Y'all hear now.

Joe Stevens

PUNK MAGAZINE

It's unbelievable that a rock group that played no more than one hundred live performances (less than 50 according to guitarist Steve Jones) and existed for only 27 months could become as internationally disliked as the Sex Pistols were.

THE SEX PISTOLS

WHAT THEY'RE REALLY LIKE

SID VICIOUS- OUTGOING, LOONEY, SELF DESTRUCTIVE. WANTS ATTENTION. SEXUAL BRAGGART. A NICE GUY.

STEVE JONES- VERY QUIET. A LITTLE RESERVED. STREET SMART - GOOD SENSE OF HUMOR. ILLITERATE.

PAUL COOK- SHY, FRIENDLY, FUN TO BE WITH. INDEPENDANT. VERY STABLE. UNAFFECTED.

JOHN ROTTEN- NASTY. KEEPS TO HIMSELF. SHY AROUND GIRLS. LIKES TO TEST PEOPLE. STUCK-UP.

McKENZIE

According to both Peter's International and Jem records, the "Never Mind The Bollocks" LP is already the biggest selling import item in memory.

Our conversation was interrupted by Paul Cook, fresh from an interview with the prestigious L.A. Times. "I said 'fuck you a few times and left.' "It's not been good," said Malcolm. "That's what they want to hear, all right." Steve Jones enters, and proudly announces that he's been farting in the reporter's face. He's hungry.

The crowd growled back and threw showers of beer cans. Sid caught a full can in the teeth. He loved it, but when someone tried to fuck with his guitar he took it off and swung it at the guy's head. A couple of security guys tried to hold him back but he did it again. The spotlights turned off and there was a silence punctuated by the babbling crowd. It looked like the show was over. It looked like the mob was going to murder the Sex Pistols.

"Oh, what a pity," Sidney dropped his guitar... John said. They played "New York," John spitting the words "You fucking little faggots" at the audience. He moved really strangely, hopping about like a cross between Groucho Marx and Quasimodo. "We don't like your fucking free gifts!" he snarled, as beer cans continued to fly around. "It's just like Iggy said—you're the fuckers who paid ten bucks to see us, so fuck you," Sid proudly shouted. "Shut up, Sidney, you're holding up the set!" John spat.

"Fuck this! Where's the hundred dollar bills?" he shouted. People handed and threw dollar bills to the group, who spent the second encore—"Liar"—picking up dollar bills and stuffing them into their pockets and mouths.

After the concert Sid picked up a glamorous blonde with big tits. Everyone wondered if it was a man or a woman. When they got back to the hotel Sid tried to kill himself, as usual. First he smashed a gin bottle against the T.V. set. The bottle didn't break so he tried to jump out the window. That didn't work so he asked if anybody had any drugs. The blonde was pulling pot out of her socks when Noel Monk barged in. He went ape shit when he saw drugs and started interrogating the blonde. "Do you have anything else on you?" No, she didn't. Noel said he'd have to search her.

There were even more security hassles than usual after the show. The L.A. punkettes complained to Malcolm that they were beaten by WB security for no reason. Two of them were holding up their friend whose face was badly bruised and could hardly stand up. Malcolm sympathised. "Those wankers. Wankers. Warner Brothers is a bunch of wankers."

"All right, Noel. O.K. Hey, Noel. I'm bein' good, aren't I? I'm doin' O.K., right?" Sid asked him sincerely. Noel, along with the bodyguards and road crew, had become close mates with Sid and Johnny. Even though they order them around like they were buck privates in the marines. John was very impressed with the bodyguards karate skill. When the Sex Pistols break up, though, the WB crew doesn't recognize Rotten's existence.

The next day the San Antonio front page headline screamed "SEX PISTOLS WIN S.A. SHOOTOUT."

Sid was really drunk as usual and started a friendly fight with Roberta after she declined to give him "a portion." Sid started slapping her, promising not to kick her with his work boots. Then Roberta began to win the fight, so he kicked her hand. "OWWWH!... "Oh, I'm sorry, did I hurt you?... I'm sorry, I feel terrible about this."... C'mon, hit me. Go ahead. I deserve it. Roberta declined. Sid consoled her. "Oh, I'm sorry, did I hurt you?... I'm sorry. I feel terrible about this."... C'mon, hit me. Go ahead. I deserve it—beat up. Next Sid came over to me and gave me an exhibition of his fighting skill, throwing punches at my face, faster and faster, missing by mere fractions of an inch. Then he punched my nose. "I'm terribly sorry... Go ahead, hit me, I deserve it." Even though Sid really wanted to get beat up.

The bodyguard was standing right back of him giving me more dirty looks so I turned down the offer. Sid whipped off his belt and left a really nice dent in the wall.

Malcolm admitted that he was sure about 1977, but he has serious doubts about 1978. "There's got to be a group out there better than the Sex Pistols so they have something to compete against besides themselves.

BY JOHN HOLMSTROM

TULSA
Roberta Bayley

THE Sun

Thursday, January 19, 1978   6p   TODAY'S TV: PAGES 12 and 13

Punk band splits up as Rotten walks out

From LESLIE HINTON in New York

BRITAIN'S top punk rock group, the Sex Pistols, have split up, said their manager early today.

The pop sensation came in Los Angeles when manager Malcolm McLaren declared: "It's all over. We will never perform again."

He spoke after lead singer Johnny Rotten quit and flew to New York.

McLaren claimed: "We had a long talk after our San Francisco concert and the other members of the band decided to kick out Johnny Rotten.

"He was just too destructive and was dragging us all down.

"I have given up as manager and we will all go our separate ways."

But Rotten, at his New York hideout, gave a different version of the break-up.

He said: "I am sick of working with the Sex Pistols. I never want to appear with them again.

It's all a publicity stunt!

SEX PISTOLS IN ONGOING CONFUSTION PROBE

". . . The fact that they are now in three different corners of the world (Stev and Paul have now, it is assumed, flown to Rio; Johnny and Sid are in New York; Malcom's in LA) could be construed as part of their continuing attempt to subvert authority and achieve world domination. It could also be construed as splitting up."

'A spokesperson for Virgin said that as far as they were concerned the band didn't exist any more but it was possible two, three or even all four of them might get back together again at some point.

RETIRED? RETIRING SOON? Have your Social Security check deposited here automatically

Save STEPS.. TIME.. WOR

Joe Stevens

'The Pistols had to end with a bang if they really meant it, man'

VIVIEN GOLDMAN writes:

A split had been in the air for some time; John and Sid's friendship has fluctuated like the light when the power's about to go for some time now, anyway. John, Paul and Steve had been feeling less and less tolerant of Sid's increasingly over the top self destruction binges.

Meanwhile, relations between Malcolm Mclaren and John were growing worse and worse — when the Pistols were first formed, John was more open to obeying Malcolm's orders, though he'd always had a mind of his own. During the American tour, John, not surprisingly, had developed enough self-confidence to be uninhibited about his dislike and contempt for Malcolm and his familiar shock horror tactics.

Malcolm retaliated by divide and conquer tactics; he singled out Steve and Paul and convinced them that the Pistols would be better off without John, and that they should kick Rotten out.

John knew what was going on, and decided to leave the band before Steve and Paul committed the act; he flew from the West Coast to New York, where he took shelter with old friends like Joe Stevens and (ex-Heartbreaker) Jerry Nolan, Warner Brothers, the Pistols' US record label, are doubtless eager to sign John independently, in whatever situation he chooses (i.e. with a new band or solo.)

Back in Los Angeles, Malcolm was described by an old associate who ran into him at the Whiskey as 'Catatonic.'

An observer from the Pistols' London organisation commented: "That's true. Malcom always tends to withdraw into himself at the crucial moment, and that's what he's doing now."

Malcolm has been trying to salvage the remnants of the Pistols' planned European tour; he ordered the Glitterbest employees to keep schtum about the split while fans in Stockholm were already queuing up — with their tickets — in blizzards days in advance to see the band.

Although now Scandinavian agents have been instructed to cancel the gigs.

Whatever they say about one another publicly, John works in a tight team with Steve, and Paul and Steve are an equally strong unit. Rumours close to the band suggest that it's not inconceivable that John, Paul and Steve may yet hook up again.

And many of the band's earliest admirers feel that at least the Pistols haven't betrayed their original militant message — they'd just reached the stage where they could have become the boring/bored papmpered rock egos the Pistols were pledged to overthrow. Better that they should spontaneously combust; the Sex Pistols had to end with bang if they really meant it, maaan . . .

SOUNDS January 28, 1978

At 4p.m. on Thursday Glitterbest issued the following statement.

"The management is bored with managing a successful rock and roll band. The group is bored with being a successful rock and roll band. Burning venues and destroying record companies is more creative than making it."

Perhaps unsurprisingly, they withdrew the statement at 6p.m.

Joe Stevens

Daily Mirror:

PUNK rockers Johnny Rotten and Sid Vicious gave their fans a couple of ugly shocks yesterday.

First, lead singer Rotten claimed that he had split from the Sex Pistols group.

Then, only hours later, Vicious was carried unconscious from an airliner after apparently swallowing a mixture of drink and rugs.

W.B. pic

FREE ALBUM

Nancy: "He plays in a Dee Dee Ramones style that some people think isn't playing. But that's damn fast, man. We were over at Phil Lynot's. He couldn't play as fast as Sid. Sid plays melodic. He missed less notes than anybody else in that band. And I'm not just speaking from bias. Ask Sid. He played shit I'd tell him. Sid use the ashtray not my foot! You've already burnt me three times!!!"

"I WAS THE ONLY GUY WITH ANY BIT OF ANARCHY LEFT".

'I'll die before I'm very old: I don't know why, I just have this feeling. There have been plenty of other times I've nearly died.'

THE SEX PISTOLS ARE AN ATTITUDE. NOT A BAND.

SOUNDS June 3, 1978
ANOTHER SIDE INCIDENT: This one at the Speakeasy, where during a set by up 'n 'comings Fischer Z, young Sid Vicious decided to get up and jam, without the band's consent. As he was putting them off their musical stroke, a roadie carried him off. En route to the exit, Sid ran into a member of the Jam. A small set-to ensued which resulted in Sid being taken to hospital. So this is news?...

We slept in the same bed for five nights before we screwed. We screwed as a joke really. He didn't appeal to me sexually then. One night I woke up and he was rubbing up and down my thigh and I said: 'Sid what to you think you are doing? He said to me, 'how is it that the birds I fancy never like me?' so the next night, when we were down the Roxy, I said to him, right, tonight we'll screw. And we went home and we did. We did it in the bathroom, we did it everywhere.

On the first night we screwed, me and Sid, he had smelly feet and he wet the bed."

Presumably, Nancy has found Sid attractive since their first meeting. What does he have now he didn't have then?

"I find him sexually attractive now. Don't you think he has a sexual aura? I've taught him everything he wants to know. I've put that sexual aura into Sid, he was pretty near a virgin before. He was turned on by me like he never was before. He had a schoolboy crush on me. You know, people have said that I've grown up a lot. Well, maybe that's true but fuck, I've grown up pretty damn fast."

"I didn't like the jam introducing 'In The City' on stage the way they did. When I saw Paul Weller was there I thought I'd teach him a lesson. But he's only a little bloke, I didn't want to hurt him too bad, so I just went over and nutted him. Then when I was walking away he smashed a glass in me face. I'll get the little cunt next time. And I won't be alone."

REMIND Sid that a couple of months back he'd told Nick Kent he thought the Pistols were "the greatest band in the universe". Had he changed his mind about that or was he just unable to work with them? Sid nods off.
Nancy awakens him with a kiss.

Ah, Sid's eyes are open. Let's leap in quick: Sid do you think the Pistols got swept up in the consequences of the aggressive way they were approached things in the first place? Sid nods (in agreement; as opposed to out): "They have." Yeah. One of the things that saved me was ...
Nancy: "Me."

ANYONE CAN BE A SEX PISTOL.

'At school I got in fights every day. I just liked the feeling of mashing someone up and splitting them open.'

I must say, Sid, this state you're in does seem to exemplify what's been said about your being the next candidate for the rock'n'roll mortuary. Obviously you know people say that about you? Sid is unable to reply because he's in the process of nodding out again.

Sid: "I had a phase of dressing up in women's clothes when I was about 14 or 15. I did it for about a couple of months. I borrowed the clothes from friends. No, not my mothers'."

London: Friday
October 13, 1978
Price: Ten pence

Evening STANDARD

CITY PRICES

Sex Pistol on murder charge

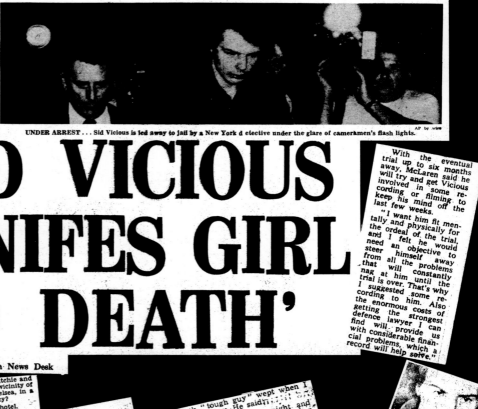

UNDER ARREST . . . Sid Vicious is led away to jail by a New York detective under the glare of cameramen's flash lights.

AP by wire

SID VICIOUS 'KNIFES GIRL TO DEATH'

Standard Foreign News Desk

With the eventual trial up to six months away, McLaren said he will try and get Vicious involved in some recording or filming to keep his mind off the last few weeks.

"I want him fit mentally and physically for the ordeal of the trial, and I felt he would need an objective to steer himself away from all the problems that will constantly nag at him until the trial is over. That's why I suggested some recording to him. Also the enormous costs of getting the strongest defence lawyer I can find will provide us with considerable financial problems, which a record will help solve."

Police said Vicious—known as John Ritchie and John Simon—was found wandering in the vicinity of one of New York's modest hotels, the Chelsea, in a semi-comatose state asking Where is Nancy?
Nancy was dead in Room 100 at the hotel.

The punk "tough guy" wept when I mentioned Nancy. He said:

"She's in my thoughts night and day. I wake in the night reaching out for her warm body, which was always cuddled next to me for two years.

DREAMING

I get in a hot sweat because I've been dreaming I'm making love to her again. The touch of her skin floats around in my brain driving me insane.

Nancy in her sexy red and black underwear never leaves me. I could never have killed her. When you love someone like I loved Nancy, life's almost impossible without them.

I'm always thinking about the good times we had together.

Nancy was great because she and I were the same — we both hated everyone. She would curse and swear and do everything I did.

OUT: Punk Sid

Free! Sid gets bail

PUNK murder suspect Sid Vicious was out on bail yesterday.

Vicious, who is accused of killing his girlfriend Nancy Spungen, was given bail at an earlier hearing, but had it revoked after a night club brawl.

Yesterday a judge freed him on condition that he reports to police daily. Vicious claims that Nancy could have stabbed herself to death.

Punk begs: Kill me

PUNK star Sid Vicious begged police to kill him.

It happened after his girlfriend "Nauseating" Nancy Spungeon was found stabbed to death in their New York hotel.

The former Sex Pistol told detectives: "Please shoot me . . . Kill me, my baby is dead."

Court papers released in New York yesterday revealed that at first Vicious claimed he did not know how Nancy died.

But later he told the detectives: "I stabbed her, but I didn't mean to kill her, I loved her . . ."

Then, under further questioning, he said that Nancy must have stabbed herself by falling on a knife when she was playing with it. He said he

From CHRISTOPHER BUCKLAND in New York

found her lying wounded before he went out to get a shot of the drug methadone, part of his treatment for heroin withdrawal.

Asked why he did not help her, he said: "I am a dog."

He is expected to be freed on £30,000 bail by a New York court today.

● Vicious has been voted "the world's most wonderful human being," in a readers' poll carried out by the New Musical Express.

Joseph Stevens, an American photographer who was one of the first on the scene, said: "Vicious told me there was a suicide pact..."

He said that he and Nancy had been planning to kill themselves for two or three weeks.

HOSPITAL

Stevens added: "There was blood everywhere when I arrived. Both his arms were badly cut."

Sun

"The first time he tried to commit suicide after Nancy's death, Sid told me: 'She's waiting for me mum. I know Nancy's just the other side. I can catch up with her if I go quickly. She's calling me from the grave.'

if Sid

Vicious gets out of jail. "I want to take karate lessons so I can defend myself. I'm getting sick of people picking on me and beating me up. There's a few geezers I've got to get even with when I get around to it, and one of them is Johnny Rotten, that boring . . ."

When Vicious was freed he put his arms round his mother to support himself. He was painfully thin, ashen-faced, and grimy, wearing filthy jeans and a T-shirt printed "I love New York."

He ripped off a black raincoat and threw it to the ground. His mother and Michele ran to cover him against the bitter cold, but he shook himself free.

Then he stretched his arms to the sky in a "good to be free" salute and made a clenched-teeth grimace which was as near as Sid Vicious could get to a smile.

His mother said: "I'm going to keep an eye on him so he won't get into trouble."

Barely 12 hours later he was dead.

They'd never give me bail if they had a strong case". Sid is currently out on $30,000 bail on condition that he avoids night clubs. This condition was imposed after he put Patti Smith's brother Todd in hospital after a disco brawl. "He (Rotten) will see who'll sell the most records when this trial is over and it won't be him. I'm the only one of the Sex Pistols left. I was always more famous than any of them. They just didn't have any bottle". . .

DEAD IN BED — Nancy Spungen, found with a knife in her stomach.

He was put back in jail for an assault on a man in a bar —soon after he first met 22-year-old Michelle Robinson.

"He had a magic kind of draw," she said.

Today, the manager of the Sex Pistols entrepreneur Malcolm McLaren, was flying to New York to help organise legal representation for Vicious.

Until Malcolm's arrival in N.Y. it had been an open and shut case. Suddenly there were at least four conflicting stories.

THE VICIOUS AFFAIR

NM EXCLUSIVE
VICIOUS PRISON INTERVIEW

ON SUNDAY, IN AN EXCLUSIVE interview with NME, Sid Vicious gave his version of the events which led up to his arrest for the for the murder of Nancy Spungen.

When we spoke to Vicious, he was undergoing heroin detoxification treatment in the hospital wing of New York's Riker's Island Prison. Although he appeared overwrought and confused about his situation, he was adamant about one thing: his innocence.

Vicious is charged with second degree murder, and intends to plead Not Guilty.

From New York, JOE STEVENS filed the following report.

RIKER'S ISLAND is a heavily guarded remand centre and short-term jail situated in the Hudson River, not far from La Guardia International Airport. The prison population consists almost exclusively of blacks and Puerto Ricans.

The Island has a tough reputation, and is supposedly a drug trafficking centre.

Accompanied by Sex Pistols manager Malcolm McLaren and Sid Vicious' mum Ann Beverly, I met Vicious in the prison hospital wing. When we told him that according to both London evening papers on Friday, Sid had "confessed" to Ms Spungen's murder, he angrily denied the reports.

"When the fuck did I make a confession?" he retorted "I was well out of it, mate!"

Over the course of our visit, Sid detailed his version of the events which took place in room 100 of the Chelsea Hotel between Wednesday evening and Thursday morning. His story is as follows:

He remembers waking up sometime during the night and seeing Nancy sitting up in bed fingering the knife they had bought earlier in the day, ostensibly to protect themselves from junkie scavengers who hung around the methodone clinic Sid frequented. Sid dozed off again

before he could ask Nancy what she was doing.

His next recollection is of waking up a few hours later and seeing blood all over Nancy's side of the bed.

"There was blood everywhere. On the sheets, on the pillow-case, all over the mattress and the floor leading into the bathroom. My first thought was that she had been killed."

He stumbled into the bathroom and found Nancy — still breathing — slouched under the bathroom sink. After a futile attempt to revive her, Sid ran out into the lobby yelling for help:

He then ran into the room and called the hotel reception desk, saying, "Get an ambulance up here quick. I'm not kidding!"

Minutes later it wasn't an ambulance but the police who arrived. When they saw the scene they turned to the dazed ex-Pistol — who, it was later revealed, had at the time been taking Tuinol — and said:

"Listen kid, why'd you do that?"

"Why'd I do what?" replied Vicious.

"Why'd you kill the girl?"

"I didn't kill her."

"If you didn't kill her why can't you look at me straight in the face?"

"All right," retorted Vicious, "I'm looking at you straight in the face. I

didn't kill her mate."

The two cops laughed at Vicious' denial, then pushed him up against the wall face first and handcuffed him.

ACCORDING TO police, Nancy died of "a stab wound inflicted after midnight on Wednesday". They later recovered the weapon, a large folding knife with a black wooden handle, and are said to be investigating reports that an unidentified young man had been with the couple until 4.00 am that morning.

Vicious was meanwhile taken to Riker's Island.

The following day he appeared in court, where he seemed understandably distressed and not a little disconnected. He was charged with second degree murder under his real name, John Simon Ritchie, and bail was set at £25,000 — much to the dismay of New York's finest, who had expected bail to be denied.

By this time Malcolm McLaren had arrived in New York — Vicious is still contracted to him — telling the British press before he left that "one of the reasons I want Sid out is to record a new album in New York. With a bit of luck the money from the record might pay for the trial."

McLaren engaged the respected New York law firm of Prior, Cashman, Sherman and Flynn to represent Vicious. Estimates of the legal fees likely to be involved are in the region of $100,000

McLaren also engaged some private investigators to follow up, amongst other leads, a theory that the death had some connection with the activities of a Puerto Rican gang that has recently taken over drug operation on the Lower East Side,

who sometimes congregate in a bar near the Chelsea Hotel.

Soon after his court appearance, Vicious was moved to the hospital wing of Riker's Island, where he is undergoing heroin detoxification.

On Sunday Sid's mother Mrs Ann Beverley arrived in New York armed with a sleeping bag and obviously ready for a long siege. We went to see Sid in hospital.

When Mrs Beverley — a very cool-headed lady who spent time on the hippie trails when Sid was ten years old — started getting a bit soft with her boy, Sid said: "Listen. I'm not a mama's boy, I'll fight my own battles."

Sid seemed to be unaware of the pressures building up around him, of the fact that the U.S. courts will probably be only too happy to make an example of him to any aspiring punk desperadoes. And, of course, Nancy's death is taking its emotional toll.

That same day Nancy's body was buried in her parents' home city of Philadelphia.

On Monday, Virgin Records telegraphed the bail money to McLaren in New York, and Sid was released on Tuesday morning.

If, when the case is heard, Vicious is convicted, the absolute minimum time he will spend in prison, with parole, is seven years. The maximum is 25.

NANCY & SID, Music Machine, earlier this year. Pic: ROSS HALFIN.

Drug cure...then killer overdose

violent streak in him. Sometimes this was turned against other people and at times against Nancy, himself in fits of self-mutilation.

Dr Michael Baden, New York's chief medical examiner, saw the body and said: "It appears he died inadvertently.

May 10, 1957
SID VICIOUS 1957-79
February 2, 1979

THE LATE Sid Vicious is featured singer on the A side of the next Sex Pistols single, a revival of the Eddie Cochran song 'Something Else'. Steve Jones handles the vocal on the flip side, 'Friggin' In The Riggin''. It's scheduled for February 23 release by Virgin, who had already planned it for that date prior to Vicious' death.

BURY ME WITH MY NANCY, SAID SID

by BRIAN WESLEY

THE body of punk junkie Sid Vicious lay in a New York mortuary last night as friends tried to make his bizarre last wish come true.

The former Sex Pistol told his mother he wanted to be buried next to Nancy Spungen, the girl he was accused of killing.

But yesterday her wealthy parents went into hiding and refused to reveal the site of her unmarked grave in Philadelphia.

The equation that Heroin = Death has been enacted enough times for it to be obvious to all.

This is definitely not a very good year for Sid Vicious' mum. She was busted on Friday night after 25 lbs of cannabis had been found in a Paddington flat. She and three others were detained at Paddington Green police station . . .

SUNDAY PEOPLE, February 4, 1979

David Black

"Look, I want to change the music business right? I want to change all that . . . But it'll take years. I'll have to do it more skilfully this time. But it'll be with a vengeance. And they won't know."

PUBLIC Image LTD

There's practically no musicians with my musical tastes. This means, oh cruel savage world, if there's any oafs going round out there who dare to consider themselves acceptable, let me know.

"And I don't mean mugs and prats and tits and liggers and wankers and madmen with pea-brained ideas about changing the musical course of history, because we all know that that's impossible."

He actually had the nerve to tell me that's what the Pistols are all about, and I had to tell him, ducky, I am what the Pistols are all about. You are not required any more. I just fail to see how going to a police state to see a failed bank robber has anything to do with us. What's the connection?"

"Singing in a band? I just thought 'Whoopee, a bumpkin like me who can hardly be bothered to talk!"

But if you're so anti-image, why call your band Public Image? "Limited. Public Image Ltd, it's a pisstake, it's ironical. Do you not understand?" — the public image is limited." That's what I hoped you meant.

As to lack of promotion on the single, Draper told me that the company had spent £8,000-£10,000 on advertising it. This, he says, is about exactly the same as was spent on any of the Sex Pistols' singles and is approximately three times what Virgin normally spend on a 45.

When did you stop being friendly with Sid?
"His attitude changed completely when he met Nancy. One hundred per cent. He was banging up all day and night. He became a total bore and just didn't recognise anyone anymore. It was pathetic. He can't play the bass. He never really could. It was horrible the noise he used to get out of it," he laughs, "about the most offensive racket ever."

CHRISTMAS WAS going to be perfect. Just fantastic. Public Image on Christmas Day, more than a gig . . . an event. I mean, they made the best single of the year and although the album was disappointing 'Lowlife' and bits of 'Religion' were good. Anyway it'll be great to see them live . . . no doubt about it, something to look forward to.

The stage looks fantastic, just like the new posters Virgin have been putting up round town. All green and black. The minute Mr Rotten walks on stage you think it's all been worth it. I mean, he looks so great. Checked suit, funny hat and shopping bags. . . you only saw me for the clothes I wore.

They start with 'Theme' from the LP. The barrage of requests for old favourites that follows is met with characteristic snot — "Listen, don't ever ask for any Pistols numbers, that's history, ya know what I mean". The sound still hasn't improved. The bass and drums are ok, very much like the album, but the guitar's virtually inaudible.

Next is 'Lowlife' which gets a bit of action out of a remarkably lethargic audience then, after about a minute of 'Attack' a huge fight breaks out at the front and the band stop playing altogether.

Another five minute wait while John throws a moody (threatens to leave) and gives us a lecture ("Don't fight among yourselves — when will you ever learn?"). Then follows a good version of 'Belsen Was A Gas' which is introduced as a song "Me and Keith Levine wrote". Funny, before we were told it was Sid, anyway I don't care who wrote it, it is the best moment of the night. The words are changed around a bit too. Then 'Religion' and 'Anna Lisa'. All through the set though it seems that the total is so much less than the sum of the parts. Kevin Levine ambles round the stage and spends an inordinate amount of time trying, but not succeeding, to tune his guitars. Jah Wobble just sits, struggling with his bass. Donut on drums is great, he's holding the whole thing together. The initial visual impact of the stage just doesn't hold up . . . in short, it gets boring.

At two minutes past twelve Rotten walks off, comes back and tells us we can have one more which is the single. As great as it is it can't seem to revive many failing spirits. Even before it's finished the house lights are flashing. They played for about 40 minutes in all. What more can I say? It didn't so much end as fizzle out.

During a two hour walk home in the early morning rain you get to think of a lot of things. Basically it's just been horrible from beginning to end. A bloody disaster. Just a bad gig, organized by and starring a group you didn't think could ever be bad. No magic. No spirit. It may be purposely anti-intellectual but it's very little fun, ya know what I mean. Christmas comes but once a year.

Did you ever get the feeling you've been conned. . .?

ROSS CRIGHTON

Public Image are more than a major force in today's music scene. You have to choose for yourself, or, in the words of John Lydon, "No gimmicks, no theatrics, just us — take it or leave it."

Public Image are possibly the most important band of the late Seventies, mainly due to the fact that they are forcing the rock audience to judge them on the music alone.

People seem terrified to admit to liking them because, at the back of their minds, they have a feeling that John Lydon is suddenly going to turn round and make complete idiots of them, by announcing that the music of Public Image is nothing but a complete parody of the rock scene.

All I can say is that this gig restored my belief that John Lydon is the finest and most compelling rock performer of the decade.

MICK MIDDLES

The Public Image Ltd singer (John insists that the group is a group and that he is only one fourth of it — hence the egalitarian songwriting credits on the eight tracks on the LP) has, after all, just been served with a tax bill for £58,000 from his days with The Sex Pistols.

A product of your society

Dennis Morris

ROTTEN v. McLAREN

JOHNNY GOES A-COURTING

ROTTEN v. McLAREN

NEW MUSICAL EXPRESS
February 24th, 1979

High Courting, that is. STEVE CLARKE (of the Court) witnesses proceedings in the case of John Lydon vs. Glitterbest Ltd., Stephen Jones, Paul Cook, John Beverley (deceased) and Matrixbest Ltd.

ROTTEN v. McLAREN

IN THE SOBER climes of court number 37 at the Royal Courts of Justice, a High Court Judge last week heard of the trials and tribulations of The Sex Pistols.

Outside, a cheerful Johnny Rotten, aka John Lydon, signed autographs for middle-aged women, and at least one well-heeled tourist ... and the court usher.

Looking the colour of chalk and in need of a course of Clearasil, Rotten was decked out in the kind of flamboyant suit favoured by circus clowns. With matching tartan tie and purple-topped brothel creepers, he brought an element of colour into the bland court room with its fluorescent strip lighting and air of taking everything at a snail's pace.

Defendant Malcolm McLaren wore the de rigeur leather strides, brown V-neck jumper, nondescript collar and tie and — for street apparel — a rather fine specimen of black fur coat.

In an action that coincided macabrely with the cremation of Sid Vicious, Lydon is seeking to appoint a receiver to sort out the Pistols financial affairs and to prevent McLaren's company Glitterbest from using the name Sex Pistols other than in connection with himself, Paul Cook, Steve Jones and the late Vicious.

Lydon is also seeking a declaration that his contract with McLaren is no longer valid and that he may no longer act as his manager or agent.

The hearing was decidedly low-key. Neither the press or public benches were full.

In the public benches there were, at various times, a collection of curious students, a party of Lydon's mates including his brother, and the odd 'respectable looking' member of the public, as well as Ari Up's mother Nora.

The legal eagles shied away from four-letter words or reading out the really juicy bits.

"I'm a little daunted at reading out 29 pages of film treatment," said Lydon's Q.C., Mr. John Wilmers, on the second day of the hearing (Thursday). And referring to how Judge Mr. Justice Browne-Wilkinson would have to read the 'treatment' at home, Mr. Wilmers added: "I'm afraid reading it won't be a pleasure."

Rotten and McLaren were impassive, although occasionally a smirk cracked their respective visages — for instance the latter couldn't suppress a smile when Wilmers read out a film script that quoted McLaren as saying: "You don't take calls from venues that want the band to play."

Despite the spicy nature of much of the material under discussion — sex and drugs and rock and roll, not to mention the alleged disappearance of substantial sums from the Pistols' coffers — the proceedings more than once plumbed the depths of boredom.

"It's boring my pants off," announced Lydon

Lydon described the Pistols' relationship until September 1976 as "highly informal".

"It was always accepted that our earnings and expenses as a group were to be shared equally between us and we just seemed to break even. We lived on virtually nothing."

At this time the Pistols had no manager, but did receive considerable assistance from McLaren. He arranged some dates for the band, though Lydon pointed out that the first gigs were organised by Matlock.

McLaren, he claimed, showed no interest in the Pistols' music then — or since.

Lydon said that all the Pistols lyrics were written by him. "The Sex Pistols style was developed by Cook, Jones, Matlock and myself, and not by McLaren.

"I was dressing and dying my hair in the way which is widely associated with me before the group was formed."

In September 1976, McLaren told the Pistols that EMI wanted to sign them, but only on condition that they had a regular manager and office. McLaren left a copy of a draft agreement with Lydon and a few days later Lydon met with McLaren and his solicitor Steven Fisher, a prominent music business lawyer.

"I did not understand much of the agreement," Lydon told the court. "But I thought it gave McLaren too much control of the group and I said so. I believe that Fisher made some changes, but I still felt I didn't understand it and I didn't like it."

Lydon alleged that McLaren told him the other three Pistols had already signed it and that if he didn't sign quickly EMI would lose interest. He therefore signed the contract, which was for five years.

Mr. Wilmers claimed that the group could not have understood the contract without help: "None of them had any serious education attainments — though my client can read very well."

Lydon told the court that he thought the agreement "one-sided and oppressive", and also said that neither the names Sex Pistols, Johnny Rotten or Sid Vicious was created by McLaren — adding that before the group formed Steve Jones had been lead singer in a group called Q.T. Jones and his Sex Pistols and that in one context or another the name Sex Pistols had been used before.

Lydon's statement pointed out that McLaren and Fisher are the only shareholders and directors of Glitterbest. Regarding Vicious joining the band, he said that he (Lydon) invited him to join and that Matlock had quit because of personal differences between the two, particularly over the material the Pistols should perform.

It was also revealed that McLaren and Fisher prepared a letter which they required Matlock to sign saying he was no longer a member of the group

ACCORDING TO Lydon's statement, Glitterbest received just under half a million pounds on the group's behalf from September 1976 until March 1978.

On top of this there was a payment of £200,000 from Warner Brothers Records in advance of a projected Pistols movie. The film was subsequently abandoned, but not until Glitterbest had spent "considerable sums on its preparation", said Mr. Wilmers.

On top of this, there was an advance of £10,000 from CPE/Barclay, the Pistols' European outlet, and two advances from Virgin Records, of £2,500 and £19,000.

Lydon's split from the Pistols came on January 16, 1978 when the group were in San Francisco on the last leg of their first American tour.

"Before the tour I had become seriously discontented with McLaren," said Lydon. "He had no interest in our music and was only interested in publicity."

One of the reasons for this disillusionment was McLaren's idea for the Pistols to make a film with the American "bombastic sex thriller" director Russ Meyer.

"I found Meyer's script and ideas objectionable."

Mr. Wilmers claimed the script was "obscene and offensive" and would have damaged Lydon's career: there were scenes of necrophillia, incest, group sex, gross violence and sexual perversion.

He described the script as "the foulest document I have ever seen."

"I am not reading the whole of it in open court. Page 52 is incest — not just incest — but incest by one of the members of the group with his mother."

Wilmers further claimed that McLaren hired another American film director, called Caplan, for the movie and then sacked him without consulting Lydon or the rest of the group.

McLaren then wrote his own script for a film called *The Great Rock And Roll Swindle*. Referring

ROTTEN v. McLAREN

Pistols to be 'exploited' yet again— by the Official Receiver...

The judge then asked whether Lydon was party to McLaren's manipulation.

Wilmers: "Bear in mind that he was precisely 20 years old."

Mr Godfried, McLaren's Q.C. later claimed that the script was meant to be a satire and not a statement of fact.

Lydon's other area of discontent with McLaren was concerned with McLaren's alleged desire to prevent the Pistols playing live gigs.

Said Lydon in his statement: "McLaren hoped that our record sales would be enhanced if the public were under the impression that we were banned from playing. That was certainly untrue. Some halls wouldn't have us, but others applied to Glitterbest for gigs during 1977 and were either refused or else received no replies."

In the end, he claimed, the Pistols resorted to doing three secret gigs under assumed names.

Mr. Wilmers then informed the court of Lydon's difficulty in contacting McLaren while in San Francisco.

Lydon claimed that McLaren set up a trip to Brazil, where the group were to be photographed with train robber Ronald Biggs, without consulting Lydon. He was exhausted and ill with bronchitis and couldn't see how the band could fit in a concert in Rio before a gig in Stockholm that had already been scheduled.

At this time Sid Vicious rang Lydon one morning at 5.00 am to inform him that McLaren had just visited him. McLaren had complained to Vicous about Lydon, and Vicious himself told Lydon that he had had enough of the Pistols.

"Vicious sounded incoherent," said Lydon's statement. "I've since heard that he took an overdose of heroin shortly after McLaren's visit." Subsequently, Wilmers claimed, Lydon and McLaren had a face to face showdown at which Lydon said he didn't like getting publicity out of a man who had left a train driver like a vegetable.

The judge asked whether Rotten had changed in view of his refusal to become involved with Biggs. "The image projected is one in which violence is not opposed," he commented.

Mr. Wilmers said that Rotten did not approve of killing people.

NME photographer Joe Stevens had joined the Pistols in Memphis, Mr Wilmers told the court, reading from Stevens' prepared statement. His immediate impression was that John and Malcolm were not getting along. Said Stevens: "It was less a situation of open hostility between them than of silence and lack of communication."

He also noticed that McLaren "had very little control over what was going on. Malcolm missed the first gig and seemed a bit disorientated. He certainly had no control over Sid, who is a strange person and given to drug excess."

As Stevens saw it, the three Warner Brothers men seemed to be more in charge. McLaren later told Stevens that he found the day-to-day running of the group boring.

Lydon, said Stevens, was unaware of the South American trip. The photographer was in fact the first person to inform Lydon of the plan. Lydon replied: "I am splitting blood and they expect me to sit on a plane for a couple of days."

In March last year Lydon had one further meeting with McLaren, at which the latter asked him to appear in a film. Lydon said he would only appear in the film if he could choose his own material, and McLaren wouldn't agree to this.

FOR McLAREN, Mr Godfried said that according to his client The Sex Pistols had choosen their name because Pistols was a brash, young name and the Sex part of it referred to McLaren's shop. Originally Steve Jones was the lead singer with the group, but he subsequently switched to guitar despite being "relatively unfamiliar with the instrument."

McLaren claimed that he approached Lydon to join the Pistols. He'd seen Lydon hanging around his shop and thought him ideal for the band. He also denied that Lydon wrote the Pistols' lyrics on his own and claimed that they were jointly inspired.

Regarding the American tour, Mr Godfried told the judge: "Things went bad in America because of Sid's drug problems and violent nature." McLaren also blamed the American public's hostility towards the group for creating intra-group tension.

He said the group had been banned in Finland, where they were due to tour immediately after America. They therefore had some unexpected free time which could be utilised by a promotional visit to South America at Virgin Records' expense. On Friday January 13 McLaren claimed he made reservations for all four Pistols to fly to Rio. He tried repeatedly to contact Lydon, but couldn't get hold of him.

ROTTEN v. McLAREN

McLaren told the cour[t he had] been informed that Lydo[n …] and, bearing in mind pers[onal] clashes between Lydon a[nd] Vicious, decided it would b[e] pointless going to Rio after Vicious had been talking ab[out] quitting, and shortly afterwa[rds] collapsed from a heroin over[dose.]

Lydon, McLaren claimed, w[as] left with a return ticket to Lon[don] and said that he would see hi[m in] London later on when he woul[d try] to sort out the band's problems. Meanwhile, McLaren alleged, C[ook] and Jones decided to go to Braz[il] with a view to Lydon and Vicious joining them at a later date.

Press cuttings were then produced, one of which quoted Lydon as saying he thought American fans boring because they weren't violent enough. Another cutting, from the London *Evening News*, was read out by McLaren's counsel. In it Lydon said he would never play with the Pistols again.

Once in London again, McLaren alleged that he tried once more to contact Lydon. He later discovered from reading a newspaper report that Lydon was in Jamaica with Virgin boss Richard Branson.

He thought McLaren had bee[n an] excellent manager and that it wasn't true to say that he had prevented the group performing. Jones reiterated Cook's stateme[nt] about the Pistols approaching McLaren to manage them. According to him, McLaren wasn['t] interested at first.

Jones alleged that Lydon approached the Pistols and asked [if] he could join the band: "John said that he sang out of tune. Malcolm thought this was a positive advantage. John mimed to a juke box and shortly afterwards joined the group."

Jones expressed the opinion that, except in the early days, Lydon never really liked McLaren.

By the time the group reached San Francisco, John had begun behaving like a prima dona donna.

In a statement, McLaren's girlfriend Vivienne Westwood claimed it was Steve Jones who was the trend-setter in the early Pistols days. He'd wear something and all the other kids would be wearing similar clothes shortly afterwards.

Peter Kodik

John Lydon dropped by the *NME* offices after the case closed clad in an exquisitely garish red towelling suit with the express intent of drinking as much of **Neil Spencer's** beer as possible, discussing things and whiling away a couple of hours, all of which was achieved quite effectively. What's actually happened is that, following the decision of **Steve Jones** and **Paul Cook** to become plaintiffs instead of defendants (i.e. to side with Lydon rather than **McLaren**), an official receiver has been appointed to sort out Glitterbest's affairs and assets (including McLaren's *Great Rock And Roll Swindle* movie). Both Glitterbest and Matrixbest (the film company) have been declared bankrupt, and Legs McLaren himself signed his rights over to Virgin and split to France, dejected and allegedly broke.

ROTTEN v. McLAREN

Worst of all, Seditionaries failed to open this weekend.

Despite the Cook-Jones volte-face (which, as John Lydon pointed out, renders the poxy pair liable for both sides' court costs — awoah!), it seems unlikely that any sudden fit of buddy-buddyness will ensue, and Legs' fear that now that he's out of the way there'll be some sort of Sex Pistols reunion seems completely out of order, out to lunch, not on etc.

Meanwhile, the burning question of the age (or at least the first burning question of the age to crop up in this week's T-Zers): where's the money? Who's got it? How much is there? Can we have some? How do you spell **Branson?** . . .

ROTTEN v. McLAREN

You may think you've been on the receiving end of heavy-duty TV saturation advertising before (whoever that is in the back row humming "Millions of parts for thousands of cars" can just get up and leave right *now*), but wait until you get whacked round the chops with the £100,000 campaign being set up for *The Great Rock'n'Roll Swindle* by **Malcolm McLaren**, currently describing the movie as "A modern *Oliver Twist*". We see, Malcolm . . . Steve Jones as the Artful Dodger, J.R. as Oliver, Sid as — sorry, have we misinterpreted the statement? Oh well. One person who we're sure will be wishing Malcolm a lotta luck on all his future ventures is **Joe Stevens** still nursing the $1700 phone bill with which Malcolm stuck him and discovering that the price of aiding and comforting **Sid Vicious** is to be unilaterally frozen out by most of the New York music business establishment . . .

Rotten objected strongly to the idea of a Pistols trip to Rio to see Ronald Biggs

Sex Pistols — From the forthcoming film THE GREAT ROCK'N'ROLL SWINDLE — A Matrixbest Production — Virgin Records

The judge had suggested that McLaren be appointed as a sub-manager to help the receiver sell the film, but McLaren informed me that, although he wanted the film to be finished, he did not currently feel that he wanted to assist someone who had forced him to leave the country. Rather than working for himself, he would then be acting for the court, the Sex Pistols partnership and Virgin Records.

"I don't mind being sold down the river, but I'm not gonna drown in it, too. It's like wiping your face in your own shit.

"The facts are that without me that group wouldn't've existed, and I feel that if I couldn't spend that money on the projects that I thought were right, then they should've thrown me out years ago."

When the band broke up and it was all over, I heard vague rumours that Malcolm wanted to film me in London. I told his lackeys at Glitterbest Ltd to drop dead 'cos I didn't want to be filmed. I made that very clear. When I found them hiding behind bushes in Jamaica I was quite disgusted. I thought that was the most basic piece of evil I'd ever seen. The crew don't know how close they come to having the camera pushed straight through the back of their brains."

Your contract with Talcy Malcy don't end for another six months, I know, but have you already split with him?

"I suppose we have, really. He was pissed off with all that stuff with retainers and that when the court said that 'The Great Rock'n'Roll Swindle' wasn't his anymore."

He's trying to get all the parts of the movie with him in it taken out, ain't he?

"Yeah, and that's most of the fucking film! That film — it's taking so fucking long to come out that by the time it's released it's gonna be soooo out of date that it ain't true . . ."

"The swindling thing ain't true, that's just McLaren's little kick of making out he's conning everybody. It's 'is ego, y'know. I mean, he's saying he got us together, but he didn't. He didn't do half the fucking things. F'rinstace, Rotten was Rotten when we first seen him, spikey 'air and ripped up t-shirts, nothing to do with McLaren.

"That's another thing, didn't write the film single 'anded either, it was abo four people. Tell you the truth I ain't got a clue ab how the film goes 'cos I ain't seen the finished version. I know there's of early film footage of playing live."

Sex Pistols — From the forthcoming film THE GREAT ROCK'N'ROLL SWINDLE — A Matrixbest Production — Virgin Records

From the forthcoming film — Sex Pistols — THE GREAT ROCK'N'ROLL SWINDLE — A Matrixbest Production — Virgin Records

"Hello Paul, it's Ray, do you fancy a chat and some snaps for the update of the book?"
"Yeah, what have you got in mind."
"A few pictures of what you're doing now and a bit of information on what you're doing next."
"Steve's here, he wants to know if he'll get paid."
"I can give him a few quid. Maybe fifteen."
"He says you're joking!"

"It's our sound. No one els

"We was just in it for

In spite of this financial disagreement Steve and Paul and I got together at Paul's Paddington Flat, drank some tea and bourbon, smoked some fags watched video clips from the movie (good stuff) and exchanged very little information.

"You said on the phone that you were broke."
"Yeah, we're fucking skint ain't even been getting our wages since the court case and won't get royalties or nothing 'til it's sorted out."
"What are you living on then?"
"Selling things, guitars and that."
"I didn't ask whose guitars."

There is a new band on the way but Paul or Steve are not saying who else is in it or what the band will be called. They will however be nastier than the Sex Pistols and have the same sound.

the piss-up and the birds

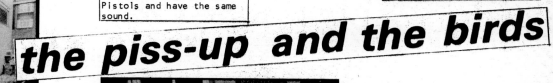

"How about Malcolm?"
"What about him....he just wanted to make money. But he wasn't that interested in money itself otherwise he would've bought a house or something and moved out of that shithouse in Clapham."
"Maybe he's got a bundle stashed somewhere."
"Nah I don't think so."

"Was the American tour responsible for the break-up?"
"It was a load of things. Sid mostly, John. We were under so much pressure all the time everywhere we went. A lot of people think the tour was bad but it wasn't, it was really a success apart from the split. Nobody had ever seen anything like it."

"I FEEL A BIT OLD. I WALK DOWN THE STREET AND SEE THESE LITTLE PUNK ROCKERS ABOUT 13 AND THEY DON'T EVEN RECOGNISE ME..."

after the show . . ."

"Would you work with Malcolm again?"
"I dunno...maybe. Yeah...we're still friends."

"Is there anything that should be said and hasn't."
"Nah, everything's bin said and so often."
"So much for my great interview with the two remaining Sex Pistols."

VIRGIN
PRESS RELEASE

21st. December, 1977

Pistols at the Nick

Editor,

Just a short note to let you know about our last group here, which was the Sex Pistols. All the lads enjoyed them very much, as they seemed to be at home amongst us. The lead singer, whose name is Johnny Rotton, lived very much up to his name — although I don't mean his singing, as that can only be described as very good — but one or two of the guys did remark to me after the show that they did feel like punching him on the nose for the way he spoke to them.

The road crew was excellent, as usual — it's funny, we have never had a band turn up late here yet, only as I explained recently it is most important that everything runs to a tight schedule in the prison. The best way I can sum everything up is to give the band a score, like on the New Faces show:

Road Crew 10 out of 10
Stage act 9 out of 10
Musically 8 out of 10
Manners 0 out of 10

— but there again I can remember the Who when they would have scored the same ratings . . . I hope that all the groups that come along and play for us for nothing get all the breaks in the world.

Peter Stunt
Secretary, Recidivists Anon
H.M. Prison, Chelmsford.

"Thirty guitars, I swiped. No one ever believes me, though . . ."

SEX PISTOLS PLAY FOR HUDDERSFIELD CHILDREN

The Sex Pistols, who last week were voted the world's top group by readers of New Musical Express, conclude their current tour of the UK by playing at a free Christmas party for children under 15 in Huddersfield on Christmas Day.

The Gingerbread Group, a nationwide association for one-parent families, have arranged for 250 local children to be collected by coach from their homes on Christmas day and taken to the club Ivanhoe's where the group is due to perform that evening.

At the party, which takes place between 3 and 6pm, festive cakes and soft drinks will be dispensed, and the Sex Pistols will perform free.

Coaches will take the children home after the party.

(Later, John said — "I don't want to put anyone down in the band because they're alright really. I don't have bad feelings at all — I mess about, I'm a sarcastic C—t. The fact that I know their weak points and they know mine is fine because we don't use them as weapons against each other. I liked working with the band — let's face it, that was my chance, and they gave it to me.")

I even saw one Swedish copper at the back of the hall on the second gig doing a restrained but joyful pogo to the lilting strains of "Pretty Vacant". Can you imagine that at a British Pistols gig — in fact, can you imagine a British Pistols gig at all these days?

I ask Jones if he thinks Malcolm could be ripping them off.
"Nah, no way."
"We trust him implicitly," claims Cook.
"And if he ripped me off," adds Steve, "I'd break his fuckin' legs."

SINGLE/EP

1 **GOD SAVE THE QUEEN, Sex Pistols, Virgin**
2 Pretty Vacant, Sex Pistols, Virgin
3 Wondrous Stories, Yes

NATTY DRESSER

1 **JOHNNY ROTTEN**
2 Freddie Mercury

NEW MUSICAL EXPRESS

"Alright, Malcolm's not looking, over the side and swim for Rio". Pistols at Golden Gate bridge, California. Pic: JOE STEVENS.

A WEEKLY EXHALATION

Ex-Pistol re-signs to EMI

November 5, 1977 SOUNDS

GLEN MATLOCK's Rich Kids have signed to EMI records. The former Sex Pistols bassist has completed the line-up of his new band and they have already recorded some songs, although nothing has been properly mixed and there are no record releases scheduled at present. The band's line-up has been completed by the addition of guitarist

Midge Ure who was formerly with Silk. The rest of the band is made up of Steve New guitar, and Rusty Egan drums. Live plans for the band are expected to be announced shortly.
Matlock and the Rich Kids were featured in SOUNDS September 3 issue.

GLENN MATLOCK: "It was like playing in The Monkees."

Over the other side of the shop, Rotten is trying on a pair of repulsive leopard-skin-topped shoes.
"They're really 'orrible," he beams. "I must have them. I could start another absurd trend . . . like safety pins."

"I never imagined the band would get anywhere. It amazed me when we got that far.

"I knew right from the start that we were going to be big, because I was sure what we were doing was right, one thousand per cent. It was the only way out for rock to go, no alternative. But to be honest, there is no mystery about music. Everything's based on the heartbeat, anyway.

BAND OF THE YEAR

1 **SEX PISTOLS**
2 Ritchie Blackmore

Protest all you like son, I'm putting you on a charge. Impersonating a Sex Pistols is a pretty serious thing . . .

"When I first met John he was really obnoxious" And now he's probably worse.

Malcolm: Well, I think it's more interesting to be hated than to be liked. It's a more invigorating idea.

I think if you can prevent them from buying records, tremendous.

and I think making what they think is hit records is pretty dopey. I really mean that.

WHAT FOR?? Who wats to sit in one's room to play some dopey rock 'n' roll record? It's boring.

MALE SINGER

1 **JOHNNY ROTTEN**
2 Ronnie James Dio, Ritchie

LP SLEEVE

1 **NEVER MIND THE BOLLOCKS, Sex Pistols,**

BORE OF THE YEAR

1 PUNK/NEW W
2 Tony Blackburn
3 Sex Pistols
4 Johnny Rotten
5 Rod and Britt

[John jumps up from the couch and lounges in front of the mirror, preening.]

"Oh, beeyootiful me!"

Why is the album not as good as the band?

ALBUM OF THE YEAR

1 **NEVER MIND THE BOLLOCKS, HERE'S THE SEX PISTOLS, Virgin**
2 On Stage, Ritchie Blackmore's

John: "What don't seem to rea that The Pistol giving them a fo entertainment W above all thin dance band."

WEEK ENDING NOVEMBER 12, 1977

1 NEW	NEVER MIND THE BOLLOCKS, HERE'S THE SEX PISTOLS	Virgin V 2086